D0687706

GLOBALISTS

GLOBALISTS

The End of Empire and the Birth of Neoliberalism

QUINN SLOBODIAN

Harvard University Press

Cambridge, Massachusetts
London, England
2018

Printed in the United States of America

First printing

Library of Congress Cataloging-in-Publication Data

Names: Slobodian, Quinn, 1978– author.
Title: Globalists : the end of empire and the birth of neoliberalism / Quinn Slobodian.
Description: Cambridge, Massachusetts : Harvard University Press, 2018. | Includes bibliographical references and index.
Identifiers: LCCN 2017050071 | ISBN 9780674979529 (alk. paper)
Subjects: LCSH: Globalization—History—20th century. | Neoliberalism—History—20th century. | Capitalism—History—20th century.
Classification: LCC JZ1318 .S595 2018 | DDC 320.51/3—dc23
LC record available at https://lccn.loc.gov/2017050071

For M & Y

Contents

Abbreviations

AAAA	American-African Affairs Association
ARA	American-Rhodesian Association
CAP	Common Agricultural Policy
CWL	Walter Lippmann Colloquium
ECLA	United Nations Economic Commission for Latin America
ECOSOC	United Nations Economic and Social Council
EDU	Eastern Democratic Union
EEC	European Economic Community
EFTA	European Free Trade Area
G-77	Group of 77
GATT	General Agreement on Tariffs and Trade
ICC	International Chamber of Commerce
ICIC	International Committee on Intellectual Cooperation
IIIC	International Institute for Intellectual Cooperation
ILO	International Labour Organization
IMF	International Monetary Fund

ISC	International Studies Conference
ITO	International Trade Organization
LSE	London School of Economics
MPS	Mont Pèlerin Society
NAFTA	North American Free Trade Agreement
NAM	National Association of Manufacturers
NBER	National Bureau of Economic Research
NIEO	New International Economic Order
TPRC	Trade Policy Research Centre
UCT	University of Cape Town
UNCTAD	United Nations Conference on Trade and Development
WTO	World Trade Organization

GLOBALISTS

Introduction

Thinking in World Orders

A nation may beget its own barbarian invaders.

—WILHELM RÖPKE, 1942

By the end of the twentieth century it was a common belief that free-market ideology had conquered the world. The importance of states was receding in the push and pull of the global economy. At the World Economic Forum at Davos in 1995, an iconic location of the era, U.S. president Bill Clinton observed that "24-hour markets can respond with blinding speed and sometimes ruthlessness."[1] Chancellor Gerhard Schröder referenced the "storms of globalization" as he announced a major reform of the welfare system in reunified Germany. The social market economy, he said, must modernize or it would "be modernized by the unchecked forces of the market."[2] Politics had moved to the passive tense. The only actor was the global economy. U.S. Federal Reserve chairman Alan Greenspan put the point most bluntly in 2007 when he declared, "It hardly makes any difference who will be the next president. The world is governed by market forces."[3] To its critics, this looked like a new empire with "globalization substituting for colonialism."[4] To its champions, it was a world in which goods and capital, if not people, flowed according to the logic of supply and demand, creating prosperity—or at least opportunity—for all.[5] This philosophy of the rule of market forces was labeled "neoliberalism" by its critics. Neoliberals, we were told, believed in global laissez-faire: self-regulating markets, shrunken states, and the reduction of all human motivation to the one-dimensional rational self-interest of *Homo economicus*. The neoliberal globalists, it was claimed, conflated free-market capitalism with democracy and fantasized about a single world market without borders.

My narrative corrects this storyline. It shows that self-described neoliberals did not believe in self-regulating markets as autonomous entities. They did not see democracy and capitalism as synonymous. They did not see humans as motivated only by economic rationality. They sought neither the disappearance of the state nor the disappearance of borders. And they did not see the world only through the lens of the individual. In fact, the foundational neoliberal insight is comparable to that of John Maynard Keynes and Karl Polanyi: the market does not and cannot take care of itself. The core of twentieth-century neoliberal theorizing involves what they called the meta-economic or extra-economic conditions for safeguarding capitalism at the scale of the entire world. I show that the neoliberal project focused on designing institutions—not to liberate markets but to encase them, to inoculate capitalism against the threat of democracy, to create a framework to contain often-irrational human behavior, and to reorder the world after empire as a space of competing states in which borders fulfill a necessary function.

How can we make sense of neoliberalism—and can we even use that name? For years many have claimed that the term is virtually meaningless. "There is for all practical purposes, no such thing" as neoliberal theory, one scholar claimed recently.[6] In 2016, however, the International Monetary Fund (IMF), making international headlines, not only identified neoliberalism as a coherent doctrine but asked if the policy package of privatization, deregulation, and liberalization had been "oversold."[7] *Fortune* reported at the time that "even the IMF now admits neoliberalism has failed."[8] The magazine's suggestion that this was a new development was somewhat inaccurate. The policies associated with neoliberalism had been challenged—at least rhetorically—for two decades. An early expression of doubt came from Joseph Stiglitz after the Asian financial crisis of 1997.[9] World Bank chief economist from 1997 to 2000 and winner of the Nobel Memorial Prize in Economics, Stiglitz became a vocal critic of neoliberal globalization. In the late 1990s other critics declared that the unregulated global free market was "the last utopia"—and the international financial institutions partly agreed.[10] They dropped their doctrinaire opposition to capital controls, the very subject of the 2016 *Fortune* article. The World Trade Organization (WTO) underwent a similar facelift. After protests shut down its 1999 meeting, it pivoted to emphasize the human side of globalization.

Even though the policies described as neoliberal had long been criticized, the IMF report was still significant for recognizing the label "neoliberalism." The term appeared poised for the mainstream, appearing in the *Financial Times,* the *Guardian,* and other newspapers.[11] Also in 2016, the Adam Smith Institute, founded in 1977 and a source of guidance for Margaret Thatcher, "came out as neoliberals," in their words, shedding their former moniker, "libertarian."[12] "Globalist in outlook" was one of the principles they claimed for themselves. In 2017 the director of the Walter Eucken Institute in Germany publicly defended the honor of what he called "classic neoliberalism" and its call for "a strong state standing above the interests of lobbies."[13] It seemed that for both critics and proponents "the movement that dared not speak its own name" could now be named.[14] This was a clarifying development. Labeling neoliberalism helps us to see it as one body of thought and one mode of governance among others—as a form or variety of regulation rather than its radical Other.

In the last decade, extraordinary efforts have been made to historicize neoliberalism and its prescriptions for global governance, and to transform the "political swearword" or "anti-liberal slogan" into a subject of rigorous archival research.[15] My narrative knits together two strands of scholarship that have remained strangely disconnected. The first strand is the work to trace the intellectual history of the neoliberal movement.[16] The second strand is the study of neoliberal globalist theory by social scientists, not historians. Scholars have shown that the term "neoliberalism" was coined first at the Walter Lippmann Colloquium in Paris in 1938 as a way to describe the desire of the gathered economists, sociologists, journalists, and business leaders to "renovate" liberalism.[17] As one scholar argues, one of the most defensible ways to study neoliberalism is as "an organized group of individuals exchanging ideas within a common intellectual framework."[18] Historians have focused, in particular, on the Mont Pèlerin Society, formed by F. A. Hayek and others in 1947, as a group of like-minded intellectuals and policy makers who would meet periodically to discuss world affairs and the contemporary condition of the political cause to which they were devoted. This group was not without its internal rifts, as the works cited have shown. Apart from monetary policy and development economics, though, the question of international and global governance has been surprisingly neglected in these histories.[19] Although there were differences among these thinkers, my contention is that we can discern the broad strokes of a coherent prescription for world order in their writings and actions. Globalizing the ordoliberal principle of "thinking in orders," their project of thinking in world orders offered a set of proposals designed to defend the world economy from a democracy that became global only in the twentieth century—producing a state of affairs and a set of challenges that their predecessors, the classical liberals, could never have predicted.

The clearest-eyed academic observers of the neoliberal philosophy of global ordering have been not historians but social scientists. For the last twenty years, political scientists and sociologists have elaborated a sophisticated analysis of the neoliberal project. They have identified efforts to insulate market actors from democratic pressures in a series of institutions from the IMF and the World Bank to port authorities and central banks worldwide, including the European Central Bank, governance structures like the European Union, trade treaties like the North American Free Trade Agreement (NAFTA), and the WTO. They have also seen efforts to insulate in the expansion of international investment law designed to protect foreign investors from diverse forms of expropriation and to provide a parallel global legal system known as the transnational law merchant.[20] They have traced the emergence of an "offshore world" of tax havens and the proliferation of zones of many types, all designed to provide safe harbor for capital, free from fear of infringement by policies of progressive taxation or redistribution.[21] "Insulation of markets" is a useful metaphorical description of the aim of neoliberalism as a specific institution-building project rather than as a nebulous "logic" or "rationality." The work of social scientists in defining this insulation has been rigorous, but their history of neoliberal theory has been less so—they often give intellectuals such as Hayek and Milton Friedman only walk-on roles.[22] The ideas of such neoliberal luminaries are said to inspire or "suggest" certain forms of global and regional governance, yet we are left to wonder how this influence actually happened and where the ideas came from in the first place. The name of Hayek, in particular, often operates as a free-floating signifier more than an index to an actual historical figure. Some label the European Union a "Hayekian federation," for example, while others call the desire to *leave* the EU a hope of "reviving Hayek's dream."[23] What exactly did thinkers like Hayek wish for, and where and when did the ideas of neoliberal globalism originate? I locate a key point of origin of neoliberal globalist thinking within the epochal shift of order that occurred at the end of empire. Decolonization, I argue, was central to the emergence of the neoliberal model of world governance.

ENCASEMENT, NOT LIBERATION

One of the obstacles to understanding neoliberals on their own terms has been an excessive reliance on a set of ideas borrowed from the Hungarian economic historian Karl Polanyi, who has become, as one scholar notes, "after Michel Foucault, probably the most popular theorist among social scientists today."[24] Across many attempts to account for neoliberal globalization, the retroactive influence of Polanyi's 1944 book *The Great Transformation* is marked. According to those who adapt Polanyi's narrative, the "market fundamentalism" of neoliberals led them to seek to "disembed" the "natural" market from society and thus realize their utopian dream of a "self-regulating market." It is noted routinely that Polanyi was actually writing about the nineteenth century, but critics often make the leap to say that this was a critique of neoliberalism before the fact. Of a piece with the Polanyian language is the idea that the goal of neoliberals is to liberate markets or set them free. The otherwise uncommon adjective "unfettered" is attached habitually to "markets" as both neoliberal goal and putative reality.[25] Against the intention of the authors of neoliberal theory, this metaphor essentializes the object of critique: the market becomes a thing capable of being liberated by agents, instead of being, as neoliberals themselves believed, a set of relationships that rely on an institutional framework.[26]

The applications of Polanyi's categories have led to key insights, and I build on the efforts of scholars since the turn of the millennium to conceive of the neoliberal project as "a simultaneous roll-back *and roll-out* of state functions."[27] Adapting Polanyi, some scholars have even written of "embedded neoliberalism."[28] Yet if we want to understand neoliberal thought on its own terms—an essential first step of critique—we should not be misled by the notion of a self-regulating market liberated from the state. Looking at the writings of the neoliberals concerned with global order, one discovers the importance of the fact that Polanyi was their contemporary. Like him, they saw the Great Depression as evidence that the old form of capitalism was unworkable, and they set about theorizing the broader conditions required for its survival. In the words of one scholar, both Hayek and Polanyi were "concerned with socio-institutional responses to the free market."[29] In fact, Hayek developed his own idea of "free markets as socially embedded."[30] If we place too much emphasis on the category of market fundamentalism, we will fail to notice that the real focus of neoliberal proposals is not on the market per se but on redesigning states, laws, and other institutions to protect the market. Legal scholars have been clear on the increasing "legalization" or "juridicization" of world trade.[31] Focusing on Hayek and his collaborators allows us to understand this within the intellectual history of neoliberal thought.

A 2006 article in the leading neoliberal journal *Ordo* clarified that the founders of the neoliberal movement "added the syllable 'neo'" because they recognized the need to establish "the role of the state both more clearly and differently," including increased attention to the "legal-institutional framework."[32] Far from having a utopian belief in the market as operating independently of human intervention, "neoliberals . . . have pointed to the extra-economic conditions for a free economic system."[33] It is an inadequately acknowledged fact that the focus of both German ordoliberalism and Austrian economics is not on the economy as such but on the institutions creating a space for the economy.[34] When Hayek referred to the "self-regulating forces of the economy"—as he did, for example, in his inaugural lecture when taking up his position in Freiburg—he followed immediately with a discussion of the need for a "framework" for the economy.[35] The overwhelming focus of his work was on the problem of designing what he called, in his next book after *The Road to Serfdom*, a "constitution of liberty."[36]

"Hayek saw clearly," one scholar writes, "that the market is a social institution embedded in a great variety of institutions in which it gains meaning."[37] Hayek himself dismissed the idea that he was calling for a "minimal state."[38] Although the shorthand phrase "strong state and free market" has its usefulness in explaining neoliberalism, how one defines strength is not self-evident.[39] One scholar has argued that it makes little sense to think of the state in quantitative rather than qualitative terms; the question of "how much" state should be replaced by "what kind" of state.[40] The chapters that follow provide an exposition through time of the neoliberal idea that markets are not natural but are products of the political construction of institutions to encase them. Markets buttress the repository of cultural values that are a necessary but not sufficient condition for markets' continued existence.

GENEVA SCHOOL, NOT CHICAGO SCHOOL

In 1983 one of Hayek's students, the leading international economic lawyer Ernst-Ulrich Petersmann, wrote, "The common starting point of the neoliberal economic theory is the insight that in any well-functioning market economy the 'invisible hand' of market competition must by necessity be complemented by the 'visible hand' of the law." He listed the well-known neoliberal schools of thought: the Freiburg School, birthplace of German ordoliberalism, and home to Walter Eucken and Franz Böhm; the Chicago School, identified with Milton Friedman, Aaron Director, Richard Posner, and others; and the Cologne School of Ludwig Müller-Armack. Then he cited a virtual unknown: the Geneva School.[41]

Who or what was the Geneva School? The following chapters present a narrative about a strain of neoliberalism that has been neglected by historians. I introduce a set of thinkers who have not been central in the English literature and reframe those like Hayek who have been. I adopt and expand the label "Geneva School" to describe a genus of neoliberal thought that stretches from the seminar rooms of fin-de-siècle Vienna to the halls of the WTO in fin-de-millennium Geneva. My goal in introducing the term is neither to invite hairsplitting about inclusion nor to litigate the roster of its members. Rather, my intention is to remedy the confusion produced when diverse thinkers are contained under the single umbrella term "neoliberal." The Geneva School offers provisional but helpful illumination of those aspects of neoliberal thought related to world order that have remained more or less in the shadows. As proposed here, the Geneva School includes thinkers who held academic positions in Geneva, Switzerland, among them Wilhelm Röpke, Ludwig von Mises, and Michael Heilperin; those who pursued or presented key research there, including Hayek, Lionel Robbins, and Gottfried Haberler; and those who worked at the General Agreement on Tariffs and Trade (GATT), such as Jan Tumlir, Frieder Roessler, and Petersmann himself. Although they shared affinities with the Freiburg School, Geneva School neoliberals transposed the ordoliberal idea of "the economic constitution"—or the totality of rules governing economic life—to the scale beyond the nation.

The distinct contributions of the Geneva School to neoliberal thought are often neglected in English-language discussions. Most histories of the neoliberal movement begin in continental Europe with the meetings in the 1930s and 1940s but shift their gaze to the United States and Great Britain ahead of the neoliberal breakthrough of Reagan and Thatcher in the 1980s. This shift is accompanied by a pointed focus on the Chicago School, and Friedman in particular. Even though some welcome attention is now being given to the field of law and economics and the public choice theory of James M. Buchanan and others of the Virginia School, the overall tendency has been toward an understanding of neoliberal thought that tilts toward the Anglo-American side.[42] What this misses is the importance of the contributions of those who remained in continental Europe or who, like Hayek, returned to Europe. Correcting this elision is critical because it was the European neoliberals who were most attentive to questions of international order.

My narrative presents a vision of neoliberal globalism viewed from Central Europe, because it was Central European neoliberals who most consistently looked at the world as a whole. Both Chicago School and Virginia School thinkers exhibited the peculiarly American quality of ignoring the rest of the world while assuming that America was a working model of it.[43] European neoliberals did not have this luxury, as they existed for most of the century under the influence of varying levels of U.S. hegemony. It made sense that Central European neoliberals were precocious theorists of world order. Their countries did not enjoy a vast domestic market like that of the United States, so they were forced to be more attentive to the question of access to the world market through either trade or annexation. The early end of empire in Central Europe after the First World War also required them to contemplate strategies for balancing state power with economic interdependence. Although the story begins in Vienna, the Swiss city on the lake, Geneva—eventually the home of the WTO—became the spiritual capital of the group of thinkers who sought to solve the riddle of postimperial order.

Most historians would claim that the question of world order had been more or less settled early in the century in favor of the idea of national self-determination offered by both Vladimir Lenin and Woodrow Wilson and demanded by anticolonial actors worldwide. In that view, the principle of self-determination, thwarted at Versailles by the unwillingness of the United States and European empires to live up to their own rhetoric, and waylaid by the fascist expansionism of Italy and Germany and later the Soviet control over its satellite states, eventually triumphed with the wave of decolonization after the Second World War and, most recently, with the end of apartheid in South Africa and Soviet rule in Eastern Europe. Geneva School neoliberals disagreed with this narrative. To their mind, commitments to national sovereignty and autonomy were dangerous if taken seriously. They were stalwart critics of national sovereignty, believing that after empire, nations must remain embedded in an international institutional order that safeguarded capital and protected its right to move throughout the world. The cardinal sin of the twentieth century was the belief in unfettered national independence, and the neoliberal world order required enforceable isonomy—or "same law," as Hayek would later call it—against the illusion of autonomy, or "own law."

Geneva School neoliberals reconciled the tension between the world economy and the world of nations through their own distinct geography. Their global imaginary was sketched by the erstwhile Nazi jurist Carl Schmitt in 1950. Schmitt proposed that there was not one world but two. One was the world partitioned into bounded, territorial states where governments ruled over human beings. This he called the world of *imperium*, using the Roman legal term. The other was the world of property, where people owned things, money, and land scattered across the earth. This was the world of *dominium*. The doubled world of modern capitalism coalesced in the nineteenth century. The ubiquity of foreign investment had made it routine for people to own all or part of enterprises in countries where they were not citizens and had never even set foot. Money worked almost anywhere and could be exchanged into and out of major currencies at the fixed rates of the gold standard. Contracts were enforced universally by written and unwritten codes of business conduct. Even military occupation did not affect private property. Unlike earlier eras of plunder, the land or business was still yours after the enemy army had swept through. To Schmitt, the division between dominium and imperium was more fundamental than the purely political distinction of foreign and domestic. The most important border did not halve the world like an orange into East and West, or North and South, but preserved overlapping wholes in suspension, like an orange's pith and peel. "Over, under and beside the state-political borders of what appeared to be a purely political international law between states," he wrote, "spread a free, i.e. non-state sphere of economy permeating everything: a global economy."[44]

Schmitt meant the doubled world as something negative, an impingement on the full exercise of national sovereignty. But neoliberals felt he had offered the best description of the world they wanted to conserve. Wilhelm Röpke, who taught in Geneva for nearly thirty years, believed that exactly this division would be the basis for a liberal world order. The ideal neoliberal order would maintain the balance between the two global spheres through an enforceable world law, creating a "minimum of constitutional order" and a "separation of the state-public sphere from the private domain."[45] In a lecture he delivered at the Academy of International Law at The Hague in 1955, Röpke emphasized the importance of the division while also pointing to its paradox. "To diminish national sovereignty is most emphatically one of the urgent needs of our time," he argued, but "the excess of sovereignty should be abolished instead of being transferred to a higher political and geographical unit."[46]

Scaling national government up to the planet, creating a global government, was no solution. The puzzle of the neoliberal century was to find the right institutions to sustain the often strained balance between the economic world and the political world. The consequences of the doubled globe for reimagining the world after empire are dismissed all too easily in narratives of modern global history as the passage from colonial subjugation to national independence. Few thinkers engaged with the consequences of this doubled world more than the group of economists and lawyers described in these pages. Convinced from the beginning of the century that there was and could only be a single world economy, they strove to reconcile mutual economic dependency with political self-determination.

In his Hague lecture, Röpke suggested that the solution could be found in the space between economics and law.[47] As the following chapters show, from its beginnings Geneva School neoliberalism has been less a discipline of economics than a discipline of statecraft and law. More than making markets, these neoliberals have concentrated on making market enforcers. When Hayek moved from the University of Chicago to Freiburg in 1962, he became the heir of the homegrown German law-and-economics tradition of ordoliberalism, and most scholars recognize him as an ally, if not a member, of the Freiburg School.[48] His 1960 work *The Constitution of Liberty* and even more so his 1970s trilogy *Law, Legislation and Liberty* (written during his time in Freiburg) justify this designation, because he became ever more focused on finding a legal and institutional fix for the disruptive effects of democracy on market processes. Unlike the ordoliberals, who called for an "economic constitution" at the level of the nation, the Geneva School neoliberals called for an economic constitution for the world. I argue that we can understand the proposal of the Geneva School as a rethinking of ordoliberalism at the scale of the world. We might call it ordoglobalism.[49]

Geneva School neoliberals offered a blueprint for globalism based on institutions of multitiered governance that are insulated from democratic decision making and charged with maintaining the balance between the political world of imperium and the economic world of dominium. Dominium is not a space of laissez-faire or noninterventionism but is instead an object of constant maintenance, litigation, design, and care. At the core of the Geneva School imaginary was a vision for what Hayek first saw in the Habsburg Empire—a model of what he called "a double government, a cultural and an economic government."[50] Geneva School neoliberals prescribed neither an obliteration of politics by economics nor the dissolution of states into a global marketplace but a carefully structured and regulated settlement between the two.

As noted earlier, social scientists have tended to use the metaphor of insulation to describe the relationship between state and market in neoliberalism. This tendency is ironic. As we will see, neoliberals from the 1930s to the 1970s used a geographic version of the metaphor to attack the belief in the possibility of "economic insulation," meaning a degree of self-sufficiency that would buffer nations from shocks of change in global markets. Neoliberals described this devotion to self-sufficiency as having the capacity to "destroy the universal society" and "shatter the world." With the switch to an electricity metaphor in the 1990s, though, it became a neoliberal norm. One of Hayek's successors at Freiburg wrote, "Hayek's principal argument is his call for an institutional arrangement that effectively insulates the rule-making authority from the short term demands of day-to-day government."[51] The semantic change was symptomatic of a larger transformation of world economic imagination: from thinking of the global economy in terms of islands *(insulae)* and territories to imagining it in terms of a unitary circuitry of a wired world. What is insulated now is not the end target of the shock of the price signal but the wire that transmits it. Yet even this metaphor is ultimately unsatisfying. The neoliberal goal is more absolute than the dampening implied by insulation. What neoliberals seek is not a partial but a complete protection of private capital rights, and the ability of supranational judiciary bodies like the European Court of Justice and the WTO to override national legislation that might disrupt the global rights of capital. For this reason, I propose the metaphor of *encasement* rather than mere insulation of the world economy as the imaginary telos of the neoliberal project—a project in which states play an indispensable role.

This narrative places neoliberalism in history. It traces neoliberal globalism as an intellectual project that began in the ashes of the Habsburg Empire and climaxed in the creation of the WTO. It shows that ordoglobalism was a way of living with the fact that the nation-state had become an enduring fixture of the modern world. What neoliberalism sought over the decades was an institutional encasement for the world of nations that would prevent catastrophic breaches of the boundaries between imperium and dominium. The right institutions, laws, and binding commitments would safeguard the well-being of the whole. This is not a narrative of triumph—the sputtering of the WTO is at best a pyrrhic victory for the specific strain of neoliberal globalism I describe in the following chapters. Instead the narrative shows that neoliberalism as a body of thought clearly originated in an early twentieth-century crisis about how to organize the whole earth.

MILITANT GLOBALISM, NOT MARKET FUNDAMENTALISM

Ordoglobalism was haunted by two puzzles across the twentieth century: first, how to rely on democracy, given democracy's capacity to destroy itself; and second, how to rely on nations, given nationalism's capacity to "disintegrate the world." The first tension is familiar to students of modern Europe. It is well known that democracy can have illiberal outcomes and can even lead to its own self-annihilation by democratic means. Many, especially in Germany, believed that the experience of the period between the two world wars had taught that democracy must be limited. It must be subject to checks and restrictions that would prevent illiberal outcomes. The idea of "militant democracy" was theorized by political scientists in the 1930s and put into practice in postwar Western Europe.[52] Constitutional courts, in particular, played a key role in fending off challenges to the liberal order from left and right. Many thinkers agreed that liberal states must show what one social democratic politician called "the courage of intolerance" toward those who rejected the constitutional order.[53]

The confrontation with mass democracy was also at the heart of the century for neoliberals. On the one hand, they embraced democracy for providing a means of peaceful change and a space for evolutionary discovery beneficial to the system at large—thus proving mistaken those who describe neoliberals as opposed to democracy as such. On the other hand, democracy bore the seed of destruction for the totality. Reflecting on the challenges to the liberal order posed by the demands of a politically mobilized working class, Röpke observed in 1942 that "a nation may beget its own barbarian invaders."[54] Histories of the neoliberal movement written from the U.S. and British perspectives—as prehistories of the Thatcher and Reagan administrations—miss the specifically post-fascist context of neoliberal prescriptions for domestic and international organization.[55] In fact, neoliberals were key articulators of what Jan-Werner Müller calls "constrained democracy."[56] The tension was always between advocating democracy for peaceful change and condemning its capacity to upend order.

If historians miss the post-fascist context, they miss the postcolonial context too. It is seldom observed that Hayek first turned his efforts toward redesigning representative government—risking the charge of inconsistency by his own confession in adopting a "made" rather than a "grown" constitution—in response to the emergence of "new nations" in the wake of decolonization.[57] His model constitution was not intended, he insisted, for Britain but for both "new nations" and fascist states such as Salazar's Portugal. Speaking of new nations as well as countries in South America with political traditions "not entirely adequate" for democracy, he wrote, "I believe that limiting the powers of democracy in these new parts of the world is the only chance of preserving democracy in those parts of the world. If democracies do not limit their own powers, they will be destroyed."[58] Historians have chronically overlooked the fact that the end of global empires was essential to the emergence of neoliberalism as an intellectual movement.

Alongside the confrontation with mass democracy, the related tension between the nation and the world was equally as central for neoliberals.

The nation could be useful insofar as it provided services of stabilization (which would often include restrictions to migration) and cultivated legitimacy in the political sphere. But like democracy, it also bore the risk of tipping into excess. Thus, it needed to be constrained just as democracy did. Neoliberals believed in what could be called militant globalism or, adapting Müller's term, constrained nationalism—the need for a set of institutional safeguards and legal constraints to prevent nation-states from transgressing their commitments to the world economic order. Neoliberals were proponents of an institutional framework in which the world economy would survive threats to its holistic integrity. Militant globalism would not displace national states but would work with and through them to ensure the proper functioning of the whole.

As will become clear in the following chapters, it is wrong to see neoliberals as critics of the state per se but correct to see them as perennial skeptics of the *nation*-state. In 1979 Hayek wrote, "It seems to me that in this century our attempts to create an international government capable of assuring peace have generally approached the task from the wrong end: creating large numbers of specialized authorities aiming at particular regulations rather than aiming at a true international law which would limit the powers of national governments to harm each other."[59] He described this as the "dethronement of politics," but it is just as obviously the dethronement of the nation. Just as proponents of militant democracy perceived a need to constrain democracy, proponents of militant globalism perceived a need to constrain nation-states and set limits on their exercise of sovereignty.

Militant globalism bears resemblances to what Hermann Heller in 1933 called "authoritarian liberalism."[60] Like him, neoliberals emphasized the need to override popular decisions when they controvert what is seen as the superior principle of the order at large. Scholars have adapted Heller's term to understand the logic of the European Union.[61] An advantage of militant globalism as an explanatory category is its attention to the question of scale, which is neglected in many treatments of neoliberal thought. As the following chapters show, the world frame was not incidental to the prescriptions of many neoliberal thinkers. Nor was their vision particularly amenable to a logic of "dimensions variable."

For the members of the Geneva School, who were attentive to problems of global systemic interdependence, only the world scale was enough. For them, capitalism at the global scale was the sine qua non of the normative neoliberal order.

I argue that the encasement of the market in a spirit of militant globalism is a better way of describing the international dimensions of the neoliberal project than the Polanyian terms of disembedding the economy according to a doctrine of market fundamentalism. Polanyi's ideas provide an elegant parable whereby the capitalist world economy progressively eliminates barriers to its own functioning, to the point that it destroys its own capacity for self-reproduction. In this narrative, the market is omnivorous, relentlessly transforming land, labor, and money into commodities, until the basis for social life has been destroyed. Capitalism, according to this analysis, needs an opposition to save it from itself. By confronting and absorbing challenges, from workers' insurance to the welfare state, capitalism secures the social conditions that allow it to persist.[62] As the following chapters show, an essential aspect of the project of neoliberalism was determining how to preempt the opposition by building an extra-economic framework that would secure the continued existence of capitalism. Rather than a self-regulating market and an economy that eats everything, what the neoliberals envisaged and fought for was an ongoing settlement between imperium and dominium while pushing policies to deepen the power of competition to shape and direct human life. The normative neoliberal world is not a borderless market without states but a doubled world kept safe from mass demands for social justice and redistributive equality by the guardians of the economic constitution.

THE THREE RUPTURES OF THE NEOLIBERAL CENTURY

A neoliberal perspective on the history of the twentieth century amounts to an alternative account of the modern era. In a neoliberal history of the century, decolonization began in 1919; fascism looked promising to some until it raised tariff walls; the Cold War was secondary to the war against the Global New Deal; the end of apartheid was seen by some as a tragedy; and countries were secondary entities subordinate to the totality of the globe. It is a history where the so-called golden age of postwar capitalism was actually a dark age, governed by Keynesian delusions and misguided fantasies of global economic equality. It is about the development of a planet linked by money, information, and goods where the signature achievement of the century was not an international community, a global civil society, or the deepening of democracy, but an ever-integrating object called the world economy and the institutions designated to encase it.

The following chapters tell the story of the twentieth century through the eyes of neoliberals who did not see capitalism and democracy as mutually reinforcing but who instead faced democracy as a problem. Democracy meant successive waves of clamoring demanding masses, always threatening to push the functioning market economy off its tracks. For neoliberals, the democratic threat took many forms, from the white working class to the non-European decolonizing world. The century was marked by three ruptures, each accompanying an expansion in what German ordoliberal Walter Eucken called in 1932 "the democratization of the world."[63] The first, and most foundational, rupture was the First World War, when nations ceased to uphold the most important condition of world trade and investment—the gold standard. The period after the war brought a crucial blurring of the division between the political and economic worlds and what neoliberals called a "politicization" of the economic, as universal suffrage spread across the West and the new nations of East Central Europe mistook the legitimate goal of independence for the hopeless project of self-sufficiency, dissolving the former regional division of labor, which itself modeled a larger interdependence of the world.

The second rupture came with the Great Depression, beginning in 1929. The thinkers who called themselves neoliberals after 1938 saw the futility of restoring the lost unity of the world economy through academic research and the coordination of international statistical experts. Not only was the task fundamentally political, but it could *only* be political. It is well known that many of the leading figures of the neoliberal movement, including Mises, Hayek, and Haberler, began their careers as researchers of what was called the business cycle, or the patterns by which economic crises occurred at regular intervals. Less frequently observed is the turn of this group away from statistics and business cycle research by the end of the 1930s. I argue that they concluded that the world economy was sublime, beyond representation and quantification. This conclusion turned them away from the documentation and analysis of the economy as such and toward the design of institutions necessary to sustain and protect the sacrosanct space of the world economy.

Hayek began to realize in the 1930s that the dispersal of knowledge throughout an entire market economy was so complete that no individual could ever gain a functional overview of it. The shock of the 1930s brought with it the realization that the world economy was basically unknowable. Any task of reconstructing the relationship between the two worlds—of many nations and one economy—would have to be a project of redesigning the state and, increasingly after 1945, of redesigning the law. The essence of this project was multitiered governance or neoliberal federalism. In the wake of the mystification of the world economy, the Geneva School neoliberals' most important field of influence was not in economics per se but in international law and international governance.

The century's third rupture came not so much with the Second World War or the Cold War—neither of which have much of a presence in the neoliberal century—but with the revolt of the Global South in the 1970s. The oil shock of 1973–1974 placed postcolonial actors at center stage. Robust demands for economic redistribution and stabilization were enshrined in the Declaration of a New International Economic Order championed by the world's poorer nations and passed by the UN General Assembly in 1974. Confronting both the Global South and the boom in computer-aided models of global reform in the 1970s, the Geneva School developed their own vision of a world economy without numbers—a world of information and rules. For the Geneva School, the period from the 1970s to the 1990s was about rethinking the world economy as an information processor and global institutions as the necessary calibrators of that processor. Trade rules, enforced through internationally enforceable constitutional laws, would ensure stability.

The rise of Geneva School globalism had little to do with the supposed free-market utopianism or market fundamentalism of which it is often accused. It was clear to the intellectuals of the 1930s that the choice was not between a governed nation and an ungoverned world economy. One of the surprises in the narrative I present may be to find thinkers like Hayek and Mises, who are commonly described as libertarian, speaking matter-of-factly about the need for various forms of international and even global governance. The withering away of the relative influence of national states was always to be accompanied by the corresponding strengthening of supranational institutions. The core of ordoglobalism is its own version of what Polanyi called re-embedding the market. The crucial difference between him and the neoliberals is the ends to which the market is being re-embedded. For Polanyi, it was to restore a measure of humanity and social justice. For neoliberals, it was to prevent state projects of egalitarian redistribution and secure competition, alternatively defined as the optimal functioning of the price-signaling system.

VERTICAL FIXES FOR A DISINTEGRATING WORLD

The twentieth century is commonly portrayed as the period of the triumph of neoliberalism. The century had proved neoliberals right, it seemed. All gods other than capitalism had failed. Communism had ended in spectacular dissolution. Despite their apparent victory, however, Geneva School neoliberals throughout the twentieth century were haunted by a vision of a world disintegrating. Sometimes accused of having a smug confidence in the resilience of capitalism, they instead were troubled by the possibility that the global conditions that sustain a capitalist world economy were fundamentally under threat. The dominant emotion felt by the neoliberals at the heart of my narrative was not hubris but anxiety. They expended all of their efforts in attempting to design fixes to stabilize what they saw as a precarious arrangement.

Although I focus on a relatively small number of individuals, I do not ascribe to them a superhuman strength or causality or treat their texts as holy writ. Neoliberal thought has not mapped directly onto reality in the era since the 1980s. I do not nominate the writings of Hayek or any other thinker as a Rosetta Stone for descrying an internal logic to a necessarily complex reality. Policies and rhetorical strategies enacted since the Thatcher and Reagan victories reflect diverse forces and constituencies that must be considered individually and that resist easy generalization. I do not attempt to deliver either the final word on neoliberalism or a magic bullet theory to summarize decades of ever-morphing global capitalism.

Instead I use the biographies of Geneva School neoliberals as a way to weave through a discussion of a series of institutions that were designed to encase the global market from interference by national governments. The following chapters offer a historical field guide to these institutions, for some of which neoliberal intellectuals were the original architects, but for most of which they played the role of advocate, adopter, or adapter. Hayek's demand to "dethrone politics" was only the first part of the neoliberal fix. The second was not to enthrone the economy but to encase it and find institutional forms to enforce the division. Neoliberals repeatedly sought solutions to the problem of order in a vertical move. The fix was found, time and again, in a scale shift for governance, including in the League of Nations, international investment law, blueprints for supranational federation, systems of weighted franchise, European competition law, and ultimately the WTO itself.

Neoliberalism is sometimes described as descending from a mountaintop, the Swiss peak of Mont Pèlerin in particular. Neoliberals themselves promote the impression of a lofty intellectual detachment through their references to Alexis de Tocqueville, Immanuel Kant, J. S. Mill, and Lord Acton. As we will see, though, the neoliberal luminaries were actually involved in very practical activity—the application of economic knowledge—getting their hands dirty in advising business, pressuring governments, drawing up charts, and gathering statistics. Across the century, neoliberals saw different bodies as potential enforcers for the world market. The following narrative begins with the period just after the First World War. Globalization talk before the Great War produced many of the tropes that still echo today. Economists spoke of the death of distance, the obsolescence of borders, the impossibility of autonomous domestic policy. That period also introduced a cluster of arguments that are central to the neoliberal imagination. The world economy was *unitary* and could not be divided meaningfully into constituent nations or empires. It was *interdependent,* because industrial nations relied on foreign markets for both raw materials and sales, and fluctuations of supply and demand were felt worldwide. It was *infrastructurally homogeneous,* comprising a material network of railroads, telegraph lines, and steamships as well as standard conventions of law, finance, and production. At the same time, it was *functionally heterogeneous,* because different regions specialized in economic activity that suited their particular endowments, producing a greater international division of labor and thus a more efficient use of the world's resources. Most importantly, the world economy had a *supranational* force, capable of overriding attempts by individual polities to influence it.

The International Chamber of Commerce (ICC) was an economically internationalist body that sought to document and propagate the idea of a single world economy. The ICC gathered international economic statistics and advocated for the removal of barriers to trade and the free movement of capital. Immediately following the First World War and the dissolution of the Habsburg and Ottoman Empires, Mises and his circle thought it looked like a good partner. Mises himself was a delegate to the ICC, and the first generation of Austrian neoliberals all worked at the Vienna Chamber of Commerce. From the beginning, the doctrine of neoliberalism reflected an intermingling with the needs of its patrons in the business community. The "world of walls" (Chapter 1) that emerged after the First World War became a counterpoint against which neoliberals imagined their open world economy.

In the 1920s the League of Nations also appeared to some of the future neoliberals as a supranational authority that might be capable of ensuring the conditions of capitalism's doubled world. Mises, Hayek, Haberler, and Röpke helped produce the first synoptic portraits of "a world of numbers" (Chapter 2) in their cooperation with the League in Geneva. By the late 1930s, though, the core of the neoliberal movements responded to the rise of what they called economic nationalism, especially in Central Europe, by denying that the economy could be seen at all. Hayek's position that the economy could not be apprehended by the senses was inconsistent with the emerging field of macroeconomics, but it also realigned the project of neoliberalism: from talking about the economy to talking about the framework that encased it.

In the 1930s and 1940s, neoliberals devised their own schemes for large-scale order, drawing up plans for international federation in blueprints of double government that would encase the ineffable market. In place of empire, Robbins, Hayek, and Mises proposed "a world of federations" (Chapter 3).

The Bretton Woods system devised in 1944 offered scarce hope to neoliberals that it would function as a guardian of the world economy. The United Nations' solution to the end of empire—granting votes to the proliferating nations of the non-European world—threatened the balance between dominium and imperium. Working again with the ICC, neoliberals helped craft a universal investment code and bilateral investment treaties that they hoped would safeguard capital in "a world of rights" (Chapter 4).

The need to defend the world economy led some neoliberals to seemingly illiberal bedfellows. The case of Augusto Pinochet's Chile is notorious; the neoliberal relationship to apartheid South Africa is less well studied. Here we encounter a split in the Geneva School. Almost all of the neoliberals discussed here rejected race as a category of analysis, especially after 1945, but Wilhelm Röpke is conspicuous for his belief that defending the world economy meant defending Western Christian—and Caucasian—principles against what fellow neoliberal William H. Hutt called "black imperialism."[64] Röpke's postwar belief in "a world of races" (Chapter 5) was in many ways a marked detour from the mainstream of Geneva School neoliberals. Figures such as Hayek, Friedman, and Hutt also criticized the diplomatic isolation of white minority governments in Southern Africa, but for reasons closer to the concerns of this book—namely, the perils of unconstrained democracy and the need to insulate world economic order from the political demands of social justice.

Far more than the segregationist solutions of Southern Africa, the most hopeful enforcer of the economic constitution in the postwar period for Geneva School neoliberals was the European Economic Community. What came into existence with the Treaty of Rome in 1957 was a compromise with Christian democracy, agricultural interests, and socialism, but some neoliberals felt that it offered a potential model for "a world of constitutions" (Chapter 6) that could trump national sovereignty in the name of competition. The multilevel model looked like an institutional means of securing market rights.

In the 1970s, Geneva School neoliberals scaled up the example of Europe to confront the demands of the world's poorer nations for a New International Economic Order (NIEO). Building on Hayek's theories, his students and followers at the GATT constructed a countertheory to the NIEO that they hoped would prevent what they called economic decolonization from disrupting world order from the margins. Hayek's students at the GATT developed an understanding of the global economy as "a world of signals" (Chapter 7) for communicating prices for which binding constitutionalized legal frameworks were necessary to preserve conditions of predictability and stability for individual economic actors. This thinking was an important intellectual stream leading into the creation of the WTO—a crowning victory of the neoliberal project of finding an extra-economic enforcer for the world economy in the twentieth century.

When the GATT moved into the former headquarters of the International Labour Organization in 1977, they renamed the building the Centre William Rappard after the Swiss neoliberal and host of the first Mont Pèlerin Society meeting, who brought Röpke, Mises, Hayek, and Robbins to Geneva in the 1930s and 1940s. When the WTO opened in 1995, it was in this building. The long intellectual prehistory of the high point of the Geneva School of neoliberalism shows that, at its origins, neoliberalism was not only a philosophy of free markets but also a blueprint for double government in capitalism's doubled world. Covering the better part of a century as it does, my account is necessarily incomplete. It focuses on the period from the early 1920s to the early 1980s, mostly ending before the breakthrough of neoliberal policies with the governments of Reagan and Thatcher. It does not explore the worthy topics of the conversion of the IMF and World Bank to the policies that became known as the "Washington Consensus." Similarly absent are the transformations in international monetary governance, including the rise of monetarism, the end of the Bretton Woods system, the introduction of the euro, and changes in central bank policy. This means leaving out the all-important question of finance, which was perhaps the single most important transformation in global capitalism since the 1970s. One reason for the omission is that these topics have been covered comprehensively by other authors, whose excellent work is cited in this Introduction's endnotes.[65] Other reasons are the constraints of space and my desire to tell one story with enough detail to avoid the generalizations that plague the social science literature.

The narrative offered here is a fairly contained story, presented largely through biography, about three generations of thinkers, from the Mises Circle in 1920s Vienna to the international economic lawyers of Geneva who helped theorize the WTO in the 1980s. Its focus is on the specific notion of a double government form designed to encase the respective fields of dominium and imperium. It finds the intellectual origins of neoliberal globalism in the reordering of the world that came at the end of empire and finds the historical roots of paradigms of international economic law and neoliberal constitutionalism more often covered by political scientists and sociologists than historians. Looking at the century from Geneva (rather than Chicago, Washington, or London), we see a strand of thought that held that, in order to survive, the world economy needed laws that limited the autonomy of nations. We see a version of neoliberalism where the core value is not the freedom of the individual but the interdependence of the whole.

It is important to note at the outset that none of the ideas proposed here ever reigned uncontested, and very few had the status of mainstream common sense. The success and failure of neoliberalism as a historical phenomenon cannot be explained only through close study of the writings of its best-known thinkers. I don't make a case for the success or failure of neoliberalism. But I do aim to shed light on a number of moments where neoliberal thought was translated into policy or institutional design through partnerships with politicians, bureaucrats, or businesspeople. As a political project, the many real-world effects of neoliberalism are documentable. One can write their histories. This book offers one such history by putting the neoliberal project into a broader framework than other scholars have provided to date. All but ignored by existing histories, the questions of empire, decolonization, and the world economy were at the heart of the neoliberal project from its inception.

❁ ❁ ❁

The fact that the paradigmatic product of Geneva School neoliberalism—the WTO—has been riven with exceptions, infractions, and ignored rules only shows that the clash of economic ideas is far from finished and that the world economy continues to be redefined.[66] As one historian notes, one of the most striking facts about the elaborate legal regime established to protect private property rights in the postwar period is that "it did not work."[67] The early twenty-first century has been marked by ever more countries refusing investment treaties or withdrawing from existing ones.[68] Ever more countries are choosing not to turn to the IMF for loans, chastened by the punishments delivered by electorates after past programs of austerity imposed by diktat. Visions of national economic sovereignty—and claims made in its name—have proven a harder nut to crack than the more optimistic neoliberal theorists believed it would be.

It should be more obvious than ever that to discuss neoliberal ideas of order, especially at the supranational level, is not to assert neoliberal omnipotence. Since the global financial crisis of 2008, so-called populist movements from left to right have multiplied and taken aim at many of the institutions described in these chapters. In the time it took to write these pages, globalism itself has gone from a rather obscure term of academic analysis to a target of right-wing opprobrium, helping to fuel the campaign of the winning candidate for the world's most powerful office. Globalists, defined (if at all) as a shifting and often shadowy combination of the financial, political, and academic elite, are routinely scapegoated for all that ails the body politic and viewed as specters of an identity dangerously unmoored from the concerns of ordinary people. The following chapters narrate the self-perception of those who would welcome being labeled "globalists." They help bring neoliberalism down to earth by casting both neoliberalism and globalism less as abstract overarching logics of history than as political projects populated by discrete individuals occupying specific places and moments in time. For all of the alternating handwringing and obituary writing of its critics, and the alternating self-congratulation and despair among its celebrants, neoliberal globalism remains one argument among many. What follows is a story, not of a victory, but of an ongoing struggle to determine which principles should govern the world economy, and, by extension, all of our lives.

A World of Walls

> For the liberal, the world does not end at the borders of the state. In his eyes, whatever significance national boundaries have is only incidental and subordinate. His political thinking encompasses the whole of mankind.
>
> —LUDWIG VON MISES, 1927

The end of the First World War delivered the first blow to the world of empires. The Austro-Hungarian Empire, which once sprawled across most of Eastern Europe, was reduced to a wisp of its former self. Austria was one-quarter of its former size and contained one-fifth of its former population. Hungary lost two-thirds of its territory and two-fifths of its population. The Ottoman Empire, which had endured over six centuries and at its height spanned Europe, the Near East, and North Africa, contracted to the peninsula of Turkey, with a footprint across the Bosporus. French and British authorities took over Ottoman territories, including Syria, Iraq, and Palestine, and claimed, at least on paper, to prepare them for self-government. Germany's African and South Pacific colonies were divvied up among the victors (with South Africa co-opting Southwest Africa for itself). These former colonies were now called mandates, with independence deferred to a future date. Although the League of Nations began its life as a "league of empires," it grew to offer a space for new claims from the global margins.[1] Even if the European world powers were far from ready to give up their overseas territories, one could see on the map of Eastern Europe, and hear in the speeches of Woodrow Wilson, V. I. Lenin, and anticolonial intellectuals such as Jawaharlal Nehru and Mao Zedong that a new principle of national self-determination was going global, readying an ambush against the old language of empire.[2]

As the concept of the nation circulated in the 1920s, so did the concept of the world. The term "world economy" entered English in the decade of the "emergence of international society."[3] It came with a raft of other "world" phrases, including "world history," "world literature," "world affairs," and, of course, "world war." Like family members and breathable air, the world economy was discussed most when it was gone. To many, the end of the First World War looked like the end of the world economy. The Austrian economist Ludwig von Mises wrote in 1922 that "shortly before the world war we were in sight of realizing the dream of an ecumenical society. Has the war merely interrupted this development for a brief period or has it utterly destroyed it? Is it conceivable that this development can cease, that society can go backwards?"[4] He wondered: "Who then would rebuild the shattered world?"[5] Liberals saw themselves in the curious position of needing to reconstruct something that had worked partly because it was taken for granted. With the war it became clear that progress was not a one-way street—the world economy could go backward. Economists, states, and businesspeople would have to work together to rebuild the shattered world of global capitalism.

One of the major ruptures in the neoliberal narrative of the twentieth century was the First World War. Scholars have observed that in the course of that war, all belligerent powers "moved in the direction of organized capitalism and war collectivism."[6] Foreign-owned property was seized, command economies replaced market supply and demand, centralized regimes of rationing and resource allocation displaced the price mechanism, and national governments and planning boards demolished the walls of corporate secrecy, intruded into private accounts and affairs of business to gather data about production and distribution, and created what some called "war socialism" and what the German statesman and entrepreneur Walther Rathenau called the *Großwirtschaft*, or "great economy."[7]

In the course of the war, the sacred nature of private property across borders was violated; the space of the private capitalist was desecrated. Private accounts were now part of state knowledge, rendered as inputs into a comprehensive plan for allocating the nation's resources. Nowhere was the collapse of the division between public and private more catastrophic than in the sites of successful socialist revolutions: the Soviet Union in 1917, the Bavarian Soviet republic of 1918, and the Hungarian revolution under Bela Kun. But the era after the First World War saw everywhere a great exposure of corporate secrets—business had to be made visible, and for its own good.

From the liberal perspective, three factors empowered the domain of politics against that of the economy after the war. First, popular sovereignty was strengthened by the generalization of universal male suffrage in Europe and North America, making it more difficult to maintain the gold standard through domestic adjustments borne by ordinary people.[8] Second, the war left a legacy of what liberals saw as misguided confidence in the power of governments to allocate resources. It is no coincidence that one of Hayek and Mises's most important antagonists in Vienna was Otto Neurath, a man who had created a moneyless plan for the Bavarian Republic. Since the war, an economy directed by central authorities looked like a viable alternative. Third, the resolution of the war in the peace treaties of Versailles and St. Germain validated the idea that the nation was the most important category for organizing human affairs. To the group that would become the neoliberals, the era after 1918 was marked by an attempt to reestablish what they saw as the correct balance between the public world of government and the private world of property and contract. Concretely, this translated into a series of projects of capitalist internationalism. There needed to be a respect for private property that trumped national law. Investment must be able to cross borders back and forth without fear of obstacles or expropriation. Capital needed to become cosmopolitan again.

In this chapter I will focus on the Austrian liberals in the Vienna of the 1920s and the institutions where they first practiced their craft and found their political worldview. The two most important international economic institutions of the period were the International Chamber of Commerce (ICC) and the League of Nations. Those two institutions organized the World Economic Conference of 1927, the first economic gathering to take the entire world as its subject. It codified an international opposition to trade obstacles and brought the metaphor of the "tariff wall" into common circulation. In an era when the United States withdrew into relative diplomatic isolation, the League of Nations took the lead in drafting blueprints for global economic governance, a series of conversations in which the later neoliberals Ludwig von Mises, Gottfried Haberler, Wilhelm Röpke, Lionel Robbins, and F. A. Hayek were all directly involved.

One challenge for the institutions was to restore free trade; the other was the domestic obstacle of labor unions. In the same year as the World Economic Conference, Mises was present for the workers' uprising in Vienna, which left close to one hundred people dead and the Palace of Justice in flames. Liberals perceived tariff walls and workers' wage demands as two kinds of barricades in the market. Achieving the liberal ideal required a state that could eliminate obstacles to trade and obstacles to the adjustment of wages. This meant a militant and, when necessary, militarized opposition to the strategies of organized labor to protect their salaries and their state-granted entitlements. The bloody suppression of the 1927 riots assured Mises that the state was willing and able to use any means necessary to prevent workers from creating political conditions favorable to their own goals.

MILITANT LIBERALISM ON THE *RINGSTRASSE*

If organized neoliberalism has a birthplace, it is Stubenring 8–10 at the eastern end of the grand boulevard of Vienna's Ringstrasse. At that address, in 1907, the Lower Austrian Chamber of Commerce and Industry (later the Vienna Chamber of Commerce) opened its new building, a massive six-story structure designed by Ludwig Baumann in a combination of neoclassicism and Jugendstil art nouveau, with the two-headed eagle of the dual monarchy on its corner with the bound fasces on a shield. One entered the building between four marble columns, then proceeded up a central stairway flanked by life-size bronze sculptures of topless Egyptian acolytes holding votive bowls aloft and backed by a geometric matrix of blue and green stained glass. After taking a job there in 1909 at age 27, Ludwig Mises walked up those stairs every working day for twenty-five years. F. A. Hayek took his first job there in 1921, working with Mises as a civil servant for eighteen months on a commission related to the St. Germain peace treaty.[9] After the mid-1920s, Mises was joined by Hayek again, along with another protégé, Gottfried Haberler, for whom Mises secured positions in the Austrian Business Cycle Research Institute, which operated in the same building. Mises's office on the second floor, facing the Ringstrasse, was also the meeting place for his private seminar, which included Fritz Machlup and visits by Lionel Robbins, Frank Knight, and John Van Sickle, becoming part of the "extra-academic cosmopolitan intellectual formation" that in 1947 would become the neoliberal Mont Pèlerin Society.[10]

Beginning the story of neoliberalism with the Stubenring in the 1920s rather than with Mont Pèlerin in 1947 deflates the self-heroizing narrative of lonely embattled intellectuals and reveals the world in which future neoliberals formed their principles. It also shows how their writing began with straightforward policy problems rather than abstract contemplation. Though Mises claimed that "no other calling was more desirable to me as that of a university professor," in many ways the Chamber of Commerce remained his most characteristic milieu, and his policy suggestions remained remarkably consistent.[11] He began his career in Austria in the last years of the Habsburg Empire, advocating strenuously for lower corporate taxes on industry, and ended it in the last years of the First Austrian Republic, arguing for the same. Taking the position of Chamber secretary in 1918, Mises was obliged to advise the government and write expert evaluations of new laws in the interwar period, a duty that peaked with leading a three-person Economic Commission in 1930.[12] Even if he is remembered for his work on social philosophy and theories of money and credit, Mises earned his livelihood for much of his adult life as a forthright advocate for the needs of business, including with the Chamber of Commerce in the 1920s and 1930s, and the National Association of

Manufacturers (NAM) and Foundation for Economic Education after his emigration to the United States.[13]

The location of the Vienna Chamber of Commerce on the Ringstrasse was heavy with symbolism and helps illustrate the milieu out of which the Austrian strain of neoliberalism emerged. The boulevards themselves were built in the wake of the revolutions of 1848 on the vacant land that had once been the medieval city walls. In his classic study of fin-de-siècle Vienna, Carl Schorske describes how the liberal city government used the Ringstrasse to showcase its vision of social order, building the parliament and city hall alongside theaters and the university.[14] The developments echoed those under way in Paris under the direction of Baron George-Eugène Haussmann. Both urban renewal projects created arteries of commerce and transportation in medieval cities, building wide streets that could serve simultaneously as sites of cultural enrichment in their opera houses and museums, expressions of state power in their monuments, and sites of consumption in their shop windows and sidewalk cafes.[15] The wide streets would also make it harder for future insurgents to build the barricades that characterized the revolutions of 1848. Both designs included arsenals and barracks for the easy deployment of troops to quell domestic threats.[16] The Ringstrasse and Haussmann's boulevards turned Vienna and Paris into modern cities, hubs of commerce capable of accommodating—and policing—an expanding population of all classes.

The Stuben Quarter was built at the tail end of the Ringstrasse in the first decade of the 1900s, "as the liberal era closed."[17] The view from the Chamber of Commerce was onto the massive seven-story War Ministry, designed by the same architect and completed in 1913. That building was topped by a bronze Habsburg eagle with a sixteen-meter wingspan, which required that an extra floor be built to undergird it. Beneath it was a slogan: "If you want peace, prepare for war." After the war, the building became a barracks for the Austrian military. The eagle remained but was literally decrowned, and the slogan was removed. The third building in the ensemble remained unchanged: the headquarters of the Postal Savings Bank, an equally massive building designed by Otto Wagner, which opened in 1906 as one of the most famous buildings in the style of Jugendstil and early modernism, built with reinforced concrete with a facade boldly free of ornament.

Mises watched the events of the decade and formed his vision of economic order from the vantage point of the Stuben Quarter. The War Ministry building across the street from the Vienna Chamber of Commerce seemed to embody what Mises would later oppose as "omnipotent government."[18] Yet his version of neoliberalism never rejected the state as such.[19] Michel Foucault's attribution of "state-phobia" to Austrian neoliberals is a misunderstanding, especially considering Mises's career as an advocate for the use of government taxes to fund business interests.[20] Mises would become a patron saint to American libertarians, but he not only worked professionally as a state-funded advisor to the government but also saw a strong role for the state in the protection of property and keeping of the peace. In a telling phrase from 1922, he called the state "a producer of security."[21] For Mises, the assessment of state action depended on the field of engagement. The imperial state itself did not concern him. His fear was of interventionist government that appealed to "the people" for its legitimacy. His state could find its legitimacy only in its defense of the sanctity of private property and the forces of competition.

We will see in Chapter 3 that Mises had no qualms about using government military power to open and secure overseas markets. And even as he condemned what he called "étatism"—state intervention into the production and supply of goods—he criticized the state for not acting more aggressively against labor unions.[22] Maintaining security often involved repressing worker demonstrations, which he saw as criminal violence outside of the law. Such undertakings were not and could not be the functions of a small state. In this sense, the transformation of the former War Ministry into a garrison for the new Austrian military after 1920 should also be seen as a necessary and appropriate component of Mises's neoliberal model.

Schorske claimed that the early twentieth century was the end of the liberal era. That might be true for party politics, but 1907 was also the year of the achievement of universal male suffrage, one of liberalism's central demands for achieving popular sovereignty. It was partly direct action, including demonstrations in 1907, that brought this about, and this shook Mises deeply. He described public demonstrations as tactics of "terror and intimidation." "Unchallenged," he wrote in his memoirs, "the Social Democrats assumed the 'right to the street.'"[23] The streets of Vienna, and the Ringstrasse in particular, were more than a symbolic space. They were the forum where popular demands were voiced, sometimes to be granted and other times to be suppressed. In moments of uprising, crowds became symbols for the people as such, and those who were skeptical of democracy often based their resistance to change on the sight of such manifestations. The city was not just the backdrop for the emergence of a particular set of ideas. Neoliberal thinkers arrived at their ideas in response to the world they saw around them. The question of democracy became more pressing in the era of universal suffrage in Austria. One could argue that the "end of the liberal era"—as the advent of a new paradigm of militarized liberalism, later to be called neoliberalism—developed precisely as a response to the growth of mass democracy. This new paradigm was centered, not in the parliament or university, but in the triumvirate of security, finance, and commerce located in the Stuben Quarter. A well-armed state and sound money flanked by business were the icons of the ideology taking shape.

THE INVENTION OF THE TARIFF WALL

After the First World War, Mises and his circle found institutional allies beyond the nation and empire. A key institution in rebuilding what Mises called the "shattered world" of the global economy was the ICC, founded in Paris in 1920. The many recent histories of international civil society have given surprisingly little attention to the international coordination of businesspeople: the global public sphere of capitalists. Only two books have been written about its most paradigmatic organization, the ICC: a dissertation in German, and a book commissioned by the chamber itself in the 1930s, with a title—*Merchants of Peace*—that suggests an in-house bias.[24] The ICC would become an important institutional partner for the Austrian neoliberals.

The ICC emerged as an amalgam of two developments in the late nineteenth century: international cartels and international statistical associations. The cartels were groups of businessmen who specialized in the same sector and would set prices and ensure collective profitability. The ICC's direct forerunners were international business federations that appeared in the decade before the First World War. These made public the formerly secretive cartel discussions and incorporated an aspect of public relations into their practice.[25] The international statistical associations began with the International Statistical Institute, which was formed in 1885 and was the first entity to collate global statistics. The Institute was overseen by two economists at the University of Vienna who were also Mises's professors: Franz Neumann-Spallart and Franz Juraschek. As F. A. Hayek's grandfather, Juraschek had a filial tie to the neoliberal circle.[26]

Without a seat at the League of Nations, American economic internationalists often relied on the ICC to make their position heard. At the 1919 meeting in Atlantic City that would lead to the formation of the ICC, the organizers explained that reestablishing world trade after the war would be a struggle in itself. The isolationist position of the U.S. government had already effected a curious reversal. European business leaders now had to come to the rescue of Americans. The chair of the Atlantic City conference, Alfred C. Bedford, said to the fifty European businessmen in attendance: "It is as if you were a relief force come to assist us in raising a blockage. For against America—as much as against Europe—a blockade by the war's havoc upon that highly sensitive mechanism of the world's trade, threatens and impends." The assembled business leaders imagined a world that should and needed to be free of walls obstructing goods and capital. As Bedford said, "not only the physical comfort and well-being but the very lives of millions of people, depend upon this modern mechanism of international trade being restored, upon the barriers which were erected in the wake of war being leveled, until the channels of commerce can be reopened so that the commodities upon which human existence depends, may flow unchecked from where they are most plentiful to where they are most needed."[27] Bedford evoked a vision of the world economy as a hydraulic landscape. Commodities flowed through the "channels of commerce" created by the infrastructure of shipping and rails, and enabled presumably by the free flow of information in the networks of communication. This was a networked world economy without centralized control, where the laws of supply and demand dictated the distribution of the world's resources and its man-made products.

Human and state facilitation was needed to realize this vision. Yet, drawing from an older classical liberal imaginary, the process was depicted as natural, stemming from the laws of physics, perhaps even gravity. Bedford condemned the "barriers" raised during the war, referring to protectionist measures throughout the world that had been designed to safeguard production and national self-sufficiency. These were portrayed by the gathered businessmen as artificial impediments to a natural state. The metaphors reflected Woodrow Wilson's own language in the Fourteen Points, one of which called for "the removal, as far as possible, of all economic barriers and the establishment of an equality of trade conditions among all the nations consenting to the peace and associating themselves for its maintenance."[28]

At its constitutive session, the members of the ICC declared that "a nation is not an independent economic unit. Every day, the facts demonstrate the interdependence of all countries in the economic domain."[29] At its first congress in 1921, the ICC already included representatives from the defeated Austria and, after 1923, Germany, with delegates from thirty-three countries.[30] By 1927 the ICC had over 2,300 members; almost half were in the field of industry, about a quarter in banking and trade.[31] After 1925 Mises was the Austrian representative to the ICC. He traveled to Brussels for the third congress in 1925 and to the United States for the first time in 1926. In his capacity as the Austrian representative, he traveled extensively and was responsible for organizing and carrying out the seventh congress of the ICC in Vienna in May–June 1933.[32]

The League of Nations also defended liberalism on a global scale, but it remained committed to the principle of political self-determination. A German newspaper referred to the ICC as the "Economic League of Nations," with the advantage that the United States was a member (it was not a member of the League).[33] U.S. businessmen and bankers with a belief in interdependence organized in the ICC. Charles Dawes of General Electric, and the American banker Owen D. Young, for example, who were involved in plans to reschedule and relieve war debts in 1924 and 1929, were both active members.[34] Willis H. Booth called the

Dawes Plan the "product" of the ICC.[35] Norman H. Davis, former under secretary of state, speaking alongside Dawes and Young before a trip to the fifth meeting of the ICC in Brussels in 1925, expressed the pragmatic attitude toward interdependence: "Whether we like it or not, we cannot any longer disregard world affairs. Our position as a creditor nation, with a growing necessity for markets, imposes a duty and an obligation upon us."[36]

Until 1926 the ICC group was primarily concerned with a task they described as economic reconstruction; after 1926 they shifted their focus to opposing both tariff and nontariff barriers to trade.[37] They received active support from the Stubenring group. Richard Riedl, an economist at the Vienna Chamber of Commerce, prepared one of the most extensive reports for the ICC with two publications calling for the sinking of tariffs.[38] At the time his was the most extensive attempt to calculate the tariff index; his calculations covered 402 commodities and fourteen countries.[39] When in 1920 the League of Nations took up the task of gathering international economic statistics, which they would eventually take to an unprecedented level of comprehensiveness, the ICC was one of the members.[40]

Arthur Salter, head of the of the League of Nations Economic and Financial Section, described the ICC's report on the reduction of trade barriers as the foundation of the World Economic Conference of 1927.[41] He described a division of labor between the two organizations, with the ICC having "direct experience of the practical effects of administrative action" and the League having "a direct and official entry into the counsels of governments and the action of departments which the Chamber, as a private institution does not possess." "If the League can offer the machinery for achieving administrative reform, it must look to you for much of the motive force," he said in an address to the ICC's members. The primary goal was the negative one of removing barriers. "The actual tasks on which we are working together nearly all consist in trying to modify policies or administrative methods which impede business."[42]

In these months, business internationalists found the most enduring symbol for their campaign against barriers. The story of the tariff wall is a telling case study in how metaphors turn into economic policy. It begins in 1926, after Clive Morrison-Bell, an English Member of Parliament

A Europe of walls. Clive Morrison-Bell at the Vienna Chamber of Commerce. Clive Morrison-Bell, *Tariff Walls: A European Crusade* (London: John Murray Press, an imprint of Hodder & Stoughton, 1930).

and former parliamentary private secretary to Winston Churchill, heard a radio report on protectionist policies that convinced him that European "countries were slowly committing suicide." He set out to find a visual means of depicting economic relationships to show that Europe was "one large community, the members of which would sink or swim together."[43]

Morrison-Bell commissioned a local carpenter to build a table-size map of Europe with miniature red brick walls circling each country. The height of each wall was to correspond to the averaged level of the country's tariffs, but Morrison-Bell found to his surprise that the government itself did not have this data. He had to turn to the League of Nations, which supplied him with the numbers that they had begun gathering at the beginning of the decade. A later version of the map had a boldface title: "Visualize the Idea." What idea was represented here? The first impression of the walls, painted red in the table-sized version, is of the European nations' hazardous and anachronistic self-encapsulation. In the foreword to Morrison-Bell's book *Tariff Walls,* the Viscount D'Abernon wrote that the continent on the map "resembles nothing so much as a group of medieval fortified camps designed to impede progress."[44]

This was precisely the situation Morrison-Bell intended his map to portray. He saw himself using the "elementary lines of mass psychology that the best hope of any progress, however moderate, depends, and for propagating this idea there can be no simpler method than through the eye by means of this somewhat novel form of cartography."[45] He explained how the visual metaphor of the bricks in the tariff wall made the economic visible—and noted that it caught on quickly. Who would have spoken, he asked

> about putting a course of bricks on a tariff wall a few years ago. It would have been necessary to go into long explanations about this simple simile. So to have accomplished even this may be of some use, for the moment the public in other countries begin . . . to be seized with the idea that they are prevented from enjoying to the full the necessaries of life, because they are walled in as though with a brick wall, the further idea might begin to take root, namely, that it might not be a very difficult operation by a concerted effort to knock a few bricks off the top of these walls.[46]

The map argued visually for the removal of the barriers to trade.

Morrison-Bell's itinerary of travels with the map traces the sites of advocacy for the flat world in the 1920s. He began with the Bank of England, where Montagu Norman welcomed and displayed the map in 1926.[47] Then he showed it at the London Stock Exchange, followed by a meeting at the headquarters of the ICC in Paris, where it was constructed in the president's room. Next he displayed it at the preparatory meeting for the 1927 World Economic Conference at the Palace of Nations, in a foyer to be seen by all delegates as they entered. The chairman of the Royal Commission on Trade, Sir Arthur Balfour, traveled to Berlin and Copenhagen with the map in pieces, assembling it on his arrival.[48] Nicholas Murray Butler, president of both Columbia University and the Carnegie Endowment for International Peace, circulated photographs of the map to 1,500 American newspapers.[49] Morrison-Bell claimed plausibly that his model brought the metaphorical term "tariff walls" into public discussion as a synonym for "tariff barriers" or "obstacles to trade."[50] An image of the map appeared across the full width of a page in the *New York Times* in late 1926, with the legend "Tariff 'walls.' "[51]

In March 1927 Morrison-Bell displayed his model in the budget room of the Austrian parliament, and then to the Chamber of Commerce on the Stubenring, which he remarked correctly was "unlike similar institutions in England, seems to be a semi-official body closely connected with the Government."[52] The members of the Chamber were so intrigued that they requested their own version of the map, which Morrison-Bell delivered in 1929 to be used as a traveling pedagogical instrument in the "struggle for an improvement of the commercial conditions in Central Europe."[53]

The most visible display was at the 1927 World Economic Conference itself. Morrison-Bell planned beforehand to scale up the map considerably. The map was to stretch over twenty square yards on the shores of Lake Geneva.[54] In this grand form the contours of countries with low tariffs would be easily recognizable from above, while others would appear warped, their shape distorted by barricades. Making the familiar profile of Europe strange was intentional. As the frontispiece to his book, Morrison-Bell reprinted a Dutch cartoon from the World Economic Conference in 1927 that depicted a towering heap of "tariff walls in Europe" that was both disorienting and daunting to the small figure in the foreground.[55]

After having troubles with construction of the large-scale map, Morrison-Bell set up a smaller-scale model in Geneva in a dedicated building on the lakeshore. While there, he received a copy of a report from the Vienna Chamber of Commerce prepared by Riedl. It included a map with shading according to relative tariff levels. The calculations were much more extensive than Morrison-Bell's previous data. The League of Nations was collecting price data on only 78 goods; the Austrian branch of the ICC on the Stubenring was collecting data on 402 goods.[56] Morrison-Bell displayed the map alongside his own. The imaginaries of Austrian and English liberals were interpenetrating, creating a common visual language for their demands for free trade.

Both the World Economic Conference in May 1927 and the Stockholm Conference of the ICC in July made opposition to trade barriers central to their message. It was key, William Rappard noted later, that "these recommendations were made on the authority not only of a few benighted liberal professors, but of a large representative gathering, including even American business men, whom no one could denounce as visionary internationalists."[57] The participation of the business community signaled an increasing willingness to take an active public role. They were also evidently more keen to draft academic expertise into the formulation of their opinions. The ICC president said, "The world turns more and more to us whenever it needs to ascertain the views of business men. Following the example of the League of Nations, great international institutions one after another, for agriculture, for communications and transit, appeal to us to assist them in their work. We claimed the responsibility of representing business and now that claim is admitted on all sides. We must not disappoint the hopes placed in us. Noblesse oblige, and if you will permit me to say so, our own interest demands."[58] Business internationalism, with the aid of economic expertise, was helping to standardize a new norm about how the world economy should operate.

A contemporary photograph shows Clive Morrison-Bell standing over his map at the Vienna Chamber of Commerce. The placard reads, in French, "A Bird's-Eye View of Economic Europe." As with the modern architects or urban planners who were often drawn to produce symmetries below pleasing to the eye in the sky, the tariff map shaped its own solutions, encouraged the realization of a world uncluttered by walls. The map did not produce this position among liberal businessmen but it crystallized and, as Morrison-Bell intuited it would, projected it in a form that made the argument more compelling to both the common person and the commentator, regardless of its actual effects on their lives.

The metaphor carried its own implications. Mises's protégé at the Chamber of Commerce, Gottfried Haberler, pointed out the legerdemain required to create a single number for the "height" (his quotation marks) of tariff walls. Beyond the reality of varying tariffs from product to product, tariffs were also usually settled on in treaties between two countries, meaning that the map would look different depending on whose perspective one saw it from.[59] The single tariff wall idea carried the idea of the Most-Favored-Nation model implicitly, that is, the idea that the reduction of a tariff toward one country would involve lowering those for all other countries automatically. This norm was enshrined at the 1927 World Economic Conference against U.S. tariffs; it would crumble in the protectionist 1930s, only to return with the creation of the General Agreement on Tariffs and Trade (GATT) after the Second World War.[60]

BARRICADES IN THE CITY, JULY 1927

In its maquette of an internally walled Europe, the tariff walls map expressed an implicit normative vision of free movement. Yet it is notable that the map reflects commodities, not people. Haberler wrote that "military language, containing expressions such as 'economic front' and 'defensive positions,' is especially inappropriate to the analysis of problems of international trade and of division of labor between countries. . . . It suggests that a 'front' of economic conflict lies always between two countries, whereas in reality the conflict is between groups having different interests *within* each country."[61] If one side of Mises's vision was removing barricades to goods to allow for price convergence, the other was the need to remove obstacles to wage convergence. The biggest challenge to this in 1920s Austria was the trade unions. In one of his first published works, Mises asked as a young student in 1906 whether "English and German workers may have to descend to the lowly standard of life of the Hindus and coolies to compete with them."[62] In 1919 he provided a mixed answer: on the one hand, in the world economy he imagined the European worker would certainly earn less than he had become accustomed to. On the other hand, the "Hindus and coolies" of the world would earn more. Once one abandoned David Ricardo's odd hesitation at expanding the scope of the spatial division of labor, Mises wrote, "then one sees a tendency prevail over the entire earth toward equalization of the rate of return on capital and of the wage of labor. Then, finally, there no longer are poorer and richer nations but only more densely and less densely settled and cultivated countries."[63]

The primary problem was the most obvious one: the unwillingness of European workers to accept lower wages for the sake of either the higher law of liberalism or, as in Mises's argument, the benefit of a distant, likely nonwhite, foreign worker. Many of the challenges to liberalism in the 1920s proceeded from this obstacle. As Mises thought globally, he had to act locally, in a city famously governed by socialists. The realities of Red Vienna were a challenge to the realization of the vision of the group that would become the neoliberals—and conflict with the socialist-run city inspired their ideas.

Mises's policy prescriptions in the 1920s always had two sides: open to the world market, and make the internal adjustments necessary to compete internationally. This required two key measures: push down wages, and cut taxes on industry. In his writings after 1918 he repeated the point that a small country like Austria had no capacity to be self-sufficient. Such a fantasy could be maintained (at least for a while) in countries with enormous domestic markets—like the United States, England with its empire and dominions, or even Germany—but the Treaty of Saint Germain had made Austria, a country of just over six million people, heavily reliant on the foreign market for raw materials. In the words of one American journalist, it had been reduced to a "mutilated torso."[64] Prefiguring many of the dilemmas that would face nations after decolonization after 1945, the end of Austria's empire meant an increased reliance on access to an open world economy.

Mises put the issue systematically in a policy program written at the request of a politician in February 1921: "Austria needs free trade." Alongside suggestions to lift prohibitions on imports and ports, Mises suggested privatizing public enterprises, eliminating food subsidies, and, consistent with his belief in free movement, lifting entry and residence restrictions for foreigners.[65] After 1920 the Chamber of Commerce had the duty of writing evaluations of laws for the government.[66] In a position statement, Mises restated the points that "Austria's future depends on free trade" and that if their goods were "to be able to compete abroad," wages would have to fall "far below their prewar level."[67]

The fight over class justice exploded onto the Ringstrasse in mid-July 1927. The precipitating event had come six months earlier when members of the right-wing militia Frontkämpfer marched in a heavily

Social Democratic area. Harassed by members of the Social Democratic militia, the Frontkämpfer fired into the crowd, killing a worker and a child. Six months later, the result of their closely watched trial was complete acquittal, enraging workers who saw it as a case of skewed standards. Though the Social Democratic Party, led by the moderate Otto Bauer, advised against a violent response, rank-and-file workers dissented. At 8:00 a.m. the following day, the electric workers stopped the streetcars, bringing the circulation of labor through the city to a halt and signaling the call to a general strike.[68] Workers marched to the Parliament on the far side of the Ringstrasse from the Chamber of Commerce. The Palace of Justice became the target of their anger at the court's verdict, and part of the crowd stormed the building and set it on fire, while others blocked fire trucks, cut hoses, and opened up other hydrants to reduce water pressure, defiantly impeding the city's functions.[69]

The authorities felt pushed to opt for a radical solution, and the police chief received emergency powers, suspended the rule of law, and gave the order to fire on the demonstrators. Police killed protesters with rifles in the center of the city, and then drove out to workers' housing complexes in the suburbs and killed more. After three days, eighty-nine people were dead and over a thousand injured.[70] The workers' movement was permanently crippled. The Social Democratic Party was unable to use the threat of mass mobilization effectively again, and, perhaps most damagingly, the days had shown that even the putatively socialist members of the police would not hesitate to fire on fellow workers.

The July 15, 1927, uprising was the deepest crisis in Vienna before the civil war of 1934. The sight of the Palace of Justice in flames shook the author and cultural critic Elias Canetti deeply, leading him to devote his life's work to understanding the relationship between crowds and power.[71] For Mises, the event was not a trauma but a great relief. He was in Vienna at the time and wrote to a friend: "Friday's putsch has cleansed the atmosphere like a thunderstorm. The social-democratic party has used all means of power and yet lost the game. The street fight ended in complete victory of the police. . . . All troops are loyal to the government."[72] "The threats by which the social-democratic party has up to now permanently tried to bully the government and the public," Mises continued, "have proved to be far less dangerous than one had believed."[73] As his biographer describes, Mises was "surprised and delighted by the failure of the general strike."[74] It appeared that he accepted lightly the means used in the suppression, which delivered a deep blow to many at the time. The right to kill with impunity under emergency powers met Mises's approval.

As with the other neoliberals we will encounter in these pages, democracy was not an absolute value for Mises. He admired it as the system most likely to produce an outcome amenable to stability and an atmosphere for free economic exchange. He did express doubts that democracy produced leaders better than those produced by autocracy or aristocracy, but he said that this was missing the point: "The significance of the democratic form of constitution is something quite different from all this. Its function is to make peace, to avoid violent revolutions."[75] If populations felt that their voice and opinion had effects on the composition of the government, then they would less frequently reach for violent means. The definition of equality must remain minimalist though, exhausting itself with equality before the law. Attempting to enforce equality beyond this would be to deny the basic fact "that men are endowed differently by nature."[76] Thus, a crucial complement to voters' democracy was what he would later call "a consumer's democracy," expressed by purchases and investments in the marketplace. "True there is no equality of vote in this democracy; some have plural votes. But the greater voting power which the disposal of a greater income implies can only be acquired and maintained by the test of election." Wealth, he wrote, was "always the result of a consumers' plebiscite."[77] Mises's functional definition of democracy had a clear implication: should democracy cease to be functional—that is, cease to secure stability—there would be no reason to maintain it.

In 1927, democracy had ceased to fulfill its primary function. It did not prevent revolution. In that case, Mises believed, it was perfectly legitimate to suspend it and enforce order by other means. The structural link between the nascent welfare state and emergency law was also clear in the uprising. In the course of negotiations, the only concession that Social Democrats were able to secure during the strike was that the government would not use its emergency powers to abolish unemployment benefits and social housing programs.[78] Yet this was precisely what Mises felt was necessary in order to make Austrian industry competitive again. In February 1930 the Chamber of Commerce, with Mises as its primary adviser, recommended cuts to unemployment benefits and to health and accident insurance. If workers wanted severance pay, it should come out of union dues rather than from the employer or state.[79]As the most influential member of a three-person Economic Commission in 1930, he argued that the terms of trade, the interest rate, and the prices of many commodities were determined by world economic conditions, and were thus out of the control of the Austrian authorities. The only thing they could change were wages and taxes. Both had to be lowered to bring down production costs.[80] The tactic of the Chamber of Commerce was to recast organized labor as illegal, and thus unable to demand protection under the law and prone to extirpation. The Chamber promoted the passage of an "anti-terror law" to be used against striking workers.[81] A similar version would be used in the civil war of 1934 when the housing estates where police had shot demonstrators were attacked again and subdued.

Critics called the Chamber of Commerce policies "class war from above" and said that the anti-terror law showed that "as always, the only means that the brains of those in power can think of to use against workers and employees is violence."[82] The recommendation of Mises's Chamber of Commerce showed his model in action. Understood functionally, democracy could be suspended when this is required for the stability of the market. The *Neue Freie Presse,* for which Mises wrote articles, called for the "actual depoliticization of the economic" *(wirklichen Entpolitisierung des Ökonomischen).*[83] Needless to say, this form of "depoliticization" was very political, and entailed a dramatic application of executive power. Foreign competition, and by extension the rhetorical weapon of invoking the world economy, was a bludgeon to beat back social policy gains in worker insurance, severance pay, and unemployment benefits.

Mises and Hayek both believed that the 1929 slump was caused by loose monetary policy and overinvestment, and that unions were the reason that the slump turned into a depression. Unemployment was voluntary. "Unemployment is a problem of wages, not of work . . . the assistance of the unemployed is what first creates unemployment as a permanent phenomenon."[84] In a lecture to German industrialists in 1931 titled "The Causes of the World Economic Crisis," Mises condemned governments that had "capitulated to the unions," which pursue their goals "by the use of violence." "Were it to proceed in its usual way and interfere with the criminals who abuse jobseekers and vandalize the machines and other of the entrepreneurs, then circumstances would be different."[85] At this exact time, he was in England in his official capacity for the ICC, seeking foreign investment in Austria. The struggle of organized labor against the reduction of their wages made this difficult. The needs of the world economy were arrayed against those of the organized workers.

In Second Empire Paris, Haussmann's mammoth project to open up pathways for trade and consumption filled the city with construction and service laborers. Marginalized and impoverished, they seized urban space for themselves in the Paris Commune, which lasted for several months, until it was ended in the so-called Bloody Week and the deaths of 20,000 communards. One could argue that liberal internationalists like Mises in the 1920s imagined the Haussmanization of the world, demolishing the brick walls that impeded commerce to permit a more productive use of the earth's resources. Their vision required that goods and capital remain in movement, pursuing profit and new sites of productivity.

Red Vienna shaped the worldview of the Austrians who would form the neoliberal movement, entrenching the idea of an armed standoff between labor and capital. In his memoirs Mises pointed out the drastic nature of the situation. The party "could paralyze all economic life at any time" with a strike. Most importantly, the Social Democrats had control of the army, which was "equipped with rifles and machine guns, light artillery, ample munitions, and manpower at least three times greater than that available to the government."[86] Mises later described collective bargaining as the "gun under the table." He might have meant it as a metaphor, but it was not a metaphor in Vienna.

By 1927 there was a well-defined and internationally organized network of pro-business forces engaged in the collection of economic information in pursuit of a common goal of negative global integration—the reestablishment of an open world economy. It was a Chamber of Commerce vision: give the businesspeople the power to govern their own affairs, and interfere as little as possible. Hidden in the mobilization, however, was a third party intervening between business and state: the economic knowledge producer. Even if the goal was to let the world economy rule, the businesspeople could not do it for themselves. They required statisticians and economists. When Morrison-Bell needed to construct his map, he started with statistics from the League of Nations. In contrast to the typical policy-minded economist in the late nineteenth century, who would have been a social reformer seeking to counteract and mollify the effects of capitalism, there emerged in the interwar period a generation of economists who sought to apply their knowledge in service of capital.

SEEING LIKE A COMMODITY

The socialization of Haberler, Hayek, and Machlup came at Mises's private seminar, which met in his office at the Chamber of Commerce on the Stubenring. Every two weeks at 7:00 p.m., a flock of young intellectuals in their twenties and thirties would pass under the leaded glass of the entrance and up the stairs past the art nouveau caryatids to Mises's office, where he would sit behind his desk with as many as twenty-five people gathered around him.[87] Discussion would last until around 10:00 p.m. and continue in the Italian restaurant nearby, and continue even further at Café Künstler. Haberler recalls that Mises was in the hard core for endurance, never leaving before 1:00 a.m.[88]

The Chamber acted as a kind of alternative university. Economists of international reputation passed through it, including Lionel Robbins, Ragnar Nurkse, and Howard S. Ellis.[89] Mises boasted that its library contained material that even the University of Vienna did not have.[90] Government offices occasionally consulted the Chamber's statistical material, which was superior to their own collection. The discussions at the private seminar were wide-ranging and became legendary for the participants. One of the participants wrote kitschy verse, later reproduced in the publication of the Mont Pèlerin Society, suggesting its sentimental power for many of the members. A sample stanza read: "I'm going tonight to Mises, because that's where I love to be, there's nowhere so nice in Vienna, to talk about economy, truth and society."[91]

At stake for the Mises Circle was the question one member asked in 1928: Is it possible "to build a bridge between economic theory and economic policy?"[92] The question of the late 1920s for the Austrian liberals was: What kind of economic information was reliable and what kind of information was politically useful? The month after the Palace of Justice burned, Gottfried Haberler was addressing this question in the Stubenring, finishing his book on "the meaning of index numbers."[93] Haberler was born in 1900 to a family of well-off civil servants, in the sylvan Viennese suburb of Purkersdorf, best known for its sanatorium designed by the Secession architect Josef Hoffmann. Built when Haberler was a toddler, the sanatorium was a gathering place for luminaries like Gustav Mahler, Arnold Schönberg, and Arthur Schnitzler. The clean white lines and geometry of the building reflected the artistic vision of the Secession, further embodied in the building in downtown Vienna with its golden leafy globe. Their goal was the *Gesamtkunstwerk,* the total work of art. Art should bring harmony and perfection to earth.

Though the distance between the sinuous forms of Klimt and Schiele and the dry texts of economists might seem vast, Haberler and his fellow Austrian liberals were engaged with something similar. Their questions were basic, and at some level also aesthetic: How should we measure the "complicated latticework of individual economic acts," and how can we represent it visually?[94] What face of economic actions should we present to the public? Haberler wrote in 1927 that economics was concerned not only with outward actions but also with internal motivations, matters of the "psyche" and the "spirit," or *Geist.* For this reason, he said, economics was one of the humanities, or *Geisteswissenschaften,* a "science of the spirit."[95]

But how to operationalize a science that tended to abstraction? Mises, Haberler, and other economists worked alongside business leaders to provide data and concepts that supported the dream of a world of commerce without walls. Haberler's earliest notable article was on the theory of comparative costs, which began as a presentation in Vienna.[96] His goal was to create a defense of free trade that worked not only in theory but also in the real-life political circumstances of the post–First World War world. His main question concerned free migration. The main argument for free trade was the international division of labor, but "freedom of migration does not exist, has never existed and probably never will exist." It would not be desirable even if it were possible. The Ruhr Valley would become unbelievably crowded, and the Alps would empty out entirely: "One need not be a nationalist for such things to be undesirable." Haberler proposed that he could prove that "free trade is beneficial for all even when there is no freedom of migration and the peoples remain firmly rooted in their countries."[97]

He did so by revisiting David Ricardo's idea of comparative advantage but recasting it without the discredited labor theory of value. In his version, workers did not need to be mobile over national borders as long as prices were. If prices accurately reflected the relative supply and demand on markets, then these would guide entrepreneurs to the most efficient use of their resources. For prices to serve their function, however, they must not encounter resistance. He gave the specific example of labor: "Here the price mechanism is partially switched off, and real frictional losses can occur in the form of strikes and unemployment." Luckily, he pointed out, "labor was the most mobile and diverse of all the factors of production."[98] Even if unemployment figures remained constant, the actual mass of unemployed usually rotated in and out as people moved from position to position. In the demand for the "faultless functioning of the price mechanism," Haberler conjured an image reminiscent of an enormous clockwork or factory apparatus, shuttling components from one location to the other. He cited earlier thinkers like Bastiat, who argued that free trade worked like invention, constantly rearranging the landscape of production, sending workers to new places of work when one has been outmoded or squeezed out by overseas competition.

The workers themselves were neutral containers of the attribute of labor, as capable of relocation as a chunk of investment capital or a carriage-load of coal. Haberler expressed the vision in an evocative geography: "Inactive production facilities are not actually witnesses to the destruction of capital, of losses that must be calculated against the advantages of the division of labor; rather, they are milestones of the economic progress produced by the international division of labor."[99] Regardless of any emotional attachment felt by people to livelihood and place, the shuttered factory was not a tombstone to a lost way of life but a monument to the forward march of the market.

Haberler thought wages in postwar Austria must fall to restore competitiveness. He put it plainly in a newspaper article in Vienna in 1933: "The dismantlement of tariffs will bring pain to a series of economic sectors . . . but the pains of transition will not be long term, they will also definitely not be worse than the unhappiness that we have been plunged into by years of tariff addiction."[100] He asked the question: "How can an economy that is more poorly equipped in almost every respect withstand the competition of an industry and agriculture working with better production conditions without protecting itself with extra-high tariffs?" The answer was simple: "The poor economy can compete with the rich when the wages and all other forms of income are correspondingly smaller." He put it bluntly: "When we have faced the necessary consequences completely, when the standard of living has sunk low enough, income has fallen far enough, then the economy can progress, business as usual. . . . When the skilled workers in export industry have moved into the coal mines, maybe into agriculture and other economic sectors too, whose products can be better exchanged for qualified export goods and the rest of the workers, insofar as possible, have emigrated, then maybe all will be employed again, granted at a pronouncedly lower standard of living."[101] For Haberler, Austria was a prototypical case of small state in the storms of globalization. As he had written a few years earlier, huge countries like the United States and the British "world empire" might be able to follow policies of stabilizing the internal price level, but small countries needed to remain attractive to foreign investment and therefore had to concentrate on stabilizing their currency.[102] There was no escape from the discipline of the world economy.

It was essential that policy makers not cave to popular demands. A case in point was the demand for stabilization of commodity prices in the wake of the stock market crash. In 1931 Haberler wrote against the idea of stabilizing the price level for certain commodities. He acknowledged that under a scheme of stabilized prices "social friction is less, since the worker can then be offered rising wages and a larger share—at the expense of rentiers—in the social product," but the outcome would be inflation. He said that he would personally rather risk the "increase of social friction" than risk inflation.[103] Here he followed his mentor Mises, who complained that governments had been captive to "public opinion, which looks for salvation in low rates of interest and rising prices." Because the business world desired cheap credit, governments encouraged banks to print money, but short-term profits "in the long run must inevitably create a situation of crisis and depression."[104] Public pressure must be resisted by the banks, schooled by economists on the consequences of their actions. Only then could international trade based on a reliable currency standard be preserved.

Faced with the imperfect world of strikes, tariffs, and democratic pressure on banks for loose credit, Haberler turned to an ideal type to defend his prescription of free trade. In his 1930s writings, he began with a model of what he called a "spaceless closed economy embracing the whole world" and introduced "one by one the circumstances which divide and disintegrate that economy."[105] He explained that he used the category of "countries" in quotation marks because the distribution of resources relevant to a model of world economic integration did not necessarily align with "political borders."[106] This optic bracketed the political, creating a vision of the world that was either pre- or postnational, depending on how one looked at it. The whole earth was a container of natural endowments over which political communities made claims. Haberler's ideal policy would make reality more closely resemble the model of a "spaceless" world economy where neither man-made nor geographical obstacles hindered the most efficient allocation of the earth's resources through the mechanisms of the free market. Imagining a spaceless world was not pure fantasy in the 1930s. In some cases it had come close to reality. Haberler pointed out that telephone and telegraph links meant that markets for currency, stocks, and commodities reacted nearly in tandem.[107] Local and world prices moved together.[108] Many goods were "international" insofar as it was more profitable to import them from overseas than produce them at home. Transportation chased communication. Both tended toward the disappearance of distance.

Haberler saw the world as a hypothetical unity and proceeded to catalog the obstacles that disrupted that unity. Distance was gradually being overcome. Man-made legal obstacles of customs duties and tariffs persisted. He wrote that the "raising of tariff walls" had "exactly the same consequences as changes in transportation cost," meaning that they created a vertical, rather than horizontal, distance for goods to travel.[109] He was repeating what had become common wisdom at the League of Nations. In 1932 Salter wrote that "the place which protective tariffs occupy in the world's economy and, regarded, as a whole and inevitable effect, are perfectly clear. They are like the natural impediments of mountain range or other obstacles to transport which increase the price paid for the benefits and economies resulting from the interchange of products of widely sundered regions."[110] The liberal geography of the League economists cast tariffs as metaphorical barriers with height to be climbed over.

Yet most mettlesome of all were the obstacles that impeded the free movement of that most essential commodity: human labor. Haberler saw labor as sticky but highly versatile when forced to move. He praised workers for their ability to adapt but condemned them for wanting to stay in place. The danger lay where labor gained allies that acted as anchors. He blamed organized labor and "state intervention in labor questions in connection with unemployment insurance and unemployment relief" for decreasing labor's "mobility and adaptability."[111] Trade unions were not only anchors. Like Mises, he saw them as walls. He described unions as "artificial obstacles to entry into certain occupations"—barriers upheld through "monopoly power" over the commodity of human expenditure of effort.[112] For free trade to work, the barriers of the trade union needed to fall. Only by being subject to the push and pull of demand within the nation-state could the nation-state container for labor remain intact.

❁ ❁ ❁

After the First World War, Austrian liberals like Mises and Haberler felt that the shattered world must be rebuilt by a process of metaphorical and literal demolition. Striking workers and tariffs to shelter domestic industries were both defined as walls to be destroyed. Paradoxically, Austrian liberals saw this demolition as a purely negative process, as if it were only a question of clearing space. But knitting commercial space back together was very much an active process. The core cohort of the neoliberal intellectual movement that had coalesced in Vienna had found their closest partners in the Businessman's International of the ICC and the League of Nations. Both of these bodies looked like partners for reestablishing the boundaries of capitalism's two worlds. Capital, goods, and wages must be free, irrespective of national frontiers. Novel in Haberler's theory was the rescue of the nation-state as a container for labor. His theory of comparative costs suggested that free trade could compensate for the absence of international labor migration as long as internal barriers established by unions were struck down. Haberler's vision revealed that the Europe of fortresses was a way of seeing like a commodity. The walls between nations were to fall for goods but not for people.

As we will see in chapter 2, the economic constitution of the world suffered a second existential blow with the Great Depression of the 1930s. The stage shifted from Vienna to Geneva as liberals fled the coming fascist wave, and the negative liberal vision of clearing space or eliminating obstacles would give way to a productive neoliberal program of finding new extra-economic conditions to protect the world economy. Mises received a Geneva professorship in 1934, and members of his seminar saw their master off with the wish that "his strong spirit will show the League of Nations the way."[113]

2

A World of Numbers

It is no exaggeration to say that the era of decay of the world economy was at the same time the era of international economic conferences.

—WILHELM RÖPKE

In 1929 the dream of a flat world economy turned into a nightmare. The Wall Street stock market crash initiated a sequence of events that led to the Great Depression, or, as it is known in German, "the world economic crisis" *(Weltwirtschaftskrise).* One historian calls the 1930s the "end of globalization."[1] After its surprising recovery after the First World War, international trade slowed again as national governments sheltered domestic production behind tariff walls of unprecedented height. In the world of money, the United States suspended the convertibility of dollars into gold in 1931, followed by the British pound. The end of the gold standard meant that one could no longer assume that today's investment, even denominated in the storied world currency of the pound, would be worth the same amount in gold tomorrow. In the minds of liberals, this was an attack on not just the sanctity of money but the sanctity of contract. One German liberal claimed that this act, more than any other, had "broken the economic unity of the world."[2]

As the gold standard dissolved, the empire principle, which had suffered a blow after the end of the Habsburg and Ottoman Empires, revived as the European powers relied on their colonies and commonwealths for raw materials traded behind tariff walls in imperial blocs. To the liberal viewer, the world of the 1930s was in segments. The barricades pictured on Clive Morrison-Bell's tariff walls map extended south from Europe to encase overseas territories like India, Algeria, the Gold Coast, and South Africa. The world economy presented as a honeycomb of walls built from "tariff fortifications."[3]

For liberals it was a painful irony that the world economy came into focus as a totality in statistics at the very moment it seemed to vanish in real life. The global economic crisis led to proposals for global economic solutions, with the League of Nations leading the way. In the words of one historian, the injunction of the 1930s was to "look at the world."[4] Economic data proliferated. The secretary general of the International Chamber of Commerce (ICC) remarked in 1937 that "there are so many different sources and centres of information scattered throughout the world having no connexion one with the other that business men and economists find themselves almost drowned by a veritable flood of pamphlets, statistical bulletins, reviews and papers."[5] The plans for the universal exposition in Paris in 1937 expressed the spirit of the decade with its plans for a Lighthouse of the World twice the height of the Eiffel Tower. Visitors would drive their own cars up ramps spiraling the concrete structure half a mile in the sky; according to a fanciful accompanying illustration, visitors would see as far as Belgium, Spain, and England.[6]

While the World Congress of Universal Documentation was held during the Paris Exhibition, nowhere was the global idea more at home than in the quaint town of Geneva, where the stripped classicist Palace of Nations stood like a secular temple to the idea of the international.[7] The tenants of a single building, the Palais Wilson, which opened on the shores of Lake Geneva in 1937, suggested the diversity of approaches to the world. Among the thirty organizations housed in the former hotel were the Carnegie Endowment for International Peace, the New Commonwealth Institute, the International Labour Organization, the World Alliance for Promoting International Friendship through the Churches, the International Council of Women, the International Bureau of Education, the International Migration Service, the World Association for Reform of the Calendar, the World Narcotic Defence Association, and the Universal Esperantist Association.[8] In the 1920s and 1930s, Geneva was confronting not only the problems of the world as individual concerns, but the problem of the world itself—how to manage the globe as a whole. "The famous 'Spirit of Geneva,'" said one observer in 1931, "may well prove to the embryo of a future world patriotism."[9] The city seemed like the only candidate for the capital of the world polity that H. G. Wells called Cosmopolis.

The world economy came into being in the 1930s in Geneva on paper and in numbers through the efforts of economists to understand the causes of the Great Depression and seek remedies for it. The head of the League of Nations economic section, Arthur Salter (who later joined the Mont Pèlerin Society), wrote in 1932 that the Depression "has at least done one thing which may in future prove of great value. It has revealed the anatomy of the world's economic structure."[10] The core group of the future neoliberal movement either relocated to Geneva or passed through the Swiss city in the 1930s. In the 1920s and 1930s, they were all involved with projects of either creating statistical portraits of the national and world economies or seeking to understand their cyclical rise and fall. In 1927 Mises and Hayek expanded their cooperation with the ICC to found a Business Cycle Research Institute in the offices on the Stubenring in Vienna. This job led Hayek to the center of global economic research in Geneva. The League hired Gottfried Haberler, a colleague of Mises and Hayek's, for a major study of the world economy beginning in 1934. In 1937 Wilhelm Röpke, a central figure in the neoliberal movement, also moved to Geneva, recruited for a global study of the effects of changes in world trade and production. Historians refer to the famous 1938 Lippmann Colloquium in Paris as the "birthplace of neoliberalism."[11] They rarely note, though, that it was only one episode in a decade of overlapping projects devoted to studying the conditions of "the Great Society," not at the national level but at the scale of the globe.

Neoliberalism was born out of projects of world observation, global statistics gathering, and international investigations of the business cycle. Why is this fact so often missed by historians? Part of the reason is that the ultimate conclusion of neoliberals about the Great Depression and its aftermath was that numbers were not enough. Even as techniques of planning gained traction both in Geneva and in the mainstream of the economics profession by the end of the 1930s, neoliberals rallied around the belief that neither statistics, nor mathematically informed theory, nor the nascent science of econometrics would suffice to forecast or stave off future crises. They even thought that the increasing sophistication of such approaches might, counterintuitively, be increasing the likelihood of another crisis by fostering the false faith that science could make the world economy crisis-proof.

As Röpke and Alexander Rüstow wrote in their contribution to the 1938 Lippmann Colloquium, "recent advances in purely economic analysis have done much to make us understand better the mechanics of economic oscillations. But here again refinement in detail has been bought at the price of blindness towards the extra-economic contexts which constitute the problem of reality."[12] Perhaps most radical was Hayek's conclusion in that decade, building on an earlier skepticism about statistics cultivated in Viennese debates, that comprehensive knowledge itself would always—and must always—elude the economist because of its necessary dispersal among all members of society. For him, to climb the Lighthouse of the World in search of a synoptic view from which to direct and plan was only the setup for a long fall.

By the end of the 1930s the Geneva School neoliberals agreed that the most important pillars of integration could not be represented or understood through graphs, charts, tables, maps, or formulas. They redirected their attention to cultural and social bonds but also to the framework of tradition and the rule of law, all of which they perceived to be disintegrating in the 1930s. The road away from statistics and business cycle research led neoliberals to, as they put it, think in orders. From that point onward they sharpened their focus on designing institutions that would best safeguard the market. The world economy must be defended, and Geneva School neoliberalism would be defined by the search for state and legal forms that were up to the task—at the level of the nation but also, more importantly, at the level of the world.

THE RISE OF BAROMETER VISION

One of the most famous images used to illustrate the Great Depression is the so-called Kindleberger spiral.[13] In an eye-catching circular graph, it tracks the relentless decline in the volume of world trade from January 1929 until June 1933. Though known by the name of the American economic historian who popularized it, the diagram might more accurately be called either the Morgenstern spiral, after the Austrian economist who created the form of representation, or the Condliffe spiral, after the first creator of a popularized version. Its parentage and its peregrinations capture the international collaboration networks of the time. Oskar Morgenstern first used the spiral to show the declining foreign trade of Austria in April 1933.[14] It then appeared expanded to the scale of the world in a newspaper notice for the World Economic Conference in London created by the Swiss Bank Corporation, and appeared soon afterward in Geneva as the lead image in the League of Nations' second ever *World Economic Survey* prepared by J. B. Condliffe.[15] By November, the globalized spiral reappeared in Vienna.[16]

The Viennese publication that featured the spiral was the monthly report of the Austrian Business Cycle Research Institute founded by Mises and Hayek in late 1926 and housed in the Vienna Chamber of Commerce building. Morgenstern took over its direction from Hayek in 1931. Understanding the business cycle was the central intellectual challenge of the 1920s and 1930s for economists. By the early 1930s, Geneva was the hub of such efforts, with spokes extending not only to Vienna but across Central Europe, over the English Channel, and traversing the Atlantic. At stake was the question of whether it was possible to predict the future. By finding the right aspects of economic life to capture and compile in numbers, would it be possible not only to comprehend but also to forecast what Columbia University economist Wesley Clair Mitchell called in his foundational work from 1913 "the complicated processes by which seasons of business prosperity, crisis, depression, and revival come about in the modern world"?[17] Although research into the business cycle began before the First World War, it boomed afterward. The U.S. government funded its study, and business

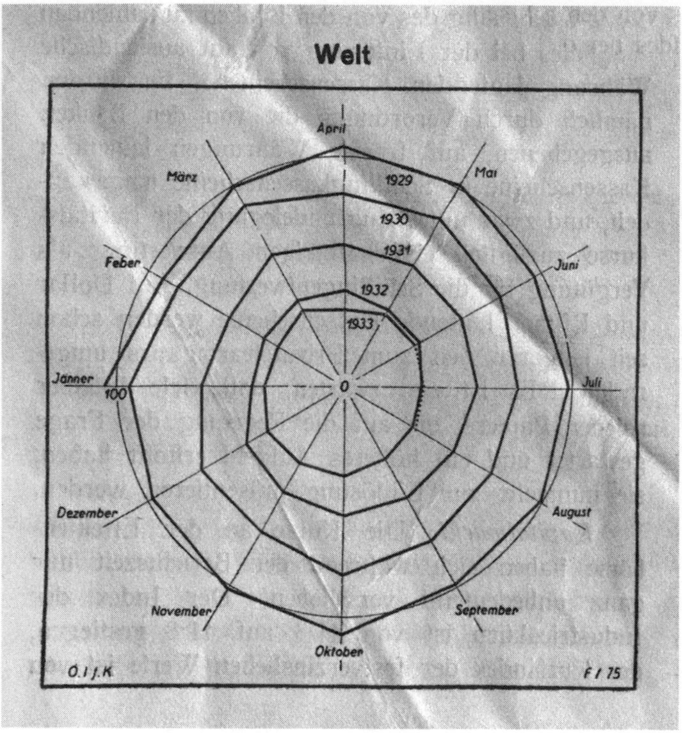

The spiral of decline in world trade. *Monthly Report of the Austrian Business Cycle Research Institute*, November 1933.

cycle research institutes were established throughout Europe and in the Soviet Union.[18]

One of the preoccupations of researchers was how to express the business cycle visually—how to make the invisible market visible. Techniques of illustrating the business cycle had originated with private services for investors. As the stock market boomed in the 1920s and ever more Americans had wealth bound up in finance, there was a ready market for advice that might offer an advantage. Charts and diagrams offered information about the direction of economic activity that could be consumed at a glance. Through such visualizations, one scholar argues, the popular reports like those of Roger Babson gave readers a sense "of 'the economy' as a complex but unified system that operated according to its own internal logic."[19] A chart of "fundamental condi-

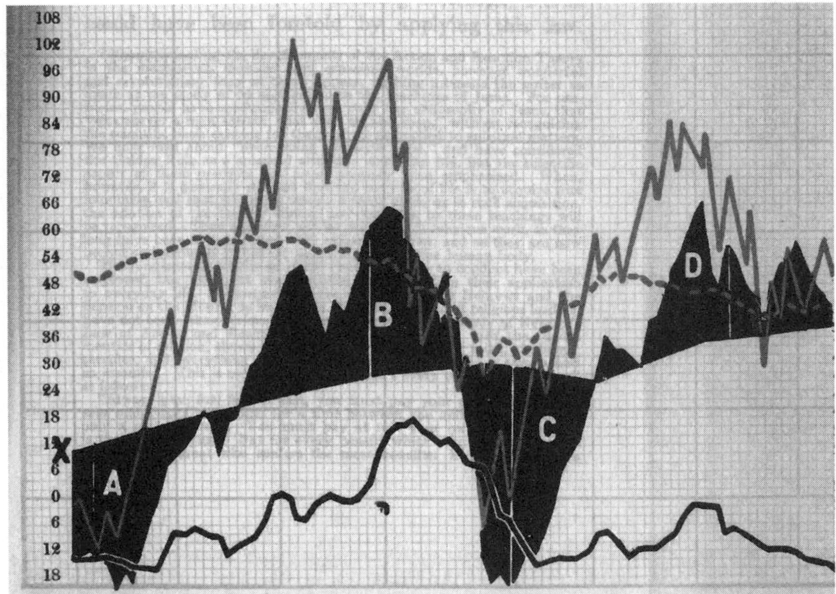

Babson's economic chasms and peaks. Roger W. Babson, *Business Barometers Used in the Accumulation of Money: A Text Book on Applied Economics for Merchants, Bankers and Investors*, 4th ed. (Wellesley Hills, MA: Babson's Compiling Offices, 1911).

tions," for example, aggregated a range of data into a single sinking and rising line, turning time into a topography of economic chasms and peaks.[20]

Predictions of the economic future based on the compilation of statistics (represented visually) were collectively called "business barometers." By the 1920s the leader in the field was the Harvard Committee on Economic Research's "three cycle" barometer. The A, B, and C curves of the Harvard barometer stood for "speculation, business, and money," roughly drawn from price movement of stocks, commodities, and the loans and credits of major banks. By observing recurrent lags between these three indicators, barometer readers believed they could forecast the change in business conditions over time.[21]

The metaphor of the barometer implied that the economy was like the weather, a sphere outside of direct human control. One could adapt Adam Smith's famous metaphor of the invisible hand to speak of the invisible *wind* of the market, captured in charts and graphs. The

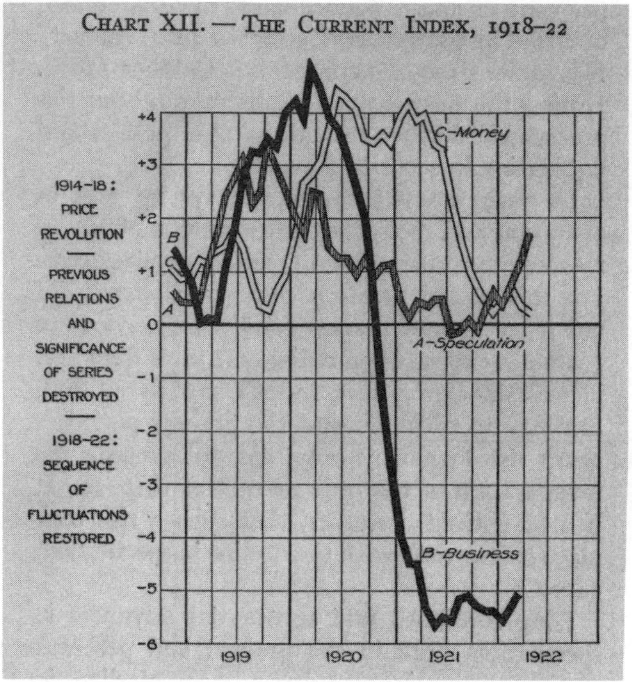

The three lines of the Harvard Economic Service Barometer. Warren M. Persons, *Interpretation of the Index of General Business Conditions* (Cambridge, MA: Harvard Economic Service, 1922).

economic conditions portrayed in three lines were experienced as a unity but were actually composed of innumerable tiny organic processes, of which we could perceive only the effects in the aggregate. The barometer metaphor went in two directions. As Hayek noted in 1927, it seemed to make the future legible to the common person. Yet the barometer "only appears to forecast the coming weather to the lay person, but actually only measures the height of the current air pressure," suggesting only a probability. A meteorologist—or economist—had access to the broader context, meaning that "the simple observation of a business barometer can never replace the judgment of a given situation based on knowledge of the causal relationships between all the available facts."[22] The "wave movement" captured in the chart "can only be explained by the autonomous laws of economic life," and, Hayek insisted, only the economist understood those laws.[23]

The goal of what one could call barometer vision was, as Austrian statistician Karl Pribram put it, "the discovery of the laws relating to the sequence of economic fluctuations."[24] The barometer metaphor helped reinforce the authority of the economist as being akin to that of a scientist, conveying the phenomena of the world in a digestible form for the layperson while preserving the economist's monopoly on the secrets of causality. In 1932 Fritz Machlup, a member of the Mises Circle, expressed the idea of economist-as-scientist in a newspaper column, writing that "the laws of economics apply even if the minister, the banker, and the parliamentarian does not know or recognize them, just as the laws of physics are not swayed based on whether some technician adheres to them or not."[25] The barometer simultaneously revealed and concealed the truth of economic life.

It is significant that barometer vision saw the world at the scale of the nation. The national economy was the object of observation and the subject of action. A related metaphor of the time, originating with the British economist (and later architect of the welfare state) William Beveridge, cast graphic depictions of the cycle as the "pulse of the nation."[26] Dutch researcher Willem Einthoven had been granted the Nobel Prize for Medicine in 1924 for his pioneering development of electrocardiography, creating a means for measuring the pulse of the human heart on a line chart over time.[27] Business cycle research—and the visual technique of the business barometer—helped place the economist alongside the medical doctor as the master of an esoteric branch of knowledge amenable to a mode of representation comprehensible to the average person. As one historian has observed, the 1920s were a time when economics became understood as a domain of technical expertise beyond politics.[28] The chart was an accessory in this shift. The suffering and thriving national economy was made visible in the line of the chart, and the root causes of individuals' pain or prosperity could be seen too.

BUSINESS CYCLE RESEARCH AND THE MODERN STATE

Institutes responsible for studying the business cycle became standard features of the modern state between the two world wars. Most European states had their own business cycle institute by the time of the Great Depression, and scholars have shown how the League began to export this model of research into Asia by the 1930s.[29] One of the most important centers worldwide was the National Bureau of Economic Research (NBER) in the United States, which took up a special role of providing economic advice during Herbert Hoover's administration. The NBER was a product of transatlantic exchange. Its first president, from 1920 to 1933, was Edwin Gay, who had studied economics for twelve years in Germany before joining Harvard in 1902.[30] Hayek visited the NBER, and its influential director of research, Wesley Clair Mitchell, during the year he spent in the United States in the early 1920s. He also met Charles Bullock, the director of the Harvard Economic Service, who recalled being favorably impressed by the young Hayek.[31] Hayek brought the idea of business cycle research back to Austria with him.[32] In his words, he imported "from America a new idea of great predictions."[33] He wrote to Mitchell in 1926 that his efforts then embodied "some of the slowly ripening fruits of my sojourn in the United States."[34]

Mises and Hayek led the campaign to establish a permanent home for business cycle research in Vienna. "In a time when the entire civilized world makes decisions and arrangements on the basis of the knowledge of economic and business cycle institutes," they wrote, Austria "would demonstrate to the world either a shameful, indolent backwardness to its own disadvantage or a mistrust-producing insincerity and secretiveness that would surely place its creditworthiness in question."[35] To be against the institute, they wrote, would be to be "against progress." Here as elsewhere, Mises and Hayek made a case for the centrality of the economist in the conduct of the modern state. Economic knowledge was a central fixture of modernity. A state unequipped with economic research was doomed to fall behind in the race of nations.

Because taking the pulse of the nation put the economist in the position of the scientist or medical doctor, on this view, the economist was entitled privileged access to the internal workings of private business. The first challenge to trying to understand the business cycle was getting access to the data. Mises and Hayek argued that it was necessary "to overcome the life-threatening secretiveness of Austrian enterprises and organizations." In their view there was no private ownership of economic knowledge. Internal operations of private business must be made transparent to the gaze of the economist. To be a good economic citizen—for one's own future prosperity—meant a necessary disclosure of internal operations.

What made the very demand of access thinkable was the rupture of the First World War. One of the pivotal figures in Central Europe was Walther Rathenau, the chairman of the AEG electrical engineering company who had held the official title "raw materials dictator" for imperial Germany during the First World War. Hayek attributed the beginning of his "interest in economics" to Rathenau and "his ideas about how to reorganize the economy."[36] Rathenau's achievement was to batter down the wall between the state and business. This was being done at almost exactly the same time in Russia in the course of the Russian Revolution. Yet Rathenau may have been the more influential in the long run because he kept the institution of private ownership intact. Rathenau created transparency of the activities of capitalists without expropriating the capitalists themselves. The kernel of private property was salvaged. Although the dictates of the wartime economy were extreme, the loss of the inviolability of business information carried over into the era after Rathenau in all the countries that had undergone the First World War. On both sides of the conflict, total war meant subordination of the entire nation's energies toward mobilization. In the case of inter-Allied cooperation, it also meant cooperation beyond the nation. Large-scale economic planning and statistics collection entered the repertoire of modern statecraft during the Great War.

As mentioned in Chapter 1, the idea of businessmen opening their account books beyond the firm represented a revision of the classical liberal vision. The privacy of the businessman was no longer sacred. In business cycle research, social science was applied to the market, but not—as had been the case of the movements of "social reform" and progressivism—in order to moderate the disruptive effects of capitalism on everyday working people. "The social" or "society" had been conceived in many ways, parallel to but in opposition to "the economy," as a domain of nonmarket values and properties that needed to be preserved against the potentially corrosive effects of unregulated private enterprise. (This implication is preserved much more clearly in German, where the term "sozial" has a normative edge, implying social reform as opposed to the more neutral category of *gesellschaftlich*.) The Verein für Sozialpolitik is the archetypical case of this form of *sozial* policy, and its lead was followed from Japan to Ireland to the United States. Much of the business cycle research of the 1920s was a different beast. Here economic knowledge was more commonly being developed to maximize rather than moderate the effectiveness and scope of the market. The business cycle research institutes were the "eyes" that would see the activities of business to help business better see itself. Hayek referred to the institutes as "business cycle observation services" and to the gathering of statistical data as a "new means of observation."[37] Charts would be mirrors that enabled deeper self-understanding.

As the metaphors suggest, the visual aspect was key. Mises and Hayek wrote that information needed to be prompt and displayed in a form that could be easily grasped.[38] Mises and Hayek described the most important thing as the "pedagogical value of constant reference to the cyclical nature of business cycle movements offered by regular business cycle reporting. It allows for a planned distribution of investments over a long period of time as well as for the selection of the time point for public works."[39] The research institute was to provide useful knowledge, providing data about the pulse of the economy in a way that could advise both the private and the public sector about how to coordinate their activity. Both the businessperson and the statesperson needed to be trained to understand the cycle.

The efforts of Mises and Hayek succeeded in late 1926. The Austrian Business Cycle Research Institute was officially constituted on December 15, 1926. Hayek became its director in January 1927, with a secretary as the only other staff member.[40] The Austrian liberals linked their work immediately to international circles. In November 1926 Mises communicated with Alexander Loveday, the head of the economic section of the League of Nations, who welcomed the new institute and promised to bring it into the circuit of distribution for the international projects organized out of Geneva.[41] In January 1927 Hayek and Richard Reisch wrote to the League about the new institute. They said that its research would be both historical and current. It would create a time series that extended well before the war, and would also continue to collect data in collaboration with neighboring countries.[42]

The Austrian Institute used the "three-cycle barometer" of the Harvard Economic Service. Like other barometers, they produced portraits of the nation in numbers and time. In their first report, they produced a three-cycle barometer chart of Austria up to the outbreak of the First World War.[43] In another chart offered as an "example of the methods of representation used in the reports," the Austrian Institute distilled the economic health of the nation down to a single line. The curve was said to "represent an average of the movement of the most important figures characteristic of the course of business in Austria."[44] The dips are explained by strikes and labor shortages, and the spikes by local and international events. For a businessperson or an interested citizen, the single line marked the passage of history through the eyes of economic data: politics subordinated to the rise and fall of an abstracted market climate.

The national frame of the business barometers made sense for the homeland of business cycle research—the United States—which had the largest domestic economy in the world. But even there the importance of global events led the Harvard Economic Service to internationalize its research in the mid-1920s. Hayek's first encounter with John Maynard Keynes came at a gathering of forecasters coordinated by the Harvard Economic Service at the London School of Economics (LSE) in June 1928.[45] For his part, Hayek realized early that the nation-state frame did not transfer well to smaller countries. Austria and other postcolonial successor states in Central Europe were much more dependent on the business cycles of neighboring countries than larger countries or empires were. The precariousness of the position of the dissolved Habsburg Empire meant that foreign economies mattered more. In 1927 Hayek wrote in an industry magazine that small countries might have economies very different from those surrounding them, but they were nonetheless interdependent.[46] Without a vast internal market or a vast overseas empire, no nation could afford to ignore its neighbor.

Hayek sought to coordinate with other Central European countries and began to think in more theoretical terms about how one could practically begin to create a synthetic statistical portrait of the region. In

March 1928 he organized a conference of Central European business cycle research institutes, which included representatives from Hungary, Poland, and Czechoslovakia, as well as Adolph Löwe from the Kiel Institute for the World Economy, and Paul Rosenstein-Rodan, one of the future founders of development economics.[47] In his invitation, Hayek pointed out that "the attention to the economic development of neighboring states is possibly as important as the economic situation of one's own country."[48] He cited the conclusion of an expert gathering in Geneva in 1926 that "in a country largely dependent upon external markets, more specially in the case of certain European states, a barometer based wholly on data referring to national phenomena would in all probability prove inadequate to foreshadow the trend of economic life, since the business of that country will tend to follow the variations in the prosperity of the market upon which it is dependent."[49] In pursuit of this portrait of economic health beyond the nation, Hayek called for a regularized exchange of economic data among the Central European states, to produce a "complete picture of the economic situation of the larger region and investigate the mutual dependency of smaller economic areas."[50] It was the very peripheral status of countries like post-imperial Austria that made it necessary to be attentive to the whole. Economic information was effectively proposed as a way of resolving problems that rose at the end of empire. In creating connections to economists in successor states, Hayek and others sought to knit back together the former Habsburg space through the exchange of data, enabling the restoration of market relationships. In the absence of the political unit of the empire, economic experts proposed a network of information.

After the stock market crash of 1929 and the onset of the Depression, funding from the United States helped to move into reality the vision of a Central Europe interconnected by streams of information. Edmund E. Day, statistician and economist, became the director of the Rockefeller Foundation in 1929 and made "scientific inquiry in the field of industrial hazards and economic stabilization" the primary focus of funding.[51] In the five years after the crash, the Rockefeller Foundation earmarked close to $18 million to research in social sciences, a colossal investment in the power of knowledge to solve social and economic problems.[52] Vienna was the first business cycle institute in Europe to receive Rockefeller funding, with a grant of $20,000 in 1931 that was a windfall in economically depressed Austria.[53] Hayek's vision of a network of Central European data sharing was brought closer to realization by funding for economic research institutes in Bulgaria, Romania, Hungary, and Poland.[54]

The League of Nations–sponsored International Studies Conference and the Carnegie Endowment for International Peace took up research on the Danubian region in the late 1930s. Studying the dissolved Habsburg Empire would provide a first version of what would be called area studies after the Second World War, with a region of formally independent states being examined as an interdependent economic unit. Hayek's collaborations were an important step in beginning to think about the business cycle and the business barometer beyond the scale of the individual nation. The predicament of post-imperial Austria directed attention outward to neighboring nations and the world beyond. The pulse of the nation was not enough. What was necessary, Hayek made clear, was the pulse of the region and the pulse of the world.

THE PULSE OF THE WORLD

F. A. Hayek's work at the Austrian Business Cycle Research Institute brought him into contact with the center of world economic research in Geneva. Alexander Loveday supported Hayek's efforts to create a network of Central European business cycle research in 1928.[55] In early 1931 Loveday invited Hayek to Geneva as the representative of the Vienna Institute for the first international gathering of economists taking the measure of the world after the stock market crash.[56] Loveday thought highly of Hayek. In March 1931 he wrote to Morgenstern, regarding the origins and causes of the Depression, that "there is nobody in Europe so well fitted to go into these points as yourself and Dr. Hayek."[57] By that year, institutions were already in the process of dissolution. As Hayek left Vienna for Geneva, the venerable Creditanstalt bank was unraveling and would declare bankruptcy by May, initiating a series of bank failures that sped the fall of Central Europe into depression. The meeting in Geneva was not a casual conclave of academics but had the urgency of economic triage. As Loveday put it, it was an attempt to cast "eyes beyond the abyss of the immediate future to the vaguer hazards of a more distant horizon."[58]

The convener of the meeting was the Swedish economist Bertil Ohlin. He had gathered reports from the invited economists about the business cycles in their respective countries. Such international coordination was felt to be necessary because "whereas a number of pre-war depressions were confined to a relatively limited area, to-day their repercussions are felt throughout the world." "The world problem," the experts concluded, "should be studied on a world basis."[59] Although phrased differently, the goal was the same as the Chilean-German statistician Ernst Wagemann had proposed in 1928: to inquire if there was "a world-economic, as well as national-economic, business cycle."[60] The conclusion of the gathered economists in 1931 was unanimous: even if solutions were still elusive, they should be sought at the scale of the world.[61]

The first step to approaching the "world problem" was to make the data comparable. The League of Nations had begun to standardize world economic statistics after the First World War. In 1920 it set up an International Statistical Commission with members of the International Statistical Institute, the International Institute of Agriculture, and the International Chamber of Commerce. It began publication of the *Statistical Year Book* in 1927.[62] In 1928 a meeting called to ratify an International Convention on Economic Statistics was attended by delegates from forty countries, and they created a Committee of Statistical Experts.[63] The process of standardizing and gathering world statistics led to the creation of a new kind of global vision. Condliffe, one of the experts in charge of the process, wrote that "the economists who do so are international not only in being drawn from different nationalities, but also in being able, nay, in being compelled, to interpret their data from a non-national viewpoint." Creating statistics was globalizing, in the sense of producing a single world picture and changing the mentality of the economists themselves. "As the data from one country fit into those from another," Condliffe wrote, "they see the world as a developing economic organism."[64]

Mises wrote in 1928 that "for the liberal, the world does not end at the borders of the state.... His political thinking encompasses the whole of mankind.[65] The statistical globalism of the League of Nations gave a numerical tangibility to this vision. Ohlin's report after the 1931 meeting reinforced the idea of what he called international "interdependencies" and the inability of states to escape the push and pull of global economic forces.[66] In 1932 Arthur Salter referred to the "collective laboratory work" on the problem of the business cycle, analogizing economists to natural scientists working on a problem that would have a definitive solution.[67] Beginning the same year, Condliffe oversaw the publication of the new annual *World Economic Survey,* which he described as a "natural sequel" to the international project of collaboration initiated by Ohlin.[68] The second survey included Morgenstern's adapted spiral of world trade; the Vienna Institute was part of the project of making the world economy seen and known as a space of unified processes. They were helping create a world economy of numbers.

Links between the Mises Circle and Geneva deepened when Haberler was appointed in May 1934, on Hayek's recommendation, to write the follow-up volume to Ohlin on theories of business cycles and the Depression.[69] As we saw in Chapter 1, Haberler used the model of the spaceless world to build his analysis, equating tariffs, distances, and the actions of organized labor as comparable obstacles to the optimal distribution of the world's resources. Even if he was unsuccessful in proving it scientifically, he saw it as a matter of fact that business cycles could be internationalized. "For a hundred years or more," he wrote, "the economic connections between most countries in the world, industrialized countries as well as agricultural and raw-material producing countries, have become so intimate and international trade so important for the various national economic systems that a closer connection between the ups and downs of the business cycle in different countries is to be expected." The "bacillus of boom or depression," he wrote, travels freely "from country to country."[70]

Even if causality remained opaque, the Great Depression had made the interconnection of world economic activity commonsense in expert circles. At the March 1931 meeting of the American Economic Conference, Ernest Minor Patterson said, "[It is] now painfully trite to observe that the world is an economic unit. Each area and each economic group is more than ever before dependent on the rest and every irregularity in the operation of any part of the world's economic machine has widespread effects." Yet despite this fact, "the approach of the economists has been largely a national approach." The exceptions he mentioned were the International Chamber of Commerce and the League of Nations.[71] Acknowledging that an interconnected world economy existed was one thing. What to do about it was another. In 1936 Loveday gathered an august group of economists to discuss the first draft of Haberler's report. The meeting included figures who would be central to the neoliberal intellectual movement, including Lionel Robbins, Wilhelm Röpke, and Charles Rist.[72] Hayek was unable to attend, as Robbins was acting as the representative from the LSE.[73]

In its form, Haberler's study and the conference convened to discuss it inaugurated something Robbins called the "Haberler-like method."[74] The method entailed group research on "a big subject" followed by a larger meeting of experts to evaluate the results. The Haberler method established a form for international collaboration and data gathering, a halfway point between abstract economics and empirical statistics with nothing less than the entire world economy as the object. It was organic and unbound to any one institution, gathering periodically to examine and exchange research results. The similarities of the Haberler method to the format of the postwar Mont Pèlerin Society were not coincidental. Part of the Geneva experiment was a belief in the halfway point between theorizing and the spadework of data collection and standardization.

Speaking at the International Statistical Institute in 1936, Karl Pribram, Mises's old acquaintance from Vienna who was now a leading figure at the International Labour Organization (ILO), tracked the descent of the economists from the clouds to the earth. Economists had begun with abstract notions of a "worldwide universal economic system" but had been forced by events to "work downward from lofty theorizing to the essential realities of economic life."[75] Wrangling with the problem of the Great Depression deepened the marriage between statisticians and economists. As Haberler put it in a letter to Loveday, he shared the goal of Mitchell and the NBER: "to bring theories and facts into closer touch."[76] The Haberler method was about expanding the ambit of economists in public life and extending economists' reach into the domain of government. Just like the business cycle research institutes sought to breach the walls around corporate secrecy, the activity of international institutions like the League sought to draw information out of national governments.

DOES THE WORLD ECONOMY EXIST?

The Haberler method was given an immediate second application after the initial conference to discuss the League report on Economic Depressions in 1936. One week after its completion, cars full of economists drove one hour south to the shores of another lake in Annecy, France. The conference, held at the Imperial Palace Hotel, was paid for by the Rockefeller Foundation.[77] Those gathered included Mises, Morgenstern, Alvin Hansen, Ohlin, Robbins, and Röpke.[78] The conference directly preceded a gathering planned for Vienna to discuss coordination among research institutes.[79] Until Ohlin and Haberler's reports on the Great Depression, most of the research on the business cycle to date had been basically national. The question the Rockefeller Foundation had for the economists in Annecy was fundamental: Did the global economy exist? As the text of the invitation put it: "Is the concept 'world economy' sufficiently real to warrant subjecting it to continuous study?"[80]

The agenda, written by the Russian-born, Sofia-based statistician Oskar Anderson, put it a bit more lengthily: "Can we say that these forces possess a certain organic unity that warrants the conclusion that there is such a thing as a 'world economy'? Or are they nothing more than a physical aggregate of unrelated and disjointed forces resulting from many conflicting national programs and policies?"[81] The immediate question for the gathered economists in Annecy was how one would measure the world economy: "If it develops that there is reasonable agreement regarding the identity of these forces, it would appear logical to ask how effectively we are now capturing, recording and analyzing them." How to capture and represent the world economy? Also, should there be a "special central institute" to do so? The economists at the conference agreed on the need for an international investigation into the effects of agricultural protectionism in industrial states and industrial protectionism in agricultural states. This was relevant because it was disrupting a core aspect of liberal globalism: the international division of labor. Those gathered proposed that the study would transition later into an "international bureau of business cycle research . . . set up to cooperate with the various national business cycle institutes and make their findings readily available."[82]

The individual nominated to lead this would-be bureau for international observation was Wilhelm Röpke, who was put forward especially by William Rappard and Robbins.[83] Röpke would be considered one of the intellectual fathers of the postwar "social market economy" in West Germany. He was also central to the organization of the transnational neoliberal intellectual movement and will be a central figure in the chapters that follow, not the least for his determinedly globalist outlook and his emphasis on extra-economic requirements for market society, including matters of race and culture. Born in the German town of Schwarmstedt near Hanover in 1899, Röpke finished his training in economics at Marburg in 1921 and returned as a full professor in 1929. He was ejected from the university for his liberal opposition to the new National Socialist government in 1933, emigrating thereafter to a post at the University of Istanbul.[84] He was seeking a return to European academic circles, and the study looked promising.

Rappard suggested that Röpke would coordinate the multicountry study from Geneva, which Jacques Polak later called "perhaps *the* leading center of applied economics in Europe" in the 1930s.[85] The institutional base would be Rappard's Graduate Institute of International Studies. While Rappard is most well-known as the director of the Mandates sections of the League, he was also central in turning his Graduate Institute into an academic home for the neoliberal group in the 1930s, inviting Mises to the faculty in 1934, Michael Heilperin in 1935, and Röpke in 1937 as well as hosting and publishing important series of lectures by Hayek and Robbins.[86]

Rappard's own biography wove through the worlds of academia, business, and international organizations on both sides of the Atlantic. Born in midtown Manhattan in 1883, he returned to Switzerland at age fifteen with dual citizenship to settle with his family in Geneva.[87] Entering university in 1901, his academic travels before the First World War exposed him to the leading figures in economics, including Gustav von Schmoller, Adolph Wagner, and Lujo Brentano in Berlin and

Munich; Edwin Francis Gay, Frank Taussig, and Charles J. Bullock at Harvard; and Eugen Böhm-Bawerk, Eugen Philippovich, and Carl Grünberg in Vienna.[88] It was through his Viennese professors that Rappard got his first position at an international institution in 1910, as one of ten employees of the International Labour Office in Basel, Switzerland, a wing of the International Association for Labour Legislation and precursor of the ILO founded in 1900.[89] In 1911 Rappard returned to Harvard to teach a course and made contacts at the Boston Chamber of Commerce, who sponsored a trip to South America.[90] He used his American connections to gain his position after the First World War as the director of the Mandates Commission.

In 1925 Rappard began conceiving of a Graduate Institute as a way to draw on the deep pool of expertise in Geneva and to cement transatlantic ties. With the notion that it might be named the Wilson Institute, Rappard saw it as a school for future American diplomats, and was consulting with Beardsley Ruml of the Rockefeller Foundation about funding.[91] In June 1926 Ruml gave him the news that the Laura Spelman Rockefeller Memorial Fund had approved $100,000 for five years of funding for the Geneva Institute.[92]

Rappard's institute offered an important institutional hub for the future neoliberals. We will see in Chapter 3 that the model of mandates he represented at the League overlapped significantly with certain visions of neoliberal federation. Always eager to secure ongoing funding, Rappard was no doubt happy in 1936 that the Rockefeller Foundation was interested in using Röpke's study as a pilot case, as it was, as their officer put it, "an interesting experiment in the organization of investigations of this type."[93] A scale model proposed for Röpke's study of the world would be the Danubian region.[94] Röpke embraced the study of what was often called "Danubia" as a starting point but also said that more needed to be done from a " 'global' point of view."[95] He dubbed a country's desire to have its own agriculture and its own industry "economic simplicism."[96] His project was about how to dissuade countries from seeking self-sufficiency and convince them of the benefits for all that can be gained from being enmeshed in a larger whole.

Taking up his position in Geneva, Röpke described his task in March 1938 as using what he called the "Haberler method" to arrive "at a better understanding of the structural crisis of the world economy."[97] Rescued from his Turkish emigration, he was to sit in Switzerland atop what the Rockefeller funder called an "international economic observation post."[98] Ironically, as we will see, even though Röpke had every intention of turning his perch into a Lighthouse of the World, gazing down upon the earth and translating it into meaningful statistics, his move back to Europe would be the first step on the road away from the world of numbers.

THE LIPPMANN COLLOQUIUM AS WORLD PROJECT

Röpke returned to Turkey after the Annecy conference to complete his contract. He remained in touch with the network of liberals from afar. In February 1937 he wrote to Lionel Robbins that he had not only been appointed to a professorship in Geneva but also had been made the "international rapporteur" for a "vast programme of research."[99] In the summer of 1937 Hayek gave Röpke the proofs of a new book, *An Inquiry into the Principles of the Good Society*, by the American journalist Walter Lippmann. Very excited, Röpke wrote to Lippmann to tell him about his own "international cooperative study on 'International Economic Disintegration' which, of course, will bring me at every point near the questions discussed in your book." He proposed that there must be "in one form or another, a discussion among the few people in the world whose thoughts in these matters have reached the necessary degree of maturity."[100] He conveyed to Robbins that "a thorough discussion of the main issues involved" in Lippmann's book "should be organized now."[101]

In August 1938 this gathering took place in Paris facilitated by Hayek, Röpke, and the host, Louis Rougier, who had published a book with Rappard's imprint in 1935.[102] The so-called Walter Lippmann Colloquium (CWL) overlapped with two major projects of seeing the world, each of which contained its own set of institutions (and acronyms). One was Röpke's International Economic Disintegration project that came out of Geneva and Annecy, funded by Rockefeller, and closely connected to the League of Nations, business cycle research, and the Vienna cohort of Haberler, Hayek, and Mises. The second was the International Studies Conference (ISC), the first international cooperative institution of the budding discipline of international relations; the conference met annually beginning in 1928.[103] The conferences were hosted by the International Institute for Intellectual Cooperation (IIIC), which originally was part of the French government but had merged with the League's International Committee on Intellectual Cooperation (ICIC) in 1926.[104] The IIIC would survive the war and morph into UNESCO. The annual International Studies Conferences were perhaps closest to the CWL in format and spirit. They followed a variation of the Haberler method, gathering for two years on a single theme dedicated to exchanging information about schemes for managing an interdependent planet. The conferences were a place to think about the problems of the world across the disciplines. In 1935 and 1936, the theme was collective security. In 1937 and 1938, it was peaceful change. In 1939, the theme was close to Röpke's own on international economic disintegration: economic policies in relation to world peace.[105] The similarity was not coincidental, as there was much movement between Geneva and the conferences. In 1937 the first compiler of the *World Economic Survey,* Condliffe, left the League of Nations to become the rapporteur for the ISC.[106]

There were important overlaps between these internationally networked groups of liberal economic experts and the CWL. Condliffe, for example, was in attendance in Paris in 1938. Hagen Schulz-Forberg has drawn attention to the importance of this context, pointing out that Mises contributed a study on raw materials to the 1936 ISC and Michael Heilperin wrote and circulated pieces for the 1937 and 1939 meetings.[107] Mises attended the May 1936 ISC meeting in Madrid as a representative of the Graduate Institute.[108] Röpke had tried to attend the ISC conference in 1936 but could not because of his German passport.[109] Also significant was the figure of Lippmann himself. The American coordinating committee for the ISC was the Council on Foreign Relations, and the group (also Rockefeller-funded) for the 1937 conference held in Paris listed Lippmann along with future secretary of state John Foster Dulles and international law expert Philip C. Jessup.[110] The Walter Lippmann Colloquium, in this sense, was not an anomalous gathering but very much of the time, a continuation of a

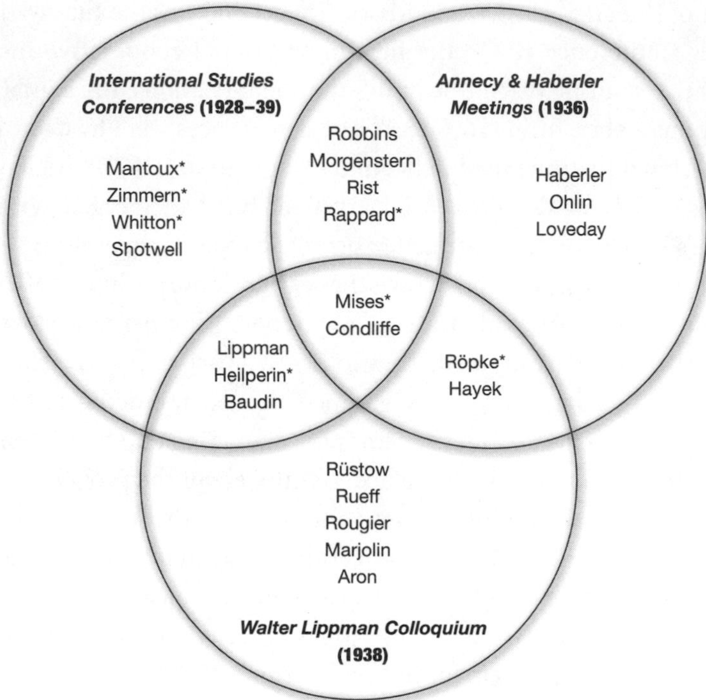

Overlap of participants in world projects of the 1930s. Asterisks mark faculty members at the Graduate Institute for International Studies in Geneva.

spirit of international liberal collaborative research funded by the ICC, the League of Nations, and U.S. philanthropic foundations.

The Walter Lippmann Colloquium lasted four days and concluded with the decision to create an International Study Center for the Renovation of Liberalism in Paris with Swiss, English, and American outposts overseen by Röpke, Hayek, and Lippmann, respectively.[111] On the suggestion of the French industrialist Louis Marlio, a major player in the creation of an aluminum cartel in the 1920s, the label on which the gathered thinkers settled for their shared ideology was "neoliberalism."[112] The French center for the new movement was to be housed in the Musée Social, a building originally created to hold the documents from the Social Economy exhibition of the 1889 Paris Exhibition. Called a "social laboratory for modern France," the building may seem like an unlikely headquarters for the just-born neoliberal movement.[113] Yet, as scholars have noted, the discussions at the CWL hardly conformed to a caricature of market fundamentalism.[114] Instead participants took a range of positions, many of which clustered around accommodation for some form of intervention and a welfare state.

Lippmann's text left itself open to such appropriation. The American journalist was scathing about what he called the "fallacy of laissez faire," by which classical liberals ended up as uninspiring apologists for the status quo.[115] In this, he reflected the interwar zeitgeist. In 1924 Keynes had already famously declared "the end of laissez faire" and suggested a rethinking of the state necessary to safeguard the market.[116] In Lippmann's view, by disavowing the need for a strong state, and especially a legal framework, to preserve the conditions of the market, nineteenth-century liberals had effectively approved of whatever conditions happened to prevail. In the phrase that was attached to the center established in his wake, Lippmann called for a "renovation of liberalism" that not only acknowledged the necessity of institutions in preserving the market but also sanctioned a startlingly broad palette of measures one would identify with the welfare state: from eugenics and education to public works and urban recreation facilities.[117] These services would be paid for through taxes on the wealthy, skimming off what he called "excess capital."[118]

The most striking feature of Lippman's book and the colloquium organized around it was that thinkers like Röpke and Hayek, who were otherwise skeptical of such forms of intervention and redistribution, would be so enthusiastic about it. One could surmise that what was most liberating about the book was not only the public attention it drew, dangling the possibility of a return to currency of the liberal cause, but also how far it was from the technical jargon of the League of Nations and the arcane details of business cycle research in which many of them had been entrenched in the late 1920s and early 1930s. By the late 1930s at the latest, it had become indisputable that all of the statistical facts in the world were not adding up to a restoration of the shattered world that Mises had identified in the 1920s.

Ahead of the conference Röpke and his co-author, the German sociologist Alexander Rüstow, put the matter most bluntly when they observed that "men and means have been mobilized during the last ten years, on an unprecedented scale. . . . Facts have been piled up sky-high, conferences have been held in endless procession, economic analysis has been brought to an ever greater degree of refinement (and incidentally to an ever greater degree of unreality), vast and detailed programs of research are being elaborated complicated machineries of institutionalized science set up and questionnaires sent to almost every country and to every section of the population" and still nations were becoming less rather than more united.[119] Röpke later remarked in a rueful line that serves as the epigraph to this chapter: "It is no exaggeration to say that the era of decay of the world economy was at the same time the era of international economic conferences."[120]

In such an atmosphere of information glut and ineffectual data overload, what was likely refreshing in Lippmann's book was his emphasis, not on the factual and economic, but on the political and sociological aspects of liberalism. While he engaged with economic matters throughout, the economy was cast not as a space of numbers and cycles but of values and order. In fact, one of the core arguments of Lippmann's book, largely adopted from his reading of Mises and Hayek, was that it was naive and damaging to try to carry out what he called the "overhead control" of the economy by "intelligent authority."[121] He drew on the Austrian thinkers extensively to critique what he called "the illusion of control" in social and economic life. He derided the attempt to fully capture and comprehend the vast coordination of human energies that was carried out, largely unplanned, by people driven only by the free movement of prices. No mass of "statistics, censuses, reports," he wrote, could add up to sufficient knowledge to plan the process from above.[122] In what could be read as an implicit critique of both socialist planning and attempts to perceive the entirety of economic life through business cycle research, Lippmann wrote that "to the data of social experience the mind is like a lantern which casts dim circles of light spasmodically upon somewhat familiar patches of ground in an unexplored wilderness."[123] He summoned the divine. "Social control," he wrote, "can never be regarded as even an approximation to the kind of mastery which men have ascribed to God as the creator and ruler of the universe."[124]

What to do in the face of a "social system" in which "innumerable elements are interdependent and interacting"?[125] Lippmann did not despair at the inherent ungovernability of a liberal capitalist society. Rather, he made the move that would define much of organized neoliberalism: he moved from the economic to the legal. "As affairs become more intricate, more extended in time and space, more involved and interrelated," he wrote, "overhead direction . . . has to give way . . . to social control by the method of a common law."[126] While it was the "historic mission of liberalism to discover the significance of the division of labor; its uncompleted task is to show how law and public policy may best be adapted to this mode of production."[127] The role of law was not limited to the nation-state. Throughout his book Lippmann used the category of "the Great Society," which he borrowed from the LSE economist Graham Wallas, to connote an interconnected space of exchange whose reach by the modern age was global.[128] Shared law must extend throughout the global Great Society. He put the point forcefully: "The necessity of common laws throughout the world economy is the necessity of all the multitudes of mankind in all their daily transactions, and its cumulative force is invincible."[129]

Lippmann followed Mises and Hayek by proposing that both socialism and liberalism faced a knowledge problem that only the free price system could solve. He went beyond Mises and Hayek in his strong emphasis on the fact that prices only worked within the uniform structure of law. Ben Jackson points out that this turn to law anticipated Hayek's own renewed interest in the rule of law from the 1940s onward.[130] Hayek and Mises also adopted the term "The Great Society" and used it throughout their careers. The fact that Lyndon B. Johnson used the same phrase to describe his suite of national welfare state programs in the late 1960s make it easy to mistake the scale of the term for Hayek, Mises, Lippmann, and indeed Adam Smith before them. For all of them, the term meant the full reach of the realm of market exchange; the Great Society, as Mises put it in 1944, embraced "all human beings."[131]

Lippmann's work was a synthesis of the Austrian perspective on the subjectivity of value with a new attention to the rule of law. For Hayek, it dovetailed with new attention he had been devoting to the question of knowledge from even before the Lippmann Colloquium. Even as they engaged in projects of statistical inquiry, the Viennese economists around Mises had always remained cautious about the limits of purely descriptive facts and the possibility of prediction.[132] The Methodenstreit of the late nineteenth century between the historical economists and the marginalists associated with Carl Menger had revolved in part around the skepticism about the possibility of capturing the totality of a national economy, let alone the world. The economists of the Mises Circle were dubious about the efforts of Ernst Wagemann in Berlin as the extension of the project of the historical school.[133] Yet until the 1930s this problem had been solved more through theoretical approaches. In the 1930s, however, Hayek returned to the so-called calculation debate to revise his own faith in the role of knowledge itself.[134]

In his presidential address, "Economics and Knowledge," at the London Economic Club in 1937, Hayek reminded his audience of the Latin definition of *datum* as "given." But the issue was, he said, "to whom the facts are supposed to be given."[135] He felt economists had fudged the difference between the things that they knew (or claimed to know) and the things that average economic actors in the world *actually* knew. His work at the Austrian Business Cycle Research Institute had been premised on the notion of economic pedagogy—the idea that the gap between the market, the economist, and the economic actor could be bridged—but now he threw that whole possibility into doubt. He pointed out that equilibrium models were based on both perfect knowledge among all actors involved and what he derided as essentially the zombie category of *Homo economicus*—"the 'economic man' whom we have exorcised with prayer and fasting, has returned through the back door."[136] Not for the last time, Hayek did something that neoliberals are often themselves accused of doing: he suggested that economists mistake their models for the real world.

To Hayek, perfect markets did not exist in reality. They could not exist because perfect knowledge is impossible. Instead one had to begin from the assumption of what, quoting Mises, he called the "division of knowledge," analogous to the division of labor.[137] He dismissed the economists' idea that "only . . . knowledge of prices" was needed. This was a clear move away from both the barometer vision and the public pedagogy role of the Viennese research institute and away from the idea of the cycle altogether as the focus of research. It was in 1937 that Hayek first gestured at what one scholar has identified as a defining feature of his philosophy: the usefulness of ignorance.[138] Hayek suggested that equilibrium exists "only because some people have no chance of learning about facts which, if they knew them, would induce them to alter their plans."[139] He concluded not only that perfect knowledge was a tautological conceit of the model inapplicable to reality but that it missed the basic point that imperfect, not perfect, knowledge was what created equilibrium in the form of economic order. As he put it later, he realized in the second half of the 1930s that "the basic function of economics was to explain the process of how human activity adapted itself to data *about which it had no information*."[140]

If humans acted in unconscious response to market stimuli, then it followed that public enlightenment was no longer the role of the economist. The business cycle chart was truly the pulse of the nation in the sense of being a record of the autonomous nervous system rather than the thinking mind. Reference to such a record of autonomous activity would be no means of ensuring greater stability over time. In fact, to assume that the chart provided actionable knowledge for the policy maker was the most seductive error of all, leading to what Lippmann called the "illusion of control." As Hayek wrote later, to even "speak of a national social or world economy . . . is one of the chief sources of the most socialist endeavor to turn the spontaneous order of the market into a deliberately run organization serving an agreed system of common ends."[141] To extend the metaphor, Hayek's solution was to remove the patient from the electrocardiograph and focus on preventative care. There was a new goal—not to cure maladies as they arose through direct action but to design a world where the patient would never fall sick in the first place. The horizon of imagination was not treatment but prophylaxis.

The emphasis on institutions and rule of law in Lippmann's book offered a perfect complement to Hayek's conclusion about limited knowledge, allowing for a turn away from attempts to capture the economy in either numbers or theoretical models and toward projects of law and statecraft. Lippmann praised the importance of selective knowledge when he conjured up a new role for the liberal as architect of order: "The thinker, as he sits in his study drawing his plans for the direction of society, will do no thinking if his breakfast has not been produced for him by a social process which is beyond his detailed comprehension. He knows that his breakfast depends upon workers on the coffee plantations of Brazil, the citrus groves of Florida, the sugar fields of Cuba, the wheat farms of the Dakotas, the dairies of New York; that it has been assembled by ships, railroads, and trucks, has been cooked with coal from Pennsylvania in utensils made of aluminum, china, steel, and glass. But the intricacy of one breakfast, if every process that brought it to the table had deliberately to be planned, would be beyond the understanding of any mind." Unlike those economists—including the later famous case of Milton Friedman and his pencil—who took the moment of phenomenological encounter as an entry point into understanding the world economy, Lippmann suggested it as a moment to forget the world economy. "Only because he can count upon an infinitely complex system of working routines," he wrote, "can a man eat his breakfast and then think about a new social order."[142] The task of the liberal intellectual was not to seek to trace the lineaments of the world economy but to take a step back and contemplate the core enabling conditions of the grander order itself. The global economy was unknowable—and this was not a dead end but the starting point for designing the order within which the world economy could thrive. This insight was foundational to the emergence of the Geneva School of neoliberalism.

The second road away from numbers in the 1930s was taken by Röpke and Rüstow. At the colloquium, Röpke advanced a theory he had floated in a letter to Robbins two years earlier that "the disintegration of the moral function of our system is the most important and the most sinister aspect of the process of the present disintegration."[143] He wrote that what liberalism had to "learn from conservatism" was to pay attention to "the imponderabilia, the vital or human element or whatever you call these elusive things."[144] Like Lippmann, Röpke and Rüstow held that the misguided belief in laissez-faire had produced adverse social effects, best expressed in the "disease called 'proletariat.' " A "narrow economic conception" of humanity had overlooked the "extra-economic" needs of humanity.[145]

Prefiguring Karl Polanyi's analysis of market fundamentalism in *The Great Transformation,* Rüstow said at the Lippmann Colloquium that "the market had become a domain of atomization" and the belief that the market "operates by itself" was a "theologico-rational error."[146] One-sided focus on efficiency, profit, and productivity had led to a sociologically damaging isolation and the degeneration of morality as the individual became detached from all community. In a cruel paradox, the experience of being severed from all social ties and set adrift in the world "appears from the point of view of the market economy as liberation from friction and extra-economic drag."[147] Without using the term "embeddedness" itself, Rüstow and Röpke effectively argued that the economy must be re-embedded in society. The individual must rediscover meaningful community relationships, including family, religion and, preferably, a connection to the rural land.

Hayek and Mises opposed Röpke and Rüstow openly at the colloquium. Mises accused Rüstow of romanticizing rural life, and Hayek argued that the proposal for a "rating scale" of "vital values" was inconsistent with the principles of liberalism.[148] This divergence would resurface again on the question of race, as Chapter 5 will show. What they all united on, however, was, first, their belief in internationalism, and, second, their skepticism about the value of numbers and models in telling the truth about the world. Röpke disparaged the declension of the social sciences into "a fact-recording machinery" and called for more synthetic collaborative work—less like the statistics-gathering of the business cycle research institutes and more like the international relations investigations of the ISC and the social philosophy of Lippmann.[149]

Perhaps the most strident attack on statistics came from the Polish economist and faculty member at Rappard's Graduate Institute, Michael Heilperin, in a book he completed the month after returning to Geneva from the Lippmann Colloquium and later condensed for his contribution to the ISC in 1939. In the book's first pages, Heilperin warned of "pseudo-quantitative concepts" and criticized the use of "statistical constructions" to understand "the heterogeneous reality they are supposed to represent." He complained that "our knowledge of economic reality tends to become an index-number knowledge."[150] Statistics offered "a comfortable way out of the perplexing multiplicity and heterogeneity presented by the economic world . . . but the multiplicity does exist and by ignoring it one falls into erroneous or meaningless statements about the world and about economic processes."[151] Once deemed the royal road to world economic insight, projects of statistics had led into a dead end.

The core neoliberals began the 1930s with a working faith in numbers but ended the decade with an antipathy toward them. Even the Austrians with their preexisting skepticism toward descriptive statistics had been willing to promote business cycle research with a public pedagogical function. Yet by the end of the decade, Hayek was speaking of the necessity of not-knowing for economic relations. What explains the collective shift? As suggested in the condemnation of the "illusion of control," over the 1930s the use of numbers had become associated with those who believed in state action to stabilize the price level and leftists like Otto Neurath and Harold Laski, whom Lippmann accused of seeking a "planetary super-state" through "economic world-planning."[152] It was a founding distinction for the newly self-identifying group of neoliberals that they did not share the belief of their opponents on the left that the economy could be seen and counted—and, thus, fine-tuned and perfected. In response to what they saw as the crippling and "degeneration" of the functioning price system, neoliberals invested heavily in the invisibility of the economy. What could not be seen could not be engineered.

If the economy was beyond representation, then the task was to find a framework to contain and protect it. The Lippmann Colloquium in 1938 yielded a normative vision of the world in which the most relevant means of intervention was not in measurement, observation, or surveillance but in the establishment of a common, enforceable law and a means of accounting for the vital needs of humanity not provided by the market. By placing the economy beyond the space of representation—and, for Hayek, beyond even reason—neoliberalism was born in the late 1930s as a project of synthetic social science in which, as surprising as it might sound, the least important disciplinary approach was that of economics itself.

Although born out of projects of global statistics and data gathering, the project of Geneva School neoliberalism would be not about seeing the world economy but about declaring its invisibility; not measuring it but casting it as sublime and beyond capture; not surveying its workings but theorizing it as a spontaneous order eluding comprehension. Geneva School neoliberalism would be a negative theology. Its program was to design the right institutions to encase the world economy without describing the world economy itself. This would be a project of law, state and organizations at the global level. It is telling that Mises's last intervention at the Lippmann Colloquium was to suggest the study of the League of Nations.[153] Far from being a paleoliberal who believed in a magical, self-organizing market, he, like all neoliberals, saw the intellectual project as finding the right state and the right law to serve the market order.

❁ ❁ ❁

In 1933 H. G. Wells published a novel, *The Shape of Things to Come,* that purported to be the dream journal of Dr. Philip Raven, an economist in the employ of the League of Nations who met an "unexpected death" in November 1930. Raven had been dreaming of the future, and his journal projected the vision of the League forward. It spoke of a Central Observation Bureau—a "complex organization of discussion, calculation, criticism and forecast" and a "World Encyclopaedia Establishment" in the "mother thought-city"—a transparent stand-in for Geneva. It was a version of the future where scientific knowledge was complete and coming events were an open book. Economists kept busy recording "irregularities and producing plans for adjustment." Raven recorded that the breakthrough for this vision had been first the Great War, after which the idea of "worldwide order" became a "working conviction" for many but really took hold after the "financial storms of the years 1928 and 1929," which gave "the World-State prophets the courage of their conviction"—"they had arrived at the realization that human society had become one indivisible economic system."[154]

The global spiral of the Great Depression had proven beyond a doubt that there was an interdependent entity called the world economy. A meeting of the ICC attended by Mises summarized the sentiment in July 1931 when they declared, "The development of the world crisis has clearly demonstrated the economic and financial interdependence of all nations."[155] The neoliberals had come to the same conclusion as Wells's fictional economist and the ICC. Yet their path did not lead to the Central Observation Bureau or the World Encyclopedia. They did not end the decade dreaming of synopsis. Indeed, they saw the fantasies of Raven—and Wells—as revealing the very root of the catastrophe that followed the Depression. From Roosevelt's New Deal to Hitler's New Order to Stalin's Five-Year Plan, neoliberals saw governments indulging in illusions of control and the misguided belief that applied scientific knowledge could make national economies transparent to an "intelligent authority" from above, enabling plans by which national economies could persist in isolation and autonomy.

In the late 1930s ever more thinkers suggested that if you could only see the economy correctly, then just as Raven wrote, "plans for adjustments" could prevent future depressions. As is now widely acknowledged, the idea of "the economy" itself as an object to be observed, modeled, and engineered only arose with the tools of national income accounting and the creation of the discipline of macroeconomics.[156] Röpke himself pointed out in 1937 that macroeconomics encouraged the national frame of policy, including what he called "self-contained national income theory."[157] The nation-state was the assumed, if not the explicit, container for projects of planning and later the distribution of the welfare state's social services and benefits. Geneva School neoliberals felt that this confidence was misplaced and drew a line around the nation when the frame of analysis should encompass the world. In a lecture at Rappard's Institute in Geneva in 1937, Hayek said that the idea of stabilizing the price level "rests largely on an illusion, based on the accident that the statistical measure of price movements are usually constructed for countries as such."[158] In a book he finished in Geneva, Mises wrote that statistics were a way of recording history, not producing theory, and had "nothing to do with economics."[159] The world of numbers and cycles gave a false impression of total vision that hid the side effects of intervention. In his inaugural lecture at the Institute in the same year, Röpke suggested that "the world has indeed come to believe that the economic system, if properly guided, can be made cycle-proof" but wondered if "those cycle-proof economies turn out to be an optical illusion, as where the unavoidable economic disharmonies will not become manifest at the place of their origin, but rather be shoved off to the periphery of the economic apparatus."[160]

Neoliberals began the 1930s studying the business cycle. By the end of the decade, the spreading belief that the business cycle could be tamed and controlled led them to see it as one of the chief causes of "international economic disintegration."[161] Röpke said at the Lippmann Colloquium: "The greatest danger is the new business cycle policy: the policy of economic autonomy, the policy of economic nationalism, combined with the planned economy and autarchy."[162] Seeing economics through statistics and cycles had fostered fantasies of management at the scale of the nation that threatened to pave the way to global disorder.

The 1930s transformed liberal thinking about the world economy. The premise of the 1920s had been that restoring the shattered global economy was a negative process. If the walls of wage demands created by unions and of tariffs created by special interests would fall, then the free market would take over. The second catastrophic collapse of the world economy in a single generation made many intellectuals think about the problem anew. The essence of the project of *neo*liberalism was that defending the world economy could not be a simply negative project but had to be a proactive project. There was a new role for law and the state. What neoliberals pioneered in the 1930s was the idea of thinking in orders, seeing the question of liberalism versus socialism as one that required a total-system perspective.

In a decade when most solutions inspired by Keynes, Moscow, and Schacht were national, and planning was in the air, Röpke and his collaborators in Paris, Geneva, and Eastern Europe thought at the scale of the globe. Their discussions came out of the same milieu as the discipline of international relations. Although globalism is now nearly synonymous with American power, the 1930s were quite different. Globalism was not an ideology that simply emanated outward from the United States. Most projects that took the world as their object were based in Paris, Geneva, and London rather than Washington or New York. Histories of international relations tend to elide its European origins in the interwar period, eclipsed as it was by the postwar paradigm. But neoliberalism was part of the questions asked at the dawn of international relations. The following chapters track the series of institutional projects, often failed, that neoliberals participated in to secure the global economy. Chapter 3 shows some of the most explicit examples as neoliberal plans for federation proposed a double government to rule over capitalism's doubled world.

3

A World of Federations

"The mines for the miners" and "Papua for the Papuans" are analytically similar slogans.

—LIONEL ROBBINS, 1937

I'm thoroughly opposed to a world government," Hayek said in a 1983 interview. When the interviewer pressed by asking "of any form," he confirmed: "Of any form."[1] If there is one certainty about the "Austrian" position in the United States today, it would be a suspicion of government, at all levels, but certainly world government. A 2002 collection on neoliberal thought and globalization posed the binary: "Will freedom or global government dominate the international marketplace?"[2] More often, the topic is simply ignored. The nearly eight-hundred-page *Oxford Handbook of Austrian Economics* includes no chapter on international order among its thirty-four chapters.[3] Yet both this interpretation and Hayek's own are either conscious disavowal of, or selective amnesia regarding, an earlier position. In the 1930s and early 1940s there was no question for neoliberals that supranational government was a possibility—and Austrians were among its most eloquent defenders.

Perhaps nothing could surprise the libertarian more than the appearance of Ludwig von Mises in an article in the *New York Times* in

1941 describing the "world government convention" of the World Fellowship Inc. at the World Fellowship Center in a small town in New Hampshire. The main speaker was Irving Fisher, the celebrated American neoclassical economist. Speaking of the "war-disease" of "Hitlerism," Fisher said that "the cure is that same cure which has worked before and the only one which has ever worked—more government." After citing the "detailed plan for a world government" of the now-forgotten journalist Clarence Streit, who was one of the world's most influential intellectuals for a short time in the 1940s, Fisher cited Mises, "who would add to the Streit plan for uniting democracies a union of Middle Europe covering a wide strip between Germany and Russia, postponing a world government to a later date."[4] What was the hero of the latter-day libertarian movement doing in the company of architects of world union and world government? Was he misquoted? Were his ideas distorted? Not at all. As we will see, Mises, Hayek, Robbins, and other neoliberals all wrote extensively about the need for strong supranational federations.

How to explain the incongruous fact that the supposed prophets of the small state were actually advocates for varieties of supranational government? Chapter 2 showed how the neoliberal movement was born out of the conviction that cycles and numbers were not enough. The cause of liberalism—and the defense of the primacy of the world economy—was too important to be left to the discipline of economics. As Röpke put it in a lecture at the Graduate Institute in Geneva, "world economy and world politics are no watertight compartments." Because their "disintegration" was interrelated, "we must also combat them simultaneously."[5] In Europe, neoliberalism emerged in the 1930s less as an economic project than as a project of politics and law. The search was on for models of governance, at scales from the local to the global, that would best encase and protect the space of the world economy. Neoliberals described this as a campaign against "interventionism," but it was clearly interventionist in its own right. Michel Foucault was correct to see neoliberalism as a project of "legal interventionism."[6] This was not a minimalist but an activist vision of statecraft mobilized to push back against the incipient power of democratically enabled masses and those special interests, including unions and cartels, who sought to obstruct the free movement of competition and the international division of labor.

The neoliberals gave a name to the enemy in the 1930s and 1940s: "economic nationalism." The term, which today is commonplace, refers to governments enacting policies that block or slow trade, and is often aimed by Northern verbal proponents of free trade at Global South countries that are seen, fairly or unfairly, as only recalcitrant participants in the global economy. The policies at issue could include tariffs—taxes on imports—as well as nontariff barriers to trade, including health and safety standards, quotas, or other voluntary restrictions. Economic nationalism was first diagnosed not in the Global South but in postcolonial Eastern Europe. Neoliberals first identified it while sifting through the shards of the former Habsburg territories. As we will see, it was one of the defining Others for the emergence of neoliberalism: it was the inverted reflection of how they saw their own policy.

Against the enemy doctrine of economic nationalism, neoliberals posed what Michael Heilperin, in his contribution to the 1939 International Studies Conference, called "economic internationalism." He defined this as "a policy intended to prevent political boundaries from exercising any disturbing effect on economic relations between areas on the two sides of the frontier."[7] Economic internationalism sought to make political borders mere lines on the map with no effect on the flow of goods and capital. By contrast, economic nationalism pursued the misguided goals of national self-sufficiency, autarky, "insulation," and "autonomy"—the latter being categories that Heilperin put in quotation marks to express his skepticism.[8] Neoliberals saw economic nationalism as a revolt against interdependence that could lead only to starvation or wars of expansion. Globalization could not be undone. To shield a national economy from the forces of world competition in any way was a sign of secession from the international community.

Neoliberals saw the root of the problem in the tension between the twin Wilsonian principles of national self-determination and economic free trade. After the Great War, the world was segmented into ever smaller political units, even as technology and exchange pushed "in the direction of a unified, world-wide economic system."[9] Louis Marlio, the French industrialist who coined the term "neoliberalism," articulated the conundrum at the Lippmann Colloquium: "It is the contrast between the shrinking of political territories and the ever-increasing necessities of economic markets that broke the liberal order."[10] The challenge for neoliberals was how to accommodate the reality of nationalism with the ongoing requirement of a supranational economic order.

Pondering a world after empire meant first taking stock of empire itself. Neoliberals were of two minds. On the one hand, they condemned the kind of empire that conflated the administration of an overseas territory with preferred access to its resources as itself being an insidious variety of economic nationalism. On the other hand, they looked wistfully back at the Habsburg Empire for supposedly balancing the demands of multiple nationalities while maintaining an internally free economic territory. They also praised the British Empire of the nineteenth century for preserving free trade in its colonial markets for all comers. The laudable model of free-trade empire was promoted at the Berlin Conference of 1884–1885, when the gathered European powers vowed to cooperate to preserve free commerce in the African continent and maintain what Mises praised in 1919 as "the open door for economic activity of all nations" in the Congo basin.[11] The spirit of Open Door empire lived on in the League of Nations mandate system, which proposed a gradual movement of colonies toward self-determination under the watchful eye of supranational authorities.[12]

The director (1920–1924) and later member of the Mandates Commission (1924–1939) was the impresario of early neoliberalism, William Rappard, director of the Graduate Institute of International Studies, who brought both Mises and Röpke to Geneva in the 1930s and hosted key lecture series by Hayek and Lionel Robbins in the same decade. As we saw in Chapter 2, neoliberalism was born out of what Rappard in 1931 called the "Geneva experiment," with its belief that the principle of "world unity" must trump "the wicked folly of the doctrine of absolute national sovereignty."[13] Neoliberals shared with the leaders of the League of Nations a belief in the need for extra-economic means to protect the liberal world economy. Arthur Salter, the head of the economics and financial section of the League, opened the International Studies Conference in 1934 by saying that the Great Depression had brought home the realization that world trade was not natural but "depends on the existence, the maintenance, the growth and adaptation of a world structure of politics, law, finance and credit and monetary system."[14] Rappard saw the seeds of future liberal world government in interwar Geneva pioneered in the League of Nations oversight over Austrian finances and the mandate supervision of African and Asian colonial territories. In their own variations on this theme, neoliberals imagined the end of empire managed by a supranational state that could override national sovereignty to protect global free trade and free capital flows.

The realization of the 1930s for neoliberals was that the self-regulating market was a myth. The foundations of world economic order—the gold standard, commercial treaties, and the Open Door policies of the British Empire—were glaring in their absence. The world economy would not reproduce itself without concerted political effort. Instead of envisioning a return to empire, however, neoliberals acknowledged that the era of the nation was irreversible. The secret was how to keep the nation but defang it. How could nations be sapped of their power to disrupt the world economy? The dream was of decolonization without the destructive desire for economic autonomy. While the liberal economist Moritz Bonn at the London School of Economics provided a striking vision of the "disintegration of world economy" in the wake of the "crumbling of empire," his colleagues Hayek and Lionel Robbins offered the most developed vision of neoliberal supranational government in their proposal of a double government for the world. They proposed large but loose federations within which the constituent nations would retain control over cultural policy but be bound to maintain free trade and free capital movement between nations. Hayek and Robbins hoped their solution would satisfy mass demands for self-representation while preserving the international division of labor and the free search for profitable markets. They also explicitly hoped that their federal schema would undermine the possibilities of both government administration of industry and popular material redistribution. By design, the denationalized state form proposed by the neoliberals would be too big to plan.

COUNTERCOLONIZATION AND THE WORLD ECONOMY

Moritz Bonn was one of the most precocious theorists of the world economy after empire. He was not part of the group that would become the neoliberal intellectual movement but was a towering figure in economic liberalism in the 1930s. In October 1933 he gave his first lecture at the London School of Economics (LSE). He had been invited to the school by, among others, Robbins, the socialist economist Harold Laski, and William Beveridge, who was the LSE's director and later one of the architects of the British welfare state. The Nazis had expelled Bonn, a Jew, from his academic post—an expulsion that was front-page news across Great Britain and the United States—and Bonn's salary at the LSE was to be paid for by donations.[15] Bonn was a student of empire. His first research, in the 1890s, had been on Ireland, where he went, as he later recalled, to "study backward economic life in the one western country where it had been preserved."[16] Before the First World War he traveled to Southern Africa and became a prominent voice for colonial reform on his return to Germany, speaking alongside Colonial Secretary Bernhard Dernburg, not against empire, but for a different kind of empire, against *métissage* (miscegenation) and the ungovernable populations he felt it produced, and for a small all-white civil service that would protect the interest of the natives and guide them into the modern world of free labor and enterprise.[17] British Basutoland was the positive example he set against German Southwest Africa.[18]

Bonn spoke to the packed lecture hall in 1933 about what to him was a deeply concerning but ultimately inevitable phenomenon with a term that he would later have a good claim to have coined—"decolonization."[19] He observed that the Great War had played midwife to two world historical processes. The first was the end of empire, the second was planning. He saw "modern planning" born in the war, when "scarcity of commodities and shortage of man power led to an attempt at substituting central state control over production and consumption for consumers' sovereignty." Planning was a secular, not a socialist, faith. "Total War and the Defense of the Realm Act, not Marx and Engels, were [its] parents."[20] In common with many recent historians, Bonn argued that war planning had permanently extended the horizon of possibility for governments, and produced what one scholar has called a *Machbarkeitswahn,* or an intoxicating, and even delusional, sense of "doability."[21]

Wartime expediency became peacetime expectation after 1918. The guiding hand of the state in economic affairs became the new normal in both capitalist and socialist states. Varieties of corporatism proliferated.[22] In the United States, the Tennessee Valley Authority and the National Recovery Act had been launched months before Bonn's speech, and the first apparently successful Five-Year Plan had just been completed in the Soviet Union. New nations were being born into an atmosphere where states coordinated enterprise and took this fact as natural. "The protection of infant industries," he said, "forced upon sometimes unwilling governments during the war, has become the economic goal of many backward and all newly organized national states. Industrialization in an already over-industrialized world is fervently followed up."[23]

Decolonization for Bonn was "a movement against political dependence" that pivoted from the empire form to the nation form. But more significantly, it also "turned against economic dependence," pivoting from what he called "international economic interdependence" toward autarky.[24] Bonn's distinction between the political and economic realms was central. Nations could have formal sovereignty while still remaining deeply connected economically. In fact, nations could even receive formal political autonomy on the condition of diminished economic autonomy. He cited the examples of Greece and China, which had been admitted as equals into the League of Nations but only with the "continuation of some sort of control over [their] finances," and the financial oversight of Austria and Hungary, which followed the same pattern.[25] Atomistic national political equality, in other words, could coexist within what Bonn called the "invisible economic empire" of trade and exchange that was global.[26] A political world of borders could coexist, and had coexisted (in the liberal imagination, if not reality) within a borderless world economy.

Bonn believed that decolonization and planning were two sides of a linked misunderstanding of the scale and form of what worked in an interdependent world. Yet the ultimate traitor to the model of one-world-economy-many-polities came not from the periphery but from the core. The central enabling condition of the invisible economic empire had been the predictability of currency value and the trust in the contract, the bill of exchange, and the loan that it created. This faith had vanished in a single day on September 20, 1931, when Britain left the gold standard. With that move, Bonn wrote, Great Britain "had broken the economic unity of the world" and accelerated the movement toward a globe of increasingly granular polities, each outfitted with its own necessarily inefficient industrial plant, misguided by the belief, promoted by John Maynard Keynes in 1933, that national self-sufficiency was a laudable goal.[27] "Up to the 21st September," Bonn wrote, "economic universalism, as a great British tradition, coincided with British economic nationalism. On that day they parted company."[28]

The imagination from which Bonn spoke on that day in London in 1933 was shared by the neoliberals, including his colleagues Robbins and Hayek at the LSE and Röpke, who praised Bonn and likely was inspired to title his 1942 book *International Economic Disintegration* partially by the subtitle of Bonn's 1938 monograph *The Crumbling of Empire: The Disintegration of World Economy*.[29] Like Bonn, the neoliberals had a differentiated attitude toward empire. They saw a chasm between, on the one hand, the many bad empires that protected their colonial trade and saw the world economy as a zero-sum container of finite resources, and, on the other hand, the single good empire of the British that promoted free trade and sound money. They saw the British Empire as the polestar of the first age of globalization from 1870 to 1914. The belief that the British had betrayed economic universalism since 1931 under the class pressures of organized labor and the intellectual seductions of Keynesianism led them to think hard about what a new organizing principle and an organizing force could be in a world after free-trade empire under the indirect rule of the City of London. What to do after the disappearance of the empire that had been so mindful, in their opinion, of the separation between imperium and dominium?

The solution that the neoliberals arrived at was supranational federation. Accepting that political frontiers could not be eliminated, and that nationalism was a force that spoke to people in an ineradicable way, they sought what Bonn called the "sterilization of frontiers." "If frontiers were no longer obstacles to international economic intercourse," he wrote, "they would lose part of their sinister significance."[30] The idea was to reconstitute the invisible economic empire of exchange and trade overlaid with a grid of externally bounded political units called nations. Their radical proposition in the 1930s was to ask—what if empire ended, and it didn't matter?

ROBBINS AND THE IDEA OF DEPLANNING

In 1935, a year and a half after Bonn's lecture, Lionel Robbins traveled to Switzerland by car to deliver a series of lectures on the topic of international economic planning. He stayed with Mises when he got there but drove through Nazi-governed Germany, seeing anti-Semitic slogans on banners in what he called "smiling Bavarian villages where you would have thought not a ripple of these political convulsions would have penetrated."[31] He had been invited to give the lectures by Rappard, who had turned his Graduate Institute of International Studies into a kind of neoliberal think tank in the 1930s, bringing Mises in 1935, Röpke in 1937, and Haberler, Hayek and Jacob Viner for stays of research and teaching. Published under the title *Economic Planning and International Order* in 1937, Robbins's Geneva talks were declared a "manifesto" by the *Economist*.[32] They took on what he called "the grand panacea of our age"—planning—a false god that he saw as responsible for among other things, the Nazism he had just seen firsthand. It also offered the first draft of a model of neoliberal federation upon which Hayek would build his own ideas.

Like Bonn, Robbins read decolonization and planning as both formally homologous and structurally reinforcing. The dissolution of empires was leading to a confusion of the categories of government and ownership: " 'the mines for the miners' and 'Papua for the Papuans' are analytically similar slogans," he said.[33] At the Lippmann Colloquium, Mises had commented similarly that "the ambiguous use of possessive pronouns frequently impedes understanding. On what grounds does a British citizen who is not a mine owner describe British coal deposits as 'ours' and those of the Ruhr as those of 'foreigners'? As a purchaser of coal, he is obliged in each case to pay the market price, whether it is British or foreign coal."[34] Robbins sought a form of human social organization that would clarify the distinction between the political and economic realms and dissolve the small, discrete collective of mutual identification—the miners or the Papuans—in a larger unity. Like Bonn, he saw the British as having provided such a transnational frame until 1931. The "open door policy" meant "that those parts of the Empire which were administered from at home were administered as if in trust for the world as a whole," he wrote. "So long as foreign goods were admitted free and foreign investment and foreign settlement not discriminated against, the Englishman was not economically better off than the foreigner because his country had wide possessions . . . The administration of the free-trade Empire is not," he said, "one of those episodes of history of which Englishmen need be ashamed."[35]

For Robbins and Bonn, the world economy provided a space of universalism, a shared arena of activity for all humanity overseen by the protective rule of the British Empire. What was necessary was a political form to fill the vacuum created by the British abdication of the role, especially after the Ottawa Agreements of 1932, which created preferential access for Great Britain to its colonies and commonwealth. Rappard condemned the agreements at the International Studies Conference in 1933. The best justification for imperial rule, he said, was "that the primitive population shall be governed in their own interests . . . and also in the interest of the whole world." The Open Door empire had "assured the natives of equality in their relations with the rest of the world, and assured the world of outlets for its industrial products and free sources of supply."[36] If the British had broken the liberal order once by leaving the gold standard in 1931, they had done so again the following year by turning colonial borders into economic walls.

Neoliberal proposals of federation came out of incredibly wide-ranging, and now largely forgotten, discussions about which political form might be used to reform, reinvigorate or replace that of empire. Transatlantic discussions of federation were given focus by the publication of American journalist Clarence Streit's *Union Now* in 1939 but had begun in earnest in the pages of *New Commonwealth Quarterly* in 1932 and the publications of the Round Table Group at around the same time.[37] In their most common variations, federation and union were proposed as Atlantic, Anglo-Saxon or Western European configurations that could bring an isolationist U.S. back into the community of the West and act as a bulwark against forces of both fascism and communism.

The focus of federation for most was moral, racial, civilizational or political. For Robbins, it was economic. "It would be the object of a liberal world federation," he said, "to create the maximum scope for international division of labor: and any restriction of trading between governmental areas would be totally alien to its intention."[38] The primary role of nation-states would be security and ensuring that "the law of property and contract the world over was unified and administered on uniform principles."[39] If the free-trade-private-property world order were put into place, then empire would be insignificant. Because "there is no conceivable repartition of the earth's surface which would be permanently satisfactory," the only lasting solution would be to make the world's resources accessible to all.[40] He uses the example of the nineteenth century when "the most important raw material of British industry . . . raw cotton—was purchased outside the Empire. Whether cotton is purchased in Carolina or the Sudan, it has to be paid for. Provided that contracts are enforceable in both places, it is a matter of indifference whether or not they are colored the same on the map."[41]

The genius of the world federation model was that, by its own power, it would begin a dynamic of what Robbins called "deplanning."[42] The most important tool of the planner in international trade—the tariff—would be taboo, meaning an end to the protection of infant industry or domestic agriculture. More meaningfully, it would also mean the dismantling of social services. As he said, "National planning involves not merely the suspension of *laissez faire* as regards movements of trade and investment. It involves also the suspension of *laissez passer* as regards the movements of men."[43] The provision of benefits by the state, he observed, means the restriction of free movement to retain control over who benefited. This was one of the reasons that the promise of equality itself was corrosive. "We must recognize," he said, that "the system would involve some inequality of income."[44] Creating economic evenness at the scale of the nation only produced a misguided sense of the origin of prosperity. The contingency of individual well-being on the flows of world economy must remain a palpable reality for national citizens. Planning muffled the bracing sounds of the global. It must always be a possibility that, as he put it in 1934, the merchant might "close down his works in Lancashire to commence operations in Japan."[45] Shared precarity could and should be the foundation of world unity.

HAYEK'S NEOLIBERAL FEDERATION

Like Robbins, Hayek was a member of Federal Union, an organization calling for federation founded in 1938 that had over 12,000 members by 1940; he and Robbins were also members of the economists' committee of the Federal Union.[46] Inspired by the work of his close friend and colleague, Hayek elaborated the free-trade world federation imaginary in its most complete form in a 1939 article in *New Commonwealth Quarterly,* where he described a political model that would undermine the "solidarity of interests" that naturally cohered when groups of people had the same economic interests.[47] Decolonization might actually work well in the sense that it would delink the political and the economic. It was the correspondence of political and economic sovereignty that produced what Hayek saw as the troubling sense of ownership that citizens of a nation felt over the products of their national territory. "In the national state, current ideologies make it comparatively easy to persuade the rest of the community that it is in their interest to protect 'their' iron industry or 'their' wheat production of whatever it be."[48] The goal of federation was to break the link between political citizenship and economic ownership.

Open economic borders would mean that constellations of interests would never be permanent nor would they become "lastingly identified with the inhabitants of a particular region." Like Robbins, Hayek described how the free flow of goods and investment would discipline economies away from intervention and planning. Because capital will move to find better interest rates and goods will come from places with lower prices, "the whole armory of marketing boards and other forms of monopolistic organizations of individual industries will cease to be at the disposal of state governments."[49] World government would by necessity focus on the task of encasing the market rather than allocating resources according to a logic of equality or social justice. The loose federation would govern narrowly but intensively, ensuring that the disciplining effect of economic flows determined the allocation of resources. Social legislation would be governed by a kind of regulatory most-favored-nation logic, whereby fewer and fewer aspects of social life would fall under planning or regulation. "We shall have to resign ourselves rather to have no legislation in a particular field than the state legislation which would break up the economic unity of the federation."[50]

The open world economy protected by political federation could be the antidote to planning and the solution to decolonization. Hayek and Robbins agreed that people would not accept either tariffs or redistributive policies for the sake of people geographically distant from them. Hayek asked: "Is it likely that the French peasant will be willing to pay more for his fertilizer to help the British chemical industry? Will the Swedish workman be ready to pay more for his oranges to assist the Californian grower? . . . Or the South African miner prepared to pay more for his sardines to help the Norwegian fisherman?"[51] Robbins observed, even more pointedly: "If, for instance, the services of the inhabitants of say Scandinavia are in part devoted to providing resources to raise the productivity of the inhabitants of China, that means, as in the case of income equalization, that they get less than they might have had in order that others may get more."[52] Reversing Adam Smith's hypothetical question about how much Western pain would be averted for the death of a Mandarin, they asked how much Western effort would be expended for the benefit of a Mandarin and concluded the answer would be: very little.[53]

Robbins wrote, "International liberalism does not bid us love humanity . . . it is merely the plan of a mechanism more efficient than the world of independent nations."[54] Anti-planning could present itself as anti-imperialist by casting empire as irrelevant, proposing instead a loose federation united by the flows of commerce and capital. World federation solved the problem of decolonization by decentering it, making the dissolution of empire secondary to a larger vision of restoring a liberal international economic order abandoned by the British after 1931. Neoliberal federation offered an alternative outcome to the "dialectics of decolonization" described by historian Frederick Cooper.[55] Where Cooper saw the demands of an increasingly empowered colonial labor force in West Africa hastening the end of empire in a post-1945 world where "social citizenship" had begun to mean more, Robbins and Hayek envisioned a further turn of the screw, in which planning measures at home were dissolved by an arrangement in which the free flow of capital and goods undercut the "communities of interest" that sustained them.[56] The social democratic state was only in utero in the 1930s. It is striking to see neoliberals already devising a scheme to counter it. In their version of federation, the discipline of the world economy would undermine planning and confine the nation-state to the field of the political.

MISES AND THE HABSBURG ORIGINS OF DOUBLE GOVERNMENT

One does not have to excavate Hayek's short 1939 article to descry his vision of world order. He devoted the whole final chapter of his 1944 best seller *The Road to Serfdom* to a reprisal of his schemes for international federation. He made it explicit that the world economy could be defended only by political means. "Far from it being true," he wrote, "that, as is now widely believed, we need an international economic authority while the states can at the same time retain their unrestricted political sovereignty, almost exactly the opposite is true. What we need and can hope to achieve is not more power in the hands of irresponsible international economic authorities, but, on the contrary, a superior political power which can hold the economic interests in check."[57] Hayek argued that only such a "powerful" "supranational authority" could prevent the mandate of individual states from expanding in ways that would damage the prosperity of the whole. The anti-planning world authority would be an agent of what other liberals called "denationalism," overseeing the member states of an international federation and enforcing standards of free trade and free investment.[58] Federation was a means of achieving the goals of militant globalism and militant democracy: it is "nothing but the application to international affairs of democracy, the only method of peaceful change man has yet invented," he wrote, "but it is a democracy with definitely limited powers."[59]

Hayek's proposals for global governance had been largely passed over until scholars recently rediscovered, in his proposals for federalism, the "reinvention of liberal internationalism" and the implicit—and even explicit—inspiration for European economic integration.[60] Wolfgang Streeck writes that Hayek's work "reads like a blueprint for today's European Union" in its design for institutions that link "internationalization" and "denationalization" with inexorable liberalization.[61] Chapter 6 weighs the claim of Hayekian inspiration for European integration, and Chapter 7 his influence on architects of the World Trade Organization.

What is notable, however, is that even those scholars who trace Hayek's internationalism forward fail to trace it backward: to the Habsburg Empire of his youth. Reflecting in 1978, Hayek wrote, "I think the first paper I ever wrote . . . was on a thing which had already occurred to me in the last few days in the army, suggesting that you might have a double government, a cultural and an economic government." He said that this occurred to him as one way to resolve "the conflict between nationalities in the Austro-Hungarian Empire." He wondered if "it might be possible in governmental functions to separate the two things—let the nationalities have their own cultural arrangements and yet let the central government provide the framework of a common economic system."[62] This idea, "the first thing I put on paper," according to Hayek, suggests the overlooked influence of the Habsburg Empire on neoliberal proposals of international order and federation.

The fact that the core neoliberal thinkers had roots in the former Habsburg Empire was far from incidental. As John Gray remarks, Hayek saw the vanished Habsburg Empire as "in some ways a model liberal regime."[63] The Habsburg Empire was a lost object of identification for many Viennese-raised intellectuals. The philosopher Karl Popper, who was one of Hayek's friends, idealized the empire in retrospect, seeing it as the space of a "cosmopolitan scientific community laboring for human progress."[64] Even during its existence, many thought fondly of the empire as representing "the international order of mankind in miniature."[65] For neoliberals, the empire's cosmopolitanism modeled and prefigured a future world. Among the most compelling aspects of the Habsburg Empire in retrospect was its separation of economics and politics. The multinational principle had made the empire a single economic space without a homogeneous language or culture. Mises was fascinated by the fact that "state and nation did not coincide" in the Habsburg monarchy. Unlike the French republics, or the post-1848 imaginaries of Germany, Italy, or Poland, Habsburg Austria did not have "the nationality principle" at its "ideological foundation."[66] A multinational state meant that every effort at intervention would threaten to upset the diplomatic balance by appearing to cater to special interests.

Though such special interests were served all the time in reality, Mises clung to the idea of a state that was denationalized in its own self-conception and thus impermeable to demands made in the language of the nation. For Mises and Hayek, the nonidentity of political and economic units in the Habsburg Empire offered a model for the world. The Austrian neoliberal vision of a decolonizing globe after 1945 would be based on their own experience and observation of decolonization at home. The vanished Habsburg Empire, ironically, became a model for the world economy after empire.

Mises's proposals for international federation followed the Habsburg example more closely than Hayek's. Indeed, Mises's most explicit proposals for supranational federation hewed closely to the borders of the former empire, and he expressed skepticism about a larger-scale "democratic world government" or a federation that would span continents.[67] Gaining an understanding of his imagination requires a brief overview of the political and economic geography that underpinned Mises's work. From his earliest publications, Mises operated with the binary opposition between a world organized by the "principle of nationality" and self-determination, and one organized by the international division of labor, indifferent to nationality, across "the entire inhabited surface of the earth."[68] The organization of the world into nations contradicted economic principles because it arranged people and other factors of production in less than optimal ways. Ideally, economic laws would trump political laws over time. "The surface of the earth is divided among nations. This division is the result of past historical processes. It does not correspond to current conditions of production and population. Under full free movement of people and goods, there are nations whose areas would be more densely and others more thinly settled. This relative overpopulation must be dissolved now through movements of migration."[69] In Mises's normative vision of economics drained of politics, populations would grow and shrink with time; and nationalities would, in some cases, be lost or absorbed through assimilation.

It is not often noticed that Mises staged the famous socialist calculation debate of the interwar period not at the scale of the nation but at the scale of the world.[70] He claimed that a hypothetical "general director of the world economy" was redundant because "what would happen under ideal world socialism by order of the general director of the world economy is achieved in the ideal of the free world economy by the reign of competition."[71] In a market system, companies, capital, and workers migrated of their own accord to better-yielding conditions. To fail to migrate would be to fail and, ultimately, to starve. Mises conceded somewhat cheerfully that his understanding of the world coincided in many ways with that of Karl Marx. He felt that Marx was a product of his time—the 1860s—when free trade reigned in Western Europe and talk of a coming world government seemed plausible. After all, he pointed out, liberalism and Marxist socialism were both cosmopolitan.[72] And the bourgeoisie, like the proletariat, was also inherently "international."[73] Where they differed was in the diagnosis of the outcome. Where Marx saw increasing immiseration, Mises saw the road to prosperity rudely interrupted by the tariff wars of the 1870s in response to the first Great Depression, then the rupture of the Great War, and the return of trade obstacles that followed.

Mises saw the earth as a vast territory of varying natural endowments that needed to be exploited as thoroughly as possible through the mobility of capital, labor, and commerce. The drive toward productivity was axiomatic. He called it the "fundamental social law" of capitalism "to draw the greatest number of human beings into the personal division of labor and the whole earth's surface into the geographical division of labor."[74] Life under "the reign of competition" left admittedly little room for individual maneuver.[75] Of the entrepreneur, he wrote, "The market controls him more strictly and exactingly than could any government or other organ of society."[76] For workers it was similar: "As producer . . . a man is merely the agent of the community and as such has to obey."[77] The space for discretionary action one had was as a consumer. Capitalist society, he said, in an analogy he would use throughout this life, was a "consumer's democracy . . . in which every penny represents a ballot paper."[78]

Mises saw the international division of labor as a process that, at least hypothetically, might one day be completed. It was, he said, "finite. When all men on earth form a unitary system of division of labor, it will have reached its goal."[79] The eventual outcome of this process would be the emergence of what he called "ecumenical society" and, necessarily, an accompanying world superstate that would realize the failed promise of the League of Nations by divorcing itself from the impracticable principle of national self-determination and taking up its proper limited—but intensive—role in safeguarding trade, investment, and migration.[80] For Mises, the demands of the world economy trumped all other political claims. In discussing colonialism, for example, he remarked that "no chapter of history is steeped further in blood than the history of colonialism" but still insisted that keeping the colonies was the first priority once Europe become dependent on the empire for raw materials.[81] Self-determination might be thinkable, but only under the control of a muscular superstate that could ensure the continuation of free trade.

For Mises, policy questions were always held to the touchstone of world economic productivity. Similarly, his preferences for democracy over dictatorship, and free labor over slavery, were purely functional. Letting people vote decreased the number of revolutions, and letting people work for a wage made them more productive than they were as human chattel.[82] The reign of competition matched human labor to the earth's natural endowments in the most optimal way. Political institutions must caretake the pathways that carry mobile factors of production to immobile ones, without seeking to "organize" them.[83] Mises believed strongly in economic principles as the most rational basis for human organization of the world while also remaining deeply mindful of the power of what he saw as its adversary—the political form of the nation. For him, the real war was not between individual nations or empires but between the world economy and the nation as forms of human organization.

If the struggle was between the principle of world economy and the nation, then Mises felt the outcome of the Great War had strengthened the hand of the latter. The dissolution of the Habsburg Empire redrew the regional map. Bulgaria and Romania expanded their territory greatly, and the former imperial heads of Austria and Hungary became freestanding nation-states. Formed from whole cloth were Poland, Czechoslovakia, and the State of Slovenes, Croats, and Serbs, which in 1922 merged with Serbia to become the new (multinational) state of Yugoslavia. In the words of one economist in 1929, the postwar reorganization had "sliced into segments the economic organism which existed under the Hapsburgs."[84] Austria was entirely cut off from its hinterland and swollen with German-speaking civil servants from the provinces.[85]

The resolution of the nationalities question after 1918 infuriated Mises. Rather than being answered, the problem had been raised to new heights. The principle of national self-determination had, disastrously, been read economically. He observed bitterly in 1927 that "the principle of national autarky wins new supporters with every day that passes. Even countries with only a few million inhabitants, like Hungary and Czechoslovakia, are attempting, by means of a high tariff policy and prohibitions on imports, to make themselves independent of the rest of the world."[86] What had been lost was the complementarity of the Habsburg Empire as a working model of a division of labor among diverse human populations. Contemporaries labeled this loss of the political and economic unity of empire "the riddle of the Danube." The riddle being: How to maintain mutually beneficial bonds of economic interdependence after the end of empire? Some even asked "whether it was not more desirable to leave the Austro-Hungarian state intact rather than destroy it."[87]

In a lecture given at Rappard's Graduate Institute, Robbins himself described the end of the Habsburg Empire as a negative example of decolonization and a cautionary tale for Britain. "The economic organization of prewar Austria, especially Vienna, was keyed up to supply the needs of the vast area of the old Austrian Empire. Suddenly, as it were overnight, the greater part of this market was cut off by almost prohibitive tariffs. The territorial division of labour of the Danube basin was destroyed by nationalist particularism." A remedy, he suggested, would have been "some form of federal constitution which would have averted the threatened disintegration."[88]

In 1938 Mises set to work drafting just such a federal constitution, and in 1940 he began to work on it in earnest. He hoped that his proposal would counter what he saw as the institutional failure of the world after Versailles, St. Germain, and Trianon. He wrote from his new home in New York City, a rent-controlled apartment at 96th street and West End Avenue on the Upper West Side where he would spend the rest of his life.[89] The focus of his work was on East Central Europe. Seeing "anarchy" in the wake of the dissolution of the Habsburg and Ottoman Empires, he proposed a new Eastern Democratic Union (EDU) that would span an enormous swath of territory, from the Baltic to the Adriatic, Aegean, and Black Seas, from the eastern borders of Switzerland and Italy to the western borders of Russia. The EDU would include all nations made independent after the First World War, from Latvia to Yugoslavia, as well as multinational parts of the German and Italian states, such as Silesia and Fiume. In all, it would "include about 700,000 square miles with about 120 million people using seventeen different languages."[90]

The core principle of the EDU was the separation of economic from cultural policy. People would have total freedom of movement, trade, and employment within the territory, which would be ruled from a centralized parliament in Vienna with an "elected president or a hereditary ruler." Recalling the tutelary practices of the Mandates Commission, the League of Nations would appoint the initial president and cabinet, to be replaced later by a vote based on universal suffrage. A version of the proposal Mises wrote in 1938 was even more reminiscent of both the mandate model and the form of financial oversight the League practiced in Austria; he suggested that certain administrative positions be permanently filled by "Englishmen and Frenchmen" and that the official language be either English or French.[91] In the 1920s Mises expressed his approval of the mandates model, writing that "the League of Nations must be given supreme authority in the administration of all those overseas territories in which there is no system of parliamentary government," calling for all colonies to be turned into mandates as a transition to self-determination.[92]

Mises was not opposed to supranational intervention as long as it served to preserve a global capitalist order based on free trade and private property. When in 1932 Austria was forced to accept a loan from the League of Nations with punitive conditions attached, he stressed its pedagogic potential: "The severe conditions under the loan may open the eyes of the entire population to the fact that the economic policy that has been followed in recent years has brought us to a situation where we really see no other way out than to accept the sort of subjugation which this loan imposes on us."[93] In this case, the League was the mechanism of an unflinching economic rationality ostensibly flouted by the policies of Red Vienna. With the compunction of League conditionality, the "measures of frugality that the economy has required for a long time—but which have always been delayed or sabotaged—be put into effect as quickly as possible."[94] In 1944 he was even more forthright, writing that the covenant for a renewed League would "have to include a rigid limitation of sovereign rights of every country. Measures which affect debts, the money systems, taxations, and other important matters have to be administered by international tribunals, and without an international police force such a plan could not be carried out. Force must be used to make debtors pay."[95] For Mises, a good version of the League had the capacity to act as an iron glove for the invisible hand of the market.

Mises's EDU proposal sought to realize a strong version of the League dream for the eastern half of Europe by radically downgrading what Rappard called the "dogma of national sovereignty."[96] His solution to the nationality problem was novel. He permitted the persistence of all the accouterments of nationhood, including flags, anthems, postage stamps, and "coins of every member state, coined with the national emblems."[97] People would be free to develop their own national culture and represent it abroad. The thorny problem of education, a major issue in the old Habsburg Empire, would be remedied through a scheme that directly anticipated the latter-day demands of U.S. neoliberals and conservatives. All schools would be private, and citizens would be granted a lump sum in the form of what are now called vouchers to spend on education.[98] Linguistic groups could establish schools anywhere in the territory there was a critical mass to form one.

Mises's EDU, which he included as the culminating chapter of his 1944 book *Omnipotent Government,* gave institutional form to his understanding of nations as protean and unmoored to any particular territory.[99] It also, to his mind, solved the problem of minorities that had bedeviled the League of Nations. Most striking in his model is the question of visibility. The constituent nations of the union would bear all the outward marks of sovereignty, yet this sovereignty would be ornamental, undermined wholly by the authority of the central government. A visitor to the territory, though, would see only the surface and not the underlying economic union. "He will not see the EDU," Mises wrote, "he will not have the opportunity to meet the agents of the EDU."[100] Consistent with the idea of an invisible realm of the economic discussed in Chapter 2, the government of the open economy would remain hidden from the public eye. Only the colorful—and powerless—representatives of national policy would be seen. A double government would serve as a model of supranational federation. That there would be free trade and free movement of labor overseen by a strong central state was primary, allowing for a shifting landscape of decentralized national and cultural institutions that would remain secondary. Mises's Habsburg Empire reborn for the twentieth century was an invisible government of the economy first, and a visible government of neutered nations second.

In 1945 Hayek endorsed Mises's idea. Expressing "some doubt as to whether the splitting of [the Habsburg Empire] up into nine independent national states was altogether a fortunate solution," he proposed instead the gathering of the nations into a federation in which "we limited the power of the national States in the interests of some central organization." Power may later be devolved, leading in the most optimistic case to "something like an Eastern European Switzerland."[101] Consistent with the Geneva School principle of constrained nationalism, it was the limiting of national sovereignty that was key. The nation-state must not be allowed its full independence.

RÖPKE, DOMINIUM, AND IMPERIUM

Hayek, Robbins, and Mises offered the most radical visions of neoliberal federation in the 1930s and 1940s. Their designs offered institutional protection for what Bonn called the invisible economic empire of free trade and free capital mobility. Their collaborator Röpke went into less detail but wrote similarly in 1942 of "the necessity for a true world union, whose structure must be genuinely federal, i.e. composed of regional and continental sub-groups."[102] He extrapolated from his newly beloved Switzerland to the scale of the global to imagine a world in which nation-states had the function of "cantons."[103] Röpke returned to the idea of federation in the spring of 1945 in a book that suggested in its concluding pages that the answer to the German Question was the decentralization of the Bismarckian state into a federal structure.[104] Hayek commended Röpke's proposal in the book's introduction. A free-trade federation, he observed, would deny Germany the "industrial and agricultural self-sufficiency on which her economic war-potential rested" and drive it "to a high degree of specialisation in the fields where she could make the greatest contribution to the prosperity of the world, and at the same time become dependent for her own prosperity on the continued exchange with other countries." As long as free trade was secured, world market demand would act as "the only kind of control which could not be secretly evaded."[105] Federation was once again endorsed as the political corollary to the putatively anonymous economic disciplinary ordering force of trade and capital flows.

Although Röpke proposed a course titled "Economics of International Federation" in Geneva in 1939, he delivered no supranational plans as concrete as those of Mises, Robbins, or Hayek before 1945.[106] Even at the high point of intellectual excitement for plans of international reordering, he delivered dismissive asides about the "lofty plans for a world community of states that are being developed from all quarters."[107] At the same time, his work before 1945 offers key insights into the neoliberal imagination of a world after empire. In his 1942 book *International Economic Disintegration,* which was the culmination of the project begun at Annecy in 1936, Röpke laid out a dynamic reminiscent of Robbins and Hayek by arguing that the international order had been undermined by the distorting demands of special interests empowered by popular democracy. He summarized this point at the Walter Lippmann Colloquium when he said, "It is not enough to say that economic nationalism is the result of a lack of intelligence among leaders; it is economic interests and professional groups that engage in nationalist policy, it is special interests that dissolve the State."[108]

Anticipating public choice theory by decades, Röpke followed the contemporary work of German ordoliberals Walter Eucken and Franz Böhm by explaining economic nationalism as an outcome of a political strategy by which elected officials embraced pluralism to buy votes with pork—promising subsidies, jobs, wage increases, tax benefits, and tariffs to interest groups in exchange for their political support. The spread of universal male suffrage after the First World War pushed this dynamic into overdrive, turning states into "loot" *(Beute)* to be divided up among clamoring special interests. Burdened with demands for trade protection, high wages, and social benefits, national economies became sluggish and unresponsive to the push and pull of global demand. Under conditions of mass democracy, the state became weak and internally divided as it sought to please all domestic groups at once. Governments overcompensated with visions of autarky and self-sufficiency and wild promises of full employment. States moved further away from what they did best from an economic point of view as industrial countries protected agriculture and agricultural countries stimulated industry.

Röpke saw special interests and the masses using nation-states as weapons to destroy the unity of the world economy and undermine the basis of human prosperity. In his inaugural lecture at the Graduate Institute in Geneva, he laid out his thesis that "planning on a national scale and the disorder on the international scale are not only parallel, but causally connected phenomena."[109] The principle of the world economy was directly at odds with that of the nation. Röpke followed Eucken in referring to the demands of interest groups for economic favors as the "politicization" *(Politisierung)* of the economic sphere.[110] Robbins used the German term to describe the effect of national planning on international economic relations.[111] Eucken used the word as early as 1932 to talk about how the state was gradually becoming an "economy state . . . whose actions become dependent on the will of economic groups that use it more or less as a tool."[112] Eucken and Röpke both referred to a "degeneration" of the relationship between economy and state. Eucken wrote that, under the pressure of "the democratization of the world and the unleashing of demonic forces in the nations that it brought with it," economic policy "dissolves into a mass of measures, each one connected to the wishes of various economic power groups, and betrays a total lack of system *(Systemlosigkeit)* rather than a unifying thought or will."[113]

In Eucken and Röpke's understanding, economic nationalism was not an irrational hysteria or an artifact of psychological manipulation but a rational attempt by the diverse groups within a nation to use their political influence—electoral and otherwise—to secure the maximum economic advantages from the state. Pushing back against this pressure would not be achieved simply through persuasion or superior argument. It would take an act of state will. Röpke used a martial metaphor to describe the task in 1942, writing that "the fortress of American protectionist policy can only be taken after the fortress of the New Deal has been taken, and after all of the theories of the 'mature economy,' of 'deficit spending' and 'full employment' have been cleared out, and the monstrous misuse of power of the large interest groups, including farmers and labor unions, has been dammed."[114] To counteract the effects of economic nationalism—and dam the power of the farmers and the labor unions—it was necessary to take the state back from the masses. As we will see in Chapter 6, Eucken and his collaborator Franz Böhm referred to this as the need to create an "economic constitution." They took the phrase directly from the conservative jurist Carl Schmitt, and described the economic constitution as a "total political decision about the ordering of national economic life."[115]

Ordoliberals Eucken and Böhm paid little attention to the international scale, but Röpke scaled their insights upward, proposing a strong state as the way to salvage the world economic order after the end of empire. In a discussion of colonialism at the Lippmann Colloquium, Röpke said, somewhat cryptically, "We must study the actual existing relations between imperialist policy and the role of private enterprise and ask if the essential point is whether, for a well-ordered system, extensive management could not be replaced by intensive management."[116]

What he might mean by this opposition is made clearer in a letter he wrote to Marcel Van Zeeland, another attendee of the colloquium:

> It is possible that in my opinion of the "strong state" *(le gouvernment qui gouverne)* I am even "more fascist" [*faschistischer*] than you yourself, because I would indeed like to see all economic policy decisions concentrated in the hands of a fully independent and vigorous state weakened by no pluralist authorities of a corporatist kind. . . . I seek the strength of the state in the *intensity,* not the *extensiveness,* of its economic policies. How the constitutional legal structure of such a state should be designed is a question in and of itself for which I have no patent recipe to offer. I share your opinion that the old formulas of parliamentary democracy have proven themselves useless. People must get used to the fact that there is also presidential, authoritarian, yes even—*horribile dictum* [horrible to say]—dictatorial democracy.[117]

Röpke floated here the possibility that forms of authoritarian government may be necessary—or are at least conceivable—to counteract the degeneration of economic policy produced by mass democracy. As with Robbins and Hayek, only such a powerful authority freed from influence by special interests could protect the conditions of free global exchange that the system of empires paired with the gold standard had done until 1914.

As we saw in the Introduction, Röpke offered useful categories from Roman law to help explain the order that the strong state would be necessary to reestablish. In a short 1934 article contending that, properly understood, capitalism itself was anti-imperialist, he argued that the doctrine of geopolitics frequently confused the principles of imperium and dominium.[118] He elaborated in 1942, saying that it was one of the contentions of economic nationalism that "political domination (imperium) is necessary for economic exploitation (dominium)."[119] In the categories of dominium, or what one scholar calls "rule over things," and imperium, "rule over people," Röpke offered legal concepts for the liberal worldview.[120] "*Imperium* and *dominium* are indeed two separate things," he continued, "but only in a liberal world. In such a world political boundaries are of little economic significance, the world market being more or less a uniform one with practically equal buying and selling opportunities for everybody, regardless of boundaries and nationality."[121] Röpke made explicit here what Eucken discussed as "the liberal separation of the spheres of the state and the economy" that was undone by the First World War and the economic nationalism that followed.[122]

Röpke's categories suggested that capitalism produce a doubled world. The ideal neoliberal order would maintain the balance between these two global spheres. These categories gave substance to the invisible. The delineation of the double world corresponded with the double government envisioned by the neoliberals: there would be one world of the economy and ownership, coexisting with another world of nations. In the ideal liberal world, nobody would mistake the lines on the map for meaningful marks in the world of dominium. A strong state—resistant to the pressures of democratic influence—would be necessary to safeguard the economic constitution of the world.

❋ ❋ ❋

In 1937 Walter Lippmann wrote that "the Good Society has no architectural design. There are no blueprints."[123] He leaned heavily on the work of Mises and Hayek, who had written two years earlier that "we are not intellectually equipped to improve the working of our economic system by 'planning.'"[124] Ironically, the response of the neoliberals to this insight was to immediately begin creating designs, blueprints, and plans, not at the scale of the nation but at the scale of the region and the world. The federation plans of Hayek, Robbins, and Mises were designed as prophylaxis—using institutions to suppress the emergence of special interest demands by design. One of the most critical special interests to suppress was the nation itself.

I have argued in this chapter that neoliberalism was born in part as a critique of national sovereignty. To neoliberals, nations were shifting, provisional, without claims on this or that patch of earth. The political identifications produced by nations led to a disruption of the balance between the economic and the political spheres as participants in democracies recklessly turned government budgets into reservoirs of personal enrichment. In Chapter 2 I argued that neoliberalism was a critique of the arrogance of a belief in omnipotence. Here I have argued that it also was a critique of what they saw as another colossal act of human arrogance—the belief that societies can create their own laws.

What did the neoliberals pose against the nation? Not only the world economy but the individual. In 1931 LSE economist William H. Hutt coined the term "consumer sovereignty." Hayek adopted the term in 1935, and Bonn used it in 1933. For Hutt it was a solution to the demands of national sovereignty. As the term implied, it was not the nation-state represented by legislatures that was sovereign but the individual within it. Hayek wrote that socialists, who allocated resources from above, were demanding the "abrogation of the sovereignty of the consumer."[125] He followed his Austrian predecessor Carl Menger by seeing the true creative force in the economy as those who either accept or reject a price, and by rejecting a price, produce a new one. At a time when nation-states were claiming more and more of something called "sovereignty," Hayek pickpocketed the term and reassigned it from the nation to the individual consumer. As national self-determination was becoming the buzzword worldwide, he reasserted the notion of individual consumer self-determination.

The apparent dissolution of the state to the granular level of the sovereign consumer, however, was always an illusion. For Hayek, individual consumer sovereignty was only made possible by the superstructure of the federation. Attacking economic and monetary nationalism did not devolve power down to the individual. Instead it split sovereignty—down to the consumer and up to the superstate. In the 1930s and 1940s neoliberal intellectuals pursued denationalization as a program, something to replace empire and tame the disruptive forces of the ascendant nation. The solution that neoliberals concocted to the joined problems of mass democracy, proletarianization, and economic nationalism was the denationalization of government. In variations on the widespread discussion of world government and federalism, Hayek, Robbins, and Mises all proposed what they sometimes called "double government," by which administration of economic issues would be separated from cultural issues and the economy would be depoliticized through a supranational state form.

Although designed with little or no input from the neoliberals themselves, the international postwar order realized some of the demands of double government. Even as the principle of national sovereignty triumphed (sometimes after long struggles of decolonization), most of the world remained within an economic framework overseen by the International Monetary Fund (IMF) and the General Agreement on Tariffs and Trade (GATT). Created in 1944 along with the World Bank, the IMF helped ensure relatively stable exchange rates and the possibility of converting money from one currency into another. The GATT, signed in 1947, worked toward the free-trade vision and, in the words of the agreement, the "reduction of tariffs and other barriers to trade and to the elimination of discriminatory treatment in international commerce." At the same time, this semblance of economic world government left much to be desired from a neoliberal standpoint. The GATT agreement began by stating its goal as "ensuring full employment"—one of the primary bugbears of neoliberals. And if the IMF was designed, in part, to expose individual nations to the discipline of the world market, its innovation was in permitting nations to insulate themselves against the vagaries of international speculation and so-called hot money flows. Policy autonomy—the ability to tailor economic policy toward the goal of the welfare state—was the hallmark of what was called the Bretton Woods system.

The Bretton Woods system realized parts of the neoliberal dream while also deviating radically in other ways. Of more concern was the transformation of the predominant world authority from the League of Nations to the United Nations. Based on the principle of one-country-one-vote, the UN would usher in the very politicization of economic activity that neoliberal visions of federation sought to prevent. The fantasy of the rebirth of the Open Door British empire in an Open Door world federation would be spoiled by special interests in the Global North and even more so in the Global South, where new nations sought self-determination beyond the supervisory mandate model. One of the most damaging additions to the language of world government after

1945 was the expansion of the idea of human rights. As we will see, neoliberals would aid in the campaign to contain demands for social and economic rights and to institutionalize a parallel global regime in which the investor and the corporation—and not the citizen or refugee—was the paradigmatic rights-bearing subject.

A World of Rights

Exchange control in time of peace should be considered an act of aggression and a violation of human rights in international law.

—PHILIP CORTNEY, 1949

Midway through *The Road to Serfdom,* the book he published in 1944 that made him famous, F. A. Hayek inserted a commentary on human rights. His target was specifically the expansive "Declaration of Rights" published by the author and public intellectual H. G. Wells in 1939, a list of eleven articles including the right to education, food, health care, and employment.[1] Hayek did not object so much to the material provisions. His own proposal included elements of a basic social safety net and even countercyclical state spending.[2] As libertarians later lamented, *The Road to Serfdom* called for "the security of a minimum income" and "a comprehensive system of social insurance."[3] What galled Hayek was Wells's combination of the language of rights with a program of centralized economic decision making. For Hayek, rights talk could not work alongside state direction of production and labor. If nebulous categories like "the common welfare" could override one's choice of employment, then individual rights could not exist.[4] Hayek defended the language of individual rights, but only insofar as those rights were negative: the freedom to move one's labor and capital where one saw fit. The rationale was based less on natural law than on utilitarianism: individual choices guided by competition would solve the riddle of the complexity of the market and ensure the best possible division of labor and allocation of resources.

Hayek and Wells moved in the same circles in 1930s Britain—an academic and cultural elite that felt obliged to rethink the foundations of a postwar world. There was a shared sense of duty among Austrian elites like Hayek, Mises, Hans Kelsen, and Hersch Lauterpacht, who had trained to serve what was now a vanished empire, and British elites like John Maynard Keynes, Lionel Robbins, Edwin Cannan, and James Meade, who were seeking to reform a still-living one. The connections were close. One of the drafters of Wells's declaration was Hayek's friend and colleague on the Federal Union's economists committee Barbara Wootton, whose own article followed his now-famous 1939 article on "inter-state federalism" in the *New Commonwealth Quarterly*.[5] Wells published in the same journal himself.[6] In the years before and during the war, Hayek participated in the broad effort of public intellectuals in the West to conceptualize what Wells called in 1940 "The New World Order" that would follow global conflict.[7] When in 1947 Hayek convened a group of intellectuals in Switzerland to form the Mont Pèlerin Society and initiate the postwar neoliberal intellectual movement, he was operating in this same spirit of visionary globalism.[8]

Although scholars routinely note Hayek's inclusion of a safety net in his normative national order, they fail to cast their gaze beyond—or above—the nation.[9] As we saw in Chapter 3, Hayek's blueprint for world order at the end of *The Road to Serfdom* prescribed international federation as an antidote, not a complement, to the expanding welfare state. His national vision balanced state duties with negative rights, but his global order concentrated exclusively on the latter. The powers of an international authority, he wrote, "must above all be able to say 'no' ": no to obstacles to the movement of goods, capital, and people, and, thus, no to protections for infant industries, increased taxation for state spending, and insulation of labor markets.[10] It is telling that the two transgressions of individual rights that Hayek cites are both related to transnational relations. The first was the expropriation of businesses in

Central Europe, where owners suddenly became foreign "minorities" in the successor nations of the crumbled Habsburg Empire.[11] The second was the control of the exchange of money from one currency into another and its transport over borders, which he called, with surprising vehemence, "the decisive advance on the path to totalitarianism and the suppression of individual liberty."[12]

Hayek's language of negative rights and the power to say no can give a false impression of a passive or inactive state in his normative global order. Yet creating and securing such an arrangement required proactive engagement. Hayek himself was explicit that the international power needed "an authority capable of enforcing [the] rules."[13] Although after the war Hayek swerved away from engagement with international order, other neoliberals did not. As we will see, neoliberals argued against adding social and economic rights to the basic list of negative rights, even as they made the case for economic rights of their own—above all, the right to keep foreign investment safe and to move capital freely over borders. Like Hayek, they focused on the expropriation of foreign-owned property and controls on capital movements as being the central violations of rights. They would help design institutions that would safeguard the "negative rights" of freedom from expropriation and capital control.

To describe the particular form of rights promoted by neoliberals, I call them "xenos rights," borrowing a term from Hayek. In his last published work, Hayek spoke of the xenos, or guest-friend, in early Greek history, "who was assured individual admission and protection within an alien territory." Hayek suggests that this practice meant that "trade must have developed very much as a matter of personal relations."[14] Elsewhere he wrote that "rules are required which make it possible at each moment to ascertain the boundary of the protected domain of each and thus to distinguish between the *meum* [that which is mine] and the *tuum* [that which is yours]."[15] The category of xenos rights helps us think about individuals having protected rights to safe passage and unmolested ownership of their property and capital, regardless of the territory. It is a right that inheres to the unitary economic space of dominium rather than the fragmented state space of imperium—yet it requires the political institutions of imperium to ensure it.

To neoliberals, the problem of the postwar period was the same problem that plagued states after the First World War: the unconstrained expansion of democracy. In 1932 ordoliberal Walter Eucken denounced "the democratization of the world." By this he meant the universal male suffrage in industrialized nations that brought "the people and their passions, the interest groups and chaotic powers of the masses" into politics.[16] The post-1945 era spread what Wilhelm Röpke called the "rabies democratica" globally.[17] As the first colonies gained independence from their imperial masters, the international institutions, and the United Nations in particular, became spaces for political claims-making.[18] As one-person-one-vote became one-country-one-vote, Global South nations found spokespeople among the very social democratic economists that the neoliberals had clashed with in the 1930s. Liberals like Haberler and Alexander Loveday had set the tone at the early League of Nations, but it was social democrats like the Swedish Gunnar Myrdal and the Hungarians Nicholas Kaldor and Thomas Balogh who dominated the young UN. The new language of "development" and the subfield of "development economics" helped legitimize worldwide demands for full employment, capital controls, and the right to nationalize foreign-owned assets and resources. As Röpke put it sarcastically, "today's 'human rights' as formulated by the UN include the sacred right of a state to expropriate a power plant."[19]

Neoliberals in the early postwar years felt that they had won the war but were losing the peace. When they gathered to take stock and talk strategies in Mont Pèlerin in 1947, Hayek suggested that they follow the example of socialists. Leftists like the Fabians, some of whom he had cooperated with in the Federal Union and as a professor at the Fabian-founded London School of Economics, had succeeded in shifting debates over time, thus capturing both public opinion and public power and making their vision reality. Scholars have noted how neoliberals began a "long-run war of position" on this understanding of the power of ideas in the postwar moment.[20]

Even as they dug in for the long struggle, neoliberals also engaged in shorter-term "wars of movement." This chapter zeroes in on a specific, little-known case of the role of neoliberal intellectuals in helping to defeat the International Trade Organization (ITO), the institution that was intended to complete the Bretton Woods system, as well as their role in writing first drafts for postwar international investment law. The key players were Michael Heilperin, Philip Cortney, and Ludwig Erhard. Geneva School neoliberals proposed their own vision of a world of rights. Against human rights, they posed the human rights of capital. Against the stateless person, they posed the investor. Against sovereignty and autonomy, they posed the world economy and the international division of labor. Their "national" was both a person and a company. As the mouthpieces of big business's two largest interest groups, Heilperin and Cortney articulated a polemical, alternative vision of human rights, created lasting precedent for international law, and made concrete Hayek's 1949 demand for a liberal utopia.

THE DANGER OF ECONOMIC DEMOCRACY

The Bretton Woods institutions were born incomplete. The International Monetary Fund (IMF) was responsible for the world's money. It helped keep currency values stable by making short-term loans to nations in trouble, and allowing states to adjust their exchange rates when necessary. The World Bank was responsible for reconstruction and development. It made low-interest, long-term loans and loan guarantees to help build infrastructure and industrial capacity, first in Western Europe and then in the Global South. What was missing was a body responsible for overseeing trade. The entity planned to fill this role was the ITO, which would complete the Bretton Woods trio. Like the IMF and the World Bank, it would be housed in the UN and provide a legal framework for international free trade. First proposed by the United States in 1945, the United Nations Economic and Social Council (ECOSOC) resolved in February 1946 to convene an international conference on trade and employment to draft a charter on world trade.[21]

The original authors of the charter were to be a group of fifteen of the major Global North nations with the addition of India and China. This allocation of decision-making power may have reflected the relative share of trade in the world economy, but it was less than representative, considering that the world contained seventy-one independent countries by 1946. Such a limited democratic principle would have reproduced the two-tier nature of governance in the UN, where a small Security Council had veto power over a large General Assembly. It would have also followed the model of the IMF and the World Bank, where votes were proportionate to a nation's share of world trade. Nudged by the UN, the ITO planning group expanded over time, adding first Chile, Lebanon, and Norway, and then others.[22] The number of nations involved in negotiations at the three meetings—in London in 1946, Geneva in 1947 and Havana in 1948—was even larger. The addition of Global South nations ended up being momentous, because Latin American and Asian delegates pushed the agenda away from free-trade orthodoxy. Without discrediting the value of international trade, these nations sought to enshrine a parallel right to deviate from the orthodox rules of free trade to protect nascent industries against foreign competition and to pursue domestic development and full employment.[23]

The expansion of the democratic principle in the planning of the ITO was a moment of revolt against the twinned imaginaries of the League of Nations and the International Chamber of Commerce (ICC) as expressed at the World Economic Conference of 1927. No longer would the simple principle of negative integration hold sway. Tariff walls did not exist only to be dismantled but to shelter aspiring infant industries. The chief U.S. negotiator at the ITO recalled a "chorus of denunciation" from the "underdeveloped nations" as they opposed uniform principles in the name of the need for special treatment in the cause of development.[24] The most important way this was expressed was in the governing principle. Unlike the IMF and World Bank, the ITO was to be organized on the principle of one-country-one-vote. Democracy was to be brought to the stage of global economic governance.

The postwar neoliberal movement was born in the midst of the ITO drama, and some of its members played a starring role in it. As delegates met in Geneva in the spring of 1947 to draft the world trade charter, a group of intellectuals gathered at the other end of the lake at the base of Mont Pèlerin. Taking their name from the location, the Mont Pèlerin Society (MPS) became the germ of what its organizer Hayek called "the neoliberal movement."[25] Among those gathered were Mises, Röpke, Robbins, and two future Nobel Memorial Prize winners,

Milton Friedman and George Stigler. The MPS picked up from the "Haberler-type" international collaborative projects of the 1930s, including the Lippmann Colloquium, the workshop on Haberler's Depression study, and the Annecy workshop on the world economy.

In Hayek's words, the intention of the MPS was to allow for "personal contact among the proponents of neoliberalism," to "erect a coherent edifice of . . . neoliberal thought, and to work out its practical application to the problems of different countries." This involved personal contact as well as translation and distribution of key texts to stimulate the "flow of neoliberal ideas."[26] Like the meetings in Geneva and Paris in the 1930s, the MPS was global in both its mandate and its object of study. Hayek felt that socialists had too long monopolized the language of internationalism. Neoliberals needed to have the courage of their convictions and exhibit the boldness to do what socialists had done for half a century: dream of a utopia. They must conceive of the world they wanted to see, even if that seemed impractical or implausible.[27]

We have already seen that socialists hardly held a monopoly on globalist thought before 1945. Economic liberals in Geneva both inside and outside of the League of Nations had dreamt big in the interwar period as they sought to reimagine and rebuild what they saw as the lost golden age of world capitalism. In many ways the MPS was a continuation of the League's spirit. Many of the figures at Mont Pèlerin—including Mises, Röpke, Hayek, Robbins, Maurice Allais, and Rappard—had either worked at Geneva or presented their work at William Rappard's Graduate Institute. Röpke had planned a meeting in Geneva to gather many of the same players for September 1939, the month the war broke out. The first gathering at Mont Pèlerin was the realization of the international meeting delayed.

Given the Genevan pedigree, it is no surprise that the MPS statement of aims was global in its perspective. Penned by Robbins, it began by observing that "over large stretches of the Earth's surface the essential conditions of human dignity and freedom have already disappeared. In others they are under constant menace from the development of current tendencies of policy." The reference here was not only to communism but also to trends toward social democracy, such as the wave of nationalizations being carried out by the recently elected Labour Party in Britain. The statement concluded by calling for study of "the creation of an international order conducive to the safeguarding of peace and liberty and permitting the establishment of harmonious international economic relations."

The broad—and somewhat vague—sentiments of the MPS statement were given substance a few weeks later when five hundred businessmen from thirty countries convened in Montreux, less than twenty kilometers from Mont Pèlerin, at the first gathering of the International Chamber of Commerce since the war. As described in Chapter 1, Hayek, Mises, Haberler, and Machlup all shared and partially adopted their global perspective from the ICC, which had been their employer through the 1920s and early 1930s; Mises had represented Austria at more than one ICC meeting in the interwar period. More proximately, the biggest single funder of the first MPS meeting was the Swiss industrialist and diplomat Hans Sulzer, who was a member of council of the ICC's executive committee in the 1930s and one of its vice presidents after 1945.[28] A main financial supporter of the MPS and later a member—and blacklisted by the British for alleged trade with the Nazis—Sulzer helped try to hire Hayek for a chair at the University of Zurich after the war.[29] He was also a member of the Joint Committee of the ICC and Carnegie Endowment for International Peace, which had sponsored major research by the world's leading economists (including Mises) on international economic reconstruction in the 1930s.[30]

If the neoliberal intellectuals spoke from the mountaintop, the ICC was its base. At Montreux, the thirty-eight-year-old Polish American economist Michael Angelo Heilperin, an MPS member who would play a major role in monetary debates of the 1960s, presented the official analysis of the ITO Havana Charter to the gathered businesspeople. Heilperin was a quintessential member of the Geneva School. Born in Warsaw in 1909, he completed his undergraduate and graduate degrees at the University of Geneva, in 1929 and 1931. His dissertation (written in French) was on the monetary problems produced by the collapse of the Habsburg Empire. In 1934 he had generated serious interest from the Rockefeller Foundation to fund the creation of an International Monetary Institute in Geneva.[31] A student of Rappard's, Heilperin took a position at Geneva's Graduate Institute for International Studies in 1935, a year after Mises.[32] For three years he worked "in almost daily contact" with Mises and also alongside Röpke, who arrived at the institute in 1937.[33] Heilperin presented on monetary issues at the Lippmann Colloquium in 1938.[34] He was a vocal member of the MPS after the war as well as an associate editor of *Fortune* magazine, a participant in Bilderberg meetings and in the Bellagio Group meetings that helped end the Bretton Woods system of fixed but adjustable exchange rates.[35]

Heilperin first became involved with international business circles in 1943, when he took a leave of absence from his position at Hamilton College to work as an adviser for the pharmaceutical and cosmetics company Bristol-Meyers, which had flagship products in laxatives and toothpastes and secured a major contract to supply penicillin to Allied soldiers during the war.[36] At the 1944 International Business Conference, which brought together the ICC, the National Association of Manufacturers, and others, Heilperin was the rapporteur for the section on international monetary relations.[37] Enjoying the highest consultative status on the UN Economic and Social Council, the ICC was a participant at every stage of the attempt to create the ITO.[38] As the ICC adviser, Heilperin was one of the few Americans attending both the Geneva and Havana conferences in an unofficial capacity.[39] When the president of Bristol-Myers, Lee H. Bristol, appeared before the U.S. Congress in 1950 to reject the ITO charter, he brought Heilperin along, drew exclusively from his analysis, and deferred to him during the session for details that he was unable to provide.[40]

Heilperin's statement of opposition to the Havana Charter at Montreux was a near carbon copy of the position of the ICC and the League of Nations at the World Economic Conference of 1927—an event that, according to Heilperin, was "the high point of international endeavor" and produced "the most comprehensive report of its kind, a well-reasoned document" but, regrettably, included no mechanism for enforcement or commitment.[41] Like the 1927 report, Heilperin demanded negative integration. For the "overall growth of productivity, trade, investment, and living standards *throughout the whole world*," a system was needed "in which goods, capital, and men can move and services be exchanged with the greatest possible freedom from country to country."[42]

Heilperin condemned the proposed ITO, using the term of critique from the 1930s: "economic nationalism." According to Heilperin, the number of exceptions, emergency clauses, and opt-outs in the Havana Charter had made it "the first international charter of economic nationalism ever written in the long history of the civilized world."[43] For Heilperin and the ICC, the ITO charter was a "dangerous document," above all in its transposition of democracy into international relations. Speaking before the U.S. Congress, Bristol said that the "one-country-one vote voting procedure is unacceptable." It threatened to create a situation in which "the rules of international commerce are being laid down by large numbers of countries who have a minor stake in international trade and often very little experience in conducting commercial policy."[44]

Heilperin expanded his critique of the ITO to general observations about the world since the end of the First World War. He noted that the period had been marked by a paradox: barriers to international trade and exchange multiplied even as awareness of global economic interdependence increased.[45] This had brought a series of quixotic hopes, such as the "insulation" promoted by Keynes and seen by many as at the heart of the postwar order. The essence of the goal of "policy autonomy" was that a nation should be free to break the rules of the game when it chose to. The Havana Conference, intended as a performance of internationalism, became a "very illuminating and enlightening seminar in present day nationalism."[46] To Heilperin, the ITO was a banner case of the failure to recognize the need for a double government for imperium and dominium.

Speaking to another gathering of industrialists, Heilperin said that a "good" ITO would "prohibit" any and all forms of blocking capital and goods, as well as more subtle forms of distorting the market through subsidizing production.[47] Heilperin put "sovereignty" in quotation marks, implying that the term had no intrinsic meaning when applied to economic matters.[48] In a paper based on a lecture delivered at the Graduate Institute in Geneva, he did the same with "autonomy," similarly discrediting the notion.[49] In Heilperin's reading, exercising economic sovereignty and economic autonomy were not simply inadvisable—they were impossible.

Heilperin phrased part of his critique in terms of what I have called capitalism's double world. One stratum of the world was that of the earth's natural endowments and the space of production, distribution, and ownership. The other stratum was the political world of nations and states. The category mistake of the sovereignty claim was to assert political control over the world of nature and economics. Heilperin elaborated on this in 1952. In physical terms, he said, "the planet is a single unit which cannot be subdivided into equivalent or self-contained parts. Politically, however, it is divided into a multitude of separate states, all bent on independence, often seeking at least partial economic self-sufficiency."[50] The resources of the earth, including climates, seas, and the earth's inner core, do "not favor the kind of political divisions which prevail on our planet." "There is no way," he wrote, "in which the political division of the planet can be reconciled with its physical structure by apportioning in some way or other the surface and the resources of the globe among individual states. The alternative is to reduce the importance of political divisions in terms of economic relationships."[51]

Heilperin's vision of order was multilateral but also unilateral: it brooked no deviations from the strictures of free trade. It was not only that he brushed away the complaint of infringement on sovereignty. Consistent with the Geneva School position of militant globalism developed since the 1930s, diminishing sovereignty was the exact point. He wrote directly that it was necessary to "subordinate" national objectives to international order.[52] He echoed the federalist vision of Mises, Robbins, and Hayek when he argued that "the importance of national boundaries . . . must be radically and drastically reduced." They must become "mere administrative demarcation lines," and national governments must "have only limited powers over their populations."[53] In its strong form, this would require what he called "geopolitics in reverse gear," reengineering national boundaries to actively *diminish* their capacity for self-sufficiency.[54]

Heilperin's demands for a muscular ITO that would bind nations to free trade and potentially shrink them to increase dependency on world trade was the first example of a postwar neoliberal utopia being articulated in full. It was also done within the world's most important business advocacy group. The solution was radical and no doubt would have been rejected by his employers within the "capitalist international." He recognized that very few nations, including the United States, would be willing to sign such a document. Given this fact, it is remarkable to note the verifiable effect that his activism, along with that of fellow neoliberals, had in sinking the ITO.

The ICC opposition to the ITO was a surprise. The organization had been close to the U.S. State Department during and immediately after the war. It stood behind Secretary of State Cordell Hull's push for free trade, and the American Council of the ICC had been one of "the keystones of bipartisan support" for his program.[55] When the Havana Charter came up for a resolution, the reflexive inclination of many ICC members was to follow their pattern of support for the U.S. State Department by signing it. Yet, as the official history of the ICC (written by a former member) recounts, Heilperin found a crucial ally for his opposition in Philip Cortney, an acquaintance of Mises who joined the MPS in 1953.[56] Cortney led the opposition and managed to convince the ICC executive committee to oppose the State Department on a major issue for the first time. The scene repeated itself at the international meeting when Cortney again led the opposition to the ITO against the British committee, who were disposed to sign the agreement. The decisive moment came when the chairman of the committee, Ernest Mercier, a French industrialist who had attended the Walter Lippmann Colloquium and was also member of the MPS, said he would tender his resignation before accepting the resolution. The resolution died on the floor.[57]

By lining up with Cortney and Heilperin, Mercier scuttled the support of the ICC for the ITO. One observer dubbed the group around Heilperin "the perfectionists" and suggested the "interesting possibility" that "in this case the businessmen were the 'hopeless idealists' while the bureaucrats and college professors who supported the Charter, without being enamored of it, were the 'realists.'"[58] Referring to a statement written by Heilperin, he said that "it is not always easy to tell when these statements are setting out utopian ideals and when they are describing a state of affairs, the business groups think is really attainable."[59] Such critiques failed to see that the utopianism was not incidental but intentional. Heilperin wrote in 1947, "We must agree to go beyond barren and complacent rationalizations of the present (in the name of what is often called 'realism') and seek goals which may appear unattainable . . . until they have actually been reached."[60] Heilperin and Cortney were fulfilling Hayek's desire from 1949 to the letter by offering a "liberal Utopia . . . which is not too severely practical, and which does not confine itself to what appears today as politically possible." It was precisely the overreach of the statements that make them amenable to the neoliberal program, which dictated polemic as a means to make liberalism "an intellectual adventure, a deed of courage."[61] What observers saw as a failing, in other words, may have been exactly Heilperin and Cortney's goal—to reject diplomacy and pragmatism and take the fight to the advocates of national economic autonomy. The ICC position statements were not just policy documents but what the Germans call *Kampfschriften,* or fighting documents. As Heilperin put it, the failed world conferences of the interwar period had taught the lesson that "in order to counteract a strong trend it is necessary to hit at it and to hit hard."[62]

In broad terms, the struggle over the ITO pitted the Global North against the Global South. Yet the official U.S. display of compromise to push the Havana Charter shows that it is important not to assume that "the West" was a single unitary actor in the postwar moment.[63] Far from being intransigent, official U.S. representatives immediately after the war showed a remarkable willingness to respond to the demands of Global South countries. To blame the U.S. failure to ratify the ITO on the unwillingness of big business to give up its sovereignty neglects the fact that the ICC's official position was not that the United States would lose too much sovereignty by participating in the ITO but that the ITO would not infringe *enough* on the sovereignty of signatories. Using the "business international" as an amplifier for a radical vision reminiscent of the federalism of Robbins and Hayek from the 1930s, Geneva School neoliberals outflanked the official government position and helped doom an organization committed to a level of decision-making parity with the poorer nations of the world.[64]

THE HUMAN RIGHT OF CAPITAL FLIGHT

Heilperin's closest ally in opposition to the ITO had been Philip Cortney, who was active within both the American Council of the ICC and the National Association of Manufacturers (NAM). One historian calls Cortney "the major spokesman for the purists" against the Havana Charter.[65] Born Philippe Cotnareanu in Romania in 1895, Cortney emigrated to the United States after taking an engineering degree in France. In 1946 he became an American citizen and president of Coty, a French perfume company. Cortney was a member of the executive committee of the U.S. Council of the ICC and would become its chairman in 1957.[66] He was also a member of the International Relations Committee of NAM, a business advocacy group that was close to the European neoliberals.[67] The committee executive was Noel Sargent, who had hired Mises to work as a paid and unpaid consultant for NAM from 1943 to 1948, when Cortney first met Mises.[68] In 1949 Cortney published his criticism of the ITO under the title *The Economic Munich*, making a polemical analogy between the Charter and Neville Chamberlain's appeasement of Adolf Hitler. Mises was extravagant in his praise, saying that the book would be "read and reread as a classic of economic freedom like the works of Cobden and Bastiat."[69]

The Economic Munich was most notable for its engagement with the language of human rights. Cortney did not reject human rights as such. He praised the UN's Universal Declaration of Human Rights as a "milestone in man's fight for liberty and human dignity."[70] It was the choice of rights he disagreed with. He condemned the way that the Havana Charter made "full employment" into a "kind of sacred human right," quoting Heilperin's Montreux statement at length in support.[71] Rather than discard the language of human rights as corrupted, Cortney added his own. In a strong statement he proposed that "exchange control in time of peace should be considered an act of aggression and a violation of human rights in international law."[72] By exchange control, Cortney meant what is better known as capital controls: the right to change money from one currency to another, specifically with the goal of transferring the money over a national border. The right to use capital controls was included in the framework of the IMF at Bretton Woods, a fact that Heilperin condemned as one of its crucial failings. Though many observers felt that the flow of "hot money" being invested by speculators back and forth across the Atlantic in the 1920s had helped precipitate the crash, Heilperin turned the problem around. "It is not the money that is 'hot,' " he said, "but the place from which it takes flight."[73] If capital controls were removed, countries that had drawn investors would have to establish conditions hospitable enough to induce foreign capital to remain.

Cortney's rhetorical move was to reframe the question from an economic matter into a matter of human rights. He linked capital control to the right to leave a country as such. Because "the right to leave a country is for all practical purposes, meaningless unless one is entitled to take with him belongings," he argued that one must under all circumstances be allowed to exchange and export capital.[74] Cortney described the right to emigrate as the "basis of all his other human rights," noting that it is included in the Universal Declaration of Human Rights (Article 13) but suggesting that this should have gone further by linking it to its necessary prerequisite: the right of free capital movement.[75] Cortney was effectively proposing the human right of capital flight.

In a postwar climate preoccupied with the rights of refugees and asylum seekers to stay once they had escaped danger, Cortney stood out for linking his claim of the human right of capital movement to the right to leave. His demand was neither spurious nor ill-informed. Cortney was a lifetime member of the American Society of International Law, and Philip Jessup, one of the fathers of transnational law, cited Cortney himself on the fact that exchange control can "effectively destroy" the right to emigrate.[76] Cortney's ingenuity was to read what was not intended as an economic right as an aspect of the economic constitution of the world, deeming money an item of property inhabiting the economic sphere that transcends political jurisdiction. Capital requires the protection of universal rights, in his interpretation. Consistent with ordoglobalism, he called for the constitutionalization of free-market principles, demanding that "exchange controls should be outlawed in the national constitutions."[77]

What seems like an act of cynicism on Cortney's part is actually consistent with the Geneva School neoliberal approach to the question of human rights in the years after 1945. Rather than reject human rights outright, the neoliberal tendency has been to undermine social democratic interpretations of human rights and international law while simultaneously co-opting them to cover clearly capitalist prerogatives. To say this was (or is) a critique of "social and economic rights" would be misleading, because the free movement of capital, goods, and labor was just as much a social and economic right as the demand for social security, employment, or nourishment. Indeed, as we will see in Chapter 6, the so-called market rights enshrined in the European Economic Community treaty were central to the neoliberal vision of Europe. Against Roosevelt's Four Freedoms—of speech, of worship, from fear, from want—neoliberals posed the four freedoms of capital, goods, services, and labor.

THE CAPITALIST MAGNA CARTA

Heilperin wore two hats at the Montreux conference in 1947. The first was as the ICC's man at the table for the ITO negotiations. The second was as the primary author of the ICC's International Code to Protect Foreign Investments. This latter document worked within Cortney's imaginary by tying business demands to the language of rights. At the conference Heilperin announced the need for "a code of fair practices in the field of international investments."[78] The draft code came out of the Committee on Foreign Investments, for which Heilperin was the rapporteur. It built on attempts made by the League of Nations in 1929 at a Conference on the Treatment of Foreigners and on a 1939 proposal from the ICC on the "legal treatment of foreign companies."[79] Picking up on prewar roots, the proposal was the first version of what would become today's regime of international investment law.

Working with rather than against the UN, Heilperin and the ICC felt that the code of investors' rights was to act as a supplement to the Universal Declaration of Human Rights. The ICC tasked ECOSOC with turning the code into "a universal convention" for later adoption.[80] The preamble, likely written by Heilperin, took direct aim at a December 1947 report by a UN subcommission submitted by Uruguay that criticized the "special danger of direct foreign investments interfering in the political and economic affairs of those countries."[81] By contrast, the ICC code called for nationals (which it defined as "not only physical persons but also incorporated or unincorporated associations") to enjoy the civil rights not of the host state but of their own state, even if this might grant them a "preferential" position.[82] Heilperin had already noted in his 1947 book that the protection for foreign investors had to exceed that for citizens. If capital controls applied to citizens, for example, they must not be allowed to apply to aliens. "Equality of treatment," he said, "does not suffice.[83] In a classic demand for xenos rights, the alien investor must actually have more rights than citizens.

The focus of neoliberals and big business on investor rights in 1947 was motivated by the perceived precariousness of private property both during and after the Second World War. The decline had begun during the First World War, when, as Röpke noted, "disregard of the private property of the enemy had become the rule among the belligerents."[84] The Soviet Union's expropriation of property after 1917 had been a signal rupture, followed by what a U.S. State Department adviser called a "dreary succession of such takings in the period between the wars."[85] It was such acts of expropriating foreign-owned property—or what was called nostrification in postimperial Central Europe when the property was given to private nationals—that Hayek complained of in *The Road to Serfdom*.[86] Even though foreign owners were often compensated at above-market price for such nationalizations worldwide, observers regularly cited cases, such as the Mexican nationalization of oil in 1938, as evidence of a global erosion of property rights.[87]

Neoliberals saw the disrespect of what were variously called "foreign rights" and "alien rights" of capitalists continuing into the postwar period. The specific sparks to their outrage were sometimes surprising. The proximate context for Cortney's call to designate exchange control a "violation of human rights," for example, was the cooperation of the U.S. and Western European governments to repatriate concealed Western European assets as part of the Marshall Plan. Cortney said that in doing this, the United States was assuming "the role of a Gestapo" in locating European assets in American bank accounts.[88] Röpke railed in a similar vein against the confiscation of German assets in Switzerland after the Second World War, saying that it undermined "the principle of the separation of sovereignty and property in the case of war."[89]

Considering the horrors of the war, it is startling to find an intellectual perceiving its lasting scandal as being the loss of foreign-owned property by citizens of the aggressor nation. Yet to Röpke and Cortney, these were not isolated grievances but symptoms of a larger malady. In demanding an economic constitution of the world, Geneva School neoliberals insisted that governing a territory did not mean owning the property within it. The campaign of the ICC and its neoliberal advisers was to create a legal framework to uphold the distinction between the imperium of government and the dominium of property. Neoliberals reached to the armory of law to rebuild the distinction between property and territory.

The ICC's proposal was taken up by an ECOSOC more sympathetic to social democratic nation-based demands than doctrinaire globalist business rights. In the postwar decades, the UN General Assembly became the "midwife" to the principle of "permanent national sovereignty over natural resources."[90] After a proposal by Uruguay and Bolivia, the UN General Assembly in 1952 passed its first resolution of many declaring that "the right of peoples freely to use and exploit their natural wealth and resources is inherent in their sovereignty."[91] Responding to a trend toward nationalization with UN sanction, the German Society for the Protection of Foreign Investment revived Heilperin's ICC code as a basis for its own Draft Convention. At the Society's inaugural meeting in 1956, MPS member Ludwig Erhard declared that "especially in the Western world, infractions against private property are eating further and further in, like a sneaking poison."[92] Erhard's placement of the danger to property in the West was consistent with the neoliberal interpretation, which held that social democracy in the Global North was working in tandem with nationalizing tendencies in the Global South to imperil the sanctity of property. At an MPS meeting in 1957, Arthur Shenfield said that "if it became clear that the capital of the West could be obtained only by those who respected the rights of capital, there would be a very salutary influence on the internal conduct of affairs in the prospective borrowing countries. But for that, of course, the

West must itself learn again to understand and respect the rights of capital owners."[93]

In 1952 Mises observed the irony of the disavowed symmetry between Global South and North when he said, "If it is right for the British to nationalize the British coal mines, it cannot be wrong for the Iranians to nationalize the Iranian oil industry. If Mr. Attlee were consistent, he would have congratulated the Iranians on their great socialist achievement."[94] Röpke wrote a year later that "the Mossadeqs appeal to the Atlees and the Bevans, who have inspired them with the idea of nationalization."[95] In fact, the British case against the expropriation of Anglo-Iranian Oil was one of the most important signals to the international business community that new standards were necessary for more robust protection of foreign property. The German Society's president, the Deutsche Bank head Hermann Josef Abs, who had overseen the expropriation of Jewish property in the Third Reich, became an international spokesperson for property rights in the second half of the 1950s. After the Society drafted an "International Convention for the Mutual Protection of Private Property Rights in Foreign Countries," Abs made his case before the American Society of International Law in 1956 and, most influentially, in a San Francisco speech at the International Industrial Development Conference on October 15, 1957, in which he cited the ICC statement. The speech, titled "The Safety of Capital," was reported in *Time* magazine under the headline "A Capitalist Magna Carta" in an issue that featured Ludwig Erhard on its cover.

Abs's proposal opened an international conversation on the rights of the investor.[96] His "capitalist Magna Carta" would oblige signees to abstain from "direct or indirect illegal interference" with "foreign capital" and would create an International Court of Arbitration to judge violations. Investors could turn to the third-party court first, without using local courts.[97] To punctuate the need for his code, Abs brought up the recent cases of the expropriation of the Anglo-Iranian Oil Company, the United Fruit Company in Guatemala, the Suez Canal, Dutch land in Indonesia, and foreign-owned power plants in Argentina.[98] For Abs, like the ICC, the UN had become an enemy accomplice of the property thieves, passing resolutions supporting the idea that "expropriations are permissible at any time without compensation."[99]

That an individual who had been an active participant in processing the expropriation of the property of German Jews would later be actively defending property was incongruous, but Abs did not act from amnesia or repentance. In his San Francisco speech he made a point of raising Cortney and Röpke's bugbear issue of foreign holders of accounts of German banks who were "still waiting for a fair settlement."[100] Abs was the man who signed the document forgiving Germany's massive war debt in 1953, and it is known that he did so in the belief that it was not forgiveness per se but instead a just settling of accounts for the German assets seized abroad. Abs's campaign for investor protection was a continuation of the dogged commitment to the economic constitution dividing the public world of states from the private world of property. Part of his original proposal, described by an observer as "idealistic," would have made alien property immune from confiscation during times of war.[101]

The capitalist Magna Carta drew interest in the United States. The chair of the judiciary committee of New York, Emmanuel Celler, declared the urgency of Abs's Magna Carta as he described a monument on a Mexico City boulevard commemorating the nationalization of oil and spoke balefully of "the law of the jungle" prevailing in Indonesia, where Dutch assets were expropriated by "wild men bent upon revenge."[102] "It would indeed be a great achievement," he said, "if West Germany could blaze a trail to the creation of such a Magna Carta under the leadership of Abs and Erhard."[103] By the late 1950s the struggle against expropriation was taking on a racialized language of the rule of law against the rule of the jungle, pitting the rational West against a Global South, with its "emotional" commitment to sovereignty.[104]

Combined with the work of a group of British attorneys under Sir Hartley Shawcross, Abs circulated a "Draft Convention on Investments Abroad" for comment in 1959. The document was concerned entirely with the protection of the property of "nationals," which were defined not as individuals but (following the ICC code) as "companies," including "both juridical persons recognized as such by the law of a Party and associations even if they do not possess legal personality."[105] The legal experts who commented on the convention were not encouraging. The preamble of the convention presented itself as a "restatement of principles," one expert noted, but "in several respects, it is clearly a good deal more than that."[106] They saw the convention as unprecedented in the protection it gave the foreign investor.[107] In every instance, it tipped toward the investor, dismissing "public interest" as a reason for expropriation, allowing investors to turn to an international court before national courts, and breaking with current practice by forcing compensation to be made in the investor's own currency and making the primary object of protection the company rather than the individual.[108]

By referring to both "direct" and "indirect" expropriation, the Abs-Shawcross convention even anticipated the later inclusion of "regulatory expropriation" in international codes. One contemporary critic noted, "It is difficult to determine where indirect deprivation of property ends and, for instance, taxation, planning legislation, or property law reform begins."[109] A former legal adviser to the State Department most sharply pointed out the lopsidedness of the convention. He wondered whether the proposition was not "to secure a commitment from a country that it must be prepared to take food from the mouth of its people in order to pay compensation in foreign exchange for property taken in exercise of its eminent domain power." He asked if this would amount to "an effort to erect 'property rights' over the 'human right' to eat."[110]

Demonstrating how far such a convention was from reality, one lawyer noted that the United States had been able to secure only "watered-down" commercial investment-protection treaties with a handful of Global South countries, and had no success at all with either recently decolonized nations or South American nations, which were major destinations for foreign capital.[111] One interpretation could be that the Abs-Shawcross convention, like the ICC Code, was not a serious proposal. It was a polemical document, outlining a dream world in which capital not only moved unobstructed globally but was encased globally by both home states and supranational third-party institutions of arbitration. What is clear is that neither of them were attempts to meet developing nations halfway. Rather, they were gauntlets thrown down to the Global South. It is symptomatic, as critics noted, that neither the ICC nor the Abs-Shawcross convention even acknowledged investment protection proposals coming from the Global South, including one in particular from Malaya, that sought to balance the needs of capital-importing and exporting countries.[112] The codes were coded threats of their own, seeking to discipline what their authors and champions saw as Third World overreach.

THE BILATERAL FIX

Given the utopian nature of the proposed international investment codes, it is a startling recognition of the long-term defeat of the bargaining power of the Global South that those codes have become reality over time. Modern international investment treaties now largely resemble the Abs-Shawcross "Draft."[113] A major difference between Heilperin's proposals and what later came into effect, however, was the switch from the mulitilateral to the bilateral approach. In 1958 U.S. representative James G. Fulton (R-PA), one of the chief negotiators for the ITO, praised the idea of the capitalist Magna Carta but conceded that the world charter had shown the difficulty of the universal demand. He suggested that bilateral treaties might be used instead.[114] From the beginning the ICC had indicated that a universal code was preferable, but their document would also work as the basis for bilateral relationships.[115] In fact, the Montreux Congress had also produced a Model Bilateral Agreement drawing on interwar templates.[116] Heilperin himself announced the failure of the "'universalist approach' to the problems of restoring the world economy to its former health."[117] When a second edition of his 1947 book *The Trade of Nations* came out in 1952, he stated that his opinion had moved in the intervening years to the quality of the bilateral treaty. State-to-state treaties were indeed much more the norm, including the Freedom of Commerce and Navigation treaties that the U.S. used up until the 1980s.[118]

The Bilateral Investment Treaty ended up offering the path that investor rights took from utopia to reality. Here, too, there was an MPS story. In 1959 the *New York Times* reported that Pakistan had "embarked upon a radical program of economic rehabilitation charted by the men behind West Germany's remarkable postwar recovery." Ludwig Erhard, economics minister for West Germany and MPS member, visited Pakistan in late 1958, and his policy advice was adopted "in toto" by General

Mohammad Ayub Khan after his seizure of power in a coup. The advice was to halt the country's industrialization campaign and to focus on agriculture to start an "all out export drive" on food crops.[119] In 1959 Egon Sohmen, another MPS member, referred in the leading American economics journal to Pakistan's "thoroughgoing reappraisal of its development planning along neoliberal lines."[120] The strategy was consistent with the development discourse in the MPS, which criticized a potential "overindustrialization" of the periphery and encouraged the Global South to keep its place in the international division of labor through agricultural production.[121]

Part of Pakistan's reform was the signing of what became the template for all future bilateral investment treaties. Signed by the West German and Pakistani governments in November 1959, Erhard submitted the "Treaty for the Promotion and Protection of Investments" to the Bundestag in 1961.[122] The treaty took language straight from the ICC Code and the Abs-Shawcross Draft, including the provision on compensation in the alien's home currency and the expanded definition of "nationals" to include "any other company or association, with or without legal personality."[123] Where the universal approach had failed, the particular approach succeeded, bringing the seemingly radical conditions of international investor protection into binding law.

❁ ❁ ❁

Hayek began one of his books by comparing the law to a knife. "Just as a man, setting out on a walking tour, will take his pocketknife with him, not for a particular foreseen use but in order to be equipped for various possible contingencies, or to be able to cope with kinds of situations likely to occur," he wrote, "so the rules of conduct developed by a group are not means for known particular purposes but adaptations to kinds of situations which past experience has shown to recur in the kind of world we live in."[124] Neoliberals took up the knife of the law in the years after 1945, relying on it to provide a framework for the market. They were compelled to do so for the same reason Hayek, over his lifetime, put increasing faith in the law: the reckless exercise and geographical expansion of democracy was corroding the principles separating politics from economics.

In the age of decolonization, neoliberals saw international organizations based on the one-nation-one-vote principle as the enemies of world economic order. They were unsuitable candidates for what Hayek called an international power with the authority to say no. The globalist Geneva of the 1930s was a lost Eden for neoliberals. In 1960 Heilperin pined for the League, "inspired by the philosophy of liberalism," which "did all in its power to promote the revival of freer trade and payments and of stable currency relations between nations." The postwar era brought "the United Nations, of which the opposite is largely true," an organization that "has so far proved singularly ineffective in helping rebuild a workable international economy."[125] In many ways neoliberals were League of Nations "lost causers," with the Genevan institution held up as the better version of international organization. Geneva School neoliberals railed against the UN not because it was world government but because it was the wrong kind of world government. It is an irony that this Edenic League, like their Edenic Habsburg Empire, was largely a fantasy, a wishful construct of their own theories. In fact, by 1945 the League had become a leading proponent for expansionary policy at a global level.[126]

One of the continuing questions regarding neoliberalism is whether it is a project to restore class power or a coherent ideology. We have seen that it was both. In the years after 1945, neoliberals worked with and alongside the International Chamber of Commerce to defend the threatened privileges of a specific class. Their imagination, however, exceeded that of their partners. Their radicalism always bore the potential of taking on a life of its own. Even though they worked with organizations grounded in *internationalism*, the *globalism* of the neoliberals often tended toward a goal that their hosts (and funders) did not necessarily share.

When in the years after 1945 neoliberals proposed a "good" ITO that would constrain national sovereignty and make investor rights stronger than civil rights, they were dismissed as dinosaurs or dreamers. Yet what was condemned by contemporaries in the 1950s as a "fallacy of nineteenth-centuryism"—believing the clock could be turned back to an earlier era—has become part of twenty-first-century reality.[127] In the 1990s the number of bilateral investment treaties, based on the original one between West Germany and Pakistan, quintupled to nearly 2,000.[128] These treaties and bodies would seek to enshrine what one scholar calls the "constitutional protection of capitalism" on the principle of "human rights as business rights."[129] Scholars see the 1970s as a time of the breakthrough of "the human rights of capital."[130] As we have seen here, that movement has an earlier history.

Defending the rights of the investor was an important early fight for neoliberal intellectuals and one they engaged in with their partners from the 1920s of the ICC. Although their campaign was framed as one for the sanctity of property rights, it is more accurately a fight for the sanctity of capital mobility. They were fighting, not for the right to own and stay, but for the right to sell and leave. In the aftermath of the Second World War, as international law was being rethought to accommodate the problem of the stateless and the refugee, international economic law was being formulated to protect the rights of what one contemporary called "refugee money" and the human right of capital flight.[131] If, as historians argue, nobody believed that the human rights of the 1940s should be enforceable at the cost of state sovereignty, it is notable that many believed that the private rights of capital should be enforceable in exactly that way. Although the actual practice of international investment law has been far from seamless, its postwar origin story provides a pointed case of the political activism of neoliberals in their quest to encase the world economy.

5

A World of Races

Let me recall Mill's dictum that there can be no liberty for "savages." Replace this harsh word by "politically and intellectually immature people" and reflect on the proposition that full democracy may not be the most suitable system of government for such people; that, for example, the unlimited right to vote and elect the men who will govern the country may lead to the destruction of many other freedoms and also of any real chance for economic development.

—FRITZ MACHLUP, 1969

Empires could end, neoliberals argued after 1945, but only if capital rights were secured and nation-states were kept from impeding the free flow of money and goods. But how to ensure this outcome in an era of decolonization when liberation, self-determination, and sovereignty were touted as the defining traits of statehood? At a Mont Pèlerin Society (MPS) meeting in Saint Moritz, Switzerland, in 1957, British economist and later MPS president Arthur Shenfield presented the paradox in two parts: First, "the liberal does not have to be a democrat but it is uncommonly difficult for him not to be." Second, "he does not have to allow the claim of dependent peoples to choose to misrule themselves but it is by no means easy for him not to do so."[1] MPS member Fritz Machlup made a similar point in a letter to Gottfried Haberler a decade later when he observed that "the cost of democracy is rather high. It makes it impossible to do what ought to be done and forces one to do what ought not to be done, in the public interest."[2]

To neoliberals, the principles of mass democracy and national self-determination were vexed. They were useful and could not be easily undone, but they also bore the potential for world economic disruption. In the postwar years the neoliberal position appeared to be losing. Like the Habsburg successor states before them, new countries in Africa and Asia, alongside older developing nations in Latin America, sought to build up their own industry and secure protection from global competition. The aspirations of new nations were aided by the prevailing economic theories. U.S. academics and policy makers, flush with postwar optimism and determined to counter the lure of communism, established an epistemology that sanctioned the political goal of what Elizabeth Borgwardt calls "a New Deal for the world," complete with full employment, transnational unionism, and opportunities for both big business and democratic governance.[3] So-called modernization theory mapped out a path for national economies to move from agricultural production to "take-off," when new technologies would increase productivity and raise the overall standard of living.[4] Coming late to development was not an obstacle but a boon, economists argued. Developing nations could enjoy the "advantages of backwardness" by adopting technologies already developed elsewhere. A Nebraskan senator reflected the zeitgeist in his memorable promise to "lift Shanghai up and up, ever up, until it is just like Kansas City."[5]

Yet modernization theory was never as hegemonic as it sometimes seems. Neoliberal critics stalked the vision of a New Deal for the world from the start. MPS members were early skeptics of foreign aid and saw postcolonial dreams of rapid industrialization as the latest variant of economic nationalism.[6] Hayek called it a "naïve fallacy" that industrialization was the only way to development.[7] Neoliberals saw the Bretton Woods system, which scholars have called embedded liberalism, as a path to isolation feeding delusions of national autonomy.[8] The neoliberal critique of mainstream development theories began with the conviction that the industrialization of formerly agricultural areas (like former colonies) and the protection of agriculture in primarily industrial areas (like Western Europe) distorted the international division of labor and led nations to specialize in branches of production for which their natural endowments were unsuited. A truly liberal world economy, in which capital and goods were exchanged freely, would result in the most efficient use of the earth's resources. Integration into the world market was a pedagogical process. Far from being permitted to shelter themselves from the push and pull of competition, postcolonial nations must be trained by the forces of the world economy to respond correctly to the guidance of market demand. The vanishing of empire meant a renewed role for what Ludwig von Mises called the reign of competition.

The neoliberal counterproposals for world economic order described in the previous chapters met with little success in the short term. Utopias of deplanning were rejected for the collective risk-pooling of the welfare state. Postwar regimes of free trade were riddled with exceptions, and capital controls were sanctioned by the International Monetary Fund (IMF). Universal investment codes ran aground on the rock of national sovereignty. Part of the problem seemed to be the failure to acknowledge that the world had changed. The Hayekian demand for xenos rights came close to the nineteenth-century principle of extraterritoriality—the immunity of foreign actors from domestic laws. Hayek himself suggested in 1953 that the U.S. government might insure American overseas investors against expropriation or the blocked repatriation of funds. Recipient nations, he said, should "allow American financial institutions to operate unhindered within their territory."[9] But who would force them to do so and why would such high-handedness be accepted? Ludwig von Mises had pointed out the problem in 1943, saying, "It is an illusion to believe that such conflicts could be settled by arbitration on the part of impartial courts. A court can administer justice only according to the articles of a code. But it is exactly these prescriptions and rules which are contested."[10]

Writing the same year, Röpke, an early critic of foreign aid, was also less than sanguine about the viability of reanimating extraterritoriality after the age of empire. Former colonial powers lacked both the will and the power to reinstate such rights, he wrote.[11] An investment code would be partially useful in creating "norms that would be dangerous to flout openly and uncomfortable to circumvent." But to believe that a solution was merely a matter of legal engineering expressed "juridicism," "false internationalism," and, with echoes of the failures of economic diplomacy in the 1930s, a delusional "conferencism."[12] Who would litigate infractions, Röpke wondered. The UN—that organization which "Western state wisdom had constructed such that Europe's voice could barely be heard in comparison to the developing countries"? The International Criminal Court at the Hague? "Just to ask such questions," he said, reflects "the bitterest sarcasm."[13] For Röpke, the postwar international system was a faulty construction. Relying on it to enforce just conduct for global capitalism would be fatal.

The chief obstacle Röpke saw was not one of design but the more intractable one of culture. He argued that the moral conditions simply did not exist in recipient nations to ensure the safety of capital and would not exist into a future "so distant that it could not be seen even with the eyes of a prophet."[14] Against what he saw as the materialism of the idea of economic development, he posed the importance of "moral infrastructure."[15] Some populations, he argued, had the traits required for success in a system of global capitalism, others did not—and little could change this fact.

My narrative thus far has focused on the ways in which law and economics complemented each other in attempts to design a world safe for capitalism. Now I will highlight a third term—the variable of race—through the overlooked example of the neoliberal relationship to Southern Africa. South Africa and Rhodesia were seen as limit cases in the reorganization of the world after the Second World War. They reasserted racial hierarchy as a formal strategy of rule even as that strategy receded globally. After introducing apartheid in 1948, South Africa left the British Commonwealth in 1961 under near-universal approbation, especially in the United Nations.[16] Rhodesia announced a Unilateral Declaration of Independence in 1965, seceding under white rule. Both countries operated through institutional arrangements that discriminated against the nonwhite population in structures of suffrage and everyday regulations.

Although condemned by international organizations and world public opinion, the alternative version of decolonization practiced by South Africa and Rhodesia had some defenders in the neoliberal movement. One finds here a split within the MPS. On the one hand, the single most high-profile champion for white South Africa in the early 1960s was one of the founders of the neoliberal movement, Röpke himself. His path to strident advocacy for South African apartheid was an idiosyncratic voyage from the moment in the 1930s when he and Alexander Rüstow called for an extra-economic framework as a necessary substrate for liberalism. Amid deepening pessimism about the potential to restore the global economic order in the age of decolonization, Röpke found an explanation in the supposedly in-built characteristics of race, and reassessed the imperialism he had once condemned.

Röpke's position on apartheid is uncomfortable for his many supporters. With one exception, recent scholarly treatments of Röpke avoid reference to his spirited defense of South Africa; an otherwise comprehensive biography makes no mention of it.[17] His rhetoric is also an ill fit with the intellectual history of the neoliberal movement from the 1920s to the 1980s, in which outright defenses of racial hierarchy play only a marginal role. Röpke's position on apartheid led him away from thinkers like Hayek, Mises, and Heilperin and toward an alliance with the traditionalist conservatives of the U.S. New Right, especially William F. Buckley, who also saw an assault on the principles of Western civilization in anticolonial movements and African American mobilizations for civil rights in the United States.[18] In the early 1960s Röpke came to see Southern Africa as the most important stand for the global front against economic disorder. In his personal fusion of neoliberalism and traditionalist conservatism, white supremacy in Southern Africa was an essential feature of the extra-economic framework securing the world economy.

No other neoliberal defended apartheid in precisely the way Röpke did, and Röpke had resigned from the MPS by the time he made his strongest statements. Yet some other neoliberal thinkers distinguished between apartheid as a comprehensive system of racial segregation and the discrete matter of suffrage for the black population. They argued, as

Machlup does in the epigraph to this chapter, that democracy might have to be restricted for certain peoples in order to preserve stability and prosperity.[19] Restricting political freedom, as commonly understood, was necessary under some circumstances to preserve economic freedom. Prominent neoliberals, including Milton Friedman, John Davenport, and Shenfield himself, followed this logic by opposing universal suffrage in Southern Africa.

The most important critic of equal voting rights was, perhaps surprisingly, the person celebrated in the libertarian movement as one of "the original and most passionate opponents of apartheid in South Africa": the British economist William H. Hutt, an MPS member since 1948 who had studied at the London School of Economics (LSE).[20] Hutt's reputation is based on his 1964 book *The Economics of the Color Bar.*[21] While the book advocated nondiscrimination in labor markets, it also proposed a revision of suffrage—inspired explicitly by Hayek—to immunize the market against the disruptive effects of an empowered population. From the 1940s until his death in the 1980s, Hutt promoted a model of weighted franchise for both South Africa and Rhodesia to counteract the negative effects of democracy. Drawing support for his interpretation from other neoliberals, Hutt promoted a color-blind market but only alongside a ballot box that saw first in black and white and then apportioned voting rights differently to the wealthy and the poor.

The last response to South Africa we will consider here is that of Hayek himself. Having visited the nation twice, Hayek was unambiguous in his public denunciation of apartheid as "both an injustice and an error."[22] Yet he saved even stronger words for the attempts by international organizations to use sanctions and embargoes against apartheid South Africa to compel it to change its internal policies. The neoliberal way of world governance was reflected more in the responses of Hutt and Hayek to apartheid than in Röpke's invocation of a world of races. Hutt offered constraints on democracy designed to lessen the likelihood of economic protectionism and redistribution, and Hayek's militant globalism affirmed that the totality must hold against the ruinous demands of a globalized morality.

RÖPKE AND THE ZAMBEZI LINE

As a nation under white minority rule, South Africa came under increasing international scrutiny as decolonization spread worldwide. After the 1960 Sharpeville massacre in the Transvaal region of South Africa, when police killed sixty-nine people who had been demonstrating against the segregationist pass laws, and the subsequent prohibition in South Africa of all anti-apartheid groups, it was ever more difficult to argue that the country was anything other than a racist police state.[23] The United States criticized the regime formally beginning in 1958, when the Eisenhower administration first signed an anti-apartheid resolution at the UN.[24] Scholars have traced the wavering line of the U.S. government as it sought to placate African and Asian opinion through symbolic actions against South Africa, including a partial arms embargo in 1963, without endangering economic ties and political relations, not least because it relied on South Africa as a source of uranium and other strategic minerals.[25]

It was in this atmosphere that Röpke wrote what he called "an attempt at a positive appraisal" of South Africa in 1964. In the pamphlet, he observed that "the South African Negro is not only a man of an utterly different race but, at the same time, stems from a completely different type and level of civilization."[26] Describing South Africa as "one of the most prosperous and—in certain respects—irreplaceable nations in the world economy," Röpke praised "the extraordinary qualities of its white population, who live under unusually favorable climatic conditions and possess a pioneering spirit that can be compared only with that found in the United States."[27] The country's most notable features were its attractiveness to tourists, its "relatively favorable tax structure," and the high returns it offered on foreign investment.[28]

The policy of apartheid was not oppressive, Röpke argued. It was instead "the specific form in which South Africa pursues the policy of 'decolonializing' and 'development aid' which corresponds to this country's needs."[29] It was necessary because the nonwhites of South Africa were "at a stage of development which excludes true, spiritual and political integration with the highly civilized Whites, and are at present in such numbers that they threaten to overwhelm the latter who are present upholders of the political, cultural and economic order."[30] Drawing a parallel to Israel, he wrote that, as with the relationship of the Jewish population to the Arabs, to provide full political equality to the black population would be to commit "national suicide."[31]

Following his corpus of writing from the 1930s and 1940s, in which race played little to no role as a category of analysis—and after his principled stance against anti-Semitism that led to his emigration from Nazi Germany—it is striking to see South Africa praised in Röpke's political geography in the 1960s as a white stronghold.[32] To prevent the country from turning into "another Congo or Indonesia," he called for "a Zambezi line" to "divide the black-controlled northern part of the continent from the white-controlled south."[33] For reasons of racial difference, economics and Realpolitik, Röpke believed that white supremacy had to persist in South Africa.

The South African government was grateful for the rhetorical ammunition. They ordered three translations and sixteen thousand copies of the book in which the article was to appear.[34] The next year they ordered twenty thousand offprints of the article for distribution in the United States.[35] Defenders of apartheid quoted Röpke's work in their own pamphlets.[36] Röpke could not rely on his usual European allies on the South Africa issue, diverging as he did from their own position. The editors of the economic-liberal Swiss newspaper *Neue Zürcher Zeitung*, with whom he had worked for three decades, did not share his zeal for Hendrik Verwoerd's regime.[37] The newspaper published a statement of protest by foreign students when Röpke delivered his paper as part of a lecture series on Africa in Zurich in July 1964.[38] "These *NZZ* intellectuals will not be satisfied until they let a real cannibal speak," Röpke wrote to his primary collaborator from the mid-1960s, Swiss businessman and former MPS European secretary Albert Hunold, who organized the lecture series.[39] Röpke himself supported the appearance of another speaker in the series, the German colonial historian Wahrhold Drascher, who faced criticism when it was made known he had published a white-supremacist monograph in the Third Reich under the title *The Ascendancy of the White Race,* alongside later postwar apologia for Western colonialism.[40] In personal correspondence, Drascher praised Röpke's article on South Africa as "outstanding."[41]

Röpke and Hunold were conscious of the fact that they were parting with the core of the MPS group on the issue of South Africa. Hunold wrote to Röpke from South Africa that their former neoliberal partner, Hayek, "now advocates one man one vote and race mixing." He concluded with contempt: "Nothing surprises me about Hayek anymore."[42] Röpke and Hunold found their primary allies on the apartheid question not in the European neoliberal milieu but in the partially overlapping circles of the U.S. New Right, a community that was often more willing to defend the principle of white rule.[43] In the 1950s Röpke was a steady source of information for the emerging U.S. conservative movement on issues of European integration, postwar reconstruction, and international economics. Buckley and Russell T. Kirk, the figureheads of the movement, corresponded and collaborated extensively with Röpke, and in 1955 his name appeared on the masthead of the first issues of both the *National Review* and *Modern Age*, the New Right's flagship publications.[44] In 1956 Buckley declared himself a "disciple" of Röpke.[45] In correspondence, Kirk expressed his indebtedness to Röpke's influence and lauded him as the best hope for "humanizing economic thought."[46] After Röpke's South Africa piece was published, libertarian newspaper columnist Lawrence Fertig wrote to congratulate him, commending Röpke's "courage" and "great integrity" in writing it, which, he acknowledged, had "contributed much" to his thinking.[47] Stanford University agricultural economist and German émigré Karl Brandt, who had suggested the name for the MPS, called the piece a "very refined and at the same time enormously strong exposition of the philosophy of freedom."[48] After Buckley published an article of his own defending the Verwoerd government, he wrote that he was "bursting with pride" over the praise Röpke paid to the piece.[49]

How do we reconcile Röpke's racism with the neoliberal discourse of world order, which accepted democratic self-determination on the conditions of free trade and free capital movement? As mentioned in Chapter 2, Röpke's reflections on the Great Depression in the 1930s led him to see extra-economic factors as essential to the preservation of the world economy. He felt that adherence to the gold standard and the free movement of capital and goods had acted before 1914 as "a sort of unwritten *ordre public international*, a secularized Res Publica Christiana, which for that reason spread all over the globe," resulting in a "political and moral integration of the world."[50] As one scholar points out, the system relied as much on "informal constraints, that is, extralegal standards, conventions and moral codes of behavior" as on national laws.[51] In Röpke's view, membership in international society was synonymous with being a responsible actor in the free market. The liberal world order, the heir of a Christian order, was defined as a system of formally ungoverned economic expectations and modes of interaction—it was a community of values, which individual economies could both join and leave, but which supranational institutions could not legislate into existence.

Peripheral to Röpke's account of the era before 1914 as the "glorious sunny day of the western world" was the fact that the nineteenth century was also the era of high imperialism, when much of the earth's territory was partitioned among the European powers.[52] What was to be done, then, in the postwar world, when both the religious basis of international society had been lost and the community of "the West" was splintered by decolonization? The quandary Röpke faced in the 1950s was shared by many other conservatives and indeed, centrists, as well: How could empire end without losing control of the nonwhite world?[53] Röpke dismissed the proposal for a democratic world government that would welcome postcolonial nations as peers as a Western death wish; the "free world," he wrote, could not be "expected to commit suicide."[54]

One of Röpke's concrete proposals was a form of federation along the lines initiated by Robbins and Hayek in the 1930s: Nations should have formal political sovereignty but a diminished economic autonomy that would be regulated by the free flow of capital and investment over borders.[55] Röpke's recommendation that a rebuilt West Germany be export-oriented stemmed in part from the idea that susceptibility to shifts in the global market would constrain attempts at large-scale and long-term planning.[56] His global vision was consistent with the "rearticulated federalism," seen by Bernhard Walpen as a basic feature of neoliberal thought, that called for the decentralization of authority to remove the collective decision-making capacity for the "emancipatory design of society as a whole."[57] As in the vision of Robbins and Hayek, a loose world federation would help prevent mass popular expectations from becoming reality because the ever-present threat of capital flight would curb campaigns of expansionary social policy. Economic actors voting with their feet—and their assets—would be the surest corrective on projects of building domestic welfare states.[58]

Röpke predicted that the disciplining function of the open world economy would be accompanied by the retrenchment of civilizational blocs in response to what he called "Hannibal at the gates," evoking an earlier moment of the West under threat.[59] Röpke's Hannibal was less the Soviet Union, often characterized as Asiatic in conservative German discourse, and more the decolonizing world. "The more the non-European great powers emerge," he wrote, "and the civilizations of other continents begin to regard us with condescending self-confidence, the more it becomes both natural and necessary for the feeling of spiritual and moral homogeneousness among Europeans to increase powerfully."[60] The borders of the besieged community extended over the ocean. He asserted that "the spiritual and political integration of Europe . . . only makes sense as part and parcel of a higher combination and organization of the resistance potential of the *entire* western world on both sides of the Atlantic."[61] A morally strengthened Fortress Occident would arise as a necessary defense against the emboldened populations of the non-West, unanchored as they were from the moral community that bound the West.[62]

Röpke's normative vision for the West and his anxiety about shifts in the global racial order overlapped considerably with the Atlanticism that historians have traced from turn-of-the-century calls for Anglo-American union to the visions of Clarence Streit for the federalist fusion of the United States with Great Britain and Western Europe in the 1930s and 1940s.[63] As we will see in Chapter 6, Röpke opposed the creation of the European Economic Community on the grounds that it would bloat bureaucracy and empower socialist tendencies in Western Europe.[64] Instead, he advocated a European Free Trade Area that would include Britain and, consistent with his federalist vision, entail free trade and convertible currencies but no supranational planning bodies.[65] As one scholar has observed, Röpke and Ludwig Erhard also believed that integration should not happen "at the expense of the Atlantic Community" and based their vision on the "Occidental concept that emphasized the political, social, and historical similarities of the West."[66]

Linked by their common Christian patrimony, Western Europe and North America, in Röpke's view, bore the responsibility for restoring the liberal international economic order lost after 1914. Other neoliberal thinkers downplayed the centrality of culture and race after 1945, but Röpke insisted on its importance. "Racial fanaticism," he wrote in 1965, "does not justify denying that there is something called ethnos, race, and it is of elementary importance."[67] The literature he footnoted was stark in its hierarchical biological essentialism. Among his recommendations for the field of "ethnopsychology" was a study that concluded that "mental capacity tends to be adequate among peoples and races adjusted to cold and temperate climates, but inadequate among those adjusted to hot climates" and warned of "lethal power in the hands of nation-states dominated by populations incapable of rational thought."[68] At a time when biological race was being either marginalized or recoded for many of the social sciences, Röpke brought it to the center of his analysis.

AGAINST THE GLOBAL NEW DEAL

The United States played a key role in Röpke's vision of a rebuilt West. Yet by the 1950s he felt that its government was doing everything in its power to accelerate the disintegration of world order. The problems had begun with the New Deal. Organized labor, protectionism, and planning had "politicized" economic processes and eroded the foundations of liberal international economic relations.[69] The interventionist state was the adversary of the liberal world economy because it sought to empower working populations and raise standards of living within national-territorial space. In the postwar moment, the U.S. government was exporting those expectations, first to Western Europe, and then to the decolonizing world. The economic constitution of the world—a firm division between the world of states and the world economy—was being eroded by American policy.

In one of his first articles in the U.S. conservative publication *The Freeman,* Röpke took aim at the wartime vision of the New Deal for the world. Citing the socioeconomic promise of Roosevelt's Four Freedoms from 1941, he remarked, "It is unlikely that the true liberal will be caught by such glib phrases as the 'Freedom from Want' by which the essence of liberty is surrendered to collectivism."[70] Since the announcement of the Atlantic Charter, Röpke had feared that "the flip side of total war," as one scholar puts it, would be the "sweeping expectation that there would be a welfare state among those mobilized for war."[71] Roosevelt had let the genie of what Röpke called "equalitarianism" out of the bottle to win the war, and it would be difficult to put back in. Filling the category of democracy with economic content would have catastrophically destabilizing effects.

The first consequence of the New Deal's internationalization was the diverse experimentation with planning that emerged in postwar Western Europe.[72] In an attack on Marshall Plan aid for Britain and France in 1950, a Missouri senator quoted Röpke's observation of the irony "that the Marshall Plan, which should have pulled Western Europe out of the muck of collectivistic, nationalist economic policy, has threatened to create a new supercollectivism on a super-state level."[73] Röpke offered colorful terms for the occasion, denouncing the U.S. support for the planning bodies of the European Economic Community (EEC) as "vulgar gigantolatry and technolatry."[74] International organizations threatened to expand the pernicious effects of planning to an even larger scale. In 1952 the American Enterprise Association (later the American Enterprise Institute) published Röpke's critique of the UN "Report on National and International Measures for Full Employment" (1949), which had been written primarily by British and French Keynesians.[75] Röpke wrote that there was "no other economic issue which appears so attractive and yet may be so dangerous as the one based on this misleading and bitterly discussed concept" of full employment and warned that the report marked the dangerous shift from "national planning" to "international planning."[76]

With the launch of Kennedy's New Frontier program in 1961, Röpke found another "New" entity to place in the crosshairs of critique. In April 1963 he published a half-page editorial in the *Wall Street Journal* titled "Washington's Economics: A German Scholar Sees Nation Moving into Fiscal Socialism." The broadside began by linking the New Deal and the New Frontier: "Thirty years ago, I published an article severely criticizing the economic policies then being pursued by President Roosevelt in the name of a 'New Deal.'" The "New Frontier" of President Kennedy, Röpke continued, was no less worrisome. "The similarity between the 'New Deal' and 'New Frontier' finds expression not only in the general decline in business confidence," he wrote, "but in an openly defiant glorification of 'big government' and in the fiscal megalomania which serves this questionable ideal." Both programs surrendered to the rising wage demands of trade unions and shared an inflationary policy of monetary expansion that expressed "the tendency for the increasingly centralized state of our times to surround like a parasitical vine both society and economy."[77]

The special danger of the New Frontier was that it was literally a global New Deal. Extending Röpke's metaphor, one could say that the vines of the state were creeping outward through an expanding foreign aid program of government loans, which had drawn in the West German partner by 1960, and the more aggressive use of trade unions, including the establishment of the American Institute of Free Labor Development as part of Kennedy's Alliance for Progress. Röpke called foreign aid "the great action by which the ideas and methods of collectivist policy are carried into the world economy" and singled out economist Gunnar Myrdal as proposing the "transposition" of the modern welfare state from the Western to what Röpke called the "undeveloped" world (consciously avoiding the normative term "*under*developed").[78]

In his article, Röpke attacked by name two authors of the Keynesian growth model and modernization theory, John Kenneth Galbraith and Walt Whitman Rostow, maintaining that the latter preached a "new version of the Rooseveltian illusionism in the dress of economic determinism . . . which is not nearly as far removed from that of Marx as Prof. Rostow seems to think." Indeed, by promoting what Röpke called "standard of life-ism," the promise of global economic evenness contained in modernization theory had "played a more important role in the advance of communism to its present power than has the whole panoply of Communist tanks, rockets and divisions."[79]

Röpke condemned, in other words, the very feature that made development a consensus internationally in the 1950s: that it concentrated on increasing output without being overly prescriptive about the route used to arrive at the goal.[80]

Röpke believed that the "one-sided economism" that exported materialist yardsticks of progress to the Global South alongside a fetish for industrialization would lead to worldwide inflation, the erosion of the world food supply, and the creation of a global urban proletariat alienated from its own traditions.[81] He believed that an economically equal world might simply be impossible, and that developing countries might have to remain underdeveloped as a way of preventing a possible "over-industrialization and underagriculturization of the world."[82] Beyond the structural imbalance of an entirely industrialized world, he added, the conditions for industrialization in the Third World did not exist. He explained global disparities in wealth through cultural essentialism, writing that "the 'rich' countries of today are rich because, along with the necessary prerequisites of modern technology and its industrial use, they have a particular form of economic organization that responds to their spirit [*Geist*]."[83] It was an "uncomfortable fact" but a reality that this spirit could be found only in "sharply curtailed areas . . . namely the fully developed industrial countries of the free world."[84] As one scholar writes, Röpke believed that the "lack of punctuality, reliability, the inclination to save and to create" in the Global South meant that industrialization schemes in the Global South were "doomed to fail."[85]

Razeen Sally describes Röpke's model as an international "liberalism from below," rooted in extralegal behavioral practices. While he is correct in this sense, he fails to observe the built-in cultural constraints of the model.[86] For Röpke, some paths to development, and thus possible futures, for postcolonial nations were disqualified from the outset. In his opinion, the right to equality encapsulated in the ethos of the welfare state was as unworkable and unwise on the global scale as it was on the national. Inequality was to be understood as an unavoidable characteristic of capitalist society. Whereas one of the greatest attractions of modernization theory has been regarded as its "promise of evenness," Röpke's model saw unevenness as the inevitable continuing status quo within an international division of labor.[87]

Three congressmen entered Röpke's anti-Kennedy polemic into the Congressional Record in a single day in 1963, and another did so in the following weeks.[88] One archconservative followed Röpke in describing the New Frontier as "continuing the master plan of the New Deal." Referring to Rostow and Galbraith, he asked, "Will our people wake up to the designs of these architects of socialism, of slavery, enough to change our course back to capitalism or not?"[89] A moderate Republican also used Röpke's article to criticize Kennedy and the "tired, unimaginative and unworkable theories of the New Deal."[90] Röpke's inflammatory critique of Kennedy and his overseas policy provided Republican policy makers with ammunition to fight the rhetorical war against the New Deal on a global level.

THE ECONOMIST-ORACLE FROM THE OTHER EUROPE

The moment when Röpke's article appeared was one of intensifying mobilization for the U.S. conservative movement. Scholars have shown that business conservatives who organized against the New Deal in the 1930s entered a more public phase of their campaign after Eisenhower's reelection and his embrace of Keynesianism in 1958 under the moniker of "modern Republicanism."[91] Arizona senator Barry Goldwater, who in his 1964 presidential bid would be advised by a coterie of émigré German-speaking economists, entered the national spotlight that year with attacks on Eisenhower's new budget.[92] Röpke himself wrote an exposé for Goldwater and described him as "a force that is changing the entire picture of American politics."[93] The John Birch Society was formed that fall, and the MPS met in the States for the first time at Princeton University, with the funding of companies including United Fruit and U.S. Steel.[94] This network of right-wing critics shared a willingness to label Eisenhower "socialist," if not "communist," for his move toward Keynesian policy tools. The election of Kennedy in 1960 only amplified the rhetoric, as Röpke's reference to "fiscal socialism" in his *Wall Street Journal* article illustrated.

The moment was also one when panicky U.S. conservatives looked to Western Europe as the bastion of market conformism. For New

Rightists, several of whom had strong affective identifications with European high culture, neoliberals like Röpke represented the "Other Europe," embodied in the policies of Economics Minister Ludwig Erhard in West Germany, President Luigi Einaudi in Italy, and De Gaulle adviser Jacques Rueff in France (all MPS members), who professed more faith in market mechanisms and more suspicion of Keynesian demand management than did most U.S. policy makers.[95] These isolated individuals were cast as brave bulwarks; Buckley said that it was Röpke's "tenacious faith in the free enterprise system [that] is largely responsible for the recovery of Western Europe."[96] In a 1963 *Wall Street Journal* article, conservative journalist and MPS member William Henry Chamberlin counted Röpke among "the leaders of the neo-liberal trend in economic thought that has been an important influence in turning European governments away from the goals and methods of collectivism and the planned economy."[97] In a dynamic that would be reversed after the 1970s, the United States seemed more "socialist" than parts of Europe—West Germany and Switzerland, in particular—in the early 1960s to members of the U.S. New Right, with credit for this going to a small group of economic luminaries.[98]

Röpke and other German-speaking economists profited from their perceived objectivity and separation from the scrum of U.S. politics. A letter to the editor after Röpke's 1963 polemic noted that "his message is the more forceful because it is delivered from a comfortable distance which permits unhurried appraisal of the situation."[99] When a business information service sent the article out to its subscribers, it included the following biographical note: "Röpke who voluntarily left Nazi Germany is deemed one of the foremost and perhaps the foremost economist and economic philosopher of Europe, if not our time. He is also for many years one who has concerned himself in depth with the United States. Obviously, he has no ax to grind; he lives in Geneva; has no political ambitions anywhere; and is a true cosmopolitan."[100] Europe and, for Röpke, Switzerland in particular, represented spatially the otherwise rhetorical redoubt from which embattled conservatives spoke at the turn of the 1960s. This was literal in the case of the MPS, which took its name from the Swiss peak of its first meeting—the "mountain where thinkers dwell" as the *Wall Street Journal* would label it in 1972.[101]

Röpke embraced the role of emissary from the "other Europe" and representative of the "other liberals" who held to principles of private property and competition rather than redistribution and social justice. Three years later he described himself as an "economist from the middle of Europe . . . who saw it as self-evident that, after all of the experiences and considerations of the last decades, one could not speak of planned economies, full employment policies, nationalization and the welfare state in anything more than a tone of sarcasm."[102] Americans informed him that they were accustomed to hearing the "commitment to the market economy and the critique of socialism . . . from the presidents of chambers of commerce and bank directors" but that Röpke had proved that "one can be 'conservative' without necessarily being intellectually crude or uneducated, and one can represent this position in a way that is worthy of an intellectual."[103] One scholar argues that identification with relatively obscure European thinkers like Röpke helped the U.S. conservative movement legitimize itself as an intellectual movement in the 1950s and 1960s.[104]

Röpke had his own theory about the dearth of U.S. intellectuals capable of defending the cause of classical liberalism. He saw the root of the problem in the "dynamic competitive economy" of the States, which was producing wealth so quickly that academics were being left behind, losing "social prestige," and expressing their resentment in anticapitalist opinions. The creation of new economic elites was happening so rapidly, Röpke noted, that a joke he told about the *nouveaux riches* during the Weimar inflation years drew blank stares from an audience of wealthy businessmen ignorant of the term.[105] He took it as a goal to bridge the gap between the "world of business and the world of intellectual life," offering himself as the *philosophe* of the *nouveaux riches.*

Röpke became part of the business conservative public relations offensive through his written work and public actions.[106] It was through these networks that he became part of the international advisory council for a plan to create a "Hall of Free Enterprise" for the 1964 New York World's Fair; its organizers claimed it would be "the first time that the totality of a free economy has ever been put together in simple, visual form."[107] The hall was a paradigmatic representation of the economist as an unerring, neutral source of information. Its central feature was a computer that would print out answers on slips of paper to questions visitors typed in. The *New Republic* reported, "There is a kind of oracular infallibility to this machine that makes it more impressive than a live pundit. A group of awe-stricken visitors punched it and read replies. What it said must be so, they seemed to feel, because after all a machine is unbiased and impartial."[108]

One could argue that German-speaking economists profited from a similar aura of "oracular infallibility" at this critical moment in the 1960s when an ambitious application of worldwide Keynesianism encountered a conservative anti-Keynesian backlash.[109] One of Röpke's correspondents from Venezuela, who studied with Haberler at Harvard and later worked with the EEC, called Röpke a "prophet."[110] One newspaper described him as "one of the high priests of free enterprise" and another compared him to "a skilled medical authority."[111] The "wise men" who advised international financial institutions and later helped direct programs of structural adjustment enjoyed a similar status, achieving a kind of superhuman detachment in their expertise. In 1960, the West German, American, and British central bankers sent to India by the World Bank to provide advice on its Five-Year Plan were referred to as the "three wise men."[112] The West German Council of Economic Experts *(Sachverständigenrat)* created in 1963, was known commonly as the Five Wise Men *(Fünf Weisen)*.[113] Scholars have noted the special prestige enjoyed by economic experts in what a book published in 1968 called "the era of the economists."[114] While it might seem superficially odd to pair the computer and the silver-haired European intellectual, they shared the claim of producing knowledge in a space ostensibly beyond politics.

TAKING THE FRONT SOUTHWARD

The Atlantic front of the conservative resistance to the export of New Deal policies extended southward in the early 1960s in an attempt to build a counterbloc to the Alliance for Progress. Röpke found allies among those who had published his work in local newspapers and translated his books and pamphlets, as well as some former students now in positions of power, such as Peruvian economics minister Pedro Beltrán.[115] In 1963 Röpke wrote to his Mexican contact, MPS member Gustavo Velasco, that he was glad his "anti-Kennedyism" had become known in his country.[116] His *Wall Street Journal* editorial appeared in Venezuela in Spanish translation one month after its original publication. His Mexican publisher, Nicomedas Zuloaga of the Institute for Economic and Social Analysis, wrote, "We are now facing a great danger in our country with the foreign policy of the U.S. toward Latin America. All that policy, we believe, is based on the writings of Mr. Raúl Prebisch of the ECLA [United Nations Economic Commission for Latin America]."[117] The shared enemy was the UN and the egalitarian economics for which it provided space and resources.

Röpke's close collaborator and funder Hunold became convinced of the need to formalize the emerging transatlantic bloc after the Peruvian Chamber of Commerce bought two thousand copies of his talk during a South American speaking tour in 1962.[118] He and Röpke began to canvass for interest in an organization they called the Forum Atlanticum. They hoped the new body would replace the MPS, from which they had both resigned in a long-simmering conflict with Hayek; Röpke described the society in 1963 as filled with "intellectual careerists and intriguers."[119] Distinguishing themselves from both the social democratic consensus and existing organized neoliberalism, they intended the forum to represent more exclusively the strain of conservatism emerging around Kirk and Buckley—which "fused" free-market principles and Christianity—rather than the philosophies of Hayek and Mises, for whom religion was peripheral if not absent. In trying to build support for the forum, they discredited the Austrians to would-be partners, describing their theories as having "no philosophy of society" and excluding "the human in his entirety."[120]

Röpke and Hunold likely hoped to steal a march on the MPS by appealing to Catholic elites. Hunold listed South Americans first among proposed members, including economics professors in Colombia, Venezuela, and Mexico. Cuban émigré businessman and founder of the first anti-Castro organization Rafael Lincoln Diaz-Balart promised to join, contribute, and raise funds for the endeavor in Latin America, no doubt disillusioned by the Kennedy administration's failure at the Bay of

Pigs.[121] Conversations with the Chilean senator and university professor Pedro Ibañez Ojeda about the threat of the Alliance for Progress strengthened Hunold's resolve to start the new organization.[122] Ibañez was the head of the Inter-American Committee on Trade and Protection, which provided the "infrastructure and network of connections" for Chicago-trained economists in Chile in the 1960s ahead of their breakthrough after Pinochet's coup.[123] Aside from Ibañez, Kirk, Buckley, Thomas Molnar, Velasco, individuals from Venezuela and Colombia, and the publisher of *U.S.A.* magazine, Alice Widener, other proposed members of the forum in the United States included Brandt, at Stanford, who, like Friedman, would become one of Goldwater's economic advisers in 1964.[124] Hunold also hoped to recruit an "African representative" during a trip to South Africa.[125]

Offering the presidency of the would-be Forum Atlanticum to Kirk, Röpke explained his idea "that the good minds of Europe and of both Americas should . . . join their forces to present and to bring into focus the common patrimony of our occidental civilization while frankly analyzing and criticizing the hostile tendencies corroding and disintegrating this civilization."[126] This was necessary, he had written earlier, "to enlighten the ever more Americanized and sinistrized Europeans about the ideological obsessions of American intellectuals, without which Kennedy's brain-damaged policies cannot be understood."[127] His old ally Erhard, formerly the West German economics minister and now chancellor, did not realize the threat Kennedy presented, Röpke said; Erhard saw world politics "like a Boy Scout" and had "entered the racket of undeveloped countries" by calling for their "supposedly necessary industrialization."[128] Röpke described Kennedy as a "vain, neo-Jacobin Hamlet, an intelligent ass, an open Germanophobe . . . surrounded by even bigger asses, a man without political will" and said that Washington's policy "could hardly be any different than if it set out to make the world communist before one could smell it coming."[129] He wrote in 1962 that Europe existed under the "terror of Kennedy."[130]

The Forum Atlanticum received encouraging signs in 1964. Hunold and Kirk met with U.S. donors John Lynn from the Lilly Endowment and Indianapolis lawyer and MPS member Pierre Goodrich, both of whom seemed supportive.[131] The difficulty came with finding a president. Röpke had suffered his second heart attack in January 1962 in the midst of his departure from the MPS, and his deteriorating health made him an unlikely candidate.[132] Kirk offered "to take the presidential office initially," but only if "no one else at all suitable can be found." He further demurred that he was "so much engaged in assailing the infidel with fire and sword that it might be better to have a president somewhat less ferocious," and also cited his lack of an institutional base and his "incessant wandering."[133] He suggested Brandt instead, who had left the MPS in solidarity with Röpke in 1962.[134] Brandt, though, had been an advisor to Goldwater and no doubt was shaken by his candidate's catastrophic loss in November 1964 and wary of new undertakings. In December of that year, Brandt wrote Röpke to tell him that MPS members (including Antony Fisher, founder of the Institute of Economic Affairs) were encouraging him to rejoin the society, and that he was seriously considering it.[135] Adopting the presidency of what was, in effect, a rival organization might alienate him permanently from the society he had helped name in 1947.[136]

The noncommittal response from would-be leaders among U.S. conservatives imperiled plans for the Forum Atlanticum.[137] Hunold suggested that they gather forces and try again in early 1966, but Röpke's health continued to decline and he died in February of that year.[138] Despite the organization's failure, we can see in the nodes of its proposed network the way Röpke went about finding his "Other America" in the conservative pundits of the North and the pro-business elites of Latin America, just as they found their "Other Europe" in German-speaking neoliberal economists. One scholar notes that Röpke most pointedly targeted the American conservatives around the *National Review* for membership in the new entity.[139] The Forum Atlanticum represented the would-be internationalization of the project fusing free-market liberalism with traditionalist conservatism, whose most effective advocates Röpke saw in the United States. Allying with the traditionalists of the New Right, he hoped to break out of what he called the "economistic ghetto" of the libertarians attracted to Mises, Hayek, and Friedman.[140] For all his criticism of the United States, Röpke implicitly admired the American New Right's capacity for what J. Howard Pew called, in the title of his postwar conservative organization, Spiritual Mobilization.[141]

THE INTEREST RATE THEORY OF CIVILIZATION

In 1964 Hunold wrote to Röpke from a speaking tour through the U.S. Midwest that he had to change the name of one of his lectures in Peoria, Illinois. The title—"European Economic Integration"—had prompted the director of the local television station to ask, "Do you fellows have a racial problem over there too?" Hunold pointed out that people in the States were preoccupied above all "with integration and segregation."[142] In fact, the intersection of questions of race and economic order were at the forefront of Röpke's concerns in this period. The economist prided himself on taking unpopular positions and being "against the tide" (as his memoir was titled when published in English by Henry Regnery).[143] This was certainly the case in the matter of South Africa. From 1964 until his death in 1966, Röpke's concerns about foreign aid and "occidental civilization" converged in Southern Africa.[144]

Historians have shown how the *National Review* tacked to the right on issues of race in the late 1950s, culminating in Buckley's 1957 editorial opposing desegregation on the grounds that whites were "the advanced race" and that science proved "the median cultural superiority of White over Negro."[145] Yet they rarely note that Buckley's editorial is couched in a defense of European colonialism in Africa. Buckley defended British actions for maintaining colonial control in Kenya (which continued until 1964) as an example to the U.S. South that "the claims of civilization supersede those of universal suffrage," and concluded with an openly antidemocratic argument for white supremacy: "It is more important for any community, *anywhere in the world,* to affirm and live by civilized standards, than to bow to the demands of the numerical majority."[146] Buckley's racial views "did not stop at the water's edge," as one scholar notes. He visited South Africa on paid fact-finding missions in the 1960s and distributed publications supporting the apartheid government.[147] Buckley's exhortation that "the South must prevail" also meant that whites had to prevail in the Global South.

Röpke's frustration with the tolerance for the claims that nonwhite actors were making on the world stage frequently tipped over into vitriol. In 1963 he expressed "disgust" at the sight of American politicians "groveling in front of the Negro chiefs on the South Africa issue." "To call for 'equality' of the blacks in South Africa is a call for suicide," he wrote, "It is saddening how few people have realized that."[148] Röpke's name continued to add European intellectual luster to the campaign of apartheid apologists after his death. For example, U.S. Representative John M. Ashbrook (R-Ohio), leader of the Draft Goldwater movement, entered a collection of documents about South Africa by the ultra-conservative American-African Affairs Association (AAAA) into the Congressional Record in 1967. Founded by *National Review* publisher William Rusher and African-American former Communist Max Yergan to advocate on behalf of white rule in southern Africa, the AAAA included the core group of New Right luminaries that Röpke had been in contact with since the 1940s, among them Kirk, Regnery, Chamberlin, and Henry Hazlitt.[149] Ashbrook cited Röpke, "the respected economist," as stating that South Africa was "not 'stupid or evil.'"[150] Ashbrook further called attention to the economic consequences of pressuring apartheid South Africa, saying that "little consideration seems to have been given by the UN to the economic disaster which would ensue for all black Africans if the most advanced and productive sector of the continent were disrupted by sanctions or war—which would incidentally concomitantly smash the British economy and end its substantial aid to Africa."[151] In Ashbrook's logic, supported by reference to Röpke, upholding the racist system that disempowered them was economically necessary for the black population itself.

As we saw earlier, Röpke described the "South African Negro" as "a man of an utterly different race" who "stems from a completely different type and level of civilization." Such crude statements of evolutionary racism were relatively rare in print. More common for Röpke was his translation of race into economics. This framework is especially evident in an article published in *Modern Age* in 1966, the year of his death. Lamenting the loss of the "republica Christiana," which could no longer be relied on as the substrate of social interaction in a secular age, he assured readers that there still was an "international order" that persisted in "Europe and the overseas countries of European settlement," although outside of this there was only "debris." He explained the principle by which he excluded the developing and decolonized world from the international order through the example of the Congo: "As long as the Congo was connected with the international order of the West through Belgium, the guarantee offered by the Belgian government made it possible to raise the enormous sums needed for the economic development and modernization of the Congo largely on the free capital markets by way of the usual loans bearing a normal rate of interest." He then contrasted this earlier moment of inclusion with the mid-1960s, by which time the Congo, "by an ill-considered and panicky act of 'decolonization,' has been severed from the international order of the West." Under this circumstance, there was "simply no rate of interest conceivable at which people in the Western countries might be persuaded to lend their money voluntarily to that country any more than they would to India, Egypt, or Indonesia."[152]

Röpke distilled the question of a nation's proximity to "the West" down to the figure of how much interest the nation would have to pay to borrow money. For him the most pertinent criterion was not culture, ideology, or geography but creditworthiness. He phrased the sentiment baldly, calling the interest rate "a quantification of one's right to membership in the bloc of the 'free world.'"[153] Because Röpke saw a perfect homology between the qualities of entrepreneurship, the civilizational category of the West, and the functioning of a free market, interest rates were not just an economic but a spiritual index, an index of *Geist.* By offering low-interest loans and state-to-state financing, the World Bank and other international financial institutions were tampering with the central mechanism of world order. This economic definition of the free world—the translation of "the West" into a financial category—underwrote Röpke's public treatment of South Africa.

Röpke's rhetoric climaxed in the wake of the white Rhodesian government's Unilateral Declaration of Independence in November 1965, along with the international criticism and British calls for sanctions that greeted it. Writing to Hunold as he entertained the South African economics minister and his wife in Geneva, Röpke observed, "[In] the revolting case of Rhodesia . . . the combination of ideology, obsession, hypocrisy, stupidity and masochism has reached a new height. If a white developing country proves that development aid is unnecessary, then [the country] has to be destroyed."[154] Hunold said he was lobbying Erhard to read Röpke's work on South Africa so that it might change his mind about Rhodesia.[155] Hunold reaffirmed that South Africa would "play an important role for the survival of the free world and the perpetuation of Western culture now and in the future."[156] He likened the happenings in Rhodesia to "the same dangerous point as thirty-five years ago, when the National Socialists achieved their first great electoral success, and after which the fronts in Germany were systematically weakened."[157] The white bloc, in other words, was wavering, signaling the potential beginning of a race war, not of Germans against Jews this time but of blacks against whites. To Hunold, the Zambezi line constituted the new Maginot Line and nonwhites were the new Nazis.

Another of Röpke's correspondents, sociologist Helmut Schoeck, who also spoke in the Zurich lecture series organized by Hunold, saw a direct relationship between the outcome of the Second World War and the decolonizing present. He felt that solidarity of Western intellectuals with nonwhite populations—or "Afrophilia" as he called it—was actually a "tardy and completely misplaced gesture of repentance of those people and groups who are ashamed because they failed to intervene at the right time and with any success in Hitler's persecution of the Jews." Schoeck averred in a letter to Röpke that because those intellectuals were seeking to make up for a past error "thanks to a strange inversion in the subconscious of many of our colleagues, the Africans (coloreds) today have been attributed all of the intelligence and cultural potential that Hitler actually did exterminate in the Jews." This attempt at a conciliatory gesture would end by accelerating the literal extinction of the white population, Schoeck believed. "You cannot bring six million Jews back to life," he cautioned, "by first putting cannibals in their place and then serving approximately the same number of Whites to them as a feast."[158]

The frequent use of the term "cannibal" in Röpke's circle of conservative acquaintances, to describe African political actors, alongside his call for a "Zambezi line" and the persistent refrain of the "suicide of the West," suggests that a racialized worldview was at the heart of Röpke's postwar philosophy of society and economy. The intersections of the categories of cultural and economic geography come to light in his writings about South Africa and their hearty approval by the New Right.

Röpke had broken with the position of Mises, who in his postwar work opposed the use of race as a category of analysis, and Hayek, who wrote his talk "Why I Am not a Conservative" explicitly to distance himself from Röpke's correspondent Russell Kirk.[159] The variety of neoliberalism pioneered by Röpke was distant from the universalist globalism we have been exploring, but as the next section shows, the neoliberal defense of white rule in Southern Africa could and did take other forms.

HUTT AND THE WEIGHTED FRANCHISE SOLUTION

Röpke's forthright statements of biological racism were not the norm among neoliberals.[160] The most notable counterpoint to the apartheid apologist would seem to be William H. Hutt, described by the *New Individualist Review* in 1964 as a "consistent opponent of the policies of apartheid."[161] Hutt's main book, *The Economics of the Color Bar,* was published in 1964 and reissued by the Institute of Economic Affairs in the late 1980s and again by the Ludwig von Mises Institute in 2007. Hutt was an exact contemporary of Röpke and Hayek. Born in 1899, he studied at the LSE with Theodore Gregory and Edwin Cannan and in 1928 joined the faculty at the University of Cape Town (UCT); he worked there with former fellow LSE student Arnold Plant, who was a founding member of the MPS and would return to the LSE as a professor in 1930.[162] One of Hutt's students at UCT was Basil Yamey, who became a prominent neoliberal critic of development aid, coauthoring articles with Peter Bauer.[163] Hutt stayed at UCT until 1966, when he moved to a series of positions in the United States. His longest stint was at the University of Dallas, where he was a distinguished visiting professor from 1972 until his death in 1988. Hutt's primary contribution to economic thought was his notion of "consumer sovereignty," as well as his work on trade unions and his "theory of idle resources."

Hutt was connected to the neoliberal intellectuals through the LSE since the 1930s. Hayek included a piece of his in the 1954 collection *Capitalism and the Historians.* Hutt became an MPS member in 1948 and from 1949 to 1984 presented at eight annual meetings, where he offered his expertise on topics such as "liberalism and racialism"

(1964) and "the image of the entrepreneur in South Africa" (1970). By his own account, he attended not only the second meeting of the MPS but the "great majority of all subsequent conferences."[164] During his time in South Africa, he hosted Hayek and was the key contact for the neoliberal movement in Africa.

In *The Economics of the Color Bar,* his most extensive application of neoliberal thought to the case of South Africa, Hutt self-consciously applied insights from Milton Friedman about U.S. racism and echoed those of Gary Becker from the same time.[165] Latter-day scholars recall the book as a "conscience-raising work" and a "profound and disturbing analysis that exposed the moral horror of apartheid in South Africa."[166] At its core, Hutt argued, racism is a form of rent-seeking analogous to trade unions defending their own privilege against the entry of non-white workers.[167] "The chief source of colour discrimination," Hutt suggested, was "to be found in the natural determination to defend economic privilege."[168] In his reading, racism was not of the market but outside of—and in opposition to—the market. In a review, fellow MPS member Enoch Powell praised Hutt's book as a testament that "the market economy . . . is the most effective enemy of discrimination between individuals, classes and races."[169]

"The market is color-blind" was the conclusion Hutt came to.[170] He celebrated the virtues of labor mobility and attacked the racialized "closed shop" of apartheid. Consistent with his earlier work, Hutt built his model around the sovereignty of both consumer and employee. Yet even as Hutt condemned apartheid, he defined it in a very particular way. For him, equality was synonymous with lifting racial barriers to employment in the workplace rather than any the fulfillment of any political demand. Tactfully avoided by his admirers—but the focus of nearly all of his other writing on the theme—is the fact that the political complement to this workplace liberation was not equality for blacks but their second-class status for the foreseeable future. Hutt's proposals for a weighted franchise ended up being just as radical as Röpke's proposition of the interest rate index of civilization.

The problem of democracy was the central theme of Hutt's writings. What he described as "the most vital point of my whole thesis" in *The Economics of the Color Bar* was not an economic but a political argument:

a warning about the "tyranny of parliamentary majorities" under systems of universal suffrage.[171] The fact that blacks were the majority population in South Africa made the situation exceptionally perilous, in his view. The apparent solution of universal suffrage would only "mean the transfer of power to a new political majority, *with no constitutional limitations to prevent retaliatory abuse.*"[172] Hutt mentioned that he sympathized with those who feared "black supremacy (a mere turning of the tables)."[173] Hutt expanded on these ideas in a piece solicited for the *National Review,* likely by Buckley himself on his state-funded trip to South Africa in the winter of 1962–1963.[174] In a draft of the unpublished piece, titled "Apartheid in South Africa and Its Foreign Critics," Hutt argued that the introduction of one-man-one-vote in South Africa would lead to what he said the Soviets were encouraging: "black imperialism."[175] Hutt expressed the need "to protect the minorities [that is, Whites] from spoliation and revenge" and suggested that the franchise be adjusted on "some principle of weighting."[176] Hutt offered more details on his proposal in a letter to the editor of the *Cape Times* in 1957. He suggested an educational requirement for franchise for European and non-European voters, but, critically, "at some time in the distant future (it would be very optimistic to assume 50 years) when the aggregate number of non-European voters equaled that of the Europeans, the value of each non-European vote would begin gradually and very slowly to diminish."[177] The model was one of degressive proportionality, and it would preserve, if not white minority rule, then a greater value for a white ballot than a nonwhite one.

The person Hutt saw as being closest to his philosophy was Hayek, with whom he shared the draft of the article ahead of hosting him in South Africa in 1963. He called Hayek's 1960 book *The Constitution of Liberty* "the greatest exposition" of the principle of the need to limit democracy.[178] In that book Hayek sketched the potential excesses of democracy, drawing on both history and the present for his argument. He invoked recent Central European history first, saying that having "seen millions voting themselves into complete dependence on a tyrant has made our generation understand that to choose one's government is not necessarily to secure freedom."[179] He followed with a subtle dig against postcolonial governments, saying that "though the concept of national freedom is analogous to that of individual freedom, it is not the same; and the striving for the first has not always enhanced the second." He observed that decolonization and democratic self-determination could have adverse outcomes: "It has sometimes led people to prefer a despot of their own race to the liberal government of an alien majority."[180]

Hayek lectured on his book *The Constitution of Liberty* during his time in South Africa. Hutt wrote up the visit under the title "The Abuse of Parliamentary Majority in Multi-Racial Society," which offers the only record of Hayek's statements.[181] According to Hutt's account, Hayek was "under no illusions about the threat which a Black-dominated electorate could constitute in the future but we do not always remind ourselves that it is the power of the state which we are really dreading."[182] Hayek argued that "it is the Whites . . . who have taught the Africans that the machinery of the State may be used to secure sectional benefits—chiefly in the form of privileges for the Whites." "Is it surprising then," he asked, "that African leaders tend, all too easily to think in terms of turning the tables?"[183] Hayek's message to Hutt and others was that a state captured by black voters would cease to be a problem if the state itself was stripped preemptively of its right to grant exemptions from the discipline of the competitive market. As with his idea of neoliberal federation from the 1930s, Hayek's proposal was to downgrade the significance of representative government by reducing its roles to the enforcement of competition and contract.

Hutt carried his proposals for weighted franchise into the publications of the U.S. New Right. In 1966 he argued in the *New Individualist Review* that in South Africa, "the prospect of an African majority, through the ultimate extension of the franchise on the basis of 'one man, one vote' created wholly justifiable fears on the part of the Whites."[184] He suggested that the only solution was to "renounce the principle of universal suffrage . . . and accept some form of weighted franchise."[185] Like Röpke, Hutt was especially enraged and mobilized by what he saw as the unjust treatment of the white-ruled country of Rhodesia after its Unilateral Declaration of Independence and departure from the British Commonwealth in 1965. Beginning in 1964 Hutt began sending letters to Prime Minister Ian Smith of Rhodesia with his advice about how to ensure that "the present regime, with all its admitted faults, shall not be replaced by an era of black domination."[186] He suggested constitutional protections of property and, again, "weighted franchise arrangements."[187] In an article on "the Rhodesian calumny," Hutt defended the property restrictions designed to protect white-minority rule as a bulwark against "'one man, one vote' tyranny," calling Rhodesia "the most promising deliberate attempt the world has ever seen at creating a wholly democratic, multi-racial society."[188] As paradoxical as it might sound, Hutt argued that it was precisely by denying universal suffrage that true democracy could be realized.

Through the 1970s and 1980s Hutt kept up a drumbeat of protest against the supposed injustice of the international mobilization against Rhodesia and South Africa. He wrote letters to Governor Ronald Reagan and President Jimmy Carter praising Rhodesia as "the only genuine anti-racist democracy in Africa."[189] After Portugal withdrew from their colonies of Angola and Mozambique, the United States hardened its position against Southern Africa, with Carter reintroducing a ban on the import of Rhodesian chrome in 1977 amid new talk of human rights and demands for moves to majority rule.[190] Sensitive to the continuing shift away from political models based on race, Hutt proposed to political leaders in South Africa an innovation of his racially weighted franchise model. He suggested instead a weighting of the franchise according to income. In a letter to South African finance minister Owen Horwood in 1978, he suggested that "[if you] weight each person's vote by the amount of taxes he is called upon to pay," South Africa could "rightly insist that Blacks, Coloureds, Indians and Whites would have the most complete equality through the dissolution of the colour bars."[191] Hutt claimed that this measure would appease enough American critics because it would amount to "absolute equality for all races."[192] The vote based on income would amount to total political nondiscrimination and yield to the greater wisdom of the market.

Hutt argued that his proposal would achieve the realization of a notion he had coined in the 1930s: "consumer's sovereignty." Hutt argued that if "every dollar was a ballot," in the phrase favored by Mises, income-weighted franchise would extend the analogy by translating one's wealth into the relative power one had in electing a representative government. "The effect of so revolutionary a reform," he argued, would be "to emphasize that citizens actually purchase the services of government and cause them to be regarded as public servants rather than as rulers."[193] Hutt's proposal was not as novel as it sounded. Beyond its obvious echoes of nineteenth-century property bars to the franchise, it is notable that such a model of weighted representation was already used at the World Bank and the IMF, both of which determined votes based on national participation in global trade. Hutt's economistic adaptation of democracy actually scaled the Bretton Woods institutions down to the level of a citizenry. He opposed apartheid in the workplace, but he advocated a new economic hierarchy of electoral privilege to replace it.

Hutt's opposition to universal suffrage in Southern Africa was shared by some others in the neoliberal camp.[194] In 1970 Shenfield invoked "the hideous dangers of totalitarian democracy" as he argued that "the limitation of the franchise in South African circumstances is not only not wrong; it is positively desirable in the interests of all races." "In South Africa," he wrote, "'one man one vote' would mean disaster for all.[195] Similar sentiments came from journalist John A. Davenport, formerly of *Fortune* and *Barron's,* and Milton Friedman. Both men had been at the founding meeting of the MPS and were active members in the neoliberal intellectual movement.[196] Like Hutt, Davenport spoke at eight MPS meetings, during the 1960s and 1970s, and Friedman had achieved international fame through his popular writing as well as the Nobel Memorial Prize he won in 1976. Hutt claimed that neither man had been engaged with Southern Africa until visiting the region in the 1970s.[197] In that decade, both became outspoken critics of universal suffrage for the region, with a focus on Rhodesia in particular.

Davenport's advocacy for white rule in Southern Africa exceeded even that of Röpke. Already in 1972 the South African Information Service had commended Davenport on his public support for the regime, including his letter to the *New York Times* defending South African rule in Namibia and demanding that the country not be "gobble[d] up by the UN" and "subjected to the indignities of so-called 'one man, one vote' democracy."[198] After the Carter administration turned definitively against the Smith regime in Rhodesia in 1977, Davenport worked with the Rhodesian Information Service to gather signatures of support from American businessman for the Smith government.[199] Davenport took two trips to Rhodesia and, as the co-chairman of the American-Rhodesian Association (ARA), hosted Smith when he visited the States in October 1978 at the invitation of segregationist senator Jesse Helms and a group of other conservative senators, including later presidential candidate Bob Dole.[200] In its mission statement, the ARA called sanctions "an aid and encouragement to barbarism" and paid homage to the "supreme gallantry and value of Rhodesia (Zimbabwe) as an outer bastion of the Free World in Africa."[201] Into the 1980s and the rise of the divestment movement on university campuses, Davenport continued to condemn the "immoral war of aggression on South Africa" driven by the "mania of majority rule" and a devotion to "the follies of doctrinaire democracy."[202] In 1985 he complained directly to the White House about sanctions and received written support from the assistant to the president, Pat Buchanan.[203] Davenport was not passively sympathetic to the opposition to majority rule in Southern Africa but instead was one of its foremost activists in the late 1970s and 1980s. Like Hutt's, his argument thrust in two directions: against sanctions and against universal suffrage. On these two points he was joined by Friedman, the most high-profile of postwar neoliberal intellectuals, and on the opposition to sanctions, by Hayek himself.

FRIEDMAN AND HAYEK'S MILITANT GLOBALISM AGAINST SANCTIONS

Milton Friedman condemned sanctions against Rhodesia in two editorials for *Newsweek*, one of which appeared first in the London *Sunday Times*.[204] In the 1976 column, published after he traveled to the region, he made the initially perplexing argument that "'Majority rule' for Rhodesia today is a euphemism for a black-minority government, which would almost surely mean both the eviction or exodus of most of the whites and also a drastically lower level of living and opportunity for the masses of black Rhodesians."[205] In defining universal suffrage as "minority rule," Friedman expressed his skepticism about the practice of democracy in the United States itself. As he argued at the University of Cape Town in South Africa in 1976, the practice of one-man-one-vote was in fact "a system of highly-weighted voting in which special interests have far greater roles to play than does the general interest."[206] Drawing implicitly on the work of theorists like Mancur Olson, Friedman argued that the "political market" favored those with the incentive and the resources to organize and militated against the interest of the public and the less powerful.[207] The economic market, by contrast, was "a system of effective, proportional representation."[208] He proposed novel solutions for the South African context. People complained that whites received free education while black students had to pay. His solution: make them both pay. "I am not in favor of egalitarianism" he reminded his audience, "in the sense of equal results."[209] Inequality was the ineradicable condition of a functioning market order.

Although Friedman followed Röpke by quoting James Burnham in saying that the isolation of Rhodesia was a sign of "the suicide of the West," his conclusions were based not on race or level of civilization but on a general critique of the practice of electoral democracy.[210] His opposition to sanctions was also based on an abstract principle: that markets succeed through "the subtlety with which they connect producers and consumers and the anonymity in which they clothe the participants." Because the ideal market does not discriminate by race, religion, or nationality, to interfere in processes of exchange to punish this or that political power through an international authority—as in the case of Rhodesia—would be to weaken "the system of free markets that is our greatest source of strength."[211] Dominium had to exist beyond the whims of diplomacy.

Hayek's public statement on South Africa echoed Friedman's. Amid widespread criticism of the visits he and Friedman paid to Pinochet's Chile in the 1970s, Hayek complained in 1977 of the "international character assassination" aimed not just at the South American nation but at South Africa too, a country he would visit for the second time the following year.[212] While condemning apartheid in strong terms, he expressed fear that the "arbitrary measures" of the UN in singling out certain nations for punishment had become one of the greatest threats to the liberal world economy. "The U.N. can only protect its influence," he wrote, "when boycotts or similar matters against individual countries are instituted according to set and posted rules, not when it lets itself be seduced through vote-catching in individual cases." Hayek warned of drastic repercussions with globally corrosive effects: "I do not know whether the representatives of the Western Great Powers that have agreed to the arms embargo against South Africa realize the danger they are courting with this decision. They have begun to destroy the international economic order."[213] The use of sanctions as an economic weapon transgressed the borders separating the world of property and the world of states. Moral demands, even those legitimized through international organizations, had no mandate to disrupt the economic constitution of the world.

Southern Africa offers a litmus test for the varying neoliberal perspectives on the questions of race, world order, and empire in the age of decolonization. Not only was there no single position in the neoliberal camp, but the major players changed their positions over time. Röpke's swerve was perhaps the most extreme. Writing from Istanbul in the mid-1930s as a scholar in exile out of principled resistance to a racist regime, he had condemned imperialism in stark terms. The history of overseas European expansion, he said, was "a history of conquest, barbarism and brutality."[214] He argued for an anti-imperialism that was not anticapitalist but liberal—one that would actively safeguard the division, as he put it, between "imperium and dominium—the economic sphere and sphere of states."[215] Three decades later, when decolonization had become a global reality, his refrain changed. Colonialism, he now claimed, had borne the "cunning of history" by bringing Western civilization to the non-Western world. Whereas he wrote in 1934 that European imperialism corresponded "to all of the irrational powers in the inner life of nations," by 1965 he was claiming that it was European patrimony that was threatened by "the monstrous forces of chaos and destruction" that opposed it.[216] Most important was his newfound conviction that "Europeanization" had turned the whole earth into a "single colony of the West."[217] Given this reality, stability and relative prosperity would come to the Global South only when they dropped their disavowal of Westernization and embraced it as an ethos, life way, and mindset. Whether genetic difference rendered this impossible was a question he left open. What was clear was that Röpke's narrative of history was no longer one of balancing public authority and private property but had instead become one of prescribing the final victory of the Western *Geist*. Empire was not an era that had ended but a task to be completed.

For Hutt, Friedman, and Hayek, the focus was not civilizations but political systems that would encourage the reproduction of a working market order. Their chief concern was that misguided morality in the demands for universal suffrage or the wielding of economic weapons such as embargoes and sanctions might upend both predictability and the facelessness on which the coordination of countless laborers, sellers, and consumers depended. Within the recognized constraints of the unwritten and even unconscious codes of conduct built into tradition, they kept a basic faith in the utility of multilevel constitutional design as a means of safeguarding property and competition worldwide. As Chapters 6 and 7 will show, the main stream of neoliberals saw a world of rules, not a world of races. And the place where this world started was in Europe.

6

A World of Constitutions

> The historical import of the European Economic Community treaty consists in its relating the internationality of law and political institutions to the internationality of economic relations. In this sense, the EEC treaty embodies an economic constitution.
>
> —ERNST-JOACHIM MESTMÄCKER, 1973

Europe is one of the riddles of the neoliberal century. Some scholars claim that the European Economic Community (EEC) was a neoliberal project from the start—that when West Germany, France, Italy, and the Benelux countries agreed to the Treaty of Rome in March 1957, they were actually signing Hayek's blueprints for federation from the 1930s.[1] Others counter with the point that Hayek himself was opposed to European federation after 1945.[2] If the EEC was a neoliberal "triumph," what to make of an observer's remark in 1962 that "economists of the so-called neoliberal persuasion have long criticized the efforts to establish a European Economic Community"?[3] Did European integration happen because of or in spite of a neoliberal vision for the continent?

Resolving the paradox requires zooming both in and out. Looking closely at the moment of Europe's institutional creation, we find that the Rome treaty split the neoliberal group into two factions. On one side was the older generation of Geneva School neoliberals, who have been labeled the universalists.[4] On the other side was another, younger cohort of neoliberals that we can call the constitutionalists. By drawing the lens back, we see the importance of empire and the world in the story. The universalists opposed to the EEC, like Wilhelm Röpke, Gottfried Haberler, and Michael Heilperin, reflected a fidelity to a prior commitment to the larger scale of global integration as defended by the League of Nations and later the General Agreement on Tariffs and Trade (GATT). Especially galling was the fact that the Treaty of Rome actually created, not "Europe," but a version of "Eurafrica." Because preferential access to the European market was extended to the French, Dutch, and Belgian empires as "associated states," 90 percent of the territorial area of the Common Market was beyond the borders of Europe itself.[5] To the universalists, Eurafrica looked like another means of disintegrating the world economy in the name of integration. The EEC created a clot the size of Western Europe plus larger parts of Africa in the network of free circulation of goods. It kept empire and protectionism alive in the supposed era of the liberal world economy.

Universalists made concrete efforts to shore up the GATT against the EEC. In 1958 Haberler coauthored a report for GATT criticizing the emerging agricultural protectionism of the EEC and agricultural subsidies in the United States. The so-called Haberler Report became a milestone in the history of GATT, and later the World Trade Organization (WTO), and won him unexpected partners in the Global South. Yet despite the universalists' zeal, their globalism contained a fatal flaw: it had no mechanism of enforcement. The goal of diminishing economic nationalism was evident, but the leap to supranational governance was less so. By pinning their hopes on the GATT, the first-generation global neoliberals put their faith in an organization without teeth.

While one faction of neoliberal globalists rejected the value of European integration, another saw it as a bridge over the gap between institutional design and implementation. In the 1960s key neoliberals including Hans von der Groeben, Ernst-Joachim Mestmäcker, and Erich Hoppmann conceived of the Treaty of Rome as an "economic constitution" and the basis for future models of multilevel governance.[6] Law was central to pro-Europe neoliberals, many of whom were trained as lawyers rather than economists. Even though Hayek's discussion of federation almost evaporated in his postwar work, the constitutionalists adapted his 1960s writings on constitutional design to reimagine supranational order. In an irony, the defining postwar project of Geneva School neoliberalism germinated inside the very project of European integration that the older neoliberals condemned. In shifting the scale of the economic constitution from the nation to the supranational federation and later the world, the neoliberal constitutionalists seeded the field of international economic law that would emerge in the 1970s and helped theorize an integrated Europe as a model for global economic governance.

THE UNIVERSALISTS: NEOLIBERALS AGAINST EUROPE

Immediately after 1945, neoliberals returned to their prewar discussions about international federation. At the first meeting of the Mont Pèlerin Society (MPS), in 1947, an entire day was devoted to "the problem and chances of European Federation." Robbins set the tone with his concern that European "economic associations might prove disruptive to the unity of the Western world."[7] Almost all of the federal ideas of the 1930s, one will recall, were based on the anchor of the Anglo-American relationship as the axial point of the Western world. Neoliberal intellectuals voiced fears that European organization might endanger the bonds of the Atlantic Community.[8] The basic problem was the patent unwillingness of nations to relinquish their own sovereignty. Writing in 1949, Haberler argued that "there will be no European union now or in our time" because it was "practically impossible that countries like Great Britain, France, Italy and Belgium should agree on a common economic policy."[9] He spoke hypothetically of the possibility of economic unification in a situation of "comparatively little state interference in economic matters as it existed before 1914," but saw no practical means of realization. The United Nations system was emphatically *inter*national rather than supranational, and the jealously guarded principle of national sovereignty was at its heart.

Against the continental dream of European integration the universalists maintained fidelity to the global vision of the League of Nations, which had envisioned an Open Door policy for the world. Even though by the end of the war the consensus at the League had shifted toward policies of full employment and Keynesian expansion, the League retained the promise of salutary liberal internationalism in the minds of Geneva School neoliberals.[10] Fatefully, however, the precondition for the League's success was always the goodwill and voluntary cooperation of the states involved. With no means to punish infractions by member states, and no means of compelling nonmembers to join, the liberal experiment had failed in the 1930s and its seemed doomed again after 1945. Many neoliberals who had been socialized in the 1920s and 1930s shared Haberler's sense of disillusionment with the large-scale solution that would involve the willing surrender of sovereignty by nations that had no desire to surrender it. Especially in light of the "paradoxical phenomenon" whereby the supposed beacon of free enterprise, the United States, was itself calling for nations to make multiyear plans to consistently disperse Marshall Plan funds, Haberler saw no route that could lead the postwar European states away from planning.[11] Although the beginnings of market liberalization in West Germany, founded in 1949, offered a praiseworthy template, there was no institutional fix whereby the other nations would be forced to follow the German lead. As we saw in Chapter 4, the best option for a neoliberal fix looked like the transnational commercial law of the investment code and the bilateral investment treaty. Concentrating on private international law would protect what I have called the xenos rights of investors without a need for multilateral inter-state arrangements of public international law.

The most vocal Euroskeptic of the 1950s was the ubiquitous Wilhelm Röpke, who enjoyed both the ear of West German economics minister (and MPS member) Ludwig Erhard and ready access to the press as a public intellectual.[12] Röpke feared that the EEC would be an extension of the "bloc solution" of the European Coal and Steel Community created in 1952, protecting the continent's products behind a shared tariff wall, sheltered from foreign competition and managed collectively by a supranational bureaucracy. He felt that the "bloc" version of Europe had no claim to be labeled "integration." It reproduced the precise symptoms of protectionism and state control that had characterized the 1930s. What looked like integration for Europe would perpetuate disintegration at the scale of the world. Such an arrangement would "turn national autarchy to a continental one and repeat the old problems at a higher geographical scale."[13]

Expressing a similar sentiment, Michael Heilperin conjured up the familiar bugbear "insulation."[14] Bloc Europe was a way to pursue the fundamentally illegitimate policy goal of being sheltered from the pressures of global competition. Furthermore, it made the fatal error described by Hayek in the 1930s: it made economic authorities a target as the source of perceived injustices. Much preferable, Erhard argued, was "a system of order that exerted what one might call an anonymous coercion on the behavior of nation-states."[15] As with the model of neoliberal federation proposed by Hayek and Robbins, the sphere of government intervention, on Erhard's view, must be self-limiting due to locked-in policies of free trade and free migration. The EEC's proposed leadership by a Commission would offer itself as a target for both the grievances and special pleading of affected parties.

Universalists defined integration not as a future vision but as a return to a former order. Wrote Röpke, "The truth [is] fundamental as it is simple and incontrovertible, that the task in front of us, is in fact, a *re-integration,* i.e., the recreation of a happier condition of European economic relations that already existed in the past and has been progressively destroyed in the storms of the world crisis since 1931."[16] The world economy, which had been unitary until 1914, needed to be reconstituted. Any talk of integration could only be talk of a means of return to that lost golden age. The universalist understanding was consistent with the etymology of the word itself. The meaning of the Latin *integratio* is not the creation of a new entity but the restoration of something lost.[17] Heilperin made a point similar to Röpke's in 1949. He disputed the fact that "integration" was an "American doctrine" imported into Europe with the Marshall Plan. In fact, it was much more at home in Europe than in the States, with its "traditional attachment to the tariff."[18] When American policy makers urge "Western Europe to integrate," they are "bringing back to the Europeans something which is not a theoretical concept alone but something which should spell to them a memory of a very prosperous past."[19]

Most early neoliberals were born around the turn of the twentieth century and were in late childhood and early adolescence during the period before the Great War. They often expressed their affective attachment to the era in elegiac terms. Röpke began one of his books by identifying himself as one of "the generation which in its youth saw the sunset glow of that long and glorious sunny day of the western world, which lasted from the Congress of Vienna until August 1914, and of which those who have only lived in the present arctic night of history can have no adequate conception."[20] World economic integration was simultaneously an ideological goal and a childhood idyll.

Neoliberals had been central in bringing the concept of *integratio* into economic discourse in the interwar period. Fritz Machlup has shown that Röpke was one of the first economists to write systematically about integration in the 1930s. After Eli Heckscher and Bertil Ohlin, Swedish economists of the Stockholm School, introduced the word "disintegration" into economic discussions in the 1920s and early 1930s, Röpke began work on his 1942 book about what was lost and what needed to be restored.[21] He first used the term "disintegration" in 1931 to describe the effect of the Great Depression's "dissolution of the stable and organic structure of international economic relations that had emerged over a century under the name of the world economy."[22] He and Mises both used the term in a 1938 publication of the Geneva Graduate Institute for International Studies devoted to "the world crisis."[23]

The Geneva School discourse of integration has been explored in preceding chapters. It perceived the world economy as an interdependent totality reliant on a series of institutional arrangements that safeguarded the division in capitalism's doubled world of imperium and dominium and allowed for both competition and the international division of labor. This vision was far different from the dream of an autonomous or self-governing market that has been falsely ascribed to neoliberals. Instead it assumed a space of trade and payments encased by universal norms and upheld by inter-state cooperation. The architectural elegance and internal consistency of the neoliberal global vision made it hard to think about partial solutions or halfway houses on the road to reintegration at the world level. Yet as Heilperin acknowledged, "universalist solutions" seemed to have failed by the 1950s.[24] He gave up on pushing the international investment code he had authored and accepted the viability of bilateral investment treaties, which had become more effective. The scandal of the International Trade Organization, which he and other neoliberals saw as tainted by the politicized special pleading of the developing world, left only what Röpke called the "modest but very useful" GATT, a relatively weak organization riddled with exceptions (including agriculture) and opt-out clauses.[25]

Euroskeptical neoliberals rallied around the GATT, despite its apparent weakness, as the best weapon at hand for attacking the new EEC. In its essence, GATT was the institutional heir of the liberal world economy model pioneered in Geneva, which was itself based on the nineteenth-century principle of the "most favored nation" treaty that extended reciprocal relaxation of trade barriers to all signees. GATT's primary architect, James Meade, had been active at the League, authoring its *World Economic Survey* in the late 1930s.[26] Röpke advocated for the GATT against French-dominated European institutions in 1958, saying that the "Coal Steel common market method of integrating Europe . . . requires a supra-national political order." "Why not leave it to GATT?" he asked, "Or if GATT is insufficiently effective, why not strengthen it?"[27] Erhard spoke in the name of "the economy" as such when he promoted the superiority of the GATT, saying that "errors and sins against the economy are not made good by proclaiming them to be European."[28]

To Röpke, the only form of integration that might be worthy of the name followed what he called the "kernel solution." Kernel Europe would not protect its goods from the outside world. Rather, it would create a free-trade zone and, eventually, a common "payment community" or currency union that would gradually expand over time, absorbing other nations into an ever-growing territory of specialization and free-market competition. This form of integration "may begin in Europe" but it "prepares for a transition into a universal world-economic integration."[29] Against the EEC, Röpke and Erhard advocated for a European Free Trade Area (EFTA), to include Great Britain, Switzerland,

Austria, Portugal, and the Scandinavian countries.[30] The failure of the EFTA model to win out over the EEC concept meant, Röpke wrote in the *National Review*, that "economic liberation . . . had to be purchased by digging a moat against the outside."[31]

Hans von der Groeben exaggerated only slightly when he wrote in hindsight that "the 'universalists' saw every regional structure as a deviation from the path of righteousness."[32] They painted the struggle over European integration in Manichaean terms, he said, with those calling for the EEC cast in the role of villains. Röpke relied on his characteristically incendiary rhetoric, urging that "the market economy" not be "sacrificed on the altar of 'Europe'" and cautioning that "what was meant to be mortar may prove to be dynamite."[33] Heilperin invoked the foundational modern battles of political economy from the nineteenth century. "Buried for many decades in intellectual and political mothballs," he wrote, "the Free Trade versus Protection controversy has, incredibly, become once again a front-page item."[34] Given such an alternative, universalists naturally sided with free trade, which, said Heilperin in the terms of classical liberal dogma, "conforms to the nature of things and to the distribution of resources and men on the globe."[35] West Germany represented the pole of free trade, under Economics Minister Erhard, and the main antagonist was France. In an article in *Fortune*, Heilperin, using a politically loaded term, denounced the French choice of "segregation," which harmed "the mass of French consumers, who are the big losers in France's essentially rich, shamefully hobbled economy."[36]

The first member of the hard core of neoliberals to deviate from opposition to European economic integration was not Röpke, who remained a staunch opponent, but an employee of Erhard's ministry, Alfred Müller-Armack. Born in 1901, Müller-Armack was a contemporary of the first generation of neoliberals. A member of the Nazi party since 1933, he held a chair in economics at the University of Münster from 1940, where he directed research on building, settlement, and textile production.[37] Some of his wartime studies tackled the Third Reich's iteration of European integration in seeking economic solutions for the Nazi empire in Eastern Europe.[38] Müller-Armack met Erhard in the early 1940s, as the future economics minister and chancellor was also researching the textile industry under Hitler's government.[39] The duo remained close after the war. Along with the Freiburg School of Walter Eucken and Franz Böhm, they helped define the foundational German neoliberal position. In 1950 Müller-Armack became a professor at the University of Cologne, and took a position as the leader of the policy department in Erhard's Economics Ministry in 1952.

Unlike Röpke and Haberler, whose academic perches protected their purism, Müller-Armack's active role in politics and administration made him more aware of the need to find practicable solutions and common ground with ideological opponents.[40] One such accomplishment was his enduring achievement in coining the term "social market economy." The term combined free-market principles with attention to welfare and labor concerns in a way that would rankle other neoliberals over time, but Müller-Armack had chosen the term precisely for its mediating "irenic" function.[41] Writing about the prospects of European integration in 1957, Müller-Armack took a similar pragmatic position. While genuflecting to the era before 1914 as a "paragon" of world economic integration, he pointed out that conditions had changed and institutions needed to adapt with them. The GATT offered one option, but its "organizational sluggishness" proved that "complicated and organizationally demanding agreements only offer success in limited circles."[42] Even while oriented at "worldwide organizations," he argued, integration would only happen "on the initiative of a tight European circle."[43]

By 1957 Müller-Armack could speak from experience. He had helped suture together opposing viewpoints within the German cabinet when he held a meeting of the principals at his summer house in May 1955.[44] At that meeting Erhard acquiesced to the project of European integration being spearheaded by Chancellor Konrad Adenauer and his Foreign Ministry. Müller-Armack and Erhard also managed to push the vision away from the Coal and Steel Community model and toward one that could protect "undistorted competition" and prioritize the "four freedoms" of goods, capital, services, and labor.[45] The concept of the competitive common market had been crafted ahead of time in the Economics Ministry, in part by the lawyer von der Groeben, who had led the Schuman Plan Department in the Economics Ministry since 1952.[46] After a meeting of delegates of the six signatories in Messina in June

1955, the Belgian foreign minister, Paul-Henri Spaak, tasked von der Groeben and Pierre Uri to draft a treaty—the so-called Spaak Report—that became the basis of negotiation beginning in the spring of 1956.[47] Von der Groeben was made the chair of the committee on the Common Market in the negotiations and Müller-Armack was made a member.[48]

After a year of negotiations in Paris and Brussels, the treaty was signed in Rome in March 1957 as children lined the roads waving miniature flags of the six signatory nations. Posters on the kiosks along the Roman streets showed six farm girls dancing in circles in blouses decorated with the national colors, foreshadowing the centrality of agriculture in the Europe that would follow.[49] The treaty itself was a product of months of negotiation and compromise. Looked at from one angle, it appeared to be a neoliberal victory. The four freedoms were enshrined in the text alongside a commitment to undistorted competition.[50] From another angle, the success was more mixed. There were no mechanisms to enforce the laws of competition regulating monopolies and cartels, and the provisions themselves bore the marks of significant compromise with the French negotiators.[51] When the unresolved issues of agriculture were addressed through the Common Agricultural Policy (CAP) passed in 1962, it included the markedly non-neoliberal measures of "politically determined prices as well as variable import levies and export subsidies for major products."[52] Never one to soften a punch, Röpke referred to the CAP as "the most grotesque system of price-fixing, subsidies, and artificial purchasing arrangements that had ever been created in a modern industrial economy."[53] The effect of the CAP was to "exacerbate the problems identified by Haberler" in 1958.[54] The Treaty of Rome, and the EEC that emerged from it, was a hybrid artifact of compromise and far from the clear-cut neoliberal "triumph . . . over remnants of French interventionism" that some scholars claim.[55]

One of the greatest deviations from neoliberal principles was on the question of empire. The fourth part of the Treaty of Rome was devoted to the euphemistically titled "non-European countries and territories which have special relations with Belgium, France, Italy and the Netherlands" (Article 131). Von der Groeben and Uri had not included the question of the colonies in the Spaak Report, but the French made their inclusion a condition of signing the Treaty.[56] As a result, the Common

Market, as a recent study put it, constituted "a territorial sphere stretching from the Baltic to the Congo."[57] Specifically, the treaty secured tariff-free access to the market for the products of the eighteen African colonies of the French, Belgian, Dutch, and Italian empires for an initial period of five years and also granted the right to infant industry protection (Article 133). Because the Common Market would have a common external tariff against third-party producers, this meant that the tropical products of the colonies would enjoy a significant advantage against competitors outside of the European empires, especially producers in Latin America, who traditionally enjoyed robust trade with Western Europe and especially West Germany.

Empire was no footnote to Müller-Armack. He devoted an entire chapter of his memoirs to the matter of the associated territories. He recounted that the French and Belgian negotiators sprang association as a "surprise" condition for ratification on the final day of negotiations, which pushed the negotiation of tariffs for individual products late into the night. Müller-Armack zeroed in on the question of bananas at the "turbulent night session . . . offering resistance to the very last" to the proposal that bananas from outside of the Common Market be burdened with a 20 percent tariff—itself an artifact of the Italian protection of their colonial Somali banana crop. Adenauer reportedly sided with Müller-Armack, delaying the completion of the negotiations in protest over the issue.[58] Even after the negotiations technically were concluded, Müller-Armack won the chance to draft a last protocol with Robert Marjolin to be included as an annex in the final version. Completed between the final negotiations in Paris and the treaty's signing in Rome, the so-called Banana Protocol created a crack in the tariff wall of the Common Market by securing renewable access for West Germany to duty-free bananas from beyond the protected African producers of the European empires and the French overseas territories in the Caribbean.[59]

Bananas became an ideological battle for Müller-Armack. "The whole thing might seem funny from the outside," he wrote, "but we wanted to emphasize our conviction in an economic policy that did not enact serious discrimination against all other banana-exporting developing countries."[60] Neoliberal fears of bloc thinking seemed most realized in the colonies. Röpke observed in 1958 that it was absurd that, "to the greater glory of the Common Market," coffee and bananas entering from Brazil, Guatemala, and Costa Rica should be made more expensive by protective tariffs. "One cannot blame such countries treated with such discrimination," he wrote, "for seeking to protect themselves by appeals to GATT."[61] Müller-Armack himself argued that excluded nations had every right to appeal to the GATT against the conditions of the Rome treaty.[62] The universalists fastened onto agriculture and Eurafrica to attack European integration at the GATT. Far from trivial, the question of bananas, coffee, and cocoa opened decades of struggle for Geneva School neoliberals against what they saw as the persistence of empire in the liberal world trading system. The famous "banana wars" of the early twenty-first century began with a fight over the Treaty of Rome.[63] The issue was the same: Had empire been displaced by the liberal world economy, or should colonial history still shape global economic relations?

GATT VERSUS EURAFRICA: THE 1958 HABERLER REPORT

The extra-European context for the creation of Europe is often overlooked.[64] By von der Groeben's own account, France's embroilment in anticolonial conflict in Algeria predisposed it to be more acquiescent to West German pressure to diverge from more state-centered approaches of *planification*.[65] Adenauer's staunch support for the military intervention of the old imperial powers of France and Britain during the Suez Crisis of 1956 also won him favor with the French.[66] Müller-Armack, who saw the Suez intervention as "political insanity," nonetheless acknowledged that the moment of French-German rapprochement in a shared moment of European defensiveness against U.S. geopolitical power helped move negotiations through a critical phase.[67] A French observer quipped later that a statue should be raised to Egyptian leader Gamal Abdel Nasser as the "federator of Europe" for nationalizing the canal and creating the conditions for the largest Western European powers to bond.[68]

For Röpke, the Suez Crisis offered a chance to reflect on the difference between the old world and the new. The Suez Canal had not been "an unresolved problem of the world economy" in the nineteenth century, he observed. Its stability was ensured by a treaty in international law underwritten by the "convictions and principles of the civilized world . . . protected by the supremacy of Great Britain." International organizations were only imperfect substitutes after the undisputed "trustee" position of imperial powers had been undermined. "It would correspond to the new principles of international order," he wrote wryly, "if an International Suez Canal Authority were to be constituted. But how is this supposed to happen? Who will oppose the volcanic force of freshly erupting nationalism?"[69] The United States was an unreliable partner. Röpke criticized it for having "fallen into the arms of a completely irresponsible oriental despot" during the Suez Crisis.[70] Although, as noted in the conclusion of Chapter 5, Röpke had combined his liberalism with anti-imperialism in the 1930s, he betrayed nostalgia for empire in an era of multilateralism and diffused authority.[71]

Röpke's plaintive tone suggests the impotence felt by universalists in the late 1950s. They were flanked by what they saw as protectionist European integration on one side of the Atlantic, an untrustworthy guardian of the world economic order on the other, and a UN steadily filling with Southern nations that were breaking the rules of the nineteenth century with their demands for sovereignty over national resources and global redistribution. As we saw in Chapter 4, neoliberals interpreted the Suez Crisis and other nationalizations as signs of a loss of the all-important division between the imperium of government and the dominium of private ownership. It was not clear to neoliberals which institutional replacements for empire were worthy of their loyalty. In the case of Europe, the most concerted stand was taken by Gottfried Haberler through the organization of the GATT.

As already suggested in the case of Müller-Armack, the association of the African states with the EEC was a special target of neoliberal critique. It collectivized the features and obligations of French colonialism by extending preferential access for agricultural imports and by cofinancing a European Development Fund. To Erhard, the commitment to Eurafrica simply "Europeanized the costs of empire" and threatened to recreate protectionist blocs that were of little use to West Germany, which purchased only a fraction of its imports from colonial West and Central Africa.[72] After being forced to accept the reconstruction of agricultural tariff walls around the borders of the six nations signatory to the treaty, neoliberals now had to swallow the extension of those walls southward to the other side of the Mediterranean and far into Africa.

Although little known today, the concept of Eurafrica circulated widely in the years before formal decolonization swept across Africa in the 1960s. It had different meanings for different populations. In France, visions of *Eurafrique* were about retaining and deepening, but also perhaps transforming, empire. Senegalese deputy Léopold Senghor supported *Eurafrique,* along with other delegates from deputies in the Indépendents d'Outre Mer bloc in the National Assembly.[73] For them it seemed a way to retain a means for voicing demands as entitlements from France "vertically" even as they created connections to other Africans "horizontally."[74] Senghor also felt it could be a route to extending social democracy to Africa in a new spirit of "cultural reciprocity."[75] During the EEC negotiations, Ivory Coast leader Félix Houphouët-Boigny came to Brussels to appeal to the national delegates to approve association for the African colonies. In Müller-Armack's recollection, it was largely the power of his persuasive defense that helped secure approval for financial aid to the French colonies as part of the Treaty of Rome.[76]

French prime minister Guy Mollet's perspective on *Eurafrique,* by contrast, was paternalistic. In 1957 he said that "all of Europe will be called upon to help in the development of Africa."[77] Mollet's formulation recalled that of the father of the Pan-European Movement, Richard Coudenhove-Kalergi, who had coined the term "Eurafrique" in 1929, proposing that the common project of creating arable land and curing disease in Africa would bring European powers together.[78] This angle on *Eurafrique* more clearly echoed the sentiment of the Berlin Conference of 1884–1885 when the European colonies expressed their unity in the common project of suppressing slavery and bringing free trade to Africa, in what Carl Schmitt calls the "last common land-appropriation of non-European soil by the European powers."[79]

Understood in this sense, Eurafrica actually exaggerated the gap between the two continents even as it combined them in a single term. The process of the project's realization suggested the continuing asymmetry in the balance of power. Despite Senghor's demand that "*Eurafrique* cannot be created without the consent of Africans," the presence of Houphoët-Boigny was the exception that proved the rule. The Treaty of Rome negotiations and debate in the French National Assembly about the treaty in 1957 happened otherwise without the presence or participation of African delegates.[80]

For the Germans, *Eurafrika* was bound up with the geopolitical thinking of the Nazi era and its ideas of territorial zero-sum economic space.[81] In the Federal Republic, *Eurafrika* was usually seen as a means for the French to sustain their colonial empire. As Ferdinand Fried, a conservative columnist and former Nazi mouthpiece, put it in 1960, "The vision of *Eurafrika* rises on the horizon—and the French have elegantly kept their old colonial legacy alive in a new era."[82] In the popular imagination, *Eurafrika* was pushed on Germany as part of the European package, a compromise accepted for the sake of integration and under pressure from the United States. Along with the Dutch, who shared their opinions, the German liberal leaders, above all Erhard, continued to hope that Eurafrica would act as a transition to an open world economy. To this end, they pushed for clauses limiting the length of aid and locking in dates for the transition to market prices for African exports—dates that ended up being pushed ever farther into the future as the years passed.

For its part, the Eisenhower administration accepted Eurafrica as a convenient means to continue to promise decolonization without taking concrete steps toward it.[83] Despite its professed liberalism, the United States placed highest priority on an agreement between the French and West Germans, regardless of the shape it took, and was even willing to tolerate agricultural protectionism if necessary. The protection of agriculture in Europe remained into the 1990s "the most important departure from the largely market-oriented economic and trade policies" of Europe, putting "farmers on welfare" as one monograph has it.[84] Ironically, the first significant policy victory of the ostensibly free-trade and anticolonial postwar U.S. order was a protected economic space in the exact shape of the European empires.

The example of agriculture shows that the right of the hegemon is the right to break the rules. Just as the U.S. subsidized its agriculture while preaching free trade, the CAP created a protectionist Europe even as it began pressuring the EEC's Associated States to transition their exports to world market prices.[85] Djeme Momar Gueye, the Senegalese ambassador to Brussels, pointed out the hypocrisy in the EEC pressuring the "Associated States to liberalize their production in the name of economic liberalism even as they protect their own agricultural production in broad daylight."[86] Free-trade talk worked to cement the customs union among the six signatory nations, but in the case of agriculture, liberal principles stopped at the borders of the EEC—that is, on the southern tip of Madagascar.

The conflict between Europe, Eurafrica, and the world economy was about the universality of the laws of economic organization. Defending *Eurafrika* in 1961, the president of the European Commission, Walter Hallstein, argued for both the importance of history and the fundamental difference of Africa. He said first that it would not make sense to ignore the remaining ties from the colonial period "for the sake of a cosmopolitan, indiscriminate, humanitarian and unfocused policy." Not only did obligations exist, but Western laws had no bearing. He used a metaphor from physics, saying that "in our relationship to the developing countries, we are entering, so to speak, a new space, which has its own dimensions, and in which our Euclidean geometry is no longer entirely applicable."[87] The rebuttal of the Euroskeptic neoliberals consisted in claiming that, in fact, the same laws did apply and the modern era required equality in the form of the economically self-determining nation-state. The West German Economics Ministry under Erhard wrote in 1961 that the new states in Africa must "achieve true independence economically as well."[88] Against the particularity of the EEC, the neoliberals held up the universal community of the GATT.

In the late 1950s neoliberals found partners for their critique of European integration in the unlikely place of the Global South. From the beginning, it was actors from Asia, Latin America, and the non–Associated States of Africa who were most openly critical of the EEC.

The forum they used to express their criticism was GATT. It was at the Geneva-based organization that the so-called "outsider" states of the developing countries drafted a probing list of 132 questions to be circulated to the EEC countries about the nature of the new economic policy.[89] At the radical end of the spectrum, at the first Afro-Asian Solidarity Conference, held at the end of 1957 in Cairo, the European Common Market was said to make colonies "the property of six European countries" and "strangle the aspirations of the people for independence from colonial domination."[90] More moderately, Eurafrica was criticized by the Latin American economists at the United Nations Economic Commission for Latin America (ECLA) and by the government of India. Their complaint was that even if the EEC's regional arrangement was in line with the letter of GATT law, the protectionism in the Treaty of Rome contradicted its liberal spirit.[91] With the United States unwilling to provoke the Franco-German alliance, which became even more tenuous with Charles De Gaulle's staunch opposition to British membership in the EEC, and also unwilling to shine a spotlight on its own comprehensive practices of agricultural subsidies, the aggrieved nations of the developing world found tactical allies in Austrian and German neoliberals.

Protests from developing countries about Eurafrica in 1957 crystallized a wider concern about the worldwide decline in commodity prices after the end of the Korean War. A review session held in 1954 prompted the executive secretary of GATT to convene a committee in November 1957 led by Haberler to investigate.[92] The Haberler Report is routinely recognized as a major turning point in the history of both the GATT and now the WTO.[93] According to the secretary in his charge to Haberler in January, 1958, the report should address three concerns, all related to developing countries: first, the susceptibility of less-developed countries to fluctuations of commodity prices on the world market; second, the disparity in growth of international trade between more and less developed countries; and thirdly "perhaps the biggest problem of all," the persistence of agricultural protectionism in developed countries.[94] Though the intention of the study was to address the concerns of developing countries, only the policies of industrialized countries would be open for criticism.

The choice of Haberler to lead the team was not surprising. At Harvard University since the 1930s, he was a leading expert in international trade as well as chairman of the National Bureau of Economic Research (NBER). The four-person team eventually expanded. New members include two other experts and active League economists—Meade, an architect of GATT who had also played a key role in formulating Britain's postwar full-employment policies, and the Dutch econometrician Jan Tinbergen, who created the first macroeconomic statistical model of a national economy while at the League. They were joined by Roberto Campos, a Brazilian economist who had been one of his nation's delegates at Bretton Woods and the head of the Brazilian Development Bank, whose U.S.-friendly policies had earned him the nickname "Bob Fields."[95] Another former League economist, Hans Staehle, had helped assemble the group. An econometrician by specialization, Staehle was a director of economic research at the League, drafting reports for the International Labour Organization (ILO) in Geneva in the 1930s and also consulted with Tinbergen on his first League volume on international trade.[96] Working for the GATT in the 1950s, Staehle corresponded with Haberler about the composition of the team. They shared a perspective on how the committee should look. Haberler expressed relief, for example, that Campos had been chosen instead of Raúl Prebisch of the ECLA, who was an advocate of liberalizing agricultural trade but also a strong advocate of industrial protection.[97] Haberler went so far as to suggest Peter T. Bauer, a fellow MPS member who was the most strident critic of both Third World industrialization and foreign aid.[98] Likely recognizing that this went too far, he then offered Meade as a compromise candidate.[99]

Haberler had no intention for his report to be used as reinforcement for projects to achieve economic evenness. He said explicitly that he was unhappy with the reference to the "further increase in the income gap" in the report's summary and further criticized the concept of a "desirable" rate of development.[100] He wrote that "it surely cannot be said so bluntly" but that that "underdeveloped countries are in the habit of blaming foreign trade and the developing countries for their own policies."[101] He also added that "some other members of the committee will not agree," thinking here likely of Tinbergen and Meade, both of whom held views close to the Keynesian principles opposed by Haberler, who remained a staunch defendant of stability over both growth and full employment. In his writings from the 1930s to the 1980s, Haberler insisted that the open world economy was important as a means of disciplining potentially inflationary social spending and rash projects of industrialization—and the potential problems of the developing nations were never far from his mind.[102] In the 1990s Paul Samuelson remembered Haberler as a "minority voice" for his advocacy of "market disciplines" rather than import substitution and state-driven development in the 1950s and 1960s.[103]

Published in October 1958, the Haberler Report could have been written in Geneva twenty-five years earlier. Far from arguing that liberalization hindered development, it concluded that liberalization had not gone far enough. The specific targets of criticism were the industrialized countries. The EEC, which formally came into existence only months earlier, on January 1, 1958, was singled out for extending agricultural protectionism to the associated territories, which would "give rise to discrimination against other overseas countries in Africa and elsewhere."[104] Along with its criticism of the just-launched EEC, the report also assailed agricultural subsidies, which were especially widespread in the United States, leading to pointed rebuttals to the report from the U.S. Federal Reserve and the U.S. Department of Agriculture.[105] Europe, above all, was cast as a test case. "If the EEC were to grow into an instrument for trade-diversion and for increased protectionism against outside agriculture or other products," the report's authors warned, "it might be the signal for a growth of undesirable discriminatory arrangements of a trade-diverting and protective character."[106] Developing countries were already "of the opinion that the rules and conventions which are at present applied to commercial policy and international trade show a lack of balance unfavorable to their interests."[107] Institutionalizing Eurafrica would send a message that the rules were there to be broken.

The executive secretary of the GATT, E. Wyndham White, told Haberler that the report had met with "great success" and "had a decisive effect on our discussions here in the GATT."[108] "Very rarely," GATT's European office wrote, "had a report by economists been so warmly received and widely acclaimed."[109] Talking about the "very considerable coverage in the British press," Staehle called it an "enormous hit."[110] The report was an especially large hit with the group that Haberler hoped to discipline: the developing countries. In May 1959 fifteen African, Asian, Caribbean, and Latin American nations, including leaders in the Non-Aligned Movement (Burma, Ghana, Malaya, India, and Indonesia), submitted a note on the "expansion of international trade."

In their interpretation, the Haberler Report had concluded that there was a tendency of "the export trade of the less developed countries to expand less rapidly than the trade of the highly industrialized countries," meaning that "special measures to assist the trade of less developed countries both in the field of primary products and manufactured goods had to be taken very early."[111] Ghana and Indonesia, along with Brazil and the United Kingdom, used the Haberler Report against the Eurafrican model of preference. In the 1990s the WTO would cut its teeth on precisely this issue as the United States brought cases against the Lomé agreement, a descendant of the original economic Eurafrica concept.[112] The case is read in popular imagination as an example of particular U.S. corporate interests being hidden in the universalist language of the free market.[113] It would present a major challenge to the Geneva School model of neoliberalism in the 2000s. Thus, it is all the more striking to see early postcolonial nations like Ghana, Indonesia, and India using the precise language of free trade with the Haberler Report as a lever, quoting it to the effect that the EEC'S preferential trade arrangements "will be trade-diverting rather than trade-creating."[114]

Against the frequently circulated cliché that Third World demands equaled the protectionist demands for tariffs, these developing nations were, in fact, using the Haberler Report to *oppose* protectionism and call for *freer* trade. Their list of "serious obstacles" included all the bugbears of the free trader: "protective quotas, subsidies and price support schemes" and quantitative restrictions. In other words, they were not asking for the right to opt out of the free world economy through barriers to protect "infant industry." Instead, they were requesting that the GATT—and by extension the industrialized world—live up to its own principles of free trade. Giuliano Garavini cites French complaints in the 1960s that the delegates from underdeveloped countries had been "seduced by liberal doctrine."[115] The demand for development and the critique of both Europe and Eurafrica was being made in the language of the open world economy.[116]

Scholars often use overly broad characterizations of Global South countries as adherents to the ideology of dependency theory, which supposedly privileged the protection of infant industry above all else to diversify the economy.[117] In that narration, the exceptions are those countries with especially close ties to the United States—Japan, Taiwan, and South Korea—whose export-oriented industrialization models are usually seen as prefiguring the direction in which development would go once the Third World snapped out of its dependency-theory-driven delusions.[118] Looking at the response to the Haberler Report, one sees that the truth is less black-and-white. In fact, developing countries were advocates of both protection and liberalization at the same time. They followed a policy of "both-and" rather than "either-or." It was not a protectionist imaginary against a free-trade imaginary, with the developing world as atavistic advocates of the failed 1930s world. Rather, weaker nations used all policy tools available to them, including GATT.[119] In the case of the Haberler Report, developing nations used the master's tools against him by suggesting that Europe and the United States adhere to their own much-preached liberal principles. The Haberler Report shows that the rise and spread of neoliberal ideas can be understood only through its piecemeal adoption by Global South nations as a development strategy.[120]

THE CONSTITUTIONALISTS: THE TREATY OF ROME AS THE BIRTH OF MULTILEVEL GOVERNANCE

The Treaty of Rome produced a crucial split in the camp of neoliberal intellectuals. To one side were those who favored what Röpke called "universalist solutions."[121] The very Austrians and Germans who had proposed federal and supranational solutions through the 1930s and 1940s opposed European integration, fearing that it would obstruct the broader approach of the GATT and lead to the contagion of French *dirigisme* in Western Europe. The Haberler Report itself was a banner case of how

Euroskeptic neoliberals not only pined for the return of a "liberalism from below," lost since 1914, but also backed the search for a neoliberal fix to secure the open world economy.[122] In a report about the European Common Market submitted to the U.S. Congress months before the Treaty of Rome came into force, Haberler emphasized the need to strengthen GATT as a "watchdog" against Europe. "It is before GATT," he wrote, "that US and the interests of other outsiders (e.g. those of the other American states and Japan) can be best defended."[123] In a key move, Haberler spoke on behalf of not only the United States but also "outsiders." In a piece written in a festschrift for Erhard the same year, Haberler spoke similarly about the outsiders, including "Latin American countries, which are much poorer than Europe," that will be injured by European trade discrimination "and had no reason to accept this injury calmly."[124] Europe itself may profit, Haberler argued, "but the world economy as a whole loses."[125] "The question about an alternative to discriminatory integration policy is easy to answer. The alternative is: overall trade liberalization [as advocated by GATT]."[126]

Even against Haberler's precise intentions, his report launched a new era at the GATT. As a follow-up to the Haberler Report, the contracting parties at their thirteenth session in November 1958 decided to establish three committees to examine various types of action to promote an expansion of international trade.[127] The working group called "Committee III" initiated a "permanent shift" in the GATT relationship to developing countries in favor of their demands for market access.[128] For the next two decades, the developing countries were able to use GATT successfully to lobby for exemptions from "disciplines" of nondiscrimination and for permission to deviate from the strictures of the treaty.[129] One scholar notes that Haberler openly opposed the interpretation of the report's finding as proof for the theory of the declining terms of trade, arguing instead that "more trade" would solve the problem in the long run.[130] In 1964 he declared confidently that "the less developed countries have greatly benefited from the expansion of world trade and that the prosperity in 'the industrial centers' has spread to 'the less developed periphery.'" Failure to grow more quickly was the fault of their own protectionism.[131] In a notable irony, the Geneva School attempt to lock in liberal trade policy through the Haberler Report ended up creating the conditions for the precise opposite: ammunition for a Global South argument against a one-size-fits-all application of trade rules.

Chapter 7 will show how the reform of the GATT against just such deviations became an essential project for Geneva School neoliberals. Yet it is important to point out that just as one group of neoliberals was attacking the EEC, another was helping to create it. Indeed, in the project of constitutionalizing the EEC, neoliberals developed an institutional fix that would transcend the GATT by providing a mechanism of oversight and, most importantly, enforcement within the nation-state. The key figures in this story were two members of what are called the "second generation" of ordoliberals, Hans von der Groeben and Ernst-Joachim Mestmäcker. It is significant that these constitutionalists were trained as lawyers rather than economists. They argued that economic integration could work without political integration as long as a well-designed treaty created legal mechanisms to move against concentrations of public and private economic power. Whereas Franz Böhm and Walter Eucken had spoken of the economic constitution only at the level of the nation, the constitutionalists suggested it could be scaled up to international arrangements.

The work of the constitutionalists was a conscious application of Hayek's work, not from the 1930s but from decades later. Beginning in the early 1960s, Hayek began to suggest using the drafting of constitutions as a way to anchor economic freedoms against the attempts of legislatures to enact protectionist or redistributive policies. He had begun this effort in *The Constitution of Liberty,* which he wrote while he was at the University of Chicago, but this book was still extremely pessimistic about the possibilities of supranational organization: "The moral foundations for a rule of law on an international scale seem to be completely lacking still, and we should probably lose whatever advantages it brings within the nation if today we were to entrust any of the new powers of government to supra-national agencies."[132]

On moving to Germany, Hayek softened this position. The problem, as he had noted, was "how to divide these powers between the tiers of authority."[133] In his inaugural speech of June 1962 for his new position at the University of Freiburg, the original institutional home of Eucken and Böhm, Hayek reminisced about having learned law alongside economics during his training in Vienna. "One is sometimes tempted to ask," he said, "whether the separation of legal and economic studies was not perhaps, after all, a mistake."[134] The importance of law became clear in the course of his presentation. He pronounced that his focus would henceforth be on "problems of economic policy."[135] Yet because of the limits of human knowledge, which had been his theme since the late 1930s, policy could not be based on the "erroneous" aggregates and forecasts of macroeconomics: "In order to interfere successfully on any point, we would have to know all the details of the whole economy, not only of our own country but of the whole world."[136] The world of numbers had been permanently discredited as the domain of the naive and the disingenuous. Given the distribution of knowledge among innumerable actors, Hayek said, "the chief task of economic policy would thus appear to be the creation of a framework within which the individual not only can freely decide for himself what he wants to do, but in which also this decision based on his particular knowledge will contribute as much as possible to aggregate output."[137] In the end, "principles are practically all that we have to contribute."[138]

Invoking the term introduced by Eucken, Hayek said both principles and measures would have to be *systemgerecht*, or "in conformity with the whole system."[139] The highest value for Hayek was not, in fact, individual freedom except insofar as it was a functional necessity for the overall reproduction and productivity of the system itself. Economic policy had more to do with setting the rules that would frame economic activity than with seeking a comprehensive overview of the economy itself, which was impossible. Ascertaining the nature of this framework necessarily led into realms of human behavior and statecraft beyond the normal ken of the discipline, which why, as he put it, "he who is only an economist cannot be a good economist."[140] Tending the system turned the task of economics into the task of institutional design.

Central to Hayek's thinking was a distinction he shared with Carl Schmitt, between law *(Recht)* and legislation *(Gesetz)*. Like Schmitt, Hayek believed that the creation of law by democratically elected state governments was leading to a degeneration of the *Rechtsstaat* into a *Gesetzesstaat,* or legislative state.[141] He wrote that "the weakness of the government of an omnipotent democracy was very clearly seen by the extraordinary German student of politics, Carl Schmitt, who in the 1920s probably understood the character of the developing form of government better than most people."[142] He quoted Schmitt's essay from 1932 to the effect that "a pluralist party state will become 'total' not from strength and force but out of weakness: it intervenes in all sectors of life, because it feels it has to fulfill the demands of all interested parties."[143] In other words, Hayek saw "unlimited" (or what Mises called "omnipotent") democracy as leading to totalitarianism out of a logic of capture. His efforts at constitutional design from 1960 onward were attempts to discover an institutional fix for the tendency of democracy to stray from economic order toward particularist rent-seeking and, as Alexander Rüstow put it, the transformation of state policy and national budgets into the "prey" of special interests.[144]

He laid out the parameters of this institutional concept first in a speech at the Chamber of Commerce in Dortmund, published in the *Frankfurter Allgemeine Zeitung*. He proposed a bicameral legislature divided into elected legislators tasked with everyday business of state, who he called "telothetes," and another set of legislators called "nomothetes" of ages forty to fifty-five elected by their peers to fifteen-year terms.[145] Putatively insulated from the pressures of interest groups by the length of their terms, the nomothetes would be responsible for the creation and interpretation of law. Hayek argued that such a change of institutions could be used as a means for "the slow production of a supranational order, in which all national governments could pursue practical goals while still being subordinated to common rules that would simultaneously protect citizens from the arbitrariness of their rulers."[146] In this model of what he later called "limited democracy," Hayek opened a door back to the supranational possibilities of the 1930s through institutional design.

Hayek's arrival in Freiburg reoriented ordoliberalism away from concerns with perfect competition, about which he was openly skeptical by the early 1960s.[147] The new direction was toward the idea of "competition as a discovery process."[148] As von der Groeben took up his position in the European Commission for Competition, he began to theorize his work in similar terms. Born in 1907, von der Groeben was almost a decade younger than the original Geneva School neoliberals Haberler, Hayek, Röpke, and Robbins. In 1965 he wrote that, on the one hand, "coordination of the economic programs of those who constitute the market is to be achieved by the play of forces in a market economy" but that this needed to happen within an institutional framework.[149] The most important aspect was "competition policy [which] does not mean laissez-faire, but the achievement of an order based on law."[150] In his own telling, in the Treaty of Rome, "the rules of competition in particular were in accordance with neoliberal ideas."[151]

How neoliberal principles were enshrined in the treaty takes some unpacking, and scholars have emphasized that its competition provisions were far from carbon copies of neoliberal doctrine.[152] From the moment of its signing, it was clear that the Treaty of Rome was only a framework of law to be shaped by political direction.[153] The original articles in the treaty related to competition (Articles 85 and 86) were rather broad and did not give a clear role to the European Court of Justice. In fact, the treaty was only provisional on the matter of competition and postponed clarification for three years (Article 87). However, von der Groeben oversaw what would become the regulation implementing the treaty that passed in 1962. The regulation was modeled explicitly on those of West Germany, which entered force in the late 1950s.[154] Regulation 17 was worded much more strongly, especially in the "unlimited jurisdiction" it granted to the court in matters of fines and penalties. The updated regulation gave the Commission new authorities of community-wide surveillance over cartels and required notification directly to the Commission—if not the administrative capacity to follow up.[155] In deference to French pressure, however, there would still be crucial exemptions—for agriculture, defense industry, transport, and nuclear energy.[156] In a critical addition, Regulation 17 also granted the right to bring cases not only to member states but to "natural or legal persons who claim a legitimate interest" (Article 3).

From early on, German neoliberals saw competition policy as central even when the French saw it in terms of flexible principles.[157] As Mestmäcker put it, the goal for von der Groeben and his team was clear: "it was about bringing the economic constitution of the EEC Treaty to life."[158] Mestmäcker was the key figure in theorizing the repercussion of the Rome treaty as a model of governance in Hayekian terms. Born in 1926, he was a whole generation younger than the original cohort of the Geneva School. Part of the so-called Flakhelfer generation, his defining young experience was not of the First but of the Second World War, and the Great Depression would have been only a dim memory from childhood. Mestmäcker studied with Böhm at the University of Freiburg and paid homage to the work of his mentor throughout his career. One scholar calls him the "leading representative of the second generation of ordoliberals."[159] His professional position was at the University of Saarland, but he was special adviser to the European Commission from 1960 to 1970. Mestmäcker saw the goal of "undistorted competition" in European Community law as "politically the most important effect of the appreciation of the legal shapability of the economic system, which in Germany was first recognized by Walter Eucken and Franz Böhm." It managed to combine the ordoliberal attention to law with Hayek's idea of "competition as a method of discovery."[160] Mestmäcker claimed to take from Böhm the idea that every economic order is the outcome of a political decision.[161] He was the most important figure in combining Hayek with Böhm and scaling up the economic constitution to the suprastate level.[162]

Gazing at the prospects for federation in postwar Europe, Haberler and other Geneva School neoliberals had invoked the ghost of the League of Nations with melancholy, arguing that an unwillingness to surrender sovereignty doomed any genuine attempt at economic integration. In a 1965 article Mestmäcker also harked back to the League—but in order to argue that Europe had found the institutional fix to transcend it. He recalled the World Economic Conference of 1927, where Clive Morrison-Bell had displayed his tariff walls map. At that gathering, the League had proposed the idea of international regulation of controls on the basis of the surrender of individual national sovereignty, but the proposal was "rejected as so extreme that 'no reasonable person' inside or outside the conference would stand for it." When one thinks about European Community law, Mestmäcker wrote, "it would be difficult to find a comparable case of involuntary prophecy" so precise.[163]

The EEC, in other words, had not only realized the lost promise of the League of Nations but surpassed it. Mestmäcker referred to Lionel Robbins's interwar federal writing, quoting his 1937 book on international order to the effect that customs unions work to decrease the "autonomy" of individual members.[164] Mestmäcker argued correctly that the distinctive nature of the EEC model was its investment in creating a political community "by means of the law."[165] It is difficult to find the presence of Hayek's thought per se in the negotiations of the Treaty of Rome, but one can see it clearly in the work of Mestmäcker. In 1973 he cited Hayek's "conclusion that a free system is possible only be renunciation of discretionary policy and by binding all action of the state to general, constitutionally guaranteed legal principles."[166] As he elaborated later, he saw Hayek's work as an expansion on "Eucken's theory of the interdependence of the legal and economic orders."[167] Seeing European integration through the lens of "economic constitutionalism," he felt that the Treaty of Rome was a starting point for creating such an arrangement.[168] Most important to Mestmäcker was the fact that the goal of the treaty was to "exclude control of interstate trade as an instrument of national economic policy."[169]

National sovereignty had been pickpocketed by the Treaty of Rome. Power was granted in two directions: upward and downward. In the upward direction, the Commission was given the power to make tariff policy. Even more importantly, the Directorate General for Competition was given the capacity of oversight and potentially antitrust measures. In the downward direction, the EEC enshrined new private rights. The "legal subjects" of the EEC were "not only the Member States but also individuals."[170] In legal jargon, this meant the Rome treaty was "self-executing" and was "directly effective." As Mestmäcker put it, "if a conflict arises national law must give way."[171] As we will see in Chapter 7, this became the core of what would later be theorized by Geneva School neoliberals as "multilevel governance."[172]

Critical for Erhard's opposition to European integration had been his unwillingness, as a good statesman, to relinquish national sovereignty to a supranational entity.[173] By contrast, this was precisely what made the EEC valuable to Mestmäcker. The critical aspect of European Community law was that it superseded national law, making "the citizens of the member states subject to the law of the community."[174] Mestmäcker's elaboration on the theory was based on two principles: the power of the court to overrule national law and the ability of individuals to make claims directly to the court. As he wrote in 1965, the European Community was a "new legal entity in International Law whose legal subjects are not only the Member States but also individuals."[175]

Mestmäcker wrote that European Community law offered "for the first time" a means to fend off "economic power and government impotence" and "expand territorially the sphere of effectiveness of public power."[176] What this permitted was the separation of public and private law, providing market actors a forum beyond their own state to make their appeals—directly now to the community level. Mestmäcker drew attention to those cases "in which access to the market is prevented or obstructed [which] make the protection of individual freedom a task of competition rules."[177]

The bifurcation of powers, upward to the community and down to the individual was essential to the constitutionalist reading of Europe. To neoliberal constitutionalists, Europe was a "supranational legal order" securing private rights enforceable by the European Court of Justice.[178] In Mestmäcker's synthesis of Hayek, Böhm, and Robbins, the emphasis is not on the surveillance rights of the Commission but on the legal relationship that placed the citizen inside the twin nested sovereignties of Europe and nation. The vertical legal relationship created from the individual to the European Court of Justice created an avenue to elude deviant exercises of national sovereignty and secure the human right to trade.

MESTMÄCKER, BÖHM, AND SCHMITT: THE ECONOMIC CONSTITUTION AND THE DECISION

An important turning point for the neoliberal discussion on Europe came in 1964 when the competition rules of the Treaty of Rome had their first significant victory as the European Court of Justice upheld the prohibition of an agreement between the German producer Grundig and the Dutch retailer Consten.[179] Von der Groeben called the Grundig-

Consten case a "sensation."[180] It was after this case that Mestmäcker began to consider the EEC Treaty as having constitutional qualities by which competition law might protect "individual freedom" even against one's own national government.[181] He declared later that the treaty "embodies an economic constitution."[182] Used first by Eucken and Böhm in the 1930s, the concept of an economic constitution had two meanings. It was both descriptive of a given sociological reality and normative of a desired legal order.[183] Ordoliberals did not mean "economic constitution" primarily in the literal form nor did they assume that it had to be embodied in a founding legal document.[184] The fact explains why Böhm gave no particular attention to the debates about the West German Basic Law in the 1940s. In the minds of neoliberals, the Basic Law was not an "economic constitution" because it did not embody a decision establishing a specific economic order, but instead was the outcome of compromise between more liberal and social democratic positions.[185] What was necessary for a genuine economic constitution was the unity of vision for an economic order, as defined first against the compromises of the Weimar Republic.[186]

Böhm took the description of the economic constitution as a "fundamental decision" directly from Carl Schmitt, who in 1928 described the constitution as a "comprehensive decision concerning the nature and form of the political unit."[187] In 1937 Böhm described it as "a normative order of the national economy" that must come into being through the exercise of a "conscious and aware political will, an authoritative decision of leadership."[188] He used martial metaphors that are worth quoting at length, declaring that "there is no longer any space for a silent growth, for an orderly formation of things out of the lap of the economy itself, that is, from the bottom up. Social Babels built of such great height and at such an accelerated tempo produce an unholy confusion of languages unless the idea of order that alone can represent the element of unity illuminates the totality down to its last details, unless the idea of order is based on the sentence: everything at my command!"[189]

Böhm's metaphors clash with those of Hayek, who specifically opposed the idea that social order followed the same model of organization as the battlefield, in the army, or inside a single firm.[190] As will be described in detail in Chapter 7, Hayek's ideas of spontaneous or "grown" orders put faith in the notion of forms of human interaction that were "the result of human action but not of human design."[191] Yet even as they were inspired by Hayek's proposals for constitutional design in the 1960s, neoliberals were frustrated by his inattention to the actual moment of implementation. For all his exercises in constitutional design, Hayek did not explicitly explain how they could be brought into action without the fallacy of what he called "constructivism."

Mestmäcker described the Treaty of Rome as a realization of the propositions of Hayek's argument for the need to bind the state through "constitutionally guaranteed legal principles."[192] Yet he saw that one of the weaknesses of law was its inability to acknowledge the politics of its own discipline.[193] He turned to Schmitt to help counter this. Looking at the evolution of liberal thought, Schmitt had argued that the nineteenth century was a time of the creation of an autonomous space of politics and economics. Mestmäcker argued that Schmitt erred by taking the doctrine at its word. For liberals, it was the apparent depoliticization that was the political project itself. Yet this should not lead to the conclusion that liberals felt this was a completed process. The ongoing depoliticization of the economic was a continual legal struggle, one that required continual innovation in the creation of institutions capable of safeguarding the space of competition.

Schmitt contended that the disavowal of politics in liberalism did not make politics disappear but only concealed a fundamental friend/enemy distinction that was all the more elemental. In the liberal claim to speak for humanity at large, any of liberalism's enemies became not only opponents but enemies of humanity as such. Mestmäcker accepted his characterization and claimed that this was precisely why liberalism must not disavow its own political nature. Against Hayek's reticence about the moment of transition, Mestmäcker argued for openness about the need for the "decisionistic" grounding of free-market principles in acts of political will. To overlook the importance of the decision, he wrote, was to miss "the political meaning of the system of undistorted competition."[194]

Mestmäcker took from Schmitt the need to remain cognizant of the explicitly political nature of the neoliberal project of depoliticizing the economy. His position was supported by another second-generation neoliberal, Erich Hoppmann. Born in 1923, Hoppmann was Mestmäcker's contemporary who succeeded Hayek in his chair at Freiburg after his retirement. He dismissed as fiction the claim that the economy was simply a machine to be maintained by apolitical minders. Because every form of economic organization presumes some prior decision about outcomes, the "apparent depoliticization of economic policy" only hid disavowed value judgments.[195] He cited Hayek's argument that to think of the economy as a machine-like apolitical entity was itself a presupposition about how market society could work. He faulted Eucken for falling into the trap of seeing the "autonomy" of the economy as a realized outcome along with delusions about the possibility of "perfect competition."[196] Like Mestmäcker and von der Groeben, Hoppmann took from Hayek the idea that competition was a "process of information, discovery and learning" whose outcome could not be determined beforehand.[197]

Maintaining competition meant resisting the fallacy of the political neutrality of economic processes and of mechanistic visions of the economy as capable of being fine-tuned and tweaked for different outputs. Competition was not an object, a structure, or an endpoint. It could not be seen. "Uncertainty," Hoppmann put it, "is the prerequisite of freedom."[198] "Because of the 'openness of the historical process,'" all that was possible to facilitate the ongoing reorganization of human life effected by competition was to formulate minimally restrictive rules enshrined in binding law.[199] Citing Hayek, he said that we were left with the choice between a "teleocratic" or purpose-governed order that stymied the promethean character of competition or a "nomocratic" or "law-governed" social order that encased competition with all its consequences.[200]

The constitutionalists took from Hayek the importance of institutional design and the idea of competition as a discovery process. What they could not find in his theory was attention to the turning point—the moment of crux where the new constitution was put into place. What those same thinkers adopted from Böhm and Schmitt was a clear sense of how that happened: it was through the moment of decision. Mestmäcker solved Hayek's problem by conceiving of the

European Court of Justice as "the guardian of the EEC Treaty"[201] and the Treaty itself as Hayek's call to bind the state through "constitutionally guaranteed legal principles."[202] The constitutionalists narrated Europe as a realization of Hayek's vision of a nomocratic society protecting the division between private law beyond the interference of democratic governments alongside the public law of states.[203]

Thus, only in its elaboration by neoliberal constitutionalists in the 1960s did the EEC offer a realization of the double government dreamed of by Hayek since the 1930s. Mestmäcker, in particular, offered a crucial bridge between the ideas of the first generation of Geneva School neoliberals and thoroughgoing theories of multilevel governance—a link more often asserted than proven by scholars. What is crucial is that Mestmäcker went further. In the Treaty of Rome as self-executing constitution and the European Court of Justice as guardian, he pioneered a model of supranational governance that had not only liberal principles at its core but a mechanism of enforcement capable of evading contamination by democratic claims-making. By 1972 Mestmäcker was suggesting a scale shift: the Rome treaty "provided the foundations for progressively restraining economic power" as "a model for the development of international economic law *not only in Europe*."[204] Though very far from the actually existing EEC of the 1960s, the neoliberal vision for Europe looked like a crucial innovation of the neoliberal fix.

❁ ❁ ❁

European integration had a Janus face for neoliberals. Looking inward, the EEC was an example of how to integrate a market with a legal structure able to enforce competition across borders. Looking outward, the EEC was a fortress that absorbed colonies as associated territories into a new trading bloc by digging "a moat against the outside," disrupting long-standing relationships with other primary producing nations, especially in Latin America.[205] The conflicting stances of the two neoliberal factions reflected the face through which they observed the continent.

The constitutionalists looked inward and found Europe to be good, having achieved new means of enforcement and oversight that the neoliberal federalists in the 1930s had not dreamed of themselves. Constitutionalist neoliberals made compromises to bring the EEC into existence but also innovated new forms of multitiered governance. The "Hayekian conversion of ordoliberalism" embodied by Mestmäcker and Hoppmann pointed to a novel variation on the neoliberal fix.[206] If nation-states accepted laws binding their own freedom of discretionary policy, then the human right to trade could be enforceable by a supranational order. The idea of the multilevel economic constitution would be central to Geneva School neoliberalism into the twenty-first century.

By contrast, the universalists observed Europe from its outer borders and saw a segmented world market. Eurafrica compromised the postwar move toward freer trade and called to mind the preferential trade agreements of the 1930s. The first generation of Geneva School neoliberals had the terrified consciousness of those who had experienced as adults the interwar collapse of world trade. Haberler warned in 1956, "Let us not forget that the Great Depression after World War I did not start until eleven years after the end of hostilities."[207]

The universalists had the advantage of purity but they lacked the mechanism of enforcement. Haberler intended his 1958 GATT report as a weapon against the growing protectionism of Europe and a clarion call to liberal order. It had the opposite effect. When the Global South used the Haberler Report to demand more market access, the Global North refused to implement free trade and cut subsidies. Instead they took the nonliberal path of less resistance and began granting preferential treatment to developing countries in the 1960s. They could thereby continue to subsidize their own production while also granting better market access to the products of developing nations. The colonial association clauses in the Rome treaty "had breached the wall" of postwar liberal norms, as one scholar put it, and the wave of preferences that followed veered from the GATT credo of nondiscrimination.[208] The result was what Gunnar Myrdal called (approvingly) a "double standard of morality in international trade"—an expectation of reciprocity between industrialized nations and "special and differential treatment" between North and South. African nations renewed their association with the EEC after the wave of decolonization in the Yaoundé Agreement of 1963, signed symbolically in Cameroon to reflect the new balance of power;

they did so again with Yaoundé II in 1969.[209] The agreement on a Generalized System of Preferences for developing nations in 1968 was another turning point as the United States followed the model of nonreciprocity pioneered by the EEC.[210] To neoliberals, it was the historically inflected model of Eurafrica, not the spaceless world of Haberler's League of Nations imaginary, that became the template for the 1960s.

Looking at the decade of the 1960s, neoliberals felt that the Eurafrica exception had let the genie out of the bottle. In his presidential address to the American Economic Association in 1964, Haberler described the EEC as an "imminent danger to worldwide integration."[211] The man who took Röpke's chair in Geneva, Gerard Curzon, called the American decision to allow the colonies in the Common Market "a case of original sin which was to cost the US dearly later on." True to Haberler's warning from 1958, the message of Eurafrica had been that "if the GATT could be ignored by its principal author for *raison d'état* it was not difficult to predict that others would soon do likewise."[212] In 1964 Haberler noted that Latin America was following the European lead, using regional integration as a "protectionist device."[213] Writing in 1970 with his partner (and future MPS president), Victoria Curzon-Price, Curzon advocated a policy of "neo-liberalism" to face the epidemic of "neo-protectionism."[214] "The wind is blowing strongly from the protectionist quarter and policy makers are giving way," the Curzons wrote. "What is needed to reverse this state of affairs is either determined political resistance or a strong wind blowing in the other direction."[215]

In a notable symmetry with critics from the far left, some neoliberals claimed that the continued links between Europe and Africa after decolonization meant a perpetuation of empire. Harry Johnson designated Europe's ongoing trade preferences as a case of "neo-neo-colonialism."[216] Another neoliberal commentator referred to "preferences as imperialism."[217] Preferences were a result of the successful mobilization of bodies like the UN Conference on Trade and Development to gain some trade concessions from the openly hypocritical "liberal" nations of the Global North. In a bold somersault, neoliberals condemned this success as a failure to fully decolonize. Without uniform trade rules across the world, empire lived on.

By the end of the 1960s, neoliberals saw an EEC that "violated GATT rules more and more openly as it advanced."[218] How did they react? Chapter 7 shows that they borrowed a page from the European playbook to find a solution by extending the economic constitution beyond Europe itself. As challenges to the uniform rules of liberal capitalism mounted from the Global South in the 1970s, Europe and its laws became a countermodel to the demands for a New International Economic Order. The universalist and constitutionalist position found a synthesis in the plans to reform the GATT of the 1970s and 1980s. The idea of the economic constitution was set to go global.

A World of Signals

Order is not an object.

—FRIEDRICH A. HAYEK, 1968

Order is adjustment.

—JAN TUMLIR, 1980

By 1970 the age of empire was almost over. Beyond the Portuguese colonies in Africa and persistent white minority rule in much of Southern Africa, a world of formerly sprawling empires had segmented into a world of nation-states. The wave of decolonization transformed the membership of international organizations. The number of countries in the United Nations had grown from the original 51 to 127, with African, Asian, and Latin American countries constituting a clear majority. Developing nations, organized as the Group of 77 (G-77), over the course of the 1960s grew from being less than half of the contracting members to the General Agreement on Tariffs and Trade (GATT) to being over two-thirds.[1]

Neither a seat in the UN nor a voice in GATT equaled automatic power. Yet national independence made new political strategies possible. Emboldened by the "commodity power" flexed by the Arab oil-producing countries in the oil embargo of 1973–1974, Global South nations came together in what economist Mahbub ul Haq called in 1976 a "trade union of the poor nations."[2] They wielded state sovereignty "as a shield and a sword," using the forum of the UN General Assembly to pass resolutions on a "New International Economic Order" (NIEO) and a "Charter of the Economic Rights and Duties of States" in 1974, demanding redistributive justice, colonial reparations, permanent sovereignty over natural resources, stabilization of commodity prices, increased aid, and greater regulation of transnational corporations.[3]

Neoliberal thinkers saw the European Economic Community's (EEC) "Eurafrican" trade preferences for postcolonial nations as evidence that colonialism had not ended cleanly. Delegates from the G-77 also argued that empire had not vanished with formal sovereignty. "Private investments, following the flag in past models, are seen now as precursors of the flag," observed Jagdish Bhagwati in 1977, "with brazen colonialism replaced by devious neocolonialism."[4] In an early influential treatise, Ghanaian president Kwame Nkrumah wrote that the abdication of administration annihilated the need for even an empty performance of accountability. Neocolonialism was "the worst form of imperialism." he wrote, "For those who practice it, it means power without responsibility and for those who suffer from it, it means exploitation without redress."[5] The rule of dominium could be even grimmer than that of imperium.

The NIEO sought to ease the sense of impotence through the leverage of UN votes. The 1974 Declaration contended that "vestiges of alien and colonial domination, foreign occupation, racial discrimination, apartheid and neo-colonialism" continued to reproduce inequality after independence. Given the patent refusal of the Global North to live up to its own liberal principles by practicing actual free trade in key sectors such as agriculture, further deviations from the liberal principles themselves were necessary to account for path-dependent inequality. As an Indian delegate to the GATT put it, "equality of treatment is equitable only among equals."[6] Because this equality did not exist substantively, Global South nations had to secure the right to bend or secure exceptions from the rules.

NIEO demands were necessarily challenges to international law. Existing principles of international law, as one expert put it in 1973, restricted "the possibility for the measures of domestic economic decolonization necessary to provide the economic complement to legal independence."[7] In 1972 the Senegalese jurist Kéba M'baye proposed a "right to development," which was adopted by the Commission on Human Rights in 1977 and the UN General Assembly in 1986.[8] In the mid-1970s the UN International Law Commission set to work on articles to give legal weight to the demands of the NIEO.[9] The NIEO aimed for new legal standards that would permit deviations from free trade and allow for nationalization of foreign-owned property. These were the very transgressions of dominium that neoliberals most feared.

Global South rhetoric was reflected in practice. Takeovers of U.S.-owned firms overseas peaked as the NIEO was declared. Seventy-nine U.S. firms were expropriated in 1967–1971; fifty-seven were expropriated in 1972–1973.[10] Investors received compensation equal to the seizure in almost every case, but the uncertainty produced by the apparent unsettling of norms of private property was a widespread concern in Northern business and government circles.[11] Opponents of the NIEO sought to fine-tune the rules for the world trading system in response to the disruption of predictability for foreign investors produced by such moves. What use were rules, after all, if the North flaunted them in its power and the South deviated from them to compensate for its relative weakness?

As we have seen, since the 1930s the Geneva School neoliberals believed that empire could end as long as private property rights—or what I adapt Hayek to call xenos rights—were protected worldwide and the free flow of capital and goods disciplined the behavior of postcolonial states. By extending the demand for sovereignty and autonomy from the realm of politics into the realm of property, the NIEO was in direct opposition to the normative neoliberal model of double government. As with the creation of the United Nations in the immediate postwar period, the scaling up of the democracy principle to the international level after the end of decolonization threatened the doubled world of global capitalism envisaged by neoliberals.

Scholars have described how neoliberals "took aim" at the NIEO in the 1970s, and defended what they called the "liberal international economic order" against its ideological challenger.[12] In conferences, articles and editorials, neoliberal thinkers presented what one called "the case against the New International Economic Order."[13] Gottfried Haberler, who had left his position at Harvard to become the first resident scholar at the American Enterprise Institute, convened one such conference in 1977. He declared the NIEO a graver threat than either communism or the resurgence of Western protectionism.[14] Hungarian-born conservative development economist and Mont Pèlerin Society (MPS) member Peter T. Bauer and W. H. Hutt's student Basil Yamey went the farthest in their polemics, claiming that the NIEO would result in not "an alleviation of the miseries of poverty, but the spread of totalitarian government."[15] A U.S. economist remarked that Bauer's vehemence had him "imagining that the Saracens were at the Pass of Roncesvalles, the Golden Horde at the Vistula, and Suleiman the Magnificent just outside Vienna, such was the enormity of the danger to Western civilization posed by the NIEO."[16]

The NIEO roused neoliberal ire disproportionate to the percentage of world trade accounted for by the G-77 countries or the means at their disposal for enforcing essentially symbolic UN resolutions. Beyond the all-important commodity of oil, attempts to build global commodity cartels were rapid failures and demands for colonial reparations fell on deaf ears in Western capitals.[17] Understanding the irritation means recognizing that the NIEO was not acting alone. They found allies among influential Northern economists and social democrats mobilized by the NIEO. Acting in solidarity with the G-77 in the 1970s, a key cadre of what one contemporary critic called "global reformists" scaled up their own ideas of Keynesian planning to the world level.[18]

The prosthetic extension of human reasoning enabled by the computer was essential to the endeavor. The first computer-aided effort at seeing the world economy's future was the Club of Rome's *The Limits to Growth* in 1972, which forecast dire consequences if there was not a reduction in global consumption—and was actually criticized by many G-77 leaders for apparently foreclosing the possibilities of development and not differentiating among the differing responsibilities of different world regions. The second Club of Rome report, published as *Mankind at the Turning Point* in 1974, was more compatible with G-77 demands, predicting a growing gap between developed and developing nations without an increase in aid.[19] It was presented in the UN explicitly as a "frame of reference in the construction of a New International Economic Order."[20] The global reformists included Jan Tinbergen, who had sparred with Haberler at the League of Nations and helped bring Keynesian language into the 1958 GATT report. In 1974 Tinbergen began research for the Club of Rome in support of NIEO demands for the "reshaping of the international order."[21]

The Russian émigré economist Wassily Leontief, trained at the Kiel Institute for the World Economy, won the Nobel Memorial Prize in Economics in 1973 for a computerized model of the world economy. The next year he called for a National Economics Planning Board, declaring that the U.S. economy was "a gigantic, intricate machine" into which one could successfully intervene.[22] In 1976 he took the plan global, publishing the so-called Leontief Report for the UN in support of the NIEO.[23] Expressing solidarity with the G-77, the global reformists argued that that the world economy could be actively "reshaped" to yield more equitable outcomes through the combination of computers, the right data, and enlightened policy.[24]

Opposing the world projects of both the NIEO and the global reformists was a formative struggle for neoliberals in the 1970s. Given what they saw as the G-77 misuse of state sovereignty to unsettle world economic order, neoliberals sought ways to circumvent the authority of national governments. By the early 1980s this manifested in renewed attention to modes of investment protection and third-party arbitration alongside the rethinking of criteria for World Bank aid and IMF assistance that would become known as the Washington Consensus.[25] Equally important was the rise of monetarism, culminating in the so-called Volcker Shock in 1979, which dramatically raised U.S. interest rates—and thus debt service payments for Global South nations—initiating the Third World debt crisis and dealing the "death blow to the NIEO movement."[26]

Scholars have tracked the rise of the Washington Consensus and shifts in ideologies of monetary governance in the United States. Yet they have overlooked the quiet counterrevolution that the NIEO challenge prompted in Geneva itself.[27] In the 1970s and early 1980s a trio of experts at the GATT, Jan Tumlir, Frieder Roessler, and Ernst-Ulrich Petersmann, explicitly applied the ideas of Hayek to rethink the international economic order and became the standard-bearers of Geneva School neoliberalism. Key was the idea of "stratified order," an isomorphism that Hayek perceived from the level of individual human cognition up to society as a whole. The Hayekians at the GATT expanded on Hayek's insight about order to propose a theory of multilevel regulation and multilevel constitutionalism that became influential in the discipline of international economic law, which coalesced in the 1970s and expanded rapidly in the 1990s. Their ideas fed an important intellectual stream that led to the metamorphosis of the GATT into the World Trade Organization (WTO) in 1995.

The 1970s staged a stark confrontation of world economic imaginaries. While the G-77 and the global reformists envisioned a world economy of nation-states in relationships of unevenness, dependency, and deteriorating exchange produced by a history of colonialism, the GATT reformers followed Hayek to propose a vision of the world economy as a "homeostatic self-equilibrating system"—an information-processing mechanism with strata of evolved laws helping to guide price signals to direct the behavior of the world's individuals.[28] At stake was the question of order. Against the NIEO vision of an end-state of redistributive justice, Geneva School neoliberals defined order as a perpetually shifting relationship of exposure to stimuli requiring response and adaptation in a necessarily unknowable future. More than simply a rearguard action to defend the status quo, the neoliberals proposed a framework and an ethos to defend the counterintuitive claim that "order is adjustment."[29]

In the Geneva School version of interdependence, rule-breakers at the margins like the NIEO could threaten the system as a whole and thus needed to be reined in. The neoliberals' remedy was the legalization of international economic relations under conditions of formal equality for states in a reformed GATT. The multilevel calibration of rules would substitute for the NIEO demands of substantive equality and preferential treatment for poorer nations. Drawing on Hayek's epistemology, they introduced what I call cybernetic legalism, which saw individual humans as units within a self-regulating system for which the lawmaker had the primary responsibility of transforming the system's rules into binding legislation. Radical in its own right, the neoliberals' own dream of a new international economic order was a world economy of signals—a vast space of information transmitted in prices and laws.

HOMO REGULARIS AND THE PRETENSE OF KNOWLEDGE

Understanding the particularity of Geneva School neoliberalism requires attention to the often misunderstood theories of their most important influence, F. A. Hayek. His theories from the 1970s were critical in linking the fields of law with the unknowability of the economy. Scholars have long argued that cybernetics, system theory, and psychology were the silent (and sometimes not-so-silent) partners in Hayek's epistemology.[30] Just as one branch of the neoliberal movement extended toward the International Chamber of Commerce after the first meeting of the MPS in April 1947, another extended to the gathering of system theorists at the European Forum Alpbach, which Hayek attended in August 1947, putting him into contact with the leading lights of the new science.[31] Hayek crossed paths again with the system theorists in the 1960s at a conference on the "Symposium on the Principles of Self-Organization" and at another meeting of the Alpbach Symposium in 1968.[32]

Hayek's work came closest to system theory in the 1970s, when he combined it with his theory of jurisprudence in his three-volume trilogy, *Law, Legislation and Liberty.* He elaborated on his particular take in 1974 when he accepted the Nobel Memorial Prize in Economics a year after Leontief had won for his computerized model of the world economy and six months after the declaration of the NIEO in the UN General Assembly. Hayek's talk struck a discordant note in a decade when confidence in a knowable future was at an all-time high. He rejected as the "pretense of knowledge" the application of the methods of the physical sciences to problems of "complex systems" like society and the economy. He cited *The Limits to Growth,* which used computer simulation to warn of the earth's dwindling resources as an example of an illegitimate argument made under the mantle of science. Instead, he emphasized the limits to knowledge. Echoing metaphors he had used since the 1930s, he referred to the market as a "communication system" whose ultimate message could not be foretold. Competition itself was a process of discovering underutilized human knowledge and earthly resources. One could not hope for concrete data about the future to be used for planning, one could only hope for "pattern predictions." He conceded this might look like a "second best" use for science in the age of grand designs, but argued that a "lesson of humility" was necessary to fend off "man's fatal striving to control society."[33]

As with his inaugural speech at Freiburg in 1962, Hayek contended that the world economy, or "catallaxy," was sublime. It operated beyond reason, but what he called the abuse of reason could lead to its ruin. To demand a preconceived idea of economic equality in pursuit of "the mirage of social justice" was to foreclose the creative capacity of competition, scramble the price signals of the market, and ultimately become "the destroyer of a civilization which no brain has designed but which has grown from the free efforts of millions of individuals."[34] The sanctity of the world economy—above statistics, mathematics, or even sensory perception—must be defended against "the synoptic delusion" of demands like the NIEO.[35]

Hayek's language sounded like the inverse of the discourse of the global reformists. Yet even as he disparaged the fallacy of computer-aided models, he drew inspiration from the same source of system theory. From the language of "pattern predictions" to his citation of Warren Weaver, Hayek did not argue against system thinking in his Nobel speech but with it. He made the case explicit when he wrote in the introduction to the third volume of his *Law, Legislation and Liberty* trilogy in 1979 that "it was largely the growth of cybernetics and the related subjects of information and system theory" that led him to modify his own categories.[36] He explained that he had adopted the idea of "self-generating order" and "self-generating structure" alongside spontaneous order; in place of order itself, he now often used "system"; for "knowledge" he substituted "information." Indeed, while Hayek disparaged the application of computers to economic policy, he offered, as scholars have observed, a vision of the world economy itself as an enormous information processor beyond the capacity of the human mind to either manufacture or comprehend.[37]

Cybernetics has its origins in the military research of self-regulating systems during the Second World War, specifically the design of anti-aircraft guns with so-called servomechanisms that could follow a target without human guidance. It is most associated with Norbert Wiener, who coined the term in 1947 and helped popularized it with his widely read book.[38] Yet despite the association of cybernetics with what Wiener called "communication and control," and the possibility of total oversight within a closed system, Hayek's approach was to see cybernetics as a humble science, eschewing omniscience to identify rules of action and reaction at the micro level, which one could only extrapolate to the macro. He even rejected the term "control," suggesting instead, in a metaphor he returned to in his Nobel speech, "cultivation, in the sense in which the farmer or gardener cultivates his plants, where he knows and can control only some of the determining circumstances, and in which the wise legislator or statesman will probably attempt to cultivate rather than to control the forces of the social process."[39] The metaphor of economic policy as akin to gardening was one of many links between his own thinking and that of Walter Eucken and Hayek's Freiburg colleague, Franz Böhm.[40] Indeed, as I have argued, Hayek's version of thinking in systems often appeared as a variation on the ordoliberal tradition of "thinking in orders" pioneered by Eucken.

Hayek arrived at his own version of system theory by looking at the place of humans in a range of complex systems that are, in a phrase he borrowed from the Scottish Enlightenment thinker Adam Ferguson, "the result of human action but not of human design."[41] Humans fumbled toward understanding without ever arriving at even an approximation of total comprehension. The best they could hope for was a set of rules that did not overly constrain or transgress the overall order—"pattern predictions" as he called them in his Nobel speech. Léon Walras said prices are discovered by groping in the dark, and Hayek saw humans as arriving at rules in a similar way, in an evolutionary process of trial and error, with more efficacious rules surviving as others passed away. He put it poetically in the 1940s, analogizing order to "the way in which footpaths are formed in a wild broken country." "At first everyone will seek for himself what seems to him the best path," he wrote, "but the fact that such a path has been used once is likely to make it easier to traverse and therefore more likely to be used again; and thus gradually more and more clearly defined tracks arise and come to be used to the exclusion of other possible ways. Human movements through the region come to conform to a definite pattern which, although the result of deliberate decisions of many people, has yet not been consciously designed by anyone."[42] An important influence on Hayek's evolutionary system thinking was a contemporary acquaintance, Ludwig von Bertalanffy, who was born in Vienna in 1901 and developed his own branch of system theory, named first in 1937.[43] Bertalanffy was careful to distinguish his "general system theory" from that of Wiener's cybernetics, emphasizing the origins he shared with Hayek in the studies of the Vienna Circle of the 1920s.[44] In the 1950s Bertalanffy founded a Society for General Systems Theory with the economist Kenneth Boulding and corresponded with Hayek about the latter's monograph on psychology, *The Sensory Order.*[45] Unlike other system theorists, Bertalanffy was not wed to the computer as the privileged tool of understanding, and he cited Hayek on the point that "explanation in principle" was often all that was possible in complex systems.[46]

The essence of Bertalanffy's theory was the proposition that there is an isomorphism in the objects of study of the various disciplines, such as biology, economics, and psychology. At a basic level, common principles and rules bound all systems of the visible and invisible world.[47] Systems were wholes composed of parts "in interaction."[48] Hayek embraced Bertalanffy's promiscuous slippage of analogy between scales and phenomena. For him, the premise of isomorphism meant that metaphor rather than mathematics was central to broader understanding. Qualitative insights about the mind, the market, and the cosmos intermingled freely as diverse instantiations of what he called emergent or spontaneous orders or complex systems.

One can approach Hayek's idea of the system by imagining a visit to the seashore. Wading in the shallow water, you may see a school of minnows approaching, traveling in a rough and shifting orb. The school is not regimented into even lines but it does cohere as a basic shape. As you approach, the orb dissipates and then reassembles before moving in another direction. Order for Hayek must be as unplanned and spontaneous as the movement of a school of fish in water. As he phrased it in 1979, against contemporary attempts at global planning, "to explain the economic aspects of large social systems, we have to account for the course of a flowing stream, constantly adapting itself as a whole to changes in circumstances."[49] Attempts to rationally coordinate such motions must fail, and they can diminish the very fluidity and capacity for improvisation that makes the order function. Hayek's successor in Freiburg, Erich Hoppmann, expanded on the metaphor, writing about the "V" formation of flying geese. One cannot predict the behavior of any individual goose, but one can discern a rule about their overall order. Thus, "pattern prediction is possible."[50] The geese themselves do not know the rules—they adhere to the formation through learned and inherited behavior.

The roots of Hayek's idea of "constitutional ignorance" are in the 1930s but he developed the theory in earnest after the Second World War. A few months after the end of hostilities, in a talk in Dublin, Hayek said that the beginning of liberalism was understanding the limits of individual knowledge: "The fundamental attitude of true individualism is one of humility toward the processes by which mankind has achieved things which have not been designed or understood by any individual and are indeed greater than individual minds."[51] Elaborating on this in one of his best-known articles, published the same year, he argued that we each possess only a small amount of information mediated by price, what he called knowledge "in an abbreviated form . . . a kind of symbol."[52] By exchanging goods and resources in the free market, we make use of that small amount of information. The sum total of all individual decisions everywhere—informed by their own small piece of the world's knowledge—adds up to a coordination of resources that would be impossible if attempted by a single individual. "The whole acts as one market," Hayek wrote.[53]

As Hayek described it in the 1960s, the knowledge problem was one of infinite regress on both the micro scale and the macro scale. Similar principles governed both the tiniest and largest imaginable orders. As one study puts it, for Hayek, "both the mind and the market are complex systems."[54] Another notes that Hayek blurred "the level that his analysis operated on, be it brains or individuals or groups."[55] One of Hayek's earliest adult experiences was a winter spent in a Zurich laboratory as a twenty-year-old in the year after the First World War, helping an anatomist trace nerve fibers in the human brain.[56] He drew on the experience for both metaphors and his understanding of cognition. To illustrate the difficulty of actually comprehending the system at work, he cited neurobiologists who found that "during a few minutes of intense cortical activity the number of interneuronic connections actually made (counting also those that are actuated more than once in different association patterns) may well be as great as the total number of atoms in the solar system."[57] Thus, the individual is not the smallest unit of study for Hayek. It is the neuron. And the highest unit of study is not the national or even the world—it is the cosmos. "There are, strictly speaking, no closed systems within the universe."[58]

As part of his attempt to prove the insufficiency of statistics and the opacity of human motivation, in 1964 Hayek conjured up the startling image of herds of computers roving the landscape. What if, he asked, "computers were natural objects which we found in sufficiently large numbers . . . whose behavior we wanted to predict"? We would need to know not only their behavior but the "theory determining their structure" in their very programming. Because humans are "much more complex structures" than computers, we cannot blithely take the individual as the unit of study.[59] The human mind is so complex as to shade off into an incalculable infinity, and the universe is too. We are never able to arrive at a satisfying observation of our selves either at the level of the neuron or at the level of the galaxy.

One of Hayek's core propositions, key to understanding the transformations of Geneva School neoliberalism since the 1970s, is that the market is built on *precognitive* responses to price signals. In a representative statement from 1963, he claimed, "Man does not know most of the rules on which he acts; and even what we call his intelligence is largely a system of rules which operate on him but which he does not know."[60] This deference to the precognitive or the pre-rational is what separated him from the rational choice and rational expectations models of Chicago School economists, who professed much more faith in the possibility of both formal mathematical modeling and forecasting. As he explained in his Nobel speech, Hayek saw such efforts as not only presumptuous but misleading. The best one could hope for was pattern prediction. Such prediction was already innate to the way we navigate in the world. In 1964 he wrote of "the intuitive capacity of our senses for pattern recognition"—"we see and hear patterns as much as individual events without having to resort to intellectual operations."[61] Appealing like Hoppmann to ethology, or the study of animal behavior, he noted that "experiments with fishes and birds . . . show that they respond in the same manner to a great variety of shapes which have only some very abstract features in common."[62] This led him to believe that basic reactions involve, not simplicity, but an unwitting abstraction, an innate ability in animals, including the human animal, to recognize complexity without realizing they are doing so. "It would seem much more appropriate to call such processes not 'subconscious' but 'super-conscious,'" he argued, "because they govern the conscious processes without appearing in them."[63]

In a key offhand statement at the Alpbach cybernetics conference in 1968, Hayek said that "order is not an object" but an "order of events."[64] His vision of the world economy is like the school of fish, a complex of neurons, a galaxy—an ever-adapting whole that the human mind can never—and must never—seek to replicate. The only way to descry the abstract principles within the system was "by what the physicists would call a cosmology, that is, a theory of their evolution."[65] "The problem of how galaxies or solar systems are formed," he wrote, "is much more like the problems which the social sciences have to face than the problems of mechanics."[66] In terms of the future, the capacity to adjust must always prepare for the unexpected. In an evocative analogy from his book on psychology from 1952, he offered the metaphor of the leaf, which "avoids being torn to shreds by a high wind by taking up a position of least resistance."[67] "What we call understanding," he wrote later, "is in the last resort simply [man's] capacity to respond to his environment with a pattern of actions that helps him to persist."[68] The system survives—and order results—through the reflexive efforts of individuals to reproduce both themselves and the totality.

On examination, one finds that in Hayek's theory the free will of the market actor is surprisingly limited. A metaphor that he returned to more than once is that of iron filings "magnetized by a magnet under the sheet of paper on which we have poured them." The filings "will so act on and react to all the others that they will arrange themselves in a characteristic figure of which we can predict the general shape but not the detail."[69] What he concluded from the analogy was that "the rules which govern the actions of the elements of such spontaneous orders need not be rules which are 'known' to these elements."[70] Another telling metaphor he favored was that of the attempt to recreate a crystal in a laboratory. We can never produce the crystal directly "by placing the individual atoms in such a position that they will form the lattice of a crystal or the system based on benzol rings which make up an organic compound," he wrote. But "we can create the conditions in which they will arrange themselves in such a manner."[71]

Hayek's argument was that humans are not as dissimilar from the components of the crystal or the individual iron filings as they might seem. "In all our thinking, we are guided (or even operated) by rules of which we are not aware."[72] He recognized that the term "knowledge" itself is misleading. "What we call knowledge," he pointed out, "is primarily a system of rules of action assisted and modified by rules indicating equivalences or differences or various combinations of stimuli."[73] We do not follow rules because they are based on a higher moral good nor because we have deduced our way to a conclusion; we follow them because we observe subconsciously that they have "secured that a greater number of the groups or individuals practicing them would survive."[74] "Man acted before he thought," Hayek wrote, "and did not understand before he acted."

It may be more accurate to see Hayek as more a proponent of the idea of *Homo regularis* than of the idea of *Homo economicus:* The first commandment of humans is not to maximize profit but to react to stimuli according to rules in a way that will maximize the chance of survival. Humans, to Hayek, are "rules-following animals."[75] Rules, like prices, are signals directing the individual, often at a "super-conscious" level. Hayek's "neuro-sensory conjecture" has been explored deeply by scholars both sympathetic to and critical of his thinking.[76] What Philip Mirowski calls Hayek's "agnotology" is echoed in the presumption of "radical ignorance" of economic actors in the work of those who seek to explain why Hayek's model is incompatible with the "rational search" implied in contemporary forms of neoclassical economics.[77]

As the above metaphors make clear, the idea of agency is diffuse in Hayek's work. One scholar speaks of Hayek's "instrumental justification of liberty, [by which] freedom is essential for the utilization of dispersed, fragmented, and habitual or tacit knowledge."[78] Freedom, in this reading, exists to discover new and better rules. The vanishing of the subject is consistent with system theory in general, where the system itself becomes the protagonist. As one scholar puts it, "the seat of causality" in Hayek's framework is not the individual but "appears to be the entire web or network."[79] Another goes even farther, saying that "the only subject is at the level of the whole system of humanity and history."[80] To Hayek, the autonomous individual is an illusory effect dependent on its relation to the whole—which, in turn, is dependent on that illusory effect.

It should be clear by now that Hayek's most famous metaphor—"the road to serfdom"—is itself strikingly un-Hayekian. The metaphor of the road is foreign to Hayek's own cache, where the more common paths are neural. His own metaphors and examples—of crystals, clouds, iron filings, pipes, and switchboards—illustrate radial and branching networks of complex interdependence characterized by uncertain outcomes, limited knowledge, and limited agency, not single-path routes of intentionality. To Hayek, the idea of an anthropomorphized collective moving purposively on a single path is itself a cognitive monstrosity—the inversion of his normative idea of order. Centralization in "what we call a nation or a state," he wrote, "is essentially the effect of the need of making this organization strong for war."[81] The problem, in other words, is not just the destination—serfdom—but the form of the metaphor itself—the nation as an autonomous agent and the basic unit of social life.

Hayek subscribed to a belief that the economist, the expert, and the policy maker had only limited knowledge. In this reading, the primary threat to order is not animal, lower-level impulses but rational, higher-level impulses. The danger is not so much the law of the jungle as the law of the engineers. Reason, if misused, is the enemy of order. Therefore, one might think that cybernetics itself would be the essence of Hayek's hated "constructivism"—coming from the Greek work for "steersman"—unless we acknowledge what my narrative has argued thus far.[82] Geneva School neoliberals did see a limited form of agency within the world economy. They saw individuals as indeed "steered" by the demands of the international division of labor. When functioning properly, the world market itself was the helmsman of human actors.

Leading ordoliberal Franz Böhm followed Hayek's cybernetic metaphors to help elucidate this vision. In his most important postwar text, he wrote that "the market price system . . . is of all the signaling systems produced by society the most mechanical or exact.[83] Citing Hayek on order, he wrote: "The principle of evaluation is, if I may draw on an expression from the field of automation and cybernetics, programmed into the steering mechanism which conforms to the program. The precondition for rational and orderly development is that all members of society are subordinated to the same steering mechanism in the same way."[84] Within both the "biological and social sphere," Hayek wrote in a key article, "spontaneous orders" form as "orderly wholes because each element responds to its particular environment in accordance with definite rules."[85]

For Hayek, Böhm, and all neoliberals who followed, the most relevant information for the reproduction of the system as a whole is prices. As Hayek put it in an interview, one of Marxism's errors was to see prices as reflective of the labor invested in an object. Actually, prices are important primarily for what he called, using a term from cybernetics, their "negative feedback effect." "The function of prices," he said, "is to tell people what they ought to do."[86] We could take the core of Hayek's philosophy to be this: "The apparent paradox that in the market it is through the systematic disappointment of some expectations that on the whole expectations are as effectively met as they are. This is the manner in which the principle of 'negative feedback' operates."[87] Hayek reveals much in this passage. What is privileged in the end is not the individual but the whole. Injustice is a functional requirement of the system. "Underserved strokes of misfortune," he wrote, are "an inseparable part of the steering mechanism of the market: it is the manner in which the cybernetic principle of negative feedback operates to maintain the order of the market."[88]

The very arbitrariness of "undeserved strokes of misfortune" increased the pressure on the individual to be as responsive as possible to price signals. The centrality of the figure of the entrepreneur for neoliberals can be understood better through this focus on danger. In a short piece on the entrepreneur from 1947, Röpke described the entrepreneur as "the node in the enormously complicated process of the market economy: he receives the impulses that the consumers send to him and translates them into the corresponding type and volume of production." In an extraordinary metaphor worth quoting at length, Röpke writes that the entrepreneur sits "at a switchgear into which a thousand currents enter to be sent out again in another direction and another form. The private economic fate of the individual entrepreneur depends on the correct operation of this switchgear . . . and it is precisely this dependency . . . that offers the best guarantee that he will operate the switchgear as conscientiously, zealously, and intelligently as the engineer of a complicated electric locomotive whom we offer the same trust and confidence because we know that the fate of the train is, at the same time, also his own."[89] By living dangerously, the entrepreneur risks the lives of others and therein risks his own life. Entrepreneurs, Röpke wrote, are "subordinated to the sovereignty of the market."[90]

Although Hayek disparaged the engineer in the sense of the scientist who believes she has sufficient overview of an entire system to build it herself, he praised the engineer in the sense of the train engineer, for reasons similar to Röpke's. He wrote in 1945 that "the price system [is] a kind of machinery for registering change, or a system of telecommunications which enables individual producers to watch merely the movement of a few pointers, as an engineer might watch the hands of a few dials, in order to adjust their activities."[91] In a near-identical metaphor from 1941, the engineer was instead "the individual entrepreneur [who] can read off, as it were, from a few gauges and in simple figures, the relevant results of everything which happens anywhere in the system."[92] The engineer and the entrepreneur became the ideal switches in the circuitry of the price system by reducing their agency to the response to stimuli in the precarious position of guiding a hurtling locomotive, churning power plant, or capitalist enterprise.

Given the above lengthy but necessary exegesis, it should be clear why the NIEO would not constitute an order in Hayek's sense. Order is not perpetuated by prescribing goals and desired end-states. Instead, the perpetuation of order requires that individuals—and states—defer to the wisdom of the system. For Hayek, the highest form of rationality is surrender to the greater knowledge of institutions, which are themselves the accretion of successful strategies determined through long-term processes of natural selection. The necessary ignorance must be preserved.

Yet where does this leave the activist neoliberal intellectual who is eager to intervene? In 1977 fellow MPS member James M. Buchanan complained that "to imply, as Hayek seems to do, that there neither exists nor should exist a guideline for evaluating existing institutions seems to me to be a counsel of despair in the modern setting."[93] John Gray contended that Hayek asks us to "entrust ourselves to all the vagaries of mankind's random walk in historical space."[94] Does Hayek's version of system theory really prescribe a kind of quietism in the face of the market? How should apparent deviations be corrected in a system of "super-conscious" rules and limited knowledge? These questions came to a head in the late 1970s as neoliberals witnessed what two of them called "the undermining of the world trade order" in the NIEO and the move of industrialized nations to the "new protectionism" of voluntary export restraints, orderly marketing arrangements, and a whole host of other measures they read as barriers to trade.[95] Interestingly enough, a key opportunity to revisit the chances for postimperial intervention—putatively against interventionism—came in one of the last remnants of the British Empire, in the crown colony of Hong Kong.

THE THIN LINE OF DELIBERATE DESIGN

The MPS meeting in Hong Kong in September 1978 was its first general meeting outside of Europe and North America. It was special also because it offered a chance for an early celebration of the eightieth birthday of the society's first president, Hayek himself.[96] Hong Kong was a remarkable example of the neoliberal fix in a basic form: a model of nonmajoritarian market economy that limited popular sovereignty while maximizing capital sovereignty with a much-touted free-trade policy, a robust bank secrecy law, and a low corporate tax rate. In many ways Hong Kong was the inverted version of the demands of the NIEO and the Global South in the 1970s. One speaker at a 1974 MPS meeting observed that because of its "exposed and dependent economic and political situation," Hong Kong was compelled to maintain "an environment conducive to profitable investment."[97] While Argentine economist Raúl Prebisch and the United Nations Economic Commission for Latin America (ECLA) theorized "dependency" as a negative state to be escaped, neoliberals openly prescribed it as a means of subjecting states to what Hayek called in the published version of his Hong Kong talk "the discipline of freedom."[98] Neither the absence of representative government nor Hong Kong's colonial status (nor, for that matter, the public ownership of all land) deterred a journalist covering the meeting from describing Hong Kong as "the most libertarian major civilized community in the world today."[99] What was admirable, in fact, was its solution to the disruptive problem of democracy.

Even as the MPS met in Hong Kong, the Chinese Communist Party was planning its own institutional fix for the People's Republic of China. At the time, mainland China as a whole exported no more than the tiny colony of Hong Kong. Deng Xiaoping's reforms started a process toward China's own form of nonmajoritarian capitalism, slowly introducing market freedoms without expanding political representation. The price mechanism was permitted without the mechanism of popular sovereignty—the multiparty election. In 1979, China opened the country's first export processing zones in the Pearl River Delta, a region of exception outside of the national tax structure that would become a defining form of neoliberal-style development by the 1990s.[100]

This future was distant in the 1970s, however, and in the decade of the NIEO, the situation still looked dire to neoliberals. The Hong Kong address presented by MPS president George Stigler was titled "Why Have the Socialists Been Winning?" The main problem he saw was the same conundrum of democracy that German neoliberals had been diagnosing since the 1930s and American public choice theorists since the

1960s: the "political process is strongly biased toward collectivism."[101] Given the possibility that the neoliberal position had become a "minority view," Stigler asked: "If in fact we seek what many do not wish, will we not be more successful if we take this into account and seek political institutions and policies that allow us to pursue our own goals?"[102] He identified a bright spot in Proposition 13, a piece of legislation passed in California that year that put a limit on property taxes and required a two-thirds majority to pass any state revenue measures.[103]

Stigler's address was published in the leading neoliberal journal, *Ordo*. It marked a turning point in the acceleration of the neoliberal search for institutional forms that would account for democratic realities but nonetheless lock in market-friendly outcomes. In the same issue, Buchanan laid out a plan for measures similar to Proposition 13 in an article titled "Constitutional Constraints on Governmental Taxing Power."[104] The advantage of tax reform in a federal state like the United States meant that the same principle applied that made Hong Kong a successful place of business—the state creates a more attractive investment climate that will encourage people "to vote with their feet, or with their mobile resources."[105] At the Hong Kong meeting W. H. Hutt met several South Africans invited by Hayek. It was after the meeting, perhaps inspired by Stigler's call for refinements of the neoliberal fix, that he wrote a seven-page single-space letter to the South African finance minister outlining his plan for weighting the franchise according to one's individual tax bracket.[106]

On the face of it, Hayek's talk had little to offer to Stigler's call for institutional design. Unlike Proposition 13, it made no call for higher bars for legislation or for binding states from redistribution. Unlike Hutt's proposal for weighted franchise, it offered no road map to link wealth to democratic power. Yet on closer examination, what one participant in the Hong Kong meeting called Hayek's "critique of sociobiology" contained clues about the application of his work to blueprints for global economic governance.[107] Hayek's paper was titled "The Three Sources of Human Values" and was published as the epilogue to *The Political Order of a Free People,* the final book of his 1970s trilogy, *Law, Legislation and Liberty.* He opened with a direct engagement with contemporary theories of complex systems, charging that sociobiologists like E. O. Wilson saw only two sources of human values: genes and human reason. Hayek made the case for a third term in the nongenetic, nonrational reservoir of culture, interpreted as "a tradition of learnt rules of conduct which have never been invented and whose functions the acting individuals usually do not understand."[108]

Scholars rightly emphasize the centrality of evolutionary rules, spontaneity, and "grown order" in Hayek's thought.[109] Yet they often miss the fact that Hayek did not replace one pair (genes / reason) with another (genes / tradition). There were "three layers of rules," he insisted. In the first layer were the unconscious, and relatively constant, instinctive rules of physiology; in the second were the unconscious and acquired rules of tradition; and the third layer, "on top of all this," was "the thin layer of rules deliberately adopted or modified to serve known purposes."[110] The first two layers of rules were unknown, more akin to "regularity," as he put it, and we follow them unconsciously, just as an iron filing follows the magnet. But the uppermost, "thin layer" of rules consisted of "the products of deliberate design: these were the rules we made through the application of our reason and which we 'have to be made to obey.'"[111]

Hayek's tripartite stratification of the rules of conduct explained both individual cognition and the social system as a whole. Like many of his models, this one could easily shift scales. In 1960 he himself had drawn the analogy between the mind and society: "Like the forces governing the individual mind, the forces making for social order are a multilevel affair"; "articulated rules" could work only because they operated on the bedrock of unspoken "common beliefs."[112] Hayek's successor in the chair at Freiburg noted that Hayek retained "rules of individual conduct in the sense of law" as "the top layer of a stratification of rules which also comprises instinctive drives and tradition."[113] The framing of the known, deliberately designed, and articulated rules as a "thin layer" or "only the top layer" can give the impression that they are dispensable or negligible. Yet while it is true that Hayek's primary intervention was to emphasize the unspoken rules, it is equally true that without the "thin layer" of articulated rules at the top of the hierarchy, his whole system would fall apart and humans would be equivalent to termites. No matter how "thin," the layer of conscious rules is necessary to reproduce social order as such. However slender it might be, what we might call Hayek's thin line of deliberate design is the lynchpin of the whole system. Pull it out and order dissolves.

It is beyond question that most of Hayek's references to design are negative, especially in his repeated insistence that orders that are "the products of human action but not human design." But it is essential to note that what he attacks are attempts to design completely. He describes his own project frankly as one of "constitutional design" in the first pages of his 1970s trilogy.[114] Though the top layer of rules may be thin, Hayek viewed it as the only place where humans can actually intervene: "Our main interest will then be those rules which, *because we can deliberately alter them,* become the chief instrument whereby we can affect the resulting order, namely the rules of law."[115]

It is helpful here to return to a distinction between planning and design offered by the philosopher Garrett Hardin in a 1969 article cited by Hayek in his Hong Kong paper. Hardin defined planning as "the making of rather detailed, rather rigid plans." By designing, he meant "much looser, less detailed, specification of a cybernetic system which includes negative feedbacks, self-correcting controls." He added that "the classical market economy is such a design."[116] Whether or not Hayek was inspired by Hardin directly on this point, the distinction helps clarify his writings. It is not difficult to argue that in the 1970s in particular, what Hayek is engaged in was a project of system design. Hayek's model is an economy of principles, or "rules of just conduct," as he called them, derived from physiology, the accretion of human tradition and—the site of action—the thin line of deliberate design.

It is thus misleading to characterize Hayek's writings from the 1970s as condemning us to, as Gray put it, "a random walk." Hayek says in black and white that "collaboration will always rest both on spontaneous order as well as on deliberate organization" and labels his project one itself of design.[117] For many scholars, Hayek's focus on the evolutionary, spontaneous, and unconscious aspects of order can distract from the fact that hard law encases the cosmos. Understood correctly, Hayek's meaning is not that we cannot design the social system *at all;* it is that we cannot design the social system *entirely*—and that we *must* design part of it.

At the end of the same volume, Hayek provides an explicit example of how this thinking might be transposed to the global level. Though his writings on federation from the 1930s and 1940s are often discussed, his return to the topic in the 1970s has all but escaped scholarly attention. In 1979, in a section calling for "the dethronement of politics," Hayek wrote, "In this century our attempts to create an inter-national government capable of assuring peace have generally approached the task from the wrong end: creating large numbers of specialized authorities aiming at particular regulations rather than aiming at a *true international law* which would limit the powers of national governments to harm each other. If the highest common values are negative, not only the highest common rules but also the highest authority should essentially be *limited to prohibitions.*"[118] Hayek offered here an indication of how his theories on international order, more or less dormant since the end of the war, could be scaled up to the global. A cadre of neoliberals would do just that by reviving Hayek's thought in Geneva. Retaliating against the G-77 with its own weapons, their solution to the NIEO was to fight law with law. The reform of the GATT would become, in part, a laboratory for Hayekian system design at the scale of the world.

NIEO AS SYSTEM ERROR

In 1977, the year before the Hong Kong MPS meeting, the GATT moved into a building newly renamed the Centre William Rappard after the impresario of the neoliberal intellectual movement at the Graduate Institute for International Studies in the 1930s and 1940s, whose wealthy family had originally donated the land. One of the first activities of the new occupants was to remove and cover over murals and tilework that had decorated the building in its previous function as the seat of the International Labour Organization (ILO). Rolled up and stashed in a gardener's cottage was a mural by Dean Cornwell; donated by the American Federation of Labor in 1956, the mural depicted female secretaries at walls of card catalogues, brass bands, and elementary schoolteachers flanking a central image of a bare-chested worker in an ironworker's apron, broken shackles dangling from his wrists.[119]

Concealed beneath linen wall panels were murals by Gustave-Louis Jaulme commissioned by the ILO in 1939 depicting figures parading in flowing garments holding palm fronds, gathering fruit, and relaxing beneath bowers.[120] Also effaced was a work of Delft tiles donated by Dutch trade unions in 1926 depicting the passage from the Versailles Treaty about the dignity of labor, translated into four languages, surrounding a stylized male worker clad in red who was building the pillars of world order after the war. Suggesting the racialization of the alternative vision of the world economic order that was replaced, WTO director-general Pascal Lamy quipped later about the art's removal: "It's a bit as if you took over from immigrants in a social housing development."[121] To the GATT's director-general Olivier Long in 1977, the art was incompatible with the spirit of his trade organization.[122] As we will see, rather than a world economy of labor, bodies, toil, and leisure, the GATT's world economy was one of price signals, rules, and, as Long declared in 1978, the "reaffirmation of the rule of law in international trade."[123]

At the time of its relocation, the GATT was in the midst of what one report called "Geneva's secret war" as the so-called Tokyo Round of negotiations (1973–1979) sought to rethink the world trade institution for an era after empire and after the dissolution of key parts of the postwar economic order. In 1971 the Bretton Woods system had ended in its original form when the United States unilaterally ceased exchanging dollars for gold. By 1973, responding in part to the diligent persuasion of Haberler and other neoliberals, the States let the dollar "float," allowing market demand (alongside targeted state interventions) to dictate its value.[124] In turn, many of the world's currencies floated too, launching an era of a variety of monetary strategies ranging from flexible exchange rates to "managed floating." Simultaneously, the end of IMF authorization for controls on capital movements brought back the "hot money" flows of the 1930s, amplified in volume by the greater global connectivity of telecommunications.[125] New investment flows were available to nations worldwide, but capital flight could also be punitive if foreign investors disapproved of costly policies like building domestic welfare states through higher taxation.[126] Neoliberals like Haberler saw the constraint as salutary because it compelled developed nations to see "the maintenance of exchange stability as something which must take precedence over all other considerations."[127] The precariousness of a territory like Hong Kong could and should be paradigmatic for a post–Bretton Woods neoliberal world.

On its face the GATT was an unlikely spot for a neoliberal legal counterrevolution. Although all of its directors were lawyers by training, the preferred mode in Geneva was economic diplomacy and ad hoc negotiation. GATT did not even have an office of legal affairs until 1983, at a time when the World Bank already employed one hundred lawyers.[128] The situation began to change first under the directorship of the Geneva-trained lawyer Olivier Long. In 1978 Long first invoked the term "rule of law" in a speech at a London-based think tank, the Trade Policy Research Centre (TPRC), founded by Australian economist Hugh Corbet in 1968.[129] Long endorsed the proposal made the previous year in another speech at the TPRC by the American lawyer John H. Jackson, on the need to develop some way to stop the tendency of governments to "disregard or side-step GATT rules."[130]

Jackson, who in 1969 had written what is often called the "GATT bible," worked with the American Society of International Law in the 1970s to shore up what he called the "flimsy constitutional basis" of the GATT and salvage "the crumbling institutions of the liberal trade system."[131] He was also credited as the inventor of contemporary trade law and the single most important figure in international economic law.[132] Jackson saw two main sources of erosion of the rules-based order. On the one hand, industrialized Northern countries were using a host of "neo-protectionist" measures to fend off competition from rising economies like Japan; on the other hand, the vast group of newly decolonized nations enjoyed "their current majority status in many organizations, when voting proceeds on a one-nation one-vote system" and used it to secure exemptions from the rule-based regime. What might appear as a salutary scaling up of the democratic principle to the level of international governance was an obstacle to order for Jackson. "There is virtually no chance of significant rule-making authority developing in any international body today," he said, "which bases its procedures on the one-nation one-vote system."[133]

Jackson's targeting of the developing nations, relatively minor actors in terms of volume of trade, might seem misplaced. Yet it is entirely emblematic of the emergent field of international economic law and GATT reform in the 1970s. The world economic imaginary of the developing world—represented by the United Nations Conference on Trade and Development (UNCTAD) and the G-77—was the Other against which GATT reform was defined. The reason was not (or, in some cases, not only) a crude neocolonialism or cultural supremacism but a backlash against concessions that the Global South had won in the 1960s. Through persuasive knowledge production, effective diplomacy, and collective mobilization, the Global South nations had secured first the so-called Part IV (1966) and then the Generalized System of Preferences (1971) that effectively freed them from GATT disciplines. This was the core of what became known as "special and differential treatment" for developing countries in the world trade regime.

The victories were tepid ones. The exclusion of agriculture from GATT meant that the primary exports of many Global South countries still had to compete against U.S. and European subsidies and protectionism. Yet the advocates of GATT reform saw concessions to the demands for mixed development as the indefensible core of decay in the rules-based global economy. After the resolution of the oil crisis led to a vast new sea of petrodollars to be recycled through Wall Street and the City of London to lenders in the Global South, the uniformity of conditions globally became all the more pressing. The TPRC and its in-house journal, *The World Economy,* became a clearinghouse for critiques of the NIEO and calls to reform the GATT in the 1970s and early 1980s.[134] One of the sharpest critics at the time was one of today's most influential economic commentators, Martin Wolf of the *Financial Times.* After beginning his career at the World Bank in 1971 (where he coauthored its first World Development Report with future MPS president Deepak Lal), Wolf was the director of studies at the TPRC in 1981 for six years before beginning at the *Financial Times.*[135] At the TPRC, Wolf criticized what he called "the desire of developing countries to create a world in which one group of countries has most of the obligations and another most of the rights."[136] By opting out of GATT disciplines, Wolf and others argued, developing countries were undermining the rule of law.

As a 1984 TPRC report that Wolf helped write put it, "Developing countries have been engaged in a sustained assault on the liberal principles of the international trading system."[137] Against special and differential treatment, the goal of NIEO opponents was to promote the idea of one rule for all in the world economy.

The three most important GATT reformers in Geneva were all devotees of Hayekian thought. First was Jan Tumlir, the head of the research division from 1967 to 1985, remembered by some as the "resident philosopher" of GATT.[138] Tumlir was born in Czechoslovakia in 1926 and studied law in Prague before emigrating in 1949. After two years in West Germany, he moved to the United States, where he earned a PhD in economics from Yale in 1964. He moved to the research position at GATT that year, and was also a faculty member at the Graduate Institute of International Studies from 1968 until his premature death by heart attack at the age of fifty-nine.[139] The library of the Graduate Institute was housed in the Centre William Rappard, and Tumlir's library of several hundred volumes is still housed as the "Jan Tumlir Legacy Collection" in the building that is now the home of the WTO.[140]

In the 1970s Tumlir was joined at GATT by two lawyers with whom he would help formulate his Hayekian theory of international order. Frieder Roessler, born in 1939, was a graduate of Freiburg University, where he had studied with Hayek. He arrived at GATT in his early thirties in 1973.[141] Ernst-Ulrich Petersmann, born in 1945, also studied with Hayek at Freiburg. Before joining GATT in 1981, he had worked as an assistant at the Max Planck Institute for International and Comparative Public Law in Heidelberg and for three years in the legal office of the Foreign Trade Department of the German Economics Ministry. In his habilitation thesis he singled out Tumlir and Hayek for their exceptional influence on his thinking.[142] By the late 1990s Petersmann became one of the most internationally visible practitioners and advocates of the field of international economic law.

Roessler and Petersmann, along with Ake Linden, were the first members of the GATT's Office of Legal Affairs, created in 1983. Roessler became the first director of the Division of Legal Affairs at the GATT in 1989 and "drafted the bulk of a series of historical decisions on the transition from the GATT to the WTO."[143] One scholar calls Tumlir and

Petersmann (along with John H. Jackson) "the GATT's major intellectual architects."[144] The GATT lawyers were worthy heirs to the Geneva School of neoliberalism. All of them either taught or researched at the Graduate Institute of International Studies. Their cohort also included Gerard Curzon, the editor of the *Journal of World Trade Law,* who assumed Röpke's chair at the Graduate Institute after Röpke's death in 1966; and his partner, Victoria Curzon-Price, who taught at the University of Geneva and would later become the first (and, thus far, only) female president of the MPS. The Geneva faction worked closely in the campaign for GATT reform with the TPRC, which launched its journal, *The World Economy,* in 1977 with a lead article by Tumlir titled "Can the International Economic Order Be Saved?"[145] Tumlir contacted Hayek personally for the first time in 1975 to send him a draft of the article. He explained that *The World Economy* was intended "to be addressed to policy-makers and political public rather than to economists" and that the "main intellectual impulse" of his article derived from Hayek's work.[146]

Geneva School neoliberals sought to save the international economic order in the 1970s and 1980s by creating a rules-based system for the world economy. They hoped to counteract the atmosphere of pragmatism and compromise that reigned at the GATT and restore the coherence of a liberal order that had been eroding continually since the granting of preferences to colonial and later postcolonial states in the Treaty of Rome.[147] The "Eurafrican" deviations from liberal principles had continued with the granting of preferences to products from the developing world through the 1960s. Following Britain's accession to the EEC in 1973, the Lomé Convention of 1975 extended affiliation to forty-six African, Caribbean, and Pacific states, replacing the previous Yaoundé conventions as well as its British counterpart, the Arusha Agreement.

When Roessler arrived as a Freiburg-trained lawyer in 1973, he was told that people at the GATT "do not believe in law. They believe in pragmatism."[148] He explained in 1978 that his goal would be to apply "arguments to world economic relations that have been made by Hayek in a broader context."[149] The question was how to calibrate the system of rules to allow price signals to operate correctly when world economic order was being disturbed by "issues of distributional equity."[150] As we have seen, Hayek offered both "grown" rules, what Roessler called "de facto norms," as well as laws of deliberate design, or what Roessler called "de iure norms." While granting the general superiority of grown norms, Roessler echoed Hayek's argument for the purposive reestablishment of principles when order was under threat. He argued for the necessity of a "transfer of decision-making to judicial or quasi-judicial bodies able to take a long-term view," suggesting that GATT as one such body that could "administer or interpret the rules in the light of broadly stated principles."[151] The GATT itself could constitute what I have called the thin line of deliberate design.

Roessler saw the Global South as the chief obstacle to a more rational organization of the world trading system. Coalitions of contracting members of the GATT with only miniscule portions of world trade were nonetheless using their votes to block or slow changes to the Charter; developing nations, as he put it, held "the key to legality."[152] Global South nations were also using the language of law proactively to pursue their own demands. The preferences they secured with GATT were one example of "principles turned into rules." Even more strident was the Declaration of the NIEO itself. Although UN declarations were technically nonbinding, they had a tendency to harden over time: "Once the principle is negotiated and written down it serves as a ready reference in debates."[153] The takeover of de jure norms by the Global South meant that industrialized nations were turning ever more to de facto norms, avoiding the forum of international organizations altogether. Such clashes, caused by the legal activism of the postcolonial and developing world, meant that, as Roessler put it in a quote from John H. Jackson, "the entire fabric of a legal structure can be . . . chewed away at the fringes over a long period of time."[154]

Petersmann's work in the 1970s was defined even more than Roessler's by a response to the apparent usurpation of international law by the nations of the Global South. Petersmann wrote more than a dozen articles on the legal aspects of the NIEO in that decade. He wrote about the "new state majority" created by the "emergence of over 80 underdeveloped new states in the course of decolonization, [and] the dominance in the General Assembly of the UN of the over 100 developing countries."[155] "Neoliberal international economic law," as he put it, was being replaced by principles of redistribution and solidarity, scaling up the welfare state and "economic and social human rights" to the global level. "The developing countries organized like trade unions," he wrote, were "demanding a total revolutionary revision of traditional international economic law."[156] The NIEO was an attempt at "the replacement of decentralized market economy mechanisms by UN planning bureaucracies (manned by bureaucrats from less developed countries)," which had been "rightly rejected" by the member countries of the Organisation for Economic Co-operation and Development.[157] In short, UNCTAD was turning the "national idea of the welfare state into an 'internationalized' welfare world."[158]

According to Petersmann's reading, "less developed and state-trading countries prevent a uniform systematic concept for the world economy and a universally recognized international economic law system."[159] The demands of the NIEO were "a cornucopia of individual economic-political demands for North–South relations without an overall concept of political order."[160] The means of carrying out the assault on liberal principles was the same as had been feared since 1945: the one-country-one-vote model of the UN. Petersmann referred to an "electoral takeover of other UN institutions" that was pushing the law of development through.[161] Like Roessler, Petersmann acknowledged that UNCTAD's resolutions were not binding, but he also pointed out that they could take on the force of law with time: "The majority resolutions of now more than 100 developing countries could seriously influence the development of international law."[162] The transformation of the world scene from a "small club of western nations" in 1945 to "a much larger number of nations representing different civilizations" had put pressure on the character of international law itself.[163] Demands for "reparations for colonial guilt," in particular, were "tantamount to an international tax obligation for industrial countries."[164]

The question was "how far universal international customary law can be . . . created anew through changing majorities even against the will of individual states."[165] Petersmann pointed out that the Charter of the Economic Rights and Duties of States had already been used as a legal argument in the nationalization of American oil concessions by

Libya.[166] As it had also been for neoliberals in the 1950s, the nationalization of foreign owned property was of primary concern. As acts of what Petersmann called "domestic economic decolonization," seizing foreign-owned property misrecognized political for economic sovereignty.[167] Decolonization itself was also a case in point, where the "right to self-determination" had become a reality "against the resistance of colonial powers."[168] If the right to escape empire could become a right, then why could the entire apparatus of existing norms not be discarded? "[Are] the over eighty developing nations, which have become independent since 1945, bound to the preexisting general international economic law, even against their will"?[169] In the 1970s the answer seemed like a clear no. The world was being created anew and international customary law along with it.

The GATT lawyers saw it as necessary to work against these developments. Petersmann used a quote from Hayek as an epigraph to an article: "It is the essence of legal thinking . . . that the lawyer strives to make the whole system consistent."[170] Petersmann described his own methodology as that of "thinking in orders," derived from what he labeled the "neoliberal *Ordo* school" of Eucken, Böhm, Röpke, and Hayek.[171] Citing work on cybernetics, he pointed out that "systems analysis" illuminated how exceptions to the "rule mechanisms can often only be understood within the total structure of the system" and "can have undesired side effects in other parts of the system."[172] Seemingly inconsequential deviations, in other words, compromised the "capacities of reaction in the system" with effects on the world economy itself.

In Petersmann's understanding, influenced by cybernetics, the complex system had to be policed at the margins where flaws could originate. The violations of GATT rules by developing countries constituted just such deviations. He wrote of the danger of "pluralism" in "world economic law," with one set of rules for the North and another for the South.[173] In a 1977 piece coauthored by Tumlir, the GATT Research Division struck a similar note, remarking that "once it is realized that any successful infraction of the rules sets a precedent, both at home and abroad . . . an accumulation of such precedents may undermine the whole order of intricately specialized yet coordinated activity."[174] For these thinkers, the biggest threat to the integrity of the world trading system in the 1970s was the activism of its least powerful economic players, most of which had just emerged as nations from a history of empire. By proposing new rules for the game rather than adhering to the liberal precepts of an earlier era, Global South actors threatened to cripple the entire system.

The most important in the trio of Hayekian GATT experts was the elder figure, Tumlir. He shared the fixation of Hayek's students on the NIEO as a global system error, describing it as a "degenerative development" in the world economic order.[175] He realized early why the changed circumstances of the 1970s made the developing countries newly important beyond their growing majority in international organizations. In a 1974 talk at the TPRC that was published as a newspaper editorial, Tumlir explained how the resolution of the oil crisis—through the quadrupling of oil revenues—presented a quandary: Where would all the extra liquidity flow? He concluded that the only noninflationary outcome would be the investment of petrodollars to the capital-hungry Global South as a spur to industrialization projects. A cartoon by Michael Heath accompanying the editorial pictured a grotesquely caricatured Arab man flipping a coin marked with the sign of industry to a supine turbaned and similarly hook-nosed beggar representing the Global South. Industrialized countries, Tumlir argued, would profit by providing "equipment, machinery, engineering and management know-how for this new massive investment" and would thereby "have an opportunity to earn their petrodollars without cutting each other's throat."[176]

Not pictured in the schematic (and racist) cartoon were the critical way-stations on the route from Middle East to Global South: Wall Street and the City of London, where the financial services sector would play a key role in directing investment Southward. It was clear in Tumlir's reading that if the Global South received a huge new pool of investment capital, the onus would be ever more on them to adhere to rules that would secure predictability for investors. Tumlir's editorial appeared in early February 1974. Less than three months later the NIEO declaration passed in the UN General Assembly, suggesting that the G-77 had no intention of cooperating with the old norms and sought to write their own rules instead.

Speaking on the occasion of Hayek's eightieth birthday, Tumlir attacked the destructive hubris of the Global South. The NIEO, he said, expressed "the confidence in modern societies' power of deliberate self-reform and self-regulation." This was not positive but negative: "Not only do nations claim to be determining their own future within a global order; now that order itself is to be transcended, the world as such [is] being mobilized to determine its own future within the order of the universe."[177] Tumlir believed that the G-77 coalition of poor nations was making the same mistake that Walter Lippman had seen in the 1930s and Hayek had diagnosed ever since. They were falling prey to the allure of "omnipotence and omniscience"—the misguided belief that one could actually change the world. Most galling for Tumlir was the appropriation of the term "order" itself. As he noted, the word has two meanings: "There is the order of observed results (the streets are safe and prices stable)," but "in a more analytical sense, the concept is used to denote the set of rules and institutions which produce the observed regularity and orderliness."[178] The goal of order was not to give the people what they want but to prevent them from taking what they want—and thereby destroying the system as a whole. His apodictic phrase could serve as a slogan for the entire Geneva School of neoliberalism: "International rules protect the world market against governments."[179] The world economy must be defended against governments themselves, which themselves need to be protected from their feckless populations driven only by self-interest.

Tumlir contended that by following these rules, states would be also salvaging their own sovereignty against internally grasping forces. He said in 1981: "The international economic order [could act] as an additional means of entrenchment protecting national sovereignty against internal erosion."[180] Also in that year he quoted Mestmäcker: "The problem is how to structure, or order, an economy so that it can become neither the servant, nor the master of the state."[181] By adopting binding rules, states would save themselves as they defended the world economy. The fact that such sovereignty would mean not unbounded autonomy but a subjection to the forces of the world market was taken as a matter of course. In a key reframing of the central category of the NIEO, Tumlir contended that order was not stability nor was it equity: instead, "order is adjustment."[182] Like Hayek's metaphorical leaf adapting to the changing wind, to thrive—and survive—was to be open to constant change. A piece he coauthored as the head of the GATT research team expressed it this way: "Adjustment to change is a necessary condition of economic growth—indeed, the growth process is little more than a sequence of adjustments."[183] The "order" of the NIEO, in short, was nothing more than "a refusal to adjust."[184] Taken together, the GATT reformers saw the G-77 demands for redistribution and special and differential treatment as producing aberrations in the uniform system of rules, which could lead to a catastrophic breakdown of the mechanism of the world economy. Order meant continual adaptation within a system, and the role of lawmakers and institutions was to transform the system's rules into binding legislation. What was needed was not only a guardian for the economic constitution but a guardian of the homeostatic system.

CALIBRATING THE STRATIFIED ORDER

At the beginning of the 1980s Tumlir reflected on the problem of world economic order in the twentieth century. Echoing Röpke and Hayek before him, he wrote that before 1914, "order functioned without being fully understood." Although this informal spontaneity was the best possible order, it could not be reproduced easily. This was made clear when "the same men who administered the international economic order before 1914 were unable to reconstitute it after 1918."[185] Tumlir observed that Robbins and Hayek had proposed their federal plans as a first solution in the 1930s. Along with other interwar liberals, including the ordoliberals Böhm and Eucken, they perceived that there was an "inherent tendency of nationalism to subvert economic policy of democratic states into a zero-sum game."[186] Tumlir adopted their insight that the masses capture the state under conditions of democracy. After this point, the state "ceases to be a government and becomes an arena for gladiatorial combats of organized interests."[187] "Where market failures are occasionally discernible," Tumlir noted, using a phrase employed by contemporary public choice theorists, "*government failure* is pervasive and massive."[188]

Tumlir's conclusion, which he shared with Petersmann and Roessler, echoed that of Stigler in Hong Kong. Asking why the socialists were winning, he conceded that perhaps democracy may simply lead by its own logic to socialism. "While the working of the economic order depends on the internal consistency of its general rules, the democratic political process is largely concerned with securing exceptions for particular groups."[189] Thus, to fend off socialism or the state's becoming, in its fragmentation, the "prey" of individual interest groups, and to defend the safety and mobility of capital, required an institutional fix. Tumlir recalled that the solution of Robbins and Hayek to this so-called government failure—by which he meant a failure of the state to protect the world economy—was in an "international authority . . . endowed with effective power to make rules, adjudicate under them and enforce the decisions."[190] Their error, however, was the absence of adequate means to enforce those rules within the nations in the federation that remained formally sovereign.

The 1930s neoliberal federalists had been optimistic about the good faith of enlightened nations capable of discerning their own self-interest in sticking to the global rules. Tumlir saw the post-1945 settlement as similar to this arrangement. Nations agreed to the rules, following the guidelines of the Bretton Woods system and largely adhering to the rules of the GATT. In some ways he saw this as a vindication of Hayek and Robbins's hope for enlightened federalism. This temporary "reintegration of the world economy was thus a result of the new discipline governing the conduct of national economic policies. This discipline was accepted by governments in the form of agreed international rules."[191] The critical turning point after which this model was no longer viable was the end of European overseas empire. Problems emerged, he noted, "when decolonization greatly increased the number of independent countries. They came to claim all kinds of dispensations from the disciplines" of the postwar international order.[192] When the industrial nations granted these exceptions, they implicitly acquiesced to the view that "discipline . . . was a luxury only the rich could afford; that it was, in fact, an obstacle to economic growth."[193] The preferential treatment of former colonial countries, the Part IV of the GATT, and nonreciprocity—these were all aspects of the North's concession that the royal road to modernization was through infant industry protection, benevolent transfers, and the right to break the rules.

At Haberler's conference on the NIEO at the American Enterprise Institute in 1977, Tumlir warned of "frightening" parallels to the 1930s.[194] In both the interwar period and the 1970s, the misstep was what Tumlir quoted Karl Popper to dub " 'the fallacy of sovereignty,' the concept of sovereignty as unlimited power, virtual omnipotence."[195] Once again we see that the neoliberal intervention was a call to think holistically—in world orders—and to be aware of the conditions of complex interdependence. Far from employing a rhetoric of personal freedom, Tumlir cast his warnings in the Hayek-inspired Geneva School rhetoric of the limits to freedom inherent in the functioning of the totality, or what he called the "costs of interdependence" by which certain "legitimate national objectives . . . have to be sacrificed to the discipline of the international order."[196]

Drawing on ideas of system theory, the GATT reformers felt that the drift from rules was contagious and perpetuated by imitation. As Tumlir put it, "Once the rules constituting the international order are seen as an obstacle to growth, the order becomes hard to defend. And it ends when the leading country itself begins to claim exceptions from the rules it has induced others to accept."[197] Despite the ever-increasing volume of global trade—which one might see generically as a sign of integration—the deviations from the legal norm had left the world order in "an advanced state of disintegration."[198]

Tumlir arrived at his solution through a scale shift. He adopted Böhm's call from the 1930s for a decisionistic "choice" of an "economic constitution" but took the step, which the German lawyer had not done, of transposing this method to the international scale.[199] In an admiring essay, Tumlir noted the scarcity of the German jurist's references to "the international matrix" and insisted that "an economic constitution is not complete without a theory of foreign economic policy and the legal control of it."[200] He proposed taking Böhm's thought in two directions of practical application. The first was to develop "a theory (and binding articulation) of private rights with respect to foreign transactions." This resonates with this narrative's earlier discussions regarding the creation of private international law as a global domain defensible regardless of national jurisdiction. International investment law and the idea of a new *lex mercatoria* can be placed in this realm. The second direction was to develop "a theory of adequate anchoring in domestic law of the international agreements and policy rules established by economic diplomacy."[201] Here Tumlir introduced what would be his lasting contribution to the institutional design of Geneva School neoliberalism: using national courts and constitutions as the means by which capital rights are locked into domestic legal systems.[202]

Like all neoliberals, Tumlir recognized that for the market to exert its salutary discipline, it needed an extra-economic framework. "The international system of trade and payments as such cannot exercise discipline over sovereign governments in the sense of compelling them to conform in their actions to the system's rules."[203] Recall here Röpke's scoffing at the "juridicism" that implied that nations would follow codes set at an international level and litigated at the Hague, the UN, or elsewhere. Tumlir's solution was different and more radical—law would not be conducted between nations but within nations, not at the border but "beyond the border," as it would become known. The system depended ultimately not on an international effort but on an "active *national* effort to conform to it and so uphold it."[204] Because "the present crisis [was] not economic . . . but political," the judiciary was a means of eluding the interference of democratically elected entities. "The courts are the agency which can bring the internationally-agreed rules to bear on legislative decisions," he wrote.[205] Domestic courts, not international courts, would enforce world economic law. Courts offered the necessary wedge and the solution to the "constitutional breach" they themselves had allowed to occur.[206]

In looking for a way to theorize a restored order, Tumlir looked in a place that superficially seems curious: Hayek's idea of stratified rules of conduct. Hayek had described a tiered system with made rules as a thin line of deliberate design resting atop the grown rules of tradition and the physiological impulses of instinct. Tumlir described the need to design rules at a series of scales "between national, regional and international systems" as a "deliberate application of Hayek's insight concerning the stratification of order."[207] The essay he cited was one of Hayek's more obscure and dealt with cybernetic questions most directly.

It was typical in its isomorphism, beginning with the statement "It does not matter . . . whether the individual members which make up the groups are animals or men" and adding in a footnote "or even whether they are living organisms or perhaps some sort of reduplicating mechanical structures."[208]

By his own testimony, Tumlir was also influenced by the text explored above, an extract from the end of the *Law, Legislation and Liberty* trilogy, which Hayek delivered as a speech in Hong Kong. In June 1979, before he wrote his most important synthetic texts on international order, Tumlir wrote to Hayek about the "marvelous ending of your third volume," which had changed his "views on a number of issues." "It is difficult to imagine," he wrote, "that anyone in this century or the next fifty years could provide a deeper foundation for a theory of justice and liberal order."[209] Tumlir signaled his acceptance of the cybernetic undertones in Hayek when he asserted that "an economy, national politics under a constitution and the international economic order can all be considered homeostatic self-equilibrating systems."[210] To Tumlir, Hayek's attention to the problems of verticality and federal forms above the nations complemented the ordoliberal focus on horizontality within the nation.[211]

Tumlir was not alone in his repurposing of Hayek's theories. Petersmann also cited Hayek's work on stratification of rules of conduct to argue that "principles and rules are designed to influence individual behavior and to promote 'spontaneous order' or deliberately created 'directed orders' so as to enable economic agents to form reasonably correct expectations regarding the future behavior of individuals (including government officials) in the economic sphere."[212] His own definition of the global economy adhered strongly to cybernetic metaphors. "A far-reaching international division of labor among billions of people is possible only by relying, to a large extent, on the informations [*sic*] conveyed by spontaneous market prices (as a cybernetic feedback mechanism) and on the free efforts of millions of people guided by general framework rules of private and public national and international law."[213] He proposed Hayek's idea of a vertical hierarchy of legal layers as reflecting both the actual historical forms of economic order, especially after the Second World War, and a normative, aspirational order.[214] It is striking that at the turn of the 1980s, before the role of cybernetics in Hayek's thought had even been acknowledged by scholars, Hayek and the GATT legal experts were writing from a shared perspective on hierarchical systems of communication and conduct. In the work of the neoliberal experts in Geneva, the multitiered metaphor that Hayek used for cognition was scaled up to rethink world economic order.

Yet how could these rather abstract Hayekian concepts be operationalized? How could the feedback mechanism between national and international systems be secured? The template adopted by the GATT reformers was the European model of multilevel governance and the "economic constitution" described in Chapter 6, as articulated by Mestmäcker.[215] Tumlir contrasted the "weakness" of the GATT in providing an "authoritative interpretation of its rules" to the "radical" solution of the EEC in creating a "uniform European law." Crucial was that "the common European law overrides the national law of member states."[216] Conceptually, he wrote, "this is the strongest possible form of implementing a supranational order. Its rules are genuine law, fully integrated into municipal law of member States, interpreted by a single authority, and creating enforceable private claims on each member State to comply with its treaty commitments."[217] What was special about European law was that it was, in the legal jargon, "directly effective" in nation-states. That meant that individual citizens—and "legal persons" (a category that crucially included corporations)—could appeal to European law within their domestic courts; the fact that "the common European law overrides the national law of member states" and that national courts enforced European Community law made it "the most radical" approach to the problem of inter-state order.[218] For Tumlir, the built-in capacity of the European Community in its ideal form to enforce smoothness of the transmission of price signals across the levels of the individual, the national, and the supranational made it "a nearly perfect example of an intermediate order in the Hayekian sense."[219]

For Tumlir, Petersmann, and others in the influential cohort of the drafters of the WTO, the goal was to scale up the "European idea" of neoliberal constitutionalism from the continent to the world economy, making the WTO into a "trade constitution" in which the Dispute Settlement Body and the Appellate Body would act as equivalents of the European Court of Justice.[220] Consistent with the development of Geneva School neoliberalism, their idea joined the thinking of Böhm and Hayek, bringing neoliberal decisionism and a vision of the strong legal enforcer to the Hayekian cybernetic construct of stratified, multilevel order. Inspired by their concern about the "degeneration" of the world trade order effected by the NIEO and its potentially contagious effects, the GATT reformers sought to fulfill the spirit of Hayek's vision by calibrating a stratified order for rules of just conduct in which prices as well as laws and rights would act as "signals and incentives for adjustment."[221]

Although Tumlir died suddenly of a heart attack in 1985 and was not alive to see some of his ideas bear fruit, his intellectual partner Petersmann was one of the leading figures promoting the idea of "constitutionalizing" the world economy in the discipline of international economic law that he had helped create, pushing precisely the issues that Tumlir identified at the turn of the 1980s.[222] The WTO that came into being in the mid-1990s was not exactly as the reformers envisioned. Nonetheless, by allowing some directly effective rights (in the case of intellectual property) and moving from enforcing the "at-the-border" issues of GATT to "beyond-the-border" issues including services, intellectual property rights, and labor, environmental, and health standards, it did fulfill some of the normative desiderata of the vertical stratified order.[223] The story told in these pages cannot substitute for reconstructing the scrum of negotiation and bargaining that led to the creation of the WTO in 1995. The road to the WTO was a twisting one of diplomacy, political economy, and power politics, with the United States, above all, as the most important player.[224] Yet often lost in the description of the WTO as a tool of American power politics or a space for disempowered negotiation by developing countries is a sense of the animating ideas behind the enterprise itself. What we recover in the writings of the Hayekians at the GATT is a genealogy of thought that linked the neoliberal world economic imaginary from the 1920s to the 1990s. For my narrative it offers the last episode of the twentieth-century neoliberal search for an institutional fix in a world they saw as always threatened by spasms of democracy and the destructive belief that global rules could be remade to bend toward social justice.

❋ ❋ ❋

If the idea of "one world" had a moment at the end of the Second World War, it had a decade in the 1970s. Visions and models of the world economy exploded in expert circles and public culture. The "blue marble" photograph of the whole earth from outer space, first available in 1968, was a symbol of the first Earth Day in 1970 and eventually became one of the most reproduced images of all time.[225] In a 1965 Geneva speech, the U.S. ambassador to the United Nations, Adlai Stevenson, coined a metaphor that would echo through the following decade. He envisioned earth's inhabitants as "passengers on a little space ship, dependent on its vulnerable reserves of air and soil; all committed for our safety to its security and peace; preserved from annihilation only by the care, the work, and I will say, the love we give our fragile craft."[226] The earth was decentered by the "awful majesty of outer space," drawing attention to the precarity of human existence and the need for global cooperation to ensure species survival.[227]

In the 1970s the exact dimensions and capacities of the "fragile craft" were turned into numbers and forecasts by the application of new technologies. As one UN official put it in 1976, "global models need no justification except that they are a natural and inevitable product of the age of the computer."[228] Econometricians threw their weight behind the demands of the G-77 nations for a NIEO in the 1970s. The efforts of global reformists to give scientific authority to projects of international redistribution culminated in the 1980 "North-South" report of the commission led by former West German chancellor Willy Brandt subtitled "A Program for Survival."[229] Through knowledge, plans—and computers—they argued, Spaceship Earth could be made a more socially just vessel.

The rise of planetary consciousness and the endeavor of left-wing economists to collaborate with Global South leaders has begun to find its historians. Less well-known is the story told in these pages of the neoliberal opposition to efforts at NIEO and computer-aided global reformism. This chapter has presented a telling fact: At the very moment when a faction of the world expert community argued that the world economy could be seen, a countermovement of neoliberals insisted that it was invisible and beyond representation. Hayek's Nobel speech about the "pretense of knowledge" and his insistence on the unknowability of the world economy underpinned the efforts of GATT reformers to introduce the "rule of law" at the global level. In so doing, they relied on a vision of the world economy without numbers. The global economy of Spaceship Earth—a domain of volumes, quantities, and disparities—vanished to make way for a Hayekian world economy of signals.

Neoliberals said yes to the nation as long as there was a larger institutional framework that would have what Hayek called the "powers to say no." When nations said no to such supranational arrangements, they became "economic nationalists" and moved beyond the pale. To neoliberals, the internationalist NIEO was an attack on internationalism itself. In the Geneva School view, the nation must recognize the precondition of its placement within global institutions and legal arrangements—and that placement consisted largely of a system of constraints. The NIEO looked like a further turn of the screw to break the bonds of neocolonialism and carry out what Petersmann described as "economic decolonization."[230] It was a monster hatched from neoliberal nightmares: a Jacobinism gone global, a trade unionism gone global, an egalitarianism gone global, derisive of the institutions of private property. *Pacta sunt servanda,* the minimum standard of treatment, the commandments of transnational economic law, were norms without weight, swept aside in the 1974 pronouncements.

At a deeper level the NIEO represented the threat of what Hayek called "constructivism." It did not take seriously enough the importance of instinctive action and the cybernetic insight that order required a neutral and uniform framework of rules for equilibrium to prevail. As mentioned earlier, Hayek saw the real danger not in the rule of the jungle but in the rule of the engineers. The NIEO in this sense was not a spasm of tribalism but a periodic upsurge of rationalist sentiment—not "mau-mauing" the West, as Irving Kristol famously put it, but Saint-Simoning the West.[231] It was hubris and overestimation of the power of the human capacity to redesign international law by fiat. The framework for reflexive action had to be defended against the campaigns of rational action.

One scholar argues that "in the 1970s noises off stage about a New International Economic Order could be faintly heard in Geneva."[232] For Geneva School neoliberals, the sounds were far from faint. Indeed, they defined their counterprogram against the strident demands of the Global South. The danger of Global South mobilization after the end of empire was that the will of the majority could become a new norm, even against the desires of the entrenched powers. The NIEO presented the prospect of a continuation and perhaps a completion of the process that dissolution of European overseas empires had begun: the fear was of the scandalous prospect of a decolonization of international law. The lack of "order" in the NIEO was a problem to be corrected by beating back the encroachment of the UN on international legal practice and the establishment of binding arbitration and adjudication, including the dispute settlement mechanisms that Roessler and Petersmann would help design for the WTO. Against the attempt of the G-77 to use law for their own purposes, the Geneva School fought to reclaim law as an enforcer of private property and competition. The neoliberal program in the 1970s was not about growth, equilibrium, optimum, equality, social justice, or prosperity. It was about the reproduction of an interdependent complex system—the defense of the totality of the world economy against an assault from nationalists that threatened to be as much of a catastrophe as the 1930s.

By the end of the 1970s, there was a Geneva School consensus in the primary international institution devoted to governing trade, the GATT, that "distortions" of the price system were not economic problems but political problems. Beginning in 1977 these were seen as best solved through processes of constitutionalization modeled on the multitiered structure of the European Community. If Hayek "frequently uses machines to illustrate his theory of mind," as one scholar observes, Geneva School neoliberals used Hayek's theory of mind to illustrate world economic order.[233] Hayek's inability or unwillingness to engage with mathematics and statistics kept him off the main road taken by economists inspired by cybernetics and systems analysis.[234] In Geneva School neoliberalism, we find Hayek's influence not in the field of economics but in the field of law. By calibrating human institutions to offer minimal resistance to the movement of the price signal, the world economy could, to use neoliberals' terms, be turned into a model of stratified order with global systems and national and regional subsystems operating in tandem to permit the smooth transmission of information and ensure predictability in commercial transactions. A GATT publication coauthored by Tumlir bore its cybernetic bona fides in 1978 when it called for the "framework of laws and policies which makes the market an effective signaling device and which allows the economy to be guided by those signals."[235] In place of the national autonomy under an NIEO and its demands for redistribution, the Geneva School offered a vision of isonomy—one law for the world economy that did not distinguish between historically poorer and richer populations or countries.

The discussions in Geneva in the 1970s and 1980s revived those of Hayek and Robbins in the 1930s. At both moments, the neoliberal vision of federation held that national independence was acceptable as long as the totality held. "Internationalism" had to prevail with respect to commercial treaties, sanctity of contract, and property. If free nations remained snug within the bonds of world economic order, then decolonization presented no problems. Indeed, the proliferation of formally sovereign territories could even be useful by multiplying the jurisdictions for investment and innovation, leading to pressure on states to create attractive climates for capital. As Tumlir said in his talk given for Hayek's birthday: "The economist sees the world of many sovereign countries as a competitive market for political ideas."[236] "Firms, and also sovereign nations, continue to learn from each other's mistakes," he noted. "This, Hayek suggests, has been the main source of progress of mankind originally structured into groups incomprehensible to each other by language and ritual."[237] What latter-day critics have dubbed the "competition state" was conceived in the neoliberal world as a node of imitative learning in a Hayekian network.[238]

Neoliberals welcomed flux as the necessary condition of a world ruled by the superior, if opaque, wisdom of the market. Order was not a steady state but an adjustment, an often painful process of learning. This was a doctrine of structural adjustment, but more to the point it was one of *perpetual* adjustment. Fine-tuning of the trade rules of the multilevel system was necessary to allow the signals to move smoothly, thus creating the conditions for the supple and eternal contortion of individual economic actors to the messages of the market.

Conclusion

A World of People without a People

If we ask what men most owe to the moral practices of those who are called capitalists the answer is: their very lives.

—FRIEDRICH A. HAYEK, 1989

Two years after the fall of the Berlin Wall and one month short of the official dissolution of the Soviet Union, George H. W. Bush granted a Presidential Medal of Freedom to Wilhelm Röpke's correspondent and the defender of racial segregation in the U.S. South, William F. Buckley. Buckley had "raised the level of political debate in this country," Bush claimed. Without irony, he followed by granting a medal to a civil rights leader. The last medal of the day was offered to the ninety-two-year-old F. A. Hayek. "We honor" Hayek, Bush said, "for a lifetime of looking beyond the horizon. At a time when many saw socialism as ordained by history, he foresaw freedom's triumph. . . . Professor von Hayek is revered by the free people of Central and Eastern Europe as a true visionary, and recognized worldwide as a revolutionary in intellectual and political thought. How magnificent it must be for him to witness his ideas validated before the eyes of the world."[1] In another irony on a day already rich with them, the man who saw his central discovery to be the fundamental unknowability of the world, the future, and the human mind was now being honored for his near-mystical foresight.

The implicit Cold War triumphalism of Bush's speech was also ironic considering how little the Cold War meant to Hayek. In his voluminous writings, the conflict scarcely appears. In one telling exception, he referred in 1979 to American foreign aid, which was "subsidizing on a large scale the socialist experiments of underdeveloped countries" because of a "silly competition with Russia."[2] An even more telling quote comes from his book *The Constitution of Liberty*, where he wrote: "While superficially it may seem that two types of civilization are today competing for the allegiance of the people of the world, the fact is that the promise they offer to the masses, the advantages they hold out to them, are essentially the same."[3] Both sides wanted prosperity and they wanted the state's help to redistribute it. "With the knowledge of possibilities spreading faster than the material benefits," Hayek wrote, "a great part of the people of the world are today dissatisfied as never before and are determined to take what they regard as their rights. As their strength grows, they will become able to extort such a redistribution."[4] Of course, the means the people of the world would use to "extort" redistribution would be democracy, and the way their strength would grow was through decolonization. In the neoliberal century, the Cold War was a sideshow to the main event of the rise of mass enfranchisement and the end of empire.

Hayek dedicated *The Constitution of Liberty* to "the unknown civilization that is growing in America." What were the parameters of the unknown civilization envisaged by the neoliberals described in these pages? It was necessarily global, designed with institutions to contain potential disruptions from the democratically empowered masses. It was a world without empires but with rules set by supranational bodies operating beyond the reach of any electorate. It was a world where the global economy was safely protected from the demands of redistributive equality and social justice. My narrative has traced a line that leads from the end of the Habsburg Empire to the foundation of the World Trade Organization. In the leading neoliberal journal *Ordo*, on the eve of the fall of the Berlin Wall, Röpke's nephew Hans Willgerodt offered a fine summation of the century of ordoglobalism. After citing Hayek and Robbins's writings from the 1930s, he wrote that "as witnesses of the international declaration of bankruptcy by communism," it was time that nation-states realized they had "made too much use of their sovereignty."[5] He wrote that the nineteenth century had achieved "world economic integration" through a "fundamental depoliticization of the economic domain."[6] Quoting Röpke from 1952, he echoed Röpke's sentiment that if "the developing countries are granted by the UN a right to expropriate foreign property, this means, when they make use of such a 'right,' they not only detach themselves from the world-economic market . . . but [take themselves] out of the international legal community of the civilized nations."[7]

For the road to world economic integration, Willgerodt looked both ahead and back: "The path to the liberation of the world market from national regulation and trade barriers can be facilitated by institutions like GATT [General Agreement on Tariffs and Trade]."[8] But he also invoked the old template of Hayek and Mises: Central European empire: "The international rule of law with curbed application of sovereignty is doubtless a difficult and unfamiliar idea for the proponents of centralist national states. The state must first forego authority over its citizens. It must also share its sovereignty downward with federal structures and bind itself upward within an international legal community. No doubt the international order is moving in this direction. It is in this context that the distorted judgment about the order of the long-lived Holy Roman Empire must be taken up again."[9] Such literal nostalgia for empire was rare. Another notable exception, though, was Mont Pèlerin Society (MPS) president Deepak Lal, who, inspired by the U.S. invasion of Afghanistan and Iraq in the name of liberal democracy, wrote a paean to empire in 2004 for its ability to bring order, institute the rule of law, and "quell ethnic conflicts."[10] He began by eulogizing the Habsburg Empire, condemning "the great deterioration of opportunities that has befallen the average citizen of the successor states."[11]

Most neoliberals, however, acknowledged that the era of the nation was irreversible. They dreamt of decolonization without the destructive desire for economic autonomy displayed by the very successor states of East Central Europe that Lal cited. This book has told stories of the neoliberal fix from the 1920s to the 1990s as institutional attempts to defend the world economy against democracy and nationalism. For Hayek, Robbins, and Mises, this meant blueprints for international federations of double government, granting political independence while preserving the reign of competition. For Heilperin, it was in the failed universal code of investment with its attempt to place law beyond the state. For Röpke and Hutt, it was forms of apartheid and weighted franchise. For Mestmäcker, it was the Treaty of Rome and the competition law that followed it. For Tumlir and Petersmann, it was the GATT reformed with a jurisdiction that reached into domestic states.

I have argued that the turn to law was the most important reorientation of German-speaking neoliberalism after the Second World War. What I have called ordoglobalism helped produce an understanding of the European Economic Community (EEC) and later the World Trade Organization (WTO) as apparatuses of juridical power to encase markets beyond democratic accountability even as it sought to create legitimacy through offering direct private rights to citizens beyond the nation. It is notable that, in the shift of ordoliberal attention to the global or international scale, their much-vaunted inclusion of aspects of the distributive state disappears.[12] Institutions like the International Labour Organization (ILO) that made workers' rights and social justice part of their mandate became the enemy again.[13] At the exact same time that Röpke was envisioning a progressive income tax and diffusion of private property within the nation, he was prescribing an international order of constraints.[14] Among other things, this shows again that the "social" in the social market economy might be seen more as a tactically necessary concession to the strength of organized labor and socialist sentiment in postwar West Germany than as an indication of a core aspect of their philosophy.[15] Beyond the nation—where the levers of democracy and organized labor are weaker—the language of the social disappeared, and only the rules remained.

Scholars have given various names to the neoliberal fix. One calls it the "constitutional protection of capitalism."[16] Another calls it the "Hayekian economic constitution" aimed at the "immunization of expanding capitalist markets against egalitarian-interventionist democratic politics."[17] In an influential coinage, Stephen Gill calls it the "New

Constitutionalism" striving to "allow dominant economic forces to be increasingly insulated from democratic rule and popular accountability."[18] As summarized by scholars, this constitutionalization "establishes a worldwide institutional grid that offers transnational capital multiple exit options."[19]

Others have written the history of the neoliberal fix in different ways. One scholar writes of the "nonmajoritarian" models of governance in port authorities and the idea of central bank independence.[20] Still others have seen this strain in the European Central Bank and the governance structure of the European Union.[21] Other scholars have described the creation of an "offshore world" of tax havens through which nations compete to offer the least possible corporate tax, the greatest possible secrecy, and the best incentives for individuals and corporations to flee the clutches of their own redistributive states.[22] Discussions in the 1990s and beyond have been dominated by "locational competition" and the idea of "policy competition."[23] At the root of the neoliberal idea of international order is the notion of so-called competitive federalism, with the possibility of capital following opportunities across borders wherever they arise. In an exploration of neoliberal federalism, one scholar notes that the American Enterprise Institute set up a Federalism Project in 2000, pursuing Buchanan's proposals from the 1990s to preserve "an effective exit option in market relationships."[24] An AEI resident scholar explained the vision of the project: "A world without borders is a world without exits. We need the exits."[25] These imaginaries are far from the borderless world or zero-state society in which neoliberals purportedly believed.[26] What has been described in these pages is much less easy to dismiss as a fanciful delusion. More realistic and, at least in theory, more realizable, is ordoglobalism's vision of a doubled world: divided and encased between imperium and dominium.

My narrative has pointed to a paradox at the heart of Hayek's thought and what I have called Geneva School neoliberalism. On the one hand, the world economy had to be defended against the excesses of democracy. On the other hand, the world economy itself was invisible and beyond reason and representation. Hayek was explicit when he wrote that "the only appropriate word" for the global market, or what he calls "the extended order," is "transcendent." In "its literal meaning," the world market "far surpasses the reach of our understanding, wishes and purposes, and our sense perceptions, and that which incorporates and generates knowledge which no individual brain, or any single organization, could possess or invent."[27] This sacred understanding of the world economy is not limited to Hayek. The word *Ordo,* in the title of the most important journal of neoliberalism, and from which the ordoliberals take their name, comes from medieval theology.[28] Hayek referred to St. Augustine's dialogues as the starting point for the concept of order.[29] In these discussions, Augustine notes that the extraordinary complexity of the universe is literally incomprehensible by any one individual. He describes not only the inevitable sense of powerlessness that humans feel in the face of this larger order but also the distortions that come from our individual and subjective perspective. "The situation," he wrote, "is akin to that of one who, confined to surveying a single section of a mosaic floor, looked at it too closely and then blamed the artisan for being ignorant of order and composition." The apparent disorder of the part is actually an artifact of the limited perspective of the viewer, who "failed to notice the larger mosaic world" that "comes together into the unity of a beautiful portrait." The individual striving for a more synoptic perspective always runs the risk of misidentifying disorder for its opposite—and vice versa. He wrote that "unable to grasp the harmony and interaction of the universe as a whole, and hurt by what is beyond their ken, such people rashly conclude that things are inherently ugly and disorderly."[30]

Augustine suggests a counterintuitive mode of observation. The viewer must guard against being deceived by a part misrepresenting the whole. There is a call here for the potential of inverse observation: that which appears as order may in fact be disorder; and that which appears as disorder may in fact be order. It was a common neoliberal critique of socialism that they failed to see the greater order. As Franz Böhm put it in an article on "the idea of Ordo," socialist thinkers "refused to catch sight of an order at all in the competitive economy, only saw anarchy and chaos, and denied the existence of any laws in it except the law of the jungle."[31] My narrative has shown that Geneva School neoliberalism is less a theory of the market or of economics than of law and the state.

Ordoglobalism can be thought of as a negative theology, contending that the world economy is sublime and ineffable.

Rather than the economism of which they are sometimes accused—in the sense of seeing the economy as machine-like, autonomous, and capable of producing certain desired outcomes—Geneva School neoliberals saw the economy as cosmic, encased in legal and political institutions, and always in an open-ended process of becoming. Hayek scoffed at the use of mathematics in macroeconomics to "impress politicians . . . which is the nearest thing to the practice of magic that occurs among professional economists."[32] He said that he always felt he should have written a critique of Milton Friedman's *Essays in Positive Economics,* "every bit as dangerous as that of Keynes."[33] Unlike the Chicago School, the Geneva School opposed the mathematization of economics and thus foreclosed the possibility of extensive forecasting and modeling of the economy. It rejected both rational expectations and perfect competition and held the claim of determining "efficiency" or "optimal" outcomes to be both quixotic and hubristic. In recent years Petersmann has even laid the blame for the financial crisis of 2008 at the feet of the "efficient markets hypothesis" of the Chicago School that "market prices reflect all relevant information."[34] As represented by Petersmann's own advocacy for the WTO as a "worldwide economic constitution," what I call the Geneva School combined the Austrian emphasis on the limits of knowledge and the global scale with the German ordoliberal emphasis on institutions and the moment of the political decision.[35]

To disavow the existence or visibility of "economies" themselves intentionally makes projects of social justice, equality, or redistribution unthinkable. But it does not make power disappear. It is sometimes claimed that the main sleight of hand for neoliberals is to hide the state, but even a cursory reading of the main theorists shows that a positive vision for the state is everywhere. The main thing the Geneva School neoliberals hide is not the state but asymmetries of power. Indeed, the invocation of complexity and unknowability is a useful practice of government. After the global financial crisis, German finance minister Wolfgang Schäuble said, "We have learned from Friedrich August von Hayek . . . that society and the economy are not machines. Anyone who believes it is possible to acquire comprehensive knowledge enabling him to control events has no knowledge, but only a pretense of knowledge."[36] Contrary to the notion of our present-day knowledge society, scholars have noted, it is professions of ignorance and unknowability that are most helpful in exonerating those putatively responsible for global systemic risk, as, for example, in the world of finance.[37]

Not knowing the totality while knowing the rules needed to maintain it is the essence of the Geneva School variety of neoliberalism described in this book. As the example of Schäuble's subsequent conduct in the Eurozone crisis showed, conceding the unknowability of the economy does not mean a willingness to exercise pragmatic open-mindedness or arrive at new management strategies through negotiation and compromise among diverse constituencies. Instead it meant an even more rigid tendency to default to the principle and the rule. Accepting the economy as an internal limit to government means inflexible adherence to the laws seen as necessary to encase the unknowable economy itself.

Looking back at the century, one notes that it was at points when there was an attempt at comprehensive oversight over the economy that neoliberals mobilized most directly. The two most prominent were in the 1930s and 1970s—both moments at the end of empire. In the 1930s neoliberals mobilized against planning at the national level and the belief that the economy could be seen and directed without a harmonized global framework. In the 1970s they criticized computer-aided reformists who sought to see the world economy as a whole. Scholars have pointed out the irony that it was at the exact moment that the world's majority of nonwhite people claimed legal equality through decolonization that influential branches of social science concluded that the individual did not exist.[38] We have seen something similar here: at the moment of the assertion of autonomy, the response of neoliberals was to assert individualism—but even more so, systemic interdependence that negated the possibility of national or regional action with a logic inconsistent with the dictates of free movement of capital and goods.

In the neoliberal vision of world order, the world economy exercises discipline on individual nations through the perpetual threat of crisis, the flight of investment that punishes expansion in social policy, and speculative attacks on currencies in reaction to increases in government spending. The competition for citizens between states remains a lasting vision. What my narrative has shown is that the declared project of liberating the market was also one of institutional design. As Petersmann put it, "Rules do not enforce themselves."[39] The Hayekian disavowal of design does not transform his proposals into anything other than precisely that. Even understood as an information processor and a self-organizing system, the world economy requires intervention to calibrate the rules. Röpke's demand from 1942 is an enduring one: "If we desire a free market, the framework of conditions, rules and institutions must be all the stronger and more inflexible. Laissez-faire—yes, but within a framework laid down by a permanent and clear-sighted market police in the widest sense of this word."[40] The moral force for an important school of the neoliberal movement came from the commitment to protect the complex and even unknowable interdependence of the global trading system through the identification of—even creation of—a market police cut to the dimensions of the world.

The essence of Geneva School neoliberalism can be summarized in a series of points. These are meant not as commandments but as propositions. Although one could split hairs by pointing to variations, they offer a basic consensus shared by the intellectuals at the core of this book:

1. There is no perfect market because no knowledge is perfect. The sublime status of the economy means that only a "thin layer" of rules can be the objects of human design.
2. Globalism trumps nationalism. Only capitalism is internationalist; socialism is always nationalist.
3. World economic order depends on the protection of dominium (the rule of property) against the overreach of imperium (the rule of states).
4. Consumer sovereignty trumps national sovereignty. The public/private distinction is more important than the foreign/domestic.

5. World law trumps a world state. International institutions should act as mechanisms for protecting and furthering competition without offering spaces for popular claims-making.
6. Democracy is a potential threat to the functioning of the market order. Therefore, safeguards against the disruptive capacity of democracy are necessary.
7. Democracy's danger is its legitimation of demands for redistribution. All world economic problems are rooted in domestic distribution struggles.
8. Laws are grown, not made. Adjudication by judges and scholars is preferable to legislation created by parliaments.
9. Isonomy (same law) trumps autonomy (own law). Humans follow rules by nature. Therefore, rules-as-regularities must be protected by rules-as-regulation.
10. Law must ensure predictability as a guide to future human action. Specifically, it must protect the role of prices in transmitting knowledge about the future.
11. Rules create the conditions for global feedback mechanisms of human action and the framework for the spontaneous order of the market.
12. Humans respond to knowledge, much of it unconscious. Central to that knowledge is the prohibition, the rule that says no. Thus, the role of international institutions is primarily negative.
13. Integration is also primarily negative, devoted to the removal of barriers between territories. Yet the project of negative integration is itself an active and ongoing undertaking. Institutions are required to keep this process functioning smoothly.
14. Trade over borders must be enshrined in legal code and is required for the coalescence of the overall order.
15. Integration is not the creation of something new but the restoration of something lost.

This book has told the story of the emergence of neoliberalism along the fault line of Global North and Global South through the genealogy of the Geneva School, whose solution to the end of empire was to promulgate one law for the world economy. Reflecting back as an elderly man in 1984 on the founding of the MPS, Hayek did not use the high-flown language of foresight that Bush would in granting him the Medal of Freedom. Instead he said that his goal in 1947 had been "to form an international association" to discuss "the problems of constitutional constraints on government."[41] In the metaphor to which he frequently returned, the goal was to tie the Ulysses of the democratic postcolonial state to the mast of the world economy through frameworks of government and law.

SEATTLE AND THE FIX FROM BELOW

It is a great irony that ordoglobalism entered a crisis at nearly the precise moment of its most significant victory. The transformation of the GATT into the WTO was the crowning moment in the twentieth century for the Geneva School. This was true despite the fact that the creation of the institution was the outcome, not of their superior intellectual vision or powers of political persuasion, but of the brute economic interests of the world's leading power, the United States. Competition from emerging economies in its traditionally strong sectors of manufacturing, and a fear that the U.S. advantage in entertainment, pharmaceuticals, and software would be bootlegged and imitated away, led the United States to cajole, pressure, and intimidate the world's countries to agree to an arrangement that clearly favored the hegemon.[42] Yet whatever the conditions were for the realization of the WTO, Geneva School neoliberals could rightly celebrate having put their stamp on the details of its structure. In the ways outlined in these pages, the world trading system under the WTO scaled up the rules and institutions governing Europe to the global scale.

Six months before 123 nations signed the agreement to create the WTO, its future director, Peter Sutherland, gave credence to this claim when he delivered the Third Hayek Memorial Lecture at the Institute of Economic Affairs in London. The drafters of the WTO, he said, "drew on two of Hayek's key insights—the role of the price system in conveying information and the importance of the rule of law."[43] Sutherland was the perfect spokesperson for the Hayekian message. An

Irishman trained as a lawyer, he took the position as European competition commissioner from 1984 to 1988 because he saw that competition law was the most powerful tool available for federal European integration. His activism earned him the nickname "the sheriff" from Jacques Delors, because he used competition law aggressively to liberalize trade within the European Community and bring individual nations to the European Court of Justice.[44] One scholar calls him the "embodiment of neoliberal ideas in the European Commission" as he used the European Court of Justice to end state funding of national industries and ramp up competition.[45]

Hayek's normative vision of the rule of law contained the features of a means of enforcement, judicial review, and isonomy. Sutherland could point to the Appellate Body as a mechanism of enforcement, the individual trading rights protected for intellectual property under the terms of the WTO Agreement, and the isonomy produced by the subjection of all nations—including those of the Global South—to trade disciplines. Sutherland's invocation of the price system connected to Hayek's belief in the world economy as a giant depository of knowledge to be accessed through the information of price signals. Hayek's argument for free trade and free movement of capital was about tapping the knowledge of the world's inhabitants. As Hayek put it at the end of his 1979 trilogy: "If we are to make use of the distinct factual knowledge of the individuals inhabiting different locations on this world, we must allow them to be told by the impersonal signals of the market how they had best use them in their own as well as in the general interest."[46] The philosophy behind the WTO reflected a Hayekian belief in the organization as the guardian of the cybernetic legal order, ensuring unimpeded transmission of price signals across the strata of nested spaces of regulation.

From this perspective the WTO looked like a triumph, offering the rule of law and calibrating the circuitry of the price mechanism to allow for ever more precise reception of information. Yet even as Hayek praised information of prices, he also conceded that knowledge was dangerous. It could imperil the system. As he put it in *The Constitution of Liberty*, it was the global spread of the "knowledge of possibilities" that required a countermovement to lock in policies of competition and perpetual adjustment. Hayek had made clear since the 1930s that two necessities for global capitalism were the invisibility and the anonymity of the world economy. The WTO transgressed those rules. Indeed, just four years after it began its work, it was the spread of knowledge *about* the organization led to a shutdown engineered from below.[47]

In 1999, massive protests led to the cancellation of the meeting of the WTO in Seattle. In a lecture series devoted to Jan Tumlir, Sutherland called Seattle a "watershed for the institution" that created "a fundamental deficit in effective political support for the WTO system." "Seattle created a generation and a legion of WTO-haters," he said, "and they have votes."[48] Martin Wolf noted in the same lecture series, "As decision-makers transformed the size, economic scope, impact and legal potency of the trading system, they also increased its political visibility. What had previously been the play thing of a limited group of highly knowledgeable policy-makers and technocrats has become the focus of fierce pressure from a wide range of non-governmental organisations." The old foe of "majoritarianism" returned as people claimed "that the present inter-governmental arrangement is 'undemocratic.'"[49]

Scholars realized only later, some ruefully, that global economic governance may have worked best when it was performed in an ad hoc, backroom manner, through negotiation, with many exit options, rather than through legalization.[50] Making the rules consistent at a global scale was such a necessarily large undertaking that the public could not help but notice. When they did, they asked why so many decisions were being made in their name with so little of their input. The very attempt to depoliticize international economic relations ended up requiring a highly visible project that could not help but make itself the object of political controversy. This was one of the core problems of the neoliberal fix that Mestmäcker was one of the few to see clearly. It was by appealing to Schmitt that he perceived the necessarily political nature of depoliticization and did not fall for the empirically falsifiable idea that simply relegating certain matters to the "rule of law" would somehow raise them permanently above the possibility of popular contestation. To deny the possibility of politics in the WTO in the interest of a notion of the guardians of the constitution of the world economy did not actually banish politics, it merely offered no frame of reference when actions like the Seattle protests did erupt. People will use their voice, it seemed, even—or especially—if no nameplate or microphone is provided.[51]

Some scholars argue that the most enduring challenge for the WTO and other efforts at encasing global markets has been the absence of a demos for the world economy.[52] Yet to look for a demos in the world economy is to pose the question wrong. It is also to commit a category error. As my narrative has shown, liberals and later neoliberals thought of the space of the world economy through the twentieth century as being a space separate from that of representative government. The many variations of the neoliberal fix were designed in the spirit, not of "undoing the demos" per se, but of sequestering and leashing it, penning it into prescribed areas.[53] If the world economy did not have a demos, this was precisely the point. It was a world of people but a world without a people.

Eager to reframe the institution after Seattle, the director-general Mike Moore declared, "We've got to get this fuckin' show back on the road. . . . We've got to rebrand!"[54] The subsequent trade round, still not completed, was dubbed the "Doha Development Round" in what participants later conceded was a blatant act of public relations. The new brand was given another name when Pascal Lamy used the term "the Geneva Consensus" for the first time in 2005 during his successful campaign for director general of the WTO.[55] He was working from his experience as the EU trade commissioner and, true to the spirit of ordoglobalism, contended that "the building of Europe is in fact the most ambitious experiment in supranational governance ever attempted" and that, as "a laboratory," "the European experience . . . offers interesting avenues for the global level."[56] Lamy claimed that the Geneva Consensus, against the Washington Consensus that it putatively replaced, would be dedicated to "humanizing globalization and establishing further justice and equity."[57] Like the IMF, which began to pay lip service to poverty reduction while continuing to focus on the old key issues of cutting public budgets, the WTO sought to add new rhetoric without changing the basic structure of the organization.[58]

Seattle was an existential crisis for ordoglobalism. It brought the sublime world economy down to earth. The prospect of a popular rejection of the encasement of markets has always posed a problem for neoliberal thought. Many critics have noted that the turn to an authoritarian solution always seems close at hand, with Hayek and Friedman's visits to Augusto Pinochet's Chile being exhibit A. Referring to Pinochet, Hayek said he would "prefer a liberal dictator to a democratic government lacking liberalism" and that "it is possible for a dictator to govern in a liberal way"—while qualifying that this should be only a "temporary transitional arrangement."[59] Hayek's statements recalled both Röpke's discussion of "dictatorial democracy" in 1940 and Mises's point in 1927 that Italian "fascism and similar movements aiming at the establishment of dictatorships are full of the best intentions and that their intervention has, for the moment, saved European civilization. The merit that Fascism has thereby won for itself will live on eternally in history."[60] Following the logic of the lesser evil, the suppression of a disruptive force from the left periodically made support for dictators thinkable for some neoliberals. Mises wrote in 1922, "Our whole civilization rests on the fact that men have always succeeded in beating off the attack of the re-distributors."[61]

The leading thinkers of the Geneva School after the assault on the WTO took neither the Pinochet option nor the recourse to a "liberal dictator" in their theorizing. Rather, they turned to the language of Pinochet's most effective opponents: that of human rights. The response of Geneva School neoliberals was one of co-optation and redefinition. With echoes of Philip Cortney's postwar calls for the human right of capital flight, they doubled down on the very language of human rights scorned by Hayek to buttress their project. This book has shown that the recasting of trading rights, market rights, and capital rights as *individual* rights was proposed by the International Chamber of Commerce (ICC) and neoliberals against the United Nations' idea of social and economic rights around 1945, incorporated as the market freedoms and market citizens of the European integration project in the 1950s and 1960s, and scaled up to the WTO in the course of GATT reform in the 1970s and 1980s. After Seattle, Ernst-Ulrich Petersmann became the most visible and vocal spokesperson for yet another renovation of liberalism with human rights at its core. In a flood of publications, he propagated the idea of a normative world economic order built of stratified institutions protecting the individual right to trade and move capital. Thrust into the public eye, the project of neoliberal federalism was reimagined as one of protecting universal human rights.

It is a revealing irony that Petersmann was a critic of the language of rights in the hands of the Global South in the G-77 and advocated rights only when redefined as free movement of capital and goods, especially in the context of European integration. One can track a similarly instrumental change in his tone after Seattle. In the last article he published before the protests—based in part on his consulting for the government of Hong Kong—Petersmann's key term was "competition." Citing Hayek three times, he denounced the absence of competition laws in less developed countries and called for " 'competition advocacy' within the WTO . . . and promoting a 'competition and entrepreneurship culture' in the WTO."[62] His first article after Seattle was framed very differently. It was titled "Time for Mainstreaming Human Rights into WTO Law."[63] Writing as a professor at the Graduate Institute of International Studies in Geneva, he wrote that the "failure of the WTO's ministerial conference at Seattle and the 'Seattle Tea Party' by violent protesters against world trade based on WTO rules, have been described as a 'wake up call' for trade diplomats who need to explain more convincingly the legitimacy and 'human rights functions' of WTO rules to domestic citizens."[64] This statement was presented in the *Journal of International Economic Law*, a publication launched in 1998 in the wake of the apparent victory of the WTO. In the journal's first issue, Petersmann had praised the "constitutional functions" of the WTO in promoting the "international rule of law," including centrally "private intellectual property rights . . . as basic individual rights."[65] His description of Seattle as a "wake up call" just two years later suggests the seriousness of the challenge to the Geneva School imagination.

After Seattle, a term appeared in Petersmann's writings that was previously almost entirely absent: "legitimacy." He responded directly to the protest, saying that "in the now regular street demonstrations at the ministerial conferences of the IMF, the World Bank and WTO, citizens are reminding governments of the need to adjust the state-centered traditional international law and international organizations to their human rights and to the emerging 'right to democracy.' "[66] He effectively agreed with the protesters but went on to interpret their language of human rights in a very particular way. It was truly a scandal, he argued, that UN human rights covenants "offer no effective protection of economic freedoms, property rights and rule of law."[67] Even as he sought to ground WTO in human rights language, he sought to insert economic language into dominant human rights talk. "The traditional disregard in WTO law of human rights is becoming as outdated as the persistent disregard in international human rights instruments for economic liberty and freedom of trade as preconditions for individual welfare."[68]

The agreement that Petersmann had praised in 1997 as a triumph of Hayekian constitutional design was, by 2001, disparaged for the fact that "many national parliaments in WTO member countries ratified the 25,000 pages of the Uruguay Round Agreements within a few hours without proper parliamentary review and transparent discussion."[69] Even though, as he put it, "from a constitutional perspective, the transition from GATT 1947 to the WTO offers an example of a successful 'constitutionalization' of international trade law," it was becoming a failure in practice.[70] The central problem people saw in the WTO was, as other legal scholars see it, "the absence of a legitimate and legitimating purpose."[71] The about-face was fascinating—the very absence of democratic pressures was now being seen as an Achilles' heel of the institution. Democratic legitimacy, it seemed, could not be designed away.

Petersmann's own solution for the legitimacy problem was to ramp up the emphasis on human rights. He claimed human rights as a new frontier for activism: "Following the 'democratic grass-root revolution of 1989,'" he wrote, "economic and legal globalization (including the global integration law of the WTO) offer the possibility for another 'human rights revolution' in favor of non-discriminatory open markets, global competition and more effective protection of human rights."[72] In an idiosyncratic interpretation, he read the string of revolts in the Arab Spring as part of just such a revolutionary demand for business and market rights.[73] Unlike the earlier form of Geneva School neoliberalism, which often saw the individual as a disruptive political actor, the multilevel constitutionalist version opened the possibility of a positive bottom-up political role for individuals. This is an angle often missed in the denunciations of the WTO as a detached distant bureaucracy and by those seeking to track the mutations of the neoliberal world project. Whereas Hayek had called for the "dethronement of politics," the Geneva School of the year 2000 was talking about a reconfiguration of politics, seeing market citizenship and its claims as the way in which the global system could be knit together from the level of the individual to the world. Petersmann wrote after Seattle, "Citizen participation in consultative WTO bodies and other multi-levelled international governance mechanisms could strengthen the legitimacy and political support for the world trading system."[74]

One scholar notes that "unlike most people, a market can function quite well without being loved."[75] But the exact reverse might be true. Many people persist without love, and experience has shown that some attention to the legitimacy of a given order is necessary for it not to descend into chaos and popular revolt. If not loved, the market needs to be accepted. The importance of the "citizen-centered" aspect is often overlooked by scholars who see the neoliberal constitution "solely as a means to impose limits on state authorities."[76] The positive side of the equation exists—it is the right to trade. One critic called this approach an attempt by Petersmann "to hijack, or more appropriately to Hayek, international human rights law."[77] Petersmann was proposing the possibility of a fix from below.

Yet what does the fix from below look like in practice? The Geneva School idea of individuals reinforcing the legitimacy of the governing structures by appealing above their own nations, or to world law within their nations, has been a path taken largely by corporations only. An inability to pay a team of trade lawyers—whose numbers have grown exponentially since the 1990s—ends up being a bar to entering this form of market citizenship. Far from being detached nomothetes above the possibility of capture by special interests, the negotiators of trade agreements like the WTO have close and formal relationships with corporate lobbies. The "private sector advisory process" in the United States, for example, comprised over thirty committees, involving nearly one thousand individuals from the private sector, that met regularly to advise the U.S. trade representative on what they needed from the legal architecture of world trade.[78] The actual existing version of the "bottom-up" legitimation described by

Petersmann included only a select slice of the world economy's market citizens.

As part of their post-Seattle rebranding, the WTO restored the old paintings that had been covered and removed when the GATT first moved into the offices of the International Labour Organization at the Centre William Rappard in the late 1970s. Murals showing heroic workers in acts of labor and leisure once again saw the light of day.[79] In 2012 Petersmann looked at the building himself and asked why nobody in his sixteen years working at the WTO had commented on the two statues at the entrance—allegorical figures of "peace" and "justice."[80] Unmentioned was the fact, which he would have surely known, that the statues were relics of the days of the ILO. The failure of employees or negotiators to remark on the statues was no mystery. WTO's mandate was not to achieve peace or justice but to lock in liberal trade rules to calibrate multilevel polities and allow for perpetual adjustment in response to price signals. For Petersmann's mentor, Hayek, the only permissible form of justice was procedural justice that treated all participants equally regardless of history. When paired with equity as social justice as in the mandate of the ILO—or in Lamy's Geneva Consensus—justice was worse than a non sequitur. Social justice was a teleocratic demand that paved the way to totalitarianism, and an atavistic spasm sending humanity from the extended order and Great Society back to the "tribal society."[81]

Petersmann's selective reading of history was displayed again in his gloss on the cover of a book he published in 2012. The cover featured Mexican painter Diego Rivera's *Calla Lilly Vendor* (1941), depicting a woman bowed under the weight of a mountain of beautiful white flowers. In the text, he called it an icon of "the freedom to sell in the market place."[82] The fact that Rivera was a card-carrying Communist best known for his workerist murals was no obstacle to Petersmann's misrepresentation of Rivera's work to reinforce his own dedication to market rights as the most fundamental of human rights.[83] A more fitting choice was made by Lamy for his book on the Geneva Consensus: one of the newer paintings that decorated the WTO's walls, from the *Danaé World Suite, 2001* by Jean-Claude Prêtre. The painting shows a Mercator projection of the world beneath a grid of crosses and flecks of

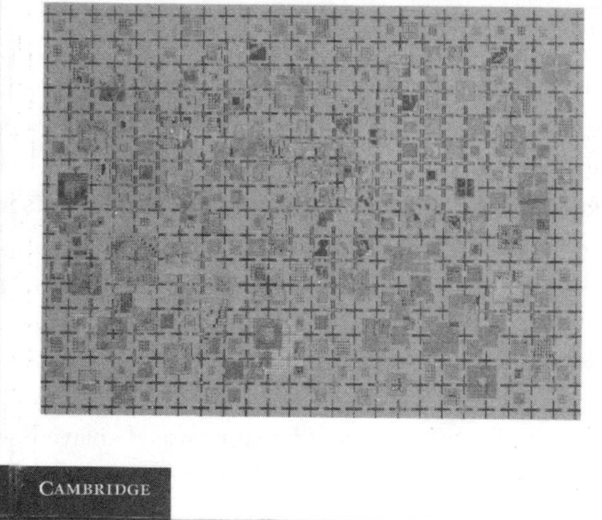

The world at the edges of representation. Pascal Lamy, *The Geneva Consensus: Making Trade Work for All* (Cambridge: Cambridge University Press, 2013). Reprinted by permission of the publisher.

colorful paint. Barely visible underneath are the outlines of the continents. The image suggests something closer to what the institution was built on. Notwithstanding the late conversion to a language of human rights, it is a conception of the world economy at the edges of representation, in a perpetual state of morphing and transformation, encased by a grid of rules.

Had Petersmann looked across the street from the Centre William Rappard past the ten-foot metal barriers and armed guards, in the traffic circle, he would have seen something that would be more difficult than the Rivera painting to transform from labor into trade. Erected in 1937, the year Hayek published his essay "Economics and Knowledge," Robbins his deplanning manifesto, and Lippmann *The Good Society*, the monument commemorated the ILO's founder, Albert Thomas. The base shows images of work: miners picking at a coalface, fishers at sea, farmers tilling and hauling crops. The four figures on top are a skull-capped Asian man carrying a rice sieve, a hooded indigenous man carrying pelts, a man in worker's apron holding pincers, and a black African man with a hoe. Etched into the plinth are words difficult to spin: "Labor exists above all struggles for competition. It is not a commodity." Small protests assemble here. In 2005 a demonstration of protesters from five continents gathered there and a Brazilian woman gave a speech about the "struggle against capitalism." One of the banners suggested the very world against which the neoliberals had organized: "Building a world of solidarity."[84]

The 1990s were the high point of neoliberal globalism as an institution-building project. In the decade's endless globalization talk, "the world economy" was granted a power beyond any single nation. Politicians grew accustomed to deferring to the world economy to justify cuts to welfare benefits and restructuring. It was convenient to have an extranational disciplinarian to which they could gesture apologetically and shrug as they shaved off another condition of the postwar settlement. Blaming the world economy was a sustainable strategy because the disciplinarian was only one of its two political faces. In its inverse incarnation, the world economy was summoned as a cornucopia of affordable consumer goods irrigated by a stream of cheap credit. The perils of this strategy were made clear only in the early 2000s and especially after 2008. When the world economy stopped giving, it was left wearing only the mask of the scapegoat. Voters reacted predictably: by voting against it.

One could argue that Geneva School neoliberals ended up being institutional determinists in spite of themselves. Though often claiming a commitment to "liberalism from below" and the need for what Röpke

Labor is not a commodity. The monument to the founder of the International Labour Organization in a traffic circle facing the World Trade Organization, Geneva, Switzerland. Photo by the author / Quinn Slobodian.

called the humus of cultural values, the most enduring intellectual contribution of these purported "anti-planners" to the twentieth century may have been their blueprints and plans. It may be that Geneva School neoliberals were so busy building crystalline fortresses for the world economy that they failed to heed Mises's advice about reinforcing a mass mentality that would favor global rather than national markets as an absolute good rather than a pragmatic good to be favored or rejected as fortunes changed. They did not plan for the downturn, nor did they ever figure out a way to placate populations cleft by vast gaps of inequality. Luckily for them, the well-being of capitalism does not rely on their interventions, and never had. But if Geneva School neoliberals saw a popular commitment to free-trade globalism as not just one feature of many but the central necessary feature, then they would have reason to worry in the early twenty-first century. These pages have told the story of the long road to the current crisis.

To diagnose a crisis of neoliberalism is not to suggest that economic inequality has ceased to advance. Nor that the application of market solutions to social problems or the calculation of all human value in monetary terms has ceased, nor that we have witnessed a return to a pattern of redistribution or a turn to Keynesian welfare state ideology. The state absorption of private debt and policies of quantitative easing have not reversed the long-standing realities of "private Keynesianism" that exacerbate the gap between the hyperwealthy and the rest.

Yet the legitimacy crises that have plagued the WTO since its creation suggest that ordoglobalism as a distinct strain of neoliberalism may have overreached. If the goal was to fine-tune the rules to prevent disruptive demands for social justice or redistribution, then victory is nowhere in sight. In a late echo of the activism following the 1958 Haberler Report, emerging countries have created global gridlock by demanding that the United States and Europe live up to their own free-trade rhetoric, thereby using the WTO in ways that the United States itself had not anticipated.[85] Other nations have begun rejecting the bilateral investment treaties designed to lock in xenos rights for foreign investors.[86] One recent book writes of "world trade law after neoliberalism."[87] Demands for evenness, sometimes expressed in inclusionary and sometimes in exclusionary ways, continue to roil the political landscape against all attempts to introduce a formal equality that disavows historically determined real inequality.

Neoliberals criticize socialists for their dream of a world economy without losers, but they had their own dream of a world economy without rule breakers and more importantly without idealistic—or, in their opinion, atavistic—alliances of rule breakers who seek to change the system of incentives, obligations, and rewards. In the mid-2010s, the popular referendum in favor of Brexit and the declining popularity of binding trade legislation suggests that even if the intentions of the neoliberals was to "undo the demos," the demos—for better or for worse—is not undone yet.[88]

NOTES

ACKNOWLEDGMENTS

INDEX

Notes

ABBREVIATIONS

CEIP	Carnegie Endowment for International Peace—Centre Européen Records, Rare Book and Manuscript Library, Columbia University Libraries
Davenport Papers	John A. Davenport Papers, Hoover Institution Archives, Stanford University
Haberler Papers	Gottfried Haberler Papers, Harvard University Archives
Hayek Papers	Friedrich A. von Hayek Papers, Hoover Institution Archives, Stanford University
Hayek Papers, Duke	F. A. Hayek Papers, Economists' Papers Archive, Duke University Library
Hutt Papers	William H. Hutt Papers, Hoover Institution Archives, Stanford University
LON	League of Nations Archive, Geneva
Machlup Papers	Fritz Machlup Papers, Hoover Institution Archives, Stanford University
RA	Wilhelm Röpke Archive, Institute for Economic Research, Cologne
Rockefeller Paris records	Rockefeller Foundation records, Rockefeller Archive Center
WWA	Vienna Chamber of Commerce Archive

INTRODUCTION

1. Bill Clinton, Remarks to the World Economic Forum, January 26, 1995, http://www.presidency.ucsb.edu/ws/?pid=51667.
2. Regierungserklärung des Bundeskanzlers Gerhard Schröder (SPD), "Mut zum Frieden und zur Veränderung," March 14, 2003, http://www.documentArchiv.de/brd/2003/rede_schroeder_03-14.html.
3. Quoted in Wolfgang Streeck, *Buying Time: The Delayed Crisis of Democratic Capitalism* (New York: Verso, 2014), 213.
4. Chakravarthi Raghavan, "Trade: The Empire Strikes Back," *SUNS—South North Development Monitor,* September 20, 1999; Michael Hardt and Antonio Negri, *Empire* (Cambridge, MA: Harvard University Press, 2000).
5. See Thomas L. Friedman, *The World Is Flat: A Brief History of the Twenty-First Century* (New York: Farrar, Straus and Giroux, 2005).
6. Rajesh Venugopal, "Neoliberalism as Concept," *Economy and Society* 44, no. 2 (2015): 181. See also Bill Dunn, "Against Neoliberalism as a Concept," *Capital and Class,* November 23, 2016, https://doi.org/10.1177/0309816816678583.
7. Jonathan D. Ostry, Prakash Loungani, and Davide Furceri, "Neoliberalism: Oversold?," *Finance and Development,* June 2016, 38–41.
8. Ben Geier, "Even the IMF Now Admits Neoliberalism Has Failed," *Fortune,* June 3, 2016, http://fortune.com/2016/06/03/imf-neoliberalism-failing/.
9. See Joseph E. Stiglitz, *Globalization and Its Discontents* (New York: W. W. Norton, 2003).
10. Andrew Gamble, "The Last Utopia," *New Left Review,* no. 236 (July–August 1999): 117–127. See also Alexander E. Kentikelenis, Thomas H. Stubbs, and Lawrence P. King, "IMF Conditionality and Development Policy Space, 1985–2014," *Review of International Political Economy* 23 (2016): 543–582.
11. Shawn Donnan, "IMF Economists Put 'Neoliberalism' under the Spotlight," *Financial Times,* May 26, 2016. The *Financial Times* followed up with an editorial denouncing neoliberalism as "the catch-all criticism of unthinking radicals who lack the skills of empirical argument." "A Misplaced Mea Culpa for Neoliberalism," *Financial Times,* May 30, 2016. Aditya Chakrabortty, "You're Witnessing the Death of Neoliberalism—from Within," *Guardian,* May 31, 2016.
12. Daniel Stedman Jones, *Masters of the Universe: Hayek, Friedman, and the Birth of Neoliberal Politics* (Princeton, NJ: Princeton University Press, 2012), 16; Keith Tribe, "Liberalism and Neoliberalism in Britain, 1930–1980," in *The Road from Mont Pèlerin: The Making of the Neoliberal Thought Collective,* ed. Philip Mirowski and Dieter Plehwe (Cambridge, MA: Harvard University Press, 2009), 90; Sam Bowman, "Coming Out as Neoliberals," *Adam Smith Institute Blog,* October 11, 2016, https://www.adamsmith.org/blog/coming-out-as-neoliberals.
13. Lars Feld quoted in Bert Losse, "Economic Neoliberalism: Philosophy of Freedom," *Handelsblatt Global,* June 10, 2017.

14. Philip Mirowski, "The Political Movement That Dared Not Speak Its Own Name: The Neoliberal Thought Collective under Erasure," Institute for New Economic Thinking Working Paper no. 23 (September 2014), 6.
15. Oliver Marc Hartwich, "Neoliberalism: The Genesis of a Political Swearword," CIS Occasional Paper 114 (2009), http://www.cis.org.au/app/uploads/2015/07/op114.pdf; Taylor C. Boas and Jordan Gans-Morse, "Neoliberalism: From New Liberal Philosophy to Anti-Liberal Slogan," *Studies in Comparative International Development* 44, no. 2 (June 2009): 137–161.
16. For pioneering studies, see Richard Cockett, *Thinking the Unthinkable: Think-Tanks and the Economic Counter-Revolution, 1931–1983* (London: Harper Collins, 1994); Dieter Haselbach, *Autoritärer Liberalismus und Soziale Marktwirtschaft: Gesellschaft und Politik im Ordoliberalismus* (Baden-Baden: Nomos Verlagsgesellschaft, 1991); Bernhard Walpen, *Die offenen Feinde und ihre Gesellschaft: Eine hegemonietheoretische Studie zur Mont Pelerin Society* (Hamburg: VSA-Verlag, 2004); Mirowski and Plehwe, *The Road from Mont Pèlerin.* For more recent work, see Angus Burgin, *The Great Persuasion: Reinventing Free Markets since the Depression* (Cambridge, MA: Harvard University Press, 2012); Pierre Dardot and Christian Laval, *The New Way of the World: On Neoliberal Society* (New York: Verso, 2014); William Davies, *The Limits of Neoliberalism: Authority, Sovereignty and the Logic of Competition* (Los Angeles: Sage, 2014); Kim Phillips-Fein, *Invisible Hands: The Making of the Conservative Movement from the New Deal to Reagan* (New York: W. W. Norton, 2009); Ralf Ptak, *Vom Ordoliberalismus zur sozialen Marktwirtschaft: Stationen des Neoliberalismus in Deutschland* (Opladen: Leske und Budrich, 2004); Philip Plickert, *Wandlungen des Neoliberalismus: Eine Studie zu Entwicklung und Ausstrahlung der "Mont Pelerin Society"* (Stuttgart: Lucius und Lucius, 2008); Ben Jackson, "Freedom, the Common Good, and the Rule of Law: Lippmann and Hayek on Economic Planning," *Journal of the History of Ideas* 73, no. 1 (2012): 47–68; Jean Solchany, *Wilhelm Röpke, l'autre Hayek: Aux origines du néolibéralisme* (Paris: Sorbonne, 2015); Stedman Jones, *Masters of the Universe;* Philip Mirowski, *Never Let a Serious Crisis Go to Waste: How Neoliberalism Survived the Financial Meltdown* (New York: Verso, 2013); Milene Wegmann, *Früher Neoliberalismus und Europäische Integration: Interdependenz der nationalen, supranationalen und internationalen Ordnung von Wirtschaft und Gesellschaft (1932–1965)* (Baden-Baden: Nomos, 2002). For studies more focused on textual analysis of neoliberal scholars, see Andrew Gamble, *Hayek: The Iron Cage of Liberty* (London: Wiley, 1996); Nils Goldschmidt and Jan-Otmar Hesse, "Eucken, Hayek, and the Road to Serfdom," *Freiburg Discussion Papers on Constitutional Economics* (2012); John Gray, *Hayek on Liberty* (New York: Routledge, 1984); Stefan Kolev, "Neoliberale Leitideen zum Staat: Die Rolle des Staates in der Wirtschaftspolitik im Werk von Walter Eucken, Friedrich August von Hayek, Ludwig von Mises und Wilhelm Ropke" (PhD diss., Hamburg University, 2011); Raymond Plant, *The Neoliberal State* (Oxford: Oxford University Press, 2010); Jeremy Shearmur, *Hayek and After: Hayekian Liberalism as a Research Programme* (London: Routledge,

1996); Manuel Wörsdörfer, "Die normativen und wirtschaftsethischen Grundlagen des Ordoliberalismus" (PhD diss., Goethe Universität Frankfurt, 2011). For leading intellectual biographies, see Bruce Caldwell, *Hayek's Challenge: An Intellectual Biography of F.A. Hayek* (Chicago: University of Chicago Press, 2004); Hans Jörg Hennecke, *Friedrich August von Hayek: Die Tradition der Freiheit* (Düsseldorf: Wirtschaft und Finanzen, 2000); Hans Jörg Hennecke, *Wilhelm Röpke: Ein Leben in der Brändung* (Stuttgart: Schäffer-Poeschel Verlag, 2005); Helge Peukert, *Das sozialökonomische Werk Wilhelm Röpkes,* 2 vols. (New York: Peter Lang, 1992).

17. See the discussion in Chapter 2. See also Serge Audier, *Le colloque Lippmann: Aux origines du néo-libéralisme, précédé de Penser le néo-libéralisme,* 2nd ed. (Paris: Éditions Le Bord de l'eau, 2012); Arnaud Brennetot, "The Geographical and Ethical Origins of Neoliberalism: The Walter Lippmann Colloquium and the Foundations of a New Geopolitical Order," *Political Geography,* no. 49 (2015): 30–39; Hagen Schulz-Forberg, "Laying the Groundwork: The Semantics of Neoliberalism in the 1930s," in *Re-inventing Western Civilisation: Transnational Reconstructions of liberalism in Europe in the Twentieth Century,* ed. Hagen Schulz-Forberg and Niklas Olsen, 13–40 (Newcastle upon Tyne: Cambridge Scholars, 2014).
18. Mitchell Dean, "Rethinking Neoliberalism," *Journal of Sociology* 50, no. 2 (2012): 2.
19. On development economics and monetary governance, see Dieter Plehwe, "The Origins of the Neoliberal Economic Development Discourse," in Mirowski and Plehwe, *The Road from Mont Pèlerin;* Matthias Schmelzer, *Freiheit für Wechselkurse und Kapital: Die Ursprünge neoliberaler Währungspolitik und die Mont Pèlerin Society* (Marburg: Metropolis, 2010). For works that do discuss international order, see Jennifer Bair, "Taking Aim at the New International Economic Order," in Mirowski and Plehwe, *The Road from Mont Pèlerin;* Jorg Spieker, "F.A. Hayek and the Reinvention of Liberal Internationalism," *International History Review* 36, no. 5 (2014): 1–24; Or Rosenboim, "Barbara Wootton, Friedrich Hayek and the Debate on Democratic Federalism in the 1940s," *International History Review* 36, no. 5 (2014): 894–918; Fabio Masini, "Designing the Institutions of International Liberalism: Some Contributions from the Interwar Period," *Constitutional Political Economy* 23, no. 1 (2012): 45–65; Jeffrey M. Chwieroth, *Capital Ideas: The IMF and the Rise of Financial Liberalization* (Princeton, NJ: Princeton University Press, 2010); Wegmann, *Früher Neoliberalismus.* For the most comprehensive overview of neoliberal ideas of international order, see Razeen Sally, *Classical Liberalism and International Economic Order: Studies in Theory and Intellectual History* (New York: Routledge, 1998).
20. For pioneering studies of this perspective, see Stephen Gill, "Economic Globalization and the Internationalization of Authority: Limits and Contradictions," *Geoforum* 23, no. 2 (1992): 269–283; Gill, "New Constitutionalism, Democratisation and Global Political Economy," *Pacifica Review: Peace, Security and Global Change* 10, no. 1 (1998): 23–38. For other key studies, see Sarah Babb, *Behind the Development Banks: Washington Politics, World Poverty, and the Wealth of Nations*

(Chicago: University of Chicago Press, 2009); Nitsan Chorev, "The Institutional Project of Neo-Liberal Globalism: The Case of the WTO," *Theory and Society* 34, no. 3 (2005): 317–355; A. Claire Cutler, *Private Power and Global Authority: Transnational Merchant Law in the Global Political Economy* (New York: Cambridge University Press, 2003); John Gray, *False Dawn: The Delusions of Global Capitalism* (New York: New Press, 1998); David J. Gerber, "Constitutionalizing the Economy: German Neoliberalism, Competition Law and the 'New' Europe," *American Journal of Comparative Law* 42, no. 1 (Winter 1994): 25–84; Christian Joerges, "What Is Left of the European Economic Constitution? A Melancholic Eulogy," *European Law Review* 30 (August 2005): 461–489; Adam Harmes, "Neoliberalism and Multilevel Governance," *Review of International Political Economy* 13, no. 5 (2006): 725–749; Alasdair Roberts, *The Logic of Discipline: Global Capitalism and the Architecture of Government* (New York: Oxford University Press, 2011); Fritz W. Scharpf, "Economic Integration, Democracy and the Welfare State," *Journal of European Public Policy* 4, no. 1 (March 1997): 18–36; David Schneiderman, *Constitutionalizing Economic Globalization: Investment Rules and Democracy's Promise* (New York: Cambridge University Press, 2008); M. Sornarajah, *The International Law on Foreign Investment,* 3rd ed. (New York: Cambridge University Press, 2010); Streeck, *Buying Time.*

21. See Keller Easterling, *Extrastatecraft: The Power of Infrastructure Space* (New York: Verso, 2014); Patrick Neveling, "Export Processing Zones, Special Economic Zones and the Long March of Capitalist Development Policies during the Cold War," in *Decolonization and the Cold War: Negotiating Independence,* ed. Leslie James and Elisabeth Leake, 63–84 (London: Bloomsbury, 2015); Ronen Palan, *The Offshore World: Sovereign Markets, Virtual Places, and Nomad Millionaires* (Ithaca, NY: Cornell University Press, 2003).
22. See, for example, Gill, "New Constitutionalism," 23; Werner Bonefeld, "Authoritarian Liberalism: From Schmitt via Ordoliberalism to the Euro," *Critical Sociology* (2016): 13.
23. Bernard H. Moss, *Monetary Union in Crisis: The European Union as a Neo-Liberal Construction* (New York: Palgrave Macmillan, 2005), 13; Owen Worth, "Reviving Hayek's Dream," *Globalizations* 14, no. 1 (2017): 105.
24. Johanna Bockman, "Socialism and the Embedded Economy," *Theory and Society* 45, no. 5 (October 2016): 386.
25. See, for example, Michael C. Dreiling and Derek Darves, *Agents of Neoliberal Globalization: Corporate Networks, State Structures, and Trade Policy* (New York: Cambridge University Press, 2016), 14.
26. For a related point, see Melinda Cooper and Martijn Konings, "Contingency and Foundation: Rethinking Money, Debt, and Finance after the Crisis," *South Atlantic Quarterly* 114, no. 2 (April 2015): 242.
27. Jamie Peck, "Neoliberalizing States: Thin Policies / Hard Outcomes," *Progress in Human Geography* 25, no. 3 (2001): 447; emphasis in the original. The work on Polanyi has yielded exceptional insights of its own. See, for instance, Fred L. Block

and Margaret R. Somers, *The Power of Market Fundamentalism: Karl Polanyi's Critique* (Cambridge, MA: Harvard University Press, 2014); Mark Blyth, *Great Transformations: Economic Ideas and Institutional Change in the Twentieth Century* (New York: Cambridge University Press, 2002); Gareth Dale, *Karl Polanyi: The Limits of the Market* (Malden, MA: Polity Press, 2010); Kari Polanyi-Levitt, *From the Great Transformation to the Great Financialization: On Karl Polanyi and Other Essays* (London: Zed, 2013).

28. See, among others, Cornel Ban, *Ruling Ideas: How Global Neoliberalism Goes Local* (Oxford: Oxford University Press, 2016); Dorothee Bohle and Bela Greskovits, "Neoliberalism, Embedded Neoliberalism and Neocorporatism: Towards Transnational Capitalism in Central-Eastern Europe," *West European Politics* 30, no. 3 (2007): 443–466; Damien Cahill, *The End of Laissez-Faire? On the Durability of Embedded Neoliberalism* (Cheltenham, UK: Edward Elgar, 2014).
29. Andrea Migone, "Embedded Markets: A Dialogue between F.A. Hayek and Karl Polanyi," *Review of Austrian Economics* 24 (2011): 357.
30. Ibid., 367.
31. Joost Pauwelyn, "The Transformation of World Trade," *Michigan Law Review* 104, no. 1 (October 2005): 1–65; Arie Reich, "From Diplomacy to Law: The Juridicization of International Trade Relations," *Northwestern Journal of International Law and Business* 17, no. 1 (Winter 1997): 775–849.
32. Hans Willgerodt, "Der Neoliberalismus—Entstehung, Kampfbegriff und Meinungsstreit," *Ordo* 57 (2006): 54–55.
33. Ibid., 69.
34. John Foster, "From Simplistic to Complex Systems in Economics," *Cambridge Journal of Economics* 29 (2005): 880.
35. F. A. Hayek, "The Economy, Science and Politics (1962)," in *New Studies in Philosophy, Politics, Economics and the History of Ideas*, ed. F. A. Hayek (Chicago: University of Chicago Press, 1978), 263.
36. F. A. Hayek, *The Constitution of Liberty* (1960) (Chicago: University of Chicago Press, 2011). There are clear resonances here with the project of "constitutional economics" associated with Mont Pèlerin Society members James M. Buchanan and Gordon Tullock. For an overview by a scholar who traveled between the worlds of ordoliberalism and Virginia School public choice, see Viktor Vanberg, *The Constitution of Markets: Essays in Political Economy* (New York: Routledge, 2001). The engagement is multigenerational. Vanberg's son, Georg, a political scientist, is currently president of the Public Choice Society.
37. Oliver Kessler, "Sleeping with the Enemy? On Hayek, Constructivist Thought, and the Current Economic Crisis," *Review of International Studies* 38, no. 2 (2012): 290.
38. F. A. Hayek, *The Political Order of a Free People*, vol. 3 of *Law, Legislation and Liberty* (Chicago: University of Chicago Press, 1979), 41.
39. The term has the advantage of originating with neoliberal thinkers themselves. In the same piece, Rüstow argued for what he called "liberal interventionism." See Alexander Rüstow, "Freie Wirtschaft—starker Staat: Die staatspolitischen

Voraussetzungen des wirtschaftlichen Liberalismus," *Schriften des Vereins für Sozialpolitik* 187 (1932). For use by scholars, see Werner Bonefeld, *The Strong State and the Free Economy* (London: Rowman & Littlefield, 2017); Andrew Gamble, "The Free Economy and the Strong State: The Rise of the Social Market Economy," *Socialist Register* 16 (1979): 1–25; Ben Jackson, "At the Origins of Neo-Liberalism: The Free Economy and the Strong State, 1930–1947," *Historical Journal* 53, no. 1 (2010): 129–151; Mitchell Dean, "Free Economy, Strong State," in *Neoliberalism beyond the Free Market,* ed. Damien Cahill, Lindy Edwards, and Frank Stilwell, 69–89 (Northampton, MA: Edward Elgar, 2012).

40. Kolev, "Neoliberale Leitideen zum Staat," 23.
41. It is worth noting the difference in my definition, which goes beyond simply identifying site of academic employment. E. U. Petersmann, "International Economic Theory and International Economic Law: On the Tasks of a Legal Theory of International Economic Order," in *The Structure and Process of International Law: Essays in Legal Philosophy Doctrine and Theory,* ed. R. St. J. Macdonald and Douglas M. Johnston (The Hague: Martinus Nijhoff, 1983), 237.
42. See Steven M. Teles, *The Rise of the Conservative Legal Movement: The Battle for Control of the Law* (Princeton, NJ: Princeton University Press, 2008).
43. It is notable, for example, that the discussion of federalism in the Virginia School around Buchanan refers largely to relations between U.S. states, whereas the thinkers I profile in my narrative speak of federalism in terms of relations between nations.
44. Carl Schmitt, *The* Nomos *of the Earth in the International Law of the* Jus Publicum Europaeum (New York: Telos Press, 2003), 235.
45. Wilhelm Röpke, "Wirtschaftssystem und internationale Ordnung: Prolegomena," *Ordo* 4 (1951): 277. For a reflection on the modern order as based on a return of the division between dominium and imperium, see Janet McLean, "The Transnational Corporation in History: Lessons for Today?," *Indiana Law Journal* 79 (2003): 373–376.
46. Wilhelm Röpke, *Economic Order and International Law* (Leiden: A. W. Sijthoff, 1955), 250.
47. Ibid., 210–214.
48. See Stefan Kolev, "F. A. Hayek as an Ordo-Liberal," Hamburg Institute of International Economics Research Paper 5-1 (2010); Viktor J. Vanberg, "Friedrich A. Hayek und die Freiburger Schule," *Ordo* 54 (2003): 3–20. For dissenting views, see Keith Tribe, *Strategies of Economic Order: German Economic Discourse, 1750–1950* (New York: Cambridge University Press, 1995), 208; Manuel Wörsdörfer, "Von Hayek and Ordoliberalism on Justice," *Journal of the History of Economic Thought* 35, no. 3 (2013): 309.
49. Wolfgang Streeck makes a similar argument: "Today's post-democratic, or better perhaps: a-democratic, Hayekian capitalism, after the victory, or almost-victory, of neoliberalism, may be regarded as a historically updated version of ordoliberalism." Streeck, "Heller, Schmitt and the Euro," *European Law Journal* 21, no. 3 (May 2015): 365.

50. "Nobel-Prize Winning Economist," oral history interview with F. A. Hayek, Oral History Program, UCLA, 1983, 46, https://archive.org/details/nobelprizewinnin00haye.
51. Vanberg, *The Constitution of Markets*, 88.
52. See Jan-Werner Müller, "Militant Democracy," in *The Oxford Handbook of Comparative Constitutional Law*, ed. Michel Rosenfeld and András Sajó (Oxford: Oxford University Press, 2012), 1253–1269; Udi Greenberg, "Militant Democracy and Human Rights," *New German Critique* 42, no. 3 (November 2015): 169–195.
53. The quote is from SPD head Carlo Schmid, in Jeremy Varon, *Bringing the War Home: The Weather Underground, the Red Army Faction, and Revolutionary Violence in the Sixties and Seventies* (Berkeley: University of California Press, 2004), 277.
54. Wilhelm Röpke, *International Economic Disintegration* (London: William Hodge and Co., 1942), 241.
55. See, for instance, Burgin, *The Great Persuasion;* Stedman Jones, *Masters of the Universe.* For a contextualized treatment, see Anthony James Nicholls, *Freedom with Responsibility: The Social Market Economy in Germany, 1918–1963* (New York: Oxford University Press, 1994); Ptak, *Vom Ordoliberalismus zur sozialen Marktwirtschaft.*
56. Jan-Werner Müller, *Contesting Democracy: Political Thought in Twentieth-Century Europe* (New Haven, CT: Yale University Press, 2011), 5.
57. F. A. Hayek, "New Nations and the Problem of Power," *The Listener,* November 10, 1960, 819. For his own statement that this was the first time he had suggested "the reconstruction of the representative assemblies," see Hayek, *The Political Order,* 192.
58. Hayek, "New Nations," 821.
59. Hayek, *The Political Order,* 149.
60. See Haselbach, *Autoritärer Liberalismus.*
61. See, for instance, the May 2015 special issue of the *European Law Journal* dedicated to Herman Heller's authoritarian liberalism. Bonefeld, "Authoritarian Liberalism"; Joerges, "What Is Left?," 467; Michael A. Wilkinson, "The Specter of Authoritarian Liberalism: Reflections on the Constitutional Crisis of the European Union," *German Law Journal* 14, no. 5 (2013): 527–560.
62. For a forceful and eloquent statement of this position, see Wolfgang Streeck, *How Will Capitalism End? Essays on a Failing System* (London: Verso, 2016), chap. 1.
63. Walter Eucken, "Staatliche Strukturwandlungen und die Krisis des Kapitalismus," *Weltwirtschaftliches Archiv* 36 (1932): 311.
64. "Apartheid in South Africa and Its Foreign Critics," undated [1963], box 31, William H. Hutt Papers, Hoover Institution Archives, Stanford University.
65. See Greta R. Krippner, *Capitalizing on Crisis: The Political Origins of the Rise of Finance* (Cambridge, MA: Harvard University Press, 2012); Schmelzer, *Freiheit für Wechselkurse und Kapital;* Carol Connell, *Reforming the World Monetary System: Fritz Machlup and the Bellagio Group* (London: Pickering and Chatto, 2013);

Chwieroth, *Capital Ideas;* Richard Peet, *Unholy Trinity: The IMF, World Bank and WTO,* 2nd ed. (London: Zed Books, 2009); Kim Phillips-Fein, *Fear City: New York City's Fiscal Crisis and the Rise of Austerity Politics* (New York: Metropolitan, 2017).

66. See Kristen Hopewell, *Breaking the WTO: How Emerging Powers Disrupted the Neoliberal Project* (Stanford, CA: Stanford University Press, 2016).
67. Vanessa Ogle, "State Rights against Private Capital: The 'New International Economic Order' and the Struggle over Aid, Trade, and Foreign Investment, 1962–1981," *Humanity: An International Journal of Human Rights, Humanitarianism, and Development* 5, no. 2 (Summer 2014): 220.
68. M. Sornarajah, *Resistance and Change in the International Law on Foreign Investment* (New York: Cambridge University Press, 2015), 1.

1. A WORLD OF WALLS

1. See Susan Pedersen, *The Guardians: The League of Nations and the Crisis of Empire* (New York: Oxford University Press, 2015).
2. Erez Manela, *The Wilsonian Moment: Self-Determination and the International Origins of Anticolonial Nationalism* (New York: Oxford University Press, 2007); Pankaj Mishra, *From the Ruins of Empire: The Intellectuals Who Remade Asia* (New York: Farrar, Straus and Giroux, 2012).
3. Daniel Gorman, *The Emergence of International Society in the 1920s* (Cambridge: Cambridge University Press, 2012). See also Quinn Slobodian, "How to See the World Economy: Statistics, Maps, and Schumpeter's Camera in the First Age of Globalization," *Journal of Global History* 10, no. 2 (2015): 308.
4. Ludwig Mises, *Die Gemeinwirtschaft* (Jena: Fischer, 1922), 294.
5. Ludwig Mises, *Socialism: An Economic and Sociological Analysis,* trans. J. Kahane (Indianapolis: Liberty Fund, 1981), 242.
6. Mary Nolan, *The Transatlantic Century: Europe and America, 1890–2010* (New York: Cambridge University Press, 2012), 57.
7. See J. Adam Tooze, *Statistics and the German State, 1900–1945: The Making of Modern Economic Knowledge* (New York: Cambridge University Press, 2001), 63–71.
8. Barry Eichengreen, *Globalizing Capital: A History of the International Monetary System* (Princeton, NJ: Princeton University Press, 2008), 4.
9. G. R. Steele, *Keynes and Hayek: The Money Economy* (New York: Routledge, 2001), 8.
10. Dieter Plehwe, introduction to *The Road from Mont Pèlerin: The Making of the Neoliberal Thought Collective,* ed. Philip Mirowski and Dieter Plehwe (Cambridge, MA: Harvard University Press, 2009), 11.
11. Ludwig Mises, *Memoirs* (Auburn, AL: Ludwig von Mises Institute, 2009), 77.
12. Alexander Hörtlehner, "Ludwig von Mises und die österreichische Handelskammerorganisation," *Wirtschaftspolitische Blätter* 28, no. 4 (1981): 142.

13. Jörg Guido Hülsmann, *Mises: The Last Knight of Liberalism* (Auburn, AL: Ludwig von Mises Institute, 2007), 822–824; Kim Phillips-Fein, *Invisible Hands: The Making of the Conservative Movement from the New Deal to Reagan* (New York: W. W. Norton, 2009), 43, 55. Mises served on the Economics Principles Commission of the National Association of Manufacturers from 1943 to 1954. Murray N. Rothbard, *Ludwig von Mises: Scholar, Creator, Hero* (Auburn, AL: Ludwig von Mises Institute, 1988), 47.
14. Carl E. Schorske, *Fin-de-Siècle Vienna: Politics and Culture* (New York: Vintage Books, 1981), 75.
15. Marshall Berman, *All That Is Solid Melts into Air: The Experience of Modernity* (New York: Simon and Schuster, 1982), 150; David Harvey, *Paris, Capital of Modernity* (New York: Routledge, 2003), chap. 4.
16. Schorske, *Fin-de-Siècle Vienna,* 66.
17. Ibid., 110.
18. Ludwig Mises, *Omnipotent Government: The Rise of the Total State and Total War* (New Haven, CT: Yale University Press, 1944).
19. See Volker Berghahn and Brigitte Young, "Reflections on Werner Bonefeld's 'Freedom and the Strong State: On German Ordoliberalism' and the Continuing Importance of the Ideas of Ordoliberalism to Understand Germany's (Contested) Role in Resolving the Eurozone Crisis," *New Political Economy* 18, no. 5 (2013): 768–778; Werner Bonefeld, "Freedom and the Strong State: On German Ordoliberalism," *New Political Economy* 17, no. 5 (2012): 633–656; Pierre Dardot and Christian Laval, *The New Way of the World: On Neoliberal Society* (New York: Verso, 2014), chap. 5; Ben Jackson, "At the Origins of Neo-Liberalism: The Free Economy and the Strong State, 1930–1947," *Historical Journal* 53, no. 1 (2010): 129–151.
20. Michel Foucault, *The Birth of Biopolitics: Lectures at the Collège de France, 1978–79* (New York: Palgrave Macmillan, 2008), 76.
21. Mises, *Socialism,* 120.
22. Quoted in Hülsmann, *Mises,* 620–621.
23. Mises, *Memoirs,* 73.
24. George L. Ridgeway, *Merchants of Peace: The History of the International Chamber of Commerce* (Boston: Little, Brown, 1959); Monika Rosengarten, *Die Internationale Handelskammer: Wirtschaftspolitische Empfehlungen in der Zeit der Weltwirtschaftskrise, 1929–1939* (Berlin: Duncker und Humblot, 2001).
25. Bob Reinalda, *Routledge History of International Organizations: From 1815 to the Present Day* (New York: Routledge, 2009), 143.
26. See Slobodian, "How to See," 313–314; Nico Randeraad, "The International Statistical Congress (1853–1876): Knowledge Transfers and their Limits," *European History Quarterly* 41, no. 1 (2011): 50–65.
27. Chamber of Commerce of the United States of America, *International Trade Conference* (n.p: n.p, 1919), 21.
28. "8 January 1918: President Woodrow Wilson's Fourteen Points," http://avalon.law.yale.edu/20th_century/wilson14.asp.

29. Quoted in Rosengarten, *Die Internationale Handelskammer,* 33.
30. Ibid., 17.
31. Ibid., 41.
32. Hörtlehner, "Ludwig von Mises," 145; Margít Von Mises, *My Years with Ludwig von Mises* (New Rochelle, NY: Arlington House, 1976), 30.
33. Quoted in Rosengarten, *Die Internationale Handelskammer,* 17.
34. Ibid., 50.
35. Ibid., 126.
36. "Predict Revival of World Trade," *New York Times,* May 20, 1925.
37. Rosengarten, *Die Internationale Handelskammer,* 124.
38. Ibid., 123.
39. Clive Morrison-Bell, *Tariff Walls: A European Crusade* (London: J. Murray, 1930), 116.
40. Charles K. Nichols, "The Statistical Work of the League of Nations in Economic, Financial and Related Fields," *Journal of the American Statistical Association* 37, no. 219 (September 1942): 338.
41. Sir Arthur Salter, Address Delivered to the Congress of the ICC at Stockholm on July 1, 1927, League of Nations Archive, Geneva (hereafter cited as LON), R390, doss. 24789, doc. 62851, p. 3.
42. Ibid., 2.
43. Ibid., 9.
44. Morrison-Bell, *Tariff Walls,* vii.
45. Ibid., 103.
46. Ibid.
47. Ibid., 26.
48. Ibid., 77.
49. Ibid., 160.
50. According to Google Ngram Viewer, the terms "tariff walls" and "*Zollmauern*" both increased precipitously in print after the mid-1920s (https://books.google.com/ngrams). The term never caught on in French, where "barrière douanière" remained the standard phrase.
51. Alfred Pearce Dennis, "Tariff Walls Block Europe's Recovery," *New York Times,* October 31, 1926.
52. Morrison-Bell, *Tariff Walls,* 42, 61.
53. Ibid., 65.
54. Ibid., 48.
55. Ibid., frontispiece.
56. Gottfried Haberler, *The Theory of International Trade with Its Applications to Commercial Policy* (London: W. Hodge, 1936), 357.
57. William E. Rappard, "Post-War Efforts for Freer Trade," *Geneva Special Studies* 9, no. 2 (March 1938): 26.
58. ICC, 25th Meeting of the Council, October 24, 1927, LON, R390, doss. 24789, doc. 62851, p. 2.

59. Haberler, *The Theory of International Trade,* 355.
60. Patricia Clavin, *Securing the World Economy: The Reinvention of the League of Nations, 1920–1946* (New York: Oxford University Press, 2013), 44.
61. Haberler, *The Theory of International Trade,* 384; emphasis in the original.
62. Ludwig Mises, "Die Rückwirkung der Entwicklung der Weltwirtschaft auf die Ausgestaltung der Sozialpolitik," *Statistische Monatsschrift* 10 (1905): 949.
63. Ludwig Mises, *Nation, State, and Economy* (1919) (New York: NYU Press, 1983), 93.
64. Dennis, "Tariff Walls Block Europe's Recovery."
65. "How Can Austria Be Saved? An Economic Policy Program for Austria," *Die Börse,* February 17, 1921, in Richard Ebeling, *Selected Writings of Ludwig von Mises,* vol. 2 (Indianapolis: Liberty Fund, 2002), 248–250.
66. Hörtlehner, "Ludwig von Mises," 142.
67. "The Restoration of Austria's Economic Situation," position statement for the Austrian Chamber of Commerce, presented on August 28, 1922, in Ebeling, *Selected Writings of Ludwig von Mises,* 267, 69.
68. Douglas D. Alder, "Decision-Making amid Public Violence; The Vienna Riots, July 15,1927," *Austrian History Yearbook* 19–20 (1983–1984): 245.
69. Ibid., 251.
70. Ibid., 254.
71. Irene Stocksieker Di Maio, "Space in Elias Canetti's Autobiographical Trilogy," in *A Companion to the Works of Elias Canetti,* ed. Dagmar C. G. Lorenz (Rochester, NY: Camden House, 2004), 183.
72. Quoted in Hülsmann, *Mises,* 580.
73. Quoted in ibid., 581.
74. Ibid., 606.
75. Mises, *Socialism,* 57.
76. Ibid., 60.
77. Preface (1934), in ibid., 20.
78. Alder, "Decision-Making," 256.
79. Grandner and Traxler, "Sozialpartnerschaft," 83.
80. Ibid., 94–95.
81. Ibid., 90.
82. Quoted in ibid., 90.
83. Ibid., 91.
84. Mises, *Socialism,* 382.
85. Quoted in Hülsmann, *Mises,* 620–621.
86. Mises, *Memoirs,* 73.
87. Ibid., 81.
88. Gottfried Haberler, "Mises' Private Seminar," *Mont Pèlerin Quarterly* 3, no. 3 (October 1961): 21.
89. Ibid., 20.
90. Mises, *Memoirs,* 79.

91. Felix Kaufmann, "Miseskreis Lied," *Mont Pèlerin Quarterly* 3, no. 3 (October 1961): 23.
92. Richard Strigl, "Wirtschaftstheorie im Dienste der Wirtschaftspolitik," *Archiv für Sozialwissenschaft und Sozialpolitik* 60 (1928): 354.
93. Gottfried Haberler, *Der Sinn der Indexzahlen: Eine Untersuchung über den Begriff des Preisniveaus und die Methoden seiner Messung* (Tübingen: Mohr, 1927).
94. Ibid., 103.
95. Ibid., 70.
96. Harald Hagemann, "The Austrian School in the Interwar Period," in *Austrian Economics in Transition: From Carl Menger to Friedrich Hayek*, ed. Harald Hagemann, Yukihiro Ikeda, and Tamotsu Nishizawa (New York: Palgrave Macmillan, 2010), 189.
97. Gottfried Haberler, "Die Theorie der komparativen Kosten und ihre Auswertung für die Begründung des Freihandels," *Weltwirtschaftliches Archiv* 32 (1930): 350.
98. Ibid., 369.
99. Ibid., 368.
100. Ibid., 370.
101. Gottfried Haberler, "Einfuhrbeschränkungen, Zahlungsbilanz und Schillingskurs (Tagblatt, 22 January 1933)," in *Machlup, Morgenstern, Haberler, Hayek: Wirtschaftspublizistische Beiträge in kritischer Zeit (1911–1934)*, ed. Hansjörg Klausinger (Marburg: Metropolis, 2005), 171.
102. Haberler, *Der Sinn der Indexzahlen*, 104.
103. Gottfried Haberler, "The Different Meanings Attached to the Term 'Fluctuations in the Purchasing Power of Gold' and the Best Instrument or Instruments for Measuring Such Fluctuations," March 9, 1931, LON, R 2961, doss. 4346, doc, 20721, p. 47.
104. Mises, "The Suitability of Methods of Ascertaining Changes in Purchasing Power for the Guidance of International Currency or Banking Policy," Gold Delegation of the Financial Committee, League of Nations, October 10, 1930, LON, R 2961, doss. 4346, doc 20721, p. 13.
105. Gottfried Haberler, *Prosperity and Depression: A Theoretical Analysis of Cyclical Movements* (Geneva: League of Nations, 1937), 303.
106. Ibid., 304.
107. Haberler, *The Theory of International Trade*, 22, 33.
108. Ibid., 35.
109. Ibid., 309.
110. Arthur Salter, *Recovery: The Second Effort* (London: G. Bell and Sons, 1932), 171.
111. Haberler, *The Theory of International Trade*, 194.
112. Ibid., 196–197.
113. Felix Kaufmann, "Abschied von Professor Mises," *Mont Pèlerin Quarterly* 3, no. 3 (October 1961): 26.

2. A WORLD OF NUMBERS

1. Harold James, *The End of Globalization: Lessons from the Great Depression* (Cambridge, MA: Harvard University Press, 2001).
2. Moritz J. Bonn, *Wandering Scholar* (New York: John Day Co., 1948), 319.
3. The metaphor comes from Wilhelm Röpke, *German Commercial Policy* (London: Longmans, Green and Co., 1934), 23.
4. This is the title of David Ekbladh's current book project on the 1930s.
5. Pierre Vasseur, "Economic Information: Essential Factor in Modern Business Organization," *World Trade*, June 1937, 69.
6. "Pleasure-Tower Half Mile High," *Modern Mechanix*, July 1933, 45.
7. Congrès Mondial de la Documentation Universelle, August 16–21, 1937, program, Carnegie Endowment for International Peace—Centre Européen Records, Rare Book and Manuscript Library, Columbia University Libraries (hereafter cited as CEIP), box 129.3.
8. The Geneva International Center at the Palais Wilson, A Record of the Inaugural Ceremony held on Monday, September 27, 1937 (1938), CEIP, box 130.
9. William E. Rappard, "The Beginnings of World Government," in *Problems of Peace: Fifth Series*, ed. Geneva Institute of International Relations (London: Oxford University Press, 1931), 20.
10. Arthur Salter, *Recovery: The Second Effort* (London: G. Bell and Sons, 1932), 173.
11. See, for instance, Stefan Kolev, "Ordoliberalism and the Austrian School," in *The Oxford Handbook of Austrian Economics*, ed. Peter J. Boettke and Christopher J. Coyne (New York: Oxford University Press, 2015), 423.
12. Reproduced in Wilhelm Röpke, *International Economic Disintegration* (London: William Hodge and Company, 1942), 4.
13. See Charles P. Kindleberger, *The World in Depression, 1929–1939* (London: Lane, 1973).
14. "Österreich," *Monatsberichte des österreichischen Institutes für Konjunkturforschung* 7, no. 4 (1933): 63.
15. League of Nations, *World Economic Survey, 1932–33* (Geneva: League of Nations, 1933), 8. My thanks to Martin Bemmann for archival material. As he notes, the Schweizer Bankverein image can be found in the German Federal Archive in Berlin, R 8034II/5885, 158. For an overview of League of Nations efforts in the 1920s, see Martin Bemmann, "Das Chaos beseitigen: Die internationale Standardisierung forst- und holzwirtschaftlicher Statistiken in den 1920er und 1930er Jahren und der Völkerbund," *Jahrbuch für Wirtschaftsgeschichte* 57, no. 2 (2016): 545–588.
16. "Österreich," 183.
17. Wesley Clair Mitchell, *Business Cycles* (Berkeley: University of California Press, 1913), vii.
18. Mary S. Morgan, *The History of Econometric Ideas* (New York: Cambridge University Press, 1990), 64.

19. Walter A. Friedman, *Fortune Tellers: The Story of America's First Economic Forecasters* (Princeton, NJ: Princeton University Press, 2014), 13.
20. On the history of the illustrated timeline, including the pioneering efforts of William Playfair, see Daniel Rosenberg and Anthony Grafton, *Cartographies of Time* (New York: Princeton Architectural Press, 2010), 136.
21. Marcel Boumans, *How Economists Model the World into Numbers* (New York: Routledge, 2005), 33.
22. "Die Methoden der Konjunkturforschung und ihre Anwendung in Österreich," *Monatsberichte des österreichischen Institutes für Konjunkturforschung* 1, no. 1 (1927): 11.
23. Ibid., 2.
24. International Labour Office, "Economic Barometers," Geneva, 1924, League of Nations Archive, Geneva (hereafter cited as LON), R406, doss. 30796, doc. 35557.
25. Fritz Machlup, "Kontingentverträge? Ein Beitrag zur wirtschaflichen Vernunft," *Tagblatt,* February 6, 1932, reproduced in *Machlup, Morgenstern, Haberler, Hayek: Wirtschaftspublizistische Beiträge in kritischer Zeit (1911–1934),* ed. Hansjörg Klausinger (Marburg: Metropolis, 2005), 71.
26. For an early use of this expression to describe a chart of economic data, see William Beveridge, *Unemployment* (New York: Longmans, Green, and Co., 1909), 44.
27. James K. Cooper, "Electrocardiography 100 Years Ago," *New England Journal of Medicine* 315, no. 7 (1986): 461.
28. Charles S. Maier, *Recasting Bourgeois Europe: Stabilization in France, Germany, and Italy in the Decade after World War I* (Princeton, NJ: Princeton University Press, 1975).
29. See Jamie Martin, "Experts of the World Economy: European Stabilization and the Transformation of Global Capitalism in the Era of Total War" (PhD diss., Harvard University, 2016).
30. Earlene Craver and Axel Leijonhufiud, "Economics in America: The Continental Influence," *History of Political Economy* 19, no. 2 (1987): 176.
31. Charles J. Bullock to Edmund E. Day, May 15, 1930, folder 36, box 4, ser. 705.S, RG 1.1, Field Offices, Paris, FA395, Rockefeller Foundation records, Rockefeller Archive Center (hereafter cited as Rockefeller Paris records). On the Harvard Economic Service, see Walter A. Friedman, "The Harvard Economic Service and the Problems of Forecasting," *History of Political Economy* 41, no. 1 (2009): 57–88.
32. Craver and Leijonhufiud, "Economics in America," 179.
33. Stephen Kresge and Leif Wenar, eds., *Hayek on Hayek: An Autobiographical Dialogue* (London: Routledge, 1994), 58.
34. Quoted in Alan O. Ebenstein, *Hayek's Journey: The Mind of Friedrich Hayek* (New York: Palgrave Macmillan, 2003), 53.
35. Entstehungsgründe des Instituts in Österreich, Wirtschaftskammer Wien (Vienna Chamber of Commerce) Archive (hereafter cited as WWA), 2627/10/262701, 1926 folder.

36. "Nobel-Prize Winning Economist," oral history interview with F. A. Hayek, Oral History Program, UCLA, 1983, 11, https://archive.org/details/nobelprizewinnin 00haye.
37. "Geschichte: Institute in europäischen Staaten," WWA, 2627/10/262701, 1926 folder.
38. "Entstehungsgründe des österr. Instituts: Zur Vermeidung der 'Verdunkelungsgefahr' für Österr. im Ausland," WWA, 2627/10/262701, 1926 folder.
39. "Entstehungsgründe des Instituts: Praktischer Vorteil," WWA, 2627/10/262701, 1926 folder.
40. Hansjörg Klausinger, "Hayek on Practical Business Cycle Research: A Note," in *Austrian Economics in Transition: From Carl Menger to Friedrich Hayek,* ed. Harald Hagemann, Yukihiro Ikeda, and Tamotsu Nishizawa (New York: Palgrave Macmillan, 2010).
41. Loveday to Mises, November 30, 1926, LON, R408, doss. 30796, doc. 55747.
42. Reisch, Hayek to Secretariat of the Committee of Experts on Economic Barometers, League of Nations, January 20, 1927, LON, R476, doss. 56987, doc. 56473.
43. "Die Methoden der Konjunkturforschung," 14.
44. Das Österreichische Institut für Konjunkturforschung, January 1931, LON, R2625, doss. 11377, doc. 172.
45. Friedman, *Fortune Tellers,* 151.
46. F. A. Hayek, "Konjunkturforschung in Österreich," *Die Industrie,* July 22, 1927, 5.
47. Verhandlungsschrift: Konferenz der mitteleuropäischen Konjunkturinstitute, 23/24 March 1928, WWA, 2627/10/262701, 1927 folder.
48. "Einleitende Bemerkungen zu der am 23 März 1928 zusammentretenden Konferenz der Vertreter der mitteleuropäischen Konjunkturforschungsinstitute," March 8, 1928, LON, R2815, doss. 2539, doc. 2539, p. 1.
49. Ibid., p. 5.
50. Ibid., p. 4.
51. Earlene Craver, "Patronage and the Directions of Research in Economics: The Rockefeller Foundation in Europe, 1924–1938," *Minerva* 24, nos. 2/3 (1986): 210–211.
52. Ibid., 214.
53. Ibid., 213.
54. Ibid.
55. Loveday to Hayek, January 21, 1928, LON, R2815, doss. 2539, doc. 2539.
56. Hayek to Ohlin, June 10, 1931, LON, R2889, doss. 23630, doc. 24135.
57. Loveday to Morgenstern, March 11, 1931, LON, R2889, doss. 23630, doc. 24135.
58. Alexander Loveday, "The League of Nations and Business Cycle Research," *Review of Economics and Statistics* 18, no. 4 (1936): 157.
59. Appendix, *League of Nations Official Journal* 12, no. 12 (December 1931): 2403.
60. Wagemann to Loveday, November 17, 1926, LON, R451, doss. 5186, doc. 52192.
61. A. M. Endres and Grant A. Fleming, *International Organizations and the Analysis of Economic Policy, 1919–1950* (New York: Cambridge University Press, 2002), 18.

62. Charles K. Nichols, "The Statistical Work of the League of Nations in Economic, Financial and Related Fields," *Journal of the American Statistical Association* 37, no. 219 (September 1942): 339.
63. Ibid., 338.
64. J. B. Condliffe, "A World Economic Survey," in *Geneva and the Drift to War,* ed. Norman Angell et al. (London: Allen and Unwin, 1938), 98.
65. Ludwig Mises, *Liberalism,* 3rd ed. (Irvington-on-Hudson, NY: Foundation for Economic Education, 1985), 148.
66. Patricia Clavin, *Securing the World Economy: The Reinvention of the League of Nations, 1920–1946* (New York: Oxford University Press, 2013), 76.
67. Salter, *Recovery,* 27.
68. League of Nations, *World Economic Survey, 1931–32* (Geneva: League of Nations, 1932), 7.
69. Annexes, *League of Nations Official Journal* 15, no. 6 (June 1934): 524; Mauro Boianovsky and Hans-Michael Trautwein, "Haberler, the League of Nations, and the Quest for Consensus in Business Cycle Theory in the 1930s," *History of Political Economy* 38, no. 1 (2006): 46.
70. Gottfried Haberler, "Systematic Analysis of the Theories of the Business Cycle," Economic Intelligence Service, August 1934, LON, R4539, doss. 12653, doc. 12653, p. 3.
71. Ernest Minor Patterson, "An Approach to World Economics," *American Economic Review* 21, no. 1 (March 1931): 147.
72. Boianovsky and Trautwein, "Haberler," 62.
73. Ibid., 63.
74. Clavin, *Securing the World Economy,* 205.
75. Karl Pribram, "How to Ascertain the Definition of Some Notions Which Are Fundamental to Business Cycle Analysis?," *Revue de l'Institut International de Statistique / Review of the International Statistical Institute* 4, no. 2 (1936): 215.
76. Haberler to Loveday, August 22, 1936, LON, R4539, doss. 12809, doc. 12653.
77. Kittredge to Condliffe, May 18, 1936, LON, R4539, doss. 12653, doc. 21852.
78. For the pioneering research on this conference, see Neil de Marchi and Peter Dohlman, "League of Nations Economists and the Ideal of Peaceful Change in the Decade of the Thirties," in *Economics and National Security: A History of Their Interaction,* ed. C. D. W. Goodwin (Durham, NC: Duke University Press, 1991), 149. The authors mistakenly place Wesley Mitchell at the conference. Though invited, he did not attend. Kittredge to Loveday, June 11, 1936, LON, R4539, doss. 12653, doc. 21852.
79. Kittredge to Loveday, February 29, 1936, LON, R4539, doss. 12653, doc. 21852.
80. Kittredge to Haberler, March 16, 1936, LON, R4539, doss. 12653, doc. 21852.
81. Draft Agenda for Conference, n.d., LON, R4539, doss. 12653, doc. 21852.
82. Rappard, "Investigation into Post-War Agrarian and Industrial Protectionism," January 1937, folder 942, box 104, ser. 100, RG 1.1, Field Offices, Paris, FA395, Rockefeller Paris records.

83. Victor Monnier, *William E. Rappard: Défenseur des libertés, serviteur de son pays et de la communauté internationale* (Geneva: Slatkine, 1995), 497.
84. Having officially been "retired" rather than fired from his post, Röpke continued to receive a pension from the German government until the outbreak of the war in 1939. Hennecke, *Wilhelm Röpke: Ein Leben in der Brändung* (Stuttgart: Schäffer-Poeschel Verlag, 2005), 89–95, 125.
85. Excerpt from memorandum from T. B. Kittredge to JVS [John Van Sickle] and SHW [Sydnor H. Walker], December 16, 1936, folder 942, box 104, ser. 100, RG 1.1, Rockefeller Paris records; Jacques J. Polak, "The Contribution of the International Monetary Fund," *History of Political Economy* 28, suppl. (1996): 214.
86. Susan Pedersen, "The Meaning of the Mandates System: An Argument," *Geschichte und Gesellschaft* 32, no. 4 (2006): 562.
87. Monnier, *William E. Rappard,* 6, 10.
88. Ibid., 28, 31–34, 43.
89. Ibid., 46; Charles Howard Ellis, *The Origin, Structure and Working of the League of Nations* (London: Allen and Unwin, 1928), 210–212.
90. Monnier, *William E. Rappard,* 51.
91. Ibid., 356.
92. Ibid., 364.
93. Excerpt from memorandum from T. B. Kittredge to JVS [John Van Sickle] and SHW [Sydnor H. Walker].
94. Kittredge to Röpke, March 31, 1937, folder 942, box 104, ser. 100, RG 1.1, Rockefeller Paris records.
95. Röpke, Investigation into Postwar Agrarian and Industrial Protectionism: Outline of the First Special Research Program, November 1937, folder 944, box 104, ser. 100, RG 1.1, Rockefeller Paris records.
96. Röpke to Fleming, March 2, 1937, folder 942, box 104, ser. 100, RG 1.1, Rockefeller Paris records.
97. Investigation into Postwar Agrarian and Industrial Protectionism: Report on the Organization and Financial Demands, February 1938, folder 944, box 104, ser. 100, RG 1.1, Rockefeller Paris records.
98. Kittredge to Van Sickle, January 28, 1937, folder 942, box 104, ser. 100, RG 1.1, Rockefeller Paris records.
99. Röpke to Robbins, February 13, 1937, Wilhelm Röpke Archive, Institute for Economic Research, Cologne (hereafter cited as RA), Panzerschrank, p. 416.
100. Röpke to Lippmann, September 14, 1937, RA, Panzerschrank, pp. 423–424.
101. Röpke to Robbins, November 17, 1937, RA, Panzerschrank, p. 429.
102. Louis Rougier, *Les mystiques politiques contemporaines et leurs incidences internationales,* Publications de l'Institut universitaire de hautes études internationales, Geneva (Paris: Librairie du Recueil Sirey, 1935).
103. David Long, "Who Killed the International Studies Conference?," *Review of International Studies* 32, no. 4 (2006): 603.

104. Daniel Gorman, *The Emergence of International Society in the 1920s* (Cambridge: Cambridge University Press, 2012), 204.
105. International Institute of Intellectual Cooperation, *Economic Policies in Relation to World Peace: International Studies Conference, Twelfth Session* (Paris: League of Nations, 1940).
106. De Marchi and Dohlman, "League of Nations Economists," 151.
107. Hagen Schulz-Forberg, "Laying the Groundwork: The Semantics of Neoliberalism in the 1930s," in *Re-inventing Western Civilisation: Transnational Reconstructions of Liberalism in Europe in the Twentieth Century,* ed. Hagen Schulz-Forberg and Niklas Olsen (Newcastle upon Tyne: Cambridge Scholars, 2014), 16.
108. Ludwig Mises, "A Draft of Guidelines for the Reconstruction of Austria (May 1940)," in *Selected Writings of Ludwig von Mises,* ed. Richard Ebeling (Indianapolis: Liberty Fund, 2000), 158.
109. Röpke to Haberler, February 25, 1936, RA, Panzerschrank, p. 462.
110. Frederick Sherwood Dunn, *Peaceful Change: A Study of International Procedures* (New York: Council on Foreign Relations, 1937), v.
111. Colloque Walter Lippmann, *Compte-Rendu des séances du Colloque Walter Lippmann* (August 26–30, 1938), vol. 1 of *Travaux du centre international d'études pour la renovation du libéralisme* (Paris: Libraire de Médicis, 1938), 110.
112. Ibid., 102.
113. Janet R. Horne, *A Social Laboratory for Modern France: The Musée Social and the Rise of the Welfare State* (Durham, NC: Duke University Press, 2002).
114. See Serge Audier, *Le colloque Lippmann: Aux origines du néo-libéralisme, précédé de Penser le néo-libéralisme,* 2nd ed. (Paris: Éditions Le Bord de l'eau, 2012); François Denord, "French Neoliberalism and Its Divisions: From the Colloque Walter Lippmann to the Fifth Republic," in *The Road from Mont Pèlerin: The Making of the Neoliberal Thought Collective,* ed. Philip Mirowski and Dieter Plehwe (Cambridge, MA: Harvard University Press, 2009), 50.
115. Walter Lippmann, *An Inquiry into the Principles of the Good Society* (Boston: Little, Brown, 1937), 201.
116. John Maynard Keynes, "The End of Laissez-Faire," in *The History of Economic Thought: A Reader,* ed. Steven G. Medema and Warren J. Samuels (New York: Routledge, 2003).
117. Lippmann, *An Inquiry into the Principles of the Good Society,* 226.
118. Ibid., 232.
119. Rüstow and Röpke, "A Note on the Urgent Necessity of Reorientation in Social Science," folder 944, box 104, ser. 100, RG 1.1, Rockefeller Paris records.
120. Wilhelm Röpke, *International Order and Economic Integration* (Dordrecht: Reidel, 1959), 14. On this period, see Patricia Clavin, *The Failure of Economic Diplomacy: Britain, France, Germany and the United States, 1931–1936* (New York: Palgrave Macmillan, 1996).
121. Lippmann, *An Inquiry into the Principles of the Good Society,* 173, 365.
122. Ibid., 33.

123. Ibid., 31.
124. Ibid., 32.
125. Ibid.
126. Ibid., 35.
127. Ibid., 174.
128. See Graham Wallas, *The Great Society: A Psychological Analysis* (New York: Macmillan, 1914), 3–4. Wallas dedicated this book to Lippmann.
129. Lippmann, *An Inquiry into the Principles of the Good Society*, 319.
130. Ben Jackson, "Freedom, the Common Good, and the Rule of Law: Lippmann and Hayek on Economic Planning," *Journal of the History of Ideas* 73, no. 1 (2012): 60.
131. Ludwig Mises, *Omnipotent Government: The Rise of the Total State and Total War* (New Haven, CT: Yale University Press, 1944), 238.
132. Hansjörg Klausinger, introduction to *The Collected Works of F. A. Hayek*, vol. 7: *Business Cycles, Part I*, ed. Hansjörg Klausinger (London: Routledge, 2009), 7.
133. Ibid.
134. F. A. Hayek, "Economics and Knowledge," *Economica* 4, no. 13 (1937): 33–54. Hayek had also revived discussion of the socialist calculation debate through his publication of some of the key essays in translation. See F. A. Hayek, ed., *Collectivist Economic Planning* (London: Routledge and Kegan Paul, 1935). For a careful reconstruction of the "Economics and Knowledge" essay, see Bruce Caldwell, *Hayek's Challenge: An Intellectual Biography of F. A. Hayek* (Chicago: University of Chicago Press, 2004), 206–230.
135. F. A. Hayek, "Economics and Knowledge (1937)," in *Individualism and Economic Order*, ed. F. A. Hayek (Chicago: University of Chicago Press, 1948), 39.
136. Ibid., 46.
137. Ibid., 50.
138. Philip Mirowski, *Never Let a Serious Crisis Go to Waste: How Neoliberalism Survived the Financial Meltdown* (New York: Verso, 2013), chap. 4.
139. Hayek, "Economics and Knowledge (1937)," 53.
140. Quoted in Ebenstein, *Hayek's Journey*, 237.
141. F. A. Hayek, "The Principles of a Liberal Social Order (1966)," in *Studies in Philosophy, Politics and Economics*, ed. F. A. Hayek (London: Routledge and Kegan Paul, 1967), 164.
142. Lippmann, *An Inquiry into the Principles of the Good Society*, 30.
143. Röpke to Robbins, May 6, 1936, RA, Panzerschrank, p. 421.
144. Röpke to Robbins, February 13, 1937, RA, Panzerschrank, p. 414.
145. Rüstow and Röpke, "A Note on the Urgent Necessity of Reorientation."
146. Colloque Walter Lippmann, *Compte-Rendu des séances*, 80–81.
147. Ibid., 81.
148. Ibid., 91.
149. Rüstow and Röpke, "A Note on the Urgent Necessity of Reorientation."
150. Michael Heilperin, *International Monetary Economics* (London: Longmans, Green and Co., 1939), viii.

151. Ibid., 267.
152. Lippmann, *An Inquiry into the Principles of the Good Society*, 314. See Neurath's contributions to International Industrial Relations Institute, *World Social Economic Planning* (New York: International Industrial Relations Institute, 1932).
153. Colloque Walter Lippmann, *Compte-Rendu des séances*, 109.
154. H. G. Wells, *The Shape of Things to Come* (New York: Macmillan, 1933), 24.
155. "Urge World Effort to End Depression," *New York Times*, July 31, 1931.
156. Timothy Mitchell, "Fixing the Economy," *Cultural Studies* 12, no. 1 (1998): 82–101. See also Daniel Speich Chassé, *Die Erfindung des Bruttosozialprodukts: Globale Ungleichheit in der Wissensgeschichte der Ökonomie* (Göttingen: Vandenhock und Ruprecht, 2013).
157. Wilhelm Röpke, *Economics of the Free Society* (Chicago: Regnery, 1963), 125.
158. F. A. Hayek, *Monetary Nationalism and International Stability* (London: Longmans, Green and Co., 1937), 7.
159. Ludwig Mises, *Nationalökonomie: Theorie des Handelns und Wirtschaftens* (Geneva: Editions Union Genf, 1940), 313.
160. Wilhelm Röpke, "International Economics in a Changing World," in *The World Crisis*, ed. Geneva Graduate Institute of International Studies (London: Longmans, Green and Co., 1938), 285.
161. Ibid.
162. Colloque Walter Lippmann, *Compte-Rendu des séances*, 59.

3. A WORLD OF FEDERATIONS

1. "Nobel-Prize Winning Economist," oral history interview with F. A. Hayek, Oral History Program, UCLA, 1983, https://archive.org/details/nobelprizewinnin00haye.
2. Richard M. Ebeling, ed., *Globalization: Will Freedom or Global Government Dominate the International Marketplace?* (Hillsdale, MI: Hillsdale College Press, 2002).
3. Peter J. Boettke and Christopher J. Coyne, eds., *The Oxford Handbook of Austrian Economics* (New York: Oxford University Press, 2015).
4. "Fisher Appeals for World Union," *New York Times*, September 1, 1941.
5. Wilhelm Röpke, *German Commercial Policy* (London: Longmans, Green and Co., 1934), 83–84.
6. Michel Foucault, *The Birth of Biopolitics: Lectures at the Collège de France, 1978–79* (New York: Palgrave Macmillan, 2008), 167.
7. Michael A. Heilperin, *International Monetary Organisation* (Paris: League of Nations International Institute of Intellectual Cooperation, 1939), 16.
8. Ibid.
9. Eugene Staley, *World Economy in Transition* (New York: Council on Foreign Relations, 1939), 35.

10. Colloque Walter Lippmann, *Compte-Rendu des séances du Colloque Walter Lippmann* (August 26–30, 1938), vol. 1 of *Travaux du centre international d'études pour la renovation du libéralisme* (Paris: Libraire de Médicis, 1938), 64.
11. Ludwig Mises, *Nation, State, and Economy* (New York: New York University Press, 1983), 106.
12. For the authoritative history of the mandates, see Susan Pedersen, *The Guardians: The League of Nations and the Crisis of Empire* (New York: Oxford University Press, 2015). For an insightful analysis of the mandates as the "economization of government," see Antony Anghie, *Imperialism, Sovereignty, and the Making of International Law* (New York: Cambridge University Press, 2007), chap. 3.
13. William E. Rappard, *The Geneva Experiment* (London: Oxford University Press, 1931); William E. Rappard, "The Beginnings of World Government," in *Problems of Peace: Fifth Series*, ed. Geneva Institute of International Relations (London: Oxford University Press, 1931), 3.
14. League of Nations, *The State and Economic Life: A Record of a Second Study Conference Held in London from May 29 to June 2, 1933* (Paris: International Institute of Intellectual Cooperation, 1934), 16.
15. For details, see Susan Howson, *Lionel Robbins* (New York: Cambridge University Press, 2011), 237–244; Patricia Clavin, "'A Wandering Scholar' in Britain and the USA, 1933–45: The Life and Work of Moritz Bonn," in *Refugees from the Third Reich in Britain (Yearbook of the Research Centre for German and Austrian Exile Studies)*, ed. Anthony Grenville (Amsterdam: Editions Rodopi B.V., 2003), 27.
16. Moritz J. Bonn, *Wandering Scholar* (New York: John Day Co., 1948), 82.
17. On Dernburg's developmentalist focus on enterprise and infrastructure, see Bradley D. Naranch, "'Colonized Body,' 'Oriental Machine': Debating Race, Railroads and the Politics of Reconstruction in Germany and East Africa, 1906–1910," *Central European History* 33, no. 3 (2000): 299–338.
18. Bonn, *Wandering Scholar*, 117; see Moritz Julius Bonn, *Nationale kolonialpolitik* (Munich: Rieger, 1910).
19. For details, see Stuart Ward, "The European Provenance of Decolonization," *Past and Present* 230, no. 1 (2016): 233–246. Todd Shepard cites precedents but acknowledges that Bonn's "reintroduction of the term into English is that which took hold." Todd Shepard, *The Invention of Decolonization: The Algerian War and the Remaking of France* (Ithaca, NY: Cornell University Press, 2006), 5. Bonn's lecture was published as "The Age of Counter-Colonisation," *International Affairs* 13, no. 6 (1934): 845–847.
20. Moritz J. Bonn, "Union Now?," *World Affairs*, July 1948, 251.
21. Detlev Peukert, *Max Webers Diagnose der Moderne* (Göttingen: Vandenhoeck und Ruprecht, 1989), 112.
22. Mary Nolan, *The Transatlantic Century: Europe and America, 1890–2010* (New York: Cambridge University Press, 2012), 118–142.
23. Bonn, "The Age of Counter-Colonisation," 846.

24. Moritz J. Bonn, "International Economic Interdependence," *Annals of the American Academy of Political and Social Science* 175 (1934): 156–165.
25. Moritz J. Bonn, *The Crumbling of Empire: The Disintegration of World Economy* (London: Allen and Unwin, 1938), 203.
26. Bonn, "International Economic Interdependence," 156.
27. Bonn, *Wandering Scholar,* 319. See John Maynard Keynes, "National Self-Sufficiency," *Yale Review* 22, no. 4 (June 1933): 755–769.
28. Bonn, *The Crumbling of Empire,* 8.
29. Wilhelm Röpke, *International Economic Disintegration* (London: William Hodge and Co., 1942), 13.
30. Moritz J. Bonn, "Planning for Peace," *American Economic Review* 30, no. 1 (1940): 276.
31. Quoted in Howson, *Lionel Robbins,* 279.
32. "An Economist's Manifesto," *The Economist,* May 15, 1937.
33. Lionel Robbins, *Economic Planning and International Order* (London: Macmillan, 1937), 67.
34. Colloque Walter Lippmann, *Compte-Rendu des séances,* 60.
35. Robbins, *Economic Planning,* 126.
36. League of Nations, *The State and Economic Life,* 90.
37. Clarence K. Streit, *Union Now: A Proposal for a Federal Union of the Democracies of the North Atlantic* (New York: Harper and Bros., 1939). *The New Commonwealth Quarterly* was created in 1932 to debate alternative models of federation and union. See David Davies, *New Commonwealth versus the Round Table* (London: New Commonwealth, 1935). For an encyclopedic overview of these discussions, see Joseph Preston Baratta, *The Politics of World Federation,* 2 vols. (Westport, CT: Praeger, 2004).
38. Robbins, *Economic Planning,* 247.
39. Ibid.
40. Ibid., 128.
41. Ibid., 124.
42. Ibid., 248.
43. Ibid., 37.
44. Ibid., 262.
45. Ibid., 210.
46. Or Rosenboim, "Barbara Wootton, Friedrich Hayek and the Debate on Democratic Federalism in the 1940s," *International History Review* 36, no. 5 (2014): 903, 906.
47. F. A. Hayek, "Economic Conditions of Inter-state Federalism," *New Commonwealth Quarterly* 5 (1939): 133.
48. Ibid., 139.
49. Ibid., 135.
50. Ibid., 143.
51. Ibid., 139.

52. Robbins, *Economic Planning,* 217.
53. On the history of this allegory, see Eric Hayot, *The Hypothetical Mandarin: Sympathy, Modernity, and Chinese Pain* (New York: Oxford University Press, 2009).
54. Robbins, *Economic Planning,* 326.
55. Frederick Cooper, "The Dialectics of Decolonization: Nationalism and Labor Movements in Post-War French Africa," in *Tensions of Empire: Colonial Cultures in a Bourgeois World,* ed. Frederick Cooper and Laura Ann Stoler (Berkeley: University of California Press, 1997), 406–435.
56. Frederick Cooper, "Alternatives to Nationalism in French Africa, 1945–1960," in *Elites and Decolonization in the Twentieth Century,* ed. Jost Dülffer and Marc Frey (New York: Palgrave Macmillan, 2011), 116.
57. F. A. Hayek, *The Road to Serfdom* (London: Routledge and Sons, 1944), 238.
58. Michael A. Heilperin, "Review: World Economic Development by Eugene Staley," *American Political Science Review* 39, no. 1 (1945): 190.
59. Hayek, *The Road to Serfdom,* 239.
60. The word "federation" does not appear in Bruce Caldwell, *Hayek's Challenge: An Intellectual Biography of F. A. Hayek* (Chicago: University of Chicago Press, 2004), in Alan O. Ebenstein, *Hayek's Journey: The Mind of Friedrich Hayek* (New York: Palgrave Macmillan, 2003), or in Edward Feser, ed., *The Cambridge companion to Hayek* (New York: Cambridge University Press, 2006). Nor does it appear in two recent overviews of the neoliberal intellectual movement: Angus Burgin, *The Great Persuasion: Reinventing Free Markets since the Depression* (Cambridge, MA: Harvard University Press, 2012), or Daniel Stedman Jones, *Masters of the Universe: Hayek, Friedman, and the Birth of Neoliberal Politics* (Princeton, NJ: Princeton University Press, 2012). It is mentioned only in a footnote in Alan O. Ebenstein, *Friedrich Hayek: A Biography* (Chicago: University of Chicago Press, 2001), 393. For recent work revisiting Hayek's supranational ideas, see Jorg Spieker, "F. A. Hayek and the Reinvention of Liberal Internationalism," *International History Review* 36, no. 5 (2014): 1–24; John Gillingham, *European Integration, 1950–2003: Superstate or New Market Economy?* (New York: Cambridge University Press, 2003); Or Rosenboim, *The Emergence of Globalism: Visions of World Order in Britain and the United States, 1939–1950* (Princeton, NJ: Princeton University Press, 2017), chap. 5.
61. Wolfgang Streeck, *Buying Time: The Delayed Crisis of Democratic Capitalism* (New York: Verso, 2014), 101.
62. "Nobel-Prize Winning Economist," 46.
63. John Gray, *Black Mass: How Religion Led the World into Crisis* (Toronto: Anchor Canada, 2008), 177.
64. Malachi Haim Hacohen, *Karl Popper, the Formative Years, 1902–1945: Politics and Philosophy in Interwar Vienna* (New York: Cambridge University Press, 2000), 6.
65. Paul Silverman, "Law and Economics in Interwar Vienna: Kelsen, Mises, and the Regeneration of Austrian Liberalism" (PhD diss., University of Chicago, 1984), 25.
66. Ludwig Mises, *Erinnerungen* (Stuttgart: Gustav Fischer Verlag, 1978).

67. Ludwig Mises, "Economic Nationalism and Peaceful Economic Cooperation (1943)," in *Money, Method, and the Market Process*, ed. Richard Ebeling (Norwell, MA: Kluwer Academic, 1990), 161–164.
68. Ludwig Mises, "Vom Ziel der Handelspolitik," *Archiv für Sozialwissenschaft und Sozialpolitik* 42, no. 2 (1916): 580.
69. Ibid., 566.
70. Mises, *Socialism: An Economic and Sociological Analysis* (New Haven, CT: Yale University Press, 1951), 224.
71. Mises, *Nation, State, and Economy*, 85.
72. Ibid., 61.
73. Ibid.
74. Mises, *Socialism*, 403.
75. Mises, *Nation, State, and Economy*, 85.
76. Ibid., 352.
77. Ibid.
78. Ibid., 351–352.
79. Ibid., 245.
80. Ludwig Mises, *Liberalism*, 3rd ed. (Irvington-on-Hudson, NY: Foundation for Economic Education, 1985), 149.
81. Ibid., 127.
82. Ibid., 21, 42.
83. Mises, *Socialism*, 231.
84. Benjamin H. Williams, "Review: Leo Pasvolsky, Economic Nationalism of the Danubian States," *American Journal of International Law* 23, no. 2 (1929): 492.
85. Kari Polanyi-Levitt, *From the Great Transformation to the Great Financialization: On Karl Polanyi and Other Essays* (London: Zed, 2013), 27–28.
86. Mises, *Liberalism*, 130.
87. Max Sylvius Handman, "Review: Leo Pasvolsky, Economic Nationalism of the Danubian States," *Journal of Political Economy* 38, no. 4 (1930): 488.
88. Lionel Robbins, *The Economic Causes of War* (London: J. Cape, 1939), 79.
89. Jörg Guido Hülsmann, *Mises: The Last Knight of Liberalism* (Auburn, AL: Ludwig von Mises Institute, 2007), 808.
90. Ludwig Mises, "An Eastern Democratic Union: A Proposal for the Establishment of a Durable Peace in Eastern Europe (October 1941)," in *Selected Writings of Ludwig von Mises*, ed. Richard Ebeling (Indianapolis: Liberty Fund, 2000), 193.
91. Ludwig Mises, "Guidelines for a New Order of Relationships in the Danube Region (1938)," in Ebeling, *Selected Writings of Ludwig von Mises*, 318.
92. Mises, *Liberalism*, 129.
93. Ludwig Mises, "An International Loan as the 'Breathing Room' for Austrian Economic Reform," in Ebeling, *Selected Writings of Ludwig von Mises*, 270.
94. Ibid., 268.
95. "Letters from Citizen Readers," *Ottawa Citizen*, August 19, 1944.
96. Rappard, *The Geneva Experiment*, 66.

97. Mises, "An Eastern Democratic Union," 197.
98. Ibid., 196.
99. Ludwig Mises, *Omnipotent Government: The Rise of the Total State and Total War* (New Haven, CT: Yale University Press, 1944).
100. Mises, "An Eastern Democratic Union," 197.
101. F. A. Hayek, "Nationalities and States in Central Europe," *Central European Trade Review* 3, no. 3 (1945): 49–52.
102. Wilhelm Röpke, *The Social Crisis of Our Time* (Chicago: University of Chicago Press, 1950), 242. The book was originally published as *Die Gesellschaftskrise der Gegenwart* (Zurich: Eugen Rentsch Verlag, 1942).
103. Ibid., 236.
104. Wilhelm Röpke, *The German Question* (London: Allen and Unwin, 1946), 198–205.
105. Hayek, in introduction to Röpke, *The German Question*, 13.
106. Wilhelm Röpke, "The Economics of International Federation (1939)," in *40ème anniversaire 1927–1967*, ed. Institut Universitaire de Hautes Etudes Internationales (Geneva: Institut Universitaire de Hautes Etudes Internationales, 1967), 95–96.
107. Wilhelm Röpke, "Die internationale Wirtschaftsordnung der Zukunft: Pläne und Probleme," *Schweizer Monatshefte* 22, no. 7 (October 1942): 375.
108. Colloque Walter Lippmann, *Compte-Rendu des séances*, 65.
109. Wilhelm Röpke, "International Economics in a Changing World," in *The World Crisis*, ed. Geneva Graduate Institute of International Studies (London: Longmans, Green and Co., 1938), 278.
110. Wilhelm Röpke, "Wirtschaftssystem und internationale Ordnung: Prolegomena," *Ordo* 4 (1951): 275.
111. Robbins, *Economic Planning*, 91.
112. Walter Eucken, "Staatliche Strukturwandlungen und die Krisis des Kapitalismus," *Weltwirtschaftliches Archiv* 36 (1932): 307.
113. Ibid., 307, 314.
114. Röpke, "Die internationale Wirtschaftsordnung der Zukunft," 382.
115. Walter Eucken, Franz Böhm, and Hans Großmann-Doerth, preface to Franz Böhm, *Die Ordnung der Wirtschaft als geschichtliche Aufgabe und rechtschöpferische Leistung* (Stuttgart: W. Kohlhammer, 1937), xix.
116. Colloque Walter Lippmann, *Compte-Rendu des séances*, 58.
117. Röpke to Marcel van Zeeland, Röpke Archive, Institute for Economic Research, Cologne, file 7; emphasis in the original.
118. Wilhelm Röpke, "Kapitalismus und Imperialismus," *Zeitschrift für schweizerische Statistik und Volkswirtschaft*, no. 3 (1934): 384.
119. Röpke, *International Economic Disintegration*, 96.
120. Timothy Mitchell, *Rule of Experts: Egypt, Techno-Politics, Modernity* (Berkeley: University of California Press, 2002), 70.
121. Röpke, *International Economic Disintegration*, 96.

122. Eucken, "Staatliche Strukturwandlungen," 314.
123. Walter Lippmann, *An Inquiry into the Principles of the Good Society* (Boston: Little, Brown and Co., 1937), 364.
124. F. A. Hayek, "The Present State of the Debate," in *Collectivist Economic Planning*, ed. F. A. Hayek (London: Routledge and Kegan Paul, 1935), 241.
125. Ibid.

4. A WORLD OF RIGHTS

1. F. A. Hayek, *The Road to Serfdom* (London: Routledge and Sons, 1944), 88. See also Roger Normand and Sarah Zaidi, *Human Rights at the UN: The Political History of Universal Justice* (Bloomington: Indiana University Press, 2008), 77.
2. See, for example, Hans-Hermann Hoppe, who writes that "Hayek's view regarding the role of market and state cannot systematically be distinguished from that of a social democrat." Hans-Hermann Hoppe, "F. A. Hayek on Government and Social Evolution: A Critique," *Review of Austrian Economics* 7, no. 1 (1994): 67.
3. Hayek, *The Road to Serfdom*, 124–125.
4. Ibid., 88. See also Normand and Zaidi, *Human Rights at the UN*, 77.
5. Barbara Wootton, "Economic Problems of Federal Union," *New Commonwealth Quarterly* 5, no. 2 (September 1939): 150–156; Jan Herman Burgers, "The Road to San Francisco: The Revival of the Human Rights Idea in the Twentieth Century," *Human Rights Quarterly* 14, no. 4 (November 1992): 465; Or Rosenboim, "Barbara Wootton, Friedrich Hayek and the Debate on Democratic Federalism in the 1940s," *International History Review* 36, no. 5 (2014): 910.
6. H. G. Wells, "The Survival of Homo sapiens," *New Commonwealth Quarterly* 7, no. 3 (January 1942): 163–171.
7. Burgers, "The Road to San Francisco," 466.
8. On this point, see Manfred B. Steger, *The Rise of the Global Imaginary: Political Ideologies from the French Revolution to the Global War on Terror* (New York: Oxford University Press, 2008), 168.
9. Angus Burgin, *The Great Persuasion: Reinventing Free Markets since the Depression* (Cambridge, MA: Harvard University Press, 2012), 90; Ben Jackson, "At the Origins of Neo-Liberalism: The Free Economy and the Strong State, 1930–1947," *Historical Journal* 53, no. 1 (2010): 145; Jeremy Shearmur, *Hayek and After: Hayekian Liberalism as a Research Programme* (London: Routledge, 1996), 140–141. For negative rights, see F. A. Hayek, *The Mirage of Social Justice*, vol. 2 of *Law, Legislation and Liberty* (London: Routledge and Kegan Paul, 1976), 103.
10. Hayek, *The Road to Serfdom*, 239.
11. Ibid., 90.
12. Ibid., 96.
13. Ibid., 239.

14. F. A. Hayek, *The Fatal Conceit: The Errors of Socialism* (Chicago: University of Chicago Press, 1989), 42.
15. F. A. Hayek, *Rules and Order,* vol. 1 of *Law, Legislation and Liberty* (London: Routledge and Kegan Paul, 1973), 132.
16. Walter Eucken, "Staatliche Strukturwandlungen und die Krisis des Kapitalismus," *Weltwirtschaftliches Archiv* 36 (1932): 297–321.
17. Röpke to Hanna Seiler, November 13, 1965, Wilhelm Röpke Archive, Institute for Economic Research, Cologne (hereafter cited as RA), file 23, p. 9.
18. This happened in spite of the conservative intentions of the UN's framers. See Mark Mazower, *No Enchanted Palace: The End of Empire and the Ideological Origins of the United Nations* (Princeton, NJ: Princeton University Press, 2009).
19. Röpke to Hanna Seiler, November 13, 1965, RA, file 23.
20. Jamie Peck, *Constructions of Neoliberal Reason* (New York: Oxford University Press, 2010), 49.
21. Rorden Wilkinson, *Multilateralism and the World Trade Organisation: The Architecture and Extension of International Trade Regulation* (New York: Routledge, 2000), 16.
22. Douglas A. Irwin, Petros C. Mavroidis, and A. O. Sykes, *The Genesis of the GATT* (New York: Cambridge University Press, 2008), 72–73.
23. Ibid., 76–78.
24. Quoted in ibid., 95.
25. F. A. Hayek, "A Rebirth of Liberalism," *The Freeman,* July 28, 1952, 731.
26. Ibid.
27. F. A. Hayek, "The Intellectuals and Socialism (1949)," in *Studies in Philosophy, Politics and Economics,* ed. F. A. Hayek (London: Routledge and Kegan Paul, 1967).
28. International Chamber of Commerce, *Resolutions Adopted by the Twelfth Congress of the International Chamber of Commerce, Quebec, 13th–17th June 1949* (Paris: International Chamber of Commerce, 1949).
29. Olivier Longchamp and Yves Steiner, "Comment les banquiers et industriels suisses ont financé le renouveau libéral," *L'Économie politique* 4, no. 44 (2009): 79; Jean Solchany, "Wilhelm Röpke et la Suisse: La dimension helvétique d'un parcours transnational," *Traverse: Zeitschrift für Geschichte* (2010): 32.
30. Joint Committee, Carnegie Endowment–International Chamber of Commerce, *The Improvement of Commercial Relations between Nations and the Problems of Monetary Stabilization* (Paris: International Chamber of Commerce, 1936), 4. For the major publication led by Bertil Ohlin, Theodore Gregory, and J. B. Condliffe, see Joint Committee of the Carnegie Endowment for International Peace and the International Chamber of Commerce, *International Economic Reconstruction: An Economists' and Businessmen's Survey of the Main Problems of Today* (Paris: International Chamber of Commerce, 1936).
31. Conversation, JVS [John Van Sickle] with Dr. Michael Heilperin, Polish Fellow, October 25, 1934, folder 482, box 12, ser. 100, RG 1.1, Officers' Diaries, FA 118, Rockefeller Foundation records, Rockefeller Archive Center.

32. Victor Monnier, *William E. Rappard: Défenseur des libertés, serviteur de son pays et de la communauté internationale* (Geneva: Slatkine, 1995), 491.
33. Quoted in Joseph T. Salerno, "Gold and the International Monetary System: The Contribution of Michael A. Heilperin," in *The Gold Standard: An Austrian Perspective,* ed. Llewellyn H. Rockwell (Lexington, MA: Lexington Books, 1985), 108.
34. Colloque Walter Lippmann, *Compte-Rendu des séances du Colloque Walter Lippmann* (August 26–30, 1938), vol. 1 of *Travaux du centre international d'études pour la renovation du libéralisme* (Paris: Libraire de Médicis, 1938).
35. Heilperin himself was an advocate of the return of the gold standard. See Anthony M. Endres, *Great Architects of International Finance: The Bretton Woods Era* (London: Routledge, 2005), 162–173. On the role of the Bellagio Group in advocating the shift to floating exchange rates, see Carol Connell, *Reforming the World Monetary System: Fritz Machlup and the Bellagio Group* (London: Pickering and Chatto, 2013); Matthias Schmelzer, *Freiheit für Wechselkurse und Kapital: Die Ursprünge neoliberaler Währungspolitik und die Mont Pèlerin Society* (Marburg: Metropolis, 2010).
36. Jim Cox, *Sold on Radio: Advertisers in the Golden Age of Broadcasting* (Jefferson, NC: McFarland, 2008), 96.
37. *Final Reports of the International Business Conference* (New York: International Business Conference, 1944), 17.
38. "Big Business at Montreux," *Economist,* June 21, 1947, 985.
39. *Membership and Participation by the U.S. in the International Trade Organization: Hearings before the United States House Committee on Foreign Affairs, Eighty-First Congress, Second Session, on Apr. 19–21, 25–27, May 1–5, 9–12, 1950* (Washington, DC: U.S. GPO, 1950), 561.
40. Ibid., 570.
41. Michael A. Heilperin, *The Trade of Nations,* 2nd ed. (New York: Knopf, 1952), 151.
42. Quoted in "Big Business at Montreux." Emphasis in the original.
43. Michael A. Heilperin, "Elephant Traps in the World Trade Charter," *American Affairs,* July 1950, 50.
44. *Membership and Participation by the U.S. in the International Trade Organization,* 569.
45. Michael Heilperin, "An Economist's Views on International Organization (1950)," in *Studies in Economic Nationalism* (Geneva: E. Droz, 1960), 181.
46. Ibid., 184.
47. "Chemical Makers Hear I.T.O. Attack," *New York Times,* February 9, 1950.
48. Heilperin, *The Trade of Nations,* 3.
49. Michael Heilperin, *Studies in Economic Nationalism* (Geneva: E. Droz, 1960), 27.
50. Heilperin, "Economic Nationalism as an Obstacle to Free World Unity (1952)," in *Studies in Economic Nationalism,* 214.
51. Ibid., 215.
52. Heilperin, *The Trade of Nations,* 133.
53. Heilperin, "An Economist's Views on International Organization," 184.

54. Heilperin, *The Trade of Nations,* 175.
55. George L. Ridgeway, *Merchants of Peace: the History of the International Chamber of Commerce* (Boston: Little, Brown and Co., 1959), 193.
56. Jörg Guido Hülsmann, *Mises: The Last Knight of Liberalism* (Auburn, AL: Ludwig von Mises Institute, 2007), 1005.
57. Ridgeway, *Merchants of Peace,* 194–195.
58. Willliam Diebold Jr., "The End of the I.T.O.," *Essays in International Finance,* no. 16 (October 1952): 22.
59. Ibid., 21.
60. Heilperin, *The Trade of Nations,* 19.
61. Hayek, "The Intellectuals and Socialism," 194.
62. Heilperin, *The Trade of Nations,* 151.
63. The tendency to treat "the West" as a homogeneous category is one of the few shortcomings of Antony Anghie's magisterial *Imperialism, Sovereignty, and the Making of International Law* (New York: Cambridge University Press, 2007), 210.
64. For more on the alternative vision of order represented by the Havana Charter, see Martin Daunton, "Presidential Address: Britain and Globalisation since 1850: III. Creating the World of Bretton Woods, 1939–1958," *Transactions of the Royal Historical Society,* 6th ser., 18 (2008): 14–18.
65. Thomas W. Zeiler, *Free Trade, Free World: The Advent of GATT* (Chapel Hill: University of North Carolina Press, 1999), 151.
66. "Philip Cortney, Ex-head of Coty," *New York Times,* June 16, 1971; "Cortney, Philip," in *Current Biography* (New York: H. W. Wilson, 1958), 4.
67. On the NAM, see Kim Phillips-Fein, *Invisible Hands: The Making of the Conservative Movement from the New Deal to Reagan* (New York: W. W. Norton, 2009).
68. Hülsmann, *Mises,* 822–825, 829.
69. Ludwig Mises, "Government vs. Liberty," *The Freeman,* May 1955, 396.
70. Philip Cortney, *The Economic Munich* (New York: Philosophical Library, 1949), 131.
71. Ibid., 27, 50.
72. Ibid., xvii.
73. Heilperin, *The Trade of Nations,* 264.
74. Cortney, *The Economic Munich,* 132.
75. Ibid., 71.
76. Philip C. Jessup, *A Modern Law of Nations: An Introduction* (New York: Macmillan, 1948), 79. See also Hersch Lauterpacht, *An International Bill of the Rights of Man* (Oxford: Oxford University Press, 2013), 129–133.
77. Cortney, *The Economic Munich,* 132.
78. "Capital Is Urged to Return Abroad," *New York Times,* June 6, 1947.
79. E. Wyndham White, "Report by the Committee of the International Chamber of Commerce on the Legal Treatment of Foreign Companies," *Modern Law Review* 3, no. 1 (1939): 55.

80. International Chamber of Commerce, *International Code of Fair Treatment for Foreign Investments* (Paris: International Chamber of Commerce, 1949), 6.
81. Ibid., 9.
82. Ibid., 14.
83. Heilperin, *The Trade of Nations*, 26.
84. Wilhelm Röpke, *International Order and Economic Integration* (Dordrecht: D. Reidel, 1959), 79.
85. Loftus Becker, "Just Compensation in Expropriation Cases: Decline and Partial Recovery," *Department of State Bulletin*, June 1, 1959, 785.
86. On nostrification, see Leo Pasvolsky, *Economic Nationalism of the Danubian States* (New York: Macmillan, 1928), 73.
87. Noel Maurer, *The Empire Trap: The Rise and Fall of U.S. Intervention to Protect American Property Overseas, 1893–2013* (Princeton, NJ: Princeton University Press, 2013), 22.
88. Cortney, *The Economic Munich*, 135.
89. Wilhelm Röpke, "Wirtschaftssystem und internationale Ordnung: Prolegomena," *Ordo* 4 (1951): 277.
90. Nico Schrijver, *Sovereignty over Natural Resources: Balancing Rights and Duties* (New York: Cambridge University Press, 1997), 31.
91. UN General Assembly Resolution 626 (VII), "Right to Exploit Freely Natural Wealth and Resources," 411th plenary meeting, December 21, 1952, https://daccess-ods.un.org/TMP/5805275.44021606.html.
92. "Vermögensschutz," *Die Zeit*, April 5, 1956.
93. A. A. Shenfield, "Liberalism and Colonialism," MPS Proceedings, 1957, box 82, Friedrich A. von Hayek Papers, Hoover Institution Archives. See also MPS member Henry Hazlitt's critique of U.S. foreign aid from 1950: "The real barrier to international loans today is not lack of potential private American investment funds but lack of proper assurances for their safety from the governments of the foreign countries that wish to borrow." Henry Hazlitt, *Illusions of Point Four* (Irvington-on-Hudson, NY: Foundation for Economic Education, 1950), 46.
94. Ludwig Von Mises, "The Plight of the Underdeveloped Nations (1952)," in *Money, Method, and the Market Process: Essays*, ed. Richard Ebeling (Auburn, AL: Praxeology Press of the Ludwig von Mises Institute, 1990), 167.
95. Wilhelm Röpke, "Unentwickelte Länder," *Ordo* 5 (1953): 69.
96. "The Capitalist Magna Carta," *Time*, October 28, 1957, 67.
97. Michael Brandon, "An International Investment Code: Current Plans," *Journal of Business Law* 3, no. 7 (1959): 14.
98. Hermann J. Abs, "The Safety of Capital," in *Private Investment: The Key to International Industrial Development*, ed. James Daniel (New York: McGraw-Hill, 1958), 72.
99. Ibid., 73.
100. Ibid., 75.

101. Becker, "Just Compensation," 789.
102. "Statement Issued by Celler in Chicago on Dec 9 Prior to Returning to NY," and "Statements Read at Press Conference Held by Celler, Amerika Haus, Frankfurt, November 21, 1957," 104 Cong. Rec. 727 (January 21, 1958), 727–729.
103. "Statements Read at Press Conference Held by Celler," 729.
104. Stanley D. Metzger, "Multilateral Conventions for the Protection of Private Foreign Investment," *Journal of Public Law* 9, no. 1 (1960): 144.
105. "Draft Convention on Investments Abroad," *Journal of Public Law* 9, no. 1 (1960): 117.
106. Richard N. Gardner, "International Measures for the Promotion and Protection of Foreign Investment," *Proceedings of the American Society of International Law at Its Annual Meeting (1921–1969)* 53 (1959): 259.
107. Metzger, "Multilateral Conventions," 133.
108. Georg Schwarzenberger, "The Abs-Shawcross Draft Convention on Investments Abroad: A Critical Commentary," *Journal of Public Law* 9, no. 1 (1960): 151–157.
109. Ibid., 157.
110. Metzger, "Multilateral Conventions," 142.
111. Gardner, "International Measures," 260.
112. Brandon, "An International Investment Code," 8.
113. Stephan Schill, *The Multilateralization of International Investment Law* (New York: Cambridge University Press, 2009), 36.
114. 104 Cong. Rec. 9959 (1958), June 2, 1958, 9959–9960.
115. International Chamber of Commerce, *Intelligent International Investment* (New York: International Chamber of Commerce, 1949), 9.
116. International Chamber of Commerce, *Resolutions adopted by the Twelfth Congress*, 26.
117. Heilperin, "Elephant Traps," 152.
118. On the earlier history of investor protection, see Kate Miles, *The Origins of International Investment Law: Empire, Environment and the Safeguarding of Capital* (New York: Cambridge University Press, 2013); A. Claire Cutler, "Artifice, Ideology and Paradox: The Public/Private Distinction in International Law," *Review of International Political Economy* 4, no. 2 (1997): 261–285.
119. "Bonn Economics Buoys Pakistan," *New York Times*, February 26, 1959.
120. Egon Sohmen, "Competition and Growth: The Lesson of West Germany," *American Economic Review* 49, no. 5 (December 1959): 1000.
121. See Röpke, "Unentwickelte Länder," 89.
122. Erhard to the German Bundestag president, February 15, 1961, Deutscher Bundestag 3, Wahlperiode, Drucksache 2495.
123. No. 6575, Pakistan and Federal Republic of Germany, Treaty for the Promotion and Protection of Investments (with Protocol and Exchange of Notes), signed at Bonn on November 25, 1959, https://www.iisd.org/pdf/2006/investment_pakistan_germany.pdf.

124. Hayek, *The Mirage of Social Justice,* 5.
125. Heilperin, *Studies in Economic Nationalism,* 43.
126. See Patricia Clavin, *Securing the World Economy: The Reinvention of the League of Nations, 1920–1946* (New York: Oxford University Press, 2013).
127. Arthur S. Miller, "Protection of Private Foreign Investment by Multilateral Convention," *American Journal of International Law* 53 (1959): 376.
128. Enrique Prieto-Rios, "Neoliberal Market Rationality: The Driver of International Investment Law," *Birkbeck Law Review* 3 no. 1 (May 2015): 59.
129. Danny Nicol, *The Constitutional Protection of Capitalism* (London: Bloomsbury, 2010); Danny Nicol, "Business Rights as Human Rights," in *The Legal Protection of Human Rights: Sceptical Essays,* ed. Tom Campbell, K. D. Ewing, and Adam Tomkins, 229–243 (New York: Oxford University Press, 2011).
130. Frederick Cooper, "Afterword: Social Rights and Human Rights in the Time of Decolonization," *Humanity* 3, no. 3 (Winter 2012): 487.
131. Quoted in Eric Helleiner, *States and the Reemergence of Global Finance: From Bretton Woods to the 1990s* (Ithaca, NY: Cornell University Press, 1994), 59.

5. A WORLD OF RACES

1. A. A. Shenfield, "Liberalism and Colonialism," MPS Proceedings, 1957, Friedrich A. von Hayek Papers, Hoover Institution Archives, Stanford University (hereafter cited as Hayek Papers), box 82.
2. Fritz Machlup to Gottfried Haberler, December 13, 1967, Fritz Machlup Papers, Hoover Institution Archives, Stanford University (hereafter cited as Machlup Papers), box 41.
3. Elizabeth Borgwardt, *A New Deal for the World: America's Vision for Human Rights* (Cambridge, MA: Belknap Press of Harvard University Press, 2005); Nils Gilman, *Mandarins of the Future: Modernization Theory in Cold War America* (Baltimore: Johns Hopkins University Press, 2003). Needless to say, there was a considerable gap between rhetoric and practice in U.S. foreign economic policy. For selections from a vast literature, see Nick Cullather, "Miracles of Modernization: The Green Revolution and the Apotheosis of Technology," *Diplomatic History* 28, no. 2 (April 2004): 227–254; Michael E. Latham, *The Right Kind of Revolution: Modernization, Development, and U.S. Foreign Policy from the Cold War to the Present* (Ithaca, NY: Cornell University Press, 2010); Greg Grandin, *Empire's Workshop: Latin America, the United States, and the Rise of the New Imperialism* (New York: Metropolitan Books, 2006); Odd Arne Westad, *The Global Cold War: Third World Interventions and the Makings of Our Times* (New York: Cambridge University Press, 2007).
4. For the central text, see W. W. Rostow, *The Stages of Economic Growth, a Non-Communist Manifesto* (Cambridge: Cambridge University Press, 1960).

5. Quoted in Michael Latham, introduction to *Staging Growth: Modernization, Development, and the Global Cold War,* ed. David C. Engerman (Amherst: University of Massachusetts Press, 2003), 1.
6. See, for instance, P. T. Bauer, "The United Nations Report on the Economic Development of Under-Developed Countries," *Economic Journal* 63, no. 249 (March 1953): 210–222; Gottfried Haberler, "The Case for Minimum Interventionism," in *Foreign Aid Reexamined: A Critical Appraisal,* ed. James W. Wiggins, 139–150 (Washington, DC: Public Affairs Press, 1958); Henry Hazlitt, *Illusions of Point Four* (Irvington-on-Hudson, NY: Foundation for Economic Education, 1950); Gaston Leduc, "Le Sous-devéloppment et ses problèmes," *Revue d'économie politique* 62, no. 2 (May 1952): 133–189; Wilhelm Röpke, *The Economics of Full Employment: An Analysis of the UN Report on National and International Measures for Full Employment* (New York: American Enterprise Association, 1952); Wilhelm Röpke, "Unentwickelte Länder," *Ordo* 5 (1953): 63–113. For an overview of MPS discussions of development, see Dieter Plehwe, "The Origins of the Neoliberal Economic Development Discourse," in *The Road from Mont Pèlerin: The Making of the Neoliberal Thought Collective,* ed. Philip Mirowski and Dieter Plehwe (Cambridge, MA: Harvard University Press, 2009), 238–279; Jean Solchany, *Wilhelm Röpke, l'autre Hayek: Aux origines du néolibéralisme* (Paris: Sorbonne, 2015), 371–383.
7. F. A. Hayek, *The Constitution of Liberty* (1960) (Chicago: University of Chicago Press, 2011), 490.
8. John Gerard Ruggie, "International Regimes, Transactions, and Change: Embedded Liberalism in the Postwar Economic Order," *International Organization* 36, no. 2 (1982): 379–415.
9. F. A. Hayek, "Substitute for Foreign Aid," *The Freeman,* April 6, 1953, 484.
10. Ludwig Mises, "Economic Nationalism and Peaceful Economic Cooperation (1943)," in *Money, Method, and the Market Process,* ed. Richard Ebeling (Norwell, MA: Kluwer Academic Publishers, 1990), 164.
11. Röpke, "Unentwickelte Länder," 102.
12. Ibid., 103. He repeated the same sentiments in a near-reprint of the same article eight years later. Wilhelm Röpke, "Die unentwickelten Länder als wirtschaftliches, soziales und gesellschaftliches Problem," in *Entwicklungsländer, Wahn und Wirklichkeit,* ed. Albert Hunold and Wilhelm Röpke (Zurich: E. Rentsch, 1961), 52.
13. Röpke, "Unentwickelte Länder," 105.
14. Ibid.
15. Wilhelm Röpke, "Die Entwicklungsländer als Partner von Morgen," in *Das Ende der Kolonialzeit und die Welt von morgen,* ed. Ludwig Alsdorf (Stuttgart: Alfred Kröner, 1961), 206.
16. Shula Marks, "Southern Africa," in *The Oxford History of the British Empire,* ed. Judith M. Brown (Oxford: Oxford University Press, 1999), 567.
17. This chapter is based substantively on Quinn Slobodian, "The World Economy and the Color Line: Wilhelm Röpke, Apartheid, and the White Atlantic," *German Historical Institute Bulletin Supplement,* no. 10 (2014): 61–87. For an extended and

informative treatment of South Africa and Röpke, published the year after, see Solchany, *Wilhelm Röpke, l'autre Hayek,* 390–404. For works with no mention of South Africa, see Samuel Gregg, *Wilhelm Röpke's Political Economy* (Northampton, MA: Edward Elgar, 2010); Hans Jörg Hennecke, *Wilhelm Röpke: Ein Leben in der Brändung* (Stuttgart: Schäffer-Poeschel Verlag, 2005); Razeen Sally, *Classical Liberalism and International Economic Order: Studies in Theory and Intellectual History* (New York: Routledge, 1998), chap. 7; Sylvia Hanna Skwiercz, *Der Dritte Weg im Denken von Wilhelm Röpke,* 2 vols. (Würzburg: Creator, 1988); Sara Warneke, *Die europäische Wirtschaftsintegration aus der Perspektive Wilhelm Röpkes* (Stuttgart: Lucius und Lucius, 2013); John Zmirak, *Wilhelm Röpke: Swiss Localist, Global Economist* (Wilmington, DE: ISI Books, 2001).

18. For an illuminating overview of this transatlantic formation, see David Sarias Rodríguez, "'We Are All Europeans': Toward a Cosmopolitan Understanding of the American Traditionalist Right," in *Transatlantic Social Politics: 1800–Present,* ed. Daniel Scroop and Andrew Heath (New York: Palgrave Macmillan, 2014), 213–234.
19. Fritz Machlup, "Liberalism and the Choice of Freedoms," in *Roads to Freedom: Essays in Honour of Friedrich A. von Hayek,* ed. Erich W. Streissler (London: Routledge and Kegan Paul, 1969), 142.
20. https://mises.org/library/economics-colour-bar; W. H. Hutt to F. A. Hayek, June 21, 1948, Hayek Papers, box 76.
21. W. H. Hutt, *The Economics of the Color Bar* (London: Andre Deutsch, 1964).
22. F. A. Hayek, "Internationaler Rufmord," *Politische Studien,* special issue no. 1 (1978): 45.
23. On the escalation of criticism, see Ryan M. Irwin, *Gordian Knot: Apartheid and the Unmaking of the Liberal World Order* (New York: Oxford University Press, 2012). A Special Committee on Apartheid was formed in the UN in 1963. Roland Burke, *Decolonization and the Evolution of International Human Rights* (Philadelphia: University of Pennsylvania Press, 2010), 60.
24. Thomas Borstelmann, *The Cold War and the Color Line: American Race Relations in the Global Arena* (Cambridge, MA: Harvard University Press, 2001), 124.
25. Ibid., 155.
26. Wilhelm Röpke, "South Africa: An Attempt at a Positive Appraisal," *Schweizer Monatshefte* 44, no. 2 (May 1964): 8. The article was published originally as "Südafrika: Versuch einer Würdigung," *Schweizer Monatshefte* 44, no. 2 (1964): 97–112. The citations follow the reprint published in English translation by the Information Service of South Africa, also in 1964. Röpke published a shorter article with similar sentiments the year before. See Wilhelm Röpke, "Wege und Irrwege der Apartheid," *Frankfurter Allgemeine Zeitung,* October 18, 1963.
27. Röpke, "South Africa," 3.
28. Ibid.
29. Ibid., 10. Röpke's use of quotation marks around these terms suggests his skepticism about their validity as categories.

30. Wilhelm Röpke, "Conceptions and Misconceptions of Apartheid," *Africa Institute Bulletin* 4, no. 1 (1964): 25. This is a translation of Röpke, "Wege und Irrwege der Apartheid."
31. Röpke, "South Africa," 13.
32. In one of the few references to racial difference, Röpke ended a chapter in a book published first in 1942 with an empathetic anecdote about an African American man traveling in Germany. Wilhelm Röpke, *The Social Crisis of Our Time* (Chicago: University of Chicago Press, 1950), 194.
33. Röpke, "South Africa," 15.
34. Hunold to Röpke, August 15, 1964, Röpke Archive, Institute for Economic Research, Cologne (hereafter cited as RA), file 22, p. 259.
35. Röpke to Hunold, August 28, 1965, RA, file 23, p. 313.
36. Afrikaans-Deutsche Kulturgemeinschaft, "Wenn die Nashörner stampfen: Deutscher Jurist über den Alexander-Prozess," ADK-Botschaft, January 1964, RA, Panzerschrank, p. 596.
37. On his partnership with the *NZZ*, see Hennecke, *Wilhelm Röpke*, 129.
38. "Zur Diskussion über den Afrika-Vortragszyklus," *Neue Zürcher Zeitung*, July 21, 1964.
39. Röpke to Hunold, January 16, 1965, RA, file 22, p. 203.
40. For Röpke's letter of defense, see Röpke to Eberhard Ernst Reinhardt, August 18, 1964, RA, Panzerschrank, correspondence 1, p. 615. See Wahrhold Drascher, *Die Vorherrschaft der Weissen Rasse: Die Ausbreitung des abendländischen Lebensbreiches auf die überseeischen Erdteile* (Stuttgart: Deutsche Verlags-Anstalt, 1936); Wahrhold Drascher, *Schuld der Weißen? Die Spätzeit des Kolonialismus* (Tübingen: Verlag Fritz Schlichtenmeyer, 1960). On the continuity and difference in Drascher's categories before and after 1945, see Katrina Hagen, "Internationalism in Cold War Germany" (PhD diss., University of Washington, Seattle, 2008), 65–71.
41. Drascher to Röpke, May 15, 1964, RA, Panzerschrank, correspondence 1, p. 584.
42. Hunold to Röpke, October 3, 1965, RA, file 23, p. 304.
43. The primary context for the U.S. New Right was domestic. Nancy MacLean has argued that "defense of white rule in the South" was a "unifying force" among the diverse strains of the conservative movement. Nancy MacLean, "Neo-Confederacy versus the New Deal: The Regional Utopia of the Modern American Right," in *The Myth of Southern Exceptionalism*, ed. Matthew D. Lassiter and Joseph Crespino (New York: Oxford University Press, 2009), 313–315.
44. Buckley's intimacy with Röpke contrasted with his relationship to Hayek, who was skeptical about the *National Review* position. Angus Burgin, *The Great Persuasion: Reinventing Free Markets since the Depression* (Cambridge, MA: Harvard University Press, 2012), 138–140.
45. Buckley to Röpke, April 25, 1956, RA, DVD 11, p. 460.
46. Kirk's biographer notes that Kirk "frequently praised" Röpke while he "rejected the moral isolation inherent in Mises' social philosophy." W. Wesley McDonald,

Russell Kirk and the Age of Ideology (Columbia: University of Missouri Press, 2004), 168; Kirk to Röpke, February 14, 1955, RA, DVD 2, p. 150.

47. Lawrence Fertig to Röpke, January13, 1965, RA, file 22, p. 96.
48. Brandt to Röpke, December 8, 1964, RA, file 22, p. 31.
49. Bill [Buckley] to Röpke, February 25 [1963], RA, file 21, p. 576. Given the timing, the article was almost certainly Buckley's report of his government-funded trip to South Africa. William F. Buckley, "South African Fortnight," *National Review,* January 15, 1963.
50. Sally, *Classical Liberalism and International Economic Order,* 74, 158.
51. Ibid., 139.
52. Wilhelm Röpke, *International Order and Economic Integration* (Dordrecht: D. Reidel, 1959), 3.
53. See Matthew Connelly, "Taking Off the Cold War Lens: Visions of North-South Conflict during the Algerian War for Independence," *American Historical Review* 105, no. 3 (2000): 753–769.
54. Röpke, *International Order and Economic Integration,* 22.
55. Ibid., 45.
56. Helge Peukert, *Das sozialökonomische Werk Wilhelm Röpkes,* vol. 1 (Frankfurt am Main: Peter Lang, 1992), 86.
57. Bernhard Walpen, *Die offenen Feinde und ihre Gesellschaft: Eine hegemonietheoretische Studie zur Mont Pelerin Society* (Hamburg: VSA-Verlag, 2004), 278.
58. On Röpke's critique of the welfare state, see Keith Tribe, *Strategies of Economic Order: German Economic Discourse, 1750–1950* (New York: Cambridge University Press, 1995), 240.
59. Röpke, *International Order and Economic Integration,* 51.
60. Ibid., 49
61. Ibid., 54.
62. It is notable that Röpke attempted to found a journal with the name *Occident* in 1944. Walpen, *Die offenen Feinde,* 99.
63. See Duncan Bell, "Project for a New Anglo Century: Race, Space and Global Order," in *Anglo-America and Its Discontents: Civilizational Identities beyond West and East,* ed. Peter J. Katzenstein, 33–55 (New York: Routledge, 2012); Clarence K. Streit, *Union Now: A Proposal for a Federal Union of the Democracies of the North Atlantic* (New York: Harper and Bros., 1939); Valérie Aubourg, Gérard Bossuat, and Giles Scott-Smith, eds., *European Community, Atlantic Community?* (Paris: Éditions Soleb, 2008).
64. Rachel S. Turner, *Neo-liberal Ideology: History, Concepts and Policies* (Edinburgh: Edinburgh University Press, 2008), 88–89.
65. Anthony James Nicholls, *Freedom with Responsibility: The Social Market Economy in Germany, 1918–1963* (New York: Oxford University Press, 1994), 341–347.
66. Milene Wegmann, *Früher Neoliberalismus und Europäische Integration: Interdependenz der nationalen, supranationalen und internationalen Ordnung von Wirtschaft und Gesellschaft (1932–1965)* (Baden-Baden: Nomos, 2002), 326.

67. Wilhelm Röpke, "Südafrika in der Weltwirtschaft und Weltpolitik," in *Afrika und seine Probleme,* ed. Albert Hunold (Zurich: Eugen Rentsch Verlag, 1965), 130.
68. Ibid., 129. The work cited was Nathaniel Weyl and Stefan Possony, *The Geography of Intellect* (Chicago: Henry Regnery, 1963), 288. For further quotes see Robert Vitalis, *White World Order, Black Power Politics* (Ithaca, NY: Cornell University Press, 2015), 152.
69. Sally, *Classical Liberalism and International Economic Order,* 139.
70. Wilhelm Röpke, "The Malady of Progressivism," *The Freeman,* July 30, 1951, 690.
71. Josef Mooser, "Liberalismus und Gesellschaft nach 1945: Soziale Marktwirtschaft und Neoliberalismus am Beispiel von Wilhelm Röpke," in *Bürgertum nach 1945,* ed. Manfred Hettling and Bernd Ulrich (Hamburg: Hamburger Edition, 2005), 152.
72. On the varieties of planning, see Tony Judt, *Postwar: A History of Europe since 1945* (New York: Penguin, 2005), 69–71.
73. 1950 Cong. Rec. 0503, May 3, 1950, p. 6222. The quote was repeated in a 1957 study sponsored by seventeen congressmen and published in the national magazine of the Chamber of Commerce: "Adverse Effects of Expanding Government," *Nation's Business* 45, no. 9 (September 1957): 39–94, at 89.
74. Quoted in Wegmann, *Früher Neoliberalismus,* 317.
75. Röpke, *The Economics of Full Employment;* J. F. J. Toye and Richard Toye, *The UN and Global Political Economy: Trade, Finance, and Development* (Bloomington: Indiana University Press, 2004), 93.
76. Röpke, *The Economics of Full Employment,* 5, 31.
77. Wilhelm Röpke, "Washington's Economics: A German Scholar Sees Nation Moving into Fiscal Socialism," *Wall Street Journal,* April 1, 1963.
78. Röpke, "Die unentwickelten Länder," 15, 59. Myrdal was often singled out for special criticism by neoliberal critics of development aid like Peter T. Bauer and Fritz W. Meyer. See Plehwe, "Origins of the Neoliberal Economic Development Discourse," 262–264; Fritz W. Meyer, "Entwicklungshilfe und Wirtschaftsordnung," *Ordo,* no. 12 (1960/1961): 279–280. On Myrdal, see William J. Barber, *Gunnar Myrdal: An Intellectual Biography* (New York: Palgrave Macmillan, 2008); Andrés Rivarola Puntigliano and Örjan Appelqvist, "Prebisch and Myrdal: Development Economics in the Core and on the Periphery," *Journal of Global History* 6, no. 1 (2011): 29–52.
79. Röpke, "Washington's Economics."
80. Toye and Toye, *The UN and Global Political Economy,* 108.
81. Wilhelm Röpke, "The Free West," in *Freedom and Serfdom: An Anthology of Western Thought,* ed. Albert Hunold (Dordrecht: D. Reidel, 1961), 76.
82. Röpke, "Unentwickelte Länder," 89.
83. Wilhelm Röpke, "Die Nationalökonomie des 'New Frontier,'" *Ordo* 9 (1963): 106.
84. Ibid.
85. Plehwe, "Origins of the Neoliberal Economic Development Discourse," 249.
86. Sally, *Classical Liberalism and International Economic Order,* 132.

87. Kristin Ross, *Fast Cars, Clean Bodies: Decolonization and the Reordering of French Culture* (Cambridge, MA: MIT Press, 1995), 10.
88. Patrick Boarman to Röpke, April 12, 1963, RA, file 21, p. 598. The congressional representatives were Steven B. Derounian (New York), Bruce Alger (Texas), Thomas B. Curtis (Missouri), and Bob Wilson (California). *Congressional Record* 1963-0401, April 1, 1963, 88-1, A1867, A1879, 5207; *Congressional Record* 1963-0422, April 22, 1963, A2339.
89. Bruce Alger (Texas), *Congressional Record* 1963-040, A1879.
90. Thomas B. Curtis (Missouri) in ibid., 5208. Curtis was one of the leaders of the "Young Turk" group of moderate Republicans in the late 1950s and early 1960s. His defense of free trade separated him from many entrenched members of the GOP. Geoffrey M. Kabaservice, *Rule and Ruin: The Downfall of Moderation and the Destruction of the Republican Party, from Eisenhower to the Tea Party* (New York: Oxford University Press, 2012), 55.
91. Kim Phillips-Fein, *Invisible Hands: The Making of the Conservative Movement from the New Deal to Reagan* (New York: W. W. Norton, 2009), 56–58.
92. Rick Perlstein, *Before the Storm: Barry Goldwater and the Unmaking of the American Consensus* (New York: Hill and Wang, 2001), 33.
93. Röpke to Paul Wilhelm Wenger, August 5, 1964, RA, file 89, p. 568.
94. Phillips-Fein, *Invisible Hands*, 57, 59. Kim Phillips-Fein, "Business Conservatives and the Mont Pèlerin Society," in Mirowski and Plehwe, *The Road from Mont Pèlerin*, 292.
95. See George H. Nash, *The Conservative Intellectual Movement in America since 1945* (Wilmington, DE: ISI Books, 2006), 69; Sarias Rodríguez, "'We Are All Europeans,'" 213; Christopher S. Allen, "The Underdevelopment of Keynesianism in the Federal Republic of Germany," in *The Political Power of Economic Ideas: Keynesianism across Nations*, ed. Peter A. Hall (Princeton, NJ: Princeton University Press, 1989); Fabio Masini, "Luigi Einaudi and the Making of the Neoliberal Project," *History of Economic Thought and Policy* 1, no. 1 (2012): 39–59.
96. William F. Buckley, "Buckley Supports DeGaulle's Views," *Boston Globe*, February 17, 1963.
97. William Henry Chamberlin, "A Powerful Argument for a Free Economy," *Wall Street Journal*, April 15, 1963.
98. On Röpke's privileging of the external liberalization policies of Switzerland and West Germany, see Sally, *Classical Liberalism and International Economic Order*, 140.
99. William R. Van Gemert, "Letter to the Editor," *Wall Street Journal*, April 22, 1963.
100. *Rundt's Weekly Intelligence: A Service to Exporters, Bankers and Overseas Investors*, April 30, 1963, RA, "Vorträge" binder.
101. Edwin McDowell, "A Mountain Where Thinkers Dwell," *Wall Street Journal*, September 20, 1972.

102. Wilhelm Röpke, "Amerikanische Intellektuelle von Europa gesehen," *Deutsche Rundschau*, February 1957, 137.
103. Ibid., 138.
104. Nash, *The Conservative Intellectual Movement*, 58–59, 69–70.
105. Röpke, "Amerikanische Intellektuelle von Europa gesehen," 139.
106. In one example of many, he recorded a piece for a program that U.S. Steel was broadcasting on Ivy League college radio stations. C. M. Underhill, Memo, U.S. Steel to Röpke, September 29, 1961, RA, file 88, p. 576.
107. Röpke to Fred Clark, September 22, 1962, RA, file 20, p. 50.
108. T. R. B., "The Fair," *New Republic*, September 25, 1965, 4.
109. Röpke's biographer refers to him as "the oracle in Geneva." Hennecke, *Wilhelm Röpke*, 182.
110. Ricardo A. Ball, Harvard University, to Röpke, December 8, 1961, RA, file 20, p. 37.
111. "Book Shelf: Anatomy of the Welfare State," *Pittsburgh Courier*, January 2, 1965; Chamberlin, "A Powerful Argument."
112. Internationale Bank für Wiederaufbau und Entwicklung, memo, April 20, 1960, Political Archive of the West German Foreign Office, B 61-411, vol. 128.
113. Christopher S. Allen, "'Ordo-Liberalism' Trumps Keynesianism: Economic Policy in the Federal Republic of Germany and the EU," in *Monetary Union in Crisis: The European Union as a Neo-Liberal Construction*, ed. Bernard H. Moss, 199–221 (New York: Palgrave Macmillan, 2005).
114. Alexander Nützenadel, *Stunde der Ökonomen: Wissenschaft, Politik und Expertenkultur in der Bundesrepublik, 1949–1974* (Göttingen: Vandenhoeck und Ruprecht, 2005), 12; Michael A. Bernstein, *A Perilous Progress: Economists and Public Purpose in Twentieth-Century America* (Princeton, NJ: Princeton University Press, 2001), chaps. 5–6.
115. Hennecke, *Wilhelm Röpke*, 219. For further details on Röpke in Latin America, see Solchany, *Wilhelm Röpke*, 383–390.
116. Röpke to Velasco, November 18, 1963, RA, file 21, p. 69. On Velasco's activities with the MPS, see Plehwe, "Origins of the Neoliberal Economic Development Discourse," 244.
117. Zuloaga to Röpke, May 9, 1963, RA, file 89, p. 318.
118. Hunold to Röpke, April 2, 1962, RA, file 20, p. 230.
119. Röpke to Karl Brandt, April 26, 1963, RA, file 21, p. 597. Beyond personality frictions, the conflict stemmed from Hunold and Röpke having a more apocalyptic diagnosis of geopolitics, a preference for greater MPS publicity, and a desire to exert more stringent control over its membership. For details, see Walpen, *Die offenen Feinde*, 145–151.
120. Hunold to Röpke, March 20, 1964, RA, file 22, p. 298.
121. Hunold to Röpke, January 1, 1965, RA, file 22, p. 206; Hunold to Röpke, January 5, 1965, RA, file 22, p. 205; Jesús Arboleya, *The Cuban Counterrevolution* (Athens: Ohio University Center for International Studies, 2000), 41.

122. Hunold to Röpke, November 13, 1962, RA, file 20, p. 178.
123. Juan Gabriel Valdés, *Pinochet's Economists: The Chicago School in Chile* (New York: Cambridge University Press, 1995), 224–225.
124. Kirk to Röpke, March 19, 1963, RA, file 21, p. 649.
125. Ibid.; Hunold to Röpke, January 1, 1965, RA, file 22, p. 206.
126. Röpke to Kirk, February 14, 1963, RA, file 21, p. 269.
127. Sinistrized is a neologism by which Röpke meant turned to the left. Röpke to Hunold, August 18, 1962, RA, file 20, p. 220.
128. Röpke to Karl Brandt, April 26, 1963, RA, file 21, p. 597; Röpke to Hunold, April 30. 1959, RA, file 18, p. 230; Röpke to Schoeck, November 17, 1958, RA, file 18, p. 623.
129. Röpke to Karl Mönch, October 18, 1961, RA, file 20, p. 397.
130. Röpke to Willi Bretscher, November 3, 1962, RA, file 89, p. 148.
131. Hunold to Röpke, March 20, 1964, RA, file 22, p. 298. On Goodrich's role in financing MPS meetings, see Phillips-Fein, *Invisible Hands*, 48–51.
132. Hennecke, *Wilhelm Röpke*, 224.
133. Kirk to Röpke, March 19, 1963, RA, file 21, p. 649.
134. For his resignation letter, see Brandt to Members of the MPS, January 8, 1962, Machlup Papers, box 279.
135. Brandt to Röpke, December 8, 1964, RA, file 22, p. 30.
136. Walpen, *Die offenen Feinde*, 108.
137. Burgin, *The Great Persuasion*, 146.
138. Hunold to Röpke, January 1, 1965, RA, file 22, p. 206.
139. Ibid., 145.
140. Röpke used the expression in a letter to Alexander Rüstow. Quoted in Philip Plickert, *Wandlungen des Neoliberalismus: Eine Studie zu Entwicklung und Ausstrahlung der "Mont Pelerin Society"* (Stuttgart: Lucius und Lucius, 2008), 189.
141. On Spiritual Mobilization, see Phillips-Fein, *Invisible Hands*, 71–74.
142. Hunold to Röpke, March 20, 1964, RA, file 22, p. 298.
143. Wilhelm Röpke, *Against the Tide* (Chicago: H. Regnery Co., 1969).
144. Nicholls suggests that Röpke shifted to the right in the 1950s, a conclusion this chapter would support. Nicholls, *Freedom with Responsibility*, 324.
145. William F. Buckley, "Why the South Must Prevail," *National Review*, August 24, 1957, 149. Such blunt statements were rare. In general, the language of states' rights and federalism served as an identifiable code in conservative publications like the *National Review* and *Modern Age* for opposition to the realization of political equality. Joseph E. Lowndes, *From the New Deal to the New Right: Race and the Southern Origins of Modern Conservatism* (New Haven, CT: Yale University Press, 2008), 50.
146. Buckley, "Why the South Must Prevail," 149; emphasis added. For an exception, see Rodríguez, "'We Are All Europeans,'" 220–221.
147. Allan J. Lichtman, *White Protestant Nation: The Rise of the American Conservative Movement* (New York: Atlantic Monthly Press, 2008), 227.

148. Röpke to Hunold, June 27, 1963, RA, file 21, p. 354. He was referring in particular to David Abner Morse, the chief of the U.S. delegation to the International Labor Conference. On Morse and the "South Africa crisis" of 1963, to which Röpke was surely alluding, see Daniel Maul, *Human Rights, Development, and Decolonization: The International Labour Organization, 1940–70* (New York: Palgrave Macmillan, 2012), 236–245.
149. Sara Diamond, *Roads to Dominion: Right-Wing Movements and Political Power in the United States* (New York: Guilford Press, 1995), 118, 346.
150. *Congressional Record* 1967-0322, March 22, 1967, 7710.
151. *Congressional Record* 1967-0322, March 22, 1967, 7711.
152. Wilhelm Röpke, "The Place of the Nation," *Modern Age* 10, no. 2 (Spring 1966): 121. For an earlier version of this argument, see Röpke, "Unentwickelte Länder," 103.
153. Röpke, "Die unentwickelten Länder," 50.
154. Röpke to Hunold, November 15, 1965, RA, file 23, p. 300.
155. Hunold to Röpke, January 4, 1966, RA, file 23, p. 104.
156. Hunold to Röpke. October 3, 1965, RA, file 23, p. 304.
157. Hunold to Röpke, November 17, 1965, RA, file 23, p. 20.
158. Schoeck to Röpke, December 16, 1964, RA, file 23, p. 551.
159. See Ludwig Mises, *Human Action: A Treatise on Economics* (1949) (Auburn, AL: Ludwig Von Mises Institute, 1998), 37; Nash, *The Conservative Intellectual Movement,* 148. One should note that Mises and Hayek both expressed reservations about immigration, for reasons of not biological racism but the social friction produced by racialized resentment. Mises wrote in 1944 that "there are few white men who would not shudder at the picture of many millions of black or yellow people living in their own countries." Ludwig Mises, *Omnipotent Government: The Rise of the Total State and Total War* (New Haven, CT: Yale University Press, 1944), 107. Hayek expressed approval of Margaret Thatcher's restrictive immigration policy in a series of articles and letters in *The Times* (London). See F. A. Hayek, "The Politics of Race and Immigration," *The Times,* February 11, 1978; Hayek, "Origins of Racialism," *The Times,* March 1, 1978; Hayek, "Integrating Immigrants," *The Times,* March 9, 1978.
160. Some prominent neoliberals did suggest links, however, between climate, cultural characteristics, and economic underdevelopment. Bauer suggested a "connection between climate and material backwardness." Peter T. Bauer, "Development Economics: The Spurious Consensus and Its Background," in Streissler, *Roads to Freedom,* 30. In 1960 Louis Rougier explained "the differences in development by the differences in mentality," citing "Arab fatalism" and the "magical pre-logical mentality" of indigenous people in Central Africa and Australasia. Quoted in Solchany, *Wilhelm Röpke, l'autre Hayek,* 381, and see also Frederick C. Benham on climate and cultural work ethic, quoted at 380.
161. "New Books and Articles," *New Individualist Review* 3, no. 3 (1964): 47.

162. For details, see "Autobiography Copy 2," August 10, 1984, William H. Hutt Papers, Hoover Institution Archives, Stanford University (hereafter cited as Hutt Papers), box 11.
163. See, for instance, P. T. Bauer and B. S. Yamey, "Against the New Economic Order," *Commentary,* April 1, 1977.
164. "Autobiography Copy 2."
165. Hutt received permission from Friedman to include a page-long quotation from *Capitalism and Freedom* in the introduction to his book. Friedman to Hutt, July 16, 1963, Hutt Papers, box 40.
166. Peter Lewin, "William Hutt and the Economics of Apartheid," *Constitutional Political Economy* 11 (2000): 255.
167. Ibid., 257. On the unacknowledged similarities between Hutt's argument and parallel discussions of public choice, see Ben Jackson, "Hayek, Hutt and the Trade Unions," in *Hayek: A Collaborative Biography; Part V: Hayek's Great Society of Free Men,* ed. Robert Leeson (Houndmills, UK: Palgrave Macmillan, 2015), 169.
168. Hutt, *The Economics of the Color Bar,* 27.
169. J. Enoch Powell, "How Money Works for Integration," *The Sunday Times* (London), June 14, 1964.
170. Hutt, *The Economics of the Color Bar,* 173.
171. Ibid., 115.
172. Ibid., 178; emphasis in the original.
173. Ibid., 180.
174. Buckley, "South African Fortnight."
175. "Apartheid in South Africa and Its Foreign Critics" undated [1963], Hutt Papers, box 31.
176. Ibid.
177. Hutt to editor, *Cape Times,* January 18, 1957, Hutt Papers, box 14.
178. "Apartheid in South Africa and Its Foreign Critics."
179. Hayek, *The Constitution of Liberty,* 63.
180. Ibid., 64.
181. Submitted as an attachment by Hutt to Victor Norton, editor, *Cape Times,* October 2, 1961, Hutt Papers, box 14.
182. W. H. Hutt, "The Abuse of Parliamentary Majority in Multi-Racial Society," Hutt Papers, box 14.
183. Ibid.
184. W. H. Hutt, "'Fragile' Constitutions," *New Individualist Review* 4, no. 3 (Spring 1966): 48.
185. Ibid.
186. Hutt to Smith, October 28, 1964, Hutt Papers, box 14.
187. Hutt to Smith, October 12, 1965, Hutt Papers, box 14.
188. W. H. Hutt, "The Rhodesian Calumny," *New Individualist Review* 5, no. 1 (Winter 1968): 3, 12.

189. Hutt to Reagan, March 9, 1977, Hutt Papers, box 14; Hutt to Carter, March 1, 1977, Hutt Papers, box 14.
190. Sean Wilentz, *The Age of Reagan: A History, 1974–2008* (New York: HarperCollins, 2008), 103.
191. Hutt to Owen Horwood, September 20, 1978, Hutt Papers, box 14.
192. Hutt to R. F. Botha, March 9, 1983, Hutt Papers, box 14.
193. Hutt to Owen Horwood, September 20, 1978.
194. It is worth noting that Fritz Machlup resisted pressure as the president of the International Economic Association to take an official stance on apartheid in 1971 with the argument that "we must stay out of ideological or political controversies." Machlup to Luc Fauvel, December 22, 1971, Machlup Papers, box 291.
195. Arthur Shenfield, "The Ideological War against Western Society," *Modern Age* 14, no. 2 (Spring 1970): 168.
196. Dieter Plehwe, introduction to Mirowski and Plehwe, *The Road from Mont Pèlerin,* 21.
197. Hutt to Susan M. Haufe, Deptartment of State, November 23, 1977, Hutt Papers, box 14.
198. Les de Villiers, Information Service of South Africa, to John Davenport, August 2, 1972, John A. Davenport Papers, Hoover Institution Archives, Stanford University (hereafter cited as Davenport Papers), box 3; John A. Davenport, "Namibia—Victim or Beneficiary of South African Rule?," *New York Times,* July 19, 1972.
199. K. H. Towsey, Rhodesian Information Office, Washington, DC, to Davenport, April 7, 1978, Davenport Papers, box 4; Towsey to Davenport, May 18, 1978, Davenport Papers, box 4.
200. Borstelmann, *The Cold War,* 256; Brenda Gayle Plummer, "Race and the Cold War," in *The Oxford Handbook of the Cold War,* ed. Richard H. Immerman and Petra Goedde (Oxford: Oxford University Press, 2013), 517; American-Rhodesian Association invitation, October 13, 1978, Davenport Papers, box 28.
201. The American-Rhodesian Association, statement of purpose, Davenport Papers, box 28.
202. John A. Davenport, "The Anti-apartheid Threat," *The Freeman,* August 1985, 454.
203. Patrick J. Buchanan, White House, to Davenport. August 28, 1985, Davenport Papers, box 28.
204. Milton Friedman, "Rhodesia," *Newsweek,* 3 May 1976, 77. The article was published verbatim the day before in the *Sunday Times.* See reprint, Milton Friedman, "Suicide of the West," in *Friedman in South Africa,* ed. Meyer Feldberg, Kate Jowell, and Stephen Mulholland (Cape Town: Graduate School of Business, 1976), 58–60. For the second article, see Milton Friedman, "Economic Sanctions," *Newsweek,* January 21, 1980.
205. Friedman, "Rhodesia," 77.
206. Friedman, "The Fragility of Freedom," 7.
207. For a founding articulation of this argument, see Mancur Olson, *The Logic of Collective Action: Public Goods and the Theory of Groups* (Cambridge, MA: Harvard University Press, 1965).

208. Friedman, "The Fragility of Freedom," 9.
209. Friedman, "The Milton Friedman View," in *Friedman in South Africa*, ed. Meyer Feldberg, Kate Jowell, and Stephen Mulholland (Cape Town: Graduate School of Business, 1976), 49.
210. Friedman, "Rhodesia," 77.
211. Friedman, "Economic Sanctions."
212. Hayek, "Internationaler Rufmord," 44. Hayek had first pitched the article to *Frankfurter Allgemeine Zeitung* but they declined to publish it. Bruce Caldwell and Leonidas Montes, "Friedrich Hayek and His Visits to Chile," *Review of Austrian Economics* 28, no. 3 (2015): 282. In addition to Caldwell and Montes, see, on Chile and the neoliberals, Andrew Farrant, Edward McPhail, and Sebastian Berger, "Preventing the 'Abuses' of Democracy: Hayek, the 'Military Usurper' and Transitional Dictatorship in Chile?," *American Journal of Economics and Sociology* 71, no. 3 (July 2012): 513–538; Karin Fischer, "The Influence of Neoliberals in Chile before, during, and after Pinochet," in Mirowski and Plehwe, *The Road from Mont Pèlerin*, 305–346. On the influence of James Buchanan on the Chilean constitution, see Nancy MacLean, *Democracy in Chains: The Deep History of the Radical Right's Stealth Plan for America* (New York: Viking, 2017), chap. 10.
213. Hayek, "Internationaler Rufmord," 45. He returned to the criticism in an interview a few years later when he complained of the use of human rights talk to intervene in other countries' policies. "People in South Africa have to deal with their own problems," he wrote, "and the idea that you can use external pressure to change people, who after all have built up a civilization of a kind, seems to me morally a very doubtful belief." "Nobel-Prize Winning Economist," oral history interview with F. A. Hayek, Oral History Program, UCLA, 1983, 439, https://archive.org/details/nobelprizewinnin00haye. Caldwell and Montes state correctly that Hayek's emphasis in this article on "the importance of following general rules" is consistent with his broader oeuvre. Caldwell and Montes, "Friedrich Hayek and His Visits to Chile," 283.
214. Wilhelm Röpke, "Kapitalismus und Imperialismus," *Zeitschrift für schweizerische Statistik und Volkswirtschaft*, no. 3 (1934): 370.
215. Ibid., 384–386.
216. Röpke, "Südafrika in der Weltwirtschaft und Weltpolitik," 158.
217. Ibid., 156.

6. A WORLD OF CONSTITUTIONS

1. John Gillingham, *European Integration, 1950–2003: Superstate or New Market Economy?* (New York: Cambridge University Press, 2003), 6; Werner Bonefeld, "European Economic Constitution and the Transformation of Democracy: On Class and the State of Law," *European Journal of International Relations* 21, no. 4

(2015): 876–877; Bernard H. Moss, *Monetary Union in Crisis: The European Union as a Neo-Liberal Construction* (New York: Palgrave Macmillan, 2005), 12, 29.

2. Milene Wegmann, *Früher Neoliberalismus und Europäische Integration: Interdependenz der nationalen, supranationalen und internationalen Ordnung von Wirtschaft und Gesellschaft (1932–1965)* (Baden-Baden: Nomos, 2002), 368.
3. Jacques Stohler, "Neoliberalismus und europäische Integration," *Europa-Archiv* 17, no. 1 (1962): 99.
4. Hans Von der Groeben, *The European Community: The Formative Years* (Luxembourg: Office for Official Publications of the European Communities, 1987), 48.
5. Peo Hansen and Stefan Jonsson, "Bringing Africa as a 'Dowry to Europe,'" *Interventions: International Journal of Postcolonial Studies* 13, no. 3 (2011): 1038.
6. Katja Seidel, "DG IV and the Origins of a Supranational Competition Policy: Establishing an Economic Constitution for Europe," in *The History of the European Union: Origins of a Trans- and Supranational Polity, 1950–72*, ed. Wolfram Kaiser, Brigitte Leucht, and Morten Rasmussen (New York: Routledge, 2009), 132. Christian Joerges, "Three Transformations of Europe and the Search for a Way out of Its Crisis," in *The European Crisis and the Transformation of Transnational Governance: Authoritarian Managerialism versus Democratic Governance*, ed. Christian Joerges and Carola Glinski (Portland, OR: Hart, 2014), 27.
7. Quoted in Susan Howson, *Lionel Robbins* (New York: Cambridge University Press, 2011), 665.
8. Wegmann, *Früher Neoliberalismus*, 326.
9. Gottfried Haberler, "Economic Aspects of a European Union," *World Politics* 1, no. 4 (1949): 434–435.
10. Patricia Clavin, *Securing the World Economy: The Reinvention of the League of Nations, 1920–1946* (New York: Oxford University Press, 2013).
11. Haberler, "Economic Aspects of a European Union," 436.
12. Stohler, "Neoliberalismus und europäische Integration," 99.
13. Röpke, "Gemeinsamer Markt und Freihandelszone: 28 Thesen als Richtpunkte," *Ordo* 10 (1958): 35.
14. Michael A. Heilperin, "Future of E.R.P.," *New York Times*, November 6, 1949.
15. Quoted in Sara Warneke, *Die europäische Wirtschaftsintegration aus der Perspektive Wilhelm Röpkes* (Stuttgart: Lucius und Lucius, 2013), 170.
16. Röpke, "Gemeinsamer Markt und Freihandelszone," 33.
17. Ludolf Herbst, "Integrationstheorie und europäische Einigung," *Vierteljahrshefte für Zeitgeschichte* 34, no. 2 (1986): 164.
18. Heilperin, "Future of E.R.P."
19. Ibid.
20. Wilhelm Röpke, *International Order and Economic Integration* (Dordrecht: D. Reidel, 1959), 3.
21. Fritz Machlup, *A History of Thought on Economic Integration* (London: Macmillan, 1977). See Wilhelm Röpke, *International Economic Disintegration* (London: William Hodge and Company, 1942).

22. Wilhelm Röpke, "Integration und Desintegration der internationalen Wirtschaft," in *Wirtschaftsfragen der freien Welt,* ed. Erwin von Beckerath (Frankfurt: F. Knapp, 1957), 494. See Wilhelm Röpke, *Weltwirtschaft und Außenhandelspolitik* (Berlin: Industrieverlag Spaeth und Linde, 1931).
23. Wilhelm Röpke, "International Economics in a Changing World," in *The World Crisis,* ed. Geneva Graduate Institute of International Studies (London: Longmans, Green and Co., 1938), 278; Ludwig Mises, "The Disintegration of the International Division of Labour," also in *The World Crisis.* See also Moritz J. Bonn, *The Crumbling of Empire: The Disintegration of World Economy* (London: Allen and Unwin, 1938).
24. Michael A. Heilperin, *The Trade of Nations,* 2nd ed. (New York: Knopf, 1952), 293.
25. Röpke, "Gemeinsamer Markt und Freihandelszone," 38.
26. Thomas W. Zeiler, *Free Trade, Free World: The Advent of GATT* (Chapel Hill: University of North Carolina Press, 1999), 28; Endres and Fleming, *International Organizations,* 126.
27. Röpke, "European Free Trade: The Great Divide," *The Banker,* September 1958, 4.
28. Quoted in Anthony James Nicholls, *Freedom with Responsibility: The Social Market Economy in Germany, 1918–1963* (New York: Oxford University Press, 1994), 345. See also Alfred C. Mierzejewski, *Ludwig Erhard: A Biography* (Chapel Hill: University of North Carolina Press, 2004), 147–150.
29. Röpke, "Gemeinsamer Markt und Freihandelszone," 39.
30. Nicholls, *Freedom with Responsibility,* 346.
31. Wilhelm Röpke, "Report on an Uneasy Common Market," *National Review,* March 10, 1964, 195.
32. Von der Groeben, *The European Community,* 48.
33. Röpke, "Gemeinsamer Markt und Freihandelszone," 32.
34. Michael A. Heilperin, "Freer Trade and Social Welfare," *International Labour Review* 75, no. 3 (1957): 173.
35. Ibid., 178.
36. Michael Heilperin, "Europe Edges toward a Common Market," *Fortune,* September 1956.
37. Ralf Ptak, *Vom Ordoliberalismus zur sozialen Marktwirtschaft: Stationen des Neoliberalismus in Deutschland* (Opladen: Leske und Budrich, 2004), 85.
38. Ibid., 86.
39. Nils Goldschmidt, "Alfred Müller-Armack and Ludwig Erhard: Social Market Liberalism," *Freiburg Discussion Papers on Constitutional Economics* 4 (2012): 16.
40. Warneke, *Die europäische Wirtschaftsintegration,* 186.
41. Ptak, *Vom Ordoliberalismus zur sozialen Marktwirtschaft,* 214.
42. Alfred Müller-Armack, "Fragen der europäischen Integration," in *Wirtschaftsfragen der freien Welt,* ed. Erwin von Beckerath (Frankfurt am Main: F. Knapp, 1957), 532.
43. Ibid., 533.
44. Alfred Müller-Armack, *Auf dem Weg nach Europa* (Stuttgart: C. E. Poeschel, 1971), 99.

45. Ulrich Enders, "Integration oder Kooperation?," *Vierteljahrshefte für Zeitgeschichte* 45, no. 1 (1997): 150.
46. Ralf Kowitz, *Alfred Müller-Armack: Wirtschaftspolitik als Berufung* (Cologne: Deutscher Instituts-Verlag, 1998), 268; Hans Von der Groeben, "Die Anfänge der Europäische Wirtschaftsgemeinschaft," in *40 Jahre Römische Verträge: Der deutsche Beitrag*, ed. Ruldolf Hrbek and Volker Schwarz (Baden-Baden: Nomos, 1998), 165.
47. Kowitz, *Alfred Müller-Armack*, 276–281.
48. Ibid., 282.
49. Details from Müller-Armack, *Auf dem Weg nach Europa*, 125.
50. David J. Gerber, "Constitutionalizing the Economy: German Neoliberalism, Competition Law and the 'New' Europe," *American Journal of Comparative Law* 42, no. 1 (Winter 1994): 73.
51. Hubert Buch-Hansen and Angela Wigger, *The Politics of European Competition Regulation: A Critical Political Economy Perspective* (New York: Routledge, 2011), 53–54; Matthieu Montalban, Sigfrido Ramirez-Perez, and Andy Smith, "EU Competition Policy Revisited: Economic Doctrines within European Political Work," *Cahiers du GREThA*, no. 33 (2011): 21.
52. Herbert Giersch, Karl-Heinz Paqué, and Holger Schmieding, *The Fading Miracle: Four Decades of Market Economy in Germany* (New York: Cambridge University Press, 1994), 174.
53. Quoted in Rachel S. Turner, *Neo-liberal Ideology: History, Concepts and Policies* (Edinburgh: Edinburgh University Press, 2008), 88.
54. Kym Anderson, "Setting the Trade Policy Agenda: What Roles for Economists?," *Journal of World Trade* 39, no. 2 (2005): 345.
55. Moss, *Monetary Union in Crisis*, 10.
56. Müller-Armack, foreword to Reinhold Biskup, Ronald Clapham, and Joachim Starbatty, "Das Bananen-Protokoll im EWG-Vertrag," *Institut für Wirtschaftspolitik an der Universität zu Köln Untersuchungen*, no. 18 (1966): 13.
57. Peo Hansen and Stefan Jonsson, *Eurafrica: The Untold History of European Integration and Colonialism* (London: Bloomsbury, 2014), 244.
58. Stefan Tangermann, "European Interests in the Banana Market," in *Banana Wars: The Anatomy of a Trade Dispute*, ed. T. E. Josling and T. G. Taylor (Cambridge, MA: CABI, 2003), 20.
59. For details, see ibid., 21.
60. Müller-Armack, *Auf dem Weg nach Europa*, 190.
61. Röpke, "Gemeinsamer Markt und Freihandelszone," 53.
62. Foreword to Biskup, Clapham, and Starbatty, "Das Bananen-Protokoll im EWG-Vertrag," 39.
63. James Wiley, *The Banana: Empires, Trade Wars, and Globalization* (Lincoln: University of Nebraska Press, 2008), 125.
64. For exceptions, along with other works cited here, see Muriam Haleh Davis, "Restaging Mise en Valeur: 'Postwar Imperialism' and the Plan de Constantine,"

Review of Middle East Studies 44, no. 2 (2010): 176–186; Giuliano Garavini, *After Empires: European Integration, Decolonization, and the Challenge from the Global South, 1957–1986* (New York: Oxford University Press, 2012).

65. Von der Groeben, *The European Community,* 33.
66. Von der Groeben, "Die Anfänge der Europäische Wirtschaftsgemeinschaft," 168.
67. Müller-Armack, *Auf dem Weg nach Europa,* 130.
68. Hansen and Jonsson, *Eurafrica,* 238.
69. Röpke, "Integration und Desintegration," 499.
70. Wilhelm Röpke, "Nation und Weltwirtschaft," *Ordo* 17 (1966): 41.
71. Wilhelm Röpke, "Kapitalismus und Imperialismus," *Zeitschrift für schweizerische Statistik und Volkswirtschaft,* no. 3 (1934): 386.
72. Thomas Moser, *Europäische Integration, Dekolonisation, Eurafrika: Eine historische Analyse über die Entstehungsbedingungen der Eurafrikanischen Gemeinschaft von der Weltwirtschaftskrise bis zum Jaunde-Vertrag, 1929–1963* (Baden-Baden: Nomos, 2000), 353.
73. Gary Wilder, "Eurafrique as the Future Past of 'Black France': Sarkozy's Temporal Confusion and Senghor's Postwar Vision," in *Black France/France Noire: The History and Politics of Blackness,* ed. Trica Danielle Keaton, T. Denean Sharpley-Whiting, and Tyler Edward Stovall (Durham, NC: Duke University Press, 2012), 70. See also Frederick Cooper, *Citizenship between Empire and Nation: Remaking France and French Africa, 1945–1960* (Princeton, NJ: Princeton University Press, 2014), 202–210; Kaye Whiteman, "The Rise and Fall of Eurafrique: From the Berlin Conference of 1884–1885 to the Tripoli EU–Africa Summit of 2010," in *The EU and Africa: From Eurafrique to Afro-Europa,* ed. Adekeye Adebajo and Kaye Whiteman (New York: Columbia University Press, 2012), 30.
74. Frederick Cooper, "Writing the History of Development," *Journal of Modern European History* 8, no. 1 (2010): 14.
75. Wilder, "Eurafrique as the Future Past," 75.
76. Müller-Armack, *Auf dem Weg nach Europa,* 119.
77. Quoted in Martin Evans, "Colonial Fantasies Shattered," in *The Oxford Handbook of Postwar European History,* ed. Dan Stone (Oxford: Oxford University Press, 2012), 493.
78. Moser, *Europäische Integration, Dekolonisation, Eurafrika,* 101.
79. Carl Schmitt, *The* Nomos *of the Earth in the International Law of the* Jus Publicum Europaeum (New York: Telos Press, 2003), 214.
80. Véronique Dimier, "Bringing the Neo-Patrimonial State Back to Europe: French Decolonization and the Making of the European Development Aid Policy," *Archiv für Sozialgeschichte,* no. 48 (2008): 441.
81. Moser, *Europäische Integration, Dekolonisation, Eurafrika,* 107.
82. Quoted in Thomas Oppermann, "Eurafrika—Idee und Wirklichkeit," *Europa-Archiv,* December 5, 1960, 700.
83. Moser, *Europäische Integration, Dekolonisation, Eurafrika,* 410–411.
84. Gerhard Pohl and Piritta Sorsa, *European Integration and Trade with the Developing World* (Washington, DC: World Bank, 1992), 18; Ann-Christina L. Knudsen,

Farmers on Welfare: The Making of Europe's Common Agricultural Policy (Ithaca, NY: Cornell University Press, 2009).

85. Martin Rempe, "Airy Promises: Senegal and the EEC's Common Agricultural Policy in the 1960s," in *Fertile Ground for Europe? The History of European Integration and the Common Agricultural Policy since 1945*, ed. Kiran Klaus Patel (Baden-Baden: Nomos, 2009), 228.
86. Quoted in ibid., 231.
87. "Vortrag des Präsidenten der EWG-Kommision Walter Hallstein, vor dem Hamburger Überseeklub am 8.Mai 1961 in Deutsche Gesellschaft für Auswärtige Politik," in *Dokumente zur auswärtigen Politik*, ed. Deutsche Gesellschaft für Auswärtigen Politik (Bonn: Auswärtiges Amt, 1961), D341.
88. Quoted in Moser, *Europäische Integration, Dekolonisation, Eurafrika*, 483.
89. Hannedore Kahmann, "Der Gemeinsame Markt im Kreuzfeuer der GATT-Kritik," *Europa-Archiv*, March 5–20, 1958, 10583.
90. *Afro-Asian Peoples' Solidarity Conference* (Moscow: Foreign Languages Press, 1958), 246.
91. Moser, *Europäische Integration, Dekolonisation, Eurafrika*, 394.
92. Robert E. Hudec, *Developing Countries in the GATT / WTO Legal System*, rev. ed. (London: Rowman and Littlefield, 2007), 43.
93. The GATT's own histories describe the Haberler Report as providing "initial guidelines for the work of the GATT." "A 40 Year Chronology of Events and Achievements," October 30, 1987, GATT Digital Library, Stanford University, GATT 40 / 2.
94. E. Wyndham White to Haberler, January 10, 1958, Gottfried Haberler Papers, Harvard University Archives (hereafter cited as Haberler Papers), box 1, "GATT Panel" folder.
95. In a well-known case, Meade had himself promoted infant industry protection for Mauritius in the 1960s. See Dani Rodrik, *The Globalization Paradox: Democracy and the Future of the World Economy* (New York: W. W. Norton, 2011), chap. 8. On Tinbergen's work at the League of Nations, see Mary S. Morgan, *The History of Econometric Ideas* (New York: Cambridge University Press, 1990), 101–133. On a constructivist reading of Tinbergen as a key figure in "the birth of the idea of the economy," see Timothy Mitchell, "Fixing the Economy," *Cultural Studies* 12, no. 1 (1998): 86–88. Dieter Plehwe calls Campos "one of the most important neoliberal intellectuals in Brazil." Dieter Plehwe, "The Origins of the Neoliberal Economic Development Discourse," in *The Road from Mont Pèlerin: The Making of the Neoliberal Thought Collective*, ed. Philip Mirowski and Dieter Plehwe (Cambridge, MA: Harvard University Press, 2009), 274.
96. Robert Leonard, "The Collapse of Interwar Vienna: Oskar Morgenstern's Community, 1925–50," *History of Political Economy* 43, no. 1 (2011), 116; Olav Bjerkholt, "Tracing Haavelmo's Steps from Confluence Analysis to the Probability Approach," Department of Economics, University of Oslo, 2001, 16, https://www.duo.uio.no/bitstream/handle/10852/17314/4845.pdf?sequence=1. According to Hagemann,

Staehle (born 1903) worked at the ILO from 1930 to 1939, at the IMF from 1946 to 1947, as director of the UN Economic Commission for Europe in Geneva from 1947 to 1953, and at the GATT from 1953 to 1961. Harald Hagemann, Claus-Dieter Krohn, and Hans Ulrich Esslinger, *Die Emigration deutschsprachiger Wirtschaftswissenschaftler nach 1933: Biographische Gesamtübersicht* (Stuttgart: Universität Hohenheim, 1992), 272.

97. Haberler to Staehle, January 28, 1958, Haberler Papers, "GATT Panel" folder.
98. On Bauer, see Plehwe, "Origins of the Neoliberal Economic Development Discourse," 262–263.
99. Haberler to Staehle, January 28, 1958, Haberler Papers, "GATT Panel" folder.
100. Haberler to Staehle, October 20, 1958, and Staehle to Haberler, May 1, 1958, both in Haberler Papers, "GATT Panel" folder.
101. Haberler to Staehle, April 11, 1958, Haberler Papers, "GATT Panel" folder.
102. For his criticism of inflationary policies in developing countries, see Gottfried Haberler, "Inflation," in *The Conservative Papers,* ed. Melvyn Laird (Chicago: Quadrangle Books, 1964); Haberler, "The Case for Minimum Interventionism," in *Foreign Aid Reexamined: A Critical Appraisal,* ed. James W. Wiggins (Washington, DC: Public Affairs Press, 1958).
103. Paul Samuelson, "Gottfried Haberler (1900–95)," *Journal of International Trade and Economic Development* 4, no. 3 (1995): 414.
104. GATT, *Trends in International Trade: Report by a Panel of Experts* (Geneva: GATT, 1958), 119.
105. A. B. Hersey, Associate Adviser, Division of International Finance, Board of Governors of the Federal Reserve, April 6, 1959, Haberler Papers, "GATT Panel" folder; J. H. Richter, "Trends in International Trade," typescript manuscript, Haberler Papers, "GATT Panel" folder.
106. GATT, *Trends in International Trade,* 122.
107. Ibid., 123.
108. Eric Wyndham White to Haberler, December 2, 1958, Haberler Papers, "GATT Panel" folder.
109. Information Service, European Office of the UN, GATT, Thirteenth Session of the Contracting Parties, October 18, 1958, Haberler Papers, "GATT Panel" folder.
110. Staehle to Haberler, October 16, 1958, Haberler Papers, "GATT Panel" folder.
111. The countries were Brazil, Burma, Cambodia, Ceylon, Chile, Cuba, Malaya, Rhodesia and Nyasaland, Ghana, Greece, India, Indonesia, Pakistan, Peru, and Uruguay. Expansion of International Trade, Note Submitted by the Less-Developed Countries, May 20, 1959, GATT Digital Library, Stanford University, W.14/15.
112. See Richard Gibb, "Post-Lomé: The European Union and the South," *Third World Quarterly* 21, no. 3 (June 2000): 457–481. Former British overseas territories did not profit from EEC preferential trade agreements until 1975 and the creation of the ACP (African, Caribbean and Pacific) Group. R. J. Barry Jones, *Routledge Encyclopedia of International Political Economy,* vol. 1 (New York: Routledge,

2001), 12. This produced a situation from 1957 to 1975 in which former British colonies, such as India and Pakistan, made common cause with the United Kingdom and Australia against the trading bloc created between EEC countries (France, above all) and their former colonies.

113. See, for instance, its depiction in the documentary film *Life and Debt* (dir. Stephanie Black, 2001).

114. "Consultation with the Member States of the EEC on Cocoa," Rome Treaty, July 10, 1959, Annex II, The Treaty of Rome, Cocoa, Submission by Ghana, Brazil, Indonesia and UK Delegations, GATT Digital Library, Stanford University, L/994.

115. Garavini, *After Empires*, 68.

116. For a similar argument about the UN Conference on Trade and Development in the 1960s, see Johanna Bockman, "Socialist Globalization against Capitalist Neocolonialism: The Economic Ideas behind the New International Economic Order," *Humanity* 6, no. 1 (Spring 2015): 110.

117. See Ankie Hoogvelt, *Globalization and the Postcolonial World: The New Political Economy of Development* (Houndmills, UK: Palgrave, 2001), 42.

118. Ibid., 241–243; Jeffry A. Frieden, *Global Capitalism: Its Fall and Rise in the Twentieth Century* (New York: W. W. Norton, 2006), 319–320. On the attempts of neoliberal economists to present export-oriented industrialization as a model of laissez-faire development economics in action, see Mark T. Berger, *The Battle for Asia: From Decolonization to Globalization* (New York: Routledge, 2004), 4–5.

119. For a similar argument, see Rorden Wilkinson, "Developing Country Participation in the GATT: A Reassessment," *World Trade Review* 7, no. 3 (2008): 473–510.

120. For a forceful version of this argument, see Raewyn Connell and Nour Dados, "Where in the World Does Neoliberalism Come From?," *Theory and Society* 43, no. 2 (2014): 133.

121. Röpke, "Gemeinsamer Markt und Freihandelszone," 37.

122. On "liberalism from below," see Razeen Sally, *Classical Liberalism and International Economic Order: Studies in Theory and Intellectual History* (New York: Routledge, 1998), 139.

123. Haberler, "Implications of the European Common market and Free Trade Area Project for United States Foreign Economic Policy," in *Foreign Trade Policy: Compendium of Papers on United States Foreign Trade Policy Collected by the Staff for the Subcommittee on Foreign Trade Policy of the Committee on Ways and Means* (Washington, DC: U.S. GPO, 1957), 478.

124. Gottfried Haberler, "Die wirtschaftliche Integration Europas," in *Wirtschaftsfragen der freien Welt*, ed. Erwin von Beckerath (Frankfurt am Main: F. Knapp, 1957), 526.

125. Ibid., 527.

126. Ibid., 529.

127. GATT, "The Launching and Organization of Trade Negotiations in the GATT," September 26, 1984, 4. GATT Digital Library, Stanford University, SPEC(85) 46,
128. Hudec, *Developing Countries in the GATT / WTO Legal System,* 43.
129. Ibid., 35.
130. Jennifer Bair, "Taking Aim at the New International Economic Order," in Mirowski and Plehwe, *The Road from Mont Pèlerin,* 359.
131. Gottfried Haberler, "Integration and Growth of the World Economy in Historical Perspective," *American Economic Review* 54, no. 2 (1964): 14, 17.
132. F. A. Hayek, *The Constitution of Liberty,* Chicago: University of Chicago Press, 2011), 379.
133. Ibid.
134. F. A. Hayek, "The Economy, Science, and Politics (1962)," in *Studies in Philosophy, Politics and Economics,* ed. F. A. Hayek (London: Routledge and Kegan Paul, 1967), 251.
135. Ibid., 253.
136. Ibid., 262–263.
137. Ibid., 263.
138. Ibid., 264.
139. Ibid., 263.
140. Ibid., 267.
141. F. A. Hayek, "Recht, Gesetz und Wirtschaftsfreiheit (1963)," in *Freiburger Studien,* ed. F. A. Hayek (Tübingen: J. C. B. Mohr, 1969), 47.
142. F. A. Hayek, *The Political Order of a Free People,* vol. 3 of *Law, Legislation and Liberty* (Chicago: University of Chicago Press, 1979), 194.
143. Ibid., 195.
144. Giersch, Paqué, and Schmieding, *The Fading Miracle,* 27.
145. Hayek, "Recht, Gesetz und Wirtschaftsfreiheit," 55.
146. Ibid.
147. F. A. Hayek, "A New Look at Economic Theory: Four Lectures Given at the University of Virginia, 1961," in *The Market and Other Orders,* ed. Bruce Caldwell (Chicago: University of Chicago Press, 2014), 425.
148. F. A. Hayek, "Der Wettbewerb als Entdeckungsverfahren," *Kieler Vorträge,* no. 56 (1968).
149. Hans Von der Groeben, "Competition Policy in the Common Market and in the Atlantic Partnership," *Antitrust Bulletin* 10, nos. 1–2 (1965): 129.
150. Ibid., 152.
151. Von der Groeben, *The European Community,* 48.
152. The debate over the neoliberal nature of competition policy is intense among specialists in European Union law. See, for example, Pinar Akman, "Searching for the Long-Lost Soul of Article 82EC," *Oxford Journal of Legal Studies* 29, no. 2 (2009); Montalban, Ramirez-Perez, and Smith, "EU Competition Policy Revisited," 21.
153. Wolfram Kaiser, "Quo vadis, Europa? Die deutsche Wirtschaft und der Gemeinsame Markt 1958–1963," in *40 Jahre Römische Verträge: Der deutsche Beitrag,* ed. Ruldolf Hrbek and Volker Schwarz (Baden-Baden: Nomos, 1998), 195.

154. Buch-Hansen and Wigger, *European Competition Regulation*, 54–55.
155. Antoine Vauchez, *Brokering Europe: Euro-Lawyers and the Making of a Transnational Polity* (New York: Cambridge University Press, 2015), 60.
156. Buch-Hansen and Wigger, *European Competition Regulation*, 54–55.
157. Vauchez, *Brokering Europe*, 60.
158. Ernst Joachim Mestmäcker, "Auf dem Wege zu einer Ordnungspolitik für Europa," in *Eine Ordnungspolitik für Europa: Festschrift für Hans von der Groeben zu seinem 80. Geburtstag*, ed. Ernst Joachim Mestmäcker, Hans Möller, and Hans-Peter Schwarz (Baden-Baden: Nomos, 1987), 11.
159. Peter Behrens, "The Ordoliberal Concept of 'Abuse' of a Dominant Position and Its Impact on Article 102 TFEU," Discussion Paper, Europa-Kolleg Hamburg, Institute for European Integration, No. 7 / 15, 2015, http://hdl.handle.net/10419/120873.
160. Ernst-Joachim Mestmäcker, "Power, Law and Economic Constitution," *German Economic Review* 11, no. 3 (1973): 182.
161. Ernst-Joachim Mestmäcker, "Offene Märkte im System unverfälschten Wettbewerbs in der Europäischen Wirtschaftsgmeinschaft," in *Wirtschaftsordnung und Rechtsordnung*, ed. Helmut Coing, Heinrich Kronstein, and Ernst-Joachim Mestmäcker (Karlsruhe: C. F. Müller, 1965), 390.
162. Christian Joerges, "The Science of Private Law and the Nation-State," in *The Europeanisation of Law: The Legal Effects of European Integration*, ed. Francis G. Snyder (Portland, OR: Hart, 2000), 69.
163. Mestmäcker, "Offene Märkte," 348.
164. Ibid., 353.
165. Ibid., 390.
166. Mestmäcker, "Power, Law and Economic Constitution," 187.
167. Ernst Joachim Mestmäcker, *A Legal Theory without Law: Posner v. Hayek on Economic Analysis of Law* (Tübingen: Mohr Siebeck, 2007), 40.
168. Fritz W. Scharpf, "Economic Integration, Democracy and the Welfare State," *Journal of European Public Policy* 4, no. 1 (March 1997): 28.
169. Ernst-Joachim Mestmäcker, "Competition Law in the European Economic Community," in *World Unfair Competition Law: An Encyclopedia*, ed. H. L. Pinner (Leyden: A. W. Sijthoff, 1965), 39.
170. Ibid., 73.
171. Ibid., 70.
172. See Adam Harmes, "Neoliberalism and Multilevel Governance," *Review of International Political Economy* 13, no. 5 (2006): 725–749; E. U. Petersmann, "Multilevel Trade Governance in the WTO Requires Multilevel Constitutionalism," in *Constitutionalism, Multilevel Trade Governance and International Economic Law*, ed. Christian Joerges and Ernst-Ulrich Petersmann (Portland, OR: Hart, 2011). For a groundbreaking article that defines the term differently, see Gary Marks, "Structural Policy and Multilevel Governance in the EC," in *The State of the European Community*, ed. Alan Cafruny and Glenda Rosenthal (Boulder,

CO: Lynne Rienner, 1993), 407. On the diverse uses of the concept, see Simona Piattoni, *The Theory of Multi-level Governance: Conceptual, Empirical, and Normative Challenges* (Oxford: Oxford University Press, 2010).

173. Kowitz, *Alfred Müller-Armack,* 271.
174. Mestmäcker, "Power, Law and Economic Constitution," 190.
175. Mestmäcker, "Competition Law," 73.
176. Mestmäcker, "Power, Law and Economic Constitution," 190.
177. Mestmäcker, "Offene Märkte," 391.
178. Joerges, "Science of Private Law and the Nation-State," 79.
179. Michelle Cini and Lee McGowan, *Competition Policy in the European Union* (New York: St. Martin's Press, 1998), 22.
180. Von der Groeben, *The European Community,* 195.
181. Mestmäcker, "Offene Märkte," 391. Although Vauchez is correct that Carl Ophüls was the first to use the term in reference to European integration, Ophüls's argument was that no such "European economic constitution" yet existed. Vauchez, *Brokering Europe,* 59. See C. F. Ophüls, "Grundzüge europäischer Wirtschaftsverfassung," *Zeitschrift für das gesamte Handelsrecht und Wirtschaftsrecht* 124 (1962): 137.
182. Mestmäcker, "Power, Law and Economic Constitution," 190.
183. Reinhard Behlke, *Der Neoliberalismus und die Gestaltung der Wirtschaftsverfassung in der Bundesrepublik Deutschland* (Berlin: Duncker und Humblot, 1961), 96.
184. Tamara Zieschang, *Das Staatsbild Franz Böhms* (Stuttgart: Lucius und Lucius, 2003), 177.
185. Behlke, *Der Neoliberalismus und die Gestaltung,* 134–135.
186. Zieschang, *Das Staatsbild Franz Böhms,* 179.
187. See, for instance, Ernst Rudolf Huber, *Wirtschaftsverwaltungsrecht,* 2nd ed., 2 vols. (Tübingen: Mohr, 1953), 24; Gerber, "Constitutionalizing the Economy," 44.
188. Franz Böhm, *Die Ordnung der Wirtschaft als geschichtliche Aufgabe und rechtschöpferische Leistung* (Stuttgart: W. Kohlhammer, 1937), 54, 56.
189. Ibid., 56.
190. John Gray, *Hayek on Liberty* (New York: Routledge, 1984), 34.
191. Hayek, "The Results of Human Action but not of Human Design" in *Studies in Philosophy, Politics and Economics,* ed. F. A. Hayek, 96–105 (London: Routledge and Kegan Paul, 1967).
192. Mestmäcker, "Power, Law and Economic Constitution," 183.
193. Ernst-Joachim Mestmäcker, *Die Vermittlung von europäischem und nationalem Recht im System unverfälschten Wettbewerbs* (Bad Homburg: Verlag Gehlen, 1969), 170.
194. Ibid., 173.
195. Erich Hoppmann, "Zum Schutzobjekte des GWB," in *Wettbewerb als Aufgabe: Nach zehn Jahren Gesetz gegen Wettbewerbsbeschrankungen,* ed. Ernst-Joachim Mestmäcker (Bad Homburg: Gehlen, 1968), 78.
196. Ibid., 97.

197. Ibid., 90.
198. Erich Hoppmann, "Wettbewerb als Norm der Wettbewerbspolitik," *Ordo* 18 (1967): 84.
199. Ibid.
200. Ibid., 92.
201. Mestmäcker, *Die Vermittlung von europäischem und nationalem Recht,* 173.
202. Mestmäcker, "Power, Law and Economic Constitution," 183.
203. Ibid., 192.
204. Ernst-Joachim Mestmäcker, "Concentration and Competition in the EEC," *Journal of World Trade Law* 6 (1972): 615–647, at 621; emphasis added.
205. Röpke, "Uneasy Common Market," 195.
206. Christian Joerges, "The European Economic Constitution and Its Transformation through the Financial Crisis," *ZenTra Working Papers in Transnational Studies,* no. 47 (2015): 10.
207. Gottfried Haberler, "Economic Consequences of a Divided World," *Review of Politics* 18, no. 1 (1956): 10.
208. Hudec, *Developing Countries in the GATT/WTO Legal System,* 49.
209. Garavini, *After Empires,* 49.
210. Ibid., 77. On the Haberler Report as a turning point, see also Andrew Lang, *World Trade Law after Neoliberalism: Reimagining the Global Economic Order* (Oxford: Oxford University Press, 2011), 45.
211. Haberler, "Integration and Growth of the World Economy," 20.
212. Gerard Curzon, "Crisis in the International Trading System," in *In Search of a New World Economic Order,* ed. Hugh Corbet and Robert Victor Jackson (New York: Wiley, 1974), 37.
213. Haberler, "Integration and Growth of the World Economy," 21.
214. Gerard Curzon and Virginia Curzon Price, *Hidden Barriers to International Trade* (London: Trade Policy Research Centre, 1970), n.p.
215. Ibid.
216. Harry G. Johnson, "World Inflation, the Developing Countries and an 'Integrated Programme for Commodities,'" *Banca Nazionale del Lavoro Review,* December 1976, 335.
217. Martin Wolf, "An Unholy Alliance: The European Community and Developing Countries in the International Trading System," in *European Trade Policies and the Developing World,* ed. L. B. M. Mennes and Jacob Kol (London: Croom Helm, 1988), 45.
218. Gerard Curzon and Victoria Curzon Price, *Global Assault on Non-tariff Trade Barriers* (London: Trade Policy Research Centre, 1972), 3.

7. A WORLD OF SIGNALS

1. Robert E. Hudec, *Developing Countries in the GATT/WTO Legal System,* rev. ed. (London: Rowman and Littlefield, 2007), 31.

2. Mahbub ul Haq, *The Poverty Curtain: Choices for the Third World* (New York: Columbia University Press, 1976), 169.
3. Balakrishnan Rajagopal, *International Law from Below: Development, Social Movements and Third World Resistance* (New York: Cambridge University Press, 2003), 79, 82. For the earlier UN history of the demand for permanent sovereignty over natural resources, see Nico Schrijver, *Sovereignty over Natural Resources: Balancing Rights and Duties* (New York: Cambridge University Press, 1997), chaps. 1–3. The NIEO has recently been the subject of renewed scholarly interest. For an overview history of the NIEO, see *Humanity: An International Journal of Human Rights, Humanitarianism, and Development* 6, no. 1 (Spring 2015). See also Umut Özsu, "Neoliberalism and the New International Economic Order: A History of 'Contemporary Legal Thought,'" in *In Search of Contemporary Legal Thought*, ed. Christopher L. Tomlins and Justin Desautels-Stein (Cambridge: Cambridge University Press, 2017), 330–347.
4. Jagdish N. Bhagwati, ed., *The New International Economic Order: The North–South Debate* (Cambridge, MA: MIT Press, 1977), 3.
5. Kwame Nkrumah, *Neo-colonialism: The Last Stage of Imperialism* (New York: International Publishers, 1965), xi.
6. N. Raghavan Pillai quoted in Amrita Narlikar, *International Trade and Developing Countries: Bargaining Coalitions in the GATT and WTO* (London: Routledge, 2003), 55.
7. E. U. Petersmann, "Die Nationalisierung der chilenischen Kupferindustrie," *Wirtschaftsrecht* 3 (1973): 278.
8. Andrew Lang, *World Trade Law after Neoliberalism: Reimagining the Global Economic Order* (Oxford: Oxford University Press, 2011), 49; Daniel J. Whelan, "'Under the Aegis of Man': The Right to Development and the Origins of the New International Economic Order," *Humanity: An International Journal of Human Rights, Humanitarianism, and Development* 6, no. 1 (Spring 2015): 224; Samuel Moyn, *The Last Utopia: Human Rights in History* (Cambridge, MA: Belknap Press of Harvard University Press, 2010).
9. Frieder Roessler, "The International Law Commission and the New International Economic Order (1979)," in *The Legal Structure, Functions and Limits of the World Trade Order*, ed. Frieder Roessler (London: Cameron May, 2000). The article was published originally under the pseudonym "Damian Hubbard" in *German Yearbook of International Law* 22 (1979): 80–99.
10. Charles Lipson, *Standing Guard: Protecting Foreign Capital in the Nineteenth and Twentieth Centuries* (Berkeley: University of California Press, 1985), 98.
11. Noel Maurer, *The Empire Trap: The Rise and Fall of U.S. Intervention to Protect American Property Overseas, 1893–2013* (Princeton, NJ: Princeton University Press, 2013), 350.
12. Jennifer Bair, "Taking Aim at the New International Economic Order," in *The Road from Mont Pèlerin: The Making of the Neoliberal Thought Collective*, ed. Philip Mirowski and Dieter Plehwe (Cambridge, MA: Harvard University Press, 2009); Özsu, "Neoliberalism and the New International Economic Order."

13. Herbert G. Grubel, "The Case against the New International Economic Order," *Weltwirtschaftliches Archiv* 113, no. 2 (1977): 284–307.
14. Gottfried Haberler, "The Liberal International Economic Order in Historical Perspective," in *Challenges to a Liberal International Economic Order,* ed. Ryan C. Amacher, Gottfried Haberler, and Thomas D. Willett (Washington, DC: American Enterprise Institute for Public Policy Research, 1979), 44.
15. P. T. Bauer and B. S. Yamey, "Against the New Economic Order," *Commentary* April 1, 1977, 31.
16. Hollis B. Chenery quoted in Amacher, Haberler, and Willett, *Challenges to a Liberal International Economic Order,* 76.
17. Bhagwati, *The New International Economic Order,* 7. On the response to the NIEO, see Daniel J. Sargent, "North / South: The United States Responds to the New International Economic Order," *Humanity: An International Journal of Human Rights, Humanitarianism, and Development* 6, no. 1 (Spring 2015): 201–216.
18. Craig N. Murphy, *Global Institutions, Marginalization, and Development* (London: Routledge, 2005), 34. The label "global reformist" comes from P. D. Henderson, "Survival, Development and the Report of the Brandt Commission," *The World Economy* 3, no. 1 (1980): 107.
19. Mihajlo D. Mesarović and Eduard Pestel, *Mankind at the Turning Point: The Second Report to the Club of Rome* (New York: Dutton, 1974), 142.
20. Sam Cole, *Global Models and the International Economic Order* (Oxford: Pergamon Press, 1977), unpaginated preface.
21. Kees van der Pijl, "The Sovereignty of Capital Impaired: Social Forces and Codes of Conduct for Multinational Corporations," in *Restructuring Hegemony in the Global Political Economy: The Rise of Transnational Neo-Liberalism in the 1980s,* ed. Henk Overbeek (London: Routledge, 1993), 36. See Jan Tinbergen et al., *Reshaping the International Order: A Report to the Club of Rome* (London: Hutchinson, 1977).
22. Wassily Leontief, "For a National Economic Planning Board," *New York Times,* March 14, 1974.
23. Wassily Leontief, *The Future of the World Economy* (New York: United Nations, 1976).
24. Tinbergen et al., *Reshaping the International Order.*
25. See Sarah Babb, *Behind the Development Banks: Washington Politics, World Poverty, and the Wealth of Nations* (Chicago: University of Chicago Press, 2009).
26. Hank Overbeek and Kees van der Pijl, "Restructuring Capital and Restructuring Hegemony: Neo-Liberalism and the Unmaking of the Post-war Order," in Overbeek, *Restructuring hegemony,* 19. See also Bair, "Taking Aim," 360–361; Martijn Konings, "Governing the System: Risk, Finance, and Neoliberal Reason," *European Journal of International Relations* 22, no. 2 (2016): 268–288; Greta R. Krippner, *Capitalizing on Crisis: The Political Origins of the Rise of Finance* (Cambridge, MA: Harvard University Press, 2012).
27. The authoritative account by Robert Hudec, although excellent and scholarly, was commissioned by the neoliberal Trade Policy Research Centre and was thus less

an outside observation and more of an actor in the counterrevolution itself. The book was dedicated to the memory of Jan Tumlir. Robert E. Hudec, *Developing Countries in the GATT Legal System* (London: Rowman and Littlefield, 1987).

28. Jan Tumlir, "Need for an Open Multilateral Trading System," *The World Economy* 6, no. 4 (1983): 407.
29. Tumlir, "National Sovereignty, Power and Interest," *Ordo* 31 (1980): 24.
30. See, for example, William N. Butos and Thomas J. McQuade, "The Sensory Order, Neuroeconomics, and Austrian Economics," in *The Oxford Handbook of Austrian Economics,* ed. Peter J. Boettke and Christopher J. Coyne (New York: Oxford University Press, 2015), 616; Bruce Caldwell, "F. A. Hayek and the Economic Calculus," *History of Political Economy* 48, no. 1 (2016): 176; Paul Lewis, "The Emergence of 'Emergence' in the Work of F. A. Hayek: A Historical Analysis," *History of Political Economy* 48, no. 1 (2016): 113; Gabriel Oliva, "The Road to Servomechanisms: The Influence of Cybernetics on Hayek from the Sensory Order to the Social Order," CHOPE Working Paper no. 2015-11 (Durham, NC: Center for the History of Political Economy, 2015); David G Tuerck, "Economics as Mechanism: The Mind as Machine in Hayek's Sensory Order," *Constitutional Political Economy* 6, no. 3 (1995): 281. For early attention to the influence of psychology on Hayek's thought, see John Gray, *Hayek on Liberty* (New York: Routledge, 1984).
31. P. A. Lewis, "Systems, Structural Properties, and Levels of Organisation: The Influence of Ludwig von Bertalanffy on the Work of F. A. Hayek," *Research in the History of Economic Thought and Methodology* (forthcoming): 11, http://dx.doi.org/10.2139/ssrn.2609349.
32. Ibid., 18.
33. F. A. Hayek, "The Pretence of Knowledge (1974)," in *New Studies in Philosophy, Politics, Economics and the History of Ideas,* ed. F. A. Hayek (Chicago: University of Chicago Press, 1978).
34. Ibid. F. A. Hayek, *The Mirage of Social Justice,* vol. 2 of *Law, Legislation and Liberty* (London: Routledge and Kegan Paul, 1976).
35. F. A. Hayek, *Rules and Order,* vol. 1 of *Law, Legislation and Liberty* (London: Routledge and K. Paul, 1973), 14.
36. Quoted in F. A. Hayek, *Law, Legislation and Liberty* (London: Routledge and Kegan Paul, 1982), xviii–xix. (Three volumes published in one, with corrections and revised preface.)
37. Philip Mirowski, *Never Let a Serious Crisis Go to Waste: How Neoliberalism Survived the Financial Meltdown* (New York: Verso, 2013), 54.
38. Peter Galison, "The Ontology of the Enemy: Norbert Wiener and the Cybernetic Vision," *Critical Inquiry* 21, no. 1 (Autumn 1994): 232. See Norbert Wiener, *Cybernetics: Or Control and Communication in the Animal and the Machine* (Cambridge, MA: MIT Press, 1948).
39. F. A. Hayek, "Degrees of Explanation (1955)," in *Studies in Philosophy, Politics and Economics,* ed. F. A. Hayek (London: Routledge and Kegan Paul, 1967), 19.

40. Viktor Vanberg, *The Constitution of Markets: Essays in Political Economy* (New York: Routledge, 2001), 46.
41. F. A. Hayek, "The Results of Human Action but not of Human Design," in Hayek, *Studies in Philosophy, Politics and Economics*, 96–105.
42. F. A. Hayek, "Scientism and the Study of Society (1942–44)," in *Studies on the Abuse and Decline of Reason: Text and Documents*, ed. F. A. Hayek (Chicago: University of Chicago Press, 2010), 104.
43. Lewis, "Systems, Structural Properties, and Levels of Organisation," 6.
44. Ludwig von Bertalanffy, *General System Theory* (New York: George Braziller, 1968), 12–15.
45. Ibid., 14.
46. Ibid., 113.
47. Ludwig von Bertalanffy, "An Outline of General System Theory," *British Journal for the Philosophy of Science* 1, no. 2 (1950): 137–139.
48. Von Bertalanffy, *General System Theory*, 19.
49. F. A. Hayek, *The Political Order of a Free People*, vol. 3 of *Law, Legislation and Liberty* (Chicago: University of Chicago Press, 1979), 159.
50. Erich Hoppmann, "Die Interdependenz der Ordnungen," *Ordo* 49 (1998): 6.
51. F. A. Hayek, "Individualism: True and False (1945)," in *Individualism and Economic Order*, ed. F. A. Hayek (Chicago: University of Chicago Press, 1948), 32.
52. F. A. Hayek, "The Use of Knowledge In Society (1945)," in Hayek, *Individualism and Economic Order*, 86.
53. Ibid.
54. Paul Lewis and Peter Lewin, "Orders, Orders, Everywhere . . . On Hayek's *The Market and Other Orders*," *Cosmos and Taxis* 2 (2015): 15.
55. Philip Mirowski, "On the Origins (at Chicago) of Some Species of Neoliberal Evolutionary Economics," in *Building Chicago Economics: New Perspectives on the History of America's Most Powerful Economics Program*, ed. Robert Van Horn, Philip Mirowski, and Thomas A. Stapleford (New York: Cambridge University Press, 2011), 262.
56. Lewis, "The Emergence of 'Emergence,'" 120.
57. F. A. Hayek, "The Theory of Complex Phenomena (1964)," in *Studies in Philosophy, Politics and Economics*, ed. F. A. Hayek (London: Routledge and Kegan Paul, 1967), 25.
58. Ibid., 27.
59. Ibid., 30.
60. F. A. Hayek, "Kinds of Order in Society," *New Individualist Review* 3, no. 2 (1964): 461.
61. Hayek, "The Theory of Complex Phenomena," 23.
62. F. A. Hayek, "The Primacy of the Abstract," in *Beyond Reductionism: The Alpbach Symposium 1968*, ed. Arthur Koestler and J. R. Smythies (New York: Macmillan, 1968), 311.
63. Ibid., 319.

64. Comment to J. R. Smythies, "Aspects of Consciousness," in *Beyond Reductionism: The Alpbach Symposium 1968,* ed. Arthur Koestler and J. R. Smythies (New York: Macmillan, 1968), 254.
65. Hayek, "Notes on the Evolution of Systems of Rules of Conduct," in *Studies in Philosophy, Politics and Economics*, ed. F. A. Hayek (London: Routledge and Kegan Paul, 1967), 76.
66. Ibid.
67. F. A. Hayek, *The Sensory Order: An Inquiry into the Foundations of Theoretical Psychology* (London: Routledge and Kegan Paul, 1952), 128.
68. Hayek, *Rules and Order,* 19.
69. Hayek, "Kinds of Order in Society," 460.
70. Hayek, *Rules and Order,* 68.
71. Ibid., 64.
72. Quoted in Steve Fleetwood, *Hayek's Political Economy: The Socio-Economics of Order* (New York: Routledge, 1995), 113.
73. Hayek, "The Primacy of the Abstract," 316.
74. Hayek, *Rules and Order,* 18.
75. Ibid., 11.
76. Manfred E. Streit, "Institutionen als Kognitionsproblem-Bemerkungen zu einer neurosensorischen Vermutung," *Ordo* 51 (2000). See also Roger Koppl, "Confessions of a Neuro-Hayekian," *Advances in Austrian Economics* 13 (2010): 391–397; J. Barkley Rosser Jr., "How Complex Are the Austrians?," *Advances in Austrian Economics* 14 (2010): 165–179; Filomena de Sousa, "Hayek and Individualism: Some Question Marks," *History of Economic Ideas* 13, no. 2 (2005): 111–127.
77. Gray, *Hayek on Liberty,* 40; Mark Pennington, "Hayek on Socialism," in *Elgar Companion to Hayekian Economics,* ed. Roger W. Garrison and Norman Barry (Cheltenham, UK: Edward Elgar, 2014), 251.
78. Raymond Plant, *The Neo-Liberal State* (Oxford: Oxford University Press, 2010), 72.
79. Fleetwood, *Hayek's Political Economy,* 112.
80. Jean-Pierre Dupuy, "The Autonomy of Social Reality: On the Contribution of Systems Theory to the Theory of Society," in *Evolution, Order and Complexity,* ed. Elias L. Khalil and Kenneth E. Boulding (New York: Routledge, 1996), 79.
81. Hayek, *The Political Order of a Free People,* 132.
82. Philip Mirowski, *Machine Dreams: Economics Becomes a Cyborg Science* (New York: Cambridge University Press, 2002), 18.
83. Franz Böhm, "Rule of Law in a Market Economy," in *Germany's Social Market Economy: Origins and Evolution,* ed. Alan T. Peacock and Hans Willgerodt (New York: St. Martin's Press, 1989), 53.
84. Franz Böhm, "Privatrechtsgesellschaft und Marktwirtschaft," *Ordo* 17 (1966): 74.
85. Hayek, "Kinds of Order in Society," 460.
86. "Nobel-Prize Winning Economist," oral history interview with F. A. Hayek, Oral History Program, UCLA, 1983, 315, https://archive.org/details/nobelprizewin nin00haye.

87. Hayek, *Rules and Order,* 104.
88. Hayek, *The Mirage of Social Justice,* 94.
89. Wilhelm Röpke, "Die Stellung des Unternehmers auf dem Markte," *Schweizer Monatshefte* (February 1947): 664.
90. Ibid.
91. Hayek, "The Use of Knowledge in Society," 86.
92. F. A. Hayek, "Planning, Science and Freedom," *Nature,* November 15, 1941, 581.
93. James M. Buchanan, *Freedom in Constitutional Contract: Perspectives of a Political Economist* (College Station: Texas A&M University Press, 1977), 34.
94. Gray, *Hayek on Liberty,* 68.
95. Gerard Curzon and Victoria Curzon Price, "The Undermining of the World Trade Order," *Ordo* 30 (1979): 383–407.
96. Though his eightieth birthday was May 8, 1979, this was the last MPS general meeting before then, so a gift was given to Hayek for the occasion. Tibor Machan, "Meeting of the (Free) Minds," *Reason,* December 1978, 47.
97. Alvin Rabushka, "How Goes the Underdeveloped World?," MPS Meeting, Brussels, 1974, William H. Hutt Papers, Hoover Institution Archives, Stanford University (hereafter cited as Hutt Papers), box 5.
98. Hayek, *The Political Order of a Free People,* 163.
99. Machan, "Meeting of the (Free) Minds."
100. Barry Naughton, *The Chinese Economy: Transitions and Growth* (Cambridge, MA: MIT Press, 2007), 382. On EPZs, see Patrick Neveling, "The Global Spread of Export Processing Zones and the 1970s as a Decade of Consolidation," in *Changes in Social Regulation: State, Economy, and Social Protagonists since the 1970s,* ed. Knud Andersen and Stefan Müller (Oxford: Berghahn Books, 2017), 23–40.
101. George J. Stigler, "Why Have the Socialists Been Winning?," *Ordo* 30 (1979): 63. See James M. Buchanan and Gordon Tullock, *The Calculus of Consent* (Ann Arbor: University of Michigan Press, 1962).
102. Stigler, "Why Have the Socialists Been Winning?"
103. Wendy Brown, "Neoliberalized Knowledge," *History of the Present* 1, no. 1 (Summer 2011): 119.
104. James M. Buchanan, "Constitutional Constraints on Governmental Taxing Power," *Ordo* 30 (1979): 358.
105. Ibid.
106. Hutt to Owen Horwood, Minister of Finance, South Africa, September 20, 1978, Hutt Papers, box 14.
107. Ernest Van den Haag, "Mont Pelerin Strikes Again," *National Review,* February 16, 1979.
108. Hayek, *The Political Order of a Free People,* 155.
109. See, for instance, Gerald F. Gaus, "Hayek on the Evolution of Society and Mind," in *The Cambridge Companion to Hayek,* ed. Edward Feser (Cambridge: Cambridge University Press, 2007); Mirowski, "On the Origins (at Chicago)," 258–265.

110. Hayek, *The Political Order of a Free People,* 159.
111. Hayek, *Rules and Order,* 45–46.
112. F. A. Hayek, *The Constitution of Liberty* (Chicago: University of Chicago Press, 2011), 268.
113. Manfred E. Streit, "Economic Order, Private Law and Public Policy: The Freiburg School of Law and Economics in Perspective," *Journal of Institutional and Theoretical Economics (JITE)/Zeitschrift für die gesamte Staatswissenschaft* 148, no. 4 (1992): 680.
114. Hayek, *Rules and Order,* 4.
115. Ibid., 45; emphasis added.
116. Garrett Hardin, "The Cybernetics of Competition: A Biologist's View of Society," in *The Subversive Science: Essays toward an Ecology of Man,* ed. Paul Shepard and Daniel McKinley (Boston: Houghton Mifflin, 1969), 295.
117. Hayek, *Rules and Order,* 46.
118. Hayek, *The Political Order of a Free People,* 149; emphasis in the original.
119. World Trade Organization, *The WTO Building: Art and Architecture at the Centre William Rappard* (Geneva: World Trade Organization, 2015), 34.
120. Ibid., 32.
121. "Socialist Realism Comes to Light at WTO after 30 Year Cover-Up," *Economic Times,* March 28, 2008.
122. Craig VanGrasstek, *The History and Future of the World Trade Organization* (Geneva: World Trade Organization, 2013), 539.
123. Olivier Long, "International Trade under Threat: A Constructive Response," *The World Economy* 1, no. 3 (1978): 257.
124. On the campaigns of Haberler, Fritz Machlup, Milton Friedman, and other economists for floating exchange rates, see Carol Connell, *Reforming the World Monetary System: Fritz Machlup and the Bellagio Group* (London: Pickering and Chatto, 2013); Robert Leeson, *The Eclipse of Keynesianism: The Political Economy of the Chicago Counter-Revolution* (New York: Palgrave, 2000); Matthias Schmelzer, *Freiheit für Wechselkurse und Kapital: Die Ursprünge neoliberaler Währungspolitik und die Mont Pèlerin Society* (Marburg: Metropolis, 2010).
125. Eric Helleiner, *States and the Reemergence of Global Finance: From Bretton Woods to the 1990s* (Ithaca, NY: Cornell University Press, 1994), 103.
126. Barry Eichengreen, *Globalizing Capital: A History of the International Monetary System* (Princeton, NJ: Princeton University Press, 2008), 178–179.
127. Quoted in Jeffrey M. Chwieroth, *Capital Ideas: The IMF and the Rise of Financial Liberalization* (Princeton, NJ: Princeton University Press, 2010), 70. Haberler had made this argument as early as 1960 in a pamphlet written for the American Enterprise Institute and republished as "Inflation" in *The Conservative Papers,* ed. Melvyn Laird (Chicago: Quadrangle Books, 1964), 175–199.
128. E. U. Petersmann, "The Establishment of a GATT Office of Legal Affairs and the Limits of 'Public Reason' in the GATT / WTO Dispute Settlement System," in *A History of Law and Lawyers in the GATT / WTO: The Development of the Rule of*

Law in the Multilateral Trading System, ed. Gabrielle Marceau (New York: Cambridge University Press, 2015).

129. Long, "International Trade under Threat," 257.
130. Ibid., 256.
131. John H. Jackson, "Crumbling Institutions of the Liberal Trade System," *Journal of World Trade Law* 12, no. 2 (1978): 95. See John H. Jackson, *World Trade and the Law of GATT* (Indianapolis: Bobbs-Merrill, 1969).
132. David Kennedy, "The International Style in Postwar Law and Policy: John Jackson and the Field of International Economic Law," *American University International Law Review* 10, no. 2 (1995): 672.
133. Jackson, "Crumbling Institutions of the Liberal Trade System," 102.
134. See, for example, W. M. Corden, *The NIEO Proposals: A Cool Look* (London: Trade Policy Research Centre, 1979); Staffan Burenstam-Linder, "How to Avoid a New International Economic Disorder," *The World Economy* 3, no. 3 (November 1980): 275–285.
135. "CBE for FT's Economics Commentator," *Financial Times*, December 13, 2000.
136. Martin Wolf, "Two-Edged Sword: Demands of Developing Countries and the Trading System," in *Power, Passions, and Purpose: Prospects for North–South Negotiation*, ed. Jagdish Bhagwati and John Gerard Ruggie (New York: Columbia University Press, 1984), 202.
137. Brian Scott, *Has the Cavalry Arrived? A Report on Trade Liberalisation and Economic Recovery* (London: Trade Policy Research Centre, 1984), 78.
138. Stuart Harbinson, "Lessons from the Launching of the Doha Round Negotiaations," Cordell Hull Institute Trade Policy Roundtable, April 18, 2002, 7. See also the lecture series established in Tumlir's honor by the European Centre for International Political Economy in Brussels.
139. "Jan Tumlir, GATT's Chief Economist, Retires," February 28, 1985, GATT Digital Library, Stanford University, GATT / 1370.
140. Peter Sutherland, "A Future for the World Trade Organisation?," *Jan Tumlir Policy Essays*, no. 1 (2010): 4.
141. Gabrielle Marceau, "From the GATT to the WTO: The Expanding Duties of the Legal Affairs Division in Non-panel Matters," in Marceau, *A History of Law and Lawyers*, 252.
142. E. U. Petersmann, *Constitutional Functions and Constitutional Problems of International Economic Law* (Fribourg: University Press Fribourg, 1991), xxxi.
143. Marceau, "From the GATT to the WTO," 252.
144. Dongsheng Zang, "Divided by Common Language: 'Capture' Theories in GATT / WTO and the Communicative Impasse," *Hastings International and Comparative Law Review* 32, no. 2 (2009): 426.
145. Jan Tumlir, "Can the International Economic Order Be Saved?," *The World Economy* 1, no. 1 (October 1977): 3–20.
146. Tumlir to Hayek, September 17, 1975, F. A. Hayek Papers, Economists' Papers Archive, Duke University Library (hereafter cited as Hayek Papers, Duke), box 53, folder 28.

147. This process is described in detail in the study commissioned by the TPRC and originally conceived by Martin Wolf. Hudec, *Developing Countries in the GATT Legal System.*
148. Frieder Roessler, "The Role of Law in International Trade Relations and the Establishment of the Legal Affairs Division of the GATT," in Marceau, *A History of Law and Lawyers,* 161–162.
149. Frieder Roessler, "Law, De Facto Agreements and Declarations of Principle in International Economic Relations," *German Yearbook of International Law* 21 (1978): 38.
150. Ibid., 39.
151. Ibid., 40.
152. Ibid., 51.
153. Ibid., 59.
154. Ibid., 56.
155. E. U. Petersmann, "Die Dritte Welt und das Wirtschaftsvölkerrecht," *Zeitschrift für ausländisches öffentliches Recht und Völkerrecht* 36, no. 16 (1976): 494.
156. Ibid., 496.
157. E. U. Petersmann, "The New International Economic Order: Principles of Politics and International Law," in *The International Law and Policy of Human Welfare,* ed. Ronald St. John Macdonald and Douglas M. Johnston (Alphen aan den Rijn: Sijthoff & Noordhoff, 1978), 466.
158. E. U. Petersmann, "Das neue Recht des Nord-Süd-Handels," *Zeitschrift für ausländisches öffentliches Recht und Völkerrecht* 32 (1972): 343.
159. Petersmann, "The New International Economic Order," 449.
160. E. U. Petersmann, "Internationales Recht und Neue Internationale Wirtschaftsordnung," *Archiv des Völkerrechts* 18, no. 1 (1978): 32.
161. Petersmann, "Die Dritte Welt und das Wirtschaftsvölkerrecht," 498.
162. E. U. Petersmann, "Völkerrecht und Entwicklung," *Verfassung und Recht in Übersee* 5, no. 2 (1972): 167.
163. Petersmann, "The New International Economic Order," 450.
164. Petersmann, "Völkerrecht und Entwicklung," 169.
165. Petersmann, "Internationales Recht und Neue Internationale Wirtschaftsordnung," 376.
166. Ibid., 36.
167. Petersmann, "Die Nationalisierung der chilenischen Kupferindustrie," 278.
168. Petersmann, "Internationales Recht und Neue Internationale Wirtschaftsordnung," 376.
169. Ibid.
170. E. U. Petersmann, "The Changing Structure of International Economic Law by Themaat, P. VerLoren van," *Verfassung und Recht in Übersee/Law and Politics in Africa, Asia and Latin America* 17, no. 4 (1984): 503.
171. Petersmann, "Internationales Recht und Neue Internationale Wirtschaftsordnung," 21.

172. Ibid., 20. He used other cybernetic terms elsewhere, including "closed circuit feedback loops," "circular causality," "spill-over," and "spill-back mechanisms." Petersmann, "Die Dritte Welt und das Wirtschaftsvölkerrecht," 513.
173. Petersmann, "Völkerrecht und Entwicklung," 161.
174. Richard Blackhurst, Nicolas Marian, and Jan Tumlir, *Trade Liberalization, Protectionism, and Interdependence* (Geneva: GATT, 1977), 5.
175. Tumlir, "National Sovereignty, Power and Interest," 21.
176. Jan Tumlir, "How the West Can Pay the New Arab Oil Bill," *Sunday Times* (London), February 3, 1974.
177. Tumlir, "National Sovereignty, Power and Interest," 2.
178. Ibid.
179. Jan Tumlir, "International Economic Order and Democratic Constitutionalism," *Ordo* 34 (1983): 72.
180. Jan Tumlir, "Notes on the Theory and Present State of International Economic Order," paper presented at the International Conference on the Free Trade Movement in Latin America, June 21–24 [1981], Haus Rissen, Hamburg, Hayek Papers, Duke, box 53, folder 28.
181. Ibid.
182. Tumlir, "National Sovereignty, Power and Interest," 24.
183. Richard Blackhurst, Nicolas Marian, and Jan Tumlir, *Adjustment, Trade and Growth in Developed and Developing Countries* (Geneva: GATT, 1978), 1.
184. Blackhurst, Marian, and Tumlir, *Trade Liberalization, Protectionism, and Interdependence,* 49.
185. Tumlir, "International Economic Order and Democratic Constitutionalism," 72.
186. Ibid., 80.
187. Tumlir, "Need for an Open Multilateral Trading System," 403.
188. Ibid.; emphasis in the original. The field of public choice and so-called constitutional economics (a term coined by Richard MacKenzie in 1982) is the silent partner in much of the discussion in this chapter, but it is not included for reasons of space. An exploration of former MPS president James M. Buchanan's idea of the fiscal constitution and federalism would serve as an important complement to the argument presented here. For an overview, see James M. Buchanan, "The Domain of Constitutional Economics," *Constitutional Political Economy* 1, no. 1 (1990): 1–18. On fiscal constitutionalism, see James M. Buchanan, *The Limits of Liberty: Between Anarchy and Leviathan* (1975) (Indianapolis: Liberty Fund, 2000), 23–24; Geoffrey Brennan and James M. Buchanan, *The Power to Tax: Analytical Foundations of a Fiscal Constitution* (1980) (Indianapolis: Liberty Fund, 2000). On Buchanan's theory of federalism, see James M. Buchanan, "Federalism as an Ideal Political Order and an Objective for Constitutional Reform," *Publius* 25, no. 2 (1995): 19–27; Lars P. Feld, "James Buchanan's Theory of Federalism: From Fiscal Equity to the Ideal Political Order," *Constitutional Political Economy* 25 (2014): 231–252; Adam Harmes, "The Political Economy of Open Federalism," *Canadian Journal of Political Science* 40, no. 2 (2007):

418–428; Richard E. Wagner, *James M. Buchanan and Liberal Political Economy: A Rational Reconstruction* (Lanham, MD: Lexington, 2017), 85–108. On the institutional history of public choice and law and economics, see Steven M. Teles, *The Rise of the Conservative Legal Movement: The Battle for Control of the Law* (Princeton, NJ: Princeton University Press, 2008).

189. Jan Tumlir, "Strong and Weak Elements in the Concept of European Integration," in *Reflections on a Troubled World Economy: Essays in Honour of Herbert Giersch*, ed. Fritz Machlup, Gerhard Fels, and Hubertus Müller-Groeling (London: Trade Policy Research Centre, 1983), 31.
190. Tumlir, "International Economic Order and Democratic Constitutionalism," 73.
191. Jan Tumlir, "International Economic Order—Can the Trend Be Reversed?," *The World Economy* 5, no. 1 (March 1982): 34.
192. Tumlir, "International Economic Order and Democratic Constitutionalism," 75.
193. Ibid.
194. Jan Tumlir, "The New Protectionism, Cartels, and the International Order," in Amacher, Haberler, and Willett, *Challenges to a Liberal International Economic Order*, 246.
195. Ibid., 256.
196. Ibid., 257.
197. Jan Tumlir, "The Contribution of Economics to International Disorder," *The World Economy* 3, no. 4 (January 1981): 399.
198. Tumlir, "International Economic Order and Democratic Constitutionalism," 74.
199. Tumlir misleadingly emphasizes the post–World War II context for this strain of Böhm's thought when the emphasis should really be on the 1930s.
200. Jan Tumlir, "Franz Böhm and the Development of Economic-Constitutional Analysis," in *German Neo-Liberals and the Social Market Economy*, ed. Alan T. Peacock, Hans Willgerodt, and Daniel Johnson (New York: St. Martin's Press, 1989), 140.
201. Ibid.
202. Heinz Hauser et al., "Der Beitrag von Jan Tumlir zur Entwicklung einer ökonomischen Verfassungstheorie internationaler Handelsregeln," *Ordo* 39 (1988): 219.
203. Tumlir, "Need for an Open Multilateral Trading System," 396.
204. Ibid.
205. Ibid., 407.
206. Jan Tumlir, "Clash of Security and Progress: The Constitutional Resolution," *Ordo* 36 (1985): 10.
207. Tumlir, "International Economic Order and Democratic Constitutionalism," 80.
208. Hayek, "Notes on the Evolution of Systems," 66.
209. Tumlir to Hayek, June 6, 1979, Hayek Papers, Duke, box 53, folder 28.
210. Tumlir, "Need for an Open Multilateral Trading System," 407. He also cited Hayek's 1952 book, *The Sensory Order*, on "the self-steering system." See Tumlir, "National Sovereignty, Power and Interest," 4.
211. Tumlir, "Strong and Weak Elements," 55.

212. Petersmann, *Constitutional Functions and Constitutional Problems,* 16.
213. Ibid., 19.
214. Ibid., 403.
215. Tumlir expressed hope that Mestmäcker would present on the idea of the economic constitution at a conference in Peru organized by Hernando de Soto, to which Tumlir successfully invited Hayek to speak. Tumlir to Hayek, April 10, 1979, Hayek Papers, Duke, box 53, folder 28. De Soto received a master's in international law and economics from the Graduate Institute in Geneva in 1967 and worked at GATT thereafter. The November 1979 conference launched his Institute for Liberty and Democracy, which in the early 2000s would lead a multimillion-dollar World Bank program to formalize property rights in Peru. Mario Vargas Llosa, "In Defense of the Black Market," *New York Times,* February 22, 1987; Peter H. Schuck and Robert E. Litan, "Regulatory Reform in the Third World: The Case of Peru," *Yale Journal on Regulation* 4, no. 1 (1986): 58; Timothy Mitchell, "How Neoliberalism Makes Its World: The Urban Property Rights Project in Peru," in Mirowski and Plehwe, *The Road from Mont Pèlerin,* 389–390. For De Soto's most influential works, see Hernando De Soto, *The Other Path: The Invisible Revolution in the Third World* (New York: Harper and Row, 1990); de Soto, *The Mystery of Capital: Why Capitalism Triumphs in the West and Fails Everywhere Else* (New York: Basic Books, 2000).
216. Tumlir, "International Economic Order and Democratic Constitutionalism," 81.
217. Ibid.
218. Ibid.
219. Tumlir, "Strong and Weak Elements," 33.
220. See, among many articles on this theme, E. U. Petersmann, "How to Promote the International Rule of Law? Contributions by the World Trade Organization Appellate Review System," *Journal of International Economic Law* 1, no. 1 (1998): 25–48.
221. Tumlir, "Strong and Weak Elements," 31.
222. Joel P. Trachtman, "The International Economic Law Revolution," *University of Pennsylvania Journal of International Economic Law* 17, no. 1 (1996): 48–49.
223. Kristen Hopewell, *Breaking the WTO: How Emerging Powers Disrupted the Neoliberal Project* (Stanford, CA: Stanford University Press, 2016), 55.
224. See, for instance, Nitsan Chorev, *Remaking U.S. Trade Policy: From Protectionism to Globalization* (Ithaca, NY: Cornell University Press, 2007); Bernard M. Hoekman and M. M. Kostecki, *The Political Economy of the World Trading System: The WTO and Beyond,* 3rd ed. (New York: Oxford University Press, 2009); VanGrasstek, *The History and Future of the World Trade Organization.*
225. Benjamin Lazier, "Earthrise; or, The Globalization of the World Picture," *American Historical Review* 116, no. 3 (2011): 606.
226. Adlai Stevenson II's Speech before the United Nations Economic and Social Council, Geneva, Switzerland, July 9, 1965, http://www.adlaitoday.org/articles/connect2_geneva_07-09-65.pdf.

227. See Jo-Anne Pemberton, *Global Metaphors: Modernity and the Quest for One World* (London: Pluto Press, 2001), 147–148.
228. Philippe de Seynes, unpaginated preface in Cole, *Global Models.*
229. Willy Brandt, *North–South: A Program for Survival* (London: Pan Books, 1980).
230. E. U. Petersmann, *Wirtschaftsintegrationsrecht und Investitionsgesetzgebung der Entwicklungsländer* (Baden-Baden: Nomos, 1974), 141.
231. Quoted in Antony Anghie, "Legal Aspects of the New International Economic Order," *Humanity: An International Journal of Human Rights, Humanitarianism, and Development* 6, no. 1 (Spring 2015): 145.
232. Sylvia Ostry, "The Uruguay Round North-South Grand Bargain: Implications for Future Negotiations," in *The Political Economy of International Trade Law,* ed. Daniel M. Kennedy and James D. Southwick (New York: Cambridge University Press, 2002), 285.
233. Tuerck, "Economics as Mechanism," 281.
234. Mirowski, *Machine Dreams,* 240.
235. Blackhurst, Marian, and Tumlir, *Adjustment, Trade and Growth in Developed and Developing Countries,* 74.
236. Tumlir, "National Sovereignty, Power and Interest," 7.
237. Ibid., 8.
238. See, for example, Philip G. Cerny, "Paradoxes of the Competition State: The Dynamics of Political Globalization," *Government and Opposition* 32, no. 2 (1997): 251–274.

CONCLUSION

1. George H. W. Bush, "Remarks on Presenting the Presidential Medal of Freedom Awards," November 18, 1991, https://bush41library.tamu.edu/archives/public-papers/3642.
2. F. A. Hayek, *The Political Order of a Free People,* vol. 3 of *Law, Legislation and Liberty* (Chicago: University of Chicago Press, 1979), 133.
3. F. A. Hayek, *The Constitution of Liberty* (Chicago: University of Chicago Press, 2011), 105.
4. Ibid.
5. Hans Willgerodt, "Staatliche Souveränität und die Ordnung der Weltwirtschaft," *Ordo* 40 (1989): 404, 407.
6. Ibid., 421.
7. Ibid., 413.
8. Ibid., 423.
9. Ibid.
10. "Far from being objectionable," he wrote, "imperialism is precisely what is needed to restore order in the Middle East." Deepak Lal, *In Praise of Empires: Globalization and Order* (New York: Palgrave Macmillan, 2004), 2–18, 33.

11. Ibid., 3.
12. For a discussion of the "synthesis of distributive and commutative justice" in ordoliberalism, see Manuel Wörsdörfer, "Von Hayek and Ordoliberalism on Justice," *Journal of the History of Economic Thought* 35, no. 3 (2013): 301–308.
13. See, for example, Wilhelm Röpke, *The Social Crisis of Our Time* (Chicago: University of Chicago Press, 1950), 224. This book was originally published in German in 1942.
14. See Röpke, *The Social Crisis of Our Time;* Röpke, *International Economic Disintegration* (London: William Hodge and Co., 1942).
15. See Ralf Ptak, *Vom Ordoliberalismus zur sozialen Marktwirtschaft: Stationen des Neoliberalismus in Deutschland* (Opladen: Leske und Budrich, 2004), 214. Hayek was notoriously displeased with Müller-Armack's coinage, referring to the phrase "social market economy" when he called "social" "one of the most confusing and harmful words of our time." F. A. Hayek, "Kinds of Rationalism," in *Studies in Philosophy and Economics,* ed. F. A. Hayek (London: Routledge and Kegan Paul, 1967), 83.
16. Danny Nicol, *The Constitutional Protection of Capitalism* (London: Bloomsbury, 2010).
17. Wolfgang Streeck, "Small-State Nostalgia? The Currency Union, Germany, and Europe: A Reply to Jürgen Habermas," *Constellations* 21, no. 2 (2014): 216.
18. Stephen Gill, "New Constitutionalism, Democratisation and Global Political Economy," *Pacifica Review: Peace, Security and Global Change* 10, no. 1 (1998): 23.
19. Neil Brenner, Jamie Peck, and Nik Theodore, "New Constitutionalism and Variegated Neo-Liberalization," in *New Constitutionalism and World Order,* ed. Stephen Gill and A. Claire Cutler (New York: Cambridge University Press, 2014), 129.
20. Alasdair Roberts, *The Logic of Discipline: Global Capitalism and the Architecture of Government* (New York: Oxford University Press, 2011).
21. Fritz W. Scharpf, "The Asymmetry of European Integration, or Why the EU Cannot Be a 'Social Market Economy,'" *Socio-Economic Review* 8 (2010): 211–250.
22. Ronen Palan, *The Offshore World: Sovereign Markets, Virtual Places, and Nomad Millionaires* (Ithaca, NY: Cornell University Press, 2003).
23. Herbert Giersch, "The Age of Schumpeter," *American Economic Review* 74, no. 2 (1984): 106. See Philip G. Cerny, "Paradoxes of the Competition State: The Dynamics of Political Globalization," *Government and Opposition* 32, no. 2 (1997): 251–274; Dieter Plehwe and Quinn Slobodian, "Landscapes of Unrest: Herbert Giersch and the Origins of Neoliberal Economic Geography," *Modern Intellectual History* (2017), https://doi:10.1017/S1479244317000324.
24. Adam Harmes, "New Constitutionalism and Multilevel Governance," in Gill and Cutler, *New Constitutionalism,* 150–151.
25. Michael S. Greve, "The AEI Federalism Project," *Federalist Outlook,* no. 1 (July / August 2000): 2.
26. For the "zero-state society" claim, see Jamie Peck, "Explaining (with) Neoliberalism," *Territory, Politics, Governance* 1, no. 2 (2013): 147.

27. F. A. Hayek, *The Fatal Conceit: The Errors of Socialism* (Chicago: University of Chicago Press, 1989), 72.
28. See Mitchell Dean, *The Signature of Power: Sovereignty, Governmentality and Biopolitics* (Los Angeles: Sage, 2013), 179–183.
29. F. A. Hayek, *Rules and Order*, vol. 1 of *Law, Legislation and Liberty* (London: Routledge and Kegan Paul, 1973), 155.
30. St. Augustine, *On Order* (South Bend, IN: St. Augustine's Press, 2007), 5.
31. Franz Böhm, "Die Idee des Ordos im Denken Walter Euckens: Dem Freunde und Mitherausgeber zum Gedächtnis," *Ordo* 3 (1950): xvii.
32. Hayek, *The Fatal Conceit*, 98.
33. Stephen Kresge and Leif Wenar, eds., *Hayek on Hayek: An Autobiographical Dialogue* (London: Routledge, 1994), 128.
34. E. U. Petersmann, *International Economic Law in the 21st Century: Constitutional Pluralism and Multilevel Governance of Interdependent Public Goods* (Portland, OR: Hart, 2012), 174.
35. E. U. Petersmann, "Theories of Justice, Human Rights, and the Constitution of International Markets," *Loyola of Los Angeles Law Review* 37 (2003–2004): 425.
36. Wolfgang Schäuble, "Germany and the Global Financial Crisis: Lessons We Need to Learn," speech presented at the London School of Economics, February 18, 2009, http://www.lse.ac.uk/website-archive/publicEvents/pdf/20090218_Schaeuble.pdf.
37. William Davies and Linsey McGoey, "Rationalities of Ignorance: On Financial Crisis and the Ambivalence of Neo-Liberal Epistemology," *Economy and Society* 41, no. 1 (2012): 65. Konings writes about "the way in which neoliberalism makes uncertainty productive." Martijn Konings, "Governing the System: Risk, Finance, and Neoliberal Reason," *European Journal of International Relations* 22, no. 2 (2016): 282.
38. Kristin Ross, *Fast Cars, Clean Bodies: Decolonization and the Reordering of French Culture* (Cambridge, MA: MIT Press, 1995), 160.
39. E. U. Petersmann, *The GATT/WTO Dispute Settlement System* (London: Kluwer Law, 1997), xiii.
40. Röpke, *The Social Crisis of Our Time*, 228.
41. F. A. Hayek, "Reflections on Constitutional Economics," in *Constitutional Economics: Containing the Economic Powers of Government*, ed. Richard B. McKenzie (Lexington, MA: Lexington Books, 1984), 237.
42. See the account in Nitsan Chorev, *Remaking U.S. Trade Policy: From Protectionism to Globalization* (Ithaca, NY: Cornell University Press, 2007).
43. Peter Sutherland, "A New Framework for International Economic Relations," third Annual Hayek Memorial Lecture, Institute of Economic Affairs, London, June 16, 1994, GATT Digital Library, Stanford University, GATT/1640.
44. John Gillingham, *European Integration, 1950–2003: Superstate or New Market Economy?* (New York: Cambridge University Press, 2003), 251.

45. Angela Wigger, "Competition for Competitiveness: The Politics of the Transformation of the EU Competition Regime" (PhD diss., University of Amsterdam, 2008), 200.
46. Hayek, *The Political Order of a Free People,* 172.
47. See Markus Krajewski, "Democratic Legitimacy and Constitutional Perspectives of WTO Law," *Journal of World Trade Law* 35, no. 1 (2001): 167.
48. Peter Sutherland, "A Future for the World Trade Organisation?," *Jan Tumlir Policy Essays,* no. 1 (2010): 6.
49. Martin Wolf, "Does the Trading System Have a Future?," *Jan Tumlir Policy Essays,* no. 1 (2009): 7.
50. Joost Pauwelyn, "The Transformation of World Trade," *Michigan Law Review* 104, no. 1 (October 2005): 17.
51. Ibid., 59.
52. Ibid., 42.
53. Wendy Brown, *Undoing the Demos: Neoliberalism's Stealth Revolution* (New York: Zone Books, 2015).
54. Quoted in Kristen Hopewell, *Breaking the WTO: How Emerging Powers Disrupted the Neoliberal Project* (Stanford, CA: Stanford University Press, 2016), 74.
55. Pascal Lamy, *The Geneva Consensus: Making Trade Work for All* (Cambridge: Cambridge University Press, 2013), vii.
56. Ibid., 9; Pascal Lamy, "Towards Global Governance," Master of Public Affairs inaugural lecture at the Institut d'Etudes Politiques, Paris, October 21, 2005, https://www.wto.org/english/news_e/sppl_e/sppl12_e.htm.
57. Statement by Pascal Lamy, January 26, 2005, WTO General Council, https://www.wto.org/english/thewto_e/dg_e/stat_lamy_e.htm.
58. On the IMF, see Alexander E. Kentikelenis, Thomas H. Stubbs, and Lawrence P. King, "IMF Conditionality and Development Policy Space, 1985–2014," *Review of International Political Economy* 23, no. 4 (2016): 543–582.
59. Quoted in Bruce Caldwell and Leonidas Montes, "Friedrich Hayek and His Visits to Chile," *Review of Austrian Economics* 28, no. 3 (2015): 298. It should be noted that the authors' overall argument is that Hayek's relationship to Pinochet has been exaggerated by critics. For further references on neoliberals and Chile, see Chapter 5.
60. Röpke to Marcel van Zeeland, October 20, 1940, Wilhelm Röpke Archive, Institute for Economic Research, Cologne, file 7, p. 729; Ludwig Mises, *Liberalism,* 3rd ed. (Irvington-on-Hudson, NY: Foundation for Economic Education, 1985).
61. Ludwig Mises, *Socialism: An Economic and Sociological Analysis* (Indianapolis: Liberty Fund, 1981), 51.
62. E. U. Petersmann, "Legal, Economic and Political Objectives of National and International Competition Policies: Constitutional Functions of WTO 'Linking Principles' for Trade and Competition," *New England Law Review* 34, no. 1 (Fall 1999): 153, 62.
63. E. U. Petersmann, "From Negative to Positive Integration in the WTO: Time for Mainstreaming Human Rights into WTO Law," *Common Market Law Review,* no. 37 (2000): 1363–1382.

64. E. U. Petersmann, "The WTO Constitution and Human Rights," *Journal of International Economic Law* 3, no. 1 (2000): 24.
65. E. U. Petersmann, "How to Promote the International Rule of Law? Contributions by the World Trade Organization Appellate Review System," *Journal of International Economic Law* 1, no. 1 (1998): 31–32.
66. E. U. Petersmann, "Human Rights and International Economic Law in the 21st Century: The Need to Clarify Their Interrelationships," *Journal of International Economic Law* 4, no. 1 (2001): 5.
67. Ibid.
68. Petersmann, "From Negative to Positive Integration," 1377.
69. Petersmann, "Human Rights and International Economic Law," 27.
70. Ibid., 24.
71. Andrew Lang, *World Trade Law after Neoliberalism: Reimagining the Global Economic Order* (Oxford: Oxford University Press, 2011), 347.
72. Petersmann, "Human Rights and International Economic Law," 30.
73. Petersmann, *International Economic Law,* 2–3.
74. Petersmann, "The WTO Constitution and Human Rights," 25.
75. Streeck, "Small-State Nostalgia?," 216.
76. Tore Fougner, "The State, International Competitiveness and Neoliberal Globalisation: Is There a Future Beyond 'The Competition State'?," *Review of International Studies* 32, no. 1 (2006): 178.
77. Philip Alston, "Resisting the Merger and Acquisition of Human Rights by Trade Law: A Reply to Petersmann," *European Journal of International Law* 13, no. 4 (2002): 816.
78. J. Michael Finger and Julio J. Nogués, "The Unbalanced Uruguay Round Outcome: The New Areas in Future WTO Negotiations," *World Economy* 25, no. 3 (March 2002): 335.
79. World Trade Organization, *The WTO Building: Art and Architecture at the Centre William Rappard* (Geneva: World Trade Organization, 2015), 9.
80. Petersmann, *International Economic Law in the 21st Century,* 9.
81. F. A. Hayek, "Adam Smith's Message in Today's Language," in *New Studies in Philosophy, Politics, Economics and the History of Ideas,* ed. F. A. Hayek (Chicago: University of Chicago Press, 1978), 269. Hayek's stark position was not shared by other figureheads of the ordoliberal tradition. On their varying definitions of justice, see Wörsdörfer, "Von Hayek and Ordoliberalism."
82. Petersmann, *International Economic Law in the 21st Century,* 2.
83. For an early elaboration of the use of multilevel governance to secure "property rights" and "private rights in non-discriminatory, undistorted foreign trade competition," see E. U. Petersmann, "Trade Policy as a Constitutional Problem: On the 'Domestic Policy Functions' of International Trade Rules," *Aussenwirtschaft* 41, nos. 2–3 (1986): 431. For critical commentary, see Robert Howse, "Human Rights in the WTO: Whose Rights, What Humanity? Comment on Petersmann," *European Journal of International Law* 13, no. 3 (2002): 654.

84. Siv O'Neall, "Stop WTO International Demonstration in Geneva on 15 October 2005," www.axisoflogic.com/artman/publish/Article_20145.shtml.
85. Hopewell, *Breaking the WTO.*
86. M. Sornarajah, *Resistance and Change in the International Law on Foreign Investment* (New York: Cambridge University Press, 2015).
87. Lang, *World Trade Law after Neoliberalism.*
88. Brown, *Undoing the Demos.*

Acknowledgments

This book is a long-simmering product of the Seattle protests against the World Trade Organization in 1999. I was part of a generation that came of age after the Cold War's end. We became adolescents in the midst of talk of globalization and the End of History. In the more hyperactive iterations of this talk, we were made to think that nations were over and the one indisputable bond uniting humanity was the global economy. Seattle was a moment when we started to make collective sense of what was going on and take back the story line. I did not make the trip north from Portland but many of my friends and acquaintances did, painting giant papier-mâché fists red to strap to backpacks and coming back with tales of zip ties and pepper spray, nights in jail, and encounters with police—tales they spun into war stories and theses. This book is an apology for not being there and an attempt to rediscover in words what the concept was that they went there to fight.

I owe debts of gratitude to the many conversation partners, friends, and collaborators who have accompanied me on this inquiry to its present point, frozen now in book form. With apologies to anyone I have forgotten, my heartfelt thanks go to: Hadji Bakara, Bruce Caldwell, Frederick Cooper, Andrew Daily, Rüdiger Graf, Eric Helleiner, Ryan Jeffery, David Kool, Leigh Claire La Berge, Boaz Levin, Molly Lynch, Owen Lyons, Ian Malcolm, James Mark, Jamie Martin, Malgorzata Mazurek, Philip Mirowski, Craig Murphy, Molly

Nolan, Subodh Patil, Dieter Plehwe, Ryan Quintana, Glenda Sluga, and Heidi Tworek. Love also to my family, especially my Baba, Stella Deloris Edgar, who passed as this book was being written and would have been tickled to see her name in print. My last thanks go to the most important people in my life, Michelle and Yann, who took his first steps earlier this morning. May he take many more.

Index

Note: Page numbers in *italics* indicate figures.

D0687698

THE BROTHERHOOD

By the same author

JACK THE RIPPER: THE FINAL SOLUTION

REQUIEM AT ROGANO (*a novel*)

THE BROTHERHOOD

The Secret World of The Freemasons

STEPHEN KNIGHT

SD

STEIN AND DAY/*Publishers*/New York

First published in the United States of America in 1984

Printed in the United States of America
STEIN AND DAY/ *Publishers*
Scarborough House
Briarcliff Manor, N.Y. 10510

Library of Congress Cataloging in Publication Data

Knight, Stephen.
The brotherhood.

Bibliography: p.
Includes index.
1. Freemasonry. I. Title.
HS395.K54 1984 366'.1 84-45208
ISBN 0-8128-2994-8

For Ma and Pa,
with love

Contents

Acknowledgements

I am free to name only a small number of the many hundreds of people who have helped me with advice and information. Most of those who helped did so only on the understanding that I would say nothing that could lead to their identification. Among these were many Freemasons who feared recrimination from other members of the Brotherhood. Others included government officials, politicians, judges, policemen of all ranks, lawyers, churchmen, past and present officers of MI5 and MI6, and people from every sector of society touched on in the book.

Some of those I can name gave me valuable assistance; some contributed a fact or an idea, did some typing, obtained press cuttings or read my notes and gave encouragement here and there. To all of them, and to all those who must remain unnamed, I am grateful. Without such people a book of this kind could not be contemplated.

Two men must be singled out for special mention: Simon Scott, managing editor of New English Library whose idea this book was and who supported me with unflagging enthusiasm all through the research and writing only to have the project snatched from him at the last moment; and my friend and agent Andrew Hewson who has never, even at the busiest moments, been unavailable.

Thank you, Simon and Andrew, and thank you, Rev Saul

Amias, Arthur Andrews, Judy Andrews, Andrew Arbuthnot, Henry Bach, Ken Barrow, Mark Barty-King, David Beal, Shirley Bennett, Victor Bretman, Ron Brown, Lord Carrington, Swami Anand Chandro, Lewis Chester, Elena Chiari, Kit Clarke, Nigel Coombs, Bill Cotton, Bernard Courtenay-Mayers, Martin Cresswell, Lord Denning, John Dickie, Athena Duncan, Robert Eagle, John Farmer, Peter Fenwick, Ray Fitzwalter, David Floyd, Laurie Flynn, Hamish Fraser, Simon Freeman, Paddy French, Sir Martin Furnival Jones, Robin Gauldie, Charles Goodman, Chris Green, Graham Greene, Karen de Groot, Martin Gwynne, Lord Hailsham, Peter Harkness, Anne Hearle, David Hearle, Cecil Rolph Hewitt, Brian Hilliard, Rt Rev Michael Hollis, Sir Geoffrey Howe, Harry Jackson, Andrew Jennings, John Johnson, Richard Johnson, Lord Elwyn Jones, Fred Jones, Ralph Jones, Tony Judge, Richard Kelly, Alistair Kelman, Rev Peter King, Robin Kirby, Philip Knightley, Feliks Kwiatowski, Barbara Land, Benedict Law, Rev John Lawrence, Leo Long, Andreas Lowenfeld, Sir Robert Mark, Tony Matthews, Doreen May, Sir Anthony Meyer, Austin Mitchell, Gerard Moate, Lesley Newson, Angus Ogilvy, Lord Justice Ormrod, June Outridge, Barry Payton, Alison Peacock, Chapman Pincher, Ronald Price, Roy Purkess, Philip Ray, Merlyn Rees, David Richardson, James Rushbrooke, Bob Satchwell, Paul Scudamore, Gustavo Selvi, Gitta Sereny, Ian Sharp, Lord Justice Sebag Shaw, John Shirley, Martin Short, Colin Simpson, Harold Smith, T. Dan Smith, Antonio de Stefano, Charles Stratton, Wendy Sturgess, Stewart Tendler, Timothy Tindal-Robertson, Peter Thomas, Peter Throsby, Fr John Tracey, SJ, Liz Usher, Alex Vincenti, Nick Webb, Peter Welling, Sir Dick White, Richard Whittington-Egan, Sir George Young.

Prologue

Freemasonry, although its leaders strenuously deny it, is a secret society. And few of its members - judges, police, politicians and royalty among them - realize that every time they attend a meeting they break the law, and (at least technically) lay themselves open to a minimum of two years' imprisonment. Under the Unlawful Societies Act of 1799 - unlikely, of course, ever to be enforced - Freemasons are permitted to hold meetings only if yearly returns providing names, addresses and descriptions of brethren are submitted to local Clerks of the Peace. This is rarely done, so most gatherings in masonic Lodges are held in breach of this law.

In England and Wales alone Freemasonry has more than 600,000 initiates, with a further 100,000 in Scotland and between 50,000 and 70,000 in Ireland. All the members of this extraordinary Brotherhood are male. All except those who are second-, third-, or fourth-generation Freemasons, who may join at eighteen, are over the age of twenty-one. All have sworn on pain of death and ghastly mutilation not to reveal masonic secrets to outsiders, who are known to brethren as the 'profane'.*

*From the Latin *pro* (before) and *fanum* (the temple); i.e. one outside the temple, not initiated to the rites performed within.

The headquarters of the Brotherhood in England and Wales is in London, where the massive bulk of Freemasons Hall squats at the corner of Great Queen Street and Wild Street like a gigantic elephant's footstool. This is the seat of the United Grand Lodge of England, the governing body of the 8,000-plus Lodges in England and Wales. These Lodges, of which there are another 1,200-odd under the jurisdiction of the Grand Lodge of Scotland and about 750 under the Grand Lodge of Ireland, carry out their secret business and ritual in a deliberately cultivated atmosphere of mystery in masonic Temples. Temples might be purpose built, or might be rooms in hotels or private buildings temporarily converted for masonic use. Many town halls up and down the country, for example, have private function rooms used for masonic rituals, as does New Scotland Yard, the headquarters of the Metropolitan Police.

The Grand Lodges control what is known as 'craft' Freemasonry, and brethren often refer to the Brotherhood as 'the Craft'. Craft Freemasonry covers the three degrees of Entered Apprentice, Fellow Craft and Master Mason. The vast majority of Freemasons rise no higher than Master Mason, and most are under the impression that there are no higher degrees. Even many of those who go on to become Royal Arch Masons, governed not by Grand Lodge but by Grand Chapter, have no idea that the masonic ladder extends a further thirty rungs above those on the third who believe they have already reached the top.

There is an important distinction to be made between *Freemasonry*, which is the movement as a whole, and *Freemasons*, which describes any number of individual Masons. This appears self-evident, but confusion of the two ideas has led to some gross misunderstandings. Take the death of Captain William Morgan in America in 1826. There is evidence to suggest that Morgan, having revealed certain masonic secrets in his book *Freemasonry Exposed*, was kidnapped and murdered by Freemasons. There have been suggestions that Mozart, a Mason, was poisoned by members of the Brotherhood, allegedly for betraying masonic secrets in *The Magic Flute.* And in 1888, the Jack the Ripper murders in the East End of London were perpetrated according to masonic ritual. Purely because people, wilfully or innocently, have regarded the words *Freemasons* and *Freemasonry* as interchangeable, these deaths have frequently been blamed, not on various individual Free*masons*, but on the whole Brotherhood. Some people, even today, look upon Freemasonry as an underground movement devoted to murder, terrorism and revolution. Hence, we read of Freemasonry as a worldwide conspiracy and watch, through the clouded vision of certain woefully mistaken writers, the whole of world history since the Renaissance unfold according to masonic machinations.

Freemasonry is not a worldwide secret society. It is a secret society that, originating in Britain, now has independent offshoots in most of the non-Communist world. And although the British Grand Lodges recognize more than a hundred Grand Lodges (forty-nine of them in the USA), they have no control over them, and most reflect the character and political complexion of the country in which they operate. Far from being revolutionary, there is no organization more reactionary, more Establishment-based, than British Freemasonry. Its members derive benefit from the Brotherhood only so long as the status quo is maintained.

Nevertheless, Freemasonry has a potent influence on life in Britain – for both good and ill.

The Brotherhood's stated aims of morality, fraternity and charity are well known. Indeed, circumspect and even secretive about all of Masonry's other doings, the average member of the Brotherhood will be eloquent on the generous donations made by United Grand Lodge and individual Lodges to charity, both masonic and profane. In 1980, for instance, Grand Lodge gave away £931,750, of which just over £300,000 was for non-masonic causes. In addition, many thousands of Masons and their relatives have benefited from the Royal Masonic Institution for Girls ('for maintaining, clothing and educating the daughters of Freemasons'), the Royal Masonic Institution for Boys, the Royal Masonic Benevolent Institution, the Royal Masonic Hospital ('for Freemasons, their wives, widows and dependent children'), and the Masonic Foundation for the Aged and the Sick.

On the other hand, there can be no doubt that many others have suffered because of Freemasonry entering into areas of life where, according to all its publicly proclaimed principles, it should never intrude. The abuse of Freemasonry causes alarming miscarriages of justice. It is one of the aims of this book to look at some of the effects of this abuse.

The Brotherhood is neither a commendation nor a condemnation of Freemasonry. Nor is it another wearisome and misnamed 'exposure' of Masonry's no longer secret rituals. Those rituals, or most of them, can be found in public libraries. In this respect the book differs from the vast majority of books written on the subject in the past 260 years. There is much here that will be unknown to the general reader, but all the verifiable facts I have obtained are presented in full, whether they are favourable or unfavourable to Masonry. Where I enter into speculation – and I do this as little as possible – I make it clear.

I am a journalist. From the beginning, I have thought of this investigation into Freemasonry in modern society as an extended piece of journalism. It is a factual report researched intensively over a relatively short period but because I was working without the benefit of a secretary or researchers the report does contain gaps. My network of contacts within Freemasonry, although extensive, represented a tiny fraction of all the Freemasons in this country. And the secret workings of Freemasonry, its use in manipulating this deal here, in getting someone promotion there, in influencing the actions of police, lawyers, judges, Civil Servants, is meat for a lifetime of study. I have therefore had to concentrate on some areas of society at the expense of others. I have devoted most time and energy to the areas of greatest concern. I trust readers will understand if this plan leaves questions where they feel there should be answers. I shall welcome comments, information and observations from anyone who has something to say. The updating process is already in hand and I expect to be able to expand and revise for as many editions as the public requires. Perhaps a better sub-title might therefore be *Freemasonry: An Interim Report*, because in addition to being wide-ranging and complicated (though always intensely fascinating), the nature of Freemasonry is changing – and the investigator has to face the problem of organized secrecy and 'disinformation'.

This latter can be crass and easily spotted, like the information passed to me covertly by a high-ranking Freemason posing as a nark, which said that at a certain degree a Candidate was required to defecate on a crucifix. This absurd sort of tactic is aimed at the gullible anti-Mason who is on the lookout for scandal and sensation, and who will believe anything that shows the Brotherhood in an unfavourable light. Such writers do exist, and in some number as I have found in the ten months I have had to prepare the report. These are the people who repeat what they are told without checking on facts and sources, and who ignore all evidence which runs counter to their own argument. And it is they who fall for the kind of disinformation tactic which several Freemasons attempted to practise upon me.* The crucifix story is just one example. There are others – including the yarn, gravely whispered to me in the corner of the Freemasons Arms just along the road from Freemasons Hall in London, that Prince Charles had been secretly initiated into a north London Lodge that practised Black Magic; and the fabrication, in support of which someone with access to Grand Lodge notepaper forged some impressive correspondence, that both main political parties had approached Grand Lodge prior to leadership elections to discuss the person most favourably looked upon by the Masons.

Nonsense.

Had I accepted any of this disinformation and published it, as was the intention of those who went to such lengths to feed it to me, the whole of this book would have been open to ridicule. What the disinformers evidently most desired was that *The Brotherhood* should be dismissed as irresponsible and unreliable and quickly forgotten.

I began my enquiry with two questions: Does Freemasonry have an influence on life in Britain, as many people believe? And if so, what kind of influence and in which areas of society? I felt from the beginning that it was important, if possible, to approach the subject from a position of absolute neutrality. In my favour was that I was neither a Mason nor an anti-Mason. But I had studied the subject in the early 1970s for my book *Jack the Ripper: The Final Solution*, and had received a large volume of letters from readers of that book, containing information, questions, theories and arguments on a range of topics associated with Freemasonry. So I did not have the open mind of one completely ignorant. I had already reached certain conclusions. Because of this, as the hundreds of Masons I have

*These individuals acted, I don't doubt, without the knowledge of Grand Lodge, which always prefers to ignore the very existence of outside enquirers.

interviewed since the spring of 1981 can testify, I probed all the more deeply for evidence that might upset those conclusions, in order to obtain as balanced a view of Freemasonry in modern Britain as I could.

But when I began writing, I very quickly discovered the impossibility of complete neutrality. I had seen, heard and discovered things that had made an impression upon me. It would have been a negation of my responsibility to the reader to deny her or him access to these impressions: I was, after all, carrying out the enquiry on behalf of those readers. Inevitably, I have reached conclusions based on the mass of new data now available to me.

Two months after I began research on this book, the United Grand Lodge of England issued a warning in its Quarterly Communication to Lodges, reminding brethren of the rule in their 'Antient Charges' concerning the ban on discussing internal affairs with outsiders. One Royal Arch Mason of thirty years' standing told me it was the first of its kind in his experience. The Quarterly Communication, according to one informant, is 'the method by which Freemasonry at its supreme level gets down to the lower levels'.

The Communication of 10 June 1981 contained this:

We have nothing to hide and certainly nothing to be ashamed of, but we object to having our affairs investigated by outsiders. We would be able to answer many of the questions likely to be asked, if not all of them, but we have found that silence is the best practice. Comment or correction only breeds further enquiry and leads to the publicity we seek to avoid. We respect and do not comment on the attitudes of other organizations. It is unfortunate that sometimes they are less respectful of ours. If therefore any of you is approached by any reporter . . . you will only be carrying out our practice if you gently decline to comment. Do not be drawn into argument or defence, however . . . Remember the Antient Charge, 'Behaviour in Presence of Strangers, Not Masons': *You shall be cautious in your words and carriage, that the most penetrating stranger shall not be able to discover or find out what is not proper to be intimated; and sometimes you shall divert a discourse, and manage it prudently for the honour of the worshipful fraternity . . .*

This warning was issued by no less a figure than the Pro Grand Master, Brother the Rt Hon the Earl Cadogan, sitting as president of the Brotherhood's Board of General Purposes. The reminder of possible disciplinary action against Freemasons who contravene Antient Charge VI.4 was not provoked solely by the United Grand Lodge's concern about my own enquiries. London Weekend Television had recently discussed in its *Credo* programme whether Freemasonry was compatible with Christianity, and the fact that several Freemasons of grand rank* had taken part in the programme had caused a storm within the Brotherhood.

A non-Mason such as I, working for information against this kind of organized secrecy, newly reinforced by stern warnings, would be hard put to obtain anything in certain areas of the subject without the assistance of at least some genuinely motivated 'moles'.

I was fortunate to have established within a few months an entire network of moles. The information this led me to was as startling as it was disturbing.

After my first book appeared in 1976, the London *Evening News*, which serialized it, received a letter from the Freemason director of a chain of bookshops, stating that he was so enraged by evidence I had produced linking Freemasons to the Jack the Ripper case that not only would he physically attack me if we should ever meet (referring to me as 'this specimen'), he would never stock the book and would do all in his power to wreck its

*Past or present holders of office in the United Grand Lodge are brethren of grand rank.

distribution to shops not owned by him. To some extent he succeeded. Although after the serialization it was in high demand, and quickly climbed to the top of the bestseller lists, I was soon receiving letters from would-be readers asking where it could be bought. Despite continuing demand for the book (it was reprinted in 1977, 1978, 1979, twice in 1981 and again in 1982) it cannot be found in branches of this particular chain. Many Freemason managers of other bookshops refuse point-blank to stock it.

Many previous books on Freemasonry have been published. Many, chiefly those by Masons themselves, are still in print after several years. It is interesting to see how many outsiders' works on the Brotherhood have gone quickly out of print despite continuing demand for them.

It is inevitable that many Freemasons will object to this book, if only because it overturns some cherished masonic beliefs. At least readers will be aware of the reason why, if it is in demand, all manner of excuses will be made by some booksellers for not stocking it.

One final point, which shows how easy it is to see masonic conspiracy where in reality there might be none. The episode is recounted in some detail because it has already been referred to in the press but not in the detail necessary for a balanced judgement to be reached. It dramatically affected *The Brotherhood*, so it is fitting that *The Brotherhood* should set the record straight.

Although the book is now being published by Granada, it was originally commissioned by New English Library. It was the idea of Simon Scott, managing editor of NEL. Scott approached my agent, Andrew Hewson, in the spring of 1981 after reading my *Jack the Ripper*, and suggested that I was the person to write it. We met, I produced a synopsis and specimen chapter, and *The Brotherhood* was commissioned. I began work in September 1981 and delivered the typescript to Scott in June 1982. It was to be the lead non-fiction title in NEL's spring 1983 catalogue.

From the first, Scott made it clear that only a handful of people within New English Library would know of the project. At the time the book was commissioned, NEL was owned by a remote American cartel which did not care what its English subsidiary published so long as it showed a profit at the end of the year. Nevertheless, Scott and editorial director Nick Webb took the precaution of confiding in their managing director, a non-Mason, and getting his full backing for the book. Scott told me that to avoid the possibility of sabotage by any hostile Freemasons within or associated with the company, *The Brotherhood* would not be entered in any schedule. Even the advance payment was obtained from the accounts department under an innocuous and misleading project title. At the time these seemed to me excessive cloak-and-dagger activities, although I knew that the publishing world had traditionally been rife with Freemasonry.

Shortly after I started work on the book, NEL was taken over by Hodder & Stoughton, whose chairman and managing director – two brothers eminent in publishing – were Philip and Michael Attenborough, also non-Masons.

After the takeover, NEL retained its own separate management structure with its existing managing director, and in practice no editorial control was exercised over NEL books by the Hodder management. So alarm bells began to ring in Webb's mind when, shortly after I delivered the typescript, Michael Attenborough asked to see it. He had not done this with any previous NEL book. Although Scott and Webb were anxious to get the book legally vetted, edited and delivered to the printer as soon as possible, and constantly pressed Attenborough for any comments he wished to make, he continued to sit on the typescript. This was baffling to Scott and Webb. The delay was by now beginning to jeopardize plans for a spring 1983 publication. Finally, after holding the script for nearly seven weeks, Attenborough asked Scott to gut the book and produce a precise summary of its content. This was done. The weeks continued to roll by, with no word from above. When Scott was in Frankfurt and Webb in New York, word came that the project was to be squashed. Scott flew back to London and a series of frantic transatlantic calls took place between him and Webb, then Webb and Attenborough. But by the time Webb was able to catch a plane home the deed was done. *The Brotherhood* was killed.

Scott's anger knew no bounds. He fought and fought for the book, even making it a resigning issue, but Attenborough was adamant. Then Attenborough told Scott that although neither he nor his brother was a Freemason, their father – John Attenborough CBE – was a senior member of the Brotherhood, and in deference to him they would not publish it.

I went to see Michael Attenborough at his Bedford Square office in January 1983, when the book was safely placed with Granada. He said he was delighted the book would be published.

'Are you?' I asked. 'Then why didn't you publish it yourself?'

He spent some time in obvious discomfort explaining that it had not been a pleasant decision and was one he genuinely regretted having to make, but that he did not feel that the sales force would be completely behind the book and it was not a title which Hodder felt it could publish with enthusiasm.

Yet I knew that the sales force had expressed great interest in the book and were looking forward to handling it. I told him so.

I was with him for three quarters of an hour, and

eventually he admitted something which he seemed nervous of confessing: he loved his father. John Attenborough, according to his son, is a devoted Freemason and a devoted Christian. In view of what I say in the book about the incompatibility of the two religions,* he and brother Philip realized they would cause their father very great pain by publishing *The Brotherhood.* Attenborough assured me that his father had not seen the script and he had not discussed the project with him.

If the incident does not demonstrate the direct power of Freemasonry over the Fourth Estate, it does offer a vivid example of the devotion that Freemasonry so often inspires in its initiates, a devotion that is nothing less than religious. So it was that the Attenboroughs made their decision to throw away £8,000 in advance royalties and thousands more in legal fees and in terms of time spent on the project by the editorial, design, subsidiary rights, promotion, sales and other departments rather than wound their father.

Stephen Knight
January 1983

*I use the word advisedly. See Chapter 25 – 'The Devil in Disguise?' – below.

PART ONE

Workers' Guild to Secret Society

CHAPTER 1

Origins

Some Freemasons claim great antiquity for Freemasonry. This is reflected in the masonic calendar which is based on Archbishop Ussher's seventeenth-century calculation that the Creation must have taken place in the year 4004 BC. For convenience, the odd four years are ignored and Anno Lucis (in the Year of Light, when Freemasonry is deemed to have begun) is four thousand years ahead of Anno Domini – so a masonic certificate of initiation bearing the date A.L. 5983 was issued in A.D. 1983. The implication is that Freemasonry is as old as Adam.

Throughout the eighteenth and nineteenth centuries, masonic writers produced vast numbers of books seeking to show that their movement had a continuous history of many hundreds, even thousands, of years. Some claimed that the ancestors of the Brotherhood were the Druids or the Culdees; some claimed they were the pre-Christian Jewish monks, the Essenes. Others insisted that Freemasonry had its origins in the religion of ancient Egypt – an amalgam of the briefly held monotheism of Ikhnaton (*c.* 1375 B.C.) and the Isis–Osiris cult.

Modern masonic historians are far more cautious. It is now accepted that Freemasonry as practised today goes back little more than three centuries. What is true, though, is that the philosophic, religious and ritualistic concoction that makes up the speculative element in Freemasonry is drawn from many sources – some of them, like the Isis–Osiris myth, dating back to the dawn of history. Rosicrucianism, Gnosticism, the Kabbala, Hinduism, Theosophy and traditional notions of the occult all play a part: but despite the exhaustive literature – one scholar estimates that some 50,000 items of Masonry had been published by the 1950s – it is impossible to determine what comes from where and when, if only because Freemasonry on its lower and more accessible levels is opposed to dogma. There is therefore no authoritative statement of what Masons believe or what the Brotherhood stands for in the first, second and third degrees, to which the vast majority of members restrict themselves. Even a 33° Mason who has persevered to attain all the enlightenment that Freemasonry claims to offer could not – even if he were freed from his oath of secrecy – provide more than a purely personal view of the masonic message and the meaning to be attached to masonic symbolism, since this remains essentially subjective.

The comparatively short documented history of Freemasonry as an institution is nevertheless quite extraordinary. It is the story of how a Roman Catholic trade guild for a few thousand building workers in Britain came to be taken over by the aristocracy, the gentry and members of mainly non-productive professions, and how it was turned into a non-Christian secret society enjoying association with offshoot fraternal societies with millions of adherents throughout most of the non-Communist world.

In many cultures and at many times humankind has been drawn to the esoteric – the conception that the great truths about life and how to control social and natural phenomena are secrets and can only be known to initiates, who pass on their privileged knowledge to the elect from generation to generation. As one highly placed Mason told me, 'Truth, to the initiate, is not for everyone; pearls must not be thrown before swine.' Equally, throughout history men have joined together in secret groups to further purely worldly ambitions. All such groups also involve initiation – the initiation ceremony involving fearful oaths of secrecy. For secrets to remain secret there must be certain and effective sanctions. Secret societies formed for essentially practical ends have commonly had religious and moral elements. The religious element creates awe and so adds to the effectiveness of the oath of secrecy. The moral element determines the fraternal way that the organization's members treat each other, which might bear small resemblance to the way they treat outsiders.

Freemasonry is both a speculative, philosophic – even religious and mystical – system, and a fraternity of those organized to help each other in material matters. For some Masons it is entirely the former, for others entirely the latter, but for most it is a mixture of the two.

Masonic historians seem as uncertain as non-Masons about who first saw in the obsolescent mediaeval Christian masonic guild an organization that could be taken over and converted into a quasi-religious, quasi-secular secret society. What evidence there is indicates that this evolution began very slowly and almost by chance, and that it was only later that the potential of the masonic guild as a clandestine power base was perceived. In other words, it appears that the original interest of the gentry in the masonic lodges stemmed from curiosity, antiquarian interest, and a kind of fashionable search for an unconventional, exclusive social milieu – rather like a jet-set fad for frequenting working men's pubs.

There are a number of reasons why the masonic guild should have attracted this genteel interest. First, the working (or 'operative') masons' craft guild was ripe for takeover: structured in the heyday of Gothic architecture in the thirteenth century,* by the end of the sixteenth century the craft was dying. King's College Chapel at Cambridge, perhaps the last truly great English Gothic building, had been completed about 1512. Secondly, the highly skilled stonemasons of the Gothic age were peculiar in that many were itinerant workers, moving from church site to cathedral site as work was to be found. They had no regular headquarters like other trades, gathering in temporary lodges on site to discuss their affairs. And, as they often did not know each other as did permanent residents of mediaeval towns, they needed some method of recognition, some way of maintaining a closed shop to protect their demanding and highly esteemed profession against interlopers who had not undergone the rigorous apprenticeship necessary to acquire the mason's skills. These, as Professor Jacob Bronowski termed them, were the 'industrial aristocrats'.

There were thus cosmopolitan romance, an exclusivity and an organized secretiveness about the masons' guild, which became increasingly moribund as baroque replaced Gothic architecture. All of this had potential fascination for men of education.

Modern Freemasonry probably originated in Scotland. The earliest known instance of a non-stonemason, a gentleman, joining a masons' lodge is John Boswell, Laird of Auchinlech, who was a member of the Lodge in Edinburgh in 1600. Apparently the first English gentleman to join an English Lodge was Elias Ashmole, founder of Oxford's Ashmolean Museum. An antiquarian deeply interested in Rosicrucianism, he joined in 1646. Masonry became so fashionable that as the seventeenth century progressed the 'acceptance' (the collective term for non-stonemasons)

*The term 'lodge' was first used, so far as can be discovered, in 1277.

became the majority in the masonic Lodges. For example, in 1670 the Aberdeen Lodge had thirty-nine 'accepted' members while only ten remained 'operative' masons. But it was not long before the novelty in participating in the quaint and venerable doings of artisans wore thin. Men of fashion saw no reason to prolong association with working men, and they began to form their own gentlemen's Lodges. Freemasonry was launched.

CHAPTER 2

Metamorphosis

The 'speculative' Masons inherited seven fundamental points from their 'operative' predecessors:

(1) An organization with the three grades of members: Apprentice, Fellow or Journeyman, and Master Mason.
(2) A unit termed a Lodge.
(3) Legendary histories of the origins of the masonic craft set out in the 100-odd manuscripts containing the so-called 'Old Charges', the oldest being the Regius manuscript of 1390, which was in verse.
(4) A tradition of fraternal and benevolent relations between members.
(5) A rule of secrecy about Lodge doings, although the Old Charges themselves were simply lists of quite ordinary rules for the guild, which members were enjoined to keep 'so help you God'. As befitted a Christian grouping there were no blood-curdling oaths.
(6) A method of recognition, notably the Scottish 'mason word' traced back to 1550: unwritten but variously rendered as *Mahabyn*, *Mahabone* or even *Matchpin*.

(7) A thoroughly Christian foundation – the Old Charges are permeated with mediaeval Roman Catholicism.

With the demise of the original 'trade union' purpose of the organization and with the eclipse not only of Roman Catholicism due to the Reformation but also the waning of Christianity with the rise of science, what was left towards the end of the seventeenth century was the framework of a secretive association, likened by one authority to a peasant's cottage ripe for extensive development as a luxury weekend home for the well-to-do.

Serious masonic historians themselves deplore the lack of documentation about the three or four critical decades before the foundation of the Grand Lodge of England in 1717. But it was during these years that the course Freemasonry was to follow was set. It was evidently then that a few men among the small number (possibly only a few hundreds in all) of 'accepted' Masons must have come to see the potential of a secret society cutting across class divisions to embrace aristocrats, gentry, professional men and elements of the expanding middle class. It was to be a brotherhood which would put a string to pull into the hand of every member, and strings enough in the hands of its shadowy controllers to manipulate events – like puppet masters behind the scenes. But who these people were and just how consciously they planned or, as some have said, even plotted, is shrouded in mystery.

One thing united a majority of politically conscious people at this time: the need to preserve the gain of the Civil War of 1642–51 – the limitation of the power of the King. The 'accepted' Masons of the last quarter of the seventeenth century would appear to have been largely drawn from the type of people most anxious to preserve and to increase the steadily growing influence in society and government of men of quite moderate wealth and standing.

Whether Lodges as such or Masons as Masons took part in the initiative to invite William of Orange and his consort Mary to become joint sovereigns in 1688 is not known, but the suggestion is plausible. All that is certain is that by the early years of the eighteenth century a number of Masons had set their sights high: they sought a maximum of reputability. In 1716, according to Dr James Anderson (of whom more later), 'the few Lodges at London resolved . . . to chuse a Grand Master from among themselves, till they should have the honour of a *Noble Brother* at their Head'. The stage was set for the system of tame aristocratic and royal figureheads that we know today, which confers an aura of indisputable approbation on everything to do with Freemasonry. When Grand Lodge was founded, George I had been on the throne only three years. The prominent in Masonry were poised to have a hand in the manipulation of the new Hanoverian dynasty.

Before the foundation of Grand Lodge in 1717, moves to transform the old guild into a true secret society were well under way. As the normal trade union business of operative masonic Lodges dwindled and eventually ceased, so the element of ritual based on the readings of the Old Charges – their legendary stories about the origins of the masons' craft and their injunctions to members to obey the traditional rules – was transformed. Lodge ritual, initiations and speculative dissertations became the main business of actual Lodge meetings. At the same time, fraternal conviviality – which in the old days of operative masonry had probably been confined to a tankard or two after meetings in a local ale house – soon became a major feature of masonic society. Much was eaten, much was drunk, and much was discussed in the privacy of masonic meeting places (usually taverns) after the rather dry formal doings in Lodge were over. The 'better' the Lodge – in the sense of social class – the 'better' the conversation and the more lavish and expensive the entertainment. Masonry was already on its way to mirroring and reinforcing the class system and the emerging social order based on strictly constitutional monarchy. Whatever it was to become overseas, where no Civil War, no Glorious Revolution had yet taken place, Masonry in England was alreaded headed towards a conservative future. The sights of its prime movers were already set on a movement underpinning a type of society admirably suited to its purposes: a stable society with limited social mobility in which a secret inner 'Old Boy' association could provide an environment where considerable benefit could be gained by members who knew how to 'play the masonic organ'.

To achieve this end, though, the confidentiality of the old guild had to be reinforced. The transformation into a secret society meant the institution of formal oaths accompanied by penalties. But once again, before the establishment of Grand Lodge, very little is known of the development of ritual, particularly the oaths. There is evidence that rituals based on various incidents in legendary masonic history were tried out in different Lodges – rituals perhaps based on stories of Noah's Ark and the Tower of Babel alluded to in some Old Charges. It is also probable that rituals based on the story of the building of King Solomon's temple, the principal subject of present-day rituals, were 'worked' (the masonic word meaning the acting out of the Brotherhood's ceremonies). But why this subject was chosen when the legends in the Old Charges give no special prominence to the story of Solomon's temple, no one has been able to explain satisfactorily.

Formal oaths of secrecy to be sworn by individual initiates appear in a number of Old Charges containing 'new orders', but as these were published five years after the establishment of Grand Lodge they are possibly spurious.

Either way, no horrific sanctions are mentioned. Even so, the inclusion of an oath in the initiation rituals can be regarded as a crucial step in the creation of a secret society from the old guild.

CHAPTER 3

Schism and Reunion

In 1717 Freemasonry enters properly into history. Four London Lodges alone formed Grand Lodge and owed allegiance to it. What is interesting is that a none-too-well-off gentleman, Anthony Sayer, was installed as Grand Master. The upper classes kept a low profile. They backed the creation of a central organization welding individual Lodges together, but evidently wanted this done before they assumed control. Of the four original London Lodges, the first three contained not one 'Esquire' between them, whereas Lodge Original No 4 was made up of seventy-one members of whom, in 1724, ten were nobles, three were honourable, four were baronets or knights, and two were generals.

In 1718 Sayer was replaced after barely a year by George Payne, a 'man of more substance', being a member of Original No 4. But he too had only one year in office – another interim while the upper classes moved in on the small gentry just as the small gentry had moved in on the 'operative' artisans a century earlier.

The third Grand Master was the Reverend John Theophilus Desaguliers, a Doctor of Law, a Fellow of the Royal Society and chaplain to Frederick, Prince of Wales, whom he admitted to the Brotherhood in 1737. He was of French extraction. A headhunter for Freemasonry, he not only visited Edinburgh to encourage the Scots along the organizational path the London Masons were following, but visited The Hague in 1731, where he admitted the Duke of Lorraine to the Brotherhood. The Duke married Maria Theresa in 1736 and become co-Regent when she acceded to the Austrian throne in 1738. How far the Duke contributed to the masonic heyday under Joseph II when Mozart, Haydn and a host of other notables were Freemasons is not known. But the cosmopolitan Dr Desaguliers certainly appears to have sparked the missionary zeal of British Freemasonry which eventually carried the movement to almost every country in the world.

Desaguliers too only held office a short time. In 1721 he gave way to the long awaited first noble Grand Master, the Duke of Montague. But, unlike his predecessors, Desaguliers was not usurped: the evidence suggests that he was the prototype of the long line of powerful masonic figures who preferred the shade to the limelight, the reality of power to mere appearances.

By 1730 when the Roman Catholic Duke of Norfolk was installed (prior to the first papal condemnation of Freemasonry in 1738), there had been nine Grand Masters, six of them nobles. The first royal Grand Master was the Duke of Cumberland, younger son of George II, who was installed in 1782, with an Acting Grand Master, the Earl of Effingham, as his proxy. In 1787 both the Prince of Wales (the future George IV) and his brother William (the future William IV) were initiated. The patronage by the Royal Family of the new secret society was thenceforth assured. Queen Elizabeth II is the present Grand Patroness.

But all the while the royals were being courted to become titular leaders of Masonry, the process of transformation of the old masons' guild continued. The Brotherhood was de-Christianized and the rituals of the various workings became formalized. Throughout the eighteenth century more and more pagan elements were brought in to replace the discarded faith.

The de-Christianization was largely accomplished by the *Constitutions* of Dr James Anderson, a Scottish Freemason who became a member of Original Lodge No 4. Anderson, a genealogist and a far from accurate historian, appears to have been put up to the task of settling the new form of the Craft by Dr Desaguliers who in 1723 presented the first version (there was a second version in 1738) to Grand Master the Duke of Montague when he, Desaguliers, had discreetly retired to the second position, that of Deputy Grand Master.

In Anderson's constitution listing the new 'Charges of a Free-Mason', the first is the most striking and had the most far-reaching consequences. It stated: ''Tis now thought more expedient only to oblige them [members of the Brotherhood] to that Religion to which all men agree, leaving their particular opinions to themselves.'

Anderson, in a long and fanciful historical preamble tracing Freemasonry back to Adam and quite unwarrantably naming many previous English monarchs as Masons, seeks to reconcile this radical departure with the spirit and tradition of the old guild by announcing, without any historical justification, that in ancient days masons had been charged in every country to be of the religion of that country where they worked – this despite the fact that virtually all the extant Old Charges were quite explicit in their Christianity.

The only reference to Christ is in Anderson's preamble when, referring to the Roman Emperor Augustus, he notes 'in whose Reign was born God's Messiah, the great Architect of the Church'. In 1815 even this historical preamble was omitted from the *Constitutions* following the Union of the 'Antients' and the 'Moderns', described later, and during the years between 1723 and 1813 the invocation of the name of Christ in the endings of prayers gradually died out. In masonic quotations of scripture (e.g. 1 Peter ii 5; 2 Thess. iii 2; 2 Thess. iii 13) the name of Christ came very pointedly to be deleted from the text. So, to Christians, the apostasy became complete. Masonry became vaguely Voltairean Deist, the 'Great Architect of the Universe' came to be invoked, and prayers ended with 'so mote it be'.

After so much activity a period of comparative neglect now followed during which the politican and littérateur Horace Walpole, himself a Mason, wrote in 1743: 'the Freemasons are in . . . low repute now in England . . . I believe nothing but a persecution could bring them into vogue again'.

There was ribaldry and mockery, and Hogarth, also a Mason, joined in making fun in his engravings of the self-indulging, self-important image the Brotherhood had earned itself. There was no persecution. Instead there was schism, partly in reaction to the de-Christianization of the Craft and other changes in its practice. Masons calling themselves 'the Antients', who had not formed part of the Grand Lodge of 1717, created in 1751 a rival Grand Lodge, also manned by aristocrats, which stood for the link with Christianity and certain other aspects of the old tradition which the 'Moderns', loyal to the 1717 Grand Lodge, had tampered with. The two Grand Lodges vied with each other to recruit provincial Lodges. To complicate matters there were also what the great masonic historian J. Heron Lepper called the 'Traditioners' who, while remaining under the jurisdiction of the London 'Modern' Grand Lodge, nevertheless did not follow its lead entirely.

There was another, later to prove most important, bone of contention between the Antients and the Moderns – the position of a masonic degree and associated working termed the Holy Royal Arch. This time it was the Moderns who objected to something new: some of the Antients had instituted this 'fourth degree', one of the first mentions of which is in 1746 when a prominent Irish Antient was 'exalted' to it. The Moderns claimed that this was a departure from unalterable tradition because the old craft, like other guild crafts, had known only a hierarchy of three degrees – Apprentice, Journeyman or Fellow, and Master Craftsman. Despite the Moderns' objections, the Royal Arch ritual grew steadily in popularity. Perhaps the turning point in the dispute came as a result of Thomas Dunckerley, a natural son of George II, a keen Mason and a Traditioner among the Moderns, coming out as an enthusiast for Royal Arch, to which he was exalted – as Masons term initiation to the Royal Arch – according to his own report in 1754. Dunckerley looms large in masonic history and other prominent Moderns soon came to share his enthusiasm.

Eventually, in 1813, tired of their long quarrel, Antients and Moderns were reconciled, the Duke of Kent, Grand Master of the Antients, giving way to the Duke of Sussex, Grand Master of the Moderns, who thus became the first Grand Master of the United Grand Lodge of England. The Moderns gave way on Royal Arch, saving face by having it declared that this was no fourth degree but simply a culmination of the other three degrees, which completed the making of a Master Mason. The Antients for their part gave way to the Moderns in accepting the total de-Christianization of the Brotherhood.

The Union's acceptance of Royal Arch workings is of great importance, for it completed in all essentials the structure of Freemasonry as it exists today. Just as the Moderns de-Christianized the movement, so with the acceptance of Royal Arch the Antients succeeded in introducing the undeniably occult – notably the invocation of the supposedly rediscovered long-lost name of God, discussed later in this book.

It is perhaps because the Freemasonic God, as revealed to Royal Arch Masons, is so far from being 'that Religion to which all men agree' that it was determined that Holy Royal Arch workings should not be conducted in Lodges but separately in 'Chapters' under the control of a Grand Chapter and not of Grand Lodge. In practice, the officers of Grand Lodge and of Grand Chapter overlap and today both bodies have their seat at Freemasons Hall in Great Queen Street, Holborn. Moreover, Chapters usually meet in the Lodge temples to which they are attached, albeit on different evenings. Today about one in five Freemasons are Royal Arch 'Companions', these constituting a more fervent, more indoctrinated, closer-knit inner circle. With the acceptance of Royal Arch, the way was open for the conferment of the bewildering mass of further even more exclusive degrees that now characterizes world Freemasonry.

During the period from the beginning of the seventeenth century to the time of the Union of Antients and Moderns in 1813, the rituals crystallized and came to approximate each other, although to this day there are a large number of somewhat different workings. The main rituals settled around the legend of King Solomon's temple. The myth mimed in the Master Mason's degree is the murder of Hiram Abiff, claimed to have been the principal architect of the temple, for refusing to reveal masonic secrets. The would-be Master Mason has to 'die' as Hiram Abiff and be 'resurrected' into Masonry. According to the myth mimed in the Royal Arch ceremony, a crypt is found in the foundations of the ruined temple in which is discovered the 'omnific word', the lost name of God. With the rituals, the oaths too became settled in the form they have today. Should he reveal the secrets of the Brotherhood, the Apprentice accepts, among other penalties, to have his tongue torn out; the Fellow Craft to have his heart torn from his breast; the Master Mason to have his bowels burned to ashes; and the exaltee to the Royal Arch accepts 'in addition' to have the top of his skull sliced off. But, as the rituals themselves express it, the 'more effective penalty' for doing anything displeasing to Masonry is to be shunned by the entire Brotherhood, a penalty adequate to bring a man to ruin, the more certainly so as Freemasonry expanded in every profession and every branch of society.

CHAPTER 4

Across the Seas and Down the Centuries

The Irish Grand Lodge was formed in 1725 and the Scottish the following year. The Scots proved at least as fervent missionaries as the English. As already mentioned, the movement had spread to the Continent at least by the third decade of the eighteenth century, often in very high society. Frederick the Great of Prussia is claimed to have been initiated in 1738, although one must be careful of accepting masonic claims of membership by the illustrious. There is no proof, for example, that Christopher Wren, often hailed as one of the brethren, was ever a member. Masonry, its undefined Deism so close to that of Voltairean rationalism, was soon the rage among the pre-revolutionary freethinkers in France: ironically, it may have been planted there by Jacobite exiles around 1725.

Freemasonry remains a power to be reckoned with in many European countries, France and Germany in particular. The French Grand Master today is Air Force General Jacques Mitterand, the President's brother, and Freemasonry's influence in politics is profound. François Mitterand owes much of his success in the 1981 election to influential Freemasons. Masonry has been closely identified with the Socialists for most of the last seventy years. According to Fred Zeller, Grand Master of the Grand Orient of France in 1971 and 1973, the 1974 presidential election would have been won by the Socialists had Valéry Giscard d'Estaing not become a Freemason and colluded with sympathetic forces in the Brotherhood, which eventually persuaded French Freemasons that it was in their best interests to vote for Giscard. He was initiated into the Franklin Roosevelt Lodge in Paris the year of the election.

Italian Freemasonry, later to play a significant role in the unification of the country (Garibaldi was a Freemason), was established in Rome by Jacobite exiles in 1735 and was already a force by 1750. Masonry among Roman Catholic prelates was one reason for the repeated papal condemnations.

No country was too small for attention: Holland, Switzerland and Sweden all had keen and influential memberships in the eighteenth century. Continental Masonry reached as far as Russia: Tolstoy in *War and Peace* describes the different motivations of upper-class Masons during the Napoleonic Wars.

Freemasonry crossed the Atlantic to the colonies of the old empire very early on: George Washington's initiation was in 1752. Today, the dollar bill bears not only Washington's likeness but also the all-seeing-eye symbol of Freemasonry. Washington refused to become head of Masonry for the whole of the newly formed United States, and US Freemasonry came to be organized on a state-by-state basis. Today, each state has its own Grand Lodge. Royal Arch Chapters come under state Grand Chapters, the first mention of Royal Arch appearing in Virginia records of 1753. A few states followed the British lead and spread the Brotherhood abroad. For example, before the Second World War there were Lodges in China under Massachusetts jurisdiction, and it was Massachusetts that warranted the first Canadian Lodge in 1749.* No fewer

*The oldest masonic Lodge room in the USA dates from 1760 and is at Prentiss House, Marblehead, Massachusetts.

than nine Canadian Grand Lodges were eventually formed. The United States proved a home from home for the Brotherhood. Eight signatories to the Declaration of Independence – Benjamin Franklin, John Hancock, Joseph Hewes, William Hooper, Robert Treat Payne, Richard Stockton, George Walton and William Whipple – were proven Masons, while twenty-four others, on less than certain evidence, have been claimed by the Brotherhood. Seventeen Presidents have been Masons: Washington, Madison, Monroe, Jackson, Polk, Buchanan, Andrew Johnson, Garfield, McKinley, both Roosevelts, Taft, Harding, Truman, Lyndon Johnson, Gerald Ford and Ronald Reagan. Seventeen Vice-Presidents including Hubert Humphrey and Adlai Stevenson have also been brethren.

But the British – the founders of Masonry – remained throughout the nineteenth and twentieth centuries the chief propagandists for the movement. Undaunted by the loss of the first empire and with it direct control over American Masonry, the British took Masonry with the flag as they created their second empire – the one on which the sun never set. For some years membership of the Lodges set up in the empire (grouped in 'Provinces' under English, Scottish or Irish jurisdiction) was confined to Europeans, apart from a handful of Indian princely exceptions. But after 1860, at first Parsees, then other Indians were brought into the Brotherhood. In British West Africa and the West Indies there were 'black' Lodges as well as 'white' Lodges (as in the USA), and eventually mixed Lodges were formed.

Associating the native upper and middle classes on a peculiar, profitable and clandestine basis with their white rulers, some historians believe, did much to defuse resentment of imperial domination. Despite his colour, any man rather better off than the mass of the people – who were not sought as members – could, by being a Freemason, feel that he belonged in however humble a way to the Establishment. Just how far Masonry reached is shown by the fact that on the small island of Jamaica there were no fewer than twelve Lodges, some in townships of little more than a couple of streets.

Freemasonry of itself is simply a secret environment tended by its various Grand Lodges, an exclusive society within society, there to be used by its members largely as they wish. Hence its influence, political, and social, can be quite different at different times and places. In the eighteenth century Masons were thin on the ground, but enough aristocrats, men of fashion and influence, were Masons to give the top Masons influence disproportionate to their numbers. And of course royal involvement ensured, as it does today, the impression of total reputability. Because of this, Freemasonry has been able to ignore all legislation dating from 1797 concerning secret societies and illegal oaths. Although regarded as subversive in some countries where the environment was less amenable, in eighteenth-century Britain the Brotherhood had the effect already alluded to – of reinforcing the development of constitutional monarchy under which its own Establishment could thrive.

Among the middle classes, though, Masonry was then too sparse in most areas to play any crucial role in local affairs. There was none of the tight-lipped apprehensive silence so common today. People could afford to ridicule the movement, and there was a lively trade in anti-masonic pamphlets. In fact, masonic 'exposures' may have done much to develop and harmonize the still unprinted rituals.

But the advantage of Masonry, in terms of cult, diversified friendships and straight worldly interest, had become evident to many. With the Union of 1813 the movement began to snowball: for the more Masons there are in any area or profession the more important it is to be a

Mason if one is not to risk losing out, as a non-member of the 'club', in one's business, one's profession and one's preferment.

Another factor was important: with the Industrial Revolution, social mobility began to increase. And Masonry, providing a ladder extending from the lower middle class to the Royal Family itself, offered great advantages to those who could learn how to climb it. There was also the loneliness of the new urban way of life: Freemasonry provided an enormous circle of instant acquaintances in most walks of life. Then too, the English public schoolboy could continue to be public schoolboy in the intimacy of the Craft.

At the end of the eighteenth century only about 320 English Lodges had been warranted. About twice as many more were formed in the next half century, No 1000 in 1864. This number was doubled in the next twenty years, No 2000 being warranted in 1883. The next twenty years maintained this rate of growth with Lodge No 3000 opening in 1903, in which year Winston Leonard Spencer Churchill, the MP for Oldham, was initiated to a masonic career that was to last more than sixty years. All this nineteenth-century explosion resulted essentially from recruitment from the middle and professional classes.

With the First World War, which led to so many of quite humble background seeking better status, the rate of growth speeded dramatically. Lodge No 4000 was formed in 1919, and No 5000 only seven years later in 1926. The Second World War, for similar reasons, led to another such period of extraordinarily rapid growth – Lodge No 6000 being formed in 1944 and No 7000 in 1950.

In 1981, Lodge No 9003 was warranted. Even allowing for Lodges that have been discontinued, taking average Lodge membership at around sixty men, a membership of at least half a million can reasonably reliably be estimated for England alone. Official masonic estimates, as already stated, put the total for England and Wales at around 600,000.

As the recruiting ground for Freemasons is primarily the not directly productive middle and professional classes, it is clear that a very high proportion of these people, occupying key roles in British society – lawyers, Civil Servants, bank managers and so on – are Freemasons. In many fields nowadays the disadvantages of being left out of the 'club' are perceived as being too serious for a great many people to contemplate, whatever they may feel personally about the morality of joining a secret society, or about the misty tenets of speculative Freemasonry.

CHAPTER 5

The Thirty-Third Degree

There is an élite group of Freemasons in England over whom the United Grand Lodge has no jurisdiction. These are the brethren of the so-called Higher Degrees, and even the majority of Freemasons have no idea of their existence.

Most Freemasons who have been raised to the 3rd Degree to become Master Masons believe they are the top of the masonic ladder. As novices they were Entered Apprentices. They were then 'passed' as Fellow Craft Masons and finally 'raised' as Masters. The very name Master has connotations of supremity. If Master Masons have ambition it will usually be to achieve office within their Lodge – eventually, with good fortune and the passing of years, to become Worshipful Master of their mother Lodge (the Lodge to which they were first initiated into Masonry). Those who have their eyes fixed on higher office will aim for rank in their Provincial Grand Lodge or in the United Grand Lodge itself. But even the Grand Master of all England is only a Freemason of the 3rd Degree. The three Craft

3° Master Mason
↑
2° Fellow Craft
↑
1° Entered Apprentice

degrees form the entire picture of Masonry for most of the

The Thirty-three Degrees of Freemasonry

33° Grand Inspector General
↑
32° Sublime Prince of the Royal Secret
↑
31° Grand Inspector Inquisitor Commander
↑
30° Grand Elected Knight Kadosh, Knight of the Black and White Eagle
↑
29° Knight of St Andrew
↑
28° Knight of the Sun
↑
27° Commander of the Temple
↑
26° Prince of Mercy
↑
25° Knight of the Brazen Serpent
↑
24° Prince of the Tabernacle
↑
23° Chief of the Tabernacle
↑
22° Prince of Libanus
↑
21° Patriarch Noachite
↑
20° Venerable Grand Master
↑
19° Grand Pontiff
↑
18° Knight of the Pelican and Eagle and Sovereign Prince Rose Croix of Heredom
↑
17° Knight of the East and West
↑
16° Prince of Jerusalem
↑
15° Knight of the Sword, or of the East
↑
14° Scottish Knight of Perfection
↑
13° Royal Arch (of Enoch)
↑
12° Grand Master Architect
↑
11° Sublime Elect
↑
10° Elect of Fifteen
↑
9° Elect of Nine
↑
8° Intendant of the Building
↑
7° Provost and Judge
↑
6° Intimate Secretary
↑
5° Perfect Master
↑
4° Secret Master

....

3° Master Mason
↑
2° Fellow Craft
↑
1° Entered Apprentice

600,000 'uninitiated initiates' of the Brotherhood in England and Wales.

The 'Masters', who form the largest proportion of Freemasons, are in most cases quite unaware of the thirty superior degrees to which they will never be admitted, nor even hear mentioned. This is the real picture, with the three lowly degrees governed by Grand Lodge and the thirty higher degrees governed by a Supreme Council.

These thirty degrees, beginning with the 4th (that of Secret Master) and culminating in the 33rd (Grand Inspector General), are controlled by a Supreme Council whose headquarters are at 10 Duke Street, St James's, London SW1. Nobody walking down Duke Street from Piccadilly is likely to suspect the true nature of what goes on inside the building, even if he or she happens to notice the small plate to the right of the entrance which says, 'The Supreme Council. Ring once'. Built in 1910–11, this imposing Edwardian mansion with fine neo-classical features might easily be taken for a consulate or the headquarters of some private institute. Nor do people thumbing through the S–Z section of the London Telephone Directory get any clue from the entry sandwiched between Supreme Cleaners and Supreme Die Cutters: 'Supreme Council 33rd Degree . . . 01-930 1606'.

Nobody looking at that fine but anonymous house from outside could suspect that behind its pleasing façade, beyond the two sets of sturdy double doors and up the stairs there is a Black Room, a Red Room and a Chamber of Death. To high Masons, the house in Duke Street is known as the Grand East.

Members of Craft Freemasonry – that is, all but a few thousand of England's Masons – often argue that Freemasonry is not a secret society but 'a society with secrets'. Although the argument is in the end unconvincing, it has its merits. But no such case can be made out for the wealthy society-within-a-society based at 10 Duke Street.

One of the regulations of ordinary Craft Freemasonry is that no Mason may invite an outsider to join. Anyone wishing to become a Freemason must take the initiative and seek two sponsors from within the Brotherhood.* The position is reversed for Freemasons of the 3rd Degree who wish to be elevated to the Higher Degrees. Initiation into the Rite is open only to those Master Masons who are *selected* by the Supreme Council. If a representative of the Supreme Council establishes contact with a Master Mason and concludes that he is suitable, the Candidate will be offered the chance of being 'perfected' and setting the first foot on the ladder to the 33rd Degree. But only a small proportion, even of the limited number of Freemasons who take the first step, progress beyond the 18th Degree, that of Knight of the Pelican and Eagle and Sovereign Prince Rose Croix of Heredom. With each Degree, the number of initiates diminishes. The 31st Degree (Grand Inspector Inquisitor Commander) is restricted to 400 members; the 32nd (Sublime Prince of the Royal Secret) to 180; and the 33rd – the pre-eminent Grand Inspectors General – to only 75 members.

While the Armed Forces are strongly represented in ordinary Freemasonry, the 'Antient and Accepted Rite of the Thirty-Third Degree' is particularly attractive to military men. Grand Inspectors General (i.e. members of the Supreme Council) have included Field Marshal Earl Alexander of Tunis, successively Commander-in-Chief in the Middle East and Allied Supreme Commander in the Mediterranean in the Second World War; Major-General Sir Leonard Henry Atkinson; Brigadier E. W. C. Flavell; Lieutenant-General Sir Harold Williams; Brigadier General

*This, at least, is the theory – and United Grand Lodge staunchly maintains that it is the practice. In reality most Entered Apprentices are recruited by existing Masons they know personally.

Edward Charles Walthall Delves Walthall; and scores more in the last two decades. Before his retirement in 1982 the Most Puissant Sovereign Grand Commander (the most senior Freemason of the 33rd Degree in England and Wales and Head of the Supreme Council) was Major-General Sir (Herbert) Ralph Hone, KCMG, KBE, MC, TD, and so on. There is no mention of Freemasonry in his entry in *Who's Who*, which lists every other decoration, award and distinction he has earned in his eighty-seven years, although becoming Britain's highest Freemason can have been of no little consequence to him. In masonic matters he would dispense with all the other abbreviations and simply sign himself, *Ralph Hone, 33°*. Born in 1896, he is also a Bailiff Grand Cross of the Order of St John of Jerusalem.

He was wounded during the First World War while serving with the British Expeditionary Force, went on to practise as a barrister-at-law in Uganda and Zanzibar in the 1920s, becoming Resident Magistrate in Zanzibar in 1928 and Crown Counsel of Tanganyika Territory two years later. In the thirties he was Attorney-General and Acting Chief Justice of Gibraltar, and Attorney-General of Uganda between 1937 and 1943. After serving as Chief Legal Adviser, Political Branch, and then Chief Political Officer, GHQ Middle East, he was appointed to the General Staff of the War Office in 1943. After the war he was Chief Civil Affairs Officer in Malaya for a year before becoming Secretary-General to the Governor-General of Malaya and then Deputy Commissioner-General in South-East Asia. In 1949 he was appointed Governor and Commander-in-Chief of North Borneo. At the end of five years there he spent seven years as Head of the Legal Division of the Commonwealth Relations Office. This took him into 1961 when he returned to the Bar. Among other posts at home and abroad in the next fourteen years he was a Constitutional Adviser to R. A. Butler's Advisers on Central Africa, to the South Arabian Government and the Bermuda Government. He was Standing Counsel to the Grand Bahama Port Authority until his retirement in 1975 at the age of seventy-nine. He succeeded Most Puissant Brother Sir Eric Studd, Bt, OBE, 33°, as Sovereign Grand Commander.

This, then, was the man who – at the time *The Brotherhood* was completed for New English Library – was truly Britain's highest Freemason, whatever might be said of the Duke of Kent, the current Grand Master of Craft Masonry. Page 39 shows the hierarchy over which the Most Puissant Sovereign Grand Commander presides, with the Duke of Kent's sub-hierarchy way down low.

Although in 1936, 1947 and 1967 Major-General Sir Ralph Hone held grand rank in the United Grand Lodge, and has achieved distinction in many fields, he is one of that brand of men who attain power without notoriety or fame. Few of the many hundreds of Freemasons I have interviewed had even heard of him, and of those few only five knew of him in his secret role as the highest Mason of the highest Degree. These five were all initiates of the Ancient and Accepted Rite: two Sovereign Princes Rose Croix of Heredom (18th Degree); one of the 180 Sublime Princes of the Royal Secret (32nd Degree); a 33rd Degree Grand Inspector General; and a former Grand Inspector Inquisitor of the 31st Degree who had renounced Freemasonry, in order, he said, to become 'a true and living Christian'. But beyond the fact that Major-General Sir Ralph was the preeminent member of the Supreme Council, none of them would say any more either about the man himself or about the rituals, the degrees or the administration of the Rite.

Sir Ralph's successor is Harold Devereux Still, former Grand Treasurer and Junior Grand Warden of the United

Grand Lodge of England, and Grand Treasurer and Grand Scribe Nehemiah of the Supreme Grand Chapter of Royal Arch Masons of England. He also attained the rank of Grand Master of the United Religious, Military and Masonic Orders of the Temple of St John of Jerusalem, Palestine, Rhodes and Malta.

The Brotherhood attracts men of distinction in the judiciary and legal profession, as will be seen later. One such man is His Honour Judge Alan Stewart Trapnell, who was appointed to the Circuit Bench in 1972. He is a Craft Freemason of grand rank, having been Assistant Grand Registrar in 1963, Junior Grand Deacon in 1971 and Senior Grand Deacon in 1979. In 1969 he became Assistant Grand Sojourner of the Supreme Grand Chapter of Royal Arch Freemasons. All these details are listed in the *Masonic Year Book*, which is now very difficult for non-Masons to come by. What is not mentioned is that he is a Freemason of the 33rd Degree and Grand Inspector General for Middlesex.

Although Craft Freemasonry is worldwide in the sense that it exists in most parts of the non-Communist world, and even underground in parts of the eastern bloc, it has no international organization. The Ancient and Accepted Rite of the Thirty-Third Degree is the only cohesive masonic group run on truly international lines. The Supreme Council in London is one of many Supreme Councils in various parts of the globe, of which the senior is the Supreme Council of Charleston, USA, which effectively operates a worldwide network of Freemasons in the most powerful positions in the executive, legislature, judiciary and armed forces as well as the industry, commerce and professions of many nations.

The English working of the Rite – sometimes known by the code name Rose Croix from the title of the initiate to the 18th Degree – differs from the American in one basic respect. In England and Wales only a few of the 33 degrees are conferred by special ritual, while in the USA each degree has its own initiation ceremony. In this country, the 4th to 17th Degrees are conferred at once and in name only during initiation of the selected Freemason to the 18th Degree. To the few who rise higher than the 18th Degree, the 19th to 29th are conferred nominally during the ritual of initiation to the 30th Degree – that of Grand Elected Knight Kadosh or Knight of the Black and White Eagle. Degrees above the 30th are conferred singly. No initiate can rise highter than the 18th Degree without the unanimous agreement of the entire Supreme Council.

PART TWO

The Police

CHAPTER 6

The Great Debate

'The insidious effect of Freemasonry among the police has to be experienced to be believed.'

With these words, David Thomas, a former head of Monmouthshire CID, created a storm of protest in 1969 and reopened a debate that had started nearly a century before, when a conspiracy involving masonic police and masonic criminals brought about the destruction of the original Detective Department in Scotland Yard.

Since then allegations of masonic corruption within the police have been rife. The Jack the Ripper murders in the East End of London in 1888 were perpetrated according to masonic ritual and a subsequent police cover-up was led by the Commissioner and Assistant Commisioner of the Metropolitan Police, both Freemasons.

There have been allegations of charges being dropped against criminal Masons by police Masons; of unfair promotions on the basis of masonic membership and not merit; of non-Masons being hounded out of the service; of livelihoods ruined; of blackmail and violence; of discipline eroded by a system in which a Chief Superintendent, Commander or even on occasion an Assistant Chief Constable or Chief Constable can be made to kneel in submission before one of his own constables; and, in recent times, of robbery and murder planned between police and criminals at Lodge meetings.

It is almost certainly true that the corruption which led to Operation Countryman, the biggest investigation of police malpractice ever mounted in Britain, would never have arisen had a masonic City of London Police commissioner in the 1970s not turned a blind eye to the activities of several desperately corrupt Freemasons under his command.

And in the purges that took place at New Scotland Yard in the early 1970s, masonic police up to the rank of Commander were found to be involved in corrupt dealings with masonic criminals.

The debate about Freemasonry in the police began in 1877 with the sensational discovery that virtually every member of the Detective Department at Scotland Yard, up to and including the second-in-command, was in the pay of a gang of vicious swindlers. The corruption had started in 1872 when Inspector John Meiklejohn, a Freemason, was introduced at a Lodge meeting in Islington to a criminal called William Kurr. Kurr had then been a Freemason for some years. One night at the Angel, Islington, the two masonic brothers exchanged intimacies. Kurr was operating a bogus 'betting agency' swindle and was sorely in need of an accomplice within the force to warn him as and when the Detective Department had sufficient information against him to move in. Meiklejohn agreed to accept £100, nearly half his annual salary, to supply information.

The Detective Department at Scotland Yard had been set up in 1842. In the 1870s there were only fifteen detectives to cover the entire capital. These were under the command of the legendary Superintendent Frederick Williamson, described by one writer as a man of 'the strictest probity, and of great experience and shrewdness'. Under Williamson, the most senior detectives in London were Chief Inspector George Clarke, Chief Inspector William Palmer and Chief Detective Inspector Nathaniel Druscovitch – all Freemasons.

The criminal partnership of Inspector Meiklejohn, who, interestingly, was 'Countryman' in various coded messages which passed between the criminals, and William Kurr continued. Eventually Kurr teamed up with Harry Benson, a psychopathic confidence trickster who had scarred and crippled himself for life by setting himself on fire in his bed at Newgate Prison. One by one, Meiklejohn corrupted nearly all the junior officers in the Detective Department, and introduced several of his most senior masonic colleagues in the department to Benson and Kurr, and they too began to accept bribes for information and services rendered.

The enterprises of Kurr and Benson came to the attention of Superintendent Williamson after they had successfully swindled the Comtesse de Goncourt of £10,000. Williamson placed the enquiry in the hands of one of his most respected men, Chief Detective Inspector Nathaniel Druscovitch. But Druscovitch was one of those who had allowed himself to be tempted into the masonic-criminal circle, and was in the pay of the very men he was now detailed to investigate. Clarke, the sixty-year-old senior officer of the department; Palmer; and a masonic solicitor named Edward Frogatt were all drawn into the conspiracy. From there the corruption spread, its full extent lost in the tangled web of deceit woven by those involved. When the men were eventually brought to justice, the Detective Department lay in ruins and the following year, 1878, saw the complete reorganization of plain clothes investigation in the Metropolitan Police with the setting up of the modern Criminal Investigation Department.

By coincidence, it was exactly one hundred years after the arrest of Meiklejohn and his brethren in July 1877 that Scotland Yard detectives were again in the dock on serious corruption charges, when once again an Old Bailey jury heard of collusion between detectives and criminals who belonged to the same masonic Lodges.

But before going on to see how history repeated itself at the Yard (see Chapter 8, below) and the startling events that affected the unique City of London Police, taking it into its darkest period, it is important to take a look at certain episodes in the years between the imprisonment of Scotland Yard Detective Inspector Meiklejohn (Freemason) in 1877 and the imprisonment of Scotland Yard Detective Chief Superintendent Moody (Freemason) in 1977.

In my book *Jack the Ripper: The Final Solution* I demonstrate how the murders of five prostitutes in the East End of London in the late summer and autumn of 1888 were perpetrated not by one person working alone but by three men operating together for a specific purpose. Four of the five women – the man in charge of the operation had been deliberately misled about the identity of the fourth victim – shared, it was later revealed by one of the killers, a dangerous secret. They had to be silenced.

It was a period when England was perilously unstable. Many believed that revolution was just beyond the horizon. The prostitutes had learned first-hand of a secret the most potent forces in the British government had been striving to maintain for nearly four years. The Prime Minister himself believed that if the secret got out, the throne itself would be in peril. In an age of fierce anti-Catholic feeling, Prince Albert Victor Christian Edward, grandson of Queen Victoria and Heir Presumptive to the throne, had illegally married and fathered a child by a Roman Catholic commoner.

In the early part of the operation, the wife of the Prince

had been bundled off to a lunatic asylum by no less a personage than Sir William Gull, Physician in Ordinary to the Queen. All this, I hasten to add, without the Queen's knowledge. When it was realized that others had to be silenced, Prime Minister Lord Salisbury turned again to Gull, never imagining that the good doctor, who was more than a little unstable, would go to the lengths he did. Gull was a Freemason. He decided that the penal oaths he had taken as a Freemason were more than mere symbolism. Gull concluded that the only safe way to silence the women was to eliminate them. And the proper way to execute them was as traitors to the nation, in which, according to one masonic writer of the period, 'true Freemasonry is about to be more powerful than Royalty'. In other words, they would be mutilated according to the penalties laid out in masonic ritual. That his intention was carried to its conclusion is borne out by the ritualized and specifically masonic nature of the injuries inflicted on the Ripper victims. Contemporary descriptions of the mutilations contained in *The Times* and the secret Home Office file on the case, to which I had full access during my investigations, compare with the mimed murders in masonic rituals and with an illustration by Hogarth of an actual masonic murder, showing startling parallels.

The importance of the Ripper murders was not so much in the individual tragedies of the five women who died at the hands of a demented Freemason and his two toadies, although those were disturbing enough, but in the national tragedy of what followed: an official cover-up of immense proportions that confirmed that Freemasonry really was the unseen power behind the throne and government alike.

The man actively responsible for concealing the truth behind the Ripper murders was Sir Charles Warren, Commissioner of the Metropolitan Police and one of the country's most eminent Freemasons. Warren impeded the investigation of the murders at every turn, caused endless confusion and delays, and personally destroyed the only clue the Ripper ever left. This was a scrawled chalk message on a wall inside a tenement block near the site of the fourth murder. Beneath the message was a blood-soaked piece of cloth which Jack the Ripper had recently cut from the apron of his latest victim. The message itself, according to a careful copy made by a conscientious PC who was at the scene early – which had been concealed in the Scotland Yard files on the case for nearly ninety years before I gained access to them – read:

The Juwes are
The Men That
will not
be blamed
for nothing

The moment he was told of this, Warren, who had not previously ventured near the East End, rushed to the place before the message could be photographed and *washed it away*. This has never been explained. The truth was that Warren, who had been exalted to the Royal Arch in 1861, had realized that the writing on the wall was a *masonic* message.

Much of masonic ritual centres on murder. At the 3rd Degree, the victim is Hiram Abiff, mythical architect in charge of the building of Solomon's temple. The ceremony involves the mimed murder of Hiram by three Apprentice Masons, and his subsequent resurrection. The three Apprentices are named Jubela, Jubelo and Jubelum – known collectively as the *Juwes*. In masonic lore, the Juwes are hunted down and executed, 'by the breast being torn open and the heart and vitals taken out and thrown over the left shoulder', which closely parallels the details of Jack the Ripper's *modus operandi*.

Warren, a founder of the Quatuor Coronati Lodge of

Masonic Research and by the time of the Ripper murders a Past Grand Sojourner of the Supreme Grand Chapter, knew only too well that the writing on the wall was telling the world, 'The *Freemasons* are the men that will not be blamed for nothing.'

The City of London Police is unique. Descended from the Watch and Ward which manned the City's walls in case of attack in the thirteenth century, the force belongs to the City and is financed largely by the City. It is controlled by a Commissioner who is equal in rank and standing with the Commissioner of the thirty-times-bigger Metropolitan Police. The Commissioner of the City of London Police is appointed by the Court of Common Council of the City Corporation and he and his force are overseen by a police committee of selected Common Councilmen (elected councillors) and Aldermen. The City of London is steeped in tradition, and it is possibly the ever-present awareness of ancient customs, of the perpetual intrusion by the past into the present, that explains why Freemasonry has been so prevalent among officers in the City of London Police.

Cecil Rolph Hewitt, criminologist, author, journalist and Vice-President of the Howard League for Penal Reform, joined the City of London Police in 1921. Writing as C. H. Rolph in the weekly news magazine *Police Review* in September 1981, he said:

> I saw enough chicanery and favouritism fostering Freemasonry in the police service to satisfy me that it ought to be barred. It wasn't so much that the Masons got actual preferment (though I'm sure some of them did); they *believed* they would, and the belief devalued their characters in a way that was as odd as it was disturbing.

Hewitt told me later, 'I was instructing City of London Police recruits from 1931 to about 1940, holding during that time the dizzily rising ranks of Sub-Inspector, Inspector and Chief Inspector. We had a school room at Snow Hill police station, opposite Holborn Viaduct railway terminus. I had to teach them rudimentary criminal law, police practice, and, I suppose, some kind of social ethics – of the kind now greeted as innovatory in the Scarman Report. The recruits often seemed to believe that if in due course they could join a Lodge their careers would be assured. I sometimes found it difficult to disabuse them, and the result was that when their time came to study for promotion, which involves a lot of hard work and is specially hard, in my opinion, on the relatively unlettered types who usually join the police, they just didn't work hard enough and they failed their exams time after time. These pre-conceived notions about the value of Freemasonry as a means to advancement had been inherited, as a rule, from parents or uncles, often policemen themselves.'

Hewitt left the City Police in 1946 and joined the *New Statesman* as a staff writer the following year. He was the editor of the Society of Authors' journal *The Author* for four years and between 1947 and 1978 produced nineteen books, mostly on the police, law and crime. The evidence of one of his contemporaries in the City of London Police is particularly valuable in building up a picture of the degree to which the high incidence of Masonry within the force influenced it between the 1920s and the late 1950s. Gilbert Stone, who joined the force in 1927, was a much-respected officer. Although a non-Mason, he is not anti-Mason, and gave a considered and self-evidently balanced account.

'I retired from the City Police early in 1959 as a 1st Class Superintendent,'* he told me. 'I served under two Commissioners, Sir Hugh Turnbull and Sir Arthur Young, and I am sure that neither of them were Masons. The Assistant

*This rank has since been upgraded to Chief Superintendent.

Commissioner in my early days was, I am pretty certain, a Mason. Quite a number of senior officers were Masons and some were not.

'I would imagine that there was a greater proportion of CID officers of all ranks in Masonry than uniformed officers, and I got the general impression without any evidence to substantiate it that Masons had a better chance of getting into the CID than non-Masons. I must say, however, that in my early days or years in the force in the late twenties I did for about a year or so work in the CID at my Divisional Station, doing clerical and admin work, and on several occasions I was invited by several CID men, including a Detective Inspector and several Detective Sergeants who were Masons, to enter the CID, which invitations I always declined. I mention this to show that the CID was not the exclusive preserve of the Masons, but I must add that I often wondered whether, if I did accept the invitations and enter the CID, I would then have been invited to become a Mason.

'A lot of constables were in Masonry, although I would not like to hazard a guess on what proportion. Some belonged when they joined the force. I think it reasonable to assume that quite a lot of them were, or became, Masons because it would confer some advantages, whether by giving them an easier "ride" in the force, or because they thought it would help them with promotion, or perhaps both.

'There is only one case, as far as I can recollect, where a Mason did reap an advantage by being one. He was a man who occasionally got drunk and in that condition often turned violent and assaulted people, including senior officers. On more than one occasion his conduct resulted in a disciplinary charge against him, and on each occasion he virtually got away with it. A small fine, 19s 6d if I remember aright, was imposed and that was that. Often he was not charged. The general view of his colleagues, which included me, was that had he not been a Mason he would have been sacked long ago.

'On one occasion a colleague invited me to think about becoming a Mason and said that if I was interested he would be pleased to propose me, but, as you can gather, I was not interested, and no pressure was brought to bear on me.

'I personally was not affected, so far as I am aware, by not being a Mason. I met and served with some Masons who were delightful colleagues and real gentlemen. I met some Masons who were quite the opposite. And that applies equally to colleagues who were not Masons.'

Ex-Superintendent Stone introduced me to Albert Treves, 'an old colleague and friend who retired as an Inspector in the City, who was a very active Mason and was also a very charming and gentlemanly person'.

Treves told me that during his fifty years' service in and with the police, the subject of Masonry was seldom if ever mentioned to him, and to his knowledge had no influence in any way. His impression was that it was a private matter that concerned only members of the Brotherhood.

I have spoken to nearly seventy former and currently serving officers of the City force, about a third of them Masons. There can be no doubt that whatever part Freemasonry played in the distant past, by the late 1960s it was very hard for non-Masons to obtain promotion above Superintendent in the uniformed branch, and above Sergeant in the CID – even under the non-masonic Commissioner Sir Arthur Young. A masonic sub-structure had grown up, which enabled Freemasons in every department and every division to come together in secret and influence decisions in the force to a remarkable degree. But more of that later.

David Gillespie (a pseudonym) joined Essex Police in 1937 as a PC and retired as Acting Detective Chief Inspector of the same force in 1963. According to several independent statements I have received from men in this force, it has been dominated by Freemasons for generations.

'The application form didn't list Freemasonry under Special Qualifications,' Gillespie told me, 'but in fact from Inspector up to and including Assistant Chief Constable, four out of every five were practising Freemasons, all promoted by one man.'

During his career, Gillespie served at Clacton-on-Sea and the adjoining area around Holland-on-Sea, in the Staff Division CID, at Tilbury Docks, Braintree, and Rochford near Southend-on-Sea. His penultimate job was a £30,000 smuggling run, and he rounded off his career with a successful investigation into murder on the high seas.

The Chief Constable of Essex for much of Gillespie's service was Sir Francis Richard Jonathan Peel, who died in 1979. A direct descendant of Sir Robert Peel, he is remembered in the force as a remote figure who would simply rubber-stamp the decisions of his most senior men. Gillespie liked Peel and reveres his memory, but says that 'he was so intent on creating a vast gulf betwixt his ivory tower and the untouchables that he left promotion to one man'. That man, Assistant Chief Constable John Crockford, was a Freemason.

'Crockford ran the promotion field for twenty years until he retired about 1953. He was a likeable man in many ways who conferred many kindnesses, although many men in the force hated him. Despite his unchallenged power in the service, he saw himself primarily as a Freemason, and one of extremely high rank.

'Of course, not all promotions of Freemasons in my force were disreputable, but many were. The most awful in my time were Walter Stephen Pope, a ridiculous little squirt, to Super, and that of James Peters. Words fail me. They were derided even by their own kidney.

'Both these men were Masons. By police standards Pope was a little man with an inverted inferiority complex, possibly for that reason. He had a high IQ in my opinion, but he was just a police clerk who climbed. He never to my knowledge caught a crook, never saw a blow struck in anger, and never looked in at Tilbury Docks on the night of the sainted Patrick when we were struggling with the Micks and the Molls outside the Presbytery or at the Sign of the Anchor Inn.

'Pope had a hectoring voice and a pompous manner, which in all charity he probably couldn't help. He was a ridiculous figure who upset the troops in every branch he entered. I had him, for my sins, in four divisions. His leadership, of how to get the best out of his men, was pathetic. I sometimes wondered if he were quite sane. Now and then men approached me for a written application *in extremis* to get them away from him. I complied. Such reports fetched up on ACC Crockford's desk and proved successful. None of this prevented them making Pope a Divisional Superintendent.

'But the case of James Peters is if anything worse, if such were possible. Peters was an amiable half-wit. He was simply one of nature's dunderheads, a twit in any company who made one cringe. And he was a congenital liar. But he had become a Freemason at twenty-one and never missed a Lodge meeting. When he was promoted to station clerk, the resultant shock waves startled even the serried ranks of the Magic Circle, which is saying something. When the promotion was published, a certain high-ranker, another Freemason, threw the relevant Force Order B across the room in a fury. He knew Peters.

'Later, on our sergeants' training course, he confided in me that during a heart-to-heart talk, Crockford had told him his future was assured. It was. His rate of promotion after that was astonishing, and he retired at a rank very very few policemen achieve.'

Detective Superintendent David Thomas, former head of Monmouthshire CID, devoted four pages of his memoirs, *Seek Out The Guilty*, to an examination of Freemasonry in the police. Before this, criticism of alleged masonic influence in the police forces of Britain had usually come from the lower ranks. Such men as did raise the question were almost invariably dismissed by their masonic colleagues as embittered failures who used Freemasonry as a scapegoat. This was not wholly unfair. Freemasons, like Communists, Jews, Gipsies and Negroes, have frequently been used as scapegoats by those simplistic souls who like to believe all society's ills have one source: a conspiracy of aliens and subversives dedicated to the overturning of the status quo. Hitler spoke of falling into a 'nest of Freemasons', and seems to have loathed them as much as he did the Jews – certainly he persecuted them as ruthlessly. Mussolini, too, hated Freemasons and during his dictatorship many were executed. On a more moderate level, the belief that no one is promoted in the police unless he is a Freemason is frequently held by non-masonic officers who would be unsuitable for promotion anyway. Unable to accept their own failings, they all too easily subscribe to the conspiracy theory and latch on to Freemasonry as a convenient scapegoat.

On the other hand, the belief that Freemasonry often exerts an improper influence is also held by many police officers who are Freemasons – because there is no doubt at all that many Freemasons have been promoted by other Freemasons for no other reason than that they are members of the same secret Brotherhood. The blanket denial that this happens, or that it can happen, issued by the United Grand Lodge, is untruthful.

The significance of David Thomas's words was that they came from a man of unimpeachable integrity and of high standing in the police and the community. Here was no hot-headed PC, freshly rejected for promotion, flinging wild allegations round the 'nick' canteen, but a successful senior officer in retirement making a reasoned statement and calling for a Royal Commission to investigate a situation he regarded as sinister and dangerous.

> During my thirty-two years' police service I saw a great deal of this secret society in action, not only in my own force but also in the many others I visited as honorary secretary of the detective conferences of No 8 Police District, which comprises the whole of Wales, Monmouthshire and Herefordshire.* Sometimes my visits took me to other areas, but wherever I went the story was the same.
>
> 'Are you on the Square?' or 'Are you on the Level?' are all naïve enquiries as to whether or not one is a Mason.

Thomas thought that of the total number of policemen in 1969, probably only a small percentage were Freemasons. 'But that small percentage forms an important and all-powerful group, the majority of whom are senior officers of the rank of Inspector, or above. Their influence on the service is incalculable.'

He assured readers that Masonry often did affect promotion, and that many sergeants and PCs became Masons for this reason. In this way, the system became self-perpetuating. Without implying that Masons will ensure the promotion of their brethren in the service, Thomas was certain that when two men of equal ability came before a promotion board, the dice would be loaded in favour of the

*The reorganization of police forces in the 1970s changed this.

Mason because of the masonic composition of many boards.

The official response to Thomas's call for a Royal Commission was predictable: like the United Grand Lodge, successive governments have adopted an ignore-it-and-it-will-go-away policy on calls to investigate any state of affairs in which Freemasonry is alleged to be playing a questionable role. An unnamed writer in the *Sunday Telegraph* said this: 'I can confirm that many detectives believe Freemasons exercise an insidious secret influence inside Scotland Yard. But it seems now the suggestion has come into the open the lie may be given to this well-entrenched belief.'

A spokesman for the Police Federation, the police 'trade union' representing all ranks up to Inspector, was quoted as saying that the Federation had never received a complaint from anyone losing promotion or being victimized for not being a Freemason. This was untrue. I have seen copies of statements of just such a nature submitted to the Federation both before and after the date of the Federation's pronouncement. Indeed, only eleven months before the publication of Thomas's book, a Northampton police Sergeant submitted a three-page typed report, every page signed by himself at the bottom and every surname typed in capitals as if it were a formal witness's statement. In it he complained of two incidents:

> In March of last year I was told in no uncertain terms by Det Insp Brian JENKINS [pseudonym] that if I did not join the lodge he would personally see to it that I was never promoted above my present rank . . . On December 24 last, just before the Christmas Party, I was called in to see Chief Insp Howard FIELD [pseudonym]. He said that life could be made very uncomfortable for officers who tried to buck the system. I asked him what he meant. He said, 'You are not on the square, are you. I won't say any more than that.'

The complainant told me the Federation never replied. He said, 'Life became intolerable after that. They treated me like a leper. I was either ignored completely by most of them or they kept picking arguments with me. Complaint after complaint was made against me. It was ridiculous. I stuck it for about a year but then I just got out.'

Now a Superintendent in the North East of England, my informant achieved very rapid promotion *without* joining the Brotherhood.

The Federation spokesman who told the *Sunday Telegraph* that complaints of this nature had never been received, went on to say: 'Under modern promotion procedures it is difficult to see how it could happen. We have national promotion exams. In London, promotion up to station sergeant is decided by exams. Boards decide other promotions. It would be gross exaggeration to say Freemason members had any undue influence.'

What the spokesman did not point out was that passing a promotion examination did not mean automatic promotion. There are many PCs and Sergeants in the country who have qualified as Inspectors, but because of a dearth of vacancies at the higher ranks, they remain at the bottom. In the 26,000-strong Metropolitan Police there is a much greater chance of early promotion, as there is for an officer prepared to move from force to force; but in country forces it is often a case of dead men's shoes. And even when a vacancy arises, applicants go before promotion boards. In suggesting that examinations eliminated favouritism the Federation was therefore being less than truthful, and the reason is perhaps not hard to find. Until very recently the majority of regional representatives of the Police Federation were Freemasons. Even today, a large proportion of its civilian staff are ardent members of the Brotherhood.

There are two other allegations which have been made so frequently, and by such well-respected officers, two Assistant Chief Constables (one a Mason) included, that they should be mentioned, although it must be said that I have yet to see undeniable evidence. One claim is that masonic officers taking exams will make some kind of mark on their paper to indicate their affiliation to the Brotherhood. The most common, it is alleged, is the age-old masonic code of writing a capital 'A' in the form of the Brotherhood's Square and Compasses symbol, thus:

Alpha

This will be meaningless to a non-masonic examiner but will be immediately recognized by a fellow Mason. The other allegation, made by scores of officers of all ranks, is that masonic promotion boards sometimes slip masonic references into their conversation when interviewing. If the candidate for promotion responds correctly, it is said, his chances are immediately elevated.

The row about Freemasonry in the police blew up again in May 1972 when *Police Review* published an article by a thirty-five-year-old Sergeant of Nottinghamshire Combined Constabulary, Peter J. Welling. The article captured the feeling of many non-masonic police officers and provoked fierce opposition and loud agreement which were publicized in the daily press and on television. Welling said that from the beginning of his police career he had been made aware by members of the general public which of his police colleagues were Freemasons. In his early years in the police he thought most masonic officers were in the higher ranks.

> This manifested itself in the instructions one would sometimes

receive regarding one's attitude to certain members of the public who held prominent positions in public life and who committed infringements, if only minor infringements, of the law. I took this to be a legacy from the old watch committee and standing joint committee days when those governing bodies virtually held the efficiency of the Service by its purse strings. It was therefore extremely important for members of the senior ranks in the Service to have close contact, not only in committee, but also socially, with such persons who were no doubt closely aligned to the Freemasonry movement.*

However, with the progress of time, the conduct and structure of the Police Service has changed, and is continuing to change at a rapid pace. But there is an increasing awareness among junior members of the Service that, after passing the appropriate examinations, a sure way to promotion is through the Freemasonry movement. Thus there is a considerable amount of canvassing to be done which appears to be creating a split in the Service itself.

Sergeant Welling was concerned with the possible long-term effects of this. He thought that if increasing numbers of serving police officers were to join the Brotherhood, 'then a saturation point will be reached when the majority, if not all police officers, will be members'.

What consequences might this have? Welling thought the best way of finding an answer was to examine 'the terms of reference and ethics behind both the Police Service and the Freemasonry movement'. He went on:

It is a fact that when a Police Officer is appointed he takes an oath of allegiance to the Queen and the community to carry out his duties 'without fear or favour, malice or ill will'. It is not commonly known that on enrolment to a Freemasonry Lodge a Freemason also takes an oath. I do not profess to know what form this oath takes or how it is administered, but it is most certainly an oath of allegiance not only to members of his own Lodge but to

*This kind of woolly phrase is misleading. Men are either Freemasons or not Freemasons. No 'close alignment' without membership is possible.

all members of the Freemasonry movement. To assist him to recognize other Freemasons he is taught secret handshakes and other secret signs. This type of association taken throughout the country forms a formidable chain of contact and associates from all walks of life.

It was in this 'formidable chain of contact' that Welling felt the danger of Freemasonry in the police lay. 'When this country has a national police service* criticism may well be levelled by minority groups against the police that the service is not impartial. The question I ask is – how can a Freemasonry Police officer be impartial? No man can serve two masters.'

The Sergeant's suggestion was for the Police Federation and the Home Office to 'join hands' on the subject of Freemasonry and press for legislation to prohibit serving policemen from taking any oath in any secret society, and to compel new recruits to renounce affiliation to any such society 'in the same manner as he would if he was an active member of a political party'.

Two days after the publication of Welling's article, the *Sunday Telegraph* ran a long story which claimed that the Sergeant's call for a ban on Masonry in the police was 'supported by thousands of policemen'. The reporter, Peter Gladstone Smith, wrote:

Sgt Welling said to me yesterday he had very good friends who were Freemasons and he had nothing against Freemasonry outside the police. He was concerned about disciplinary proceedings when it came to complaints.

'If a person who is a Freemason complains against a police officer and that complaint is investigated by a senior officer who is a Freemason, then that cannot be an impartial enquiry.' His attitude was not 'sour grapes' and he himself was promoted early.

Cdr Ray Anning, head of Scotland Yard's new 60-strong

*Which it still doesn't have, more than eleven years on.

round-the-clock complaints branch, told me that he was not a Freemason. At the same time he believed the suggestion was 'utter nonsense'.

The *Daily Telegraph*'s crime correspondent, T. A. Sandrock, wrote a similar story the following day, which ended with this observation:

> I have discussed this subject myself during many years' association with policemen, asking on hundreds of occasions if they would be restricted as Freemasons in investigations into a criminal act if the suspect was also a Freemason. Invariably their answer has been that they would continue to do their duty as police officers.

Can this distinguished journalist have imagined that if any masonic officers did feel restricted in this way, they would openly have admitted it? It was nonsense to intimate such a thing.

On the next day, Tuesday 9 May, Welling was interviewed on BBC Television's *Nationwide* programme. Also in the studio was Brian Bailey, a local government officer and former Freemason.

Presenter Michael Barratt asked Bailey, 'What do you say to these charges that a sure way to promotion in the police force is through the Freemasonry movement?'

The ex-Mason replied, 'I don't think there's any substance in this. I lapsed my membership of the masonic movement for various reasons, but it seems to me that you might as well say that if the Chief Constable is a keen Rugby enthusiast and you play a good game of Rugby, you are on the inside track.'

And then he added a comment which seems to run counter to his main argument. 'I think one gets all sorts of ideas that there are ways of getting preferment. I think that Freemasonry is just one of them. I doubt very much *these days* if there is any real substance in it.' (My italics.)

The admission that Freemasonry did have an undesirable influence 'up to about ten years ago', 'until only recently', 'not since the last war', 'up until a year or so ago', 'around five years back' has been made to me by scores of Freemasons and former Freemasons. Most are prepared to say it had an influence 'then' – never now. It is interesting to note that in a period when, according to many of my masonic informants, Masonry *was* exercising undue influence in the police, there were those who even then were denying its existence except in the past.

The 'Rugby enthusiast' point of view was taken up by Welling, who replied: 'If Freemasons were as open as a member of a Rugby club would be, then I would have no objections. It's the secrecy that surrounds the whole movement which I object to.'

Bailey did not like the secrecy either. 'One of the things I disliked in the Craft was its secrecy. I think it's bound to give rise to suspicion. It doesn't follow that this suspicion is well founded, however.'

The controversy arising from Welling's article continued in the correspondence columns of *Police Review* for the next three months.

Chief Superintendent T. W. A. Lucas, who became a Freemason after achieving senior rank in the police, said that nothing would influence him to show favour to anyone. 'Neither do I hope to seek such favour, and, while obviously I cannot speak for all, those of senior rank whom I know in many forces hold the same views.' He said:

Everyone who enters Freemasonry is, at the outset, strictly forbidden to countenance any act which may have a tendency to subvert the peace and good order of society; he must pay due obedience to the law of any state in which he resides or which may afford him protection, and he must never be remiss in the allegiance due to the Sovereign of his native land. At no time in his capacity as a Freemason is he permitted to discuss or to advance views on theological or political questions.*

A PC from Neath in Glamorgan wrote to say that he had been a Freemason since 1955. He had qualified for promotion in 1963 but was still at the lowest rank. Further evidence that the police service was not totally the domain of Freemasons came from John Williamson, CBE, QPM, President of the Christian Police Association in Northampton. He said Welling's article 'moved me strangely', and continued:

> After 45 years in the service I have found that being a Christian – that other brotherhood – stood me in better stead when it came to promotion interviews, particularly in the old days. On one occasion I was able to quote a verse from the 75th Psalm: 'Promotion cometh from neither the east nor the west but from the Lord'. I have always believed that it is the worker bees that keep the hive working and strong. I do not think that Freemasonry was that powerful for I made my way through the ranks to become Chief Constable of Northampton at 33. Never was I approached by anyone to become a Mason . . . I went into the service in 1910 fearing God and the Sergeant, and came out in 1955 fearing God.

A Freemason who signed himself T. M. T. described Welling's article as 'a load of rubbish . . . on a subject he obviously knows nothing about'. There were many letters in a similar vein. 'Freemasons,' declared T. M. T., 'are the backbone of the community. They are the most public spirited and charitable people he [Welling] will find. That is if he cares to look. Why has he picked on Freemasons when there are other "secret societies" he could expose?'

One of those phrases admitting that the Brotherhood

*It is perfectly true that the Brotherhood forbids its members to discuss business, politics or religion, but there is ample evidence from present and past Masons that this is rarely obeyed.

had influence but only in the past reared its head in a letter from C. P. Cheshire. This time it was: 'Since Edwardian days Freemasonry has not had the influence ascribed to it.' The majority of Freemasons who know anything about the police admit that the Brotherhood has until some point in the past – remote or recent, depending on the individuals – exerted influence within the police forces of this country. None of them has been able to answer satisfactorily why, at the particular moment in history they have chosen, the Brotherhood's influence either dwindled appreciably or ceased altogether.

In this connection the view of *Police Review*, or at least its then editor Brian Clark, is worthy of note:

> *In pre-war days* [my italics] it was a power to be reckoned with in the Police Service and in many Forces, membership of the 'square' was virtually a qualification for promotion. The falling off of the influence of the movement is related to the 'liberalization' of the Police Service and the Freemasons who remain tend to be found in the senior ranks of the Service – particularly those with pre-war service. Young men are not interested in the pseudo religiosity of Freemasonry and all its secret ritual.

Even if this decline in interest among young policemen was apparent in 1972, and I have found no evidence of it, it is most certainly untrue today. Freemasonry in the police is as high today as ever. And while a great number of senior officers are members of the Brotherhood, so too are many Constables and Sergeants. Back to Clark's assessment of the situation a decade ago:

> Nepotism, through Freemasonry, may still be a factor in promotion, albeit to a decreasing degree, but what is still a serious matter is that Freemasons (and come to that Rotarians, Lions, Roundtablers) tend to expect favours from fellow members who are police officers. A few policemen have been so embarrassed by what is expected of them that they have been obliged to dissociate themselves from Freemasonry.

A former Sergeant of the City of London Police, Frederick E. Moore, a non-Mason, had this to say:

> As a young Constable, despite my keeping an open mind on the subject, it became increasingly evident that the suspicion, not without foundation, was right: membership of one of these fraternities [i.e. secret societies] was an advantage especially for those seeking promotion, for defaulters in disciplinary cases, and when top brass belonged to your Lodge, who could go wrong?

Freemason PC Robert Glencross of Fife replied thus to Sergeant Welling's criticisms:

> There are Freemasons in every trade and not only the Police and there could be those who have reached high ranks in those fields. If junior members of the service feel that the road to success is paved with handshakes they are in for a big disappointment. Among any group of people some will take advantage of whatever benefits are going but there are others who further the aim of the group itself, and one seldom hears from them.
>
> While I am not at liberty to divulge the form of oath taken by Freemasons it in no way conflicts with an officer's duty . . . Freemasonry is not so secret that it is impossible to find out who its members are. Its secrets are there for anyone to learn who wants to join.

This last comment holds true for the Mafia and the Ku Klux Klan, of course, so does not answer Welling's point about the secrecy of Masonry breeding suspicion among the uninitiated. And as for finding out who its members are, a non-Mason has only to ask for help at United Grand Lodge to be told, 'It is not our policy to make membership lists of our Lodges available to enquirers.' (See Epilogue, page 307.)

But one point made by PC Glencross, and by a multitude of Masons before and since, is true up to a point: the oaths, or obligations to use the masonic term, if properly interpreted, should not create the kind of dual allegiance most 'profane' policemen are concerned about. (See Appendix 3.)

Eight weeks after the publication of the original article, a letter appeared from a former police officer, a non-Mason of Malvern Link, Worcestershire. 'The letters on Freemasonry in the service filled me with remorse,' began ex-Detective Chief Inspector Ralph Jones ironically.

> When I joined a large force before the war three-quarters of divisional Superintendents and above belonged to the Craft, a position that still obtains. I see now that most of their appointments only *appeared* bizarre, but were really based on merit.
>
> The tradesmen who whispered down the years, 'Met your Super last night. Don't you want your stripes?' were having me on . . . What shamed me was the revelation that all those old mates who climbed like blue meteors from PC to the top in quick time just *happened* to belong to the Craft but were in fact devoted to Christianity and charitable works. They could have fooled me.
>
> As a practising Christian with a son an Anglican priest, I doubt if I have quite got the moral fibre to qualify. But now I realize that the parcelling out of promotions and the dispensing of rough justice on delinquents behind closed doors is merely benevolent paternalism. Long may it reign.

The fact that the Police Federation was dominated by Freemasons did not inhibit the editor of the Federation's journal *Police* from publishing this complaint from Metropolitan Police Sergeant Robin Kirby in 1977:

> All my service, I have been aware that it is a distinct advantage to be a Freemason. Doors are opened, rank structures are broken down and men normally destined to perform shiftwork all their service are spirited on to 9 A.M. to 5 P.M. jobs, often never to return to the mundane vulgarity of early, late and nights.

The following issue of *Police* contained one of the most serious allegations about Freemasonry in the police to have appeared in print up to that time. Blair Watt, a Thames Valley PC for sixteen years, wrote:

> I speak from personal experience of no less than three occasions on which I have been approached, and even threatened, by more senior officers who sought to influence my dealing with fellow Freemasons and relatives of fellow Freemasons, with regard to offences committed by them.

Watt said later, 'I'm either very brave or an idiot. I was approached by senior officers on quite serious offences. But it must be said that nothing came of their pressure.'

He was not prepared to name the individuals involved, he said, for fear of repercussions. Depending chiefly on whether they are Masons or non-Masons, people have said that Watt's reluctance to give full details was quite understandable, given the power of Masonry in the police, or that it indicated he was inventing the story. Watt himself died shortly afterwards, of natural causes, so a conclusive investigation of his claim is impossible.

CHAPTER 7

The Men at the Top

There are fifty-two police forces in England, Wales, Scotland and Northern Ireland. These comprise ten combined forces in England and Wales, two combined forces in Scotland, thirty-one county forces in England and Wales, six Scottish regional forces, the two London forces and the Royal Ulster Constabulary. I wrote in 1981 to every one of the fifty Chief Constables and both London Commissioners. From this survey, and from private enquiries involving more than 200 informants between the ranks of Chief Inspector and Chief Constable in forces all over the UK, I have been able to identify with certainty only fourteen as non-Masons.

These are C. James Anderton (Greater Manchester); Ronald Gregory (West Yorkshire); R. Birch (Warwickshire); A. F. C. Clissitt (Hertfordshire); G. E. Fenn (Cheshire); Robert Sim (Tayside); A. Morrison (Grampian); Sir George Terry (Sussex); Sir Kenneth Newman (Metropolitan Commissioner since October 1982); Peter Marshall (City of London); G. Charlton (Norfolk); Philip Myers (North Wales); Peter Imbert (Thames Valley); and W. G. Sutherland (Bedfordshire).

The consensus among my most reliable, high-ranking informants is that of the remaining thirty-eight Chief Constables, no fewer than thirty-three members are of the

Brotherhood. If this is correct, more than sixty per cent of all police chiefs in the UK are Freemasons. According to sources within the Police Federation, the Association of Chief Police Officers, the Scottish Police Federation, the Police Superintendents' Association, police forces all over the country and also within the Police Authority for Northern Ireland as well as retired senior police officers and former Chief Constables, this figure is about ten or twelve per cent lower than it was before the amalgamation of police forces.

Police chiefs who replied to my enquiry but refused to answer the question 'Are you a Freemason?' included C. F. Payne (Cleveland) and Alex Campbell (Dumfries and Galloway). Campbell told me, 'I consider that whether or not a man is a Freemason or for that matter whether he is an Orangeman, a member of the Black Preceptory or a member of the Ancient Order of Hibernians is a matter for him alone. Likewise his religious persuasion, be he Protestant, Roman Catholic, atheist or agnostic is a matter for him. I would point out, however, that in my police experience extending over forty-three years, irrespective of the persuasion of senior officers I have found them performing their duties and accepting their responsibilities with complete impartiality.'

Another Chief Constable told me, 'I am well aware of the traditions of Freemasonry and I agree with you there is much misunderstanding, and yet it is not always what exists that is important but other people's perception of what exists. For professional reasons I have never thought it right for a senior police officer in particular to be associated with any political, religious, social or cultural group to the extent where decisions may be seen to be biased or actually to be biased, even if subconsciously.

'I can say that from time to time decisions which have

been made concerning advancement or discipline have often been perceived, however rightly or wrongly, as having been influenced by the bonds of Freemasonry. I do believe that sometimes the "reds under the beds" theory can apply to Freemasonry as it can to politics and religion . . . It is my impression that the proportion of police officers who belong to the movement becomes higher as you reach the higher echelons of the service. I am not however suggesting that this is cause and effect, but merely noting the phenomenon.

'I think my own views could be summed up by saying that what a man does with his private life in these matters of religion, politics or culture is part of the freedom of our society, but where such beliefs manifest themselves as influencing decisions against people who are outsiders or are perceived to do so this can cause problems for those concerned.'

Another Chief Constable, a non-Mason, said, 'Freemasonry is not *so* much a problem today in the police service as it was twenty years ago. Even so, it is still a problem. It certainly still has some controlling influence, and any amount of influence is wrong. Over the years a lot of policemen have been Masons. It's not so fashionable today, although it's as strong as it ever was in one or two quarters of the country.

'Its influence in the police was strongest in the days pre-amalgamation of forces when the promotion stakes relied on this kind of thing in the days of Watch Committees and local political influence on the police. This is what I am very fearful of today – that we don't move back into the era of Watch Committees in spite of the fact that some elements of society are calling for a greater accountability of the police. Accountability is OK but if it's going to be accountability with too much political influence then it will lead us back into worse problems with Freemasonry than we have now. If it's bad now, you should have seen Masonry at work pre-1964 and pre-1947.'

One Chief Constable was particularly frank. His reputation, record and standing in the police service lend particular weight to his testimony. He told me, 'I went to London as a Chief Inspector and it was at that stage that I became a Mason, for no real reason other than the people who invited me to join were friends who I respected very very much.

'Masonry did me a great favour because public speaking didn't come easy to me. I'd lose sleep for two nights beforehand, get very tense and then make a botch of it. And Masonry – the fact that one has to get up on one's feet on occasions, the occasional after-dinner speech or vote of thanks or what-have-you – fulfilled a need that in retrospect I see was very very important to me in terms of character building.

'I joined a very small, friendly Lodge in London, and eventually within a period of about eight years I became Master of that Lodge, which was a tremendous thing. I thoroughly enjoyed it. But then when I left London and moved to B— [a provincial city force], because of the sheer logistics involved, I dropped off. I was three years in B— and gradually my attendances were declining until I got the Deputy Chief Constable's job in this force. My predecessor here was also a Mason and was very heavily involved locally. In fact he subsquently became Master of a Lodge not far from where we're sitting now. But I thought as Deputy Chief when I came here, I would not – certainly for the first year – take part in it at all. I received countless invitations to go out – genuine invitations, for no underhand motives but people genuinely wanted me to go out and visit various Lodges. But I declined this for a year. The year became two years, the two years became four years and so I've never

ever set foot in a Lodge in the area covered by this police force.

'I've also ceased to be a full member in London; although I'm still a member it's on what we call a Country List. That means if ever I do go back I pay for my meal on the night as opposed to paying a large annual subscription.

'I've not stood back because I've got any guilt complex or conscience at all about Masonry, but because of what people think of Masonry. If one is in the position to (a) influence promotions and (b) take decisions on discipline, then quite obviously one is open to the allegation that Masonry is a factor in one's decisions – although I can assure you that I've locked up Masons in my time and sent police officers and others to prison, and been very pleased to have done it.

'Masonry *is* fairly strong in the police service. In my service, which will be twenty-five years next year, therefore relatively modern, I can honestly say that I don't know of any occasion when Masonry has been a fundamental issue in promotion or any other aspect for that matter.

'I think it's not wholly to be unexpected that police are quite heavily involved because we are very conservative by nature. Like attracts like. Freemasonry is a very conservative organization, all about the Establishment, all about the maintenance of the status quo, which is bound to attract a certain sympathy with police officers.

'A lot of nonsense is talked about promotion and so on, and the way I always answer that is this: if you and I went to the same school together, or played for the same Rugby club, or our fathers did whatever together, and then we come to a situation where I am interviewing you and A. N. Other for a job, I've got to make a judgement on your characters, and I've got to take a gamble. I've got to choose the best man to manage this branch or the best man to do this job, or what-have-you. And the more I know about you that causes me to be in sympathy to your cause – the school, the Rugby club, the golf club, Freemasonry or whatever it may be, the more I will be inclined to take a chance – life is all about taking chances when you give appointments – on you as opposed to the man that I know nothing about.'

I wrote to every senior officer at New Scotland Yard in 1981 when Sir David McNee was Commissioner. With the exception of two Deputy Assistant Commissioners, Sir David and all his men ignored my letters to them about Freemasonry. One of the DACs wrote: 'I understand that several of my colleagues have not answered your letter of 21st August. Lest you get the wrong impression that this relates to Freemasonry I am replying just to state that I am not, never have been or ever will be, a Free Mason.'

His colleague told me, 'I am not a Mason, so it is *possible* to get promotion right up to Commissioner without being one. But it is unlikely. Nearly all of my colleagues and seniors are Masons. It's not enough to say that senior police officers are the kind of men who like Freemasonry, or that the sort of men who join Freemasonry are senior officer material. A lot of people at the Yard have got into positions they shouldn't be in purely and simply because they've got Masonry behind them. But if you think anything can be done about it, you're wasting your time.'

CHAPTER 8

Worshipful Masters of Conspiracy

Corruption among Scotland Yard detectives, always a problem, grew enormously during the 1960s. One cause of the trouble was that conventional methods of detection were becoming less and less effective in the face of the burgeoning crime rate. Many policemen believed in a surer way of securing convictions that necessitated a blurring of the 'them and us' divide between the law enforcers and the law breakers. The belief was that to combat crime adequately, the police had to be intimately acquainted with the ways of individual criminals and the day-to-day workings of the underworld. This meant cultivating certain smaller villains, who in return for favours could be counted upon to 'grass' on the bigger men the Yard regarded as its prime quarry. The idea was not new. London police for generations had known that brilliant detective minds which required only sketchy clues and a warm fireside to solve the most bizarre crimes were fine for 221b Baker Street and 10a Piccadilly – but in the cold reality of life at Scotland Yard, things did not work out so neatly. Real-life detectives had to some extent to depend on informers; and informers were usually criminals. In the past it had been an unpalatable necessity, never officially recognized. By the 1960s it was the norm. The system inevitably brought temptation to many police officers, who would be offered money to keep quiet about so-and-so's activities, or a cut in the takings if they made sure the regular police patrol was diverted or unavoidably delayed on a particular night when a job was planned.

The question to be asked is: were there any masonic elements in this corruption, and but for Freemasonry would the corruption have been less likely to have occurred or more easily discovered?

In forces all over England, Freemasonry is strongest in the CID. This had been particularly noticeable at Scotland Yard, and the situation remains the same today. Between 1969 and the setting-up of the famous Operation Countryman in 1978 there were three big investigations into corruption in the Metropolitan Police. These were:

(1) An enquiry into allegations of corruption and extortion by police, first published in *The Times*. This resulted in the arrest, trial and imprisonment of two London detectives in 1972.
(2) An enquiry by Lancashire Police into members of the Metropolitan Police Drug Squad. This led to the trial of six detectives, and the imprisonment in 1973 of three of them.
(3) An enquiry into allegations of corruption among CID officers responsible for coping with vice and pornography in London's West End. Over twenty detectives were sacked from the force during the three-year investigation in the early 1970s, which led eventually to the notorious Porn Squad trials.

There were corrupt masonic policemen involved in all these cases, but this report is not concerned with corrupt policemen who just happen to be Freemasons any more than it is with corrupt policemen who happen to be Roman Catholics, Rotarians or members of their local lawn tennis club. Many people see the discovery of a corrupt Freemason as proof of the corrupting influence of Masonry. This is about as sensible as condemning Christianity because a murderer is found to be a regular churchgoer. There might well be grounds for criticism of Freemasonry in the police, but where Freemasonry has clearly played no part in the corruption of an officer, where his membership of the Brotherhood is incidental, it must not be brought as evidence. Only one of the three major cases of corruption investigated in the seventies can be said to have had any serious masonic elements – the activities of the Porn Squad. This section of the Metropolitan Police was, in the words of the present Lord Chief Justice, 'involved in wholesale corruption. The very men employed to bring the corrupt to book were thriving on the proceeds of corruption.'

The worst of these men was Detective Chief Superintendent William 'Bill' Moody, former head of the Obscene Publications Squad. Moody, an exceedingly corrupt policeman, was an active Freemason. He was gaoled for twelve years, the heaviest sentence meted out to the 'bent' members of the Porn Squad. Moody and ten others, who had received sentences ranging from three years upwards, were told when their appeals were dismissed that 'the individual sentences properly reflected the degree [of responsibility] and complicity and wickedness'.

Moody still protests his innocence from behind bars. Ironically, it had been Moody who in 1969 had been placed in charge of the first of the major enquiries into corruption while himself extorting vast sums of 'protection money' from Soho pornography racketeers. In one transaction alone Moody received £14,000. Almost the entire Porn Squad was in on the racket, openly collecting huge bribes – at one stage estimated at £100,000 a year – from porn shop proprietors in return for the freedom to flout the law unmolested.

Moody lived at Weybridge in Surrey. He and several

other Freemason members of the Porn Squad who lived in the area were members of the same Lodge. So, incidentally, were a number of pornographers. These included a small-time pornographer who used to work in the nearby village of Cobham; another whose home was at Walton-on-Thames; and others who lived or worked at Hampton Wick, Weybridge and Hersham.

John Shirley, co-author of *The Fall of Scotland Yard*, who gave oral evidence before the Royal Commission on Standards of Conduct in Public Life, chaired by Lord Salmon, told me, 'It's fairly certain that the basis of a corrupt network, of the corrupt relationship between that particular group of police officers and those particular pornographers, was either formed or developed within that masonic Lodge.

'The point I was trying to make to the Salmon Commission was that, yes, police officers had private lives but in the nature of it the privacy of their lives needed to be more clearly known to their superiors. If it had been spotted that Moody was a member of the same Freemasonry Lodge as a number of well-known pornographers, on whom the police would have had files, then I think the link between them would have been established much earlier than it was.'

The major breakthrough in stamping out corruption on a grand scale within the Metropolitan Police was the appointment of Robert Mark as Commissioner in 1972. As Chief Constable of Leicester until 1967 he was unhampered by long-standing personal loyalties, untainted by the years-old corruption at the Yard, and a man who loathed nothing so much as a bent copper. Within a very short time, Mark, a non-Mason, had turned Scotland Yard on its head. One of his first reforms was to set up the 'ruthlessly efficient' department A10 to investigate complaints against police officers. In *The Fall of Scotland Yard*, the authors explain:

The setting-up of A10 broke the absolute control of the CID over the investigation of all major crime, whether it occurred inside or outside the Metropolitan Police. For the first time, uniformed officers were to be empowered to investigate allegations of misconduct - whether disciplinary or criminal - not just against their uniformed colleagues but also against the CID. This was a complete reversal of the status quo, where only CID officers had been able to investigate complaints against the uniformed branch *and* their own tight fraternity.

That tight fraternity, as has been mentioned, was and is heavily masonic. And despite A10's success in ridding the Yard of suspect detectives - nearly 300 had been forced to resign by spring 1975 - it was constantly obstructed in its attempts to obtain evidence solid enough to make charges stick. Even in cases of obvious criminality, fellow officers whose evidence was vital clammed up and obstinately refused to make statements, or co-operate in any other way. Some would not speak at all. It rapidly became clear why. The 'honest' men needed as witnesses were members of the same Brotherhood as the 'bent' officers. Many shared the same Lodges.

CHAPTER 9

Operation Countryman

Operation Countryman, the biggest investigation ever conducted into police corruption in Britain, would never have come about if the Commissioner of the City of London Police between 1971 and 1977 had not been corrupted and unduly influenced by Freemasonry. Indeed, there seems little doubt that if James Page had refused to join the Brotherhood, he would not have been appointed Commissioner in the first place.

Page transferred at the rank of Superintendent from the Metropolitan Police to the tiny, 800-man City Force in 1967, at first simply for experience as Commander of B Division based at Snow Hill police station. An excellent communicator and a good host, Page brought a style of administration to Snow Hill that can rarely, if ever, have been matched in any force in the country. It was the style he had learned in the disreputable old Blackpool City Force, where he had served under disgraced Chief Constable Stanley Parr (pages 99–102). Coachloads of policemen would arrive at Snow Hill for darts matches, boozing sessions and parties of all kinds. This earned him popularity with 'the lads' in the lower ranks, most of whom, even the lowliest PCs, were encouraged to address him as 'Jim'. Two months before his forty-fourth birthday in March 1969, he was promoted to Chief Superintendent. At this stage, so far as is known, he had never set foot inside a masonic temple. Eight months later the then Commissioner, Sir Arthur Young, was seconded to the Royal Ulster Constabulary and Page transferred to Old Jewry, the force headquarters, as Acting Commissioner. Page's successor at Snow Hill, Chief Superintendent Brian Rowland, was astonished at what he found. 'It was,' said one of the most senior officers in the force at that time, 'like running a huge pub.'

By now Page had set the pattern of his relations with the public and the force. In stark contrast to the aloof and dignified manner of the man he was standing in for, 'good old Jim' would be right in there with the lads – drinking, guffawing over a bar-room joke, out within the hallowed purlieus of the City of London opening pubs, and all too frequently getting so inebriated that he had to be carried home in a patrol car. He was liked and respected as 'one of the boys', a very different kind of respect from that enjoyed by the absent Commissioner. In the minds of senior officers, Page's extravagant *bonhomie* was marring his undoubted abilities. 'He had a very good brain,' I was told by one of the top men of the time. 'He could think on his feet in crises and was a staunch supporter of his men.'

Although a significant proportion of City policemen had been Freemasons since the twenties and there had been a masonic element in many promotions over the decades, there is no evidence that before the early 1970s the consequences had been more serious than occasional miscarriages of justice, a distortion of values, and a disgruntlement among non-Masons, inevitable whenever less able men are given preferential treatment. All this was bad enough but what flourished under Page was iniquitous.

In 1969, on the eve of Page's taking over as Acting Commissioner, a private meeting took place at his office at

Old Jewry. One of the highest-ranking officers in the force, whom I shall call Commander Dryden, had some urgent advice for his new chief. Dryden warned Page about two City police officers he knew to be corrupt. Because the Countryman investigations in the City have still not been completed – whatever offical statements say to the contrary – I shall give these men pseudonyms and refer to them as Tearle and Oates. Both were Freemasons.

'If you are ever going to run this force,' said Dryden, 'watch Oates and Tearle very closely. If you ever promote them you'll have so much trouble you won't know where to turn.'

Dryden told me, 'I'd not been long off the shop floor and was still closely in touch with events at grass roots. Everyone said that Oates and Tearle were corrupt. They would duck and dive with villains, take bribes to put in false reports on cases so that charges would be reduced or dropped altogether. One night, Oates was called to a jeweller's shop which had been found to have a broken window. He helped himself from the stock and reported that it had been missing when he arrived. Tearle was looked upon as being "swift", very shrewd and quick to make a few bob in league with criminals. A suspect man in all respects, he too would square a job up for a price.'

Dryden felt 'quite pleased' that he had alerted Page. It was a load off his mind, and he felt he'd done his duty.

So the matter rested . . . for a while.

Sir Arthur Young was due to retire on 30 November 1971, so applications were invited for his successor. The process by which the City of London Corporation appoints a new Commissioner begins with the police committee, one of twenty-seven committees whose membership is drawn from the Court of Common Council, setting up a sub-committee. The sub-committee vets applications and draws up a short list which it passes to the main committee. Short-listed applicants are later interviewed by the entire Common Council, at which each delivers a prepared speech on his own behalf. Voting then takes place and the applicant with the highest number of votes is appointed, subject to ratification by the Home Secretary and the Queen.

Inevitably, Page applied for the job, but he knew he was skating on thin ice. On the grounds of his now notorious drinking habits alone, few in the force thought he had a chance. Everyone knew that the former City Assistant Commissioner, John Duke, had been groomed for Sir Arthur's job and had meanwhile transferred to Essex Police to await the day the office fell vacant. Duke had duly applied and the force waited for his appointment to be announced.

When the short list was down to two and Page let it be known that he was on it, his colleagues felt sure the police committee had already reached its decision, but had kept Page's name on the list until the very latest stages out of consideration for his feelings. Duke was the man. Then, to everyone's astonishment, it came through the grapevine that Duke was not on the short list, that Page, incredibly, had beaten him. Still, the force were confident Page would not be appointed because it was learned that his rival was no less a figure than John Alderson (who resigned as Chief Constable of Devon and Cornwall in April 1982).

Not only had Alderson been personally recommended by Sir Arthur Young himself, his achievements cast a long shadow over those of Page, who was almost exactly three years his junior. Then Commandant of the Police College at Bramshill in Hampshire, Alderson had served in the Highland Light Infantry between 1938 and 1941, and after five years as Warrant Officer with the Army Physical Training Corp in North Africa and Italy, he had joined West Riding Constabulary as a constable in 1946. He had been promoted to Inspector in 1955, and given command of a sub-division in 1960. Between 1964 and 1966 he was Deputy Chief Constable of Dorset, after which he transferred to the Metropolitan Police as Deputy Commander, Administration and Operations. Appointed second-in-command of No 3 Police District in 1967, he was promoted again the following year to Deputy Assistant Commissioner (Training), which gave him a two-year lead-up to running the Police College from 1970. In 1971, the year he applied for the Commissioner's job in the City, he became a member of the BBC General Advisory Council. In addition he was a qualified barrister, having been called to the Bar of the Middle Temple. He was a Fellow of the British Memorial Foundation of Australia, he held an Extension Certificate in Criminology from the University of Leeds, and was a Fellow of the British Institute of Management. He had contributed to the *Encyclopaedia of Crime and Criminals* (1960), and written numerous articles for newspapers and professional publications.

This, then, was James Page's opponent. The outcome of the Common Council's vote seemed a foregone conclusion.

But neither the general run of officers in the City, nor probably even Page himself, reckoned on the power of Freemasonry within the Square Mile.

It became clear that influential Freemasons had decided that Page was the man for the job, for various reasons. For one thing, he was a known quantity. His sense of duty was more malleable than Alderson's, his loyalty to those who helped him very easy to exploit. In many ways, Page was as trusting as a child.

One eminent Mason in the City had been courting Page on behalf of the Brotherhood for a long time, and by early 1971 knew he was within an ace of being recruited. Page had never been hostile to the idea in principle, but until now he had not committed himself.

He was made aware that if he did commit himself, he was virtually assured of victory. He agreed, and the Masons who had set their sights on him were triumphant. Although it has been shown that his *formal* application to join City Livery Club Lodge No 3752 post-dated Page's election as Commissioner in July, strings were pulled and he was involved in meetings at several lodges from June onwards.

'It was astonishing,' said Dryden. 'When I heard that Alderson had lost to Page, it was as big a shock as when Kennedy was shot. I can remember exactly where I was and what I was doing on both occasions. Others felt the same.'

And there the trouble, which led eventually to the multi-million-pound Countryman operation, began.

Page quickly demonstrated his unsuitability for the post, although his achievements should not be glossed over lightly. He is remembered, for instance, as Director of Police Extended Interviews between 1975 and 1977. He became a Fellow of the British Institute of Management in 1975 and an Officer of the Légion d'honneur in 1976. But he was promoted above his ability. Attending more than 600 social functions in a single year, he became known as a heavy drinker not only in the force but in other organizations and institutions within the City, both august and common. He would turn up to almost every birthday, retirement or promotion party in the force. He would even be found at the lowliest office celebrations, when for instance a uniformed constable was transferred to the CID.

James Page had much to thank Freemasonry for, and he showed his gratitude by proving an enthusiastic Mason. 'He was mad about his Masonry,' said one uniformed superintendent. Others of all ranks, some Freemasons among them, have confirmed this. When the already highly masonic City force learned of the new Commissioner's passionate commitment to the Brotherhood, many more officers joined the Lodges. Page had a simple faith in Masonry's power for good: officers who were Masons were good officers because Masonry was good.

Dryden liked Page as a man, but he did not like the way he was running the force. He did not heed the warning about the two bad apples, Tearle and Oates. Far from keeping them down and watching them with an eagle eye, he openly fraternized with them. The answer was not hard to find. Both Tearle and Oates were Freemasons, so in Page's view Dryden must be mistaken about them. Things went from bad to worse: Tearle introduced Page to his own Lodge, where as Worshipful Master he was superior in rank to the Commissioner.

Eventually, Dryden confided in Chief Superintendent Brian Rowland, who was still in command at Snow Hill and was secretary of the National Police Superintendents' Association. They agreed something had to be done and decided to speak of their fears to Assistant Commissioner Wally Stapleton, who had influence with Page. They received a cheering reply.

'Don't worry,' said Stapleton. 'Those men will get promotion over my dead body.'

Dryden told me, 'He satisfied both of us that he had the measure of the situation, and that nothing wrong would get past him.'

Page ignored even Stapleton and subsequently promoted Tearle not once but twice. Oates later received even higher promotion.

'A lot can happen to a force in ten years,' I was told by a sorrowing Detective Sergeant at Old Jewry. Himself a Freemason since 1957, he is 'appalled' by what has happened in the City: 'I've seen Masonry used for rotten things in the force in recent years. I'd never have believed it was possible if I hadn't seen it and heard it myself. What sickens me is the filthy distortion of the principles of

Freemasonry. It's not meant to be for this, it's really not. But Masons are being promoted over the heads of non-Masons left, right and centre. I've been to most of the police Lodges in the City area and in the last few years it seems to me that the ritual and purpose of Masonry is getting less and less important. It's forbidden to talk about politics, religion or business in the Temple, but these yobbos – they shouldn't be in the police, let alone the Craft – they're using the secrecy to get into corners and decide who's next for promotion and who they can place where to their own advantage. Most of the time it's about how to protect themselves, having someone in the right place to cover up if they skive off. That's bad enough, and it's shown itself in the fallen standards of the force as a whole. But I've seen one or two things worse than that – actual criminal stuff. Nothing really terrible when you consider some of the things Old Bill Masons are supposed to have done here – I don't have any personal knowledge of that. But nevertheless I know people in the Craft who have had charges dropped as a result of little conferences at Lodge meetings: things like acts of gross indecency, taking and driving away and, once, a GBH [grievous bodily harm].'*

Page was now immersed in the whole Freemasonic life of the City, and he had been corrupted by it to the extent that the 'without fear or favour' part of his oath as a policeman no longer took precedence. I have been told by several senior officers who served under Page that there were numerous occasions when his judgement on relatively minor issues was called into question. All of them related in some way to Masonry. He was once challenged by a high-ranking officer as to why he had ordered the suspension of certain proceedings against an organization whose Freemason head had appealed to him for help. Page explained: 'I owe them

*This statement is culled from a long interview which took place on 30 September 1981.

three more years yet,' meaning that he owed his position to the Masons, and in return for that, wherever he could, he would see to it that his first allegiance was to the Brotherhood.

On at least seven occasions he is alleged to have contacted Grand Lodge for advice on how to act in purely internal matters, or *for permission* to take a course of action if it related in any way to Masonry.

Another non-Mason in the City related how he had once sat with Page on a two-man interviewing panel considering the application of a man who had already been rejected by two other forces as a police probationer. It was decided that he would be given a try, but he proved highly unsatisfactory. I have seen a four-page report in which the officer who sat with Page on the interviewing panel describes various incidents in which the PC became involved – offences as serious as threatening violence to a member of the public, absenting himself from duty while on reserve during a sensitive Old Bailey trial and later abusing an Inspector who found him drunk at home, and phoning the force control centre in the middle of the night and demanding to be put through to Page. This was roughly comparable to a drunken private in the army insisting on an audience with his General.

Convinced the probationer was unstable, the officer recommended to Page that his services be dispensed with, which is possible at any time within a PC's first two years of service. The recommendation was supported by other senior officers *and* the Assistant Commissioner.

Bearing in mind the strength of the condemnation, and the standing and integrity of the officer who made it, it was unthinkable that the recommendation could be ignored.

But the erring PC was a Freemason. The masonic cogs began to move and Page was prevailed upon to do the unthinkable. He vetoed the recommendation and simply transferred the PC to another division. Thus Page's incomplete understanding of the obligation he had taken to assist fellow Masons in distress led not only to the retention of a known dangerous element within the force, but to undermining the authority of one of the most senior men below the rank of Assistant Commissioner. In the event, the decision proved disastrous as the PC went from bad to worse, finally leaving the force after Page's own less than happy exit in 1977.

The first of three serious crimes in the City Police area, which led eventually to the Countryman investigation into police malpractice, occurred in May 1976 at the offices of the *Daily Express* when £175,000 in wages was stolen. This was followed sixteen months later by a £520,000 robbery at the City headquarters of Williams and Glyn's Bank in Birchin Lane, off Lombard Street. Six men in balaclava helmets armed with shotguns ambushed a Securicor van about to deliver the money to the bank, and blasted one of the guards in the legs. Two other members of the gang waited nearby in getaway cars. The third crime took place at the *Daily Mirror* in May 1978 when three robbers, two disguised as printers, staged a daring raid on a Securicor van after it had actually been locked inside the loading area beneath the *Mirror* building. The gang escaped with £197,000 in banknotes after shooting the driver of the van at point-blank range through the heart. He died on the way to hospital.

These crimes would never have occurred if Page had not committed himself to Freemasonry to assure himself of the Commissioner's job. If he hadn't done so, he would not have become Commissioner in 1971. If Page had not been a Freemason, he would have heeded Dryden's 1969 warning never to promote Tearle and Oates, when both of them were in the less influential rank of detective chief inspector. As it was, he promoted them because he and they were part of the same Brotherhood. They achieved high rank under Page. Commander Dryden told me: 'If Tearle and Oates had not been promoted, others would not have been promoted because they – Tearle and Oates – came to have influence over other promotions. Once they were in a position of control, they then promoted their masonic brethren, many of whom were in on the corruption with them. This brought about an ease of communication and a whole corrupt masonic network was set up within the force. Tearle and Oates colluded with some of these newly promoted Masons and played a part in setting up the Williams and Glyn's and the *Mirror* jobs, and they helped out after the event at the *Express*. Mason police shared out around £60,000 from one job.'

Oates and some of the worst of their accomplices have now gone from the force, but Tearle remains, terrified that his name will be connected publicly with the crimes in which he has taken part if one of his former colleagues decides there is no longer anything to be gained by protecting him. One of the men who is thinking very seriously of 'shopping' Tearle, Oates and the rest of the crew told me, 'One word from me and they go down for a long, long while.'

So far that word has not been forthcoming.

CHAPTER 10

The Brotherhood Misjudged

In 1978, following one of several appearances I made on Australian television, the studio's switchboard was jammed with calls from viewers who wanted to talk to me about the masonic aspects of the Jack the Ripper case. One man subsequently wrote to me saying, 'I have a story which confirms yours. The same secret society is still doing the same things here (Sydney). I cannot begin to even outline events that have taken place here, but misdeeds ranging from murder to cannibalism have taken place. Persons involved include some famous, wealthy and politically powerful people, including a person in one of the top political offices in Australia. This story is still current and desperately needs someone to write/expose it.

'If you are outside Australia when you get this letter, *please* write back at once, as time is getting short in many ways.'

The letter ended with the postscript, 'Help! Please.'

I had my reservations, not only because of the extreme nature of the allegations but also because of the tone and presentation of the letter, which was handwritten on flimsy lined paper. However, I was intrigued, and in view of the man's plea I decided it would do me no harm to listen and might well do him some good to have a listener. Although it was hard for me to picture Malcolm Fraser sitting down to breakfast off a human arm and orange juice, it was just possible there was a story in it somewhere. I phoned the man and we met at the Melbourne Hilton.

I sat and listened to a convoluted tale of crime and wickedness in high places, partly involving the corruption by way of 'the secret brotherhood of Freemasonry' of all levels of the police in Sydney. The allegations of criminal activity might or might not have been well founded. But apart from the fact that several unconnected cases involved men who were Masons, he offered no evidence except his own 'absolute certainty' that Freemasonry played any part at all.

Logic can very quickly go out of the window if a clear distinction is not made between incidents caused by Freemasonry and incidents merely involving Freemasons. As I have already said, the difference between the two is often ignored or not appreciated. There are several examples of alleged police malpractice involving Freemasons which show the importance of this point.

One bullish Welsh PC told me at great length how an Inspector had once intervened and stopped him when he, the PC, was dealing with a charge of obstruction against a detective sergeant of a nearby force whose private car had blocked the pavement in the town's main street for more than an hour on a busy Saturday afternoon. The Inspector and the Sergeant were Masons in the same Lodge, said the non-Mason PC.

So, here we have a clear case of one police officer with masonic loyalty to another stepping in and preventing the law taking its course. Or do we?

If the only reliable test – beyond reasonable doubt – is

applied, the PC's case does not stand up for five minutes. The PC was convinced that had the other two not been Freemasons, the incident would not have occurred. But his argument begins from the premise that Freemasonry is corrupting, and cites an example of dubious conduct on the part of a Freemason to prove it. The argument is circular and therefore specious.

The plain fact is that embarrassing incidents of this sort are being covered up all the time, and nobody takes much notice until someone says, 'They're both Masons, of course,' and everyone nods sagely and grumbles about the Great Conspiracy.

This incident would have occurred whether or not the men were Freemasons, because they were also brothers-in-law, something the PC failed to tell me when he was cracking on about masonic corruption.

Stanley Parr, the sixty-year-old Chief Constable of Lancashire, was suspended on full pay in March 1977 following a top-level enquiry into allegations of malpractice, including the misuse of his position to show favours. Ten months later he was sacked amid a welter of publicity. The case of Parr, who was a Freemason, has been quoted as one which provides strong evidence of the corrupting influence of Masonry. Unfortunately for the anti-Brotherhood lobby, this is not strictly true.

The trouble began when a Blackpool Sergeant, Harry Roby, made a complaint to an Inspector of Constabulary. Further allegations were made that certain motorists known to Parr were given preferential treatment after being accused of speeding and parking offences. The most serious suggestion was that Parr had altered a charge made against a motorist whose car had mounted the pavement on the main Blackpool–Preston road in August 1975 and killed two young mothers.

Sir Douglas Osmond, the then Chief Constable of Hampshire, was appointed to investigate and report on the allegations. He was assisted by a highly respected detective, Norman Green, who is now Assistant Chief Constable of Bedfordshire. Both men were non-Masons.

The three-month investigation resulted in the confidential 150-page Osmond Report, part of which examined the alleged undesirable associates of Chief Constable Parr. Before the reorganization of police forces in England and Wales, Parr had been Chief Constable of Blackpool. Even after the reorganization, when Blackpool Force had been absorbed into the new Lancashire County Force with headquarters in Preston, Parr continued to live in Blackpool and spent a great deal of his time, both on and off duty, in the town. It was the relationships which Parr maintained in Blackpool which proved his undoing. He fraternized with a number of people who were considered undesirable company for a Chief Constable, either because they were themselves criminals or associates of criminals, or because they were proprietors of businesses which required some kind of police-approved licence to operate.

These characters included the owner of a Blackpool hotel. Parr was regularly in this man's company, and the two men and their wives went on holiday to Tenerife together. One of thirty-seven disciplinary charges against Parr alleged that he had intervened improperly to prevent the hotel owner being prosecuted for traffic offences. A tribunal set up in the wake of the Osmond Report heard how the hotel owner's son had collided with another vehicle while driving his father's Jaguar on the day the two families returned from Tenerife. The son had told the police who interviewed him: 'My father is on holiday in Tenerife with Stanley Parr and I'll see Mr Parr when he returns home tonight.' He was not prosecuted. His father, who was the holder of a Justice's Licence and therefore subject to police observation and supervision, was considered 'untouchable' by the local police because of his friendship with the Chief Constable. This meant that although he committed frequent traffic offences he was effectively immune from prosecution.

Other acquaintances of the Chief Constable included a 'swag shop' operator, the joint owner of a large 'bingo' business, two bookmakers, a former bookmaker, two club owners, two amusement caterers, a holiday-camp proprietor and a licensee.

These 'unwise' relationships were formed and developed in various organizations in Blackpool – Freemasonry among them. The main one was Sportsmen's Aid, a crypto-masonic organization which over a period of ten years raised more than £70,000 for various local charities. As the original complainant, Sergeant Roby was grilled for two full days by Detective Superintendent Green. At one point, Green, who suspected a Freemasonic link between Parr and those who benefited from his improper conduct, asked Roby outright what part Masonry had played in the whole affair. To Green's surprise, Roby said, 'Oh, nothing whatever. In fact I am a Mason myself.'

Sources close to the investigation told me that at the end of the enquiry, Osmond and Green concluded that a lot of people who were involved were, like Parr, Freemasons. But they were also members of other organizations like the Rotary Club and more particularly Sportsmen's Aid. And although Freemasonry played a part in building relationships which were not 'kept at the proper level', there was no real reason to suspect that Freemasonry alone was to blame.

It is widely appreciated that some journalists will go to inordinate lengths to get a 'good story'. One case, involving the police and the Brotherhood, illustrates how far many people go to malign Freemasonry unwarrantably. The *News of the World* carried a story by a freelance reporter in some editions of its 3 January 1982 issue under the headline ROW OVER COP CAUGHT IN VICE TRAP. It must be said that the newspaper published the story in good faith. It ran:

A detective who is a Freemason has caused a storm in a county's police force after being caught with a prostitute in his car by the Vice Squad.

Detective Sergeant Alpha Beta [a pseudonym], who is married with a family, has been officially reprimanded by Assistant Chief Constable David East, of Devon and Cornwall force.

But a senior detective said last night: 'Ordinary policemen feel that if it were them they would have been put back into uniform or transferred.

'It has led to a sincere belief that there's one rule for Masons and another for the rest.'

The incident involving Detective Sergeant Beta, who is stationed in Paignton, happened in Plymouth's red light district.

Vice Squad officers watched as he picked up prostitute Janice Hayes, 18, in his car. Then, after he had handed over £10, they pounced.

The policemen recognized the sergeant, who was previously stationed in Plymouth, and they called in their duty inspector.

A report was made to Police HQ in Exeter and the reprimand followed.

At her bedsit home in Devonport, Janice said: 'We agreed £10 for straight sex and drove to a nearby car park.

'I hadn't even got my knickers off when there was a tap on the window. It was the Vice Squad.

'They seemed to know him and said Hello. One of them told

me to be on my way so I just ran. If it had been any other punter I'd have been done.'

When a local paper inquired about the affair, Assistant Chief Constable East wrote to the editor admitting the sergeant had been reprimanded, but asking for the story not to be used because it might damage his marriage.

A police spokesman said yesterday: 'This was an internal matter that did not involve a complaint from the public.'

When I read this story, I naturally sought further information because of its relevance to my research. I went first to the *News of the World*, and second to a reporter on the Devon News Agency who had had a hand in producing it. According to this man the story was even better – which was journalese for sensational – than was suggested in the *News of the World.*

I was told that Detective Sergeant Beta, aged thirty-seven, had been initiated to the Princetown Lodge about two years previously on the recommendation of none other than David East, his own Deputy Chief Constable (wrongly described as ACC in the newspaper report).* I was told that East was a former Worshipful Master of a Lodge in Somerset and that Beta's superiors in the CID right up the line were all brethren of his Lodge. Not only that, they had all been to a Lodge meeting together the night Beta was picked up by the Vice Squad. The journalist told me: 'After the arrest in Plymouth, the girl was sent home and after the duty inspector was called Beta was taken to Charles Cross Police Station in Plymouth and later released. No disciplinary action was taken against him and he never appeared before a disciplinary board, which he should have done. It was East's statutory duty to discipline the man but he let him off. All he got was a reprimand, which means he goes back in seniority a year. Anyone but a Mason would have

*East succeeded John Alderson as Chief Constable of Devon and Cornwall in 1982.

been back on the beat. That copper was aiding and abetting a criminal offence.'

I asked the reporter to get further details for me and he assured me that he would arrange for me to talk to someone within the police who knew all the details of the 'masonic corruption' and could provide evidence to back up what he said. Days passed. I phoned again. He told me the contact was unavailable. This state of affairs persisted for nearly two months, then the first reporter passed on to me another reporter in Torquay. I met with similar promises and an identical lack of results. Eventually I investigated the story myself. This is the truth of the case.

Detective Sergeant Beta was a Freemason, and a member of Benevolence Lodge No 666 at Princetown, Devon. A number of his colleagues and superiors were brethren in the same Lodge, and on the night of his misconduct he had been to a Lodge meeting with them. The truth about what happened in Plymouth is quite at variance with the account that appeared later in the *News of the World*, however.

One vital point is that the prostitute Janice Hayes quoted by the newspaper *was not the prostitute who was found with the detective sergeant.* Nor could the real prostitute have said, 'One of them told me to be on my way so I just ran. If it had been any other punter I'd have been done,' because the prostitute found with Beta *was* done. She was not sent on her way but was arrested and taken by the two Vice Squad officers along with Beta to the police station, where she was officially cautioned. 'Janice Hayes' was either a figment of the reporters' imagination dreamed up for the purpose of making a good story or, less likely, was another prostitute who agreed to lend her name to the untruthful quote. The reporters are known to have been talking to prostitutes in the red light district of Plymouth after Beta was found in the compromising position.

A man who consorts with a prostitute does not commit a

criminal offence. The lawbreaker is the woman, the offence 'soliciting for the purpose of prostitution'. In order to prove soliciting to the satisfaction of the courts, it is established practice all over the country that a woman be cautioned twice and only on the third time be taken before the court. An element of the offence is *persistent* soliciting. The two cautions were devised in order to prove that element. This was the first time the woman involved with Beta had been cautioned, so there was no offence by her. Logically, there was no offence by Beta. Had she committed an offence, Beta would then technically have been aiding and abetting, but no policeman or lawyer I have spoken to on the subject has heard of any man in Beta's position being charged with aiding and abetting a prostitute.

Because a policeman was involved, and because the Vice Squad officers quite properly informed their superiors, the matter came before Deputy Chief Constable David East. East was a Freemason but had not been active for years and had no connection with Benevolence Lodge No 666 or any other in Devon and Cornwall. It was up to East to decide how to deal with Beta. There had been no criminal offence by the woman, therefore none by the man, so the case was outside the ambit of the Director of Public Prosecutions. Therefore it was a matter of internal police discipline. The only offence within the disciplinary code which was even remotely relevant was discreditable conduct - bringing discredit upon the force.

When this is analysed, it is not difficult to see East's dilemma. There had been no member of the public involved, the prostitute did not know Beta was a policeman, and the only others involved were two police officers. In technical terms it would have been extremely difficult to press a charge of bringing discredit on the police when the arresting officers were the only witnesses. Adding to the difficulty were the facts that he was off-duty, in his own time, and over forty miles away from the place of his work, Torquay. Taking all this into consideration, East had little choice but to decide that it was not a case for formal discipline but for parading Beta in his office, one means at a DCC's disposal for dealing with less serious disciplinary cases, and really going to town on him verbally.

Beta was severely reprimanded by East and the admonishment was formally entered in his personal file, which meant that he was barred from promotion for three years. Having applied that not insignificant punishment, East had to decide whether to leave the officer where he was or transfer him back to uniform. There were problems. CID officers have more freedom than uniformed police. The plain clothes man is far more on personal trust, out of the immediate scope of organized routine supervision. Some officers have told me the answer was clear: Beta could not be trusted, so he should have been back in uniform without delay.

One aspect to be considered was that his wife and family knew nothing of the incident. In itself, that would be no justification for East failing to transfer Beta if a transfer was the only proper course. The main problem was that if the Sergeant was moved back to uniform on the grounds that he required greater supervision, he would have to go either to Exeter or Plymouth. A move to Exeter would mean that he would become responsible for young probationary constables. A move to Plymouth would put him right back in the midst of one of the biggest red light districts in the West Country. Bearing in mind both the nature of the incident and the punishment already meted out by East, most senior police officers – non-Masons to a man – I have tackled about this case are of the opinion that the action taken in leaving Beta in plain clothes at Torquay was the correct one.

This case has been treated at some length because it is an admirable example of how the anti-Mason's view of any incident can be coloured by his prejudices. This goes further than interpreting ordinary events in a masonic way simply because Freemasons happened to be involved - it actually leads people, as in this instance, to *invent* details that turn happenstance into masonic conspiracy.

CHAPTER 11

Birmingham City Police

What I really needed at the outset of my investigation into Masonry in the police was a masonic 'mole' who was a policeman of rank and integrity. Eventually, as has been shown, I built up a large network of such men. None was so earnest or more scathing than those contacts, Masons and otherwise, who spoke to me about Birmingham City Police.

One informant spoke of his experiences in Birmingham dating back many years. He was on the point of entering the first of the three chairs of his Holy Royal Arch Chapter. He had, he told me, been considering becoming a Knight Templar, the branch of Freemasonry which admits only Christians, but was becoming increasingly disillusioned with the abuse of Masonry within the police and had come to realize that he had to resign from one or the other.

He explained that in Birmingham City Police before the reorganization of police forces in England and Wales, it was next to impossible for non-Masons to reach any rank above Chief Inspector. The then Chief Constable, Sir Derrick Capper, was an officer of the Warwickshire Provincial Grand Lodge, and he saw to it as far as possible that non-Masons were kept to the lower and middle ranks. In Capper's time, according to my informant, it was impossible to be a civilian employee at higher level unless you were a Mason. This became the accepted way of life.

In 1974 Birmingham City Police was amalgamated with other nearby forces to become West Midlands Police. My informant continued, 'The old masonic system still pertains within the Birmingham City area. Within the wider scope of West Midlands, which now includes places like Coventry and Wolverhampton, it does not pertain. But in the City area there is not one of the divisional commanders or their deputies who is not a Freemason.'

I pressed him about his motive for talking to me. He replied, 'I've always been conscious of democracy and I just don't see why many good men who joined with me have never reached the same rank as me because they have the misfortune not to be Freemasons.'

I felt there must be something closer to home. If he had been an active Freemason for ten years, as he had told me, he must have been aware for a long time that the existence of Masonry in the police could put non-Masons at a disadvantage. I put the point to him.

'I've had to rack myself recently as to whether I'm going to stay in the job,' he said, 'or abandon Masonry. I don't find them compatible at all.

'In theory, Masons are not supposed to show favour to a man just because he's a Mason. But in practice it doesn't work that way at all. You go to a London Lodge where the Met Police meet, and the next promotions in every department are discussed. It's the same in Birmingham. You cannot possibly rise in the CID, for instance, in the old Birmingham City area, which is a considerable area, unless you're in a Lodge. And it even has to be the right Lodge. The centre of it all is the Masonic Temple at 1 Clarendon Road, Edgbaston.'

But wasn't there something more particular?

'Yes. I'm not finding it particularly good having colleagues in my rank and the two above me getting promoted because they are Masons. I don't see that it's necessary as a criterion for promotion that you're from a masonic Lodge. I'd rather have the men who qualify and get there by hard work. I have two deputies, both promoted because they're Masons. They really are shockers at their job. I suddenly realized they would never have got there if they hadn't been Masons, and that worried me considerably. That's why I'm speaking to you.'

A Birmingham Detective Chief Inspector, also a Mason who wished to remain anonymous, contacted me on 10 October 1981. He said he would try to write but probably would not. In the event he didn't and that one conversation is the only contact I had with him. Even so, he impressed me as genuine and in the light of the information given by my first informant, whose identity I do know, the DCI's conflicting comments should be noted.

He said, 'I'm not an avid Mason. I joined when I was doing a two-year stint at Scotland Yard. I was in a big town where nobody talks to you and I was lonely. I'd been along to a Ladies' Night* at a friend's masonic Lodge and been impressed with the really genuine people there. So I decided to join.

'I didn't join the Masons until I reached my present rank, so it wasn't Freemasonry that got me there. It's sheer hard work that gets you promotion, whatever non-Masons tell you. I had a lad in my department just a while ago who was transferred into uniform because he had transgressed. He was a Mason. It just doesn't make any difference. All this talk of allegiance to two masters is based on ignorance.

'I once met a retired Detective Chief Inspector in Birmingham. He was a good policeman. He'd have rated a Detective Chief Superintendent today. I met him wander-

*Most Lodges hold a Ladies' Night once a year. It is the only occasion when women (wives, daughters or girl friends) are permitted at a gathering of brethren.

ing aimlessly around the streets of the city. His wife had died, he had lost all drive, he was not looking after himself properly. His clothes were patched, he had nothing to live for. I bought him a drink and we talked. He sounded hopeless. Some years later when I had joined the Masons I saw him again – at a Lodge meeting. It had been the making of him. Someone had bumped into him just as I had done, and, being a Mason, had pointed him in the right direction. He was smart, enthusiastic about life, a completely changed man, very enthusiastic about Masonry. Freemasonry alone had given him a reason for living, and that's quite something.'

Quite something indeed. But few people would deny that there are many men, women and children in the world who benefit directly and indirectly from Freemasonry. The movement's contributions to charity, and the work of the Royal Masonic Hospital and the Masonic schools are examples of how non-Masons as well as Masons benefit from the existence of the Brotherhood. This good, and there are other examples, as will become apparent, should not be taken lightly. But neither should it be seen as an answer to those aspects of Masonry which are alleged to be bad. 'The good justifies the bad' is as dangerous a philosophy as 'The end justifies the means'.

But to return to Birmingham, one other masonic policeman who has seen no harm come from so many police officers swearing allegiance to the Brotherhood is former Superintendent David Webb, well known for his championing of 'community policing' in the Birmingham ghetto districts. He resigned from the police in December 1981 and spoke to me shortly after.

'In the City of Birmingham there are hundreds of policemen who are members of Freemasonry,' he said, 'including plenty of divisional commanders. I am a Past Master of more than one Lodge.

'I can honestly say that in the police service I've never found anyone that's ever tried to use Masonry – just the opposite. Amongst the policemen that I know in Masonry, if anyone tried that bloody game on, he'd get clonked well and truly. It's never gained me anything.'

However, hearing various allegations about Birmingham which had been reported to me by informers, he said, 'I'm not saying it *doesn't* happen, the same as when I say to people about police beating people up. I don't say it doesn't happen, but I've never experienced it.'

A Birmingham Chief Inspector, another Mason, said, 'Policemen are very isolated socially. I'll admit that my whole life, because I'm a Mason in a police Lodge, is tied up with the same people. There is a lot of jiggery-pokery among police Masons in Birmingham, I don't mind saying as long as you won't quote me on it. But I doubt if it's any better anywhere else. There's nothing specially bad about Birmingham, it's a good force. The worry is that if I know about one or two of my colleagues who are involved in one or two little – let's say, they've got some fingers in a few pies they shouldn't have—'

'You mean corruption?'

'No, nothing like that. Just *involvements* outside the force. Certain people they don't arrest for certain things. The worry is that as a Mason policeman myself, if I report them I will put my whole work and social life in jeopardy, all my friendships and work relationships will be at stake. So it's better to say nothing. That's the only problem with Masonry. You can get too involved.'

CHAPTER 12

Conclusion

An independent enquiry into Freemasonry in the police should be initiated at the earliest possible moment. Even though the majority of police, including masonic officers, are not corrupt, it is clear that corrupt police can and do use Freemasonry to effect and further their corruption. There are now so many allegations about masonic corruption within the service that even if ninety-nine per cent of them were wholly groundless – and no one who has investigated it could accept that for one moment – we are still left with a disturbing situation. Why successive Home Secretaries have ignored or refused calls for an enquiry is not known. Not all have been Freemasons, but all have had masonic advisers in the persons of their senior Civil Servants.

In September 1981 and again in April 1982 there were claims in court of criminal conduct on the part of Freemason police. At Knightsbridge Crown Court on Tuesday, 22 September 1981 an ex-Metropolitan Police Detective accused of trying to bribe a senior Drugs Squad officer said they were both members of the same masonic Lodge. The detective told the court that he had seconded the application of the Drugs Squad man – a Superintendent – to join the Lodge when they were both stationed at King's Cross Road. The Superintendent admitted that he was a member of the Brotherhood and that he had visited the Lodge when the detective was there, but denied he had ever been a member of the Lodge. And the detective denied, along with a co-defendant, paying the Superintendent £2,800 as an inducement to return sixteen million diethylpropion hydrochloride tablets. Prosecuting counsel told the court that when the attempted bribe had taken place, the conversation had been secretly recorded.

In the later case, a police informer named Michael Gervaise claimed at the Old Bailey that policemen in the same masonic Lodge as criminals involved in a multi-million-pound silver bullion robbery had warned them that they were about to be arrested. As a result of this masonic act, one of the men involved in the £3.5 million robbery fled and has never been traced. Gervaise, who had been involved in the robbery himself, told the court, 'certain officers were Freemasons. Certain criminals belonged to the same Lodge. There were eight or nine officers in the same Lodge as the people involved in the silver bullion robbery.'

Unrest about the undoubted misuse of Freemasonry by policemen is spreading and demands for an enquiry will continue to grow. The worst possible thing would be a masonic witch-hunt, and the surest way of avoiding that would be to institute a proper, sober enquiry before the issue becomes a tool in the hands of political extremists.

Many people want to see Masonry banned in the police. This would inflict damage to the personal happiness of many thousands of upright masonic policemen and to the principle of individual freedom that might outweigh any good effect. But a compulsory register on which police officers have to list their affiliation to secret societies, and their status within such societies, is the minimum requirement if a grave situation is to be improved.

PART THREE

Inside Information

CHAPTER 13

The Rabbi's Tale

Despite the ban on speaking to outsiders, many Freemasons allowed me to interview them. Some were extraordinarily frank, some going so far, having secured my promise not to reveal their identities, as confiding the most secret workings of the Brotherhood. Some said very little at all. Most were prepared to give me candid answers to as many questions as they felt were not within the areas of secrecy. Only a few, however, had the courage to be quoted by name and, while remaining faithful to their masonic obligations of secrecy, spoke openly of the little-known aspects of Masonry which, properly speaking, are not covered by the oaths, however hysterical some grand officers might become in insisting that everything masonic is for Masons alone. Among these honourable men was an eminent Freemason of long standing and grand rank: the Rev Saul Amias, MBE, a London rabbi who was Assistant Grand Chaplain to the United Grand Lodge in 1973. I interviewed him at his home in Edgware in 1981.

'Before I joined Freemasonry there were members of my community in Edgware who were members, and we used to discuss it. A few of them were fighting to have the honour to introduce their minister to their own particular Lodge. I asked them to tell me about it. They said, "No, we can't tell you, but there's nothing bad about it. It's only good, it's only a movement to do good, and there are a lot of Jewish people in it as well as non-Jewish. There's nothing that you say a Jew shouldn't be." In fact, the late Chief Rabbi was a very foremost Mason, and it did not take away from his position as a Chief Rabbi.

'I'm not sorry that I came into the Work because apart from being a brother amongst Masons, if I have to see somebody – say in hospital – and he's a Freemason, I can talk to him and we talk about Freemasonry, take away his mind from his illness. But I don't ask. My first question isn't, "Are you a Freemason?", that would be silly. You're not supposed to do that.

'Anyhow, there's another thing that I want to say. People say Freemasons only help each other. If my brother, my blood brother, comes to me and asks me to advise him or help him, I drop everything, I go, because he's my brother. Or if there's a member of my congregation – although I'm retired they still come to see me – who says, "Look, I need help", I don't say, "Look, I'm retired, go somewhere else." I give help because I *know* him. Mr Cohen. I know him, so why should he go to strangers when he knows Mr Amias? And the same thing, if a man is a Mason, and another Mason comes to him, why shouldn't he help? It doesn't mean to say that I do not help non-Masons, or non-brothers of my family or non-members of my Synagogue.'

'There is, however, a widespread belief that Masons are helped to the detriment of non-Masons,' I said.

'This excites us very much! It's absolutely not a fact – *not* to the detriment. Look, I was looking only this morning – I got a letter from the Royal Benevolent Organization of the Freemasonry. There are about eighteen homes for old people, retired people, for Masons or their relatives, their dependants, their wives, or their widows. Right? Should we not help them? But I help other homes, non-Jewish and Jewish, for old people too. There's no saying I'll only help the masonic ones. No, not at all. But if people come to me through an organization which in this case is the organization of the Brotherhood of Freemasonry, why should I not help him? Or his widow, or whomever? There's a hospital of which I am chaplain, the Royal Masonic Hospital at Hammersmith. I go there very religiously each week. Now all those patients are Freemasons or dependent relatives, that is to say a wife or a son under twenty-one, or an unmarried daughter. So why should I not go? But it doesn't mean that I am not going this afternoon to the Edgware Hospital because I heard the wife of one of my people is there. Or tomorrow I will go to St Albans Hospital where I am a chaplain and to Napsbury Hospital where I'm a chaplain and to Hill End Mental Hospital. It's *absolutely false* to say otherwise.'

'Yes,' I said, 'it's absolutely false to say that Freemasonry *sets out* to help its members to the detriment of non-members, or that any Freemason swears in his oath to help any other Mason to the detriment of a non-Mason, but it does happen. Only this week a man senior in local government admitted to me that he doesn't see anything wrong with showing favour to his fellow Masons. He thinks this is what Freemasonry is about. If he is on a panel interviewing people for posts in the council, assuming there wasn't a great deal of difference in the ability of two applicants, he would choose the Mason every time.'

'Well, I think that's wrong,' replied Amias. 'I know it does happen. All things being equal, you are saying. But if he's not the best candidate and he chooses him as a Freemason then it's . . . un-moral, and it is against all the precepts of Freemasonry where we've got to help *people*, and we keep on stressing that we must practise outside the Lodge, not only with Freemasons, those things which we say and we do inside the Lodge. There is no question.

'It is *true* that people help their brother Masons. Let me put it this way: Freemasonry for some people, who are quiet, who don't take part in local affairs, don't go to church, don't go to Rotary, who don't belong to Toc H, or all the usual – or the tennis club, you know, people who are quiet, who perhaps haven't the opportunity – they work long hours and they haven't got the opportunity of any social work, and so on. For *them* Freemasonry is an avenue through which they walk to the path of helping . . . of unselfish deeds – that means charity, that means helping, that means lending the car to somebody, taking them into hospital, or . . . helping it might be with money, it might be with a job, as you say. It might *be*. But people don't go and say, "I'm a Mason, can you help me?"

'I cannot . . . I will *not* accept that Freemasons help *only* Freemasons to the detriment of others.'

CHAPTER 14

Five Masters and a Lewis

'A Freemason is not supposed to use Masonry for selfish reasons. But there is no doubt that a percentage of people do try. Accepting that, do you think they can succeed?'

I was speaking to a Master Mason, a retired barrister, at his home on the top floor of a Middle Temple chambers. He looked into his sherry and said, 'Oh, I should think to a very limited degree. If you join any club there are always some people who hope to gain something by their membership apart from the normal things in the club. Yes, I'm sure some people do, but it's very indirect, you know?

'You might say, "That's a nice doctor in our Lodge. Perhaps I'll go and see him when I'm ill; that chap's a nice estate agent – yes, well, who should I put my property in to sell with? Oh, well, there's Joe in our Lodge, I'll give it to him to do." That sort of thing. That does crop up. It applies to some more than others, probably solicitors more than barristers. Estate agents, doctors, tradesmen, people like that.

'This doesn't happen so much in London. It's more likely to apply in a smaller, more integrated local place – but then they know each other anyway, so I expect Freemasonry doesn't mean anything one way or the other.

'I think if someone's really hard up, then Freemasonry

comes into its own. "Joe's very hard up, can't you put a bit of business his way?", or something like that.

'I'm not a very enthusiastic Freemason. In fact I suppose I'm a very *unenthusiastic* one, because I like having the dinner with my friends but I get rather bored with the little ceremonies they go through before. I can't be bothered to learn it, anyway.'

'What happens if you don't learn it?'

'Oh, well, you just sit back and don't take an active part in it. They don't like you to write it down. Well, quite frankly, I can't be bothered to memorize it. I wouldn't mind doing it if I could have a sheet, a sort of brief in front of me. That's my attitude to it, so you can see I'm not a very good Freemason.'

A former Worshipful Master of several Lodges of the Hampshire and Isle of Wight Province, a master builder, told me how after a lifetime of devotion to Masonry, he no longer took any part in it because he had become so despondent about its deteriorating standards.

'There was a time,' he said, 'up to about twenty years ago, when it was a proud thing to be a Freemason. They didn't let just anybody into it in those days like they do now. There was a real feeling of comradeship. And we had real power then, as well.

'All the top-notch people in the community or parish or whatever would be in it – the police chief, the magistrates, the coroner, the doctors, tradesmen, solicitors, architects, builders, dentists and the like. And a lot of good men of lower station. It didn't matter what you earned, it was your *character* which mattered. That meant that if anything ever happened in the community, we would have the authority to do something about it.

'Like when, years ago in the fifties, there were some

attacks by a pervert on some young girls. I phoned up the senior policeman in the district (he was in the Lodge), and a deputation of us Masons went to see him to find out what we could do. All the Lodges in the area formed into vigilante groups and we did house-to-house searches. We found him all right and by the time we'd finished with him he was in no state to interfere with anyone again.

'But we can't do those sort of things now. All the same people are in the Lodges but they've gone namby-pamby. With all this talk about rehabilitating criminals and leaving the law to take its course. It can still happen in some places where standards haven't dropped so much, but the old fellowship and trust isn't there any more. It's got bad all over. They are even taking blacks and Jews into it now.'

A Warwickshire Mason of Provincial grand rank, a leading figure in the construction industry, had different reasons for suggesting that Freemasonry was in decline.

'If you became interested enough in Freemasonry after what I tell you tonight to want to join, and asked me to sponsor you, I would say no. If you came back to me in two years I would say no. If you came back in five or eight years I would say no. I would want to know you well for at least ten years before I would consider supporting your application for membership. That's the way it always was, but it's not like it any more with most Masons.

'Interest in the Craft has been steadily decreasing among young men for the past twenty or twenty-five years. Because Lodges wanted to reverse this trend and give recruitment a boost, they gradually began to lower their standards. Now it is very easy to become a Freemason. Some members sponsor people they hardly know, or workmates of only a few months. It is not possible to know someone enough in a short time to be certain he genuinely has the values of a real Mason. Because of that, the Craft is now full of people who have joined because of what they can get out of it, not for what the Craft can get out of them.'

'I never found Freemasonry the least bit of use to me. I don't think in this country people understand it. It has a reputation that is completely misinformed,' said one of my informants, who has been a Master Mason for thirteen years. 'Obviously, if one belongs to a club, and I wouldn't put Freemasonry much higher than a dining-club incidentally, one meets people. If one meets people who get to know you, they probably give you their business. I happen to be a barrister so I don't really seek business. I never sought business or expected to get anything out of it except comradeship.'

'And you got that?'

'I belong to a Lodge which includes most of my friends anyway, so it's just another occasion where I meet my friends.'

'Would you agree that the majority of Freemasons do put it higher than a dining-club? There's the ritual, for instance . . .'

'I've noticed people do seem to like ritual, and I've been surprised once or twice how seriously some Masons do take all that side of it . . . One of the problems with Freemasonry is that you don't really know what it is before you join.'

'Does that worry you at all?'

'No, not if you're being introduced by your friends. I mean, some people think it's a secret society, but it's not a secret society because a secret society is one that you don't know exists.'

This definition of a secret society, repeated to me so often by Freemasons I interviewed, is inaccurate. The existence of many secret societies is known. What makes them secret is that their inner workings are unknown to outsiders, and their secrets are protected by initiation ceremonies which impose penalties on those who betray secrets. There is usually some ritualistic element to the secret society. These elements in Freemasonry justify the application of the term to Freemasonry just as they do to societies which are generally thought more sinister like the Ku Klux Klan, the Italian Carbonari or the Chinese Triads, whose ritual has much in common with English Masonry.

When a man seeks admission to Freemasonry he must find two sponsors within the Brotherhood. In theory, a Mason must not approach an outsider with an invitation to join. In practice, an invitation from a friend or business associate in the Craft is the most common kind of introduction, although United Grand Lodge steadfastly denies this.

One of my contacts within Grand Lodge, a man who thinks of the secrecy with which Masonry surrounds itself as ludicrous and childish, told me what follows a would-be candidate's application to join a particular Lodge.

'We have a little preliminary committee of senior Lodge members who interview the Candidate informally, to look at him and to ask questions like, "Why do you want to come into Freemasonry?" and "Why particularly this Lodge?"

'He might say, "An uncle of mine recommended this one," or a business associate, or a neighbour spoke about it.

'The very first question he is asked is: "Do you believe in God?" and invariably they answer, Yes. Maybe they were told by other Freemasons that they'd better, but they do. I had one case only in all my long experience in Freemasonry when a man began to vacillate, saying, "I'm not really sure, I don't know . . ."

'*We wouldn't have anything to do with him.*'

It would seem, therefore, that atheistic or agnostic Candidates canny enough to know the rules in advance and to lie about their beliefs are preferred to those who have genuine doubts and are honest enough to say so. My informant continued:

'After that, we send one or two of our committee to go into his home, by appointment, to see how he lives, that he is living in a *decent* way. I mean, I'm not a judge and you're not a judge, but if we go to his house and it looks reasonable, lived in, and it's nicely decorated, we know that we've got a man of standing. And I don't mean in the material sense. I mean that he is living as a human being should. He can be very modest, in two rooms, very modest. But, you see, a man in two rooms won't be a Mason because the fees are a bit costly, and you're expected to give charity. We don't say how much, but you're expected to give. If it's a pound or a thousand pounds, you give charity. Nobody will query.

'So we go into his home. We speak to his wife, if he's married. And we ask if she approves of her husband coming into the movement.

'We see if there are children. We ask him, "What about family life?" We're entitled to ask. If you want to come into my club, I'm entitled to ask you certain questions. If you resent it then it's a shame, then you can't come in. Same everywhere. This is how we accept people. If a man is a bankrupt we don't accept him. It sometimes happens that after joining, a man becomes bankrupt. That's too bad. We ask if the Candidate has any convictions. Someone who has been fined for speeding or not putting two bob in the parking meter is not rejected, they aren't criminal acts. But if a man has had a criminal record, we don't accept him. It's a pity, because a man might perjure himself to get into Masonry and say he does not have convictions. But if he admits he has, we don't accept him because we want men of standing, or stand*ards*. Not standing so much as standards. The ones that you and I try to live up to.'

I asked if a would-be Freemason in England had to be 'whole', or was there a rule here, as there is in America, forbidding the initiation of people with serious illnesses, or those who are chairbound for any reason.

'We've got men with wooden legs, we've got men who are lame. There is a lame man at one of the Lodges I go to. No, I suppose in parts of the ceremonies which are to do with legs it may be difficult, but we make special allowances, even if they don't do exactly what is laid down in the ritual. The Lodge committee will discuss this kind of difficulty and find ways to cope with it. So, yes, we accept people with a physical disability. If you had a mental disability you wouldn't want to be a Mason, and it would be embarrassing for a mentally handicapped person, and for members of the Lodge.'

As a Lewis, or son of a Freemason, author and *Sunday Times* feature writer Philip Knightley was able to join the Brotherhood at eighteen instead of twenty-one. When I contacted him he said that he had been wanting to tell someone about his masonic experience for years. He said, 'My father had been a Mason for years. I don't know how he joined. I think he was invited by friends.

'In Australia, the Masons have to single *you* out and invite you to join – it's the opposite to the system in England. If you make the approach first then you're likely to be turned down.

'After being initiated as an Entered Apprentice in

Sydney, I was to do my Second Degree in Fiji, where I'd gone. And so I switched from the jurisdiction of the New South Wales Lodge to the jurisdiction of a British colonial one. When the time approached for my Second Degree I was indirectly informed that they were not prepared to put me through the Second Degree. When I say indirectly, instead of telling me, the Lodge, which I'd visited several times, told the Australian Grand Lodge who told my Lodge who wrote to me via my father. The reason was that I had been associating with what were considered undesirable elements in the island – namely people who weren't white. So for the first time I realized that all the business about the brotherhood of man and brotherly love and all that applied largely to white Anglo-Saxon Protestants. And with the help of a Jehovah's Witness on the island who was brilliant in digging up references from the Bible, I composed a bitter letter of complaint about the behaviour of the Lodge, which I sent to the secretary of the Grand Lodge of New South Wales, quoting various references in the Bible about the brotherhood of man which had come up in various sections of the ritual. He didn't answer my letter. He told my father that the best thing to do was to wait until I came back to Australia and they'd continue with the process of making me a Master Mason there. His only excuse for the behaviour of the Fiji Lodge was to say that customs varied from country to country and I shouldn't be too harsh on local customs. I returned to Australia, took the second degree, third degree, became a Master Mason, continued to go to Lodge with my father, more as a social thing than anything else. But I eventually found it more and more boring, particularly because there was so much memorization. I thought that if I really wanted to tax my brain with remembering things, I could remember things of more use to me – like learning another language or something, instead of running through this endless ritual. And apart from the fact that one month it would be first degree, one month second degree, one month third degree, the *repetition* became boring. The food afterwards was lousy and I began to see little or no use in it intellectually.

'I continued as a Mason, but very intermittently. I went to live in Britain then in India. I didn't visit Lodges in India. I returned to Australia after about eight weeks as virtually a non-practising Mason, and I fell ill with a tropical fever, and was in hospital. This was in the early days of transistor radios, and the hospital had no radio sets or anything like that. One of our brother Masons owned a radio shop and he had a lot of transistors. My father asked him as a brother Mason, could he lend me a radio for my spell in hospital, and he said no. He said I might break it or something. That was just the final straw. It seems a trivial thing but I thought if he couldn't even lend me a radio, what the hell was the whole Brotherhood of Masonry about? And I just lapsed and let my subscriptions run out, and all that sort of thing. But, because it's once a Mason always a Mason, I could, no doubt, by reinstating my standing with the Lodge in Sydney, visit Lodges here and continue to be a Mason if I wanted to.'

CHAPTER 15

Jobs For the Brethren?

The traditional outsider's view of Freemasonry as a self-help organization is certainly an important facet of the Brotherhood in real life not, as many masonic apologists maintain, only in the imaginations of the 'profane'. Although a new initiate to Freemasonry declares on his honour that he offers himself as a candidate 'uninfluenced by mercenary or other unworthy motives', there can be no doubt that the majority of businessmen who become Masons do so because they believe it will assist them in business – as indeed it frequently does. Those who suggest that no selfish motive is ever present in the mind of the prospective Mason speak conscious humbug. One only has to speak to a handful of Freemasons and ex-Masons to realize how widespread the desire to 'get on' is in those who turn to the Brotherhood. This is not to denigrate the often very real desire for the legitimate privileges of Masonry – brotherhood, morality and charity – of many members. Many Freemasons, in addition to admitting that they joined primarily in the hope of having the edge in business and at job interviews, have told me they also think of Masonry as an insurance policy. If they become ill, they have the Royal Masonic Hospital. If they die, they feel confident that their wives and children will be taken care of financially. One man, the proprietor of a butcher's shop, a bakery and a launderette in a humble part of Cambridge, told me that he looked upon Masonic dues in precisely the same way as he did his National Insurance contributions, and as the union fees he had paid before becoming self-employed.

The exploitation of masonic membership, which, it must be said, most outsiders who are not directly affected by it accept as a part of the British way of life, comes into its own in the business world. Whether on the level of local trade or national commerce and industry, the Brotherhood plays a varying, often considerable, part in the awarding of contracts and in promotion.

On the local level, there is much cross-fertilization between Masonry and other groups of business people such as Round Table, Lions Clubs, and Rotary Clubs as well as Chambers of Commerce. Most of the male members of these organizations – and Chambers of Commerce at least contain an increasing number of women – are Freemasons as well. Men in business on their own account – for example, accountants, architects, builders, estate agents, restaurateurs, taxi firm proprietors, travel agents and shop keepers of all kinds – are strongly represented in Lodges up and down the country.

Commercial travellers frequently become Freemasons in order to be able to visit Lodges all over the country and to cultivate potential clients within the unique secret atmosphere of the Temple or the post-ritual dinner. There are no fewer than five Lodges named Commercial Travellers Lodge: in Darlington, Liverpool, London, Newcastle, and Preston.*

Ron Price, an insurance agent and a former Master Mason and Junior Deacon of a Lodge in Worcestershire, told me, 'Membership of Freemasonry is used considerably in the field of industry and commerce – because of the sign

*Nos 5089, 2631, 2795, 3700 and 3493 respectively.

one can give which is unnoticeable by anyone else. You can make it known to the other person that you are what they call on the square, and if the other person is on the square he will recognize the sign, and that can influence either your being able to make a sale or, if you are applying for a job, it can make the difference between whether you get the job or not.'

The sign by which a Mason may secretly make himself known to others in the room involves a particular arrangement of the feet. This arrangement is outlined in the ceremony of initiation to the First Degree. The Worshipful Master tells the Candidate, 'I shall, therefore, proceed to entrust you with the secrets of this degree, or those marks by which we are known to each other, and distinguished from the rest of the world . . . You are therefore expected to stand perfectly erect, your feet formed in a square, your body being thus considered an emblem of your mind, and your feet of the rectitude of your actions.' This is one of several bodily arrangements by which a Brother proclaims his affiliation to unknown brethren. If he is in a position to shake hands with the person to whom he wishes to identify himself, recognition becomes much easier. There are three basic handshakes in daily use, one for each of the first three degrees. The Entered Apprentice applies distinct pressure with his right thumb on the knuckle of the other man's forefinger. The Fellow Craft does the same thing with the second knuckle. The Master Mason applies distinct pressure with his right thumb between the knuckles of the other's middle and third finger.

Price went on, 'I have got business from two people as a result of being a Mason – not because I asked or made myself known particularly. Once it was actually in Lodge after dinner. I was sitting next to a man and he said, "Well, what is your business?" and I told him and he said, "Well, you can come along and have a chat with me," and I went along and had a chat and did some business. But after I came out of Freemasonry he didn't want to know. I had another case where I didn't really intend to convey that I was a Mason in any way but I obviously did so quite inadvertently because it was the natural way for me to shake hands. And as a result of that I got that particular client, but it faded when I resigned.'

A Grimsby restaurant owner told me that his one motive in joining Freemasonry was to 'ease the passage' of licence renewals. He said that before he became a Mason he had to contend with objections from the police and others, mainly individuals acting on behalf of his rivals. After becoming a Brother there were no further police objections because the majority of senior officers belonged to his Lodge, and such objections as were raised by others were from then on ignored by the local justices – because they, too, were members of the Lodge. He said, 'We help each other. Why not? It's what it's all about innit? I mean, you come to me, you scratch my back and I'll scratch yours. I'd be a bloody masochist if I didn't take advantage like everyone else, wouldn't I? We're all human.'

A Past Master of Eden Park Lodge No 5379 in Croydon told me he had worked for many years as a consultant for Taylor Woodrow, the construction, home building and property development group of companies. He said, 'Looking back, although I didn't think anything about it at the time, I suppose it was wrong. But quite a few times I know I got contracts because I gave a masonic grip. The whole board of directors of Taylor Woodrow were Freemasons then. I don't know about now.

'You'll find that nine out of ten architects are Masons – and there is no getting away from it, I would put in a tender and when I did so, I'd shake the architect by the hand. "Oh," he'd say, "you're a Mason. The contract is yours."

'Looking back on it now I can see that it was a bit too "wheels within wheels" to be right. I probably shouldn't have done it, but that's the way Masonry works. If there's a contract going from an architect, the chances are he's a Mason, so the chances are a Mason will get it.'

John Poulson, the notoriously corrupt architect whose activities in bribing local government officers, councillors, Civil Servants, officials of nationalized industries and others created a scandal which has been described by more than one commentator as the British Watergate, was an avid Freemason. Nothing surprising in itself, perhaps, but Poulson did use Masonry as a back door to obtaining business. In *Web of Corruption*, the definitive story of Poulson and his infamous PR man T. Dan Smith, the authors state:

> If the Church was one of the focal points in Poulson's life, the Freemason's Lodge was another. In business much of what he did was behind closed doors, and he was naturally attracted to the secret society of Freemasonry, which practised morality, charity and obedience to the law and yet offered its members enormous political and business advantages. In the Middle Ages, you had to be a cathedral builder to become a Freemason but, in Poulson's Pontefract, the rule had been stood on its head, and an architect really needed to be a Freemason to design a block of flats. Poulson joined two lodges, De Lacy, code number Pontefract 4643, and Tateshall, code number 7647.* Together these lodges had recruited most of the town's business and professional people.

Poulson, say the authors, 'liked the ritual of Freemasonry, the rites and trappings and chivalric brotherhoods. He became master of both his Lodges and capped his underground career by being elected Provincial Grand Deacon of Yorkshire.' He exploited Masonry to the full in

*This is a typographical error in *Web of Corruption*. Tateshall Lodge, which meets at the Masonic Hall, Carleton Close, Pontefract, is numbered 7645.

advancing his professional interests and establishing contacts in all fields of potential advantage.

Banking is another stronghold of Freemasonry in the world of business. I have met bank employees at all levels from clerks in small local branches to directors of national clearing banks. It is generally accepted that promotion, although far from impossible for the non-Mason, less so now that so many women are entering banking, is nevertheless much more likely for the man who joins a Lodge early in his career. This is especially true of promotion to branch manager level and higher, where very few women or non-Masons reach even today. The Bank of England is rife with Masons and has its own Lodge.

I have been told by several informants how details of their bank accounts have been obtained by parties with no right to the information by way of masonic contacts in banks. The high proportion of bank managers and bank staff who are Freemasons can make the acquisition of this kind of confidential information relatively easy for a Mason, having as he does the right of access to every Lodge in the country. One man wanted to discover how much his twenty-nine-year-old daughter had in her two bank accounts, and to whom she had written cheques over the past year. He paid several visits to the Lodges in the town, about thirty miles away, where his daughter lived. Eventually he found a brother Mason who worked in a bank. It was an easy task for this Mason to telephone – through the legitimate inter-bank enquiry system – the branch where the other Mason's daughter had her accounts. When he obtained the information, the bank employee passed it to the father, doubtless convinced it was for good reasons as the request had come from a fellow Freemason. Indeed, the father himself believed it was for good reasons because he suspected that his daughter was involved with a man who was draining her of all she had. In fact, the daughter had a steady and long-term relationship with a man four years her junior who was studying for a PhD in London. They intended to marry when he got his doctorate. Meanwhile the woman was supporting him. This arrangement infuriated the father, whose view of life dated from the sterner 1920s. He traced the fiancé through the cheque records illicitly obtained from the bank, and wrecked the relationship by revealing to the man that his daughter had been pregnant by someone else when she met him, and had later, without his knowledge, had an abortion. This information had also been gleaned from clues obtained from cleared cheques from the masonic contacts in the bank.

In industry, Masonry is far stronger among white-collar workers and management up to the highest echelons, although once men on the shop floor attain the position of foremen or its equivalent, there is usually distinct advantage in joining the appropriate Lodge. The nationalized industries are rife with Freemasonry, especially the British Steel Corporation, the National Coal Board, British Rail, the Post Office, the regional gas and electricity boards and the Central Electricity Generating Board, the Atomic Energy Authority and London Transport. Mr Raymond B. Mole (Past Assistant Grand Director of Ceremonies, 1977), chief executive of the Royal Masonic Hospital at Hammersmith, told journalist Robert Eagle, 'You often find that when a man with London Transport gets promotion and a bit of gold braid on his uniform, he then starts thinking of becoming a Mason.'

Eagle's investigation was centred on Masonry in the medical profession, which is prevalent, especially among general practitioners and the more senior hospital doctors. Hospital Lodges prove useful meeting places for medical staff and administrators. Most main hospitals, including all the London teaching hospitals, have their own Lodges. According to Sir Edward Tuckwell, former Serjeant-

Surgeon to the Queen, and Lord Porritt, Chairman of the African Medical and Research Foundation, both Freemasons and both consultants to the Royal Masonic Hospital, the Lodges of the teaching hospitals draw their members from hospital staff and GPs connected with the hospital in question. Tuckwell and Porritt are members of the Lodges attached to the teaching hospitals where they trained and later worked – Porritt at St Mary's, Paddington (St Mary's Lodge No 63), which has about about forty active members out of a total of 300, half of them general practitioners; and Tuckwell at St Bartholomew's (Rahere Lodge No 2546), with about thirty active brethren. Other London hospital Lodges include King's College (No 2973); London Hospital, Whitechapel (No 2845); St Thomas's (No 142) and Moorfields (No 4949).

Many of the most senior members of the profession are Freemasons, especially those actively involved with the Royal College of Physicians and the Royal College of Surgeons, which has benefited from a massive £600,000 trust fund set up by the Brotherhood for medical research. Masonry does seem to have had an influence over certain appointments. Tuckwell emphatically denied that membership of the Brotherhood ever helped any doctor's career, telling Eagle that there was not the slightest truth in the rumour '. . . whereas Lord Porritt more circumspectly said that "it would be hard to deny that some people have been helped"'.

Although the governing bodies of most major hospitals are formed largely of Freemasons, the one overriding consideration in medicine, at least in the non-administrative areas, seems to be placing the best person in the job, whether Mason or otherwise. This is perhaps best illustrated by the staffing of the Brotherhood's own hospital. The Royal Masonic Hospital is not staffed exclusively by Freemasons, although most of its consultants are Brothers.

Chief executive of the hospital Raymond Mole says that Masonry is not a criterion for appointment. The only qualification demanded is that a Royal Masonic consultant be a consultant at a teaching hospital. Robert Eagle again:

> . . . registrars at the hospital are not usually Masons . . . one of the few women doctors to work at the Royal Masonic Hospital told me that during the several years she held the job she heard very little mention of the subject.
>
> 'Obviously no one asked me to join; but I had no idea whether even my closest colleague there was a Mason.' As she subsequently became a consultant at the hospital she does not seem to have been the victim of Masonic misogyny either.

Freemasonry plays a significant but declining role in the field of education. It is common for junior and secondary school headmasters and college lecturers to be Brothers. There are as many as 170 Old Boys Lodges in England and Wales, most of which have current teaching staff among their members.

The ambulance and fire services are strongly represented in Masonry, and there is a higher proportion of prison officers than police officers in the Brotherhood. Unlike the police, though, there is little fraternization between the higher and lower ranks in the service. The senior officers of prisons have their Lodges, the 'screws' theirs, and rare the twain shall meet. One premier London Lodge has in a matter of a few years completely changed its character due to an influx of prison officers from Wormwood Scrubs Prison. Lodge La Tolerance No 538, consecrated in 1847, until recently considered something of an élite Lodge, was in need of new members. One of the brethren knew a senior officer at the Scrubs who was interested in joining the Brotherhood, and it was agreed that he should be considered. The prison officer was interviewed and accepted into the Lodge. Such was the interest among the new initiate's colleagues that one by one the number of prison officers in Lodge La Tolerance increased. As more and more joined, so more and more older members left because they were unhappy with the changing character of the Lodge. Lodge No 538 is now dominated by prison officers from the Scrubs, where it is strongest in D Wing, the lifers' section. Although I have heard no allegations that promotion at the Scrubs is difficult for non-Masons, claims throughout the service of masonic favouritism are more common than in the police.

It is not possible in the space available to give more than a general survey of the part played by the Brotherhood in the field of business and work. The specific allegations investigated produce a picture of undeniable masonic influence over appointments, contracts and promotions in many areas, but also of widespread suspicion of masonic collusion where none exists. Certain strongly masonic areas of life not covered in this chapter are looked at in some detail elsewhere in the book.

CHAPTER 16

The Dissidents

One of my major sources of information was a former Grand Inspector Inquisitor Commander of the Thirty-First Degree of the Ancient and Accepted Rite who had withdrawn from Masonry in 1968 for religious reasons. As with so many other people in the labyrinthine world of Freemasonry, I was led to him by way of a series of contacts. He agreed through a third party to be interviewed by me concerning his conviction that no active Christian could in all conscience remain a Freemason.

When I met him I learned that he was a judge, and a particularly quick-tempered one. Although I had heard of him, I had hitherto known little about him.

We spent a long time talking about Masonry and religion, but after a while I began to ask him about the Ancient and Accepted Rite of the Thirty-Third Degree. He was, after all, only the fourth initiate to the Rite who had agreed to see me. He answered quickly. 'No, I dare not go into that,' he said. 'We'd better stick with religion.' It seemed a perfectly normal answer – I had received many such replies over the months of my investigation. It *sounded* like the usual rebuff. But I thought immediately afterwards how strange it was that he had used the words '*dare* not'. Most people said, 'I'd *better* not', or 'I'd *rather* not'. I remarked on his use of the word. He said, 'Anyone in public life has to be cautious.'

'Cautious,' I repeated. 'That's a masonic word of recognition.'

'You've obviously delved into the ritual, so you know,' he said. 'But I mean cautious in the sense everybody understands it.'

'What must you be cautious about?'

'Mr Knight, I don't like this line of questioning. I agreed to speak to you in general terms about why my commitment to Jesus is incompatible with the masonic religion. I do not wish to be drawn into discussion of matters covered by whatever undertakings I have . . . taken.'

'By undertakings, do you mean masonic oaths?'

He paused. 'Yes, I do. I prefer the word obligation to oath. It's not the same.'

I remember thinking as I turned the conversation back on to the track I wanted it to follow that it would be interesting later on to return to this question of the distinction between an obligation and an oath. I never did.

'*Why* do you have to be cautious, careful?' I said. 'You're not a Mason any more. I've got copies of all the rituals of the 4th to 33rd degree. There is no obligation which could possibly be interpreted to forbid you from telling me what you meant when you used the word "dare" in an ordinary conversation.'

'This isn't about my religious convictions, is it?'

'Many of your former masonic colleagues are very powerful people in this country. Do you think there would be some kind of reprisal if you gave away any secrets?'

'Not of the kind you write about in your book about Jack the Ripper.' He laughed. A bit hollowly, I thought.

'Well, not murder, no, I wouldn't have thought so.' I, too, laughed. I felt oddly embarrassed. 'But there is *some* kind of reprisal to be feared then? Something more . . . subtle?'

He began to look angry. He had made a slip. 'That was a

figure of sp— I was making a joke. A very bad joke.'

'But you said—'

'I know, I know! And I do not believe for one moment that what you suggest in your book has happened in real life – then or ever.'

I could see the rattled ex-Mason automatically slipping back into the practice of a lifetime. *Sometimes you shall divert a discourse, and manage it prudently for the honour of the worshipful fraternity.* I would not be diverted into defending the evidence and arguments in my first book. I felt I was close to something. I pressed on.

'Leaving murder aside, can I ask you . . .' And then it hit me. 'Can I ask you, *as a Christian*, have you ever seen at first hand any sort of reprisals carried out by Freemasons using masonic influence against any non-Freemason or anti-Freemason?'

All at once, he seemed to relax, or to somehow collapse into a smaller man as he let all the anger go out of him. 'As a Christian . . .' He paused thoughtfully, and I noticed how very many times he blinked his eyes during this hiatus. I wondered at one point if he was praying for guidance. He drew a long, slow, deep breath. 'As a Christian, I have to tell you that I have never in my whole life witnessed or heard about a single act of hostility by a Freemason or group of Freemasons *that was sanctioned by Grand Lodge or Supreme Council.*' He looked at me significantly as he laid stress on that qualifying clause. 'There,' he said. 'I have said nothing which betrays my obligations.'

'I have heard from quite a lot of contacts about organized action by groups of Freemasons that have resulted in the financial or social ruin of certain people,' I said.

'So have I,' he said, still looking me straight in the eye as if telling me this was important. '*So have I, Mr Knight.*'

'Have you any direct knowledge of such happenings?'

'Not of such happenings *which had the backing of official Freemasonry.*'

'But of action which was *un*official? In other words, Masons abusing the Craft for their own ends?'

'You know the answer to that, from the way I have said what I have said.'

'I have also heard about people who have "crossed" certain Masons and finished up in prison . . .'

He stopped me in mid-sentence by placing a finger on his lips.

'If I told you everything I know about Freemasonry being betrayed by its members, it would surprise even you,' he said. 'It would make your hair stand on end. I can't tell you any more.' Then, as if it was an afterthought, but I don't believe it was, he said, 'Give me your phone number. You might hear from someone in a few days.'

I gave him the number. 'Who?' I said.

The finger went back to his lips and he went to fetch my coat.

'God bless,' he said as I left, and I ran pell-mell to a sandwich bar in nearby Chancery Lane to scribble down the notes on which this account of our meeting has been based.

Four days later I received a phone call from a man who told me he had seen my advertisement for people with information about Freemasonry in an old copy of the *New Statesman.** He said he had read my *Jack the Ripper: The Final Solution* and would very much like to meet me. I tried, as I tried with all my callers, to get him to say something concrete on the phone, but he would not even tell me whether or not he was a Mason. I had already

*This advertisment had appeared for four weeks in the summer of 1981, some nine months earlier.

received a dozen or so similar calls, some of which had proved useful, some wild goose chases. But the researcher's world is the natural habitat of wild geese and red herrings, and one accepts the necessity of chasing them. Despite his unwillingness to talk – perhaps, in a way, because of it – I arranged to meet him the following Saturday in the vestibule of the Café Royal. From there we would go to his club. He said his name was Christopher. Whether this was his Christian name or his surname I didn't know.

When I arrived, he was sitting in the armchair to the right of the fireplace just inside the entrance, smoking a small cigar in a holder and reading that day's *Times*. He was tall, more than six feet, slim and aged about fifty. Everything about him spoke of affluence, except his plain National Health Service glasses. We went to his club, which he pledged me not to name as it could be used to identify him. It turned out that Christopher was one of his three Christian names and that he was a very senior Civil Servant in Whitehall. He had contacted me, he said, not as a result of seeing the *New Statesman* advertisement – although he had seen it when it appeared – but at the request of my cautious Christian judge. He asked me what I wanted to know. I said I took it that he was a Freemason. He nodded and took some papers out of his slimline briefcase. He wanted me to be in no doubt as to his bona fides.

After examining the papers I told him I was interested to know what a person might have to fear from a group of influential Freemasons if circumstances made him, for instance, a threat to them in the business world; or if he discovered they were using Masonry for corrupt purposes; or had fallen a victim of their misuse of Freemasonry and would not heed warnings not to oppose them.

'It is not difficult to ruin a man,' he said. 'And I will tell you how it is done time and again. There are more than half a million brethren under the jurisdiction of Grand Lodge.

Standards have been falling for twenty or thirty years. It is too easy to enter the Craft, so many men of dubious morals have joined. The secrecy and power attract such people, and when they come the decent leave. The numbers of people who would never have been considered for membership in the fifties are getting larger all the time. If only five per cent of Freemasons use – *abuse* – the Craft for selfish or corrupt ends it means there are 25,000 of them. The figure is much closer to twelve or thirteen per cent now.'

It transpired that Christopher was one of a small and unpopular group within Masonry who some time in the early seventies had decided that either they had to get out of the Brotherhood or they had to do something 'to stop the rot' which the blinkered officers of Great Queen Street refused to admit was there. His reason for talking to me was to assure me that the Brotherhood was an essentially good body of men devoted to all that was best in the British social system and which promoted brotherly love and contributed to the wellbeing of the country and to the relief of suffering. He wanted this put firmly across to the public, and his group wanted pressure brought to bear on those in positions of responsibility within the Brotherhood to put Freemasonry's house in order – to institute proper policing, to close down Lodges used for shady dealings and to root out corrupt brethren and expel them. The group – it had no name – also wanted the whole business of masonic secrecy looked into by Grand Lodge, most of them believing that secrecy was more harmful than helpful to Masonry.

Christopher explained that Masonry's nationwide organization of men from most walks of life provided one of the most efficient private intelligence networks imaginable. Private information on anybody in the country could normally be accessed very rapidly through endless permutations of masonic contacts – police, magistrates, solicitors, bank managers, Post Office staff ('very useful in supplying copies of a man's mail'), doctors, government employees, bosses of firms and nationalized industries etc., etc. A dossier of personal data could be built up on anybody very quickly. When the major facts of an individual's life were known, areas of vulnerability would become apparent. Perhaps he is in financial difficulties; perhaps he has some social vice – if married he might 'retain a mistress' or have a proclivity for visiting prostitutes; perhaps there is something in his past he wishes keep buried, some guilty secret, a criminal offence (easily obtainable through Freemason police of doubtful virtue), or other blemish on his character: all these and more could be discovered via the wide-ranging masonic network of 600,000 contacts, a great many of whom were disposed to do favours for one another because that had been their prime motive for joining. Even decent Masons could often be 'conned' into providing information on the basis that 'Brother Smith needs this to help the person involved'. The adversary would even sometimes be described as a fellow Mason to the Brother from whom information was sought – perhaps someone with access to his bank manager or employer. The 'good' Mason would not go to the lengths of checking with Freemasons Hall whether or not this was so. If the 'target' was presented as a Brother in distress by a fellow Mason, especially a fellow Lodge member, that would be enough for any upright member of the Craft.*

Sometimes this information-gathering process – often

*I discovered from other sources that this system has been long established within Masonry for the 'legitimate' purpose of bringing succour to a distressed Brother Mason or to the family of a departed Mason. It is common for details of a Freemason's debts, for instance, to be passed to his Lodge by his masonic bank manager. This 'invasion of privacy' is for no more sinister reason than for his brethren to club together and pay off his debts. This occurs most often after the death of a Mason, but by no means always. And this, apparently, is just one example of the many methods by which Freemasons obtain information *about each other* for genuine purposes.

involving a long chain of masonic contacts all over the country and possibly abroad – would be unnecessary. Enough would be known in advance about the adversary to initiate any desired action against him.

I asked how this 'action' might be taken.

'Solicitors are very good at it,' said Christopher. 'Get your man involved in something legal – it need not be serious – and you have him.' Solicitors, I was told, are 'past masters' at causing endless delays, generating useless paperwork, ignoring instructions, running up immense bills, misleading clients into taking decisions damaging to themselves.

Masonic police can harass, arrest on false charges, and plant evidence. 'A businessman in a small community or a person in public office arrested for dealing in child pornography, for indecent exposure, or for trafficking in drugs is at the end of the line,' said Christopher. 'He will never work again. Some people have committed suicide after experiences of that kind.'

Masons can bring about the situation where credit companies and banks withdraw credit facilities from individual clients and tradesmen, said my informant. Banks can foreclose. People who rely on the telephone for their work can be cut off for long periods. Masonic employees of local authorities can arrange for a person's drains to be inspected and extensive damage to be reported, thus burdening the person with huge repair bills; workmen carrying out the job can 'find' – in reality *cause* – further damage. Again with regard to legal matters, a fair hearing is hard to get when a man in ordinary circumstances is in financial difficulties. If he is trying to fight a group of unprincipled Freemasons skilled in using the 'network' it will be impossible because masonic Department of Health and Social Security and Law Society officials (see pp 189–90) can delay applications for Legal Aid endlessly.

'Employers, if they are Freemasons or not, can be given private information about a man who has made himself an enemy of Masonry. At worst he will be dismissed (if the information is true) or consistently passed over for promotion.'

Christopher added, 'Masonic doctors can also be used. But for some reason doctors seem to be the least corruptible men. There are only two occurrences of false medical certificates issued by company doctors to ruin the chances of an individual getting a particular job which I know about. It's not a problem that need greatly worry us like the rest.'

He continued for about half an hour to list examples of the ways in which corrupt members of the Brotherhood could defeat opposition, repeating every few minutes that these kinds of circumstances involved a minority of the brethren and that most would be utterly appalled at even the suggestion that such things were happening, let alone countenance them. That they were happening at all reflected the deterioration of the Craft inasmuch as its entry requirements were no longer stringent enough. Those in power in Freemasons Hall knew something of what went on, but they felt defeated by it and preferred to look the other way rather than take steps to eradicate it. If Christopher and his group failed to force the issue into the open, he said, the organization would become so morally polluted that it would simply cease to exist. But he was not solely concerned with the Brotherhood. It was the victims of those who used Masonry as a source of personal power who had to be helped as well.

'Only the fighters have any hope of beating the system once it's at work against them,' he told me. 'Most people, fighters or not, are beaten in the end, though. It's . . . you see, I . . . you finish up not knowing who you can trust. You can get no help because your story sounds so paranoid that you are thought a crank, one of those nuts who think the whole world is a conspiracy against *them.* It is a strange phenomenon. By setting up a situation that most people will think of as fantasy, these people can poison every part of a person's life. If they give in they go under. If they don't give in it's only putting off the day because if they fight, so much unhappiness will be brought to the people around them that there will likely come a time when even their families turn against them out of desperation. When that happens and they are without friends wherever they look, they become easy meat. The newspapers will not touch them.

'There is no defence against an evil which only the victims and the perpetrators know exists.'

PART FOUR

The Law

CHAPTER 17

The System

A large number of people who have contacted me in the past seven years have been concerned that Freemasons in the judiciary and legal profession exercise a pernicious influence over the administration of justice. Allegations of collusion between judges and lawyers, on behalf of their brethren in the dock, have been rife. The impartiality of Freemason judges has been called into question. There have been claims of huge masonic conspiracies between rival firms of solicitors and suggestions that Freemasonry is such a Grey Eminence that proceedings in open court are merely outward show, while everything is decided in advance, long before cases involving Masons reach court. I have heard many claims of civil battles lost and won on the basis of masonic signs made in court. Even the odd murderer is said to have got himself off by pulling the trick at an opportune moment.

But are any of these fears grounded in truth?

The legal system of England and Wales has certainly been a bastion of Freemasonry for generations. For a first opinion on whether this poses any kind of threat I approached the head of the judiciary, the Lord High Chancellor of Great Britain.

One of the most powerful men in the country, the Lord Chancellor is responsible for the appointment of High

Court judges, Recorders, Circuit judges and magistrates, as well as having a host of other duties. In his office come together the three powers of government - judicial, legislative and executive - which in all other individual constitutional positions except that of the Sovereign are kept separate as a safeguard against tyranny. As head of the judiciary he is the most powerful man in the first of the three spheres of power; as President of the House of Lords he exercises legislative power; and as a member of the Cabinet he exercises executive power. At the time of writing, this position - eighth in order of precedence after the Sovereign - is occupied by the Rt Hon Lord Hailsham of St Marylebone. So fervent is Hailsham's faith in the incorruptibility of the legal system over which he presides that when I tackled him on the subject he swept aside the widespread concern that a Freemason judge might be tempted to show favour to members of the Brotherhood who appear before him. Freemasonry is irrelevant in the administration of justice in England, says Hailsham. He told me he was not a Mason and declared that my research was 'worthless activity' and my book 'a valueless project'.

Lord Gardiner, Labour's Lord Chancellor in the four years prior to Hailsham's first appointment to the office in 1970, was a senior Mason. Lord Elwyn-Jones, Lord Chancellor in the Labour years between 1974 and 1979, when Hailsham was reappointed on the advice of Margaret Thatcher, was not a Freemason.

After the Lord Chancellor, the highest judicial appointments are to the Supreme Court of Judicature. These are:

Lord Chief Justice: Head of the Court of Appeal (Criminal Division); Head of the Queen's Bench Division of the High Court; Member of the House of Lords. Current incumbent: Lord Lane of St Ippollitts in the County of Hertfordshire (Life Peer, born 1918).

Master of the Rolls: Lord Chancellor's deputy. Head of the Court of Appeal (Civil Division). In charge of superintending the admission of solicitors to the Rolls of the Supreme Court. Current incumbent: the Rt Hon Sir John Donaldson, PC (born 1920).

President of the Family Division: Head of the High Court division which handles matters including matrimonial appeals from magistrates' courts (maintenance, separation orders, etc.), marriage of minors, divorce, and non-contentious probate. Current incumbent: the Rt Hon Sir John Lewis Arnold (born 1915).

Vice-Chancellor of the Chancery Division: Head, after the official President (the Lord Chancellor), of the High Court division dealing with matters that include private, public and charitable trusts, the administration of the estates of those who have died, dissolving and winding up companies and other company-related matters, mortgages and land charges, wards of court, revenue, bankruptcy, contractual disputes, and commercial partnership matters. Current incumbent: the Rt Hon Sir Robert Megarry (born 1910).

I wrote to all these men asking if they were members of the Brotherhood. My first letter to Lord Lane received no reply; my second was opened and returned to me without comment. Sir John Donaldson, before he succeeded Lord Denning, a non-Mason, as Master of the Rolls, told me, 'I do not really feel that the question of whether or not I am a Mason is a matter of public concern . . . It is a totally irrelevant consideration in our work.' Sir John's wife is tipped as the first woman Lord Mayor of London, an office that membership of the Brotherhood is usually helpful in obtaining. Sir John Arnold, who did not reply to two letters, is a Freemason of grand rank. He was an Assistant

Grand Registrar in 1970 and was promoted to Past Junior Grand Warden in 1973. Sir Robert Megarry did not reply to two letters. If he is a Freemason, and most people I have spoken to who know him think it unlikely, he is not of grand rank.

Lord Lane's predecessor as Lord Chief Justice, Lord Widgery, was an extremely enthusiastic Freemason of grand rank, holding office as Past Junior Grand Warden and Past Senior Grand Warden.

CHAPTER 18

The Two-Edged Sword

A former High Court judge who had been a member of the Brotherhood for more than fifty years told me, 'Yes, I knew which judges were and which judges were not Freemasons in my time. I am speaking of the High Court and Court of Appeal only – and of course the Law Lords. I know, I think, most of the judges who are Freemasons who currently sit in those courts. I am not at liberty to give you names, you understand. If they wish you to know they will tell you themselves. For myself, I can't see why you shouldn't know. Being a Freemason is the last thing I would wish to hide. I *can* tell you that there were many judges in my time who were members of the Craft. Probably fifteen years ago, sixty or seventy per cent of us were Masons. It's lower now – probably not much above fifty per cent – and that's not necessarily good.'

I asked if in his view Masonry exerted any influence over judges.

'Of course it does. Freemasonry cannot fail to influence a man. It has a very great influence for good.'

'And ill?'

'Only very occasionally.'

'Can you be more specific?'

'Yes I can. Freemasonry teaches a man to love his fellow men. Now, that might sound twee, but it isn't. It's perhaps more important than anything else in the world.'

'The good it brings or can bring is like the good that can come from Christianity, then? Or Buddhism?'

'Yes. But it's bigger than Christianity. Bigger than all religions because it embraces them all.'

'You said it occasionally has a bad influence.'

'Judges are men. Freemasons are men. Being a Christian doesn't make you like Christ, try as you might. The problem is in understanding what your religion, be it Christianity, Buddhism, Hindu or whatever you like, is all about, isn't it? It's a misunderstanding of the tenets of Freemasonry's aims, which can cause serious moral problems sometimes. But judges are less likely to misunderstand or misinterpret than most other people. The problem of the judge, and you realize this every day you sit, is that he's human.

'I have known two cases in my entire life at the Bar and on the Bench when Freemasonry influenced a judge in a way he should not, properly speaking, have been influenced. Bear in mind this is two cases out of perhaps twenty or thirty occasions when I have seen a man indicate by a movement or form of words that he was a Freemason.'

'That sort of thing does happen, then?'

'Of course it does. But we ignore it.'

'Most judges who are Freemasons say it doesn't happen.'

'It can't truly be said that people don't try these things because some people do. And who can blame them? I think part of Freemasonry's problem is that it tries to pretend that men in the Craft are above using it for their personal benefit. That's rubbish. Many wouldn't consider using it – most I would say. But thousands do every day, in all areas of life.'

'So some Freemasons who appear in court do try to use their membership to help them.'

'I've said so. Some, but in my experience not many.

Hundreds of Masons must pass through the courts without anyone knowing if they are in the Craft or not.'

'How can a Freemason make it known that he is a Mason without non-Masons in the court being aware that he is doing or saying something strange?'

'I am not at liberty to tell you these things because they are covered by our pledge of secrecy. There are certain words, certain phrases, certain motions. If you weren't a Freemason you wouldn't notice. They are not big gestures or anything like that, or strange mumbo-jumbo words.'

'What happened on the two occasions when the judge was swayed by the knowledge that the man before him was a Freemason?'

'It happened years and years ago when I was defending two brothers on charges of larceny. After re-examination of the younger of the two, the judge started asking him some particularly awkward questions which hadn't been raised by the prosecution. My client began to stumble over his words and contradicted himself on a fundamental point. The judge – who I should point out was a bit eccentric anyway and was retired prematurely – spotted it straight away and said that what my client had just said meant he could not have been speaking the truth before. Before he had finished speaking, my client made a sign which told the judge he was a Mason. Instead of ignoring it, he reacted.'

'How?'

'He looked surprised and very disconcerted.'

'What did he say?'

'Nothing. And he did not ask the questions which should naturally have followed.'

'What happened?'

'In his summing-up to the jury, the judge turned the incident back-to-front and referred to my client's sincerity. He went as far as suggesting that the jury might well consider that any apparent contradiction in his evidence was due not to a wish to befog the truth but to a confusion arising from the strain of a long hearing and natural nervousness.'

'Couldn't that have been true?'

'My client was lying. I knew it and the judge must have known. Nobody can say that the judge's summing up does not influence a jury, and on all but the main charge the Freemason was acquitted. The brother, who had not been the prime mover, was found guilty on all charges. In sentencing them, the non-Mason received two years and the Mason a year – for the same crime.'

'The other case?'

'Was when I was on the Bench, but it wasn't a case of mine. The judge was a very eminent Freemason, now dead. A man said something which made it clear he too was a Freemason. The judge told me afterwards that he had imposed a much more severe sentence than he would otherwise have done for that offence.'

'Why?'

'Because, as he saw it, the crime was the more reprehensible because a Freemason had committed it, and the defendant had compounded this "betrayal" of Freemasonry by abusing the masonic bond of brotherhood that existed between himself and the judge.'

'Do you agree with the judge's action?'

'No, I do not. But it does show that Freemasonry among the judiciary can be a two-edged sword.'

CHAPTER 19

The Mason Poisoner

'Frederick Henry Seddon, you stand convicted of wilful murder. Have you anything to say for yourself why the Court should not give judgement of death according to law?'

'I have, sir.'

Reading from notes, the poisoner calmly spoke of his innocence of the murder of his middle-aged spinster lodger Eliza Barrow. Then, turning to the judge, Seddon made a masonic sign. 'I declare before the Great Architect of the Universe I am not guilty, my lord.'

The Hon Mr Justice Bucknill, PC, who was approaching his sixty-seventh birthday, was a senior Freemason. In all his thirty-seven years as barrister, Recorder, and finally Judge of the Queen's Bench Division of the High Court of Justice, he had never encountered anything like this. He was appalled. He had no alternative but to sentence this avaricious killer to death. And now, at the very last moment, that killer had revealed himself as a fellow Mason – one of those whom Bucknill had sworn on bended knee and on pain of being 'severed in two, my bowels burned to ashes', to assist in adversity and to 'cheerfully and liberally stretch forth the hand of kindness to save him from sinking . . .'

This incident at the Old Bailey on 12 March 1912 passed

quickly into legend. Like most legends, it has grown, changed, and become confused in the telling. There are now almost as many versions of it as there are people who quote it. I have heard versions set as early as the 1850s and as late as the 1940s. I have heard it applied to murderers as diverse as William Palmer, Crippen, Haigh, Christie, Armstrong and Buck Ruxton. In 1972 a man being interviewed about Freemasonry on television applied the story to Rouse, the blazing car murderer who was hanged in 1931. In this version it was embellished to the point where the prisoner in the dock produced his full masonic regalia and appealed to the judge to free him! The judge in the case has been variously named as Sir James Fitzjames Stephen, Lord Justice Avory and others. Most people who repeat the yarn do not identify the characters involved. To them it is the story of the masonic murderer who made secret signs to the masonic judge and as a result . . .

The dénouement is another variable. Countless people have told me that the murderer was saved from execution as a direct result of the judge learning he was a Freemason. Many more, mainly Masons, denounce this as a lie.

It is important that the truth of this most famous of all stories about Freemasonry perverting the cause of justice within a court of law should be understood at the outset.

When Bucknill realized that Seddon was a Mason he was speechless. He seemed completely dazed as the black cap was placed on his head and oblivious to the usher crying out the traditional, 'Oyez! Oyez! My lords, the King's justices do strictly charge and command all persons to keep silence while sentence of death is passing upon the prisoner at the bar, upon pain of imprisonment. God save the King!'

Even now Bucknill sat as if struck dumb for a full minute. When he had composed himself enough to speak, he said, 'Frederick Henry Seddon, you have been found guilty of the wilful murder of Eliza Mary Barrow. With that verdict I am bound to say I agree. I should be more than terribly pained if you thought that I, in my charge to the jury, had stated anything against you that was not supported by the evidence. But even if what you say is strictly correct, that there is no evidence that you ever were left at a material time alone in the room with the deceased person, there is still in my opinion ample evidence to show that you had the opportunity of putting poison into her food or in her medicine. You have a motive for this crime. That motive was greed of gold. Whether it was that you wanted to put an end to the annuities or not, I know not. You only can know. Whether it was to get the gold that was or was not – but which you thought was – in the cash box, I do not know. But I think I do know this: that you wanted to make a great pecuniary profit by felonious means. This murder has been described by yourself in the box as one which, if made out against you, was a barbarous one; a murder of design, a cruel murder. It is not for me to harrow your feelings.'

All through the admonition, the judge was visibly shaken. The prisoner meanwhile listened calmly to Bucknill's quiet, gentlemanly tones. 'I do believe he was the most peaceful man in the court,' wrote Filson Young, a journalist who was there.

'It does not affect me, I have a clear conscience,' said Seddon.

'I have very little more to say,' went on Bucknill, struggling with the powerful emotional conflict Seddon had brought about by that one reference to the Great Architect of the Universe, 'except to remind you that you have had a very fair and patient trial. Your learned counsel, who has given his undivided time to this case, has done everything that a counsel at the English Bar could do. The Attorney General [prosecuting] has conducted his case with remarkable fairness. The jury has shown patience and intelligence I have never seen exceeded by any jury with which I had to do.'

Every now and again, the judge's voice dropped to a whisper. It did so now. 'I, as minister of the Law, have now to pass upon you that sentence which the Law demands has to be passed, which is that you have forfeited your life in consequence of your great crime. Try and make peace with your Maker.'

'I am at peace.'

'From what you have said,' and the judge was now all but sobbing, 'you and I know we both belong to one Brotherhood, and it is all the more painful to me to have to say what I am saying. But our Brotherhoood does not encourage crime. On the contrary, it condemns it. I pray you again to make your peace with the Great Architect of the Universe. Mercy – pray for it, ask for it . . .'

He continued speaking for about half a minute before pausing and bracing himself. 'And now I have to pass sentence,' he said, looking across the hushed courtroom at his Brother with tears filling his eyes. Another long pause. 'The sentence of the court is that you be taken from hence to a lawful prison, and from thence to a place of execution, and that you be there hanged by the neck until you are dead. And that your body be buried within the precincts of the prison in which you shall have been confined after your conviction. And may the Lord have mercy on your soul.'

This, then, is the real story about the Freemason murderer and the Freemason judge. But getting the facts straight is only half the battle. Only by perceiving what was behind the facts can we decide if this so-called 'classic' case is even relevant. Freemasons will say that Bucknill's reaction to Seddon's appeal for help is proof positive that there is no masonic influence on the execution of justice. Anti-Masons will argue that Seddon made his appeal too late, that by the time he made clear the esoteric bond between himself and the judge he was beyond help because the jury had already declared its verdict. Thus, although Bucknill might have wanted desperately to 'save him from sinking', his hands were tied.

Both these arguments are specious: the Bucknill–Seddon case proves nothing. The reason for this is simple. Seddon was *not* trying to exploit the masonic bond between them to influence the judge's actions.

This must be clear to anyone who returns to the original transcript of the trial. First, if he had intended to influence the judge in his favour, he would have made his membership of the Brotherhood clear at an earlier stage – certainly before the verdict had been returned, and before the judge's summing-up, by which a jury might conceivably be swayed. And if he had expected his Masonry to help him, he would surely have communicated the fact that he was a Brother to the judge in a way which would not have been noticed by others. There are methods, as I found out for myself, for Masons to identify themselves to one another without incongruous signals and invoking aloud the Great Architect. No, it is clear that Seddon was not saying to Bucknill, 'I am a Freemason like you. Help me,' but that he was using the masonic term for God to reinforce the usual oath he had taken on entering the witness box to speak the truth, the whole truth and nothing but the truth. It came as a natural culmination of his carefully thought-out speech in his own defence:

> . . . The prosecution has not traced anything to me in the shape of money, which is the great motive suggested by the prosecution in this case for my committing the diabolical crime of which I declare by the Great Architect of the Universe I am not guilty, my lord. Anything more I might have to say I do not suppose will be of any account, but still if it is the last words that I speak, I am not guilty of the crime of which I stand committed.

As he said, 'I declare . . .', he lifted up his hand to accompany the oath and to show it was his solemn word. Yes, it was a masonic sign. Yes, they were masonic words. But they were the natural words of a Freemason wishing to convey with all possible gravity that he was speaking the truth. That Seddon's action was perfectly natural and quite lacking in the sinister undertones ascribed to it by anti-Masons and others is shown by the openness with which it was performed. Because there was nothing hidden in the interaction between Seddon and Bucknill, it remains interesting to the student of Freemasonry only in the depth of brotherly feeling which was either inborn in Judge Bucknill or which Freemasonry had instilled in him. It tells us nothing of any alleged influence by Masonry in the courts.

CHAPTER 20

Barristers and Judges

Where Freemasonry does play a big part – and this is why so many judges are Masons – is in the process by which appointments to the Bench are made. I discovered this as a result of acting on the advice of a London Circuit judge who wrote to me:

> Apart from the professional judiciary, I would think it just as important to ascertain the position in respect of the lay magistrates who decide the overwhelming number of cases, especially outside London . . . I would not hold out much hope of success, but it might be worth asking the Lord Chancellor's Department if any consideration is given to Masonry when applicants for the Magistracy are interviewed.

There would have been no hope of getting a straight answer to the question by a direct approach, but after some weeks I established contact with an acquaintance of an acquaintance of a contact of a trusted fellow writer. This man, as a senior official in the Lord Chancellor's Department, knew a great deal of the behind-the-scenes wheeling and dealing which culminates in the appointment of a judge, magistrate or other member of the judiciary.

Judges are appointed from the ranks of those barristers and solicitors who have been in practice for at least ten years. Although there is a growing tendency for solicitors to be given preferment to the judiciary, the great majority of judges are former barristers.

To understand why Freemasonry is so powerful in the law, it is helpful to be familiar with the distinct roles of the two branches of the legal profession.

The barrister is the only member of the profession who has the right of audience in any court in the country. Whereas solicitors may be heard only in Magistrates' Courts, County Courts and, in certain circumstances, Crown Courts, a barrister can present and argue a client's case in all these as well as in the High Court, the Court of Appeal, and the House of Lords. But unlike the solicitor, the barrister cannot deal with the client direct. Contact between client and barrister is supposed always to be through the solicitor, although this does not always work out in practice. The etiquette of the profession demands that the solicitor, not the client, instructs the barrister. Thus the barrister is dependent on the solicitor for his living.

In England, the rank of barrister-at-law is conferred exclusively by four unincorporated bodies in London, known collectively as the Honourable Societies of the Inns of Court. The four Inns, established between 1310 and 1357, are Lincoln's Inn, Gray's Inn, the Middle Temple and the Inner Temple. Prior to the establishment of the latter two Inns, the Temple, which lies between Fleet Street and the River Thames, was the headquarters of the Knights Templar, declared heretics by King Philip IV of France and wiped out during the early fourteenth century. There is a modern-day Order of Knights Templar within British Freemasonry which claims direct descent from the medieval order. From the beginning the men of law were linked with Freemasonry.

Each Inn has its own library, dining-hall and chapel. Thousands of barristers' chambers are crammed into the large, impressive eighteenth- and nineteenth-century houses. There are cobbled alleys, covered passages, Gothic arches and winding stairs. There are gardens, swards, opulent residences and courtyards, all turning their backs on the outside world and looking into their own small world, redolent of dusty ledgers, moth-eaten wigs, public school mores, black gowns, scarlet robes and all the ponderous unchanging majesty of the law of old England.

Each Inn is owned by its Honourable Society and is governed by its own senior members – barristers and judges – who are known as Benchers. The Benchers decide which students will be called to the Bar (that is, made barristers) and which will not. Their decision is final. As with so much else in British Law, ancient customs attend the passage of students to their final examinations and admission. Candidates must of course pass examinations, which are set by the Council for Legal Education. But in addition they must 'keep twelve terms', which in everyday language means that on a set number of occasions in each legal term (Hilary, Easter, Trinity and Michaelmas) for three years, candidates must dine at their Inn. If they do so without fail, pass their exams and pay their fees they will then be called, and the degree, or rank, of barrister-at-law will be bestowed upon them.

The Scottish equivalent of a barrister is an advocate, and the Scottish equivalent of the Inns of Court is the Faculty of Advocates in Edinburgh. King's Inn, Dublin, is the Irish counterpart of the English Inns.

In 1966 a Senate of the Inns of Court was set up as an overall governing body. Its first president was, not unexpectedly, a Freemason of grand rank: Mr Justice Widgery. Widgery had been Junior Grand Warden in the United Grand Lodge in 1961. In Masonry he went on to become Senior Grand Warden in 1972, and in the non-secret world to become the first Lord Chief Justice of England to have been a solicitor as well as a barrister.

The Senate itself was superseded in 1974 by a new body which combined the functions of the Senate with the General Council of the Bar. This was given the name of Senate of the Inns of Court and the Bar and to its ninety-four members including six Benchers from each Inn devolved the duty to oversee the conditions of admission, legal education and welfare, and the authority to discipline and disbar, which was previously vested in each Honourable Society. The presidents since 1974 have been Lord Justice Templeman, Lord Scarman, Lord Justice Waller, Lord Justice Ackner and Lord Justice Griffiths. Of these, Waller is a Freemason of grand rank; Templeman did not respond to letters of enquiry; Ackner, asked if he was a Mason, could 'give . . . no information at all concerning Freemasonry'; Griffiths, in reply to the same question, regretted that he was unable to enter into correspondence on the matter raised; and Scarman did not reply.

Gray's Inn has its own Craft Lodge – No 4938 – which has its own Royal Arch Chapter and which meets at Freemasons Hall on the third Monday of January, March and October (its yearly installation meeting) and on the first Monday of December.

Some specialized sections of the Bar have their own Lodges, such as the Chancery Bar Lodge (No 2456), constituted in 1892, whose membership comprises barristers dealing mainly in chancery matters and judges of the Chancery Division of the High Court. The Lodge meets in Lincoln's Inn Hall. Masonic barristers are among the hardest Masons of all to persuade to talk, or even admit to being part of the Brotherhood. Take, for example, the barrister with chambers in Gray's Inn who, unable in truth to deny his membership, told me, 'I don't know in what circumstances you may or may not have been told and I am not in a position to discuss the matter with you in any shape or form.' While the Bar remains a masonic stronghold, there is not such a high proportion of masonic barristers as masonic solicitors, who are looked at in Chapter 21.

One reason there was always less need for a barrister to join the Brotherhood is that barristers traditionally had the compensation of circuit life. One barrister told me: 'We are already a brotherhood in a sense. We are a small profession and are therefore very close to each other in any event, and don't really need the additional qualification of being Freemasons in order to be known among ourselves.' Despite this, Masonry remains strong. Why?

The Bar is a strange profession in many ways, not least because most of the very top people *do not want* preferment, thus creating great opportunities for second-raters. I was first given insight into this phenomenon by an experienced barrister, a non-Mason, who had excellent contacts in Masonry. He told me, 'A top silk can earn between a quarter and half a million pounds a year. He will not thank you if he is promoted to being a High Court judge, because his income will drop by ninety per cent.* And with the prestige and respect in which he is already held, the automatic knighthood that goes with an appointment to the High Court would be neither here nor there. This applies to half a dozen, perhaps a dozen of the really household names.

'And there has been considerable evidence, certainly since the war, that the appointments to the High Court bench have been – with a few notable exceptions – if not second eleven members, at least not the first rank of the first division.

'This was underlined with the appointment of Henry Fisher to the Queen's Bench Division of the High Court in

*The annual salary of a High Court judge in 1982–3 was £42,500.

1968. Fisher had been an absolute top practitioner in City matters – commercial law and the like. He accepted the appointment to the High Court Bench, then two years later made legal history by resigning to go back into commercial life. He couldn't return to the Bar of course, but he went into the City as a company director. In 1973 he became Vice-President of the Bar Association for Commerce, Finance and Industry, and he has conducted several important enquiries, notably into the operations of Lloyd's. It has been said by his friends, although he hasn't said it, that it was not just the loss of financial income that led him to resign, it was the horror at suddenly moving away from the most eminent businessmen in the country and their really intellectually stimulating problems, and just sitting there trying criminals and listening to old ladies who get hit by motor cycles and claim a couple of thousand pounds' damages. He didn't even have the patience to wait for promotion to the Court of Appeal as he was bound to get. And even if he *had* got to the Court of Appeal, only one case in twenty is of any intellectual stimulation.'

The top lawyers who don't want preferment are the specialists, those with outstanding ability and long experience in specialized branches of the law like patent law, Common Market law, restrictive practices, Revenue, Chancery, shipping, and so on. These are the first rank of specialists, and for the most part have no ambitions to become judges.

There are therefore never enough people of ability to fill all the posts such as circuit judges, stipendiary magistrates, chairmen of employment tribunals, National Health Service commissions, and so on. First, the pay is a fraction of what people of outstanding ability can command; secondly, they are often soul-destroying occupations. That of circuit judge was described to me thus:

Can you imagine sitting there for eleven months of the year listening to people repeating the same old excuses as to why they have committed crimes? And then you can't even make a decision for yourself – you sum up to the jury, then the jury makes the decision guilty or not guilty. Even when it comes to your discretion on passing sentence, it's all on a scale, and if you exceed the scale you're either going to be reversed by the Court of Appeal or the Home Secretary is going to say the judges are not doing what they're told.*

Oh, they give them a bit of prestige. They dress them up in colourful robes and call them, 'your Honour' and the like. One of the few reasons for a lawyer of real ability to want to become a circuit judge is the very attractive pension arrangements.

But of course, preferment becomes *extremely* attractive to people who do not have that level of personal ability that they are going to maintain their professional career up to retirement age. Because once you're a little bit over the top, you're fifty or fifty-five, if you haven't made it, or unless you are offering a specialist service, you are what is called a *general* practitioner. And all the general practitioners always have young and attractive men and women following behind them and they get pushed out as has-beens. Therefore there is *terrific* competition on the part of the second-rate barrister to get what I call 'minor' preferment. And these second-rate barristers are the people who are prepared to join a Bar Lodge of Freemasons.

There are of course circuit judges who are of the first order of ability. And among the London stipendiary magistrates there is a small number who have chosen that particular appointment in preference even to being a High Court judge or a circuit judge because they feel it more rewarding to work *in* the community. Equally, there are individual circuit judges who feel they can best serve society in that capacity. There are several outstanding examples in men who have specialist knowledge – particularly of family law. There are some extremely compassionate circuit judges in this field who feel they are more

*Under the separation of powers, of course, judges are not supposed to do what politicians tell them.

valuable dealing with divorce, custody and related matters in the County Courts than they would be higher up. There are also circuit judges of the first ability who have accepted what many regard as a second-rater's appointment because they resent the dogmatic or Establishment-mindedness, even the narrow-mindedness of the typical authoritarian circuit judge and want to dilute that quality.

Be this as it may, the vast majority of 'top' lawyers do not want preferment. They are, by the nature of brilliance, rare men of law in any case – probably not more than a hundred in number.

So what of the others, the second- and third-raters? Beneath the first rank of specialists there is another rank of specialists. These barristers are not highly specialized in that they are not dealing in extremely erudite and abstruse subjects which require a high level of qualification. They are in areas where, because of experience, they are able to practise in a limited field where there is a degree of mystique and expertise, where the longer they go on the more they are going to know, and where the youngster can never achieve the older man's knowledge by ability alone, only by passage of time. This second group of specialists can do moderately well by the standards of the legal profession – and can be reasonably confident that they can continue in practice beyond what barristers call the 'has-been age' in life because their knowledge will always be saleable.

The spectre of the 'has-been age' drives many barristers into Freemasonry. Those who most dread it are the general practitioners with no specialist knowledge. Some of this largest of all groups will do extremely well because they have a degree of success, one good case, and they become fashionable. But most, of course, don't become fashionable. Because they do not specialize in a particular field, they feel under constant threat by brilliant young people coming up behind them. If a young barrister is talented and gets the opportunity for experience, it will probably take him or her no more than five years to be as good in general practice as a man or woman twenty years older. As a barrister gets older, his cases do not get better. He is briefed in exactly the same kind of cases when he is sixty as when he was thirty.

It is at this level that barristers live in fear of not getting preferment. They realize that if they are not appointed to the Bench in their early fifties, they probably will not have a practice after they are fifty-five. The only way they can hope to maintain their earning capacity into their late sixties or early seventies is by being appointed to the circuit bench, the stipendiary magistracy, to a chairmanship of tribunals or such like.

These are the men who turn in large numbers to Freemasonry,* because initiation unlocks a door and allows them admission to the right place where they can be seen by the right people. There is a euphemism at the Bar for this 'right place'. If a barrister is seeking preferment and wishes to see and be seen by judges and executives and Civil Servants of the Lord Chancellor's Department, he must 'join the Bar Golfing Society'.

I was told by a leading QC who is a Freemason, 'There is a legitimate Bar Golfing Society, but most people who talk about being members of the Bar Golfing Society can't play golf at all. They are Masons. Why this childish code has come into being I do not know. They behave as if they are ashamed of being Freemasons. Using Masonry as a stepping stone to the Bench is not wrong. Why do people pretend they don't do it? It *would* be wrong if on becoming judges

*There is nowhere for women barristers in the same position to turn.

they were tempted to abuse it, but I don't believe for the most part they do.'

Although it is not essential for candidates for the judiciary to be QCs, it is a big move in the right direction, and there is no doubt at all according to sources both masonic and otherwise that joining the Brotherhood, while not a prerequisite, certainly helps in getting to be a QC. Of course, first-rate barristers will be successful in their applications whether they are Masons or not. In fact, the most successful practitioners have to become QCs or the amount of their work becomes impossible. A barrister in the Inner Temple told me; 'At the risk of over-simplification, it can be said that a QC does a smaller number of larger cases. If a successful barrister remains a junior barrister [a barrister who is not a QC, not necessarily very junior in years], his practice becomes so top heavy that he just cannot cope. You can't start refusing work otherwise your practice disappears. Indeed, you become a QC if only to protect your position.'

But these men rarely want preferment, as said before. It is the second-raters, those who want to become QCs in their late forties in the hope that it will help them to attain other appointments, who join the Bar Lodges.

My masonic contact among the senior executives of the Lord Chancellor's Department told me, 'When a barrister joins the right Bar Lodge he can be certain of getting on intimate terms with scores of influential judges, big names many of them, and with large numbers of my colleagues in the Lord Chancellor's Department. And this is right and correct, a right and proper method for men of integrity to come to the Bench. Being a judge is an important, exacting task. Strength of character, personal probity, courage, are all qualities a good judge should have in full measure. And compassion. Where better to find out if a man has these qualities than in Lodge? Can you tell me? This is why most judges are Freemasons. Because Freemasons make the best judges.'

I asked him in whose opinion it was that the best people to be judges were Masons. He replied, 'By those whose job it is to select and recommend. By those who are judged the best people to know.'

Which, of course, was a way of saying, 'Freemasons'.

I asked him about the Lord Chancellor's position in all this, about how Lord Hailsham's not being a member of the Brotherhood affected the procedure. Surprisingly, he had not known whether Hailsham was a Mason or not. But it seemed a matter of indifference to him. 'The Lord Chancellor is in a very peculiar position,' he said. 'Hailsham is good. Absolutely brilliant, whether he's a Mason or not. I hope you don't think I'm saying that *only* Freemasons make good judges. Of course, the Lord Chancellor has the final say in the appointment of puisne judges, but as he should and is only right, he takes note of the recommendations of existing judges and of the Department. I am sure Hailsham doesn't care whether a man's a Mason or not.'

The fact is, Hailsham as a non-Mason does not know who among the judges he appoints are Freemasons or otherwise. By his own admission, he does not think the issue worth considering. Without knowing it he is fed recommendations of Freemasons by Freemasons. Perhaps there is no great ill in this. Perhaps Masons *do* make the best judges, although men like Lord Denning and the few women judges such as the Hon Mrs Justice Heilbron in the Family Division of the High Court indicate the calibre of some of the non-Masons in the law.

There is surely something more admirable in a woman or man who has proven her or his ability and reached the Bench of the High Court without having to resort to the secret ladder of Freemasonry. In this sense, it could be argued with some force that it is non-Masons who make the best judges.

The best potential judges are, of course, to be found both within the Brotherhood and outside it, and the very best are going to be appointed regardless. But so long as the system that allows Freemasonry to be a factor in the appointment of judges persists, those of 'second division' ability within Masonry will always have the advantage over their equals outside the Brotherhood – and the majority of judges in this country will continue to be Freemasons.

Most of the non-Mason judges I spoke to knew nothing that pointed to any secret influence in the courts. But, many of them added, as outsiders they would be unlikely to know even if it existed unless it was blatant. Two non-Mason judges were particularly strong in denying the Brotherhood had influence. One, a London judge, told me, 'If the judiciary is at all under the influence of Freemasonry it is a very well kept secret as I have never heard the subject mentioned during eight years as a Metropolitan Stipendiary Magistrate and nine years as a Circuit Judge. To be truthful, the thought has never crossed my mind. In my seventeen and a half years' experience on the full-time bench I do not think the subject of Freemasonry has ever been discussed in front of me by my colleagues and I have never been aware of any influence it has had in their appointment, promotion, or their professional lives.'

The strongest statement disputing allegations of untoward influence in the courts I received from a non-masonic judge (I received some much stronger ones from Masons, as might be expected) was from Judge Rodney Percy of the North Eastern Circuit: 'Although I was in practice at the Newcastle Bar for thirty years from 1950 onwards, I never became aware that Freemasonry played any part in "influencing" any decisions made either in or between counsel themselves or counsel and judges. I am sure that I should have recognized and remembered such occasions, but I can recall none.'

A Hertfordshire judge whose father and father-in-law are both Freemasons, but who is not one himself, told me, 'I have not experienced anything in my profession as barrister or judge to indicate any sinister influence at work by Freemasons.' A judge currently serving on the North Eastern Circuit, which covers courts in Leeds, Newcastle-upon-Tyne, Sheffield, Teesside, York, Bradford, Huddersfield, Wakefield, Durham, Beverley, Doncaster and Hull, was representative of many non-Mason judges in his view: 'In the whole of the time I have been in the legal profession I have never been conscious of Freemasonry playing any part in any decision.'

There is, of course, a natural disinclination by anyone who has spent his life dispensing justice to the best of his ability to acknowledge the possibility that some of his colleagues, whoever they are, might not be doing the same. And a judge not being aware of a certain phenomenon does not necessarily mean it isn't there, as evidenced by the Kent judge who does not know '*any* member of the judiciary to be a Freemason', although they are all around him. This judge, too, has 'no reason to think that Freemasonry plays any part in the administration of justice'.

One of the most eminent judges in the Queen's Bench Division of the High Court, who associates with masonic judges daily, has this to say: 'I am not a Freemason although I have had numerous opportunities of becoming one. I have a fundamental objection to any secret society, which has the power of influencing decisions affecting its members in a manner which would otherwise not have occurred, and/or to the disadvantage of non-members.'

Strong stuff, but to the chagrin of those seeking evidence

of the masonic influence in the courts, he adds, 'I have, of course, no evidence that Freemasons exercise such a power in that way.'

A former Lord Justice of Appeal stressed how general ignorance of the existence of masonic influence was no guarantee that it did not exist. 'I had chambers for many years in Lincoln's Inn,' he said. 'I was not aware of any masonic activity whatsoever. I then learned what a thriving centre of Masonry the Inn was. They kept the secret so well that I never knew there was any secret being kept. We mix with people all the time and still after many years know nothing about them. One heard of the occasional bad judgement – in civil cases – and as a barrister one saw them also. Later, many more bad judgements came one's way. I know personally of one judgement on the part of a judge in the Family Division of the High Court, who is a Freemason, that I can explain only in terms of this organization.'

This case was also brought to my notice independently by one of the main participants. The outline that follows is based on the documents of the case; interviews with the main participant; the former Lord Justice of Appeal who made behind-the-scenes enquiries after first hearing of the case, two barristers who were present during the proceedings, and other well-known and highly respected witnesses involved in the case; and upon my own observations during part of the hearings.

The first point to be stressed is the integrity and standing of the main participant, whom I shall call Randolph Hammond. Hammond had been unjustly deprived of all rights over his only child, a girl aged four. Custody of the child has been awarded to his wife, from whom he is legally separated, and access to his daughter has been made so inhumanly difficult for him by a judge that in practice he is never likely to see her again.

I shall call Hammond's wife Olivia, née Denbeigh. Her main witness was her father, a doctor, for our purposes to be called Roland Denbeigh. According to the evidence I have seen and heard it was Denbeigh who is to blame for breaking up Randolph and Olivia's marriage, and Denbeigh who instigated the custody action. Olivia herself has described her father to several people as being 'insanely' jealous and possessive of her, having broken up all her previous relationships, some with well-known and respected people who were willing to testify to the truth of Hammond's statements. But the judge in the case refused to hear the evidence of these vital witnesses. Olivia has spoken to many people over the years of her father's complete domination of her, of her inability to resist him and of her lifelong desire to 'escape' from him. He had only to forbid her to marry her previous lovers for her to comply helplessly with his demand. There is evidence that Denbeigh still has this sinister Svengali-like influence over Olivia, although she is well into her thirties. Now, Hammond fears, he is exerting that influence over his granddaughter as well.

During his cross-examination at the trial, it became apparent what a peculiar man Denbeigh was. At a crucial stage in the questioning it came out that he had subjected Olivia to internal examinations every day when she was pregnant, although a Harley Street specialist was in regular attendance. Skilful questioning was beginning to chip away at his upright, moral image and hint at the unnatural relationship he had with his daughter. This in turn showed what a morally and psychologically tainted atmosphere the child would be raised in if Olivia were to be awarded custody. Counsel for Hammond was getting close to showing that the father–daughter relationship was at least mentally incestuous, and was going on to find out the likelihood of there having been actual incest in the past.

Hammond was confident he was on the point of gaining custody of his child, that the judge could not fail to see what an undesirable and even sinister home his daughter would be raised in if custody were awarded to Olivia. But one of the barristers in court was by no means so sure. He told me afterwards, 'That whole case had a bloody strange feel to it. The whole atmosphere of it gave me a very bad gut feeling. All my instincts told me that Hammond was in the right but that he would go down, and that's what happened. The decision went the wrong way for no obvious reason I could gauge. But from the evidence in court and the papers of the case, Hammond was in the right.'

This barrister either did not see or thought nothing of a movement made by Denbeigh at what was for him the most perilous moment of his cross-examination. He suddenly placed his left arm stiff at his side, his finger tips pointing to the floor, and at the same time craned his head round over his right shoulder, his right hand above his eyes as if shading them. 'It was as if,' said Hammond later, 'he was watching an aeroplane in the back corner of the court.' At the time it happened, Hammond thought nothing of it other than as evidence of the old man's strangeness. Only later, thinking back over the judge's inexplicable behaviour immediately afterwards, did he recall Denbeigh's action. Asked by a friend to describe the action, Hammond imitated it and was astonished to be told that it was a Freemasonic signal. As soon as the judge saw the signal, he jumped forward in his seat and ordered counsel to cease his questioning of Denbeigh, utterly mystifying Hammond.

From that moment Hammond's case was doomed. Counsel was blocked at every step in his questioning and, as stated, was refused permission to call necessary witnesses.

Before the first mention of Masonry to him by the friend he told about the sign, Hammond knew virtually nothing of the Brotherhood. Later, when he aped Denbeigh's courtroom antic for my benefit, I was able to tell him that he was making the masonic sign of Grief and Distress, which is associated with the fourth of the Five Points of Fellowship, sacred to the Brotherhood: 'When adversity has visited our Brother, and his calamities call for our aid, we should cheerfully and liberally stretch forth the hand of kindness, to save him from sinking, and to relieve his necessities.'

In other words, Denbeigh was appealing to the judge to save him from the disastrous cross-examination and to make certain that custody was awarded to Olivia. When Hammond told me the name of the judge I was able to tell him that he was indeed an advanced Freemason. The name of that judge appears nowhere in this book, but will I hope later feature prominently in the report of whatever official enquiry is set up to examine this case.

The other barrister I spoke to signed this statement:

> I had known [Randolph Hammond] for about six months when he asked me to come in and listen to his case, which I agreed to do. I attended court during most of the action and took notes. I tried to remain objective throughout.
>
> I have no hesitation in stating that in my view the judge showed strong bias from the start. [Hammond's counsel] outlined his case, made his points, successfully took apart the testimony of [Olivia Hammond's] witnesses, placed certain cases with clear judgements before the court but was never heard in any real sense. The judge's findings in his judgement are totally contradicted by the evidence of many examples.
>
> [Mr Hammond's] suggestions concerning the masonic aspects of his action are matters which warrant consideration. I have no knowledge of Masonry but having sat through the action feel that something very funny was going on.

The former Lord Justice of Appeal was in no doubt, finally, that the judgement was 'so bad, so wrong' that Freemasonry, not Right, was the ruling factor in this case. But he could only give an opinion, he said. He could produce no *evidence* to an enquiry that this was so, and he doubted if it were capable of proof.

I was reminded about the story of the judge who told a prisoner still protesting his innocence after sentence, 'These are not Courts of Justice, they are Courts of Law.'

An enquiry into this case at the earliest possible time is clearly essential.

There are occasions, of course, when the masonic boot is on the other foot. One masonic judge, for instance, stopped a case mid-way, turned to the jury and told them that the defendant had just indicated to him that he was a Freemason. As the judge, too, was a Mason he felt it would be proper to withdraw from the case, and did so.

One of my 'moles' in the higher echelons of West Midlands Police, a Freemason, insisted, however, that the masonic link between judges and police officers was 'most damaging to society and to Masonry'. He added, 'The connection between us – the police – and the judiciary is very wrong. I'm not against judges being Masons. It's this unseen intimacy between the groups that is bad.

'I really don't like the way the organization [Freemasonry] is going, particularly with the judges and an overwhelming majority of the magistracy being Freemasons. I have seen policemen indicate to judges that they are Masons. They usually do it by making a deliberate mistake when taking the oath – "I swear by the Great Archit— oh, I'm sorry, I swear by Almighty God . . ." Every Freemason in court then knows he's a Brother.'

I asked him what a police officer could possibly hope to achieve by this.

'Oh, I've seen it so often,' he said. 'If the policeman has a sticky case where he's been under heavy pressure, it certainly won't do him any harm for the judge to know he's a fellow Mason. He will hold back on the criticism he might have of the officer's handling of the case, for instance. He will also take the word of the police officer as gospel, where he would not necessarily do so if neither of them were Masons.'

'And you've seen this happen?' I asked.

'As recently as last Thursday, yes.'

'How often does it happen?'

'I don't really know these days. I don't go to court very often now. I used to see it a lot when I did. I was listening in at Birmingham Crown Court on another matter and I saw it happen. I had a quiet smirk to myself actually. There was no need for it because it was no open-and-shut thing. This rather nattily dressed Detective Superintendent did it in court. There was not a lot of benefit in it, if that's what you're thinking. It's just that I can't see that this famous impartiality of judges can exist under these circumstances.'

If the perversion of justice by masonic judges were at all frequent, I am confident that my research would have produced direct evidence of it. There have, as we have seen, been cases of obvious masonic abuse, several reported to me by men of integrity and standing in the law. There are instances where Freemason judges are influenced by their loyalty to the Brotherhood to act in a way they otherwise would not, either to the detriment or benefit of the defendant. Such cases, in whichever direction the judge is influenced to bend or stretch the law, are nothing less than dereliction of duty. They are by their very nature dishonourable and always detrimental to society. But it can safely be stated that such incidents are rare exceptions in the higher courts, although those courts are presided over by a majority of Freemasons.

It is only common sense that if there was a single

Freemason judge in England who regularly tried to influence juries in favour of masonic prisoners, who showed favour to masonic litigants, or who regularly passed the lowest permissible sentence on his masonic brethren, he would have been exposed long ago, given the large number of assiduous journalists, honest and otherwise, this country boasts.

CHAPTER 21

Solicitors

Masonry is very powerful among solicitors in England and Wales. According to a survey in which I questioned all the solicitors in twenty selected towns, and a cross-section of London solicitors, it is less prevalent in the capital than it is in the provinces. This assessment of the situation from a Cambridgeshire lawyer who, although not a Mason, knows a great many Freemasons and receives regular unofficial briefings from members of the Brotherhood, rings true:

> In London there are plenty of other things to do. Life is much more impersonal and Freemasonry is not necessarily going to do a solicitor a great deal of good. What is more, good solicitors are so thin on the ground that if you are really good, you don't need to be a Freemason to get your clients. And if you're not any good, being a Freemason is not going to impress your client.

Solicitors, especially those outside London, have a particular incentive for becoming Freemasons. By the rules of their profession they are forbidden to advertise. They are therefore reliant upon passing trade, which is often sparse, and recommendation, which is hard to get. I have interviewed countless solicitors who joined Freemasonry purely to get on close terms with the businessmen and worthies of their community, and to gain personal contact with police, JPs, magistrate's clerks and any local or visiting members of the judiciary – men they could rely upon either to put business their way or whose good offices would be professionally valuable.

One young ex-Home Counties solicitor told me that after he began to practise in his town he was regularly advised by local Freemasons to join the Brotherhood. He resisted because of his religious convictions – he was a practising Christian – and because he was repelled by the idea of being unable to succeed on his own merits alone. But business was so bad that he eventually relented to the continuing pressure of his colleagues in the firm and to their promises that by becoming a Mason he would get all the clients he needed. He said: 'I was initiated and within days clients began to contact me out of the blue. Within a few weeks I had more than I could cope with. That went on for some months, but it troubled me, and I left Masonry before being made up to the second degree. Most of my clients melted away as fast as they had appeared. They were all Masons. So I moved to London. You don't need Masonry or advertising if you're good here – there's more litigation than all the London solicitors can deal with.'

The governing body of the 40,735 solicitors in England and Wales is the Law Society, which has its headquarters at 113 Chancery Lane, London WC2. The Society controls the admission of solicitors and the education for trainee solicitors. Although no solicitor may practise without certification by the Law Society, membership of the Society is not compulsory. At the end of March 1982, 33,226 practising solicitors were members of the Society and 7,509 were not.

The Law Society is one of the most masonic institutions in the world. This has proved an almost insurmountable obstacle to certain 'profane' individuals involved either willingly or unwillingly in litigation with Masons, because it is the Law Society whose job it is – with the Department of Health and Social Security – to decide who will be awarded legal aid and who will not. It also dictates the conditions on which legal aid is granted in each separate case. The difficulty is compounded if the subject of any proposed action by an applicant for legal aid is not only a Mason but a solicitor as well. There are cases where the decision whether or not an individual should be granted financial aid in order to pursue his case or defend himself against a case being brought against him has been in the hands of close colleagues of the applicant's counsel.

A great many of the sixty-odd members of the Law Society Council as well as a high proportion of the Society's staff and committees – one estimate puts it as high as ninety per cent of all male staff above the age of thirty – are ardent Freemasons.

I have thousands of papers on one case alone, a case so well documented it can be followed in minute detail. It involves one of the many masonic members of the Law Society Council, who had personally committed an act of gross negligence which caused one of his clients to lose a £100,000 inheritance. Deliberate action on the part of several other firms of masonic solicitors – some of the biggest names in the legal profession – acting in collusion with the original solicitor and with each other to cover up the negligence, brought the client to the edge of financial ruin. Having mortgaged his home, spent £15,000 in legal fees to lawyers who deliberately ignored his instructions, wasted valuable time and generated hundreds and hundreds of expensive, unnecessary documents, he was forced to apply to the Law Society, of which his chief opponent was an influential member, for legal aid. Finally, in 1982, after fighting masonic manipulation of the legal aid system for more than a year, and only after a direct appeal to a senior and non-masonic official in the Department of Health and Social Security, which works in tandem with the Law

Society on legal aid applications, he was granted a legal aid certificate – but on extremely onerous conditions. As this case is still not closed, and far from lost following recent unexpected developments in the client's favour, no further details can be disclosed as yet.

The term 'masonic firm' is used more often in the law than in any other profession. This is because there is a greater preponderance of companies which are exclusively run by members of the Brotherhood in this area of society than elsewhere. It refers to those firms of solicitors whose senior partners are, without exception and as part of a deliberate policy, Freemasons. In such firms, and this is equally true in London as in the provinces, most of the junior partners will also be 'on the Square'. Some masonic firms will not allow the possibility of a non-masonic partner. In these cases only existing brethren will be taken on. In some larger masonic firms there will be one, perhaps two, of the junior partners who are not Masons. These non-Masons generally never even suspect the secret allegiance of their fellow partners. At a certain stage in their career they might receive an approach from one of the Brothers within the firm – not a blunt invitation to join, but a subtle implantation of an idea, a curtain twitched gently aside. Usually if this is passed over nothing further will occur. If it is recognized and rebuffed, the non-Mason will probably be actively looking for a partnership elsewhere shortly afterwards, as work becomes unaccountably more demanding and as he finds he no longer seems to measure up to the standard expected of him. Most will not realize that it is the standard which has moved in relation to them rather than vice versa. This does not often occur as the senior men in masonic firms 'have been taught to be cautious', and do not make overtures to outsiders without having first established that the odds are in favour of a sympathetic response.

Many of the largest and most prestigious firms of solicitors in London are masonic firms. During my research for my book *Jack the Ripper: The Final Solution*, I was introduced to Ben K——, an elderly Royal Arch Freemason who had been a partner of one of these firms for more than thirty years. An avid and jocular Mason, Ben told me often how appalled he was by the frequent misuse of masonic influence, especially in his own profession. He gave me a lot of help in my researches in the early seventies and we have kept in touch since. In 1980, the year before I was commissioned to write *The Brotherhood*, he mentioned a case which had been brought to his attention by one of his friends at another top London (masonic) firm. This friend was likewise infuriated by the corruption of Masonry's precepts. The case involved blatant misuse of Freemasonry to conceal criminal conduct on the part of a senior partner in another, even more prestigious, masonic firm. At that time I was in the middle of my second novel and was convalescing from a major operation, so I did not follow it up.

In June 1981 I saw Ben again, and asked if he could get me further details. Meanwhile, I went to see the main casualty of the alleged masonic conspiracy. He was visibly shocked at how much I knew of his case. He was also a very frightened man, and told me that he was thinking of joining the Brotherhood himself for his own protection. As a result of harrowing personal experience, he had come to hate the power of Freemasonry, but believed that becoming part of it was his only hope of survival in the highly masonic world of the law. Whether or not he was right in this, it does indicate the tremendous power certain cliques of Masons can exert. It was clear that he wanted very much to speak about his experiences, that his conscience told him he should. But in the end his own sense of self-preservation triumphed and he told me regretfully that he could not help me to publicize the evils which had nearly ruined him.

All was not lost. Ben, my Royal Arch companion, phoned me late in July and said he had 'a little something' for me. We met in the Freemasons Arms in Long Acre that evening. His 'little something' was a bundle of photocopies tied up in red tape: the complete file on the case.

The story begins in 1980 at the offices of one of the most celebrated firms of solicitors in London. A fashionable yet long established company, it counts several well-known members of the nobility among its clients. Only one partner of this firm whom I shall call Gamma Delta LLB, was not a Freemason. Delta, who had been with the company for seven years, handled general litigation.

One of his senior colleagues had to take an unexpected period of leave. Delta was asked to handle the Mason's work during his absence. As he worked through the documents, familiarizing himself with the various cases, Delta became increasingly puzzled. Finally, to his horror, it dawned on him that his absent partner was engaged in corruption on a large scale. The papers made it clear that the solicitor, acting in case after case on behalf of clients seeking compensation from insurance companies, was in fact in league with the insurance companies. He would settle out of court for sums much lower than he and the insurers knew could be obtained, and he would then receive a rake-off from the insurance companies. Delta at first found it impossible to believe. 'I had no idea such things could happen,' he told another of my informants, a client of his colleague and a victim of his deliberate malpractice.

Stunned by what he had found, Delta at first did not know what he should do. At last, having checked and rechecked the papers to make certain there was no other explanation, he approached the senior partner of the firm and showed him what he had found. The senior partner immediately called a partners' meeting – and Delta was sacked on the spot. There was no explanation given, merely that his services had been dispensed with, and within two days he was on the street. Why the partners had not been as horrified as he by the conduct of his criminal colleague he could not imagine. It was only then, when he approached a barrister friend who was a Mason, that he learned that the company he had worked for had, without his ever giving it a moment's consideration, been a masonic firm. He had had the temerity to attempt to expose not a crooked and negligent lawyer, but a crooked and negligent *Freemason* lawyer. Having been found out, that Freemason was in distress. And his colleagues were all of that mould of Mason which takes it as read that, no matter what qualifying clauses appear in Masonic ritual, a fellow Mason must be extricated from distress at all costs. There was also, of course, the consideration that if the case came into the open, the inevitable publicity would harm the whole company.

The manner in which Delta was dismissed was designed to give him no credence should he talk about the documents he found. When an instant dismissal of that kind occurs in the legal profession, there is usually only one inference: the person sacked has had his hand in the till.

Delta's first move was to approach another of the leading firms in London, another 'big name' company much involved in the world of international finance. The company agreed to act for Delta in his claim against his erstwhile employers for compensation for termination of partnership. But according to an informant within this second company, which also turned out to be a masonic firm, the senior partner of the first company contacted his masonic colleagues at the top level of the second firm, and this firm (this is also documented) dropped Delta like a hot potato. Not only did they drop him after they had agreed to act, they actually then agreed to defend the first firm in any case brought against them by Delta!

Eventually, though, Delta found a solicitor who was not a Mason and, evidently fearing adverse publicity, the original firm settled out of court, paying Delta £50,000 compensation.

But even after he got his money, and set himself up in his own practice elsewhere in the country, Delta was still aware of the potential power of Masonry to ruin him, and decided that the only safe place was within.

This 'if you can't beat 'em . . .' attitude is prevalent, especially among tradesmen and the proprietors of small businesses in all parts of the country.

PART FIVE

Powers Temporal and Spiritual

CHAPTER 22

Government

Almost every local authority in the country has its own Freemasonic Lodge, the temple often situated actually within the Town or County Hall. These local government Lodges are known variously as '*A* Borough Lodge', '*B* County Lodge, '*C* Town Hall Lodge' or '*D* Council Lodge', depending where they are. In London alone there are no fewer than twenty-four Lodges which from their names in the Masonic Year Book can be identified as being based on local authorities.* There are at least as many again in Greater London whose identity is cloaked under a classical or other obscuring title like 'Harmony'.

In addition to these there are the Lodges based upon the City of London Corporation, with which I deal in Chapter 24, and the Greater London Council Lodge No 2603 for officers and members of the GLC, originally consecrated as the London County Council Lodge in 1896.

In the provinces, virtually every County Council, district council and parish council has its own Lodge.

*The boroughs of Acton, Bethnal Green, Camberwell, Finchley, Finsbury, Greenwich, Hackney, Islington, Newham, St Pancras, Shoreditch, Stepney, Woolwich; Barnet London Borough Council; City of London; City of Westminster; Greater London Council; Guildhall; Holborn Boro' Council; Lambeth Boro' Council; St Marylebone Borough Council; Tower Hamlets; Wandsworth Borough Council; Westminster City Council.

One thing is clear: the vast majority of councillors and officials join these Lodges, rather than a Lodge based on a geographical area or on an institution or profession, because they believe it increases their influence over local affairs.

How realistic is this belief, strongly denied by some but generally acknowledged by the more honest of local authority Masons, especially after one or two whiskies?

The basis for what criticism there has been of the concept of local authority Lodges is that they undermine the process of democracy.

For democracy to work at its best there has to be a party system, preferably with at least two strong parties politically at odds. The British system of democracy avoids widespread corruption in government by a series of checks and balances. One of the most important of these is an official Opposition party. The Opposition has a duty to oppose the majority party that forms the government. Only by the criticism and constant watchfulness of an Opposition can a government be kept up to the mark. The bad points of the ruling party are by this means constantly shown to the public, and if its strengths do not outweigh its weaknesses the government will eventually, in theory, fall.

This efficient system of keeping government inefficiency and corruption to a minimum can scarcely be threatened when it comes to central government, where there are so many checks and balances and where both Press and public are vigilant in the extreme. But on a local level journalists are usually in their teens or early twenties and do not have the experience or wherewithal to keep such a critical eye on the processes of democracy, and the majority of residents do not take much interest in their local authority beyond its decisions about the annual rate increase.

The parliamentary system works as well in the local council chamber as it does in the Commons – except, say the critics, where Freemasonry rears its head in the shape of a Town Hall Lodge.

Within the Lodge three things which are generally considered undesirable can happen:

(1) There is fraternization between council officers and elected members, who in the public interest should keep each other at arm's length.
(2) Party differences are broken down and men who have a duty fiercely to oppose each other in the council chamber and in all their actions on behalf of the electorate are brought together in intimate harmony.
(3) There is undesirable contact with local businessmen – builders, architects, etc. – who often join such Lodges blatantly to curry favour and exploit the masonic bond to canvass for local authority contracts.

None of these objections would be valid, perhaps, if all Freemasons scrupulously avoided discussing business, politics or religion with each other within the Temple. But of course Freemasons are human, and no matter what claims are made that such talk never goes on at masonic gatherings, there is ample evidence that it does. Additionally, there is no bar against talking business, religion or politics at the customary drinking session up which follows the ceremonies in the Temple.

The critics say that Lodges where leading members of the majority party swear an oath of allegiance to leading members of the Opposition party, and vice versa, destroy the two-party system. From there on, especially when council officers belong to the Lodge as well, democracy is finished. Whatever debate occurs in public is a façade that covers the disturbing truth that everything has been decided in advance.

Are the critics right? In 1974 Prime Minister Harold Wilson presented to Parliament the findings of his committee on local government rules of conduct. The committee had been set up in the wake of the Poulson scandal and amid growing public concern about corruption in local government. Under the chairmanship of Lord Redcliffe-Maud, the committee had produced a seventy-two-page report that analysed the problems and ended by recommending a National Code of Local Government Conduct.

On the question of fraternization between council officers and elected members, the code had this advice for councillors:

> (i) Both councillors and officers are servants of the public, and they are indispensable to one another. But their responsibilities are distinct. Councillors are responsible to the electorate and serve only so long as their term of office lasts. Officers are responsible to the council and are permanently appointed. An officer's job is to give advice to councillors and to carry out the council's work under the direction and control of councillors.
>
> (ii) Mutual respect between councillors and officers is essential to good local government. *Close personal familiarity between individual councillor and officer can damage this relationship and prove embarrassing to other councillors and officers.* [My italics.]
>
> (iii) If you are called upon to take part in appointing an officer, the only question you should consider is which candidate would best serve the whole council. You should not let your personal or political preferences influence your judgement. You should not canvass the support of colleagues for any candidate and you should resist any attempt by others to canvass yours.

Elsewhere the report deals with proper declaration of interests by councillors. Numerous minor cases of failure to declare pecuniary interests can be cited: where, for instance, a councillor discussed and voted on the arrears of rent by Council tenants without admitting that he was himself a Council tenant in arrears with his rent; or where a councillor voted on the question of his own expenses.

Failure to declare pecuniary interest is illegal. But failure to declare non-pecuniary interest is not against the law and is therefore hard to combat. Even so, a councillor can be influenced in his decisions by his connection with an organization or a person just as strongly as he can by financial considerations.

A councillor should never take part in debate or voting on such matters as a relative or friend seeking planning permission, rehousing, or employment with the council or where any other conflict of interest exists.

The report goes on:

> There are other interests which are less easily defined but where the same principles of disclosure, and usually, of non-participation, should apply. Trusteeship in a charitable body, membership of a religious denomination, a trade union, a professional association or *a society such as Freemasonry* [my italics], or even ordinary friendship, can all create situations where it is to the member's credit, and for the health of local government, if he is quite open about them.

The committee did not think that these matters needed to be covered by standing orders because what was involved was a principle rather than a procedure. And the principle should be for councillors *to treat non-pecuniary interests on the same lines as pecuniary interests* – which means very seriously indeed.

In its final recommendations, the committee again refers to kinship, friendship, membership of an association or society (Freemasonry, etc.) and other bodies and states where such membership 'can sometimes influence your judgement or give the impression [it] might do so'.

So it is acknowledged that the dangers are real enough.

But has Freemasonry ever actually undermined local democracy to any extent worth worrying about?

One does not have to look too far for the strongest evidence that it has.

In its report to the Royal Commission on Standards of Conduct in Public Life, chaired by the Rt Hon Lord Salmon between 1974 and 1976, the Society of Labour Lawyers makes this statement:

We regret the timidity of the Redcliffe-Maud Committee in their recommendations relating to the disclosure of interest. We think it essential that there should no loopholes; oral and public disclosure of all direct and indirect interests, financial and otherwise, must be made (for example) by local councillors at every meeting of council or committee in addition to a comprehensive written record; this obligation should not be avoided by a councillor absenting himself from a meeting. In case of absence his interest must be declared at the meeting at the instance of the councillor concerned by the chairman or clerk. We say 'financial or otherwise' because it is well within the experience of our members that secret decisions or understandings are reached in places which would not exist if generally known. In particular, we refer to 'town hall Lodges' which, we know, existed at each and every one of the local authorities concerned in recent criminal proceedings and almost all of the defendants were members. These Lodges take into membership leading councillors across the political divide together with a limited number of senior officers, to the prejudice of the justification of the two-party system – that of public dispute and decision – and to the prejudice of the proper relationship between councillor and officer. It is no part of our message to decry the traditions and charitable good work of the masonic movement; we imagine that the national leaders would be as distressed as anyone if they knew of the extent to which the town hall Lodges were used, at the very least, to ease communication of matters which would never have been communicated at all in the full glare of publicity. Membership of such groups as these must be subject to disclosure and if this should offend the rules and practices of an organization of the nature of Freemasons, the remedy is to dissolve Lodges based upon restricted membership of those in a local field of public life. If those concerned complain that it limits their opportunity to engage in the honourable and altruistic activities of their movement, their desires can, no doubt, fructify in the company of like-minded persons elsewhere than in or about the town hall.

The authorities referred to as being involved in criminal proceedings and all having a masonic thread running through the corruption were, among others, Bradford, Birmingham, Newcastle and Wandsworth.

The town hall Lodge at Wandsworth in south-west London was consecrated in 1903 as Wandsworth Borough Council Lodge No 2979. Its members are not only current officers and members of the council (now the London Borough of Wandsworth) but also past members and officers and others associated with local government. A number of builders, architects, civil engineers and such like belonged to the Lodge in the 1960s when masonic corruption starting there spread outwards until it engulfed and ruined national figures like former Home Secretary Reginald Maudling, himself a Freemason. As former Wandsworth Town Clerk Barry Payton told me: 'The real seriousness of the Wandsworth affair was the incestuous relationship between the two opposing leaders, Sidney Sporle and Ronald Ash. Sporle was the Labour leader. He had no visible means of support, he didn't have a job, but he nevertheless lived at a fair old rate, always having rolls of five-pound notes in his pocket. Although his home life was not in any great style, he really enjoyed entertaining and going out and being the grandiose host. He got his income through his association with certain dubious activities. Ash, the Conservative leader, was the proprietor of Lewis of Balham, a builders' merchants.'

One example of the oddity of the relationship between

Sporle and Ash was in relation to an organization called the South London Housing Consortium. This had been formed by a group of south London local authorities who were engaged in a lot of building work at that time. The object of forming the consortium was to enable the authorities to buy building materials in bulk direct from the manufacturers, thus making big savings and also being sure of obtaining materials when they were required. For a reason that has never been discovered the consortium employed Lewis of Balham as an intermediary. This negated the reason for forming a consortium in the first place: there is small point in a consortium if a middle man is used. It is interesting to speculate that if Lewis of Balham earned only one per cent for acting as intermediary, which is an improbably low rate of commission, this previously modest business would, on a turnover of £10 million, have made £100,000. And that sort of money in the late sixties was a very great sum indeed.

In the municipal election in 1968 Labour was defeated in Wandsworth and Ash became the Leader of the Council. Shortly afterwards, the new Tory controllers of the council had their first meetings to appoint committees and nominate members to outside bodies. The Conservatives' first group meeting was to consider whom to nominate as the council's representatives on the South London Housing Consortium. Ash fought tooth and nail to nominate the Labour leader, Sidney Sporle. Finally, Ash forced the issue by threatening to resign if he didn't get his way, and his members reluctantly voted for Sporle. It was not known to them that the two 'opponents' were close friends, and that their friendship had sprung from the deep ties of being Brother Masons in the same Lodge.

Sporle, now dead, was a corrupt man who used the Lodge at Wandsworth unashamedly for setting up crooked deals. Among seven charges of corruption for which he was later jailed for six years, Sporle was found guilty of taking a job from T. Dan Smith, PR man and fellow conspirator of architect John Poulson. It is generally thought that Smith, who did so much to further the interests of Poulson (himself known to have exploited his masonic membership at every opportunity), was also a member of the Brotherhood. According to what he told me, and I have no reason to disbelieve him, he is not and never has been a Freemason, however. This is what he said when we met for a cup of tea at the Charing Cross Hotel: 'People have always assumed that I am a Mason, so gradually I found the way they shook hands and the way they made the next move – and because I virtually detested them (for no reason other than that I hate that kind of organization) I always used to give them the handshake back. Still do. I met a journalist last week from the *Daily Mirror*. He gave me a Freemasonic handshake and I gave him one, and he said, "Oh, you're on the Square." He said, "As you're on the Square, why didn't you pass the money to Ted Short* *that* way?"

'I said, "Well, how do you do it that way?" He said, "Very simply. *You just pass it through the organization.*"'

There are clues that there is a well-established system within Freemasonry for passing money untraceably from one Mason to another. No fewer than seven informants within the Brotherhood as well as T. Dan Smith on the outside have told me of the system. If such a system does exist, it is probably connected with the method by which the vast sums of money collected in charity by individual

*Edward Short, MP for Newcastle Central, was an old friend of Smith's and a Freemason. He accepted £500 from Smith 'for the work you have done on behalf of the firm'. The DPP later considered prosecuting Short for accepting a bribe but decided there was no case to answer. Eleven years after the event, when it all came out, Short, by then deputy Prime Minister and Leader of the House, astonished Parliament by not resigning despite dissatisfaction with his explanation.

Lodges each year is transmitted to Grand Lodge. Until further clues come to light, however, I am unable to say more than this. It seems highly unlikely that the officers at Great Queen Street are in on the secret – unless, of course, they have some legitimate purpose for operating such a system, and this can be used by corrupt members without the knowledge of the hierarchy or the Charity trustees.

At any one time there seems to be only about thirty to sixty Freemasons in Parliament, and there is no real discernible influence by Freemasonry on voting in the Commons: even if there were a large number of masonic MPs, debates so rarely touch issues masonic that any kind of cross-party collusion by members of the Brotherhood is inconceivable. There are far greater and more important vested interests than Freemasonry at Westminster.

The majority of MPs who are Masons – witness Cecil Parkinson, Paymaster General and Chairman of the Conservative Party* – have no time to attend Lodge meetings. Those who do have the time tend to pursue their Masonry on a local level with no connection with Parliament. So far as I have been able to discover there is no House of Commons or parliamentary Lodge. Members of Margaret Thatcher's post-Falklands Cabinet* who have told me they are not members of the Brotherhood include Lord Hailsham (see pp 153–4 above), the Lord Chancellor; Sir Geoffrey Howe, Chancellor of the Exchequer; James Prior, Secretary of State for Northern Ireland; John Nott, Secretary of State for Defence; George Younger, Secretary of State for Scotland; John Biffen, Secretary of State for Trade; David Howell, Secretary of State for Transport; Leon Brittan, Chief Secretary to the Treasury; and

*Again reshuffled by Thatcher in June 1983.

Norman Tebbit, Secretary of State for Employment. Lord Carrington, Foreign Secretary before the Falklands crisis, told me he is not and never has been a Freemason. Those who ignored my letters include Home Secretary William Whitelaw, almost certainly a Mason, Sir Keith Joseph, Francis Pym, Peter Walker and Michael Heseltine. Neither Humphrey Atkins, Lord Privy Seal, nor Patrick Jenkin, Industry Secretary, wished to comment.

In the Labour, Liberal and Social Democratic parties, no senior member owns to being a Freemason now or in the past. And even Tony Benn, whom one would expect to make political capital from anything getting close to masonic influence in Parliament, has 'never heard Freemasonry mentioned'. None of the main parties has any particular policy on Freemasonry, although a Labour Party assistant information officer did say the party regarded the Brotherhood 'as a secret and select club and object to the way it undermines the National Health Service by providing private hospital beds', a reference to the Royal Masonic Hospital at Hammersmith, West London. The officer then took the sting out of her bold accusation by saying, 'The problem is that we do not know enough about it to be critical.' Even the Communist Party can muster insufficient enthusiasm to talk about the subject, and simply dislike it because in their view it reinforces the class structure.

Two men in particular seemed to have achieved high office in the Labour Party directly through membership of the Brotherhood: Attlee, Prime Minister from 1945 to 1951, and Arthur Greenwood, Deputy Leader of the party from 1935. On 22 November 1935 a masonic Lodge whose members included Transport House officials and several Labour MPs held one of its regular meetings. The party meeting to select a new Leader was fixed for 26 November. Three men were in the running. Even though Attlee was a Mason, it was Greenwood, a member of the Transport

House Lodge, who was, according to Hugh Dalton, Labour Chancellor of the Exchequer between 1945 and 1947, 'the Masons' Candidate'. In his book *The Fateful Years* Dalton wrote:

> Most members of the Lodge were closer friends of Greenwood than they were of the other two candidates, Attlee and Morrison. On the first ballot the result was Attlee 58, Morrison 44, Greenwood 33. As had been decided in advance, the bottom candidate, Greenwood, dropped out. On the second ballot, all but four of Greenwood's supporters voted for Attlee, giving him a victory over Morrison of 88 to 48.

First, of course, this is not an example of Freemasonry at work in Parliament but inside an individual party, which is quite different. Secondly, considering the facts coolly, it is hard to see much that is sinister in them. Freemasons getting together in secret to decide whom they as a group want to have as leader seems no different from the Tribunites, the Manifesto Group or any other sub group within a party doing the same thing. Were there a secret non-party band of Freemasons influencing matters behind the scenes and manipulating this Mason into power in this party and that Mason into power in that party, the matter would be somewhat different.

There have been several attempts in Parliament to initiate official enquiries into the effects of Freemasonry on society. Every one of them has failed.

On 11 April 1951, Fred Longden, MP for the Small Heath district of Birmingham, stood up in the Commons and asked Prime Minister Clement Attlee whether 'in the interests of all sides' he would move for the appointment of a Royal Commission to enquire into the effects of Freemasonry on the political, religious, social and administrative life of the country.

Foreign Secretary Herbert Morrison, a non-Mason, said, 'I have been asked to reply. No, sir. This is not a matter for which the government are responsible, and my right honourable Friend the Prime Minister does not think that an enquiry of this kind would be appropriate.'

To this, Longden said, 'As I have received a large number of letters on this question might it not be good for Freemasons themselves if, apart altogether from their rites and ceremonies, the suspicions and accusations concerning their influence on personal appointments and interference with our constitutional institutions were brought to the light of day?'

'I understand the point made by my honourable friend,' said Morrison, 'but I really think we have enough troubles without starting any more.'

Masonic MP for Kidderminster Gerald (later Sir Gerald) Nabarro sprang to his feet and said, 'Would not such an enquiry be an infringement of human liberties?', and the House passed on to the car mileage allowance of threepence-ha'penny per mile for army chaplains, the cheese ration, and to a question about a speech given in South Shields by the Home Secretary in which he had said, 'We cannot control General MacArthur because we do not pay him.'

Whitehall and the Civil Service generally is the side of central government where Freemasonry plays a part. Membership of the Brotherhood can be an important factor in promotion, especially to the ranks of the powerful Permanent Secretaries. In some ministries, Defence for example, it can be a distinct disadvantage not to be a Mason. Several people have recounted how when they were interviewed for senior positions at the Ministry of Defence, they were suddenly, in the middle, asked how they interpreted a certain biblical quotation. One of my informants, a non-Mason, could not remember the exact quotation. Both the others, one a Mason, did remember. The two quotations were not quite accurate, but amended as Masons amend them for use in their ceremonies. The Mason identified himself as such and was appointed. The two non-Masons, not knowing what to make of a request to interpret a biblical reference, were not. This might all, of course, be coincidence. We do not know how able the individuals were and how well or ill they suited the posts for which they were applying. What is certain is that the Civil Service has real and continuing power in the administration of this country, in that it remains while governments come and go; and that power is largely in the hands of members of the Brotherhood. This area of masonic influence warrants a book in itself, and will, I hope, command an entire section in future editions, when more detailed research is completed.

CHAPTER 23

The Highest in the Land

On 5 December 1952 His Royal Highness the Duke of Edinburgh, consort of the new Queen Elizabeth II, as yet uncrowned, was initiated into the secrets of Freemasonry by the Worshipful Master of Navy Lodge No 2612. He joined against his will. His uncle, Earl Mountbatten of Burma, was – in the words of an impeccable source close to the Royal Family – 'fiercely opposed' to Freemasonry, and had strongly advised Philip to have nothing to do with it. But in 1947 when Philip became engaged to Princess Elizabeth, his future father-in-law King George VI had made it plain that he expected any husband of his daughter to maintain the tradition of royal patronage of Freemasonry. George was an ardent Mason and finally extracted a promise from Philip to join the Brotherhood. George died before Philip was able to fulfil the promise, but despite his own reservations (he regarded the whole thing as a silly joke) and his uncle's hostility, he felt bound to honour his promise to the dead King.

But having been initiated to Freemasonry as an Entered Apprentice, Philip felt honour was satisfied and he was free to act as he chose – which was to forget the whole business as quickly as possible. and while still nominally a member of the Brotherhood, the Duke has taken no active part for thirty years and has refused all invitations to climb the masonic ladder and achieve grand rank.

His determination to rise no higher in the masonic hierarchy has meant that, in masonic terms, Philip is inferior in rank to thousands of commoners. This has caused much irritation in the sealed rooms of Great Queen Street, and annoyed the masonic elders considerably in the 1960s when a successor to the Earl of Scarborough, who had taken office as Grand Master the year before Philip was initiated, was being discussed. The monarch's husband, the Freemason of the highest standing in the non-masonic world, was considered the natural successor. But Philip would not have it.

Finally, in 1966, after much speculation both within Masonry and outside, the new Grand Master was named – in the William Hickey column of the *Daily Express.* He was to be the thirty-year-old Duke of Kent, the Queen's cousin, who was a major in the Royal Scots Greys stationed at Hounslow. The Duke, who was initiated into Masonry in 1964, would be following in the footsteps of his father who had been Grand Master between 1939 and 1942, when he was killed in action. Hickey's prediction came to pass and the Duke was installed as Grand Master by the Earl of Scarborough at the greatest masonic spectacular of all time – the 250th anniversary celebrations at the Royal Albert Hall in June 1967 when Masons from all over the world attended in full regalia and Arab Mason walked with Israeli Mason only ten days after the Six Day War.

Philip's apathy and Mountbatten's antipathy have had their effect on Prince Charles, the heir to the throne. Mountbatten, as Charles' favourite uncle, made a lasting impression on the future King and Charles remains adamant, despite rumours to the contrary, that he does not wish to become a Freemason. A greater influence in this direction than either his father or his uncle, however, has been his grandmother, Queen Elizabeth the Queen Mother, who had much of the responsibility for Charles' upbringing when his parents were travelling. The Queen Mother, despite – perhaps because of – being the wife of a devoted Freemason, does not approve of the Brotherhood. She is a committed Bible-believing Christian and, largely due to her influence, Prince Charles too is a committed (as opposed to nominal) Christian.

Great pressure was brought to bear on Charles when he was in his early and mid-twenties to follow family tradition and become a Freemason. It was assumed by high Masons that when Charles reached his twenty-first birthday in 1969, he would be initiated and take over from the Duke of Kent. He refused to be pressed into doing so, and when approached he gave an emphatic 'No', adding, 'I do not want to join any secret society.' When he was twenty-five the *Sunday Mirror* published an article by Audrey Whiting, described in her byline as 'an authoritative writer on Royal affairs'. She said that the pressure brought to bear on Charles to become a Mason had been 'considerable'. She continued:

> If he persists [in refusing] he will become in due time the first monarch in centuries who has not been the titular head of Freemasonry in Britain . . . Freemasonry will survive and flourish, as it does today, without a monarch as its titular head – but the Prince's refusal to adopt the traditional role in [the] ranks of Masonry as heir to the Throne was and is a great blow to a body of men who are above all traditionalists.

But by this time there was talk that Charles 'was not strictly against Freemasonry', but that he simply had no wish to become involved. According to Whiting, he wanted to prove himself as a man 'who can meet and beat all the tests which could face a fighting man and an adventurer'.

A senior court official told me: 'The answer is that without benefit, if you can call it that, of wartime experience, Charles is determined to be as good as his father – and perhaps even better.'

The question remains: Will Charles, in the end, conform to tradition?

Despite rumours that the Prince had suggested that 'if' he joined the Brotherhood, it would be as an initiate to the Royal Air Force Lodge No 7335, there is still no indication that Charles has changed his attitude.

I failed miserably to ascertain more clearly Charles's current thinking on the subject. The Court is brimming with Freemasons and my own enquiries never got past Charles's masonic private secretary, the Hon Edward Adeane. Adeane, son of Lt-Col the Rt Hon Lord (Michael) Adeane, former private secretary to the Queen and Freemason of Grand Rank, refused to ask the Prince if he would be prepared to say why he had decided to go against tradition. He told me: 'The basis for the suggestion that His Royal Highness has any view on the matter at all depends purely on speculative statements in the press, and the Prince of Wales does not comment on other people's speculation.'

The first part of this statement was really not true for anyone who had contacts within the Grand Lodge, the Palace or at Windsor. The suggestion that the Prince had views on the matter was *not* a matter of speculation. However, I wrote back asking if I might rephrase my question in the light of Adeane's statement: 'Rather than asking why the Prince has taken a stand, which I now realize to be in doubt, can I ask the Prince what his thinking is on the subject of Freemasonry, not necessarily whether he intends joining the movement or not, but simply his thoughts on the organization?' I received a two-line reply. The first line thanked me for my letter. The second said: 'I am afraid that I cannot assist you in this matter.'

It is an interesting anomaly that the Queen, as a woman, is banned from entering a masonic temple – yet she is Grand Patroness of the movement. Her two younger sons are already marked down by the elders of Great Queen Street as possible future Grand Masters, should they not go the way of their brother Charles. Prince Michael of Kent is already a Brother of Grand Rank, having been Senior Grand Warden in 1979.

CHAPTER 24

The City of London

As darkness closed in on the City of London in the late afternoon of 16 February 1982, a number of influential men converged on the ancient Guildhall, seat of the City's medieval-style government. They came in taxis, in chauffeur-driven limousines, and on foot. They came from all parts of the City - and beyond. Between them they represented a wide spectrum of wealth and power. Their decisions, in the worlds of high finance, the law, industry, international trade and commerce and politics, affected the lives of thousands.

Each of the men, beneath his outer garments, wore a dark lounge suit, and most of them carried small oblong cases, some inscribed in gold leaf with the owner's initials. These cases contained the regalia the men would put on when they reached their destination. The men came from different directions and entered the Guildhall by various entrances. Some came across Guildhall Yard, some along Aldermanbury, some by way of Masons Avenue. Once inside the Hall, each turned his steps towards the Crypt, which was cordoned off so that no intruder could make his way down the stair and report the goings-on to any 'Gentile'. A Tyler, or Outer Guard, was posted at the door to block the path of any stranger who might slip past the Guildhall commissionaire.

At precisely 5.15 P.M. the participants in the drama which was to be acted out had gathered in the Crypt, which had been transformed into a Masonic Temple. The brethren of Guildhall Lodge No 3116 took their places. Outgoing Worshipful Master Brother Frank Nathaniel Steiner, MA, knocked once with his gavel. The sound echoed around the East Crypt with its low vaulted ceiling and clustered pillars of Purbeck marble. The coat of arms of Sir Bernard Waley-Cohen, a member and former Worshipful Master of the Lodge, had pride of place at one of the six intersections of the vaulting, because he had been Lord Mayor when the Crypt was restored in 1961. Other coats of arms included those of Edward the Confessor, Henry IV, in whose reign the Crypt was built, and Queen Elizabeth II. A masonic prince among royal princes.

Two knocks, like echoes of the first, followed in quick succession from the Senior Warden and the Junior Warden.

'Brethren,' said Worshipful Brother Steiner solemnly, 'assist me to open the Lodge . . .' Addressing the Junior Warden, Steiner continued, '. . . what is the first care of every Mason?'

'To see that the Lodge is properly tyled.'

'Direct that duty to be done.'

The installation ceremony of Worshipful Brother Charles Richard Coward, JP, as Worshipful Master of the Lodge for 1982–3 had begun.

The Guildhall Lodge was consecrated at the Mansion House, the official residence of the Lord Mayor of London, on Tuesday, 14 November 1905. Since then, no fewer than sixty-two Lord Mayors have been Masters of the Lodge, whose membership comprises both elected members of the Corporation of London and its salaried officers.

The Worshipful Master of the Lodge both in 1981–2 and 1982–3 was not the Lord Mayor, because neither was a

Freemason. So Steiner, Common Councilman for Bread Street Ward and Deputy Grand Registrar of the United Grand Lodge, was elected in place of Col Sir Ronald Gardner-Thorpe, and Coward in what would have been the natural place of the Lord Mayor, the Rt Hon Sir Christopher Leaver, had he been of the Brotherhood.

The Lodge was opened in the First Degree. The ritual dismissal of the Entered Apprentices was intoned. The Lodge was opened in the Second Degree. Worshipful Brother Coward, Senior Grand Deacon of the United Grand Lodge, stood waiting to be presented to the Installing Master. He wore a lambskin apron lined with garter-blue, ornamented with gold and blue strings and bearing the emblem of his rank. A four-inch-wide band of garter-blue ribbon embroidered with a design combining an ear of corn and a sprig of acacia lay on his shoulders and formed a V on his breast.

Among the brethren in the temple were Anthony Stuart Joliffe, Alderman and Sheriff of the City of London, director of numerous companies including SAS Catering Ltd, Nikko Hillier International Trading Co Ltd, Capital for Industry Ltd, Marlborough Property Holdings (Developments) Ltd, and Albany Commercial and Industrial Developments Ltd. Joliffe, Senior Warden of the Lodge for the current year, has been vice president of the European League for Economic Co-operation, Hon Treasurer of Britain in Europe Residual Fund, and a trustee of the Police Foundation, and he has held many other influential positions.

Also in the Crypt that night was the Lodge Chaplain, Christopher Selwyn Priestley Rawson, chairman and managing director of Christopher Rawson Ltd, an underwriting Member of Lloyd's, and an honorary member of the Metal Exchange. As a Freemason of London Grand

Rank, he wore a collar of garter-blue ribbon with narrow edging.

Installing Master Steiner proceeded with the ceremonial listing of qualities which Worshipful Brother Coward would need as Master: to be of good report, well skilled in Masonry, exemplary in conduct, steady and firm in principle. The secretary of the Lodge then addressed the Master Elect and recited a fifteen-point summary of the Ancient Charges and Regulations.

Steiner then asked Coward, 'Do you submit to and promise to support these Charges and Regulations as Masters have done in all ages?' Coward replied by placing his right hand on his left breast with the thumb squared upwards. This, the 'sign of fidelity', meant 'I do', and the ceremony continued as he swore on the Bible faithfully to discharge the duties of Master and to abide by Masonry's 'Landmarks'.

The ritual went on and on. When all but Installed Masters had been dismissed from the Crypt, the 'secrets of the Chair' were communicated to Worshipful Brother Coward. Bent on both knees, he took a second oath, with his hands resting on the Bible. There had been no penalty attached to the first obligation. But now Coward faced having his 'right hand struck off and slung over my left shoulder, there to wither and decay', if he betrayed his oath. After more ceremony he was told the secret sign of the Installed Master (a beckoning movement made three times with the right hand); the secret grip (whereby two Installed Masters place their left hands on each other's left shoulder while keeping their arms straight); the secret word (Giblum, meaning Excellent Mason); and finally the sign of Salutation ('Bowing and saluting with the right hand from the forehead three times, stepping backwards with the right foot').

At the end of this long ceremony, with all those of lower degree recalled from the Crypt, Worshipful Brother Coward, now Master of the Lodge, invested the officers of the Lodge for 1982–3 as follows:

IMMEDIATE PAST MASTER: W. Bro. Frank N. Steiner, MA, Deputy Grand Registrar of the United Grand Lodge 1981–2; Common Councilman, Bread Street Ward.

SENIOR WARDEN: Bro. Alderman and Sheriff Anthony S. Joliffe, Fellow of the Institute of Chartered Accountants; Justice of the Peace; Alderman for Candlewick Ward.

JUNIOR WARDEN: Bro. Rev Basil A. Watson, OBE, MA, RN.

CHAPLAIN: W. Bro. Alderman Christopher Rawson, Former City Sheriff; Common Councilman (Bread Street) 1963–72; Alderman (Lime Street); Associate of Textile Industries; Associate of the Institute of Marine Engineers.

TREASURER: W. Bro. Frank N. Steiner, MA.

SECRETARY: W. Bro. Deputy H. Derek Balls, Justice of the Peace; Deputy (Cripplegate Without).

DIRECTOR OF CEREMONIES: W. Bro. Sir John Newson-Smith, Bt, MA, former Lord Mayor of London; Deputy Lieutenant, City of London, 1947; Member of HM Commission of Lieutenancy for the City of London; Deputy Chairman, London United Investments Ltd.

SENIOR DEACON: W. Bro. Michael H. Hinton.

JUNIOR DEACON: Bro. David M. Shalit, Common Councilman (Farringdon Within).

CHARITY STEWARD: W. Bro. Richard Theodore Beck, Fellow of the Royal Institute of British Architects; Fellow of the Society of Antiquaries; Fellow of the Royal Society of Arts; Member of the Royal Town Planning Institute; Deputy (Farringdon Within); Sheriff of the

City of London 1969–70; Prestonian Lecturer (*the* annual masonic lecture delivered at Freemasons Hall, London), 1975.

ALMONER: W. Bro. Matthew Henry Oram, TD, MA, Common Councilman (Cordwainer).

ASSISTANT DIRECTOR OF CEREMONIES: W. Bro. Colin Frederick Walter Dyer, ERD, Past Assistant Grand Director of Ceremonies and Past Junior Grand Deacon of the United Grand Lodge; Common Councilman (Aldgate); Prestonian Lecturer 1973.

INNER GUARD: W. Bro. Gerald Maurice Stitcher, CBE; Past Grand Standard Bearer of the United Grand Lodge; Common Councilman (Farringdon Without).

STEWARD: Bro. Deputy Arthur Brian Wilson; Deputy (Aldersgate).

Between them, these men play vital roles in all aspects of the running of the City – including police, housing, education, social services, town planning and the courts of law.

As Senior Warden of the Guildhall Lodge, Anthony Joliffe was the front runner for Master of the Lodge in 1983–4. This was no accident as he was to be and became Lord Mayor during the same period.

Ancient institutions survive and hold sway in the City of London more than anywhere else in Britain. Although the City is one of the most important financial and business centres in the world, medieval custom and tradition are apparent everywhere. Even the Bank of England, the nationalized central bank which holds our gold reserves, conducts the government's monetary policy, regulates lending and finances the national debt, retains its 'Old Lady of Threadneedle Street' image, its messengers or waiters wearing pink waistcoats and top hats as they go about their time-honoured business. Once a year the Worshipful Company of Butchers presents the Lord Mayor with a boar's head on a silver platter, exactly as it did in the fourteenth century. The Port of London Authority's garden in Seething Lane is leased to the Corporation as a public amenity for an annual rent of a nosegay. Every October at the Royal Courts of Justice the Corporation's legal officer – the Comptroller and City Solicitor – pays the Queen's Remembrancer a hatchet, a bill hook, six horses and sixty-one nails – the so-called Quit Rents for two of the City's holdings, the Forge in St Clement Danes and the Moors in Shropshire. 'The City's institutions are as varied as they are ancient,' wrote the late Blake Ehrlich.

> Five 'wise men' set the world price of bullion in the opulent Gold Room of N. M. Rothschild and Sons,* St Swithin's Lane, at 10.30 each morning, but, before these gentlemen are out of bed, the gentlemen from the Fishmongers Guild, their boots silvered with fish scales, are exercising their immemorial functions down by the river at Billingsgate, London's fish market. On the other side of the City, predawn buyers eye hook-hung carcasses at Smithfield, the world's largest dressed-meat market. Nearby nurses begin to prepare patients for surgery at St Bartholomew's ('Bart's), London's first hospital (founded 1123) and the place where, in the 17th century, William Harvey first demonstrated the circulation of the blood. Closer to St Paul's Cathedral, the vans begin to deliver prisoners whose cases will be heard that day at Old Bailey, as the Central Criminal Court is known, where most of Britain's sensational murder trials have been held.

These daily occurrences, the mundane modern mingled inextricably with the flavour of the Middle Ages, are what lend the City its unique life.

Only the sovereign takes precedence over the Lord Mayor within the City's square mile. Even the Prime

*The Rothschilds have been Freemasons for generations.

Minister – *even* Margaret Thatcher – will walk behind the Mayor in official processions through the City.

The City is not entirely an island in the river of time. It is rather a place where two historical clocks are running: one which for the past thousand years has been going so slowly that its hands have picked up the ceremonial dust of the centuries, of which very little has been lost; the other which operates with the impeccable efficiency of quartz crystal. It is the continuing belief in the importance of ancient tradition which is largely responsible for the undying strength of Freemasonry: for Freemasonry underpins all the great and influential institutions of the Square Mile. According to confidential statistics from Great Queen Street, there are 1,677 Lodges in London. Hundreds of these are in the City. Between the hours of eight in the morning and six at night when the City's residential population of about 4,000 swells to 345,000 with the influx of commuters, the Square Mile has the highest density of Freemasons anywhere in Britain.

The Royal Exchange, the Corn Exchange, the Baltic Exchange, the Metal Exchange, the Bank of England, the merchant banks, the insurance companies, the mercantile houses, the Old Bailey, the Inns of Court, the Guildhall, the schools and colleges, the ancient markets, all of them have Freemasons in significant positions. Among the institutions with their own Lodges are the Baltic Exchange (Baltic Lodge No 3006 which has its own temple actually in the Exchange in St Mary Axe); the Bank of England (Bank of England Lodge No 263); and Lloyd's (Black Horse of Lombard Street Lodge No 4155).

Like any local authority – and like central government itself – the City Corporation is formed of a council of elected representatives (the Aldermen, Deputies and Common

Council) and of salaried permanent officers whose job it is to advise the council and execute its decisions. For administrative purposes the City is divided into twenty-five wards. Ten of these wards have their own Lodges.* Five of the six Common Councilmen representing Aldersgate Ward – Arthur Brian Wilson (Deputy), Hyman Liss, Edwin Stephen Wilson, Bernard Joseph Brown, JP, and Peter George Robert Sayles – are Freemasons. Only Michael John Cassidy is, at the time of writing, not a member of the Brotherhood. Every ward, without exception, has at least one Freemason among its representatives.

One Common Councilman who openly admits he is a Freemason spoke to me about the commonly held belief that there is an immense Freemasonic influence on affairs in the City. He asked me not to identify him as it would put him in 'bad odour' with his brethren.

'I have never noticed any direct masonic influence. It's always *there*, one accepts that, always just beneath the surface as it were, but I would say the City is run more on an Old Boys network than on a Freemasonry network, just as somewhere you meet people and get to know them and presumably get chummy with them. I wouldn't have thought there's much influence. You see, we read about that scandal in Italy – P2 wasn't it? – I can't believe it's true. I don't think Freemasonry had anything to do with it.' (See Chapter 26, below.)

I asked if he knew how many of his fellow Common Councilmen were Freemasons.

'No, but I'd have thought the majority. Certainly if you

*Aldgate Ward Lodge No 3939; Billingsgate Lodge No 3443 (mainly for those associated with Billingsgate Fish Market); Bishopsgate Lodge No 2396; Cordwainer Ward Lodge No 2241; Cornhill Lodge No 1803; Cripplegate Lodge No 1613; Farringdon Without Lodge No 1745; Langbourn Lodge No 6795; Portsoken Lodge No 5088; and Tower Lodge No 5159.

count out the Roman Catholics and the women I should think the great majority. Probably some of the younger ones aren't. It's rather an old man's game, let's face it. Youngsters don't really want to get involved in these sort of things. They've got more interesting things to do. I should have thought two-thirds of the older ones are Masons. By older, I mean those past fifty. I certainly know personally a lot who are. A lot in the Lodge I'm in are on the Common Council.'

'*Do all Freemasons vote together?*'

'If the strength of the vote I've often got when I've put up is any indication, I'd have thought that none of them voted for me. I don't think there's anything in that suggestion. I've had some very bad votes when I've put up for things and I'm quite a prominent member, and if Freemasonry had done me any good I'd certainly have got a great many more votes than I got.'

Frederick Clearey, CBE, Deputy of Coleman Street Ward, told me, 'I have been a member of only one Lodge, Old Owens No 4440, my school Lodge, but I think Freemasonry engenders a very fine spirit, cementing members of the Lodge with the school. I believe too many people feel that Freemasonry is some secret society where members rush about making signs and getting business from each other which, of course, is utterly untrue. In my experience it has generated an enormous amount of friendship, goodwill and charity, which is what Freemasonry is about.'

All the main salaried officers of the Corporation are Masons. Indeed, it is virtually impossible to reach a high position in Guildhall without being an active Brother, as three senior officers currently serving and two past officers have informed me. The subject of Masonry is spoken about openly in interviews for high posts. At the time of writing, the Town Clerk, the Chamberlain, the City Marshal, the

Hall Keeper, the City Solicitor, the City Architect and the City Engineer are all members of the Brotherhood.

One of the first steps I took in looking into the extent of Freemasonry within the Corporation of London was to write to every male member of the Common Council including all Deputies, Aldermen and Sheriffs, setting out the purpose of my book and asking each recipient if he would be prepared to tell me if he was, or ever had been, a Freemason. I telephoned the general enquiry office at the Guildhall and explained I was writing to each member in connection with a book which included a section on the City – studiously avoiding any reference to Masonry. I asked if I might deliver the letters by hand, rather than separately post 153 letters to the same address. The lady I spoke to assured me I could, that it would cause no problems whatever, and, after checking with her superior, she said that when I arrived at the Guildhall I should ask for a particular official. I followed these instructions and later that day a commissionaire showed me into the appropriate office.

The official remained seated, looked up as if irritated that I should have disturbed the sanctity of his glass-sided booth overlooking Guildhall Yard, and said nothing.

'Hello,' I said, in my friendly way.

'Yes?' he said curtly. 'What is it?' Even then I thought he might ask me to take a seat, but I was disappointed.

'I wonder if you'll help,' I began. 'I'm writing a book which will have a section devoted to the City of London and a lady in your enquiry office said I could deliver these letters to the members of the Common Council by hand to you.'

'Oh, no,' he said, looking dismissively back at the papers on his desk. 'We can't accept them.' It was apparent that he regarded that as the final word in the matter and that he expected me to withdraw.

I sat down and, hail-fellow-well-met, asked him how one went about writing to the members.

'I can't help you,' he said.

'Presumably, if I posted all these to the Guildhall, they would arrive in a bundle like this and be distributed to the people concerned?'

'Presumably.' Still he didn't look up.

'I can't see the difference between the GPO delivering them in a bundle and me delivering them in a bundle. Do you have a Post Room to which I could deliver them . . . ?'

'That's impossible. If I accept your letters, I'll have to accept everyone's.'

'But the Post Room . . . ?' No, I knew I was flogging a dead horse. On impulse, as I rose to leave, I thrust my hand into his and gave him the handshake of the Master Mason, applying distinct pressure with my thumb between his second and third joints.

His attitude changed completely.

Now he was giving me all his attention. 'I'm sorry,' he said, with a sheepish sort of grin, and got up from his chair. He came round to my side of the desk and said, 'I think the best thing you can do is go upstairs to the enquiry office, tell them I sent you and say you'd like a list of the addresses of all members of the Council. That will be much the quickest way of contacting them all.'

Now very solicitous and quite the genial host, he accompanied me to the door, repeated the directions, shook my hand again and wished me well. I followed his advice and it proved sound.

Brother official had helped another member of the Brotherhood – or thought he had.

The influential Livery Companies are almost entirely peopled by Freemasons. Like the Brotherhood, the Livery

Companies – the name derives from the ceremonial dress of members – have developed from the medieval craftsmen's guilds and from religious or social fraternities. Some companies are involved in education and some are influential in the operation of their trade. There are close links between the guilds and livery companies and the Corporation: the City and Guilds of London Institute, set up in 1878 to promote education in technical subjects and set examinations, is a joint venture. And the Lord Mayor of London is selected each year from two of the city's twenty-six aldermen who are nominated by the 15,000 liverymen. To qualify for membership of one of the livery companies, a man must be a Freeman of the City, an honour generally awarded by Freemasons to Freemasons, although there are many notable exceptions. A number of Livery Companies have their own Lodges* and the City Livery Club has its own temple. A masonic alderman told me: 'There are so many competing bodies, especially in the City. What with Livery Companies, Rotary, Chamber of Commerce, Ward clubs, there are so *many* competing clubs. I would have thought that most people in the City attach much more importance to their Livery than they do to their Freemasonry – although of course the majority of Livery Club members are Freemasons as well.'

The Corporation of the City of London is so strongly masonic that many connected with it, some Masons included, think of it as virtually an arm of Grand Lodge. But it must not be forgotten that the City is first and foremost a financial centre. And money to a successful financier – Freemason or not – speaks louder than anything. When it comes to a choice between serving

*Basketmakers Lodge No 5639; Blacksmiths Lodge No 7175; Cutlers Lodge No 2730; Farriers Lodge No 6305; Feltmakers Lodge No 3839; Paviors Lodge No 5646; Plaisterers Lodge No 7390; Needlemakers Lodge No 4343, etc., etc.

Mammon and serving the Brotherhood, all but a few Freemasons in the City act upon the masonic principle enshrined in the fifth paragraph of *The Universal Book of Craft Masonry*, which declares, 'Freemasonry distinctly teaches that a man's first duty is to *himself*...'

CHAPTER 25

The Devil in Disguise?

Enemies of the Brotherhood have been denouncing its rituals as devil worship for more than 250 years. One of my purposes was to discover if these denunciations were true or false. Another was to try to resolve, by taking an entirely new approach, the continuing problem of whether or not Masonry was compatible with Christianity.

For the average reader, the difficulty of overcoming any religious objections to Freemasonry is increased rather than lessened by the very abundance of printed matter on the subject. Much of the vast literature of Masonry is devoted to religious issues. The problem is further aggravated by the extreme unreliability of a large portion of this bibliography, wherein scurrilous tirade frequently masquerades as learned treatise.

Almost everything written so far on Freemasonry and religion has fallen into one of two categories: arguments attacking Masonry by non- or anti-Masons, and arguments defending Masonry by committed Masons. There is virtually nothing from neutral outsiders. This, then, would be my approach: as a neutral investigator holding no brief for Christianity and no automatic aversion to devil worship. For the purposes of the investigation, I would suspend moral judgement, admit no good, bad, right or wrong because these could only confuse the issue further. The questions were: Is Freemasonry compatible with

Christianity? and, Is masonic ritual, or any element of it, diabolism? By sticking to these and looking unemotionally at facts, both questions were surely capable of a yes or no answer. The reader could then make his or her own moral judgements.

Another part of my 'new approach' was to avoid the sophisticated theological arguments which have inevitably entered – in fact dominated – the debate. In fact the answers can be arrived at simply and on strictly logical grounds. One does not have to be a theologian – nor even a Freemason or a Christian – to recognize that Christians and Freemasons would have to worship the same God for the two to be compatible. The question simply, then, is do they? If Freemasonry were found, despite its protestations to the contrary, to be a quasi-religion and to have a different god from the Christian god, then the two would naturally be incompatible.

It has been said that these issues are of no concern to Freemasons, but hundreds of members of the Brotherhood have spoken to me of the turmoil they experience in attempting to reconcile their religious views with the demands of masonic ritual. It is of obvious importance to a section of those interested in Freemasonry, whether they be initiates or among the ranks of the 'profane', to attempt to find some answers which can be understood without profound religious knowledge.

First, then, is Freemasonry a religion?

The Rev Saul Amias takes the official masonic line in saying that Freemasonry is neither a religion nor a substitute for religion.

'There are Christians, there are Moslems, there are members of every religion in Freemasonry,' he told me. 'Catholics are not allowed by their own church to become Masons, although some do come in. There's nothing incompatible with my religion as a Jew, as an orthodox

Jew, in Freemasonry, nothing at all. It is not a religion.'

Other Masons told me that Freemasonry is no more a religion than are Rotary Clubs or tennis clubs. Amias agreed with this.

'But,' I objected, 'the Rotary Club and the tennis club do not meet in such solemn environs. You have a masonic *temple*. You have an *altar*. You *kneel* before your *deity*, the Great Architect. You swear oaths on your *Volume of Sacred Law* – the Bible, the Koran, whatever is deemed most appropriate. All these are surely religious trappings?'

He replied, 'Agreed. But these are to *enhance* the individual Mason's belief in his God. *Vouchsafe Thine Aid, Almighty Father, Supreme Governor of the Universe, to our present convention, and grant that this candidate for Freemasonry may so be endowed* . . . and so on. This is a prayer to the *Almighty* that is said by the chaplain, in the case of my Lodge, by myself. A prayer to Almighty God in whom Jews and Christians believe. This is to enhance it, to encourage it. But we do not pray and worship to a masonic God. There is no idol.'

A former Freemason, City of London merchant banker Andrew Arbuthnot, was also able to speak on the question with the knowledge of an initiate. He told me: 'If you take a purely objective view of religions in the plural, one has to accept that Freemasonry is a religion. It induces a sense of brotherhood and togetherness by means of a secret society, which always gives that sense, but it leads people towards the thought of a Supreme Being, to the transcendental. It is at least as much a religion as the average, dry Church of England conventional matins service.'

When Walton Hannah's *Darkness Visible* appeared in 1952, it caused a sensation. This book alone deals conclusively with the matter of whether or not Masonry is a religion as well as reproducing word for word the entire ritual of Freemasonry in the three Craft degrees and concluding that Masonry and Christianity are not compatible. Following its publication, an Anglican vicar who, unlike Hannah, was a Freemason, wrote a book under the pseudonym Vindex, which was entitled *Light Invisible*. This was subtitled: *The Freemason's Answer to Darkness Visible*, and sought to disprove Hannah's assertion that Masonry and Christianity were incompatible. Where the book is valuable, however, is in confirming that Masonry does in fact regard itself as a religion, whatever it might tell outsiders:

> We now come to the core of the matter. What *is* the religion of Freemasonry?
>
> *It is the oldest of all religious systems, dating from time immemorial* [my italics]. It is not in itself a separate religion, and has never claimed to be one, but it embodies in itself the fundamental truths and ancient mysteries on which every religion is based. Taunts that it worships a 'common denominator' God are rather wide of the mark if the phrase indicates any inadequacy or limitation in nature or title of the God we worship, for we worship and believe as a first principle in the fullness of the Godhead of which other religions see only in part.

This 'Total God' which Freemasonry claims for itself is not presented to potential initiates as such. Thousands of practising Christians in Britain today worship the Freemasonic God believing it to be precisely the same as the Christian God, *if they will it*. This is perhaps the most prevalent misunderstanding by the average Freemason of his own Brotherhood.

Candidates for initiation are told that one of the basic qualifications for membership is belief in a Supreme Being of some kind – Jehovah, Allah, the Holy Trinity of Christianity, it does not matter. So long as this belief is present, then whichever divine creator an individual Freemason wishes to follow can be accommodated under the masonic umbrella term for all Supreme Beings (the impossibility of more than one Supreme Being is ignored), that of Great Architect of the Universe,* or sometimes the Grand Geometrician, who created everything with one sweep of His divine compasses. As Vindex puts it in his general downgrading of all the Faiths as mere parts of the Masonic Whole:

> As Masons, we believe in God, the Father, Almighty. As Christian Masons we may believe in a symbolical triune essence, and that Jesus Christ is His Son, Our Lord. As Moslem Masons we are equally entitled to believe that Mahomet is His prophet. With these subsidiary and secondary beliefs Masonry has nothing to do, giving her members a perfect liberty to interpret the Godhead as they please.

This is what Freemasons are taught, and this is what the majority of Freemasons believe. Even if it were true, there is enough in this statement to show that Masonry and Christianity are mutually exclusive. Because in this official view propounded by Vindex for public digestion, the very essence of Christianity is obliterated. In Masonry, we learn, Christ is not God but man – in Vindex's estimation the man who showed 'more than any other man who ever lived' what God is like. He later adds: 'I for one can never understand how anyone who takes an exclusive view of Christ as the only complete revelation of God's truth can become a Freemason without suffering from spiritual schizophrenia.'

There are many people who would agree with this non-exclusivity of Christ's teaching. But Christianity does not agree with it. The definition of a Christian is one who believes in Christ's teachings. And Christ taught, rightly or wrongly, '. . . no one cometh unto the Father, but by me'.

Therefore Vindex, although an Anglican cleric, was not a

*Denoted in printed masonic rituals as TGAOTU.

Christian. And the Freemasonic God he describes is not a Christian one.

Earlier I used the words 'even if it were true' when referring to the statement made by Vindex and by Freemasonry of the nature of the Masonic God. I did this because the assurance given to candidates that the name Great Architect of the Universe can be applied to whatever Supreme Being they choose is worse than misleading: it is a blatant lie.

In fact the Masonic God – cloaked under the description Great Architect – has a specific name and a particular nature, which has nothing to do with Christ, Vishnu, Buddha, Mohammed or any other being recognized by the great faiths of the modern world.

Two-thirds of Freemasons never realize the untruth of the line they are fed as to the identity of the Great Architect, because it is deliberately kept hidden from them. It is no overstatement to say that most Freemasons, even those without strong religious convictions, would never have joined the Brotherhood if they had not been victims of this subtle trick.

The true name, although not the nature, of the Masonic God is revealed only to those Third Degree Masons who elect to be 'exalted' to the Holy Royal Arch. The Royal Arch is often thought of as the Fourth Degree (but as explained in Chapter 5, the Fourth Degree is that of Secret Master), by others as a 'side degree'. In fact the Royal Arch is an extension of the Third Degree, and represents the completion of the 'ordeal' of the Master Mason. Only about one-fifth of all Master Masons are exalted. But even these, who are taught the 'ineffable name' of the masonic God, do not appreciate its true nature. This is basically because of deliberate obfuscation of the truth by some of those who know, and a general acceptance that everything is as they are told by most members of the Brotherhood.

In the ritual of exaltation, the name of the Great Architect of the Universe is revealed as JAH-BUL-ON – not a general umbrella term open to any interpretation an individual Freemason might choose, but a precise designation that describes a specific supernatural being – a compound deity composed of three separate personalities fused in one. Each syllable of the 'ineffable name' represents one personality of this Trinity:

JAH = Jahweh, the God of the Hebrews.
BUL = Baal, the ancient Canaanite fertility god associated with 'licentious rites of imitative magic'.
ON = Osiris, the Ancient Egyptian god of the underworld.

Baal, of course, was the 'false god' with whom Jahweh competed for the allegiance of the Israelites in the Old Testament. But more recently, within a hundred years of the creation of the Freemason's God, the sixteenth-century demonologist John Weir identified Baal as a devil. This grotesque manifestation of evil had the body of a spider and three heads – those of a man, a toad and a cat. A description of Baal to be found in de Plancy's *Dictionary of Witchcraft* is particularly apposite when considered in the light of the secretive and deceptive nature of Freemasonry: his voice was raucous, and he taught his followers guile, cunning and the ability to become invisible.

In 1873, the renowned masonic author and historian General Albert Pike, later to become Grand Commander of the Southern Jurisdiction of the Supreme Council (of the 33rd Degree) at Charleston, USA, wrote of his reaction on learning of Jah-Bul-On. He was disquieted and disgusted by the name, and went on: 'No man or body of men can make me accept as a sacred word, as a symbol of the infinite and eternal Godhead, a mongrel word, in part composed of the name of an accursed and beastly heathen god, whose name has been for more than two thousand years an appellation of the Devil.'

I have spoken to no less than fifty-seven long-standing Royal Arch Freemasons who have been happy to talk to me, to help me in my ambition to give Freemasonry 'a fair crack of the whip'. Most of them spoke quite freely, explaining without hesitation their views, reactions and answers to the criticisms and queries I raised. However, all but four lost their self-assurance and composure when I said, 'What about Jah-Bul-On?' Some, although they had previously told me they had been exalted to the Royal Arch, and therefore must have not only received the lecture on the name but also studied the passages and enacted the ritual relating to Jah-Bul-On, said they had never heard of it. In most cases the interviewees very rapidly brought the meeting to a close when I asked the question. Others laughed unconvincingly and extricated themselves from having to reply by jauntily saying such words as, 'Oh, that old chestnut', and passing quickly on to some other subject, normally going on the offensive with something like, 'Why are you so interested in Freemasonry in particular? Why don't you look into Christianity or something? Why do people always pick on Freemasonry?' – thereby diverting the conversation from the course I had plotted. If I insisted on returning to Jah-Bul-On, almost invariably the interview would be unceremoniously terminated. Others said that although they had heard of the word, they did not know what it meant. To them it meant God, and previously erudite Freemasons, with a precise knowledge of every other aspect of Masonry we had discussed, suddenly became vague and claimed ignorance of this most central of all Freemasonic subjects. While professing an almost total lack of knowledge of Jah-Bul-On, several dismissed it as of no real importance.

Charles Stratton, one Royal Arch Freemason for whom I have the utmost admiration, told me this of Jah-Bul-On: 'No one ever has time to think about its meaning, you're too busy trying to remember your words. As far as I know it's just another name for Jehovah.'

Acute silences, chiefly of embarrassment, followed my question on many occasions, as happened when I spoke to a most co-operative officer both of Grand Lodge and Grand Chapter.

We had been discussing whether or not Freemasonry was a religion, and I had run through my customary list of religious terms used in Freemasonry. Then I added, 'One comes across the phrase, "the *sacred* tenets of Freemasonry". This seems to imply that Masonry thinks of itself as a religion.'

The Grand Officer replied, 'No, I haven't said that . . . the *sacred* tenets?'

'Yes.'

'Well, the word sacred means holy.'

'Yes. Then there's the "Holy" Royal Arch.'

He paused. When he began to speak again it was much more slowly.

'Yes. The Holy Royal Arch. They are all expressions of . . . religion in its fullest sense, not in a masonic sense. I cannot stress too strongly the fact that there is no masonic religion, no masonic god, deity or someone or something to which a Freemason must swear loyalty. No.'

'What about Jah-Bul-On?'

He was obviously taken off-guard. He said nothing for nearly ten seconds and looked most discomfited. At length, proceeding with the extreme caution of a man feeling his way through a thicket of thorns, he said: 'These are . . . Hebrew words which are . . . murdered from their original. And *Jah* is the Hebrew word for God, so it's God again. You come back to God, the *real* God. But these – ha!

[he chuckled] – these are ways in which we express our *loyalty* to God.'

'It's interesting you should choose only to define the first syllable, which is of course the most acceptable to those with religious convictions. But what about the other parts of that word which are, are they not, Baal and Osiris?'

Another long pause. 'I don't know them. That's the higher echelons of Freemasonry.'

'That's in the Royal Arch, isn't it?'

'I don't do Royal Arch. I do Chapter, but not Royal Arch.'

This was the first lie he had told me, and I could see it was unpleasant for him.*

I continued: 'It is established that Jahbulon is a composite name for God, made up of Jah—'

'What's Bul-On?'

'Bul is Baal and On is Osiris, the Ancient Egyptian god of the dead.'

'Well . . .'

'Pike was outraged when he heard that name for the first time and saw it associated with Freemasonry, which of course was so dear to him. He said that nothing would induce him to accept as the name of God a word which is in part the name of a pagan god and for more than two thousand years an appellation of the devil.'

'I agree on that, but I . . . I . . . I don't know about it. It's not that I don't want to. I don't know about it so I really can't comment. You'll have to ask someone who knows.'

'Does it worry you?'

'In one of the higher degrees they use Jesus Christ.'

'Yes, there are several masonic orders which are exclusively Christian – the Knights Templar, the Ancient

*See Mackey's *Revised Encyclopaedia of Freemasonry*, Volume I, p 191.

and Accepted Rite, the Societas Rosicruciana, the Knights of Malta, the Order of Eri. But does the name Jah-Bul-On worry you?'

'Many Masons wouldn't subscribe to those Christian degrees.'

The implication was clear: if Christ was an acceptable part of Freemasonry even to a non-Christian, why not the devil as well? Unacceptable though he might be to most initiates, he has his place.

The Church of England has been a stronghold of Freemasonry for more than two hundred years. Traditionally, joining the Brotherhood and advancing within it has always been the key to preferment in the Church. This situation has altered in the past twenty years and today there are fewer Masons within the Church than ever before. Even so, the Church is still rife with members of the Brotherhood. This is why, despite overwhelming evidence of Masonry's incompatibility with Christianity and the shattering revelation as to the nature of the Masonic God, no amount of pressure from inside or outside the Church has so far succeeded in forcing an enquiry into the subject.

Thirty years ago a thirty-eight-year-old Anglican clergyman, the Rev Walton Hannah, gave up his living in Sussex to devote himself to studying and writing about Freemasonry. In January 1951, Hannah launched his attack on clergymen Freemasons in an article in *Theology*. The article created a fissure through which poured the pent-up anxieties and suspicion of non-masonic Anglicans, which had been rumbling beneath the surface for years. The controversy spread far beyond the pages of theological journals as spin-off 'shock-horror-sensation' pieces appeared in the popular press. The furore led to a debate in the

Church Assembly and it began to look as if the whole subject of Freemasonry in the Church might be brought before the Convocation of Canterbury. But as the Archbishop of Canterbury himself (Fisher) was a powerful Freemason, the Brotherhood had little trouble in blocking the attempt, and it was ruled out of order on a technicality.

Hannah later published his condemnation of Freemasonry and his arguments against its compatibility with Christianity in his book *Darkness Visible*, in which he pointed out that every Christian Church that had studied Freemasonry has declared that it was incompatible with Christianity. These condemnations ranged from the famous papal pronouncements, the first of which was in 1738, to an instruction of General Booth, founder of the Salvation Army, that 'no language of mine could be too strong in condemning an Officer's affiliation with any Society which shuts Him outside its Temples'. The Greek Orthodox Church, pointing out that Lutheran, Methodist and Presbyterian communities had also declared Masonry incompatible with Christianity, condemned the movement formally in 1933 in part and significantly because 'it constitutes a mystagogical system which reminds us of the ancient heathen mystery-religions and cults – from which it descends and is their continuation and regeneration'.

Dr H. S. Box, author of *The Nature of Freemasonry*, attempted to raise the issue of Freemasonry in the Canterbury Convocation of the Church of England in 1951. 'Due largely,' Hannah says, 'to the persuasive influence of the Masonic Bishop of Reading, Dr A. Groom Parham, this was never debated.' There was, though, a debate in the Church Assembly in 1952. Hannah records that the 'critics of Masonry were frankly out-manoeuvred by the unexpectedness and speed with which Masons acted': the motion for an enquiry was overwhelmingly rejected. The Church of England has still never considered the matter officially.

Hannah's conclusion, echoed today by several deeply concerned Church of England clergy and bishops in private conversation, is that 'the Church . . . dares not offend or provoke thousands of influential and often financially substantial laymen by enquiring into the religious implications of Freemasonry'.

The present Archbishop of Canterbury, Dr Robert Runcie, is not a Freemason and a recent survey suggests that many fewer bishops are Freemasons today than in the 1950s, when it would have been hard to find half a dozen bishops who were not Masons.

One great difficulty, today as in the 1950s, is for non-Masonic clergy and laity – and indeed the general reader – to obtain reliable information about the religious implications of Freemasonry. The vast – though often inaccessible – masonic literature is contradictory and full of gaps. It is all but impossible to know which books and what parts of them reflect the inmost beliefs of the masonic leadership.

To take one striking example: in the first three degrees – the 'blue' Craft Masonry conducted in Lodges – the initiate is introduced right away to 'The Great Architect of the Universe' as the masonic deity. He will doubtless assume according to his upbringing that this is merely a quaint way of referring to Jahweh, Allah, or the triune God of Christianity. If he should wonder why this title is a masonic secret and why masonic texts therefore cryptically refer to the 'GAOTU' instead of simply to God with a capital 'G', he will probably see no more than a little harmless clandestinity, maybe guessing (incorrectly) that it is a time-honoured vagary deriving from the days of 'operative' masons.

The average Christian man who has not studied the theological implications of the oaths, rituals and lectures usually experiences a certain initial moral and religious disquiet about what he has done in joining. Many have admitted to being somewhat ashamed by the initiation ceremony they have undergone. But all this is allayed by the reassurance that so many of the eminent and reputable have for centuries done the same and that the masonic system somehow enjoys an immunity in these matters sanctioned by tradition. As already stated, it is only when a Master Mason is 'exalted' to the Royal Arch and becomes a member of a Royal Arch Chapter, that the real name of the 'GAOTU' – Jahbulon – is communicated to him. Even then, carried so far by his experience of the first three Craft degrees, and being used by that time to the ambivalence surrounding all masonic ritual and symbolism arising from the fact that the one masonic dogma is that there are no immutable truths, most fail to appreciate that they have been deliberately misled into thinking 'GAOTU' is the one God of the great monotheistic religions. No one will enlighten the duped Royal Arch Masons for no one has the authority to do more than sketch his own personal interpretation of what the attributes of Jahbulon may be.

Those that have a feeling for the occult – the true adepts – recognize each other: they appreciate the real significance behind the deliberate masonic ambiguities. They develop a confidence in drawing their own deductions, making their own interpretations of symbolism and ritual. Such people come slowly to be accepted into the inner sanctum of the Brotherhood. But even among themselves – to judge by what senior masonic defectors have reported, and by the rare esoteric literature solely for advanced Masons – there is no mention of anything openly suggestive of satanism. There is no need: long practice of the masonic system ensures that the understanding is on another level. In just the same way, in worldly matters, all Masons at their initiation are required to 'declare on your honour that – uninfluenced by mercenary or other unworthy motive, you freely and voluntarily offer yourself . . . for the mysteries and privileges of Freemasonry'. Most candidates fully understand that this is humbug: they know full well that many join primarily or at least partly in the hope that membership will forward their worldly ambitions. But they give their word – and so, right from the beginning, they enter into the double-speak of Masonry. A double-speak some learn to talk like a guided missile homing on its target. It is a double-speak the student of Masonry must learn to recognize and not allow to confuse him.

Against all this, the Church of England's Society for the Propagation of Christian Knowledge (SPCK), for example, even today carries no literature examining Freemasonry and discussing whether a Christian should be a Mason. Hannah states that the SPCK issued a directive to their bookshops that his book *Darkness Visible*, probably still the most accurate and scholarly general work on the matter, should not be stocked. The Archbishop of Canterbury is the President of the SPCK. The Archbishop of Canterbury responsible for banning Hannah's book was Dr Geoffrey Fisher – a Freemason of long standing.

There is no doubt that Freemasonry is extremely anxious to have – or to appear to have – good relations with all Christian Churches and, knowing that no serious masonic scholar and no Christian theologian has been prepared to argue compatibility, the Movement remains silent. There is evidence of very considerable efforts being made by Masons – including pressures on publishers, distributors and libraries – to suppress works critical of the Brotherhood.* Hannah related how a mysterious gentleman invited him to the foyer of the Savoy Hotel where he offered the author £1,000 in notes for not publishing *Darkness Visible* or any other attack on Masonry. It should be stated that there is no evidence of this particular incident except Hannah's word.

Hannah ends his review of the attitudes of the Christian Churches towards Freemasonry by remarking: 'There is fear on both sides, hence the search for truth is stifled, and the religious bigamy continues. Only Rome can afford to smile at the situation, and continue to win converts.' For once, Hannah – who became a Roman Catholic after the Church of England had failed to examine Masonry and pronounce upon it – was wrong.

The Church of Rome, traditional arch-enemy of Freemasonry, is even more the object of masonic attention than the Church of England.

Roman Catholics of the older generation remember pamphlets published by the Catholic Truth Society (the Roman Church's equivalent of the SPCK) about the incompatibility of Freemasonry and Catholicism at every church bookstall. They understood that a long line of Popes had declared Freemasonry illicit and that Catholics who were Freemasons were automatically excommunicated by the mere fact of membership.

The situation today has mysteriously changed. Like the SPCK, the CTS has ceased publishing any guidance on

*This even extends to the Brotherhood's own publications. When the British Library applied in the normal way to Freemasons Hall for two copies of the *Masonic Year Book* for the Reading Room in 1981, it was informed that it would not be permitted to have copies of the directory then or in the future. No explanation was given. See also pp 9–12 on the prepubliction adventures of *The Brotherhood.*

Freemasonry. Priests, although perhaps better trained today than ever before, are commonly ignorant about the subject and are themselves unaware of their Church's present position.

I have discovered that there is a deliberate policy in operation within the English hierarchy of the Roman Catholic Church to keep its members in ignorance of the true standing of the Church on the question of Freemasonry. This policy is intended to cover up a huge mistake made by the English Catholic Bishops in 1974 which led to Catholics in Britain being informed that after two hundred years of implacable opposition from Rome, the Holy See had changed its mind and that with the permission of their local Bishop Catholics could now become Freemasons. As well as covering up what I can now reveal as this blunder on the part of the English hierarchy, the wall-of-silence policy conceals, perhaps inadvertently, a more sinister situation in Rome, where I have evidence that the Vatican itself is infiltrated by Freemasons.

In 1982 I asked a trusted friend, a Roman Catholic and like myself an author and journalist, to raise the matter of the widespread ignorance of Catholics with the present Archbishop of Westminster, Cardinal Basil Hume. The Archbishop's response was: 'I think it would be wise to wait for the publication of the new Canon Law before taking any public stance on the questions of Freemasons.' His General Secretary, Monsignor Norris, wrote in amplification: '. . . we have been informed that Freemasonry in this country has no connection with Freemasonry of an unpleasant kind on the Continent'. He went on to add that a Catholic's Bishop could give permission for a man to join the Brotherhood if 'convinced [membership] will have no bad effect on the person's Catholicity'.

Only now, after independent investigation by my Roman Catholic friend and myself, and contact with the Roman Church's hierarchy in Rome, can this statement be revealed as inaccurate. Norris's comment that '... we have been informed ...' begs the question – *who* convinced the English hierarchy that English Freemasonry is fundamentally different? What happened to the Canon Law automatically excommunicating Freemasons? The story is a strange one.

By the 1880s eight Popes had already condemned Freemasonry when Freemasons urged that these condemnations had been based on erroneous information and were excessively severe. This led Pope Leo XIII to issue his famous encyclical *Humanum Genus* in 1884. Leo XIII classed Freemasonry as a grouping of secret societies in the 'kingdom of Satan' and, like the Greek Orthodox Church half a century later, stated that it wished 'to bring back after eighteen centuries the manners and customs of the pagans'. He qualified Masonry as subversive of Church and state, condemned it for its rejection of Christian revelation, and for its religious indifferentism – the idea that all religions are equally valid. He warned against the effectiveness of masonic organization, its use of figurehead leaders, and its subtle use of 'double-speak'. He urged the bishops to whom the Encyclical was addressed 'first of all to tear away the mask of Freemasonry, and let it be seen for what it really is'.

There were further condemnations in 1894 and 1902. Then the Canon Law promulgated in 1917 provided in Canon 2335 that '*ipso facto* excommunication' is incurred by 'those who enrol in the masonic sect or in other associations of the same sort which plot against the Church or the legitimate civil authorities'. One reason for the unusual frequency of these papal condemnations is that Freemasonry has always had sympathizers, even members, clerical as well as lay, in the Roman Catholic Church.

From the 1920s Freemasons increasingly urged that British Freemasonry (and indeed other Freemasonry which did not accept the avowed atheism of the French and certain other 'Grand Orients' which had cost them recognition by the British Grand Lodges) was different from what the Popes had had in mind and so was unjustly condemned: they insisted that this British-type Freemasonry did not plot against either Church or state. The Vatican paid no attention, but three Jesuits with masonic contacts (Gruber, Bertheloot and Riquet) successively urged study of the possibility for a rapprochement.

Then came Vatican II and the great impetus this gave to the ecumenical movement – the reconciliation of all Christians. Senior members of the Brotherhood saw an opportunity to exploit this enthusiasm and used its ecclesiastical contacts to renew its call for an end to Catholic hostility. In America, France and Germany, notably, there were a number of small indications that the Catholic attitude to Masonry was softening. These were enough for Harry Carr,* one of those leading Freemasons who, like Dr Theophilus Desaguliers in the eighteenth century, exercise immense influence from a discreet position some rungs below the top of the Grand Lodge ladder. Carr spoke of the possibility of reconciliation to the London Grand Lodge Association in February 1968.

As related in his book *The Freemason at Work*, a questioner asked Carr how there could be any such move while 'defamatory and inaccurate' anti-masonic literature was on sale at Westminster Cathedral bookstall. Carr

*Past Junior Grand Deacon; Past Master of Quatuor Coronati Lodge No 2076 and of four other Lodges – 2265, 2429, 6226 and 7464; Hon. Member of six Lodges – 236, 2429, 2911, 3931, 7998 and 8227; Hon. Member of eight Lodges in France, the USA and Canada.

wrote to Cardinal Heenan, then Archbishop of Westminster, who undertook to have the offending literature, if indeed inaccurate, withdrawn. It was. Heenan saw Carr on 18 March 1968.

Carr stressed the old distinction between British and atheistic Continental Freemasonry and said that both as a Jew and a Mason he hoped the time had come for a reconciliation. According to Carr, this led Heenan to offer himself as 'intermediary' between English Freemasonry and the Vatican. Carr says he saw Heenan again on the eve of the Cardinal's departure for Rome. There was talk of a revision of Canon 2335 and of meetings between the Brotherhood and the Holy See.

On the surface nothing happened for nearly three years until the spring of 1971 when the Jesuit Father Giovanni Caprile, a leading and very hostile Catholic expert on Freemasonry, changed tack and wrote a number of conciliatory articles in the quasi-official *Civilta Cattolica*. It was widely believed that Caprile's new line was backed by none other than Cardinal Villot, then Vatican Secretary of State. The story is that Villot, dubbed a 'progressive', used Father Caprile's articles to overcome the resistance to any change in the Church's teaching on Masonry by Cardinal Franjo Seper, Prefect of the Sacred Congregation for the Doctrine of Faith.

Against this background Carr saw Heenan a third time on 26 April 1971 and Heenan related how the Holy See had granted dispensations to two English Masons to remain members of the Brotherhood after their reception into the Roman Catholic Church.

On 12 June 1973 Heenan felt able to warn his priests that a change in Rome's policy towards Masonry was imminent. He was right. After years of procrastination Cardinal Seper felt obliged on 19 July 1974 to authorize the Sacred Congregation for the Doctrine of the Faith to write a confidential letter to certain Episcopal Conferences, the English among them, commenting on the interpretation to be given to Canon 2335.

Seper said no more than he had to: someone had pointed out that, as there was no comma in the definitive Latin text of Canon 2335, it was not clear whether *all* Freemasons were automatically excommunicated, or *only* those Freemasons whose particular group plots against Church or legitimate civil authorities. Wherever a Canon provides for penalties, Seper was obliged to point out, the most restrictive interpretation had to be given in the case of ambiguity. Therefore, the Canon reserved automatic excommunication only for the plotters.

Of itself the cautious letter signalled no change in the Church's attitude to the Brotherhood. But Caprile in *Civilta Cattolica* published what was allegedly an 'authorized commentary' suggesting that the Church now officially accepted that there were masonic associations which did not conspire against Church or state, that the Church now intended to leave it to local Episcopal Conferences to decide whether their local Masons were in this category – and if they were, there need be no ban on Masonry.

The English bishops accepted this view and issued a statement of general guidance which reads in part:

> Times change. The Holy See has reviewed the Church's present relationship with Freemasonry . . . the Congregation has ruled that Canon 2335 no longer automatically bars a Catholic from membership of Masonic groups . . . And so a Catholic who joins the Freemasons is excommunicated only if the policy and actions of the Freemasons in his area are known to be hostile to the Church.

The Catholic News Service announced that the effect of this guidance 'is to move from a ban on Catholics belonging to the Masonic Movement to a cautious procedure whereby such membership may in some cases be sought'.

For Carr and for Masonry this was the definitive breakthrough: the reconciliation so long sought by the Masons had been achieved. As Carr puts it, 'There must be hundreds of dedicated Masons all over the world who have played some part in the achievement of this long desired end. We have seen masonic history in the making . . . the sad story which began in 1738 is happily ended.' Masons hastened to spread the word that Catholics could at last be Freemasons without incurring their Church's displeasure.

Inside sources have informed me that behind all this disarray in the Vatican there may well have been a small number of masonic prelates - specifically an Archbishop who in July 1975 was dismissed from his post when 'unquestionable proof' of his being a Freemason was submitted to the Pope. *Prima facie* evidence of a few such cases does certainly exist, but as Paul VI, fearing scandal, ordered no enquiry to establish the truth, rumour has taken over and spurious lists of high-ranking 'masonic prelates' have been passed around, making the facts more than ever difficult to establish.

Everywhere there was confusion. In Brazil, on Christmas Day 1975, at the request of the Masonic Lodge Liberty, Cardinal Abelard Brandao Vilela, Primate of Brazil, celebrated Mass to commemorate the Lodge's fortieth anniversary. For his attitude towards the Brotherhood the Cardinal next year received the title 'Great Benefactor' of the Lodge.

All this happened under Pope Paul VI who, whatever

his other virtues, is widely considered to have been a weak man unable to face scandal if need be to keep masonic influence out of the Vatican and national Episcopal conferences.

With the advent of Pope John Paul II it soon became clear that Harry Carr had been over-sanguine in suggesting that the story was at an end. On 17 February 1981 the Sacred Congregation for the Doctrine of the Faith issued a 'declaration' stating that the 1974 letter had given rise to 'erroneous and tendentious' interpretations. It insisted: '. . . canonical discipline regarding Freemasonry remains in force and has not been modified in any way, consequently neither excommunication nor the other penalties envisaged have been abrogated'.

The 1974 letter had merely drawn attention to the fact that the Church's penal laws must always be interpreted restrictively. In evident reproof of the English bishops, the Congregation declared that it had *not* intended Episcopal Conferences to issue public pronouncements of a general character on the nature of masonic associations 'which would change the position of the Church in regard to Freemasonry'.

The 1981 declaration pulls the rug from under the new understanding of the relationship between the Roman Catholic Church and Masonry. Yet it has had virtually no publicity and the myth that canon law on the subject was changed in 1974 persists.

Roman Catholics seeking a true answer to the question of the Church's position on Freemasonry can find it only in the pages of this book. A high Vatican official, well qualified to explain the present position of the Holy See, said I should make four points:

First: the purpose of the Vatican letter of 19 July 1974 was simply to point out that only the restrictive interpretation of

Canon 2335 should be applied: in other words only those Freemasons whose organization plots against the (Roman Catholic) Church, or the legitimate civil authorities are automatically excommunicated, a matter which it is of course extremely difficult to determine in the case of a secret society where the thinking of its clandestine leading members is not known to the ordinary membership.

Secondly: the Church wishes to reduce wherever possible the offences that incur automatic excommunication. Consequently the new Canon Law now before the Pope may very well end automatic excommunication for Freemasons even under the restrictive interpretation of the present Canon 2335.

Thirdly, and most important: *it does not follow that because some action may no longer attract automatic excommunication it becomes licit.* If something is contrary to Divine Law it is illicit even though the Church may apply no extraordinary sanctions. The Vatican draws particular attention to the findings of the German bishops as recently as May 1980. After prolonged study in co-operation with German Freemasonry of only the first three 'Craft' degrees, the German bishops concluded that 'Masonry has not changed' and can in no way be reconciled with Christianity. The position of the Catholic Church is thus that, as Freemasonry is essentially similar in Britain and Germany, the German bishops' conclusions that Freemasonry is contrary to Divine Law *applies to British as much as to German Freemasonry.*

Fourthly: there are moral as well as theological and political issues. It is unChristian to join any secret organization which systematically benefits its own members to the detriment of the legitimate interests of non-members. Insofar as Freemasonry is guilty of this, Roman Catholics obviously should not join it.

The Vatican's position is thus plain enough for anyone able to travel to Rome and obtain an audience with an eminent official. As most Catholic clergy and laity are not in a position to do this, it is curious that the English hierarchy have left English Catholics in ignorance. It is impossible to guess how long they would have remained ignorant had not New English Library decided to commission this investigation into Freemasonry.

An eminent prelate in Rome, who enthusiastically welcomed the prospect of this book and described the project as 'work of great importance', disclosed how the English Roman Catholic hierarchy, far from hastening to 'tear away the mask from Freemasonry' as urged by Pope Leo XIII, is in practice out on a limb in its toleration of Freemasonry and its unwillingness to give any guidance to Catholics, even to its own priests. He explained, 'The English bishops are anxious to give an English face to Catholicism. So, because Freemasonry is so English, they feel they must come to terms with it. The bishops wish for silence.'

Effectively, then, the true position of the Roman Catholic Church is not unlike that of the Church of England. Faced with the prestige, influence, and prevalence of Freemasonry in British society, both are similarly paralysed. The Vatican contact said, 'The Catholic hierarchy are well aware too of the pressures on the Roman Catholic laity in many walks of life to join Freemasonry if their worldly interests are not to be too gravely prejudiced in an increasingly masonic world. If the English Bishops do not consider they should demand that the faithful make the sacrifice required by the official Vatican position, it is hardly surprising that Freemasonry among Catholics is on the increase. It is certainly no longer safe to assume that Roman Catholic professional men are not Freemasons.'

The people and places in the following episode have been given obvious pseudonyms to make identification impossible and so to protect my informant, an Anglican vicar. For more than five months after I first heard of this man's plight, he was guarded about what was happening to him. Eventually, though, he decided that the disturbing events which took place in and around his parish during 1981 should be widely known – if only to warn other clergymen of the trouble in which they might become embroiled if they did not handle their local Freemasons skilfully. At this time the vicar requested that I did not disclose his name. Less than two days later, after much contemplation and soul-searching, he decided that he must stand up and be counted even if it meant placing himself in jeopardy again. But his fear overcame him once again and the pseudonyms were inserted into his story.

The Parish Church of Epsilon lies between the Berkshire villages of Zeta and Theta. From the porch there is a beautiful view of the Kappa valley and the highway beyond. For the Vicar of Epsilon, however, all beauty ends when he enters his church. He strongly suspects, from his experiences since taking up the living in 1980 and from his own observations and research, that the building called Epsilon Parish Church is not a church at all, but a pagan temple. It is full of masonic symbols. The Rev Lamda Mu says he came close to being driven out of his parish and his livelihood after opposing plans, on Christian grounds, for a service in the church for members of the two local masonic Lodges. When I met the Rev Mu he told me, 'In May 1981 I knew almost nothing about Freemasonry, but I have since come to understand the spiritual implications of this whole secret society, religion, or whatever you may care to call it.'

On 5 May 1982, before deciding finally that it would be too dangerous to be named, he wrote to me, 'Apart from my testimony, there are two principal reasons why I have decided to contribute to your work on Freemasonry.' He asked that I list these reasons in full in his own words:

(1) A number of people for one reason or another in contributing to this book were unwilling to give their names and I am told that some of the evidence had to be disguised. This in fact would make it possible for people to criticize the book as sheer fabrication. I was impressed by the author's motives in preparing this book on Freemasonry as he wanted to examine the subject from all points of view so that the reader might be able to make his own judgement on Freemasonry. I have learned that Freemasonry is very big indeed and I am only describing *my* contact with Freemasonry.

(2) I am contributing as a member of the established Church, that has had strong contacts with Masonry for a very long time. In this day and age it is fashionable to criticize the establishment, and my very real fear is that should anything vaguely comparable happen in this country with regard to Freemasonry as happened with the P2 Lodge in Italy [see Chapter 26], it could not only seriously undermine but possibly destroy confidence in authority and the use of authority in this land. I therefore wish to dissociate myself from all those who desire to use criticism of Masonry for their own ends.

Mu wished it to be said that he bore Masons no animosity or ill-will. He said that in whatever contacts he had had over the events so far, the Freemasons themselves had been courteous and polite. 'I must also add that there are a number of Masons in my parishes, some of them are very close friends of mine, and some of them played a very active part in saving one of my churches from certain closure.'

This is the Rev Mu's story.

'I remember as a small boy that my mother announced after seeing a postcard that somebody had gone to the "Grand Lodge Above". She then showed me my father's masonic apron. In 1967 at theological college, there was a discussion about Freemasonry among some of the students. I had no idea what Freemasonry was. I was given a book on heresies by one of the students which contained eight pages on Freemasonry. I read it and this in fact has coloured all my thinking on Masonry. I felt, as a Christian believing in Jesus Christ, I could not become a Mason as this would mean denying Jesus Christ as the Saviour of the world.

'Before I became Vicar of [Epsilon] in Berkshire in 1980, I was told that the Freemasons had an annual service once a year in [Epsilon] Church. I raised this with the Bishop, who advised me to allow the Masons to have their service but ask to see the order of service beforehand and to insist on every prayer being said "in the name of our Lord Jesus Christ". In May 1981, I received a letter from the [Theta] Lodge requesting a service in [Epsilon] Church. The letter gave no indication as to what exactly the Masons wanted and I was concerned that I would be involved in all sorts of bizarre rituals. I later discovered that they had only wanted Prayer Book Evensong. The surprise for me on the letter was a masonic symbol, *which I recognized immediately as being like a sign in [Epsilon] Church.* I had to reply to the letter fairly quickly, but I had no idea what to do. The one person I felt I could talk to about this was away on holiday. I did not know who were Masons and who were not. I did not know what the feelings of the local clergy were on Masonry, and I was not absolutely certain if even the Bishop was a Mason. (As it turned out he most certainly was not.) I remembered hearing something of a clergyman who was driven from this country to Canada or somewhere because he opposed Masonry. I later discovered that this was Walton Hannah. I had no wish to follow him but I was extremely reluctant to be involved in any way with a society that wanted a service in church but wanted the Founder of the church excluded. It took me four or five days to summon up enough courage to reply to the Masons. I said that all my knowledge of Masonry was second hand, I knew very little about Masonry, except that Masons had services which did not allow the name of Jesus Christ to be used, and for that reason I was not happy about them having a service. I did not flatly refuse to give them a service, but made the same conditions as those suggested by the Bishop, only adding that *I* should preach the sermon. Had I known then the kind of hymns Masons sing, I would have wanted to see those in advance as well.

'Over a period of time, I became aware of a gathering storm, and I began in desperation to search for books about Masonry. I found one which only confirmed my views and made me even more aware of the true nature of Freemasonry. Also I began to find out who were Masons in all three of my parishes, and this provided me with many surprises. I sensed a major storm was brewing and I felt totally ill equipped to face what was about to happen. I had become aware that a number of Popes had condemned Masonry and I discovered a number of books on the subject at Douai Abbey. I had practically no time to read them before I was given six days' notice that the only subject on the agenda for the next Parish Church Council meeting at [Epsilon] was the Annual Freemasons' Service. In that brief period of time I tried to prepare as convincing a case as possible as to why I knew a Christian could not be a Mason. I used some information from the recent *Credo* television programme, and I even quoted from the 39 Articles the relevant articles which should convince any Anglican that he cannot be an Anglican and a Mason. I was not allowed to explain anything about the rituals of Masonry as the meeting suddenly exploded in uproar. Some of the members were very angry with me and felt that I had insulted their relatives dead and living. In the end the PCC passed a resolution asking me to consider writing to the Masons inviting them back again. If I did not do this, I was told that they would all resign, and one person warned me that I might become "a Vicar without a Parish". They then decided to have a further meeting two weeks later.

'What surprised me most of all was that they could not accept or could not hear me say that Masonry was contrary to the first three of the Ten Commandments and denied Christ. They said that as many clergy were Masons, including bishops, there was nothing wrong with it. I do not recount all this in order to criticize the way the PCC reacted. I felt that for many decades the PCC had been badly let down by the clergy who have been Masons and believed that it was compatible with their allegiance to Christ. It grieves me to think of those times and the only reason why I relate all this is hopefully to spare some other vicar and PCC the kind of experience we all suffered at that time. The next morning, I wrote to the Bishop and said that I had no intention of sending any letter to the Masons. One of my churchwardens came to see me. He was greatly distressed by all that had happened and asked me to reconsider writing to the Masons and he told me how upset many people were, and that unless I wrote a letter they would all resign. I wrote a further letter to the Bishop suggesting how I proposed to resolve the crisis. The Bishop replied with a very tough letter condemning Masonry in no uncertain terms. He supported my actions, adding that had he been in my position he would have done as I did. The letter displayed his deep loyalty to Christ. Nevertheless at the next meeting, I did produce a letter which was not accepted. I produced another letter, in which I regretted the upset I had caused everyone and that I had not realized that all they wanted was Evensong. I also said that I thought that they had wanted a masonic service. Even with the letter that I finally sent to the Masons I had to omit the one and only reference I made to Jesus Christ. One of my churchwardens worked overtime to restore peace and harmony, and he succeeded.

'I felt very puzzled by all that had happened. I could not understand why the PCC acted in the way it had. Why had they been so angry and upset? What puzzled me most of all was that none of them were Masons! There had to be a reason behind it all and I just did not know the reason. The Bishop came to see me. At first I was worried as he had told me before I became a vicar that he would support me in my parishes but if he felt that I was wrong over something he would tell me privately. I need not have worried, his real concern was how I had taken everything, and he only came to support me and my wife. In retrospect I feel she suffered most of all through the crisis. We had a long and happy time with the Bishop over a meal discussing all that had happened; he also told me to expect further consequences of my actions. I did not understand at the time what he meant, and to a certain extent, I still do not understand. I had only just weathered a major crisis. Without the firm support of the Bishop, it is unlikely that I would still be Vicar of [Epsilon]. I was still very puzzled by all that had happened and I just did not appreciate the spiritual implications of Freemasonry.

'If ever I faced another crisis over Freemasonry, I felt that I had to know what Freemasonry was. I came up against another problem: nearly all the books that I had borrowed on Freemasonry had been out of print for many years. It took many months even to obtain one or two of the books. Someone lent to me a copy of Richard Carlile's *Manual of Freemasonry.* This was the first masonic book I ever saw that gave full details of the rituals of Masonry. Although produced early in the last century, it remains a very important document on Freemasonry. I also wrote to London Weekend Television in the hope of obtaining a copy of the German Bishops' Report on Freemasonry from James Rushbrooke, a scholar who had appeared on the *Credò* programme. On the same day, I received not only James Rushbrooke's translation of the Report, but also another translation from some other source. Not only that but the Rev John Lawrence, who had also been involved in the *Credo* programme, contacted me, and not long afterwards, I was also visited by James Rushbrooke. James impressed upon me how large a thing Masonry was and considered that I had acted bravely in taking the action I did, "... because you know they will put your name down on their list of clergymen who are actively opposed to Freemasonry".

'There were two other things that happened. One was that the local Masons went to another church and the preacher at the service made some unpleasant comments about my attitude towards Freemasonry. The Vicar of the parish came and apologized to me afterwards. I felt very sorry for him and tried to ease his conscience, but I also pointed out that I as a Christian could not accept Masonry. The other incident was that a member of one of my parishes, a Mason, asked to see me. I had made a point of seeing the churchgoing Masons and I thought I had reassured them that I had no intention of driving Masons out of church. The minute you drive any sinner out of church you go against the principle that the church exists to reform penitent sinners through our Lord Jesus Christ. Freemasonry does not operate on that principle and therefore I explained that I was against the *system* but not the people involved in it. This parishioner was still worried and confused by my actions. We had a very long conversation in which I began to have the feeling that Masonry really did have a false spirit behind it. The fellowship of Masonry was a counterfeit of the fellowship of the Holy Spirit. I was taken by surprise for a moment when he told me that if I wanted to join a Lodge, I would be made very welcome!

'I have only told you the bare bones of what happened. I have deliberately avoided as far as possible giving theological opinions about Masonry or indeed details about the rituals of Masonry as there is plenty of information available to anyone who wishes to find it. The books on Masonry are endless. During the following months, I learnt more and more about Masonry and discovered many more symbols of Masonry in [Epsilon] Church to the extent that now I really wonder if it is a church at all.

'I have also learned that the last family owner of [Epsilon] Court had been a top Mason. I found this out from an old masonic book which listed two pages of his many masonic connections. I have also become alarmed by the deep occult connections there are in Masonry.'

The one fortunate discovery Mu has made, he told me, was the testimony of former Masons who have renounced the Brotherhood and turned 'wholeheartedly to Christ'.

In May 1981 – a month of controversial masonic activity in a number of disparate areas – another clergyman was sacked from his church and ordered to leave the manse. He later claimed before an industrial tribunal that the Presbyterian Church of Wales had dismissed him purely because he had preached against Freemasonry. The Rev William Colin Davies of Whitchurch, Cardiff, requested through his lawyer that there should be no member of the Brotherhood on the tribunal, which was agreed.

The minister's duties called for him to preach thirty-six Sundays of the year at his own church and twelve Sundays in other churches without a regular minister. In August

1979 Davies wrote to the Church's rota secretary stating that he did not wish to be seen to be helping in the teachings of tenets of Freemasonry, which he believed to be 'a challenge to the discipleship of Jesus Christ'. He enclosed a cheque for £108.00 to cover his absence from certain churches where he felt his presence had been both unexpected and unwanted because of his views on Freemasonry. When I spoke to him about his case in May 1982, Davies said that the Presbyterian Church of Wales was particularly strongly influenced by members of the Brotherhood among its own members and administration. He explained, 'I became a minister in 1974 and Cardiff was my first pastorate. I had two churches. In one of them I encountered some Freemasons. I did not know then what I know now. I researched into Masonry and found it entirely incompatible with faith in Jesus Christ. I spoke privately to some men in the church, and without making it a bee in my bonnet I did some comparisons between Freemasonry and Christianity during the course of some sermons. I compared, for example, the meaning of faith in Christianity and the masonic meaning of faith.

'In February 1980 I discovered a booklet called *Christ, the Christian and Freemasonry* which I circulated among the members of the church.

'By this time I had been reported to the local church governing body – the presbytery – and a committee of seven men came to see me. I know now that some of them were Freemasons. They accused me of being an evangelical Christian, which I am, 'intolerant of un-Biblical teaching and in particular Freemasonry'. They accused me of being un-compassionate, which presumably meant I had upset Masons' and their relatives' feelings. It was said that membership of my church was going down, but I had had about fifty of the elderly members die and had introduced twenty-six new members. They said I was not ecumenically minded enough in that I didn't join in local services of other churches, which was not true. It is true that I have reservations about the present moves towards church unity but we did have ecumenical meetings with local churches roundabout. And I was accused of allowing the children's work to decline when it is actually expanding. I knew then that the rest of the charges had been trumped up by Masons determined to end my opposition to Masonry. I was not allowed to answer the charges. And then when I next met them a month later on 20 June 1980 they presented a report before the governing body without any warning – and I was dismissed.

'I received information several days later from a member of my other church who made some enquiries of some masonic friends that a Lodge meeting had taken place in March at which it was decided that pressure had to be brought to bear to have me removed. I have made this charge in public and it has never been rebutted.

'I was dismissed from the pastorate, not from my ministry. These are technically different, in practice the same. I then appealed to the highest body in the church, the Association, which appointed a panel of men to look into it. They said that a period of twelve months should be allowed to see if a reconciliation could be achieved between me and the local people who wanted me sacked. I agreed to this but they made no attempt at reconciliation.

'I won my appeal but it was not implemented because my local church would not accept it. I was sacked and told to leave my house within six weeks.'

The elders of the church claimed before the industrial tribunal that Davies had not been an employee of the Church but self-employed, and as such ineligible to claim unfair dismissal. They cited the case of a minister dismissed from Scunthorpe Congregational Church in 1978 as a precedent. But the non-masonic tribunal decided that Davies had been an employee and therefore had the right to seek a ruling.

Meanwhile, after six months on the dole, he works (at the time of writing) as minister for an independent church he has formed at Whitchurch along with members of both his former churches.

PART SIX

The KGB Connection

CHAPTER 26

The Italian Crisis

A masonic conspiracy of gigantic proportions rocked Italy to its foundations in the spring and summer of 1981. Known as the 'P2' case, this imbroglio of corruption, blackmail and murder brought down the coalition government of premier Arnaldo Forlani and decimated the upper echelons of Italian power.

P2 is the popular abbreviation of Masonic Lodge *Propaganda Due*, which had become, in the words of the leader of Italy's Republican Party, 'the centre of pollution of national life – secret, perverse and corrupting'.

The moment this 'scandal of scandals' hit the headlines, individual members of the United Grand Lodge hastened to point out that English Freemasonry was fundamentally different from that practised in Italy. But in spite of the perfectly sincere disclaimers emanating from Great Queen Street, the mysterious P2 case has a direct bearing on events in Britain today.

If the solution to the mystery of P2 is as I suspect, Britain stands in danger of a social calamity at least as great as that which struck Italy. Data and clues garnered from many sources, including the British Secret Intelligence Service (MI6) and the Security Service (MI5), suggest that without yet knowing it the British government faces an impossible dilemma. Evidence published here for the first time indicates that British Freemasonry, without realizing it, has become a time-bomb which could explode at any moment.

But first P2: how it began, what it seemed, and what it really was.

Freemasonry was introduced to Italy in about 1733 by an Englishman, Lord Sackville, but because of its open involvement in politics and religion Italian Freemasonry was not recognized by the United Grand Lodge of England until 1973.

A 'Propaganda' Lodge was constituted in Turin a century ago under the Grand Orient of Italy. This élite Lodge, which counted among its members the King himself, was in some ways similar to the English Quatuor Coronati Lodge No 2076 in that its purpose was to further research into Masonry. Despite several reports to the contrary, there was no connection save the name between this Lodge and the sinister masonic group of the present day. In fact, Lodge Propaganda Due was not even a Lodge in the true sense. It was a secret grouping of Masons but it was never officially constituted and never held regular meetings of all members.

P2 was formed in 1966 at the behest of the then Grand Master of the Grand Orient of Italy, Giordano Gamberini. The Grand Master's plan was to establish a group of eminent men who would be sympathetic and useful to Freemasonry. The man chosen to create this élite band was a rich textile manufacturer from the town of Arezzo in Tuscany. He had entered Masonry two years before and had risen to the Italian equivalent of Master Mason. His name was Licio Gelli.

Gelli, the first Italian to have been accredited with dual Italian–Argentinian nationality, had fought for the

Fascists in the Spanish Civil War and later been a passionate supporter of Mussolini. Later, having been involved in the torture of Italian partisans, he was forced to flee the country, winding up in Argentina. There he met President Juan Perón and a long and close friendship began. Perón eventually appointed Gelli to the position of Argentina's economic adviser to Italy. Years passed, and Gelli returned to his native country, settled at Arezzo and became a Freemason.

The group of men Gelli was ostensibly getting together on behalf of Grand Master Gamberini was called Raggruppamento Gelli Propaganda Due – P2 for short. The members came to be known as *Piduisti* – 'P2-ists'. Gelli had ambitions for P2 which the Grand Master had never so much as imagined.

By 1969 P2 was being spoken of as a Lodge, and Gelli as its Venerable Master. He had a genius for convincing people he had immense influence in public affairs, and many men joined P2 because they believed the Venerable Master's patronage was indispensable to the furtherance of their careers. By this self-perpetuating process, Gelli's purported power became real. Others joined the Lodge because Gelli used ruthless blackmail. The 'masonic dues' Gelli extracted from the brethren of Lodge P2 were not primarily financial. What the Venerable Master demanded – and got – were secrets: official secrets which he could use to consolidate and extend his power, and personal secrets he could use to blackmail others into joining his Lodge. This most sensitive information from all areas of government was passed to him by his members, who seem to have obeyed him with unquestioning devotion. In 1975 a legitimate Freemason, Francesco Siniscalchi, made a statement at the office of the Rome Public Prosecutor, alleging that Gelli was involved in criminal activities. He was ignored, partly because of Gelli's already formidable reputation, which intimidated two officers responsible for processing the complaint.

Soon after this, Gelli came to the notice of the police after his friend and P2 member Michele Sindona, Italy's most influential private banker, had fled to the United States leaving financial chaos behind him. Wanted on charges of fraud in Italy, Sindona was arrested in New York. Gelli flew to America and testified that Sindona was an innocent victim of Communist intrigue. It was Sindona, widely believed to have links with the Mafia, who introduced Gelli in Washington, DC, to Philip Guarino, a director of the US Republican Party's National Committee and Ronald Reagan's campaign manager in the 1980 Presidential Election. It was thanks to Guarino that Gelli was able to attend the inauguration of Reagan as President in January 1981, two months before the P2 bomb exploded.

In 1980, facing fraud charges in New York following the collapse of his Franklin National Bank - reputedly America's worst banking disaster - Sindona appealed to his Venerable Master for help. Meanwhile in Italy magistrates were still investigating Sindona's fraudulent activities and also the events behind the murder of the liquidator of his financial empire. After the appeal to Gelli, a fake kidnapping was staged in New York and Sindona disappeared. Evidence came to light that implicated Gelli in the escape and on 18 March 1981 two Milan magistrates ordered a police raid on his villa outside Arezzo.

Gelli, as always, had been one step ahead. By the time the police reached the Villa Wanda, named after his wife, they had both disappeared. A warrant was later issued for Gelli's arrest on charges of political, military and industrial espionage, and endangering the security of the state.

Among the documents left behind at the abandoned villa were the membership files of P2. A list of members drawn up by Gelli contained the names of nearly a thousand of Italy's most powerful men. One prosecutor's report later stated: 'Lodge Propaganda Due is a secret sect that has combined business and politics with the intention of destroying the country's constitutional order.'

Among the names were three members of the Cabinet including Justice Minister Adolfo Sarti; several former Prime Ministers including Giulio Andreotti who had held office between 1972 and 1973 and again between 1976 and 1979; forty-three Members of Parliament; fifty-four top Civil Servants; 183 army, navy and air force officers including thirty generals and eight admirals (among them the Commander of the Armed Forces, Admiral Giovanni Torrisi); nineteen judges; lawyers; magistrates; *carabiniere*; police chiefs; leading bankers; newspaper proprietors, editors and journalists (including the editor of the country's leading newspaper *Il Corriere Della Sera*); fifty-eight university professors; the leaders of several political parties; and even the directors of the three main intelligence services.

All these men, according to the files, had sworn allegiance to Gelli, and held themselves ready to respond to his call. The 953 names were divided into seventeen groupings, or cells, each having its own leader. P2 was so secret and so expertly run by Gelli that even its own members did not know who belonged to it. Those who knew most were the seventeen cell leaders and they knew only their own grouping. Not even Spartaco Mennini, the then Grand Secretary of the Grand Orient of Italy, knew the entire membership of the Lodge. Only Licio Gelli knew that.

P2 was the very embodiment of the fear that had haunted Italy's Under Secretary of State in 1913 when he had called for a law that 'declared the unsuitability of members of the Masonic Lodge to hold certain offices (such as those in the Judiciary, in the Army, in the Education Department, etc.), the high moral and social value of which is compromised by any hidden and therefore uncontrollable tie, and by any motive of suspicion, and lack of trust on the part of the public'.

In 1976 an official in Italy's Interior Ministry had declared that Gelli controlled 'the most potent hidden power centre' in the country. It took five more years, *and Gelli's own connivance*, for the real extent of his power to be revealed. As the magistrates ploughing through the files from the Villa Wanda stated, Gelli had 'constructed a very real state within the state', and was attempting to overturn the Republic.

Of the many political groupings in Italy, Gelli's files showed that only the Communist Party had no links with P2. All the others - Christian Democrats, Socialists, Republicans, Radicals, Neo-Fascists - had members in the Lodge.

When the magistrates finally presented the Gelli papers to the Italian Parliament in May 1981, they had sorted them into ten heavy piles. There was immediate uproar and calls for the four-party coalition government of Christian Democrat Prime Minister Aldo Forlani to resign. As it became clear how completely Gelli had infiltrated not only the corridors but the most secret and vital centres of power, increasing pressure was applied to Forlani to have the documents published. He was finally forced to agree, but fought to hold on to the premiership by a mere reshuffle that would expel the *Piduisti* from the Cabinet. But the Communists, the second largest political grouping in the country, now doubly strong by virtue of the fact that only they among Italy's parties were completely free of involvement in P2, resisted furiously.

And the Socialists' leader, Bettino Craxi, although he had thirty-five P2 members within his own party, seized his opportunity and refused to be part of any coalition headed by a Christian Democrat. After seventeen days of desperate negotiations with his former political allies, Forlani reached the end of the road. The government fell and Craxi made his bid for the premiership.

When Craxi, too, failed, the eighty-five-year-old President Alessandro Pertini invited Republican Party leader Giovanni Spadolini to attempt to form a new coalition. Spadolini succeeded, becoming Italy's first non-Christian Democrat premier since the Second World War, and heading a government made up of five separate parties.

As more and more documents were scrutinized it became clear that Gelli had his Freemasons in every decision-making centre in Italian politics, and was able to exert significant influence over those decisions. Even top secret summit meetings between the leaders of the coalition had not been secret for Gelli because of the substantial presence at the meetings of Social Democrat leader Pietro Longo, who was P2 member 2223. P2 had reached the very heart of government activity in the Palazzo Chigi. Mario Semprini, the Prime Minister's closest collaborator and his Chief of Cabinet, had been a member of P2 for over four years (membership No 1637), and was regularly passing secrets to his Venerable Master.

Another Christian Democrat officer, Massimiliano Cercelli, a former minister and a friend of masonic Justice Minister Sarti, was also a spy for P2. Lodge member 2180, Cercelli worked at the Office for the Co-ordination of the Secret Services.

Many P2 members were close associates of Forlani.

These included Enzo Badioli, the powerful chief of the Christian Democrat Co-operatives, and Gianni Cerioni, MP for Ancona.

Others were close to the President of the Senate, Amintore Fanfani, who was from Gelli's home town of Arezzo.

The catalogue of the powerful becomes tedious by its very length. A typical example of the enormity of Gelli's own influence over the lives of these men is the case of Mario Pedini who had suddenly been appointed a minister when he joined P2 and as quickly dropped by the government when his Lodge membership lapsed in 1978.

Other P2 members included the Minister of Employment, the Under-Secretary for Industry, the Under-Secretary for Foreign Affairs and the Foreign Commerce Minister.

It became apparent that nothing of vital importance had occurred in Italy in recent years which Gelli had not known about in advance or shortly after. Many vital developments were the result of his covert actions from the centre of his secret web. At the height of his power, the most bizarre actions were taken by successive governments, each of which were in Gelli's pocket.

Magistrates sifting the documents from the Villa Wanda found hundreds of top secret intelligence documents. Colonel Antonio Viezzer, the former head of the combined intelligence services, was identified as the prime source of this material and was arrested in Rome for spying on behalf of a foreign power. Following his interrogation, police raided the offices of a fashionable Tuscan lawyer and two suitcases crammed with incriminating documents were discovered. Dr Domenico Sica, head of the enquiries into P2 in Rome, was confident the papers had belonged to Gelli. They backed up the evidence in the Villa Wanda papers in the form of receipts for subscriptions paid to P2 by its members, and also receipts for bribes paid to Lodge members for 'services rendered'.

The extent to which P2 had destabilized Italy is exemplified by the events following President Pertini's actions immediately he was informed of the scandal. Among the members of the Lodge were two of his own executives, men he had liked and trusted. They were Sergio Piscitello (Master of Ceremonies of the Quirinale) and Francesco Gregorio, Pertini's diligent secretary for many years. Without hesitation the President suspended Piscitello and demoted Gregorio to typist. Three government ministers who believed the P2 lists were genuine wanted to follow Pertini's example. They couldn't. As one observer put it:

> The trial of strength with the concealed power of P2 has been exhausting for the weakened Forlani government. For days and days the ministers have been asking for some sign of good will (from Lodge members in high office), even simply to go on leave or to be available to the committee of enquiry, or to delegate their tasks to subordinates.
>
> But the 'Piduisti' have turned down every request, especially those within the military establishment.

On the weekend of 16 and 17 May, generals and admirals included on the membership lists met to work out a common strategy for their own survival. They decided to declare themselves victims of a plot and sit tight, defying the investigators to find concrete evidence against them.

At this point the fearful power of Gelli was found to have undermined not only the national security of Italy, but to have struck at the roots of western strength in southern Europe and the Middle East. NATO was forced to support the attitude of the corrupt Freemasons in Italy's armed forces. Officials in Brussels and Washington suggested discreetly that it was not the right moment to create a vacuum of power in the Italian army, navy and secret services. To replace the Defence Chief of Staff (P2 member No 1825), the Chief of Military Counter-espionage (P2 member No 1603), and the Chief of National Security (P2 member No 1620) might, said NATO, have grave repercussions on NATO's south flank forces, where the Lebanese crisis had taken a dangerous turn.

CHAPTER 27

The Chinaman Report

A bizarre incident occurred in early July 1981. Gelli's daughter Maria flew into Italy under her own name, knowing she would be instantly recognized. She was arrested at Fiumicino Airport, Rome, and her luggage was seized. In a compartment in a false-bottomed suitcase, Customs officers discovered five packages of documents relating to P2. They included statements from several Swiss banks in the names of Italian politicians and political parties, and also a document which appears to have been a forged 'secret report' by the CIA on attempts to subvert western Europe in general and Italy in particular. Why would Signora Gelli return to Italy with incriminating P2 documents that had already been safely removed from the country? What motive was so pressing that she took the step knowing she would be imprisoned on charges of espionage? For an answer to this, and to the question of what Gelli really was up to, we must also look at what was *not* contained in all the bundles of documents from the Villa Wanda, nor in Maria Gelli's suitcase, nor any of the other P2-related papers.

Without the benefit of inside information such as I was later to have, journalist Peter Hebblethwaite came close to the truth in his article 'Gelli's Babies', which appeared in *The Spectator* on 6 June 1981:

We know that he [Gelli] did business with east European countries. . . . As we have already seen, he boasted about his friendship with Ceausescu. Yet there are no names of any Italian Communist politicians or any east Europeans in this vast store of material. But no one can do business with a Communist country without such intermediaries. It follows that their names have been deliberately suppressed. By whom? Not by the Italian Government, which would have every interest in revealing them. By Gelli himself? If so, the suspicion would be aroused that Gelli deliberately 'planted' all this material, arranged for his disappearance, and is now observing the fascinating consequence of his handiwork from some safe villa on the Black Sea coast.

Licio Gelli - ruthless Fascist, torturer of partisans in the Second World War, friend and adviser of Perón and co-ordinator of right-wing corruption in Italy - was an agent of the KGB. This alone answers all the questions that rise up around his sinister figure. It explains how a document describing the structure of the KGB came to be among the Venerable Master's files; why Maria Gelli returned to Italy - to throw the country, and its attempts to recover from the scandal, into further confusion. She even brought with her a forged letter to her father that alluded to purported arrangements for bribing the members of the judiciary actually investigating P2. It explains how the P2 affair, described by many as the most damaging of all Italy's scandals, was linked with the attempted assassination of the Pope on 13 May 1981, even as P2 was coming to the boil. Western intelligence experts are now generally agreed that the attempted killing was inspired by the KGB.

Loyal to no one, obsessed with power for its own sake, Licio Gelli was determined to use whatever means he could to achieve his ambition: the ruin of those colourless weaklings, the Christian Democrats, who for nearly forty years had run the country which had spawned him, then spurned him for his turpitude. A man filled with such hatred can become a precision instrument in the hands of the Soviet Secret Service, intent as it is on implanting the seeds of disruption wherever it can in the West. According to an impeccable source within British Intelligence, Gelli was recruited by the KGB soon after he set about the task of building up *Raggruppamento Gelli Propaganda Due.* Britain's Secret Intelligence Service (MI6) has closely monitored P2 since its inception. It detected KGB involvement in the affair at an early stage.

From the beginning, Lodge P2 was a KGB-sponsored programme aimed at destabilizing Italy, weakening NATO's southern flank, sweeping the Communists into power in Italy and sending resultant shock waves throughout the western world. It achieved its first aim, partially succeeded in its second, came close to realizing the third, and all but failed in the fourth.

MI6 and other western intelligence services have been trying to convince their governments of the enormous growth of the KGB's activities since 1965 (P2 was formed in 1966). Senior officers in British Intelligence regard the KGB as the 'biggest conspiracy in the world', according to one well-placed informant. But their warnings have so far fallen on muffled ears. Even the more hawkish western leaders like Reagan and Thatcher are reluctant to accept the enormity of the threat as it is assessed by MI6 and America's Central Intelligence Agency (CIA).

I have obtained a copy of a secret memorandum written by a British diplomat who worked with MI6 for nearly twenty years during the Cold War, largely in South-East Asia. A First Secretary in the Diplomatic Service, this officer had a secret service training, chaired several sub-committees of the Joint Intelligence Committee (JIC) and worked closely with the legendary former head of MI6, Sir

Maurice Oldfield. He is a specialist in the methods of secret societies and an expert on China, in which he has travelled widely.

The document is fourteen pages long and is typed on ordinary plain A4 paper with a manual typewriter. It is dated 4 June 1981, a time when there was much undercover activity by MI6, the CIA and Israel's Mossad focused on P2. For reasons of security I shall refer to the author of the document by a codename: 'Chinaman'.

By way of background he states:

> . . . as a result notably of the loss of the war in Vietnam, and the economic problems of the non-Communist countries which have been exacerbated by the cost of oil, the Soviet Union – despite grave and presently growing problems of its own – has embarked on a further phase in its major concerted effort to exploit to its own advantage the weakness and confusions in the non-Communist world by all means short of war. It can be argued that the Soviet leadership itself has come to regard the Cold War as a race to determine who buries whom – accepting that *both* sides, not just the 'capitalist' side, suffer severe internal 'contradictions' and vulnerable areas.

Writing on information received up to 4 June 1981, Chinaman was unable then to state with certainty that the KGB had been behind P2, but merely confirmed that 'the affair has so far been to the considerable advantage of the Soviet Union and of the Communists, which alone of the political parties has no known members among the listed names published by order of the [Italian] Prime Minister'.

Since then I have had many long meetings with him and developments have persuaded him that the original strong suspicion that the KGB was responsible for P2 is now inescapable.

Freemasonry has been a factor in Russian political thinking since long before the establishment of the Soviet state.

The February 1917 Revolution was provoked by Freemasons and was operated from the few masonic Lodges left after decades of persecution from Tsarist Secret Police. Alexander Kerensky, Justice Minister in the provisional government of Prince Georgi Yevgenievich Lvov, was a Freemason. After the Petrograd uprising in July 1917 which led to the resignation of Lvov, Kerensky took over as Prime Minister and appointed exclusively Masons to the government. When, chiefly because of Kerensky's inability to control the economy and his refusal to withdraw from the European war, the Bolsheviks took over the country in October, Kerensky and most of the Masons involved in the earlier revolution fled to France, where they established Lodges under the aegis of the Grand Orient of France.

As soon as the Bolshevik State was declared, Freemasonry was proscribed. This anti-masonic stand was enshrined in a resolution of the fourth Congress of the Communist International:

> It is absolutely necessary that the leading elements of the Party should close all channels which lead to the middle classes and should therefore bring about a definite breach with Freemasonry. The chasm which divides the proletariat from the middle classes must be clearly brought to the consciousness of the Communist Party. A small fraction of the leading elements of the Party wished to bridge this chasm and to avail themselves of the masonic Lodges. Freemasonry is a most dishonest and infamous swindle of the proletariat by the radically inclined section of the middle classes. We regard it as our duty to oppose it to the uttermost.*

*Quoted by Eugen Lenhoff, *The Freemasons*, 1934.

Freemasonry was thoroughly investigated by the CHEKA, the first Soviet intelligence organization, as a matter of priority. This enquiry led to the formal outlawing of the Brotherhood in 1922. It is known that in its successive incarnations as GPU, NKVD, GUKR ('Smersh'), KGB and the rest, the Soviet espionage machine has made a priority of infiltrating every kind of organization in every country of the world. Its prime target, in every country where it existed, was inevitably Freemasonry. 'Any organization, and in particular any secretive organization,' says Chinaman, 'must come to the notice of the KGB, whatever its political, social, spiritual, criminal or subversive aims.'

There is abundant evidence not only that this has been true from the very beginning of the Soviet state, but that it is a continuing phenomenon, and that the Russian government is pouring ever more funds into the KGB coffers to expand this penetration and manipulation of foreign organizations. KGB defector Dr Vladimir Sakharov describes modern KGB operatives as the 'crème de la crème of Soviet society', top experts in the language, customs, religion and way of life of the country in which they operate.*

The exploitation of Freemasonry by the KGB is not restricted to Italy. I can reveal that senior officers of British Intelligence are concerned that the KGB has been using Freemasonry in England for decades to help place its

*It has recently been revealed that the KGB runs its own religious centres for training appropriate agents to be sent to western and Third World countries. These centres are at Feodosia in the Crimea, Lvov in the Ukraine and at Constanza. In Lithuania there is a school for agents bound for Britain and other English-speaking countries. The Lithuanian centre is almost certain to be the centre of any training in the exploitation of English Freemasonry. Bulgarian defector Mikhail Gloechov has disclosed that Stalin had the centres set up as early as 1936.

agents in positions of responsibility and influence. The areas the KGB is most interested in penetrating are delineated by Chapman Pincher in his controversial study of Russia's infiltration of the West's secret defences, *Their Trade is Treachery*: '. . . when Soviet Intelligence secures a promising recruit, he or she is urged to get a job in MI5, the Secret Service, Government Communication Headquarters (the radio-interception organization), *The Times*, the BBC, the Foreign Office or the Home Office - in that order of preference'.

According to the evidence now available the undoubted 'jobs for the brethren' aspect of British Freemasonry has been used extensively by the KGB to penetrate the most sensitive areas of authority, most spectacularly illustrated in the years since 1945 by its placing of spies at the highest levels of both MI5 and MI6. Even today, members of the security services privately admit that they have no idea of the extent of this penetration.

Although one senior and decorated MI6 officer, based in London, has been actively researching Freemasonry's influence in Britain since the Chinaman Report came into his hands, no investigation has so far been started by MI5, which as Britain's internal security service must conduct any *official* enquiry. MI6 is empowered to act only abroad.

Former KGB officers who have defected to the West confirm the endless patience the organization expends on gathering information on every aspect of life in Britain. Even the tiniest details are filed away at the great KGB headquarters building at 2 Dzerzhinsky Square, Moscow, for possible use in its vast programme of destabilization in the West.

These facts are known, but what MI6 failed to appreciate before the Chinaman Report was the vital corollary to its knowledge that organizations, especially of a secretive nature, were being used by the KGB: a fact so obvious it was never even considered – that the largest and most important organization of a secretive nature in Britain was Freemasonry.

The 'old boy network', the favouritism and the use of Masonry for professional and social advancement – all proscribed by the Constitutions but all nevertheless widespread, as this book has shown – are of obvious value to Englishmen recruited to spy for a foreign power.

I have spoken to five currently serving officers of MI6, two of them senior men but not of the highest stratum. Posed the question, 'If you were a KGB agent in England, given the nature of Freemasonry, what would you do?', four them agreed independently that becoming a Freemason would be an obvious priority. The fifth said, 'I haven't heard of this, but obviously if there hasn't already been an enquiry there should be now. I know of only two Masons in 6. Naturally, it's not often spoken of.'

This is an interesting point. As I learned from a former Home Secretary (the Home Secretary is responsible for MI5), it is forbidden for any member of either of the intelligence services to be a Freemason.

Pages three to four of the Chinaman document contain this:

> I was required when I joined the Foreign Service and when I was given access to increasingly delicate material to 'sign the Official Secrets Act' and make declarations that I was not and never had been a member of certain listed extreme organizations of both left and right wing aims. But I was never required even orally to state whether I was or ever had been a member of any secret society whether of the Masonic type or not. This is less surprising given the social respectability of Freemasonry and the assumption by both members and non-members alike that it could not possibly come to represent in any way a threat to the established order.

This assumption is well illustrated by a comment made by

James Dewar, author of a book on Freemasonry entitled *The Open Secret*, when interviewed by the *Sunday Telegraph* in May 1981 at the height of the publicity about P2. He said, 'Any secret society has in it the seeds of menace. But it is very unlikely that a similar clique could operate here, as the movement is headed by so many people of obviously good repute . . .' And Judge D. H. Botha, who carried out an enquiry into Freemasonry in South Africa in 1964, had to rely largely on the evidence of four Freemasons. He entertained no doubts about their evidence as to what occurred at masonic meetings because of the 'exceptionally high esteem in which each of these persons is held in society and because of their obvious integrity'. Referring to this, Chinaman states:

This cannot be the view of any trained intelligence officer. It is of course inconceivable that, given the present composition of the British Grand Lodges and indeed other Lodges and chapters, the movement as a whole could possibly be suborned or persuaded to act consciously in any way to Soviet advantage. The dangers arise from numerous possibilities for covert exploitation of a movement which is almost conterminous with 'The Establishment' in common parlance:
(a) Any KGB officer with an agent recruited, say at university, must be concerned to arrange for that agent to have access to the highest priority on the list of targets provided by KGB headquarters that the particular agent is considered suitable to work against. If it is believed by so many Masons themselves that recruitment to many organizations, promotion, and other forms of success can be assisted by membership of Freemasonry, there can be little doubt but that the KGB shares this view. It must be expected therefore that the KGB instructs any agent, whom it believes could benefit from doing so, to become a Freemason.
(b) Equally clearly the KGB, if it recruits an agent who already has some access to a target, must consider whether membership of Freemasonry could assist in improving his access.
(c) In any long-term penetration the question of 'the Succession' is always in a case officer's mind. In addition to the ordinary risks of life and inevitable ageing, espionage and other covert

activity carries its own risks of being 'blown', and mental strain leading to breakdown. Therefore an agent in place who is a Mason may very well be considered more likely to be able to assist in placing his own successor to best advantage.

(d) The KGB must consider in each case whether membership of Freemasonry would afford any particular agent increased protection. For example, whether membership would confer on the agent additional respectability which would stifle or help to stifle suspicion, and whether membership could provide useful cover for other secret activities; or indeed, whether membership would assist in any necessary cover-up – other members of the Fraternity doubtless believing they were only assisting a brother over some dereliction of duty or other relatively minor infringement.

(e) The KGB will also consider whether Fraternal relationships can be used to obtain information or to cause actions desired by its headquarters. That is to say, to use the masonic bond apparently for the normal purposes of mutual advancement and mutual protection, but in fact for the benefit of the KGB. In particular the KGB will be aware that Masons may well be less on their guard when talking outside the Lodge to other Lodge members and other Masons generally than they would be speaking to others about their professional and personal concerns.

(f) It follows from this that the KGB may through masonic contacts come by information which would greatly assist in any blackmail attempt against an individual. Indeed, were the KGB to become aware of any improper actions by two or more Masons in regard to cover-ups, e.g. in the administration of justice, such blackmail could be applied to a group. The threat of exposure could then lead to further masonic involvement in order to preserve the movement's good name. As Watergate showed, cover-ups generally start small but tend to grow uncontrollably.

(g) An agent in any movement enjoying such diverse support at such varying levels of the social hierarchy provides (a) ideal opportunities to 'talent spot', and (b) the means to contact some specialist in almost every field where assistance may be needed, and in a manner most conducive to obtaining any 'favour' required.

It will be noted that in all these cases there is no need for Freemasonry as an institution, or indeed for any other member of the movement to be 'conscious' to KGB's use of Masonry. KGB will simply be riding the 'lift' that Masonry supplies ready installed to enable its members to arrive at higher floors more quickly and with less effort than those, perhaps better qualified, who are hurrying up the stairs. During the 'lift ride', others in the 'lift' may be examined and contacted in a relaxed atmosphere. It is clearly unlikely that once KGB found . . . the masonic 'lift' they would not use it again several times. But once again there is no need for one conscious KGB agent within Masonry to know or even know *of* any other. Unless there is some overriding 'need to know', the KGB will obviously make every effort to prevent this happening.

Through an intermediary, I asked former KGB spy Ilya Grigevich Dzhirkvelov, who defected to the West in 1980, about Freemasonry. The Soviet authorities are well aware of the size and influence of Masonry in the West. Dzhirkvelov was based in Geneva for most of his thirty-year career as a KGB agent, so was not in direct touch with espionage activities in Britain. Switzerland's Grand Lodge 'Alpina' is based at Lausanne. The entire country has only fifty-two Lodges – compared with London's 1,677. There are about 3,450 Swiss Masons. Dzhirkvelov spoke of the 'vast' scale of the KGB's espionage activities in the UK, and said that if Freemasonry was such an important part of the Establishment as I said, *there was no doubt at all that the KGB was exploiting it, even to the extent of instructing its British recruits to become Masons.*

Among the currently serving and former officers of both services I met was one much respected officer of MI6, recently retired, who was more cautious. We met next to the fish pond on the first floor of Coutts & Co in the Strand early in 1982. He had agreed to meet me only on the understanding that we did not discuss matters covered by the Official Secrets Act. He was not a Freemason. He said that he had never been aware that Freemasonry could be an advantage in government service, nor felt the need to become a Mason to advance his career. He added, 'But perhaps that is because I have never thought about it.'

He told me that he had never come across a case of the KGB using Freemasonry in England, and added, 'But of course that does not mean it has not happened.' The fact that he had never even considered such an obvious possibility did not surprise me. It seems that nobody prior to Chinaman had. Even Sir George Young, former Vice Chief of MI6, told me that the extent of his knowledge about Freemasonry was that 'the Royal Family are all in it'.

My contact pointed out that Masonry would not be used by a KGB agent as a cover, in the sense that Guy Burgess joined the Anglo-German Fellowship before the war to conceal his Communist sympathies, because by its very nature membership of Freemasonry is not something one can boast about without giving rise to suspicion. He paused and set his mind to work on the problem. At length he said: 'The records of Freemasonry in Tsarist Russia would have fallen into the hands of the CHEKA, the KGB's predecessor, in 1917. A close study of Freemasonry would certainly have been made by Soviet intelligence officers then.*

'If the KGB had a target in England – somebody they wanted to "turn" or from whom they wanted to obtain information by one of a number of means – and this person was a Freemason, I have no doubt that it would instruct an agent to join the same Lodge. That would be an obvious move. If being a Freemason makes a man more likely to bare his soul to another Freemason than to an outsider [there is ample evidence that this is the case], any intelligence service worth its salt would exploit that. Once

*This was the case, as already explained.

again, I have no evidence that this has happened. The fraternity most often exploited of course is the homosexual one – the homintern we used to call it.'

Towards the end of our meeting, my contact said, 'Is there any evidence that any of the known people were Freemasons?'

By 'people' he meant traitors, British subjects who had been recruited by the KGB either before they were in positions where they had access to delicate material, while they were rising in their careers towards such positions, or after they had arrived.

One case particularly bears examination.

Few people in MI5 now doubt that Sir Roger Hollis, director-general of the service in the crucial years 1956–65, was a Russian spy for nearly thirty years. This has been convincingly demonstrated by veteran investigative journalist and espionage expert Chapman Pincher. The government in the person of Margaret Thatcher has denied this, and a number of Hollis's old colleagues have jumped to his defence, but their evidence is weak and contradictory.

I shall not rehearse the case against Hollis here. It is proven beyond reasonable doubt in the revised edition of Pincher's book, which appeared in fuller form after various official attempts to discredit the evidence and arguments contained in the first edition.

As one MI5 officer of long standing confided to me: 'We've known about Hollis for years. Pincher has excellent sources within the service and an excellent brain. He is *so close* to the truth.'

Hollis was not a member of the 'homintern'. The same MI5 source told me baldly, 'Hollis was certainly a Mason.'

Of the many mysteries surrounding Sir Roger Hollis, one of the most baffling is how he was ever accepted into MI5 in the first place. He was quite *the opposite* of what was required. In MI5, as opposed to MI6 which operates abroad, there is a reluctance to accept candidates who have travelled widely out of the UK. In the 1930s when Hollis was recruited this stipulation was more easily met than it is today. For this and other reasons, Hollis was a most unlikely recruit. Doing badly at university, he threw in the towel in 1926 after only two years, worked in a London bank for a while and set off for China. Stranded with only £10 in his pocket in Malaya, he got a job with an international tobacco company in Penang and was later transferred to the company's offices in Shanghai. He moved around China for the next nine years, working at Peking, Hangkow and Dairen. After this, he became tuberculous, and travelled to a Swiss sanatorium by way of the Trans-Siberian Railway from Vladivostok, spending some time in Russia. All this, especially his time in Russia, should have been an insuperable obstacle to any hopes he had of joining MI5.

And so it proved . . . at first. Even after his treatment his health was not strong enough for him to continue working for the tobacco company, so early in 1936 he was back in England. 'Even his friends agree that he was not particularly talented,' wrote Chapman Pincher, who describes him at the time of his return to England as 'basically a broken man': 'Though surprisingly athletic, he was to retain the look of someone who had been tuberculous and became progressively so round-shouldered that he looked almost hunched . . . He had no degree, his health was suspect and his experience in China was not likely to be helpful in securing a post in England. The only work he could find was as a clerk–typist.'

However, through an army major he met, he secured an interview with MI5. He was turned down and told that his experience abroad might be useful to MI6. He applied and was turned down for health reasons by that service.

When he applied to MI5 for the second time later that

year nothing had changed . . . except the mind of MI5. This time he was taken on. The director-general of MI5 then was Major General Sir Vernon Kell, who happened to be a Freemason.

With almost everything going against him, Hollis got in. What is even more remarkable was the rate at which he was promoted within the service once he had got in. This astonished his colleagues then, and still cannot be explained by any of the MI5 officers, current and retired, with whom I have had contact either directly or through intermediaries. This is one of the great mysteries of Roger Hollis, even to those who, because they were not involved in particular events and because they liked the man, are not convinced that he was a spy.

Even though it was against the regulations for any officer to be a Freemason – and this, incidentally, must presumably indicate that membership was regarded as a threat to security – several officers were in the Brotherhood. Among them was a man called Potter, who was in charge of the huge MI5 card index, now computerized. Such a man would be good to have as a friend.

But was it Freemasonry that got Hollis against all odds into the service and took him, the unlikeliest of all its officers, to the very top? I believe it was. The likeliest key to the mystery of Hollis is Shanghai and the time he spent there working for the British American Tobacco Company in the 1930s.

The European community in Shanghai was small. The English-speaking community was of course smaller and very tight-knit. Virtually every Englishman arriving in Shanghai gravitated to the Masonic Hall at 1623 Avenue Road. Freemasonry had flourished among the British expatriates here and at the previous Masonic Hall at 30 The Bund, Shanghai, since the mid-1800s. In the twenties and thirties, when Hollis was in Shanghai, the tradition of Freemasonry there was at its zenith. A man who was not a Mason was at a grave disadvantage in achieving whatever social or professional ambitions he had.

Almost everyone I have contacted who knew Hollis, including MI5 officers past and present, has reacted similarly to the suggestion that the former director-general was a member of the Brotherhood – that he was just the kind of man, extremely secretive by nature, with few open friendships and with small prospect of advancement – who would join Masonry in order to exploit its covert advantages. Freemasonry, said the contacts, offered the first explanation to the Hollis mystery, his otherwise inexplicable acceptance and his phenomenal rate of promotion. This would be especially likely, I was told, if Hollis's immediate predecessor as director-general of the Security Service, Sir Dick Goldsmith White, had been a Mason. The one notable voice of dissent was that of Sir Dick White himself, whose own formidable career contains one striking anomaly. White is the only man ever to have been head of both MI5 and MI6. He moved from 5 in 1956 to take over the Secret Service from Sir John 'Sinbad' Sinclair. Despite his impressive record and qualifications, the unprecedented transfer was viewed by many within MI6 as dangerous and as something which, once again breaking all the traditional rules governing the secure operation of the two services, should never have been allowed. It was White who, on his appointment as Secret Service Chief, recommended Hollis as his successor to premier Anthony Eden. When I put it to Sir Dick at his retirement home near Arundel that Hollis's period in Shanghai made it virtually certain that he had been a member of the Brotherhood, he laughed and said, 'Oh dear me, I wouldn't have thought so at all. I can't guarantee it, but it seems to me most unlikely.' When I asked why not, he said exactly the opposite of what others had told me – that Hollis 'really didn't seem the type'. When I asked him if he himself was or ever had been a Freemason, Sir Dick seemed amused, and told me genially that he never had, adding that he hoped I 'reached the right conclusion' about Hollis.

Hollis's treachery should have come to light in the late 1940s when Sir Percy Sillitoe was director-general of MI5. As A. W. Cockerill, Sillitoe's biographer, points out, 'practically the entire effort of the Service from 1946 on, and until long after Sillitoe's retirement, was directed at identifying and weeding out Communists from positions in which they posed a threat to national security'. Cockerill states that one of Sillitoe's first actions after getting settled into the job as MI5 chief was to carry out a purge, for which he had something of a reputation in his former career in the police.

> In the case of MI5, he was primarily interested in the political reliability of his staff, and a number of employees were forced to leave for one reason or another . . . Beginning with those whose credentials were 'impeccable', he carried out a systematic security check of the entire establishment. This was a programme in which the internal security officers combed through each personal file as though the person concerned was a newcomer; the individuals's history was checked and rechecked, membership in clubs, societies and social organizations was investigated anew to ensure that the service itself was 'clean'.

But Sillitoe, without knowing it, was fighting an impossible battle. With the man in charge of all the personal records being a member of the Brotherhood, Sillitoe would never be allowed to learn that Hollis's means of entry to the service had been by way of a masonic Lodge in China and a masonic director-general.

It is an interesting fact that the membership lists of the

Shanghai Lodges between the wars are among the most closely guarded secrets of the United Grand Lodge. Several attempts by concerned members of the Brotherhood to get hold of these files through the ordinary channels have been blocked. It is evident that those lists of names contain something so explosive, so potentially damaging to the Brotherhood, that it will not permit them to be examined even by senior Masons. Whose name is being concealed, if not Hollis's?

CHAPTER 28

The Threat to Britain

The Chinaman Report goes further than drawing attention to the KGB's almost certain use of Freemasonry for placing operatives in positions of authority, most damagingly achieved, so far as we know, in the case of Hollis. The Report also expresses concern that British Freemasonry as a whole is, quite unknown to its members, a major target for so-called 'Special Political Action' by the KGB. It states:

> . . . sheer prudence demands that the lessons of the P2 affair receive the attention of all who have the interests of the UK and the West at heart, Masons and non-Masons alike . . . The affair has so far been to the considerable advantage of the Soviet Union and of the Communists, which alone of the political parties has no known members among the listed names published by order of the Prime Minister. Had P2 continued its secret growth and unacceptable activities, the inevitable eventual scandal could have brought down with it non-Communist government in Italy. Yet Italian Freemasonry has been estimated as of the order of under 100,000 – a mere tenth of the supposed UK total for a roughly similar population.*

*This includes England and Wales, Scotland *and* Ireland. Even so, the commonly quoted figure of a million Freemasons in Britain is about 250,000 too high.

It could be argued that Italy's laws regarding secret associations differ from Britain's, and that there is far more prejudice against Freemasonry in Italy because of strong Roman Catholic and Communist opposition than there is in the UK where, on the contrary, the Brotherhood enjoys the inestimable advantage of royal patronage. Thus the reaction in Britain to a masonic scandal would be nothing like so extreme as in Italy. But Chinaman suggests that 'the Italian affair is a serious warning from which important lessons can be drawn . . . The UK could well prove very much more vulnerable to exposure of improper activities by a group of Freemasons than is Italy.'

There are two reasons for this:

First, Masonry so permeates so many revered British institutions from the Crown downwards, that a grave masonic scandal could in modern circumstances involve popular revulsion against the whole established order, Government and business. Second, the proportion of Masons to non-Masons in some professions and other walks of life, including areas of Government, appears to have reached a critical point: the point at which people believe themselves obliged to join Freemasonry, no longer voluntarily, but from a feeling of compulsion.

This statement is certainly accurate, as my own enquiries have revealed.

Masons and non-Masons alike seem increasingly to fear the potential of the fraternity to ruin them. At such a point it becomes hard to find in certain areas vital to the state an adequate number of competent persons who are non-Masons to prevent such a vacuum as now threatens Italy were all the officers of the armed forces of General rank named in the P2 documents to be required to retire. Third, there is much circumstantial evidence that more ruthless elements have joined Freemasonry and are using up the fund of respectability that Royal patronage confers to indulge in activities which reputable members would find quite unacceptable were they aware of the extent of the abuse. This, of course, is a danger inherent in all secretive societies for their cellular form devised by the founders for the security of the movement, can as readily be used to 'hoodwink' the leadership, who thus become unwitting 'front men' for activities they would never countenance.

The Report alludes to the argument that there has not been a masonic scandal of major proportions in modern times and the contention that should one occur, it could readily be contained by the Brotherhood by means of both public expulsions and cover-ups. It continues:

This may possibly be so. But British society as a whole is changing rapidly. The established order of things developed over the past thousand years is no longer so widely and so automatically accepted as in even the recent past. Many, of all political hues, consider some of our institutions archaic and in need of reform. This view is fuelled by the loss of national self-confidence and national pride following from the loss of Empire and our very poor showing in the list of advanced industrial societies. Disrespect for those in authority is already considerable and is increasing at an accelerating rate: such rife dissatisfaction soon comes to seek a scapegoat, such as 'the Establishment' provides. But our institutions – both public and private – seem incapable of reforming themselves and performing the *aggiornamento* the thoughtful of all moderate persuasions are increasingly coming to expect.

Against this worsening background it would be rash to suppose that the methods of the past to contain scandals and irregularities in Masonry (or indeed in anything else) will still be adequate by, say, the end of this decade. And this is to count without the attentions of the KGB.

The possibility that the KGB has a long-term interest in British Freemasonry must be taken seriously. For to any trained intelligence officer, Freemasonry offers an ideal vehicle for the destabilization of the United Kingdom. To make two points: there has for some time been practically no mention of Freemasonry in the media: for so widespread and important a movement this almost amounts to a taboo – any serious, well-documented exposure of substantial malpractices could be expected to have a disproportionate shock effect. We are not yet so cynical and so inured to scandal as the Italians. Second, the KGB – itself growing out of a clandestine movement's seizure of state power, well understands the organization, motivation and other problems of secret societies (particularly of communications, records, and the use of a reputable 'front') and is thus ideally qualified to exploit Freemasonry for its own ends.

Here Chinaman constructs, from his thirty-year knowledge of the KGB's political methods and of the inner workings of British Freemasonry – with the P2 conspiracy forming a bridge between the two – a scenario which to my certain knowledge senior officials of both MI5 and MI6 regard with the utmost gravity. The man code-named Chinaman suggests that the most likely method of attack would follow the pattern of P2 – in other words, the KGB, doubtless through Czech intelligence, would attempt to hive off a promising area of Freemasonry and encourage its growth.

The more prominent those unwittingly involved, the greater the ultimate effect – provided the top echelon [of Freemasonry] were carefully preserved untainted. Another phase would be deliberately to encourage and exacerbate existing abuses for personal advancement at the expense of non-Masons. Arrogance would be inflated to a point where the Masons concerned would become over-confident and incautious . . . the KGB would then obtain and collate documentary and circumstantial evidence in as many spheres of activity as possible.

Once sufficient material had been gathered, the KGB would be prepared to wait years if required until directed to mount an exposure at a politically appropriate juncture. Then the 'fuse' would be lit, for example by arranging for a blackmail operation to fail, or a Soviet 'defector' to arrive perhaps in the US, and point conclusively to KGB involvement in Masonry. Media and Government enquiries could then be fed with supplementary evidence garnered for the purpose over the years. Names would be called. Confusion would be sown by including the righteous (chosen for their effectiveness in opposition to Soviet designs) with the guilty (chosen for their publicity value): in such circumstances lies mixed with incontrovertible truths would be hard to winnow.

If the right moment for 'ignition' were chosen the disaster could be very great. One need only to remember the effect on each occasion of the news of Fuchs's* espionage, the Maclean and Burgess defections, the Philby case, the Blunt exposure and the recent public allegations regarding the late Sir Roger Hollis, to appreciate the effect of well documented exposures at one time of even fifty prominent persons – let alone nearly a thousand as in the Italian case.

Chinaman makes it plain that short of information from some formerly well-placed genuine defector, there is no certain means of knowing whether the Soviet Union is operating such a plan – nor, if so, how long it has been in preparation. And if it is in preparation, we cannot know how much time is likely to elapse before it could be 'ignited'.

I have no idea whether Communist bloc defectors have been questioned on the subject or what were their replies. I simply suggest that it is self-evident that the possibility should be taken seriously and appropriate defensive action taken if this has not already been done adequately.

I can reveal that no such defensive action has yet been taken because prior to the submission of the Chinaman Report, no one had considered the possible exploitation of Masonry. No one knew enough about the Brotherhood for it to present itself as a possibility. Chinaman suggests measures to minimize the effects of any KGB-promoted exposure in two main ways:

*Klaus Emil Julian Fuchs, convicted in 1950 of passing British and American atomic research secrets to the Soviet Union.

First, by ensuring that we are not 'caught' with persons holding certain key delicate positions being Masons . . . From my own experience (as well as reports of the P2 case) I would hope for example that the heads of both the Secret Intelligence Service and the Security Service are not permitted to be Masons, and that the regulations of these two services now provide for any Masons to declare their adherence to the head of the service concerned personally.* I believe that the same should apply to Special Branch. Masons who are members of these branches of Government could however provide a valuable link to Freemasonry in the service of the state if they are not so acting already. In other Departments, arrangements could be made to ensure that heads of personnel sections be non-Masons, and that they have a right of access to the Director-General of the Security Service. The legal profession – presently the object of increasing public disquiet because of its alleged tendency to protect its own – is a particular problem given the large number of Freemasons . . . The second direction I would concentrate upon would be legislation. It seems to me, for instance, far less likely that any deliberately organized exposure would cause serious and lasting damage to the benefit of the pro-Communist left and the Soviet Union, if all citizens had the legal right, if they so elected, to a written assurance that any professional person they consulted is not a member of any secret society, including the Freemasons and similar or related groupings: an untrue denial rendering the professional person liable to criminal proceedings. I appreciate the very great difficulties, but possibly in the not too far distant future in the wake of the P2 affair, some measure along these lines might be passed . . . In the Government service Masons in delicate areas would come to know that for security reasons a few positions were closed to them: this too would help shift the balance of advantage.

Such measures could, I believe, also incidentally lead to a significant improvement in Britain's performance in many places, lessening the possibility that the more dynamic, more forward-looking and better qualified may be passed over to the detriment of governmental and industrial efficiency. I repeat, though, that I am well aware that I have not the qualifications for suggesting counter-measures, that I have for setting out the dangers.

*As already stated, MI5 officers are banned from joining the Brotherhood, but this has not prevented several from doing so.

I have discussed this Report in general terms and off the record with several highly placed officials and with three former Cabinet Ministers, all of whom told me that if such a report came into their hands when they were in office they would have initiated an enquiry. In March 1982, having contacted Foreign Secretary Lord Carrington and been assured by him that he was not nor had ever been a member of the Brotherhood, I was on the point of raising it with him. Then Argentina invaded the Falkland Islands and Britain lost one of its most able ministers.

And here another link is forged between Licio Gelli, his Soviet masters, and the important task P2 had been created to perform in the continuing programme to destablize the West. After his flight from Italy, Gelli did not go into hiding beyond the Iron Curtain as suggested by the perspicacious Peter Hebblethwaite. Most informed sources believed he was in Argentina, where he had exercised so much influence in the past and where, I suggest, General Galtieri was his new Perón. It cannot be a coincidence that Admiral Emilio Massera, the commander of the Argentine Navy and one of the three-man junta that launched the Falklands invasion, and the commander of the Argentine First Army, General Carlos Suarez Mason, were both secret members of Lodge P2.

Epilogue

On 18 June 1982 the dead body of a middle-aged man was found hanging by the neck from a rope suspended from scaffolding beneath Blackfriars Bridge, London. The pockets of his black suit contained nearly £23,000 in various currencies and were weighted with 12 pounds of builder's bricks. He was Roberto Calvi, president of Italy's Banco Ambrosiano, who in 1981 had been named a member of Licio Gelli's illegal Freemasonic Lodge, Propaganda Due. Calvi was later found guilty by an Italian court of illegally exporting $26.4 million to Switzerland and received a four-year suspended prison sentence and ordered to pay a fine equivalent to £7.3 million. A week later he was confirmed as chairman of Banco Ambrosiano. In April 1982 Calvi's deputy at the bank was wounded by a would-be assassin. Known as 'God's banker', Calvi had ben closely linked with Instituto per le Opere di Religione (IOR), the Vatican Bank, for years. A number of highly questionable transactions involving the Vatican Bank, Calvi and Banco Ambrosiano subsidiaries in Latin America and elsewhere led the Bank of Italy to launch an investigation. On the last day of May 1982 the Bank of Italy demanded an explanation for loans of $1,400 million made by Banco Ambrosiano subsidiaries to several companies registered in Panama owned directly or indirectly by the Vatican Bank. This precipitated a run on Ambrosiano's shares, and eleven days later Calvi disappeared in Rome. Using a false passport, he fled to Austria and then England, arriving at Gatwick on 15 June and travelling straight to London where he remained for several days in an apartment in Chelsea Cloisters. On 17 June the Bank of Italy seized control of Banco Ambrosiano and trading in its shares was suspended after they had dropped twenty per cent in value in one day. Ambrosiano's directors resigned and Calvi's secretary, Graziella Corrocher – who kept the books of Lodge P2 – jumped, or was pushed, to her death from a fourth-floor window at the bank. She left behind her what was obviously intended to be taken as a suicide note, although there is more than a small doubt that this was genuine. The note said: 'May Calvi be double cursed for the damage he has caused to the bank and its employees.'

The following night Calvi's body was found hanging from the scaffolding beneath Blackfriars Bridge, four miles from the apartment in Chelsea Cloisters. Even as the *Daily Express* postal clerk who found the body was hastening to call the police, Italian police were busy chartering a plane and a party of high officials arrived at Gatwick a few hours later.

There were many rumours: the Mafia, with whom Calvi had connections, had murdered him; frightened and despairing, he had committed suicide; he had been ritually done to death by Freemasons, a masonic 'cable-tow' around his neck and his pockets filled symbolically with chunks of masonry, the location of the murder being chosen for its name – in Italy, the logo of the Brotherhood is the figure of a Blackfriar.

But a City of London inquest later decided that Calvi had committed suicide, a verdict the banker's family immediately announced its intention to challenge. Italian police, and a number of City of London police associated with the case, are convinced it was murder.

The inquest was told that Calvi had been a 'frightened man, fearful of his life' before flying to London in June. And it was never explained why, even if Calvi had decided to do the work of those he feared, he would travel four miles across London late at night to Blackfriars Bridge, fill his pockets with bricks, climb on to the bridge and over the side on to scaffolding he could not possibly have known was there – all this in a man who suffered extreme vertigo – and perform the elaborate task of arranging a heavy rope, presumably brought with him for the purpose, and launch himself off the scaffolding. It would have been easier by far to throw himself from his office window in Italy, or if the idea of suicide only came to him when he reached London – an awfully long way to go just to kill yourself – why not do it with his belt in the comfort of his Chelsea apartment?

The mystery of Calvi's death deepens rather than clarifies with time. It is inextricably bound up with the riddle of P2, the KGB penetration of Freemasonry, and Freemasonry's penetration not only of the Roman Catholic Church but the Vatican itself.* At the time this book goes to press, investigations are continuing into Banco Ambrosiano's links with the enigmatic president of the Vatican Bank, Archbishop Paul Marcinkus, and into the continuing international reverberations of the P2 conspiracy.

Meanwhile, Licio Gelli has since been arrested in Switzerland where he was attempting to withdraw nearly $100 million from several numbered accounts at Geneva's Union Bank – money belonging to Banco Ambrosiano. Gelli awaits the outcome of extradition proceedings.

*At a second inquest in June 1983, the jury returned an open verdict.

Meanwhile, too, Yuri Andropov, head of the KGB when the P2 plot was hatched, now sits at the pinnacle of Soviet power and diverts ever more funds towards the KGB's activities in the West, the exploitation of Freemasonry included.

There are several clear areas which call for an investigation into the use of Freemasonry's secrets and its network of contacts. Why is it that, although the United Grand Lodge has powers to revoke the charter of any Lodge found to be conducting itself in an unworthy, immoral or criminal way, this provision is never implemented? Why is it that individual Masons, who betray the Brotherhood by proving daily they have joined for pecuniary or other advantage and by constantly exploiting the unique privileges which Masonry confers, are hardly ever expelled, as the Brotherhood's *Book of Constitutions* provides? Grand Lodge remains obdurately silent.

I approached United Grand Lodge early in my investigation explaining my aims and how in its own interests the Brotherhood should surely at least talk of its attitude to those 'bad apples' that all but a few Freemasons readily admit are there. I received a courteous rebuff and was told, nicely but firmly, to mind my own business.

This stubborn refusal to speak to outsiders and Grand Lodge's traditional silence in the face of criticism, even when corruption has been traced to members of a Lodge or group of Lodges abusing Masonry for their own ends, does nothing but heighten suspicion.

It is time for Freemasonry to put its house in order, to operate openly, to comply with the laws relating to it, and to be seen to condemn those within its ranks who are 'traitors' to its stated highly moral aims.

No one who has investigated Freemasonry in Britain

with a clear brain can fail to be impressed by the goodness it contains and which is manifested in many ways. I have met many men who would otherwise be without purpose or self-respect who have found that Masonry brings out all that is most admirable in them.

But the rot must be cut out ruthlessly, because it is spreading. And as it spreads more and more of the 'good' brethren get out and are replaced by the 'bad'.

In the end is the beginning. Although this first edition of *The Brotherhood* has reached its final paragraph, it represents barely a glimpse beneath the surface of Freemasonry in modern society. I am still at the start of my investigations, which will continue, and future editions will not only look at the Brotherhood's influence in fields hardly touched on here - like education, the Civil Service, the Press, agriculture, science and many others - but will include further case histories, and any arguments either in favour of or against Masonry which readers of this edition think relevant and cannot find here.

APPENDIX ONE

Information For Candidates

(from *The Universal Book of Craft Masonry*)

Freemasonry consists of a body of men banded together to preserve the secrets, customs and ceremonials handed down to them from time immemorial, and for the purpose of mutual intellectual, social and moral improvement. They also endeavour to cultivate and exhibit brotherly love, relief and truth, not only to one another, but to the world at large.

Freemasonry offers no pecuniary advantages whatever, neither does there exist any obligation nor implied understanding binding one Mason to deal with another, nor to support him in any way in the ordinary business relations of life.

Freemasonry teaches us to remember our common origin; it also distinctly enjoins us to respect all social distinctions, so that while some must rule, others must obey and cheerfully accept their inferior positions.

Freemasonry has certain charities, but it is not in any sense whatever a benefit society, nor is it based on any calculations which would render this possible. The charities are solely for *those who having been in good circumstances* have been overtaken by misfortune or adversity, and they are quite insufficient to meet even these demands now made upon them.

Freemasonry distinctly teaches that a man's first duty is

to *himself, his wife, his family and his connections*, and no one should join the Order who cannot well afford to pay the initiation fees and subscriptions to his Lodge as well as to the Masonic charities, and this without detriment in any way to his comfort, or to that of those who have any claim upon his support.

Freemasonry recognizes no distinctions of religion, but none should attempt to enter who have no religious belief, as faith in a Deity must be expressed before any can be initiated, and prayers to Him form a frequent part of the ritual.

Freemasonry, therefore, demands that everyone before offering himself as a candidate, should be well assured in his own mind:

1. That he sincerely desires the intellectual and moral improvement of himself and his fellow creatures, and that he is willing to devote part of his time, means and efforts to the promotion of brotherly love, relief and trust.
2. That he seeks no commercial, social nor pecuniary advantages.
3. That he is able to afford the necessary expenditure without injury to himself or connections.
4. That he is willing to enter into solemn obligations in the sight of his God.

APPENDIX TWO

The Officers of the Lodge

Each Lodge elects the following officers every year:

Worshipful Master Chairman of the Lodge.
Immediate Past Master Last year's Worshipful Master.
Senior Warden Personal officer of WM; next year's WM in most lodges.
Junior Warden Personal officer of WM and next in seniority.
Chaplain The officer who conducts prayers. Can be a man of any profession in the outside world, not necessarily a clergyman.
Treasurer The senior officer in charge of the Lodge funds.
Secretary
Director of Ceremonies In charge of the ritual element of Lodge business.
Senior Deacon
Junior Deacon The Deacons – with their wands – play an important part in Lodge ritual, including acting the role of messengers.
Charity Steward Officer in charge of the Lodge's donations to charity.
Almoner Officer in charge of collecting and spending the Lodge's benevolent funds.
Assistant Director of Ceremonies Self-explanatory.
Inner Guard Officer who guards the door of the Lodge on the inside and ensures that only Freemasons enter.
Tyler The outer guard who stands outside the Lodge door with a dagger as the first line of defence against non-Masons trying to enter.

APPENDIX THREE

Initiation to the First Degree up to the end of the Obligation

The Tyler prepares the Candidate in a room outside the Lodge room where he is to be initiated by divesting him of all metal articles. The Candidate removes his outer clothing until he stands in socks, his left shoe, trousers and shirt only. His shirt is unbuttoned to reveal his left breast, his right sleeve is rolled up to reveal the elbow, his left trouser leg is rolled up above the knee and a slipper is placed on his unshod foot. A hangman's noose is then placed around his neck, the end of the rope hanging down behind him. He is blindfolded.

He is then led by the Tyler to the door of the Lodge and the Tyler knocks.

The Inner Guard, moving with the prescribed step and making the First Degree sign, says, 'Brother Junior Warden, there is a report.' After several ritual responses, the Inner Guard opens the door and asks the Tyler, 'Whom have you there?'

'Mr John Smith, a poor Candidate in a state of darkness,' says the Tyler, 'who has been well and worthily recommended, regularly proposed and approved in open Lodge, and now comes of his own free will and accord, properly prepared, humbly soliciting to be admitted to the mysteries and privileges of Freemasonry.'

There follow several repetitious exchanges, the Inner

Guard places the point of a dagger to the Candidate's left breast. He is asked, 'Do you feel anything?'

'Yes.'

The Inner Guard raises the dagger in the air, and the still blindfolded Candidate is led by the right hand by the Junior Deacon to the kneeling-stool before the Worshipful Master, who then addresses the Candidate for the first time.

'Mr John Smith, as no person can be made a Mason unless he is free and of mature age, I demand of you, are you a free man and of the full age of twenty-one years?'

'I am.'

'Thus assured, I will thank you to kneel, while the blessing of Heaven is invoked on our proceedings.'

The Candidate kneels. The Brethren move in the prescribed manner, the Lodge Deacons crossing their wands above the Candidate's head, while the Worshipful Master or the Chaplain prays aloud, 'Vouchsafe Thine aid, Almighty Father and Supreme Governor of the Universe, to our present convention and grant that this Candidate for Freemasonry may so dedicate and devote his life to Thy service, as to become a true and faithful Brother among us. Endue him with a competency of Thy Divine Wisdom, so that, assisted by the secrets of our masonic art, he may be the better enabled to unfold the beauties of true Godliness, to the honour and glory of Thy Holy Name.'

The Immediate Past Master says or sings, 'So mote it be.'

'Mr Smith,' continues the Worshipful Master, 'in all cases of difficulty and danger, in whom do you put your trust?', and the Candidate replies, 'In God.'

'Right glad I am to find your faith so well founded. Relying on such sure support you may safely rise and follow your leader with a firm but humble confidence, for where the name of God is invoked we trust no danger can ensue.'

The Candidate rises to his feet with the help of the Deacons. The Worshipful Master and the Brethren sit. The Worshipful Master then gives a single knock with his gavel. 'The Brethren from the north, east, south and west will take notice that Mr John Smith is about to pass in view before them, to show that he is the Candidate properly prepared, and a fit and proper person to be made a Mason,' says the Master.

There then follows various ritual motions and the Candidate is led in a procession around the Lodge. Arriving at the place where the Junior Warden stands, the Junior Deacon takes the Candidate's right hand and taps the Junior Warden's right shoulder with it three times.

The Junior Warden asks, 'Whom have you there?'

'Mr John Smith,' replies the Junior Deacon, 'A poor Candidate in a state of darkness, who has been well and worthily recommended, regularly proposed and approved in open Lodge, and now comes of his own free will and accord, properly prepared, humbly soliciting to be admitted to the mysteries and privileges of Freemasonry.'

'How does he hope to obtain those privileges?'

'By the help of God, being free and of good report.'

The Junior Warden then takes the Candidate's right hand, and says to him, 'Enter, free and of good report,' and he is led to the Senior Warden, before whom a similar exchange takes place. The Senior Warden moves to the Worshipful Master. 'Worshipful Master,' he says, making the appropriate sign, 'I present to you Mr John Smith, a Candidate properly prepared to be made a Mason.'

'Brother Senior Warden,' replies the Worshipful Master, 'your presentation shall be attended to, for which purpose I shall address a few questions to the Candidate, which I trust he will answer with candour.' He turns to the Candidate. 'Do you seriously declare on your honour that, unbiased by the improper solicitation of friends against your own inclination, and uninfluenced by mercenary or other unworthy motive, you freely and voluntarily offer yourself a Candidate for the mysteries and privileges of Freemasonry?'

'I do.'

'Do you likewise pledge yourself that you are prompted to solicit those privileges by a favourable opinion preconceived of the Institution, a genuine desire of knowledge, and a sincere wish to render yourself more extensively serviceable to your fellow creatures?'

'I do.'

'Do you further seriously declare on your honour that, avoiding fear on the one hand and rashness on the other, you will steadily persevere through the ceremony of your initiation, and if once admitted you will afterwards act and abide by the ancient usages and established customs of the order?'

'I do.'

'Brother Senior Warden, you will direct the Junior Deacon to instruct the Candidate to advance to the pedestal in due form.'

'Brother Junior Deacon, it is the Worshipful Master's command that you instruct the Candidate to advance to the pedestal in due form.'

The Junior Deacon complies, leading the Candidate to the pedestal and instructing him to stand with his heels together and his feet at right angles, the left foot facing east and the right foot south. He continues: 'Take a short pace with your left foot, bringing the heels together in the form of a square. Take another, a little longer, heel to heel as before. Another still longer, heels together as before.'

The Candidate is now standing before the pedestal, with the Junior Deacon to his right and the Senior Deacon to his left.

'It is my duty to inform you,' says the Worshipful Master, 'that Masonry is free, and requires a perfect freedom of inclination in every Candidate for its mysteries. It is founded on the purest principles of piety and virtue. It possesses great and invaluable privileges. And in order to secure those privileges to worthy men, and we trust to worthy men alone, vows of fidelity are required. But let me assure you that in those vows there is nothing incompatible with your civil, moral or religious duties. Are you therefore willing to take a Solemn Obligation, founded on the principles I have stated, to keep inviolate the secrets and mysteries of the order?'

'I am.'

'Then you will kneel on your left knee, your right foot formed in a square, give me your right hand which I place on the Volume of the Sacred Law, while your left will be employed in supporting these compasses, one point presented to your naked left breast.'

This done, the Candidate is then made to repeat the 'Obligation' after the Worshipful Master, 'I, John Smith, in the presence of the Great Architect of the Universe, and of this worthy, worshipful, and warranted Lodge of Free and Accepted Masons, regularly assembled and properly dedicated, of my own free will and accord, do hereby (*WM touches Candidate's right hand with his left hand*) and hereon (*WM touches the Bible with his left hand*) sincerely and solemnly promise and swear, that I will always hele, conceal and never reveal any part or parts, point or points of the secrets or mysteries of or belonging to Free and Accepted Masons in Masonry, which may heretofore have been known by me, or shall now or at any future period be communicated to me, unless it be to a true and lawful Brother or Brothers, and not even to him or them, until after due trial, strict examination, or sure information from a well-known Brother, that he or they are worthy of that confidence, or in the body of a just, perfect, and regular Lodge of Ancient Freemasons. I further solemnly promise that I will not write those secrets, indite, carve, mark, engrave or otherwise them delineate, or cause or suffer it to be so done by others, if in my power to prevent it, on anything movable or immovable, under the canopy of Heaven, whereby or whereon any letter, character or figure, or the least trace of a letter, character or figure, may become legible, or intelligible to myself or anyone in the world, so that our secret arts and hidden mysteries may improperly become known through my unworthiness. These several points I solemnly swear to observe, without evasion, equivocation, or mental reservation of any kind, under no less a penalty, on the violation of any of them, than that of having my throat cut across, my tongue torn out by the root, and buried in the sand of the sea at low water mark, or a cable's length from the shore, where the tide regularly ebbs and flows twice in twenty-four hours, or the more effective punishment of being branded as a wilfully perjured individual, void of all moral worth, and totally unfit to be received into this worshipful Lodge, or any other warranted Lodge or society of men, who prize honour and virtue above the external advantages of rank and fortune. So help me, God, and keep me steadfast in this my Great and Solemn Obligation of an Entered Apprentice Freemason.

Further Reading

BEHA, Ernest, *A Comprehensive Dictionary of Freemasonry* (Arco Publications, 1962).

BOX, Hubert S., *The Nature of Freemasonry* (Augustine Press, 1952)

CAHILL, E., *Freemasonry and the Anti-Christian Movement* (Gill and Son, Dublin, 1952).

CARLILE, Richard, *Manual of Freemasonry* (Wm Reeves, London, 1845).

CARR, Harry, *The Freemason at Work* (Lewis Masonic, 1976).

COVEY-CRUMP, Rev, *The Hiramic Tradition*, (London, 1937).

COX, Barry, SHIRLEY, John and SHORT, Martin, *The Fall of Scotland Yard* (Penguin, 1977).

DEWAR, James, *The Unlocked Secret* (William Kimber, 1966).

FITZWALTER, Raymond and TAYLOR, David, *Web of Corruption* (Granada, 1981)

GOULD, R. F., *History of Freemasonry* (Caxton, 1951).

HANNAH, Walton, *Darkness Visible* (Augustine Press, 1952); *Christian by Degrees* (Britons Publishing Co 1954).

JONES, Bernard E., *Freemasons' Book of the Royal Arch*

(Harrap, 1957); *Freemasons's Guide and Compendium* (Harrap, 1950).

'JUBELUM', *Freemasonry and the Church of England Reconciled* (Britons Publishing Co 1951).

KNIGHT, Stephen, *Jack the Ripper: The Final Solution* (Harrap, 1976).

LAWRENCE, Rev John, *Freemasonry – A Way of Salvation?* (Grove Books, 1982).

LAWRENCE, Rev John T., *Masonic Jurisprudence* (A. Lewis, 1923).

LENNHOFF, Eugen, *The Freemasons* (A. Lewis, 1934).

LEPPER, J. Herron, *The Traditioners* (Ars Quatuor Coronatorum, vol 56, Quatuor Coronati Lodge, no 2076).

LEO XIII, POPE, *Humanum Genus, 1884* (Britons Publishing Co, 1952).

MACKENZIE, Norman (Editor), *Secret Societies* (Aldus, 1967).

MACKEY, Albert G., *Encyclopaedia of Freemasonry* (3 vols) (Macoy Publishing and Supply Co, Richmond, Virginia, 1946).

MORGAN, William, *Freemasonry Exposed* (Glasgow, 1836).

NEWTON, Joseph Fort, *The Builders: A Story and Study of Freemasonry* (Hogg, 1917; Allen and Unwin, 1918).

PICK, Fred L. and KNIGHT, G. Norman, *The Pocket History of Freemasonry* (Frederick Muller, 1953).

PINCHER, Chapman, *Their Trade is Treachery* (Sidgwick and Jackson, 1981).

RAINSBURY, Rev A. W., *Freemasonry – of God or the Devil?* (substance of a sermon preached in Emmanuel Church, South Croydon, 1959).

RUMBLE, Dr L., *Catholics and Freemasonry* (Catholic Truth Society pamphlet).

THURSTON, H., *Freemasonry* (CTS pamphlet).

'VINDEX', *Light Invisible, A Freemason's Answer to Darkness Visible* (Britons Publishing Co, 1952).

VOORHIS, H. V. B., *Facts for Freemasons* (Macoy Publishing Co, 1951, revised 1979).

WHALEN, William J., *Christianity and American Freemasonry* (Bruce Publishing Co, Milwaukee, 1958).

MASONIC PERIODICALS

Freemasons' Magazine and Masonic Mirror
Freemasons' Monthly Remembrancer
Freemasons' Quarterly Review
Masonic Square

CONSTITUTIONS of the Antient Fraternity of Free and Accepted Masons under the United Grand Lodge of England (UGL, London, 1917).

Index